FEDERAL AVIATIC

EXPLAINED

Parts 1, 61, 91, 141, and NTSB 830

MW01286490

Kent S. Jackson

© Jeppesen Sanderson, Inc., 1993, 1994, 1995, 1997, 1999, 2000, 2002
All Rights Reserved
55 Inverness Drive East, Englewood, CO 80112-5498

JS319012-006
ISBN 088487-173-8

The Author

Kent S. Jackson is a partner in the law firm of Jackson & Wade, L.L.C. The firm promotes and fosters the aviation industry by guiding clients through the conflicting requirements of the FAA, IRS, and other international, federal and local governing bodies. The firm represents pilots and companies in enforcement actions before the FAA, IRS, U.S. Customs and other agencies. Jackson & Wade, L.L.C. provides extensive assistance in structuring the acquisition, ownership and operation of aircraft. Jackson & Wade, L.L.C. has represented clients in acquisitions from all major aircraft manufacturers, including Augusta, Bell, Boeing, Bombardier, Pilatus, Cessna, Dassault, Fairchild Dornier, Galaxy, Gulfstream, Learjet, Raytheon and Sikorsky.

A type-rated airline transport pilot and flight instructor, Kent S. Jackson participated on the Fractional Ownership Aviation Rulemaking Committee. Mr. Jackson is past Chairman of the National Business Aviation Association's Tax Committee. He frequently speaks at seminars on behalf of aviation groups, and he writes a legal column for Business & Commercial Aviation.

The authors welcome comments, suggestions, and information which will aid in the development of the *Federal Aviation Regulations Explained*. Information may be sent to the author in care of

Jeppesen
55 Inverness Drive East
Englewood, CO 80112-5498
Tel: (303) 328-4495

or, the author may be contacted directly at
(913) 338-1700
FAX: (913) 338-1755
email: kjackson@jetlaw.com

Acknowledgments

For nearly ten years, Joseph T. Brennan co-authored this book. Joe Brennan was an FAA attorney for 27 years. His perspective as an advocate for the FAA, and his "tribal knowledge" of the history of FAA policies made an invaluable contribution to this book. Although his name and photograph no longer grace the cover, this book will always benefit from Joe's contributions.

The Author would also like to thank the many friends at the FAA, NTSB, and in the aviation industry whose help and support continue to make this book possible.

The Author would also particularly like to thank the following for their contributions, and for putting up with the strain of keeping this book up-to-date:

Cathy Jackson
Elizabeth Jackson
Paul Jackson
Schuyler Jackson
Steve Blanck
Melissa Gowin
Heather Paul
Michelle Wade

The Author would particularly like to thank Lori Edwards for her prodigious research and assistance, and Jim Mowery for his editing of this book.

Cover design by Stephanie Malcy
Cover Photograph by Jamie Paul, J. Andrew Photography

Preface

When Captain Jeppesen began writing letdown procedures in his "little black book," flying was less complicated and far less reliable. The demand for dependable schedules and safety in increasingly congested airspace has forced pilots to give up the romance of silk scarves and face the realities of complex, and sometimes confusing, regulations.

Intended to increase safety and make common sense of the law, the Federal Aviation Regulations have become so detailed and complex that pilots have found themselves saying "I know what it says, but what does it mean?" To help pilots answer the question "what does it mean?" the *Federal Aviation Regulations Explained* looks at Federal Register Preambles, FAA Advisory Circulars, the *Aeronautical Information Manual*, Cases, FAA Chief Counsel opinions, and other regulatory background. *Federal Aviation Regulations Explained* is the only publication that also provides cross references and an index to help pilots see the regulatory "big picture."

This book contains the regulations for FAR Parts 61, 91, 141, and NTSB 830. FAR Part 1 is included as a reference source for the other regulations. Each regulation has the following interpretive resources:

- The regulation itself
- An explanation, unless it is self-explanatory
- Preamble Information
- Cross-references to other regulations
- Related advisory circulars
- The location in the *Aeronautical Information Manual* where related information can be found
- Case excerpts associated with the regulation
- FAA Chief Counsel opinion excerpts

Not all the areas are covered in each regulation, only those areas which are pertinent are included.

Note: Regulation numbers mentioned in case discussions and FAA Chief Council opinions enclosed in brackets "[ ]" indicate the present designation not the designation that was included in the original discussion or opinion.

Although it would be nearly impossible to locate **every** FAA interpretation of every issue presented by the FARs, the authors have endeavored to select NTSB decisions and FAA opinions that are representative of common interpretations. The authors have also selected some of the more conservative FAA interpretations to inform pilots of the FAA's position.

A Word of Caution

No book can replace the advice and counsel of an attorney experienced in aviation law. Federal Aviation Regulations Explained is intended to help pilots understand how the FAA and the NTSB have interpreted the regulations based on past incidences and circumstances. Since not every Flight Standards District Office interprets regulations in precisely the same way, a simple phone call to the local FSDO can often prevent expensive and time-consuming misunderstandings.

FEDERAL AVIATION REGULATIONS

PART 1 — DEFINITIONS AND ABBREVIATIONS

TABLE OF CONTENTS

INTENTIONALLY

LEFT

BLANK

1.1 GENERAL DEFINITIONS

As used in Subchapters A through K of this chapter, unless the context requires otherwise:

Administrator means the Federal Aviation Administrator or any person to whom he has delegated his authority in the matter concerned.

Aerodynamic coefficients means non-dimensional coefficients for aerodynamic forces and moments.

Air carrier means a person who undertakes directly by lease, or other arrangement, to engage in air transportation.

Air commerce means interstate, overseas, or foreign air commerce or the transportation of mail by aircraft or any operation or navigation of aircraft within the limits of any Federal airway or any operation or navigation of aircraft which directly affects, or which may endanger safety in, interstate, overseas, or foreign air commerce.

Aircraft means a device that is used or intended to be used for flight in the air.

Aircraft engine means an engine that is used or intended to be used for propelling aircraft. It includes turbosuperchargers, appurtenances, and accessories necessary for its functioning, but does not include propellers.

Airframe means the fuselage, booms, nacelles, cowlings, fairings, airfoil surfaces (including rotors but excluding propellers and rotating airfoils of engines), and landing gear of an aircraft and their accessories and controls.

Airplane means an engine-driven fixed-wing aircraft heavier than air, that is supported in flight by the dynamic reaction of the air against its wings.

Airport means an area of land or water that is used or intended to be used for the landing and takeoff of aircraft, and includes its buildings and facilities, if any.

Airship means an engine-driven lighter-than-air aircraft that can be steered.

Air traffic means aircraft operating in the air or on an airport surface, exclusive of loading ramps and parking areas.

Air traffic clearance means an authorization by air traffic control, for the purpose of preventing collision between known aircraft, for an aircraft to proceed under specified traffic conditions within controlled airspace.

Air traffic control means a service operated by appropriate authority to promote the safe, orderly, and expeditious flow of air traffic.

Air transportation means interstate, overseas, or foreign air transportation or the transportation of mail by aircraft.

Alert Area — An alert area is established to inform pilots of a specific area wherein a high volume of pilot training or an unusual type of aeronautical activity is conducted.

Alternate airport means an airport at which an aircraft may land if a landing at the intended airport becomes inadvisable.

Altitude engine means a reciprocating aircraft engine having a rated takeoff power that is producible from sea level to an established higher altitude.

Appliance means any instrument, mechanism, equipment, part, apparatus, appurtenance, or accessory, including communications equipment, that is used or intended to be used in operating or controlling an aircraft in flight, is installed in or attached to the aircraft, and is not part of an airframe, engine, or propeller.

Approved, unless used with reference to another person, means approved by the Administrator.

Area navigation (RNAV) means a method of navigation that permits aircraft operations on any desired course within the coverage of station-referenced navigation signals or within the limits of self-contained system capability.

Area navigation low route means an area navigation route within the airspace extending upward from 1,200 feet above the surface of the earth to, but not including, 18,000 feet MSL.

Area navigation high route means an area navigation route within the airspace extending upward from, and including, 18,000 feet MSL to flight level 450.

Armed Forces means the Army, Navy, Air Force, Marine Corps, and Coast Guard, including their regular and reserve components and members serving without component status.

Autorotation means a rotorcraft flight condition in which the lifting rotor is driven entirely by action of the air when the rotorcraft is in motion.

Auxiliary rotor means a rotor that serves either to counteract the effect of the main rotor torque on a rotorcraft or to maneuver the rotorcraft about one or more of its three principal axes.

Balloon means a lighter-than-air aircraft that is not engine driven, and that sustains flight through the use of either gas buoyancy or an airborne heater.

Brake horsepower means the power delivered at the propeller shaft (main drive or main output) of an aircraft engine.

Calibrated airspeed means the indicated airspeed of an aircraft, corrected for position and instrument error. Calibrated airspeed is equal to true airspeed in standard atmosphere at sea level.

Canard means the forward wing of a canard configuration and may be a fixed, movable, or variable geometry surface, with or without control surfaces.

Canard configuration means a configuration in which the span of the forward wing is substantially less than that of the main wing.

Category:

  (1)   As used with respect to the certification, ratings, privileges, and limitations of airmen, means a broad classification of aircraft. Examples include: airplane; rotorcraft; glider; and lighter-than-air; and

  (2)   As used with respect to the certification of aircraft, means a grouping of aircraft based upon intended use or operating limitations. Examples include: transport, normal, utility, acrobatic, limited, restricted, and provisional.

Category A, with respect to transport category rotorcraft, means multiengine rotorcraft designed with engine and system isolation features specified in Part 29 and utilizing scheduled takeoff and landing operations under a critical engine failure concept which assures adequate designated surface area and adequate performance capability for continued safe flight in the event of engine failure.

Category B, with respect to transport category rotorcraft, means single-engine or multiengine rotorcraft which do not fully meet all Category A standards. Category B rotorcraft have no guaranteed stay-up ability in the event of engine failure and unscheduled landing is assumed.

Category II operations, with respect to the operation of aircraft, means a straight-in ILS approach to the runway of an airport under a Category II ILS instrument approach procedure issued by the Administrator or other appropriate authority.

Category III operations, with respect to the operation of aircraft, means an ILS approach to, and landing on, the runway of an airport using a Category III ILS instrument approach procedure issued by the Administrator or other appropriate authority.

Category IIIa operations, an ILS approach and landing with no decision height (DH), or a DH below 100 feet (30 meters), and controlling runway visual range not less than 700 feet (200 meters).

Category IIIb operations, an ILS approach and landing with no DH, or with a DH below 50 feet (15 meters), and controlling runway visual range less than 700 feet (200 meters), but not less than 150 feet (50 meters).

Category IIIc operations, an ILS approach and landing with no DH and no runway visual range limitation.

Ceiling means the height above the earth's surface of the lowest layer of clouds or obscuring phenomena that is reported as "broken", "overcast", or "obscuration", and not classified as "thin" or "partial".

Civil aircraft means aircraft other than public aircraft.

Class:

(1)   As used with respect to the certification, ratings, privileges, and limitations of airmen, means a classification of aircraft within a category having similar operating characteristics. Examples include: single engine; multiengine; land; water; gyroplane; helicopter; airship; and free balloon; and

(2)   As used with respect to the certification of aircraft, means a broad grouping of aircraft having similar characteristics of propulsion, flight, or landing. Examples include: airplane; rotorcraft; glider; balloon; landplane; and seaplane.

Clearway means:

(1)   For turbine engine powered airplanes certificated after August 29, 1959, an area beyond the runway, not less than 500 feet wide, centrally located about the extended centerline of the runway, and under the control of the airport authorities. The clearway is expressed in terms of a clearway plane, extending from the end of the runway with an upward slope not exceeding 1.25 percent, above which no object nor any terrain protrudes. However, threshold lights may protrude above the plane if their height above the end of the runway is 26 inches or less and if they are located to each side of the runway.

(2)   For turbine engine powered airplanes certificated after September 30, 1958, but before August 30, 1959, an area beyond the takeoff runway extending no less than 300 feet on either side of the extended centerline of the runway, at an elevation no higher than the elevation of the end of the runway, clear of all fixed obstacles, and under the control of the airport authorities.

Climbout speed, with respect to rotorcraft, means a referenced airspeed which results in a flight path clear of the height-velocity envelope during initial climbout.

Commercial operator means a person who, for compensation or hire, engages in the carriage by aircraft in air commerce of persons or property, other than as an air carrier or foreign air carrier or under the authority of Part 375 of this title. Where it is doubtful that an operation is for "compensation or hire", the test applied is whether the carriage by air is merely incidental to the person's other business or is, in itself, a major enterprise for profit.

Controlled airspace means an airspace of defined dimensions within which air traffic control service is provided to IFR flights and to VFR flights in accordance with the airspace classification.

> **Note**: Controlled airspace is a generic term that covers Class A, Class B, Class C, Class D, and Class E airspace.

Controlled Firing Area—A controlled firing area is established to contain activities, which if not conducted in a controlled environment, would be hazardous to nonparticipating aircraft.

Crewmember means a person assigned to perform duty in an aircraft during flight time.

Critical altitude means the maximum altitude at which, in standard atmosphere, it is possible to maintain, at a specified rotational speed, a specified power or a specified manifold pressure. Unless otherwise stated, the critical altitude is the maximum altitude at which it is possible to maintain, at the maximum continuous rotational speed, one of the following:

(1)   The maximum continuous power, in the case of engines for which this power rating is the same at sea level and at the rated altitude.

(2)   The maximum continuous rated manifold pressure, in the case of engines, the maximum continuous power of which is governed by a constant manifold pressure.

Critical engine means the engine whose failure would most adversely affect the performance or handling qualities of an aircraft.

Decision height, with respect to the operation of aircraft, means the height at which a decision must be made, during an ILS or PAR instrument approach, to either continue the approach or to execute a missed approach.

Equivalent airspeed means the calibrated airspeed of an aircraft corrected for adiabatic compressible flow for the particular altitude. Equivalent airspeed is equal to calibrated airspeed in standard atmosphere at sea level.

Extended over-water operation means:

(1)   With respect to aircraft other than helicopters, an operation over water at a horizontal distance of more than 50 nautical miles from the nearest shoreline; and

(2)   With respect to helicopters, an operation over water at a horizontal distance of more than 50 nautical miles from the nearest shoreline and more than 50 nautical miles from an off-shore heliport structure.

External load means a load that is carried, or extends, outside of the aircraft fuselage.

External-load attaching means means the structural components used to attach an external load to an aircraft, including external-load containers, the backup structure at the attachment points, and any quick-release device used to jettison the external load.

Fireproof:

(1)   With respect to materials and parts used to confine fire in a designated fire zone, means the capacity to withstand at least as well as steel in dimensions appropriate for the purpose for which they are used, the heat produced when there is a severe fire of extended duration in that zone; and

(2)   With respect to other materials and parts, means the capacity to withstand the heat associated with fire at least as well as steel in dimensions appropriate for the purpose for which they are used.

Fire resistant:

    (1)   With respect to sheet or structural members means the capacity to withstand the heat associated with fire at least as well as aluminum alloy in dimensions appropriate for the purpose for which they are used; and

    (2)   With respect to fluid-carrying lines, fluid system parts, wiring, air ducts, fittings, and powerplant controls, means the capacity to perform the intended functions under the heat and other conditions likely to occur when there is a fire at the place concerned.

Flame resistant means not susceptible to combustion to the point of propagating a flame, beyond safe limits, after the ignition source is removed.

Flammable, with respect to a fluid or gas, means susceptible to igniting readily or to exploding.

Flap extended speed means the highest speed permissible with wing flaps in a prescribed extended position.

Flash resistant means not susceptible to burning violently when ignited.

Flightcrew member means a pilot, flight engineer, or flight navigator assigned to duty in an aircraft during flight time.

Flight level means a level of constant atmospheric pressure related to a reference datum of 29.92 inches of mercury. Each is stated in three digits that represent hundreds of feet. For example, flight level 250 represents a barometric altimeter indication of 25,000 feet; flight level 255, an indication of 25,500 feet.

Flight plan means specified information, relating to the intended flight of an aircraft, that is filed orally or in writing with air traffic control.

Flight time means:

    (1)   Pilot time that commences when an aircraft moves under its own power for the purpose of flight and ends when the aircraft comes to rest after landing; or

    (2)   For a glider without self-launch capability, pilot time that commences when the glider is towed for the purpose of flight and ends when the glider comes to rest after landing.

Flight visibility means the average forward horizontal distance, from the cockpit of an aircraft in flight, at which prominent unlighted objects may be seen and identified by day and prominent lighted objects may be seen and identified by night.

Foreign air carrier means any person other than a citizen of the United States, who undertakes directly, by lease or other arrangement, to engage in air transportation.

Foreign air commerce means the carriage by aircraft of persons or property for compensation or hire, or the carriage of mail by aircraft, or the operation or navigation of aircraft in the conduct or furtherance of a business or vocation, in commerce between a place in the United States and any place outside thereof; whether such commerce moves wholly by aircraft or partly by aircraft and partly by other forms of transportation.

Foreign air transportation means the carriage by aircraft of persons or property as a common carrier for compensation or hire, or the carriage of mail by aircraft, in commerce between a place in the United States and any place outside of the United States, whether that commerce moves wholly by aircraft or partly by aircraft and partly by other forms of transportation.

Forward wing means a forward lifting surface of a canard configuration or tandem-wing configuration airplane. The surface may be a fixed, movable, or variable geometry surface, with or without control surfaces.

Glider means a heavier-than-air aircraft, that is supported in flight by the dynamic reaction of the air against its lifting surfaces and whose free flight does not depend principally on an engine.

Ground visibility means prevailing horizontal visibility near the earth's surface as reported by the United States National Weather Service or an accredited observer.

Go-around power or thrust setting means the maximum allowable in-flight power or thrust setting identified in the performance data.

Gyrodyne means a rotorcraft whose rotors are normally engine-driven for takeoff, hovering, and landing, and for forward flight through part of its speed range, and whose means of propulsion, consisting usually of conventional propellers, is independent of the rotor system.

Gyroplane means a rotorcraft whose rotors are not engine-driven, except for initial starting, but are made to rotate by action of the air when the rotorcraft is moving; and whose means of propulsion, consisting usually of conventional propellers, is independent of the rotor system.

Helicopter means a rotorcraft that, for its horizontal motion, depends principally on its engine-driven rotors.

Heliport means an area of land, water, or structure used or intended to be used for the landing and takeoff of helicopters.

Idle thrust means the jet thrust obtained with the engine power control level set at the stop for the least thrust position at which it can be placed.

IFR conditions means weather conditions below the minimum for flight under visual flight rules.

IFR over-the-top, with respect to the operation of aircraft, means the operation of an aircraft over-the-top on an IFR flight plan when cleared by air traffic control to maintain "VFR conditions" or "VFR conditions on top".

Indicated airspeed means the speed of an aircraft as shown on its pitot static airspeed indicator calibrated to reflect standard atmosphere adiabatic compressible flow at sea level uncorrected for airspeed system errors.

Instrument means a device using an internal mechanism to show visually or aurally the attitude, altitude, or operation of an aircraft or aircraft part. It includes electronic devices for automatically controlling an aircraft in flight.

Interstate air commerce means the carriage by aircraft of persons or property for compensation or hire, or the carriage of mail by aircraft, or the operation or navigation of aircraft in the conduct or furtherance of a business or vocation, in commerce between a place in any State of the United States, or the District of Columbia, and a place in any other State of the United States, or the District of Columbia; or between places in the same State of the United States through the airspace over any place outside thereof; or between places in the same territory or possession of the United States, or the District of Columbia.

Interstate air transportation means the carriage by aircraft of persons or property as a common carrier for compensation or hire, or the carriage of mail by aircraft in commerce:

(1)   Between a place in a State or the District of Columbia and another place in another State or the District of Columbia;

(2)   Between places in the same State through the airspace over any place outside that State; or

(3)   Between places in the same possession of the United States;

Whether that commerce moves wholly by aircraft of partly by aircraft and partly by other forms of transportation.

Intrastate air transportation means the carriage of persons or property as a common carrier for compensation or hire, by turbojet-powered aircraft capable of carrying thirty or more persons, wholly within the same State of the United States.

Kite means a framework, covered with paper, cloth, metal, or other material, intended to be flown at the end of a rope or cable, and having as its only support the force of the wind moving past its surfaces.

Landing gear extended speed means the maximum speed at which an aircraft can be safely flown with the landing gear extended.

Landing gear operating speed means the maximum speed at which the landing gear can be safely extended or retracted.

Large aircraft means aircraft of more than 12,500 pounds, maximum certificated takeoff weight.

Lighter-than-air aircraft means aircraft that can rise and remain suspended by using contained gas weighing less than the air that is displaced by the gas.

Load factor means the ratio of a specified load to the total weight of the aircraft. The specified load is expressed in terms of any of the following: aerodynamic forces, inertia forces, or ground or water reactions.

Long-range communication system (LRCS) — A system that uses satellite relay, data link, high frequency, or another approved communication system which extends beyond line of sight.

Long-range navigation system (LRNS) — An electronic navigation unit that is approved for use under instrument flight rules as a primary means of navigation, and has at least one source of navigational input, such as inertial navigation system, global positioning system, Omega/very low frequency, or Loran C.

Mach number means the ratio of true airspeed to the speed of sound.

Main rotor means the rotor that supplies the principal lift to a rotorcraft.

Maintenance means inspection, overhaul, repair, preservation, and the replacement of parts, but excludes preventive maintenance.

Major alteration means an alteration not listed in the aircraft, aircraft engine, or propeller specifications:

(1)	That might appreciably affect weight, balance, structural strength, performance, powerplant operation, flight characteristics, or other qualities affecting airworthiness; or

(2)	That is not done according to accepted practices or cannot be done by elementary operations.

Major repair means a repair:

(1)	That, if improperly done, might appreciably affect weight, balance, structural strength, performance, powerplant operation, flight characteristics, or other qualities affecting airworthiness; or

(2)	That is not done according to accepted practices or cannot be done by elementary operations.

Manifold pressure means absolute pressure as measured at the appropriate point in the induction system and usually expressed in inches of mercury.

Maximum speed for stability characteristics, VFC/MFC means a speed that may not be less than a speed midway between maximum operating limit speed (VMO/MMO) and demonstrated flight diving speed (VDF/MDF), except that, for altitudes where the Mach number is the limiting factor, MFC need not exceed the Mach number at which effective speed warning occurs.

Medical certificate means acceptable evidence of physical fitness on a form prescribed by the Administrator.

Military operations area. A military operations area (MOA) is airspace established outside Class A airspace to separate or segregate certain nonhazardous military activities from IFR Traffic and to identify for VFR traffic where theses activities are conducted.

Minimum descent altitude means the lowest altitude, expressed in feet above mean sea level, to which descent is authorized on final approach or during circle-to-land maneuvering in execution of a standard instrument approach procedure, where no electronic glide slope is provided.

Minor alteration means an alteration other than a major alteration.

Minor repair means a repair other than a major repair.

Navigable airspace means airspace at and above the minimum flight altitudes prescribed by or under this chapter, including airspace needed for safe takeoff and landing.

Night means the time between the end of evening civil twilight and the beginning of morning civil twilight, as published in the American Air Almanac, converted to local time.

Nonprecision approach procedure means a standard instrument approach procedure in which no electronic glide slope is provided.

Operate, with respect to aircraft, means use, cause to use or authorize to use aircraft, for the purpose (except as provided in §91.13 of this chapter) of air navigation including the piloting of aircraft, with or without the right of legal control (as owner, lessee, or otherwise).

Operational control, with respect to a flight, means the exercise of authority over initiating, conducting or terminating a flight.

Overseas air commerce means the carriage by aircraft of persons or property for compensation or hire, or the carriage of mail by aircraft, or the operation or navigation of aircraft in the conduct or furtherance of a business or vocation, in commerce between a place in any State of the United States, or the District of Columbia, and any place in a territory or possession of the United States; or between a place in a territory or possession of the United States, and a place in any other territory or possession of the United States.

Overseas air transportation means the carriage by aircraft of persons or property as a common carrier for compensation or hire, or the carriage of mail by aircraft, in commerce:

(1) Between a place in a State or the District of Columbia and a place in a possession of the United States; or

(2) Between a place in a possession of the United States and a place in another possession of the United States; whether that commerce moves wholly by aircraft or partly by aircraft and partly by other forms of transportation.

Over-the-top means above the layer of clouds or other obscuring phenomena forming the ceiling.

Parachute means a device used or intended to be used to retard the fall of a body or object through the air.

Person means an individual, firm, partnership, corporation, company, association, joint-stock association, or governmental entity. It includes a trustee, receiver, assignee, or similar representative of any of them.

Pilotage means navigation by visual reference to landmarks.

Pilot in command means the person who:

    (1)   Has final authority and responsibility for the operation and safety of the flight;

    (2)   Has been designated as pilot in command before or during the flight; and

    (3)   Holds the appropriate category, class, and type rating, if appropriate, for the conduct of the flight.

Pitch setting means the propeller blade setting as determined by the blade angle measured in a manner, and at a radius, specified by the instruction manual for the propeller.

Positive control means control of all air traffic, within designated airspace, by air traffic control.

Powered-lift means a heavier-than-air aircraft capable of vertical takeoff, vertical landing, and low speed flight that depends principally on engine-driven lift devices or engine thrust for lift during these flight regimes and on nonrotating airfoil(s) for lift during horizontal flight.

Precision approach procedure means a standard instrument approach procedure in which an electronic glide slope is provided, such as ILS and PAR.

Preventive maintenance means simple or minor preservation operations and the replacement of small standard parts not involving complex assembly operations.

Prohibited area — A prohibited area is airspace designated under part 73 within which no person may operate an aircraft without the permission of the using agency.

Propeller means a device for propelling an aircraft that has blades on an engine-driven shaft and that, when rotated, produces by its action on the air, a thrust approximately perpendicular to its plane of rotation. It includes control components normally supplied by its manufacturer, but does not include main and auxiliary rotors or rotating airfoils of engines.

Public aircraft means an aircraft used only for the United States Government, or owned and operated (except for commercial purposes), or exclusively leased for at least 90 continuous days, by a government (except the United States Government), including a State, the District of Columbia, or a territory or possession of the United States, or political subdivision of that government; but does not include a government-owned aircraft transporting property for commercial purposes, or transporting passengers other than transporting (for other than commercial purposes) crewmembers or other persons aboard the aircraft whose presence is required to perform, or is associated with the performance of, a governmental function such as firefighting, search and rescue, law enforcement, aeronautical research, or biological or geological resource management; or transporting (for other than commercial purposes) persons aboard the aircraft if the aircraft is operated by the Armed Forces or an intelligence agency of the United States. An aircraft described in the preceding sentence shall, notwithstanding any limitation relating to use of the aircraft for commercial purposes, be considered to be a public aircraft for the purposes of this Chapter without regard to whether the aircraft is operated by a unit of government on behalf of another unit of government, pursuant to a cost reimbursement agreement between such units of government, if the unit of government on whose behalf the operation is conducted certifies to the Administrator of the Federal Aviation Administration that the operation was necessary to respond to a significant and imminent threat to life or property (including natural resources) and that no service by a private operator was reasonably available to meet the threat.

Rated 30-second OEI power, with respect to rotorcraft turbine engines, means the approved brake horsepower developed under static conditions at specified altitudes and temperatures within the operating limitations established for the engine under part 33 of this chapter, for continued one-flight operation after the failure of one engine in multiengine rotorcraft, limited to three periods of use no longer than 30 seconds each in any one flight, and followed by mandatory inspection and prescribed maintenance action.

Rated 2-minute OEI power, with respect to rotorcraft turbine engines, means the approved brake horsepower developed under static conditions at specified altitudes and temperatures within the operating limitations established for the engine under part 33 of this chapter, for continued one-flight operation after the failure of one engine in multiengine rotorcraft, limited to three periods of use no longer than 2 minutes each in any one flight, and followed by mandatory inspection and prescribed maintenance action.

Rated continuous OEI power, with respect to rotorcraft turbine engines, means the approved brake horsepower developed under static conditions at specified altitudes and temperatures within the operating limitations established for the engine under Part 33 of this chapter, and limited in use to the time required to complete the flight after the failure of one engine of a multiengine rotorcraft.

Rated maximum continuous augmented thrust, with respect to turbojet engine type certification, means the approved jet thrust that is developed statically or in flight, in standard atmosphere at a specified altitude, with fluid injection or with the burning of fuel in a separate combustion chamber, within the engine operating limitations established under Part 33 of this chapter, and approved for unrestricted periods of use.

Rated maximum continuous power, with respect to reciprocating, turbopropeller, and turboshaft engines, means the approved brake horsepower that is developed statically or in flight, in standard atmosphere at a specified altitude, within the engine operating limitations established under Part 33, and approved for unrestricted periods of use.

Rated maximum continuous thrust, with respect to turbojet engine type certification, means the approved jet thrust that is developed statically or in flight, in standard atmosphere at a specified altitude, without fluid injection and without the burning of fuel in a separate combustion chamber, within the engine operating limitations established under Part 33 of this chapter, and approved for unrestricted periods of use.

Rated takeoff augmented thrust, with respect to turbojet engine type certification, means the approved jet thrust that is developed statically under standard sea level conditions, with fluid injection or with the burning of fuel in a separate combustion chamber, within the engine operating limitations established under Part 33 of this chapter, and limited in use to periods of not over 5 minutes for takeoff operation.

Rated takeoff power, with respect to reciprocating, turbopropeller, and turboshaft engine type certification, means the approved brake horsepower that is developed statically under standard sea level conditions, within the engine operating limitations established under Part 33, and limited in use to periods of not over 5 minutes for takeoff operation.

Rated takeoff thrust, with respect to turbojet engine type certification, means the approved jet thrust that is developed statically under standard sea level conditions, without fluid injection and without the burning of fuel in a separate combustion chamber, within the engine operating limitations established under Part 33 of this chapter, and limited in use to periods of not over 5 minutes for takeoff operation.

Rated 30-minute OEI power, with respect to rotorcraft turbine engines, means the approved brake horsepower developed under static conditions at specified altitudes and temperatures within the operating limitations established for the engine under Part 33 of this chapter, and limited in use to a period of not more than 30 minutes after the failure of one engine of a multiengine rotorcraft.

Rated 2 1/2-minute OEI power, with respect to rotorcraft turbine engines, means the approved brake horsepower developed under static conditions at specified altitudes and temperatures within the operating limitations established for the engine under Part 33 of this chapter, and limited in use to a period of not more than 2 1/2 minutes after the failure of one engine of a multiengine rotorcraft.

Rating means a statement that, as a part of a certificate, sets forth special conditions, privileges, or limitations.

Reporting point means a geographical location in relation to which the position of an aircraft is reported.

Restricted area — A restricted area is airspace designated under Part 73 within which the flight of aircraft, while not wholly prohibited, is subject to restriction.

RNAV way point (W/P) means a predetermined geographical position used for route or instrument approach definition or progress reporting purposes that is defined relative to a VORTAC station position.

Rocket means an aircraft propelled by ejected expanding gases generated in the engine from self-contained propellants and not dependent on the intake of outside substances. It includes any part which becomes separated during the operation.

Rotorcraft means a heavier-than-air aircraft that depends principally for its support in flight on the lift generated by one or more rotors.

Rotorcraft-load combination means the combination of a rotorcraft and an external-load, including the external-load attaching means. Rotorcraft-load combinations are designated as Class A, Class B, Class C, and Class D, as follows:

(1) Class A rotorcraft-load combination means one in which the external load cannot move freely, cannot be jettisoned, and does not extend below the landing gear.

(2) Class B rotorcraft-load combination means one in which the external load is jettisonable and is lifted free of land or water during the rotorcraft operation.

(3) Class C rotorcraft-load combination means one in which the external load is jettisonable and remains in contact with land or water during the rotorcraft operation.

(4) Class D rotorcraft-load combination means one in which the external-load is other than a Class A, B, or C and has been specifically approved by the Administrator for that operation.

Route segment means a part of a route. Each end of that part is identified by:

(1) A continental or insular geographical location; or

(2) A point at which a definite radio fix can be established.

Sea level engine means a reciprocating aircraft engine having a rated takeoff power that is producible only at sea level.

Second in command means a pilot who is designated to be second in command of an aircraft during flight time.

Show, unless the context otherwise requires, means to show to the satisfaction of the Administrator.

Small aircraft means aircraft of 12,500 pounds or less, maximum certificated takeoff weight.

Special VFR conditions mean meteorological conditions that are less than those required for basic VFR flight in controlled airspace and in which some aircraft are permitted flight under visual flight rules.

Special VFR operations means aircraft operating in accordance with clearances within controlled airspace in meteorological conditions less than the basic VFR weather minima. Such operations must be requested by the pilot and approved by ATC.

Standard atmosphere means the atmosphere defined in U.S. Standard Atmosphere, 1962 (Geopotential altitude tables).

Stopway means an area beyond the takeoff runway, no less wide than the runway and centered upon the extended centerline of the runway, able to support the airplane during an aborted takeoff, without causing structural damage to the airplane, and designated by the airport authorities for use in decelerating the airplane during an aborted takeoff.

Takeoff power:

(1)   With respect to reciprocating engines, means the brake horsepower that is developed under standard sea level conditions, and under the maximum conditions of crankshaft rotational speed and engine manifold pressure approved for the normal takeoff, and limited in continuous use to the period of time shown in the approved engine specification; and

(2)   With respect to turbine engines, means the brake horsepower that is developed under static conditions at a specified altitude and atmospheric temperature, and under the maximum conditions of rotor shaft rotational speed and gas temperature approved for the normal takeoff, and limited in continuous use to the period of time shown in the approved engine specification.

Takeoff safety speed means a referenced airspeed obtained after lift-off at which the required one-engine-inoperative climb performance can be achieved.

Takeoff thrust, with respect to turbine engines, means the jet thrust that is developed under static conditions at a specific altitude and atmospheric temperature under the maximum conditions of rotorshaft rotational speed and gas temperature approved for the normal takeoff, and limited in continuous use to the period of time shown in the approved engine specification.

Tandem wing configuration means a configuration having two wings of similar span, mounted in tandem.

TCAS I means a TCAS that utilizes interrogations of, and replies from, airborne radar beacon transponders and provides traffic advisories to the pilot.

TCAS II means a TCAS that utilizes interrogations of, and replies from airborne radar beacon transponders and provides traffic advisories and resolution advisories in the vertical plane.

TCAS III means a TCAS that utilizes interrogation of, and replies from, airborne radar beacon transponders and provides traffic advisories and resolution advisories in the vertical and horizontal planes to the pilot.

Time in service, with respect to maintenance time records, means the time from the moment an aircraft leaves the surface of the earth until it touches it at the next point of landing.

True airspeed means the airspeed of an aircraft relative to undisturbed air. True airspeed is equal to equivalent airspeed multiplied by $(\rho_0/\rho)^{1/2}$.

Traffic pattern means the traffic flow that is prescribed for aircraft landing at, taxiing on, or taking off from, an airport.

Type:

(1) As used with respect to the certification, ratings, privileges, and limitations of airmen, means a specific make and basic model of aircraft, including modifications thereto that do not change its handling or flight characteristics. Examples include: DC-7, 1049, and F-27; and

(2) As used with respect to the certification of aircraft, means those aircraft which are similar in design. Examples include: DC-7 and DC-7C; 1049G and 1049H; and F-27 and F-27F.

(3) As used with respect to the certification of aircraft engines means those engines which are similar in design. For example, JT8D and JT8D-7 are engines of the same type, and JT9D-3A and JT9D-7 are engines of the same type.

United States, in a geographical sense, means (1) the States, the District of Columbia, Puerto Rico, and the possessions, including the territorial waters, and (2) the airspace of those areas.

United States air carrier means a citizen of the United States who undertakes directly by lease, or other arrangement, to engage in air transportation.

VFR over-the-top, with respect to the operation of aircraft, means the operation of an aircraft over-the-top under VFR when it is not being operated on an IFR flight plan.

Warning area — A warning area is airspace of defined dimensions, extending from 3 nautical miles outward from the coast of the United States, that contains activity that may be hazardous to nonparticipating aircraft. The purpose of such warning areas is to warn nonparticipating pilots of the potential danger. A warning area may be located over domestic or international waters or both.

Winglet or tip fin means an out-of-plane surface extending from a lifting surface. The surface may or may not have control surfaces.

1.2 ABBREVIATIONS AND SYMBOLS

In Subchapters A through K of this chapter:

AGL means above ground level.

ALS means approach light system.

ASR means airport surveillance radar.

ATC means air traffic control.

CAS means calibrated airspeed.

CAT II means Category II.

CONSOL or CONSOLAN means a kind of low or medium frequency long range navigational aid.

DH means decision height.

DME means distance measuring equipment compatible with TACAN.

EAS means equivalent airspeed.

FAA means Federal Aviation Administration.

FM means fan marker.

GS means glide slope.

HIRL means high-intensity runway light system.

IAS means indicated airspeed.

ICAO means International Civil Aviation Organization.

IFR means instrument flight rules.

ILS means instrument landing system.

IM means ILS inner marker.

INT means intersection.

LDA means localizer-type directional aid.

LFR means low-frequency radio range.

LMM means compass locator at middle marker.

LOC means ILS localizer.

LOM means compass locator at outer marker.

M means mach number.

MAA means maximum authorized IFR altitude.

MALS means medium intensity approach light system.

MALSR means medium intensity approach light system with runway alignment indicator lights.

MCA means minimum crossing altitude.

MDA means minimum descent altitude.

MEA means minimum en route IFR altitude.

MM means ILS middle marker.

MOCA means minimum obstruction clearance altitude.

MRA means minimum reception altitude.

MSL means mean sea level.

NDB(ADF) means nondirectional beacon (automatic direction finder).

NOPT means no procedure turn required.

OEI means one engine inoperative.

OM means ILS outer marker.

PAR means precision approach radar.

RAIL means runway alignment indicator light system.

RBN means radio beacon.

RCLM means runway centerline marking.

RCLS means runway centerline light system.

REIL means runway end identification lights.

RR means low or medium frequency radio range station.

RVR means runway visual range as measured in the touchdown zone area.

SALS means short approach light system.

SSALS means simplified short approach light system.

SSALSR means simplified short approach light system with runway alignment indicator lights.

TACAN means ultra-high frequency tactical air navigational aid.

TAS means true airspeed.

TCAS means a traffic alert and collision avoidance system.

TDZL means touchdown zone lights.

TVOR means very high frequency terminal omnirange station.

V_A means design maneuvering speed.

V_B means design speed for maximum gust intensity.

V_C means design cruising speed.

V_D means design diving speed.

V_{DF}/M_{DF} means demonstrated flight diving speed.

V_{EF} means the speed at which the critical engine is assumed to fail during takeoff.

V_F means design flap speed.

V_{FC}/M_{FC} means maximum speed for stability characteristics.

V_{FE} means maximum flap extended speed.

V_H means maximum speed in level flight with maximum continuous power.

V_{LE} means maximum landing gear extended speed.

V_{LO} means maximum landing gear operating speed.

V_{LOF} means lift-off speed.

V_{MC} means minimum control speed with the critical engine inoperative.

V_{MO}/M_{MO} means maximum operating limit speed.

V_{MU} means minimum unstick speed.

V_{NE} means never-exceed speed.

V_{NO} means maximum structural cruising speed.

V_R means rotation speed.

V_0 means the stalling speed or the minimum steady flight speed at which the airplane is controllable.

V_{S0} means the stalling speed or the minimum steady flight speed in the landing configuration.

V_{S1} means the stalling speed or the minimum steady flight speed obtained in a specific configuration.

V_{TOSS} means takeoff safety speed for Category A rotorcraft.

V_X means speed for best angle of climb.

V_Y means speed for best rate of climb.

V_1 means the maximum speed in the takeoff at which the pilot must take the first action (e.g., apply brakes, reduce thrust, deploy speed brakes) to stop the airplane within the accelerate-stop distance. V1 also means the minimum speed in the takeoff, following a failure of the critical engine at V_{EF}, at which the pilot can continue the takeoff and achieve the required height above the takeoff surface within the takeoff distance.

V_2 means takeoff safety speed.

$V_{2\ min}$ means minimum takeoff safety speed.

VFR means visual flight rules.

VHF means very high frequency.

VOR means very high frequency omnirange station.

VORTAC means collocated VOR and TACAN.

1.3 RULES OF CONSTRUCTION

(a)   In Subchapters A through K of this chapter, unless the context requires otherwise:

    (1) Words importing the singular include the plural;
    (2) Words importing the plural include the singular; and
    (3) Words importing the masculine gender include the feminine.

(b)   In Subchapters A through K of this chapter, the word:

    (1) Shall is used in an imperative sense;
    (2) May is used in a permissive sense to state authority or permission to do the act prescribed, and the words "no person may *   *   *" or "a person may not *   *   *" mean that no person is required, authorized, or permitted to do the act prescribed; and
    (3) Includes means "includes but is not limited to".

FEDERAL AVIATION REGULATIONS

PART 61 CERTIFICATION: PILOTS, FLIGHT INSTRUCTORS AND GROUND INSTRUCTORS

TABLE OF CONTENTS

SUBPART A — GENERAL

SUBPART A — GENERAL (continued)

SUBPART B — AIRCRAFT RATINGS AND PILOT AUTHORIZATIONS

SUBPART C — STUDENT PILOTS

TABLE OF CONTENTS

SUBPART D — RECREATIONAL PILOTS

SUBPART E — PRIVATE PILOTS

SUBPART F — COMMERCIAL PILOTS

TABLE OF CONTENTS

SUBPART G — AIRLINE TRANSPORT PILOTS

SUBPART H — FLIGHT INSTRUCTORS

SUBPART I — GROUND INSTRUCTORS

SUBPART A — GENERAL

61.1 APPLICABILITY AND DEFINITIONS

(a) This part prescribes:
  (1) The requirements for issuing pilot, flight instructor, and ground instructor certificates and ratings; the conditions under which those certificates and ratings are necessary; and the privileges and limitations of those certificates and ratings.
  (2) The requirements for issuing pilot, flight instructor, and ground instructor authorizations; the conditions under which those authorizations are necessary; and the privileges and limitations of those authorizations.
  (3) The requirements for issuing pilot, flight instructor, and ground instructor certificates and ratings for persons who have taken courses approved by the Administrator under other parts of this chapter.
(b) For the purpose of this part:
  (1) *Aeronautical experience* means pilot time obtained in an aircraft, flight simulator, or flight training device for meeting the appropriate training and flight time requirements for an airman certificate, rating, flight review, or recency of flight experience requirements of this part.
  (2) *Authorized instructor* means—
    (i) A person who holds a valid ground instructor certificate issued under part 61 or part 143 of this chapter when conducting ground training in accordance with the privileges and limitations of his or her ground instructor certificate;
    (ii) A person who holds a current flight instructor certificate issued under part 61 of this chapter when conducting ground training or flight training in accordance with the privileges and limitations of his or her flight instructor certificate; or
    (iii) A person authorized by the Administrator to provide ground training or flight training under SFAR No. 58, or part 61, 121, 135, or 142 of this chapter when conducting ground training or flight training in accordance with that authority.
  (3) *Cross-country time* means—
    (i) Except as provided in paragraphs (b)(3) (ii), (iii), (iv), and (v) of this section, time acquired during a flight—
      (A) Conducted by a person who holds a pilot certificate;
      (B) Conducted in an aircraft;
      (C) That includes a landing at a point other than the point of departure; and
      (D) That involves the use of dead reckoning, pilotage, electronic navigation aids, radio aids, or other navigation systems to navigate to the landing point.
    (ii) For the purpose of meeting the aeronautical experience requirements (except for a rotorcraft category rating), for a private pilot certificate, a commercial pilot certificate, or an instrument rating, or for the purpose of exercising recreational pilot privileges (except in a rotorcraft) under §61.101(c), time acquired during a flight—
      (A) Conducted in an appropriate aircraft;
      (B) That includes a point of landing that was at least a straight-line distance of more than 50 nautical miles from the original point of departure; and
      (C) That involves the use of dead reckoning, pilotage, electronic navigation aids, radio aids, or other navigation systems to navigate to the landing point.

(iii) For the purpose of meeting the aeronautical experience requirements for any pilot certificate with a rotorcraft category rating, or an instrument-helicopter rating, or for the purpose of exercising recreational pilot privileges, in a rotorcraft, under §61.101(c), time acquired during a flight—
   (A) Conducted in an appropriate aircraft;
   (B) That includes a point of landing that was at least a straight-line distance of more than 25 nautical miles from the original point of departure; and
   (C) That involves the use of dead reckoning, pilotage, electronic navigation aids, radio aids, or other navigation systems to navigate to the landing point.

(iv) For the purpose of meeting the aeronautical experience requirements for an airline transport pilot certificate (except with a rotorcraft category rating), time acquired during a flight—
   (A) Conducted in an appropriate aircraft;
   (B) That is at least a straight-line distance of more than 50 nautical miles from the original point of departure; and
   (C) That involves the use of dead reckoning, pilotage, electronic navigation aids, radio aids, or other navigation systems.

(v) For a military pilot who qualifies for a commercial pilot certificate (except with a rotorcraft category rating) under §61.73 of this part, time acquired during a flight—
   (A) Conducted in an appropriate aircraft;
   (B) That is at least a straight-line distance of more than 50 nautical miles from the original point of departure; and
   (C) That involves the use of dead reckoning, pilotage, electronic navigation aids, radio aids, or other navigation systems.

(4) *Examiner* means any person who is authorized by the Administrator to conduct a pilot proficiency test or a practical test for an airman certificate or rating issued under this part, or a person who is authorized to conduct a knowledge test under this part.

(5) *Flight simulator* means a device that—
   (i) Is a full-size aircraft cockpit replica of a specific type of aircraft, or make, model, and series of aircraft;
   (ii) Includes the hardware and software necessary to represent the aircraft in ground operations and flight operations;
   (iii) Uses a force cueing system that provides cues at least equivalent to those cues provided by a 3 degree freedom of motion system;
   (iv) Uses a visual system that provides at least a 45 degree horizontal field of view and a 30 degree vertical field of view simultaneously for each pilot; and
   (v) Has been evaluated, qualified, and approved by the Administrator.

(6) *Flight training* means that training, other than ground training, received from an authorized instructor in flight in an aircraft.

(7) *Flight training device* means a device that—
   (i) Is a full-size replica of the instruments, equipment, panels, and controls of an aircraft, or set of aircraft, in an open flight deck area or in an enclosed cockpit, including the hardware and software for the systems installed, that is necessary to simulate the aircraft in ground and flight operations;
   (ii) Need not have a force (motion) cueing or visual system; and
   (iii) Has been evaluated, qualified, and approved by the Administrator.

(8) *Ground training* means that training, other than flight training, received from an authorized instructor.

(9) *Instrument approach* means an approach procedure defined in part 97 of this chapter.

(10) *Instrument training* means that time in which instrument training is received from an authorized instructor under actual or simulated instrument conditions.

(11) *Knowledge test* means a test on the aeronautical knowledge areas required for an airman certificate or rating that can be administered in written form or by a computer.

(12) *Pilot time* means that time in which a person—
   (i) Serves as a required pilot flight crewmember;
   (ii) Receives training from an authorized instructor in an aircraft, flight simulator, or flight training device; or
   (iii) Gives training as an authorized instructor in an aircraft, flight simulator, or flight training device.

(13) *Practical test* means a test on the areas of operations for an airman certificate, rating, or authorization that is conducted by having the applicant respond to questions and demonstrate maneuvers in flight, in a flight simulator, or in a flight training device.

(14) *Set of aircraft* means aircraft that share similar performance characteristics, such as similar airspeed and altitude operating envelopes, similar handling characteristics, and the same number and type of propulsion systems.

(15) *Training time* means training received—
   (i) In flight from an authorized instructor;
   (ii) On the ground from an authorized instructor; or
   (iii) In a flight simulator or flight training device from an authorized instructor.

EXPLANATION

The addition of definitions was designed to clarify the terms used in Part 61.

PREAMBLE

Amendment No. 61-100 redesignated §§61.2, 61.3, and 61.5 as §§61.3, 61.5, and 61.6, respectively. In addition, that amendment added a new section, §61.2, Definition of terms. In this final rule, §61.1 includes both the applicability provisions and the definitions of terms currently found in §61.1 and §61.2. Accordingly, §§61.2, 61.3, 61.5, and the preamble discussion of those sections in this final rule reflect the structure of part 61 prior to the adoption of Amendment No. 61-100 and the organization of part 61 proposed in Notice No. 95-11. (62 FR 16222).

61.1(a): In response to the cited comments, the FAA acknowledges that certain definitions would not clarify part 61. Therefore, the FAA has decided to not include the definitions for "airman certificate," "authorized ground instructor," "authorized flight instructor," and "supervised pilot in command" in the final rule. The FAA agrees that the definition of "airman certificate" conflicts with the U.S. Code and the FAR, and should be deleted. The FAA has removed the definitions for "authorized flight instructor" and "authorized ground instructor" and replaced them with a single definition for "authorized instructor" as explained in the analysis of §61.1(b)(2) below. The concept of supervised pilot in command was created only to permit the logging of student solo time as pilot-in-command time under §61.51. The proposed definition created difficulty in determining when supervision was occurring, and has been removed.

61.1(b)(2) Authorized Instructor: The FAA has removed the definitions of "authorized flight instructor" and "authorized ground instructor" and replaced them with a new term, "authorized instructor," which encompasses commercial lighter-than-air pilots and ATP certificate holders who may also provide training. Additionally, the FAA has modified the definition to include persons providing training under part 142. With respect to the commenters' fear that the term "certificated flight instructor" will no longer be valid due to the change, the FAA stresses that flight and ground instructors are still certificated under part 61, and therefore will remain certificated instructors.

61.1(b)(3) Cross-country time: In response to the commenters' concerns, the FAA has modified the definition of "cross-country time" to remove any distinction between flight and actual flight. The definition was also modified to permit flights of 25 nautical miles for a private rotorcraft rating to be considered as cross-country flights. The definition was modified to include references to future navigation systems rather than restricting cross-country navigation to present methods and systems. In response to comments received, the FAA modified the definition of cross-country time to permit a commercial pilot, airline transport pilot, or military pilot qualified for a commercial pilot rating to log cross-country time without requiring a landing at a point 50 nautical miles from the original point of departure.

61.1(b)(6) Flight training: The intent of the section is to ensure more consistent use of terms throughout Part 61. The FAA believes the definition achieves this goal and should be adopted as proposed with a modification to remove any distinction between flight and actual flight in response to commenters' concerns.

61.1(b)(9) Instrument approach: To address the public's concerns, the definition of "instrument approach" was modified to remove any requirement that the approach be conducted to DH, MDA, or to a higher altitude selected by ATC in order to be considered an instrument approach.
61.1(b)(10) Instrument training: Training received in flight simulators is outside the scope of the rule, and is addressed in another rulemaking project (Notice No. 92-10), as explained in section II. The term "authorized instructor" is used as explained in the analysis of §61.1(b)(2), and the definition of instrument training has been modified to reflect this change.

61.1(b)(11) Knowledge test: Since the early 1980's, the FAA has recognized the importance of flight simulators and flight training devices, and has issued over 30 exemptions to provide for the use of simulators and flight training devices. Therefore, the final rule reflects established FAA policy.

61.1(b)(15) Training time: The definition of "training time" was modified in the final rule to remove any distinction between flight and actual flight. Taxi and run-up time performed for the purpose of flight can be logged as training time. (62 FR 16234 – 16236).

CASES

Because this section states that "no person may act as pilot in command," it applies to any person piloting an aircraft, regardless of whether or not he holds an airman certificate. *Administrator v. Green*, 1 NTSB 1751 (1972).

61.3 REQUIREMENT FOR CERTIFICATES, RATINGS, AND AUTHORIZATIONS

(a) *Pilot certificate.* A person may not act as pilot in command or in any other capacity as a required pilot flight crewmember of a civil aircraft of U.S. registry, unless that person has a valid pilot certificate or special purpose pilot authorization issued under this part in that person's physical possession or readily accessible in the aircraft when exercising the privileges of that pilot certificate or authorization. However, when the aircraft is operated within a foreign country, a current pilot license issued by the country in which the aircraft is operated may be used.

(b) *Required pilot certificate for operating a foreign-registered aircraft.* A person may not act as pilot in command or in any other capacity as a required pilot flight crewmember of a civil aircraft of foreign registry within the United States, unless that person's pilot certificate:

    (1) Is valid and in that person's physical possession, or readily accessible in the aircraft when exercising the privileges of that pilot certificate; and

    (2) Has been issued under this part, or has been issued or validated by the country in which the aircraft is registered.

(c) *Medical certificate.*

    (1) Except as provided for in paragraph (c)(2) of this section, a person may not act as pilot in command or in any other capacity as a required pilot flight crewmember of an aircraft, under a certificate issued to that person under this part, unless that person has a current and appropriate medical certificate that has been issued under part 67 of this chapter, or other documentation acceptable to the Administrator, which is in that person's physical possession or readily accessible in the aircraft.

    (2) A person is not required to meet the requirements of paragraph (c)(1) of this section if that person—

        (i) Is exercising the privileges of a student pilot certificate while seeking a pilot certificate with a glider category rating or balloon class rating;

        (ii) Is holding a pilot certificate with a balloon class rating and is piloting or providing training in a balloon as appropriate;

        (iii) Is holding a pilot certificate or a flight instructor certificate with a glider category rating, and is piloting or providing training in a glider, as appropriate;

        (iv) Except as provided in paragraph (c)(2)(iii) of this section, is exercising the privileges of a flight instructor certificate, provided the person is not acting as pilot in command or as a required pilot flight crewmember;

        (v) Is exercising the privileges of a ground instructor certificate;

        (vi) Is operating an aircraft within a foreign country using a pilot license issued by that country and possesses evidence of current medical qualification for that license; or

        (vii) Is operating an aircraft with a U.S. pilot certificate, issued on the basis of a foreign pilot license, issued under §61.75 of this part, and holds a current medical certificate issued by the foreign country that issued the foreign pilot license, which is in that person's physical possession or readily accessible in the aircraft when exercising the privileges of that airman certificate.

(d) *Flight instructor certificate.*
    (1) A person who holds a flight instructor certificate issued under this part must have that certificate, or other documentation acceptable to the Administrator, in that person's physical possession or readily accessible in the aircraft when exercising the privileges of that flight instructor certificate.
    (2) Except as provided in paragraph (d)(3) of this section, no person other than the holder of a flight instructor certificate issued under this part with the appropriate rating on that certificate may—
        (i) Give training required to qualify a person for solo flight and solo cross-country flight;
        (ii) Endorse an applicant for a—
            (A) Pilot certificate or rating issued under this part;
            (B) Flight instructor certificate or rating issued under this part; or
            (C) Ground instructor certificate or rating issued under this part;
        (iii) Endorse a pilot logbook to show training given; or
        (iv) Endorse a student pilot certificate and logbook for solo operating privileges.
    (3) A flight instructor certificate issued under this part is not necessary—
        (i) Under paragraph (d)(2) of this section, if the training is given by the holder of a commercial pilot certificate with a lighter-than-air rating, provided the training is given in accordance with the privileges of the certificate in a lighter-than-air aircraft;
        (ii) Under paragraph (d)(2) of this section, if the training is given by the holder of an airline transport pilot certificate with a rating appropriate to the aircraft in which the training is given, provided the training is given in accordance with the privileges of the certificate and conducted in accordance with an approved air carrier training program approved under part 121 or 135 of this chapter;
        (iii) Under paragraph (d)(2) of this section, if the training is given by a person who is qualified in accordance with subpart C of part 142 of this chapter, provided the training is conducted in accordance with an approved part 142 training program;
        (iv) Under paragraph (d)(2)(i), (d)(2)(ii)(C), and (d)(2)(iii) of this section, if the training is given by the holder of a ground instructor certificate in accordance with the privileges of the certificate; or
        (v) Under paragraph (d)(2)(iii) of this section, if the training is given by an authorized flight instructor under §61.41 of this part.
(e) *Instrument rating.* No person may act as pilot in command of a civil aircraft under IFR or in weather conditions less than the minimums prescribed for VFR flight unless that person holds:
    (1) The appropriate aircraft category, class, type (if required), and instrument rating on that person's pilot certificate for any airplane, helicopter, or powered-lift being flown;
    (2) An airline transport pilot certificate with the appropriate aircraft category, class, and type rating (if required) for the aircraft being flown;
    (3) For a glider, a pilot certificate with a glider category rating and an airplane instrument rating; or
    (4) For an airship, a commercial pilot certificate with a lighter-than-air category rating and airship class rating.

(f) *Category II pilot authorization.* Except for a pilot conducting Category II operations under part 121 or part 135, a person may not:

    (1) Act as pilot in command of a civil aircraft during Category II operations unless that person—

        (i) Holds a current Category II pilot authorization for that category or class of aircraft, and the type of aircraft, if applicable; or

        (ii) In the case of a civil aircraft of foreign registry, is authorized by the country of registry to act as pilot in command of that aircraft in Category II operations.

    (2) Act as second in command of a civil aircraft during Category II operations unless that person—

        (i) Holds a valid pilot certificate with category and class ratings for that aircraft and a current instrument rating for that category aircraft;

        (ii) Holds an airline transport pilot certificate with category and class ratings for that aircraft; or

        (iii) In the case of a civil aircraft of foreign registry, is authorized by the country of registry to act as second in command of that aircraft during Category II operations.

(g) *Category III pilot authorization.* Except for a pilot conducting Category III operations under part 121 or part 135, a person may not:

    (1) Act as pilot in command of a civil aircraft during Category III operations unless that person—

        (i) Holds a current Category III pilot authorization for that category or class of aircraft, and the type of aircraft, if applicable; or

        (ii) In the case of a civil aircraft of foreign registry, is authorized by the country of registry to act as pilot in command of that aircraft in Category III operations.

    (2) Act as second in command of a civil aircraft during Category III operations unless that person—

        (i) Holds a valid pilot certificate with category and class ratings for that aircraft and a current instrument rating for that category aircraft;

        (ii) Holds an airline transport pilot certificate with category and class ratings for that aircraft; or

        (iii) In the case of a civil aircraft of foreign registry, is authorized by the country of registry to act as second in command of that aircraft during Category III operations.

(h) *Category A aircraft pilot authorization.* The Administrator may issue a certificate of authorization for a Category II or Category III operation to the pilot of a small aircraft that is a Category A aircraft, as identified in §97.3(b)(1) of this chapter if:

    (1) The Administrator determines that the Category II or Category III operation can be performed safely by that pilot under the terms of the certificate of authorization; and

    (2) The Category II or Category III operation does not involve the carriage of persons or property for compensation or hire.

(i) *Ground instructor certificate.*

    (1) Each person who holds a ground instructor certificate issued under this part or part 143 must have that certificate in that person's physical possession or immediately accessible when exercising the privileges of that certificate.

(2)   Except as provided in paragraph (i)(3) of this section, no person other than the holder of a ground instructor certificate issued under this part or part 143, with the appropriate rating on that certificate may—

    (i)   Give ground training required to qualify a person for solo flight and solo cross-country flight;

    (ii)   Endorse an applicant for a knowledge test required for a pilot, flight instructor, or ground instructor certificate or rating issued under this part; or

    (iii)   Endorse a pilot logbook to show ground training given.

(3)   A ground instructor certificate issued under this part is not necessary—

    (i)   Under paragraph (i)(2) of this section, if the training is given by the holder of a flight instructor certificate issued under this part in accordance with the privileges of that certificate;

    (ii)   Under paragraph (i)(2) of this section, if the training is given by the holder of a commercial pilot certificate with a lighter-than-air rating, provided the training is given in accordance with the privileges of the certificate in a lighter-than-air aircraft;

    (iii)   Under paragraph (i)(2) of this section, if the training is given by the holder of an airline transport pilot certificate with a rating appropriate to the aircraft in which the training is given, provided the training is given in accordance with the privileges of the certificate and conducted in accordance with an approved air carrier training program approved under part 121 or 135 of this chapter;

    (iv)   Under paragraph (i)(2) of this section, if the training is given by a person who is qualified in accordance with subpart C of part 142 of this chapter, provided the training is conducted in accordance with an approved part 142 training program; or

    (v)   Under paragraph (i)(2)(iii) of this section, if the training is given by an authorized flight instructor under §61.41 of this part.

(j)   *Age limitation for certain operations.*

(1)   *Age limitation.* Except as provided in paragraph (j)(3) of this section, no person who holds a pilot certificate issued under this part shall serve as a pilot on a civil airplane of U.S. registry in the following operations if the person has reached his or her 60th birthday—

    (i)   Scheduled international air services carrying passengers in turbojet-powered airplanes;

    (ii)   Scheduled international air services carrying passengers in airplanes having a passenger-seat configuration of more than nine passenger seats, excluding each crewmember seat;

    (iii)   Nonscheduled international air transportation for compensation or hire in airplanes having a passenger-seat configuration of more than 30 passenger seats, excluding each crewmember seat; or

    (iv)   Scheduled international air services, or nonscheduled international air transportation for compensation or hire, in airplanes having a payload capacity of more than 7,500 pounds.

(2)   *Definitions.*

    (i)   "International air service," as used in paragraph (j) of this section, means scheduled air service performed in airplanes for the public transport of passengers, mail, or cargo, in which the service passes through the airspace over the territory of more than one country.

    (ii)   "International air transportation," as used in paragraph (j) of this section, means air transportation performed in airplanes for the public transport of passengers, mail, or cargo, in which the service passes through the airspace over the territory of more than one country.

(3)   *Delayed pilot age limitation.* Until December 20, 1999, a person may serve as a pilot in operations covered by this paragraph after that person has reached his or her 60th birthday if, on March 20, 1997, that person was employed as a pilot in operations covered by this paragraph.

(k)   *Special purpose pilot authorization.* Any person that is required to hold a special purpose pilot authorization, issued in accordance with §61.77 of this part, must have that authorization and the person's foreign pilot license in that person's physical possession or have it readily accessible in the aircraft when exercising the privileges of that authorization.

(l)   *Inspection of certificate.* Each person who holds an airman certificate, medical certificate, authorization, or license required by this part must present it for inspection upon a request from:

(1)   The Administrator;

(2)   An authorized representative of the National Transportation Safety Board; or

(3)   Any Federal, State, or local law enforcement officer.

EXPLANATION

61.3(e): There is a difference between serving as pilot in command (PIC) and logging PIC time. A noninstrument-rated pilot who is taking instrument instruction in IFR conditions may log that as PIC time, but may not actually serve as the PIC. The other pilot must be the PIC, as that term is defined under §1.1 of FAR.

61.3(l): There are some common misconceptions about how to "present" a certificate if requested. An FAA inspector will not snatch the certificate away and claim that it was voluntarily surrendered. Absent an order issued by the Administrator through one of his attorneys under 49 U.S.C. §44709, the certificate can not be retained by an FAA inspector or other authorized person beyond the time necessary to copy the information on the certificate. By allowing the authorized person to take temporary possession of the certificate you are not giving up any of your rights.

Where an airman certificate is suspended or revoked, the suspension or revocation is effective as of the date stated in the order unless an appeal is filed. If no appeal is filed, the suspension is effective on the date noted and continues until such time as the airman certificate has been in the possession of the FAA for the period of suspension set forth in the order. In the case of a revocation, the one year period before another certificate will be issued does not start to run until the certificate is in the possession of the FAA. A certificate is considered to be in the possession of the FAA as of 12:01 AM on the date of the postmark of the envelope containing the certificate or the date the certificate is physically surrendered to the FAA.

If an airman certificate has been lost or misplaced, the FAA will accept a properly notarized affidavit to that effect in lieu of the surrender of the actual certificate. The affidavit does not replace the procedures set forth in 61.29.

Don't fly with an expired medical. Operation of an aircraft without a current appropriate medical certificate can result in a suspension of your airman certificate.

PREAMBLE

61.3(a): The FAA is persuaded by the public comments that contend the proposed section could create difficulties in certain situations. As provided for in §61.29, the FAA will permit a pilot to use a facsimile received from the FAA to satisfy the requirements of §61.3(a). In response to AOPA's comment regarding instructors who act as safety pilots not being required to have a medical certificate, the FAA notes that §91.109 specifies that a safety pilot is required to conduct simulated instrument flight, which makes the safety pilot a required crewmember. Therefore, an instructor in such situations would be required to hold a medical certificate. In addition, AOPA requests that safety pilots operating under §91.109 be excepted from holding medical certificates. The FAA has decided not to address this request here, as it is beyond the scope of this rulemaking.

61.3(c): The FAA has considered the public comments that indicate the proposed section could create difficulties for certificate holders who are awaiting the replacement of lost or destroyed certificates. Therefore, the phrase "or other documentation acceptable to the Administrator" has been added to the final rule. With regard to AOPA's concern over medical certificate requirements for pilots flying powered gliders, as explained in section IV, F, the FAA is not adopting the proposed separation of the glider category into powered and nonpowered classes.

61.3(d): Based on public comments that argue the proposed section could create difficulties in situations where flight instructor certificates are mailed in upon completion of a renewal course, the FAA has decided to add the phrase "or other documentation acceptable to the Administrator," which would permit a flight instructor to use a copy of a graduation certificate from a CFI refresher course and a copy of the completed application for renewal to meet this requirement. The FAA also agrees with ATA's comment, because the practice that ATA refers to is currently permitted, and the FAA did not intend to revoke it. Therefore, the FAA has changed the final rule to permit an air carrier conducting operations under part 121 or 135 with an approved training program to train another air carrier's pilots. Additionally, the FAA has added provisions stating that a flight instructor certificate is not necessary for certain training given by the holder of a commercial pilot certificate with a lighter-than-air rating, a person qualified in accordance with subpart C of part 142, a person as provided in §61.41 of this part, and the holder of a ground instructor certificate.

61.3(j): The FAA has treated the age 60 rule in the past as both an operational rule (§121.383(c)) and a certification rule (§61.77). Annex 1 places the limitation in its certification standards. Part 61 contains not only general aviation rules, but also rules that apply to airline transport pilots and commercial pilots. The FAA has decided to include the age limitation in §61.3(j) as a convenient location where affected persons may easily find it. (62 FR 16237 – 16238).

CROSS REFERENCE

61.29, Replacement Of Lost Or Destroyed Airman Or Medical Certificate Or Knowledge Test Report; 61.51, Pilot Logbooks; 61.75, Private Pilot Certificates Issued On Basis Of A Foreign Pilot License; Part 67, Medical Standards And Certification; 91.189, Category II And III Operations: General Operating Rules; 14 C.F.R. Part 375, Navigation Of Foreign Civil Aircraft Within The United States; 6010(a)(2) Of The Federal Aviation Act Of 1958, as amended (49 U.S.C. App. 1430(a)(2)).

ADVISORY CIRCULARS

AC 60-26B *Announcement of Availability: Flight Standards Service Airman Training and Testing* (2000)

AC 61-65D *Certification: Pilot and Flight Instructors* (1999).

CASES

In a case where an airman acted as pilot in command and as flight instructor while his certificates were suspended, the Board sustained a violation of §§61.3(a), 61.3(d) and 61.19(f). It further held that under the circumstances, revocation of the certificates was warranted. It did not accept the pilot's position that, since he was not present at the earlier hearing when the certificates were suspended, he was not aware of their suspension. The Board held that where he willfully keeps himself in the dark regarding the results of an action against him they will not accept the argument that he was unaware of suspension as a valid excuse for the subsequent violations. *Administrator v. Morse*, EA-3659 (1992).

Failure to have airman and medical certificates in his personal possession resulted in an air carrier pilot receiving a 7-day suspension which was upheld by the Board. *Administrator v. Munson*, EA-3663 (1992).

Pilot was found to be in violation of §61.3(a) and §61.3(c) for failing to have his airman and medical certificates in his personal possession. However, the Board held that his failure to have the certificates was due to the mistaken but reasonable assumption that they were in his luggage and held that no sanction was required. *Administrator v. Miller*, 5 NTSB 407, (1985). **Editor's Note:** The Board referred to this case in the *Munson* decision referred to above, but indicated that the "unique" facts of the *Miller* case were not present in the *Munson* case.

The Board has held that the mere fact that a pilot, who does not hold a license at the time of the flight, ascertains that some other person in the plane is a rated pilot does not make the other person the pilot in command. Rather, a pilot in command is the individual who has overall responsibility for, and control of, a flight. In this case the Board held that the extent to which the respondent, from the left seat, exercised direct control over significant aspects of the flights, i.e., start-ups, radios, checklists, take off, landing, and the flight controls during most of airborne portion of the flights stamped him as pilot in command. Respondent, whose certificate was under suspension, was found to be pilot in command and in violation of §61.3(a). *Administrator v. McCartney*, 4 NTSB 925 (1983).

Board affirmed a relatively short 10-day suspension for a violation of §61.3(c) on the basis that the pilot was not actually unqualified medically at time of accident, it happened only 8 days after the expiration of the certificate, and he obtained a new medical certificate shortly thereafter. *Administrator v. Meyering*, 5 NTSB 924 (1986).

In a case where a pilot undertook a flight when he had been without a medical certificate for two years, the Board sustained the Administrative Law Judge's finding that the operation of a passenger carrying flight under these circumstances was "reckless". *Administrator v. Thompson*, 4 NTSB 1112 (1983).

The Board sustained a 60 day suspension for a pilot conducting 18 flights during a 10-month period when he did not hold a medical certificate and could offer no factors which could justify any mitigation. *Administrator v. Levingston*, 4 NTSB 1704 (1984).

A pilot's argument that a signature in a logbook is not an endorsement, coming within the provisions of §61.3(d) merely because it is not coupled with some indication that a certain level of proficiency has been achieved or some statement attesting that a student has completed the prerequisites "required to qualify" him to progress to the next step in his training was held by the Board to be an untenable position, and the pilot was held to be in violation of §61.3(d). *Administrator v. Schlagenhauf*, EA-3611 (1992).

The Board found that a 6-month suspension of the airline transport pilot certificate of the respondent for giving flight instruction (other than that allowed by §61.167) was warranted because he knew he was not qualified for a flight instructor's certificate, having failed to pass the requalification standards. *Administrator v. Dickinson*, 5 NTSB 235 (1985).

The Board reinstated a 90-day suspension for violations of §§61.3(e) and 91.13(a). The non-IFR rated pilot filed an IFR flight plan and operated pursuant to that plan with three passengers on board. While never actually in clouds, he operated above a cloud cover and required the assistance of ATC in order to descend below it and make a safe landing. The Board further held the filing of an IFR flight plan without entry into IFR conditions is not to be considered a "technical" violation. *Administrator v. Ragland*, EA-3358 (1991).

A pilot who did not have his airman certificate in his personal possession was charged with violating §61.3(i) when he refused, without explanation, to present his certificate for inspection by a deputy sheriff. The Board sustained the violation. It was the Board's finding that an unexplained refusal to present the certificate establishes a breach of that obligation without regard to the respondent's ability to comply. *Administrator v. Sturman*, 4 NTSB 1752 (1984).

The Board affirmed a 180 suspension for a pilot who after mistakenly landing on an active taxiway was found to have not held a current medical certificate for seven years and had failed to meet the requirements for a biennial flight review for several years. *Administrator v. Grant*, EA-4827 (2000).

Believing that the 240 day suspension of his private pilot certification was not valid, a pilot chose to operate an aircraft in violation of the order. Because the pilot failed to file the proper appeal challenging the suspension before the incident, his suspension was changed to a revocation and upheld by the Board. *Administrator v. Mauch*, EA-4881 (2001).

In a case where the holder of third-class medical certificate who had not yet received his private pilot certificate was found to have operated an aircraft with a passenger on board in an air commerce operation, the Board determined that the defense of not being a U.S. citizen was not sufficient to avoid the revocation of his certificate. The respondent claimed that the Administrator could not take certificate action against him for this reason to which the Board replied that the certificate was issued by the Administrator, and that the respondent recognized the Administrator's authority in this matter by filing an appeal. *Administrator v. Lemrick*, EA-4914 (2001).

§61.3(a) explicitly provides that a pilot who holds a foreign pilot's license may operate a U.S.-registered aircraft in the country that issued the license. Therefore, a foreign airline transport pilot certificate may constitute an "airline transport pilot certificate" under §135.243(a)(1) because this regulation does not specifically require that the pilot must hold a U.S.-issued certificate. *FAA v. Evergreen Helicopters of Alaska, Inc.*, FAA Order No. 2000-12 (6-2-2000).

FAA CHIEF COUNSEL OPINIONS

When operating a U.S.-registered aircraft within a foreign country §§61.3(a) and 61.3(c) require only that the pilot hold a current pilot certificate issued by that country and evidence of current medical qualification for that certificate issued by that country. However, that pilot can not operate the aircraft outside that country. (1-28-85).

A CFI giving flight instruction need not possess a valid medical certificate if the instructor is not exercising pilot privileges as pilot in command or a required crewmember. It would be necessary for the CFI to act as pilot in command if the person being instructed was not qualified to so act, e.g., if that person had not had the flight review required by §61.57(a). Similarly, if the type certificate of the aircraft in which instruction is being given requires more than one pilot crewmember, the CFI would have to act as a required crewmember, unless another qualified pilot is in the aircraft. (10-5-78).

There is a difference between serving as PIC and logging PIC time. §61.3(e)(1) provides in part that no person may act as pilot-in-command of a civil aircraft under instrument flight rules, or in weather conditions less than VFR minimums unless that person holds an instrument rating. A noninstrument-rated pilot who is taking instrument instruction in IFR conditions may log that as PIC time, but may not actually serve as the PIC. The other pilot must be the PIC, as that term is defined under §1.1 of FAR. (12-9-92).

A person that holds a current and valid pilot certificate issued under 14 CFR part 61 may operate a foreign-registered aircraft within the United States. Please note that the person's pilot certificate must be current, which means that the pilot meets the flight review requirements of 61.56, the appropriate flight experience requirements of 61.57, and has a current medical certificate appropriate to the operation being conducted as required under 14 CFR section 61.23. (5-18-99).

A person who does not hold a flight instructor certificate issued under part 61 may give instruction and endorsements for a pilot certificate or rating issued under part 61, provided the instruction is given in a flight simulator or flight training device under an approved part 142 training program. (9-15-99)

61.4 QUALIFICATION AND APPROVAL OF FLIGHT SIMULATORS AND FLIGHT TRAINING DEVICES

(a) Except as specified in paragraph (b) or (c) of this section, each flight simulator and flight training device used for training, and for which an airman is to receive credit to satisfy any training, testing, or checking requirement under this chapter, must be qualified and approved by the Administrator for—
   (1) The training, testing, and checking for which it is used;
   (2) Each particular maneuver, procedure, or crewmember function performed; and
   (3) The representation of the specific category and class of aircraft, type of aircraft, particular variation within the type of aircraft, or set of aircraft for certain flight training devices.
(b) Any device used for flight training, testing, or checking that has been determined to be acceptable to or approved by the Administrator prior to August 1, 1996, which can be shown to function as originally designed, is considered to be a flight training device, provided it is used for the same purposes for which it was originally accepted or approved and only to the extent of such acceptance or approval.
(c) The Administrator may approve a device other than a flight simulator or flight training device for specific purposes.

EXPLANATION

Only those flight simulators and flight training devices used by persons to satisfy training, testing or checking functions, as may be necessary to meet FAA regulatory requirements, must be qualified by the FAA.

CROSS REFERENCE

61.1, Definitions.

ADVISORY CIRCULARS

AC 61-126 *Qualification and Approval of Personal Computer-Based Aviation Training Devices* (1997).

AC 61-65D *Certification: Pilots and Flight and Ground Instructors* (1999).

AC 120-40B *Airplane Simulator Qualifications* (1993).

AC 120-45A *Airplane Flight Training Device Qualification* (1992).

61.5 CERTIFICATES AND RATINGS ISSUED UNDER THIS PART

(a) The following certificates are issued under this part to an applicant who satisfactorily accomplishes the training and certification requirements for the certificate sought:
  (1) Pilot certificates—
    (i) Student pilot.
    (ii) Recreational pilot.
    (iii) Private pilot.
    (iv) Commercial pilot.
    (v) Airline transport pilot.
  (2) Flight instructor certificates.
  (3) Ground instructor certificates.
(b) The following ratings are placed on a pilot certificate (other than student pilot) when an applicant satisfactorily accomplishes the training and certification requirements for the rating sought:
  (1) Aircraft category ratings—
    (i) Airplane.
    (ii) Rotorcraft.
    (iii) Glider.
    (iv) Lighter-than-air.
    (v) Powered-lift.
  (2) Airplane class ratings—
    (i) Single-engine land.
    (ii) Multiengine land.
    (iii) Single-engine sea.
    (iv) Multiengine sea.
  (3) Rotorcraft class ratings—
    (i) Helicopter.
    (ii) Gyroplane.
  (4) Lighter-than-air class ratings—
    (i) Airship.
    (ii) Balloon.
  (5) Aircraft type ratings—
    (i) Large aircraft other than lighter-than-air.
    (ii) Turbojet-powered airplanes.
    (iii) Other aircraft type ratings specified by the Administrator through the aircraft type certification procedures.
  (6) Instrument ratings (on private and commercial pilot certificates only)—
    (i) Instrument—Airplane.
    (ii) Instrument—Helicopter.
    (iii) Instrument—Powered-lift.
(c) The following ratings are placed on a flight instructor certificate when an applicant satisfactorily accomplishes the training and certification requirements for the rating sought:
  (1) Aircraft category ratings—
    (i) Airplane.
    (ii) Rotorcraft.
    (iii) Glider.
    (iv) Powered-lift.
  (2) Airplane class ratings—
    (i) Single-engine.
    (ii) Multiengine.

       (3)   Rotorcraft class ratings—
           (i)   Helicopter.
           (ii)   Gyroplane.
       (4)   Instrument ratings—
           (i)   Instrument—Airplane.
           (ii)   Instrument—Helicopter.
           (iii)   Instrument—Powered-lift.

(d)   The following ratings are placed on a ground instructor certificate when an applicant satisfactorily accomplishes the training and certification requirements for the rating sought:
       (1)   Basic.
       (2)   Advanced.
       (3)   Instrument.

61.7 OBSOLETE CERTIFICATES AND RATINGS

(a)   The holder of a free-balloon pilot certificate issued before November 1, 1973, may not exercise the privileges of that certificate.

(b)   The holder of a pilot certificate that bears any of the following category ratings without an associated class rating may not exercise the privileges of that category rating:
       (1)   Rotorcraft.
       (2)   Lighter-than-air.
       (3)   Helicopter.
       (4)   Autogyro.

61.11 EXPIRED PILOT CERTIFICATES AND REISSUANCE

(a)   No person who holds an expired pilot certificate or rating may:
       (1)   Exercise the privileges of that pilot certificate or rating; or
       (2)   Act as pilot in command or as a required pilot flight crewmember of an aircraft of the same category and class specified on the expired pilot certificate or rating.

(b)   The following pilot certificates and ratings have expired and will not be reissued:
       (1)   An airline transport pilot certificate issued before May 1, 1949, or an airline transport pilot certificate that contains a horsepower limitation;
       (2)   A private or commercial pilot certificate issued before July 1, 1945; and
       (3)   A pilot certificate with a lighter-than-air or free-balloon rating issued before July 1, 1945.

(c)   A pilot certificate issued on the basis of a foreign pilot license will expire on the date the foreign license expires unless otherwise specified on the U.S. pilot certificate. A certificate without an expiration date is issued to the holder of the expired certificate only if that person meets the requirements of §61.75 for the issuance of a pilot certificate based on a foreign pilot license.

(d)   An airline transport pilot certificate issued after April 30, 1949, that bears an expiration date but does not contain a horsepower limitation may be reissued without an expiration date.

(e)   A private or commercial pilot certificate issued after June 30, 1945, that bears an expiration date may be reissued without an expiration date.

(f)   A pilot certificate with a lighter-than-air or free-balloon rating issued after June 30, 1945, that bears an expiration date may be reissued without an expiration date.

CROSS REFERENCE

61.75, Private Pilot Certificates Issued On Basis Of A Foreign Pilot License.

61.13 ISSUANCE OF AIRMAN CERTIFICATES, RATINGS, AND AUTHORIZATIONS

(a) *Application.*
  (1) An applicant for an airman certificate, rating, or authorization under this part must make that application on a form and in a manner acceptable to the Administrator.
  (2) An applicant who is neither a citizen of the United States nor a resident alien of the United States—
    (i) Must show evidence that the appropriate fee prescribed in appendix A to part 187 of this chapter has been paid when that person applies for a—
      (A) Student pilot certificate that is issued outside the United States; or
      (B) Knowledge test or practical test for a airman certificate or rating issued under this part, if the test is administered outside the United States.
    (ii) May be refused issuance of any U.S. airman certificate, rating, or authorization by the Administrator.
  (3) Except as provided in paragraph (a)(2)(ii) of this section, an applicant who satisfactorily accomplishes the training and certification requirements for the certificate, rating, or authorization sought is entitled to receive that airman certificate, rating, or authorization.
(b) *Limitations.*
  (1) An applicant who cannot comply with certain areas of operation required on the practical test because of physical limitations may be issued an airman certificate, rating, or authorization with the appropriate limitation placed on the applicant's airman certificate provided the—
    (i) Applicant is able to meet all other certification requirements for the airman certificate, rating, or authorization sought;
    (ii) Physical limitation has been recorded with the FAA on the applicant's medical records; and
    (iii) Administrator determines that the applicant's inability to perform the particular area of operation will not adversely affect safety.
  (2) A limitation placed on a person's airman certificate may be removed, provided that person demonstrates for an examiner satisfactory proficiency in the area of operation appropriate to the airman certificate, rating, or authorization sought.
(c) *Additional requirements for Category II and Category III pilot authorizations.*
  (1) A Category II or Category III pilot authorization is issued by a letter of authorization as a part of an applicant's instrument rating or airline transport pilot certificate.
  (2) Upon original issue the authorization contains the following limitations:
    (i) For Category II operations, the limitation is 1,600 feet RVR and a 150-foot decision height; and
    (ii) For Category III operations, each initial limitation is specified in the authorization document.

(3)   The limitations on a Category II or Category III pilot authorization may be removed as follows:
  (i)   In the case of Category II limitations, a limitation is removed when the holder shows that, since the beginning of the sixth preceding month, the holder has made three Category II ILS approaches with a 150-foot decision height to a landing under actual or simulated instrument conditions.
  (ii) In the case of Category III limitations, a limitation is removed as specified in the authorization.
(4)   To meet the experience requirement of paragraph (c)(3) of this section, and for the practical test required by this part for a Category II or a Category III pilot authorization, a flight simulator or flight training device may be used if it is approved by the Administrator for such use.

(d)   *Application during suspension or revocation.*
  (1)   Unless otherwise authorized by the Administrator, a person whose pilot, flight instructor, or ground instructor certificate has been suspended may not apply for any certificate, rating, or authorization during the period of suspension.
  (2)   Unless otherwise authorized by the Administrator, a person whose pilot, flight instructor, or ground instructor certificate has been revoked may not apply for any certificate, rating, or authorization for 1 year after the date of revocation.

EXPLANATION

Section 61.13(c) does not apply to Part 121 or Part 135 operators.

CROSS REFERENCES

61.3, Requirements for Certificates, Rating, and Authorization; 61.59, Falsification, Reproduction or Alteration of Applications, Certificates, Logbooks, Reports, or Records; 61.67, Category II Pilot Authorization Requirements; 61.68, Category III Pilot Authorization Requirements; 67.40, Special Issuance of Medical Certificates; Appendix A, Part 187; 18 U.S.C. 1001; 602 and 609 of The Federal Aviation Act of 1958, as amended (49 U.S.C. App. 1422 and 1429).

ADVISORY CIRCULARS

AC 61-65D *Certification: Pilots and Flight and Ground Instructors* (1999).

AC 61-126 *Qualification and Approval of Personal Computer-Based Aviation Training Devices* (1997).

AC 120-40B *Airplane Simulator Qualification* (1993).

AC 120-45A *Airplane Flight Training Device Qualification* (1992).

61.14 REFUSAL TO SUBMIT TO A DRUG OR ALCOHOL TEST

(a)   This section applies to an employee who performs a function listed in appendix I to part 121 or appendix J to part 121 of this chapter directly or by contract for a part 121 air carrier, a part 135 air carrier, or for a person conducting operations as specified in §135.1(a)(5) of this chapter.

(b)   Refusal by the holder of a certificate issued under this part to take a drug test required under the provisions of appendix I to part 121 or an alcohol test required under the provisions of appendix J to part 121 is grounds for:

    (1)   Denial of an application for any certificate, rating, or authorization issued under this part for a period of up to 1 year after the date of such refusal; and

    (2)   Suspension or revocation of any certificate, rating, or authorization issued under this part.

EXPLANATION

This regulation authorizes FAA action against any certificate or rating held by a pilot who refuses to take a test for a drug specified in Appendix I to Part 121, or an alcohol test specified in Appendix J to Part 121.

CROSS REFERENCES

1.1, definition of "Operator;" 61.15, Offenses Involving Alcohol or Drugs; 61.16 Refusal to Submit to an Alcohol Test or to Furnish Test Results; 91.17, Alcohol or Drugs; Appendix I, Part 121, Drug Testing Program; Appendix J, Part 121, Alcohol Misuse Prevention Program; 135.1(d), Applicability.

CASES

Refusal to submit to an alcohol test resulted in emergency revocation of pilot's certificate. *Administrator v. Pittman*, EA-4678 (1998).

A specimen collected as a part of a Department of Transportation random drug test from an airman holding an Airline Transport Pilot Certificate was found to have an unnaturally high level of nitrate, indicating that the specimen had been adulterated. As a result all of the pilot's airmen certificates were revoked. On appeal to the Board, it was revealed that the testing facility did not follow all of the steps in analyzing the specimen, and therefore, the results could not be reliably evaluated. As a result, the Board reversed the order of revocation. *Administrator v. Bosela*, EA-4928 (2001).

61.15   OFFENSES INVOLVING ALCOHOL OR DRUGS

(a)   A conviction for the violation of any Federal or State statute relating to the growing, processing, manufacture, sale, disposition, possession, transportation, or importation of narcotic drugs, marijuana, or depressant or stimulant drugs or substances is grounds for:

    (1)   Denial of an application for any certificate, rating, or authorization issued under this part for a period of up to 1 year after the date of final conviction; or

    (2)   Suspension or revocation of any certificate, rating, or authorization issued under this part.

(b)   Committing an act prohibited by §91.17(a) or §91.19(a) of this chapter is grounds for:

    (1)   Denial of an application for a certificate, rating, or authorization issued under this part for a period of up to 1 year after the date of that act; or

    (2)   Suspension or revocation of any certificate, rating, or authorization issued under this part.

(c) For the purposes of paragraphs (d), (e), and (f) of this section, a motor vehicle action means:
   (1) A conviction after November 29, 1990, for the violation of any Federal or State statute relating to the operation of a motor vehicle while intoxicated by alcohol or a drug, while impaired by alcohol or a drug, or while under the influence of alcohol or a drug;
   (2) The cancellation, suspension, or revocation of a license to operate a motor vehicle after November 29, 1990, for a cause related to the operation of a motor vehicle while intoxicated by alcohol or a drug, while impaired by alcohol or a drug, or while under the influence of alcohol or a drug; or
   (3) The denial after November 29, 1990, of an application for a license to operate a motor vehicle for a cause related to the operation of a motor vehicle while intoxicated by alcohol or a drug, while impaired by alcohol or a drug, or while under the influence of alcohol or a drug.
(d) Except for a motor vehicle action that results from the same incident or arises out of the same factual circumstances, a motor vehicle action occurring within 3 years of a previous motor vehicle action is grounds for:
   (1) Denial of an application for any certificate, rating, or authorization issued under this part for a period of up to 1 year after the date of the last motor vehicle action; or
   (2) Suspension or revocation of any certificate, rating, or authorization issued under this part.
(e) Each person holding a certificate issued under this part shall provide a written report of each motor vehicle action to the FAA, Civil Aviation Security Division (AMC-700), P.O. Box 25810, Oklahoma City, OK 73125, not later than 60 days after the motor vehicle action. The report must include:
   (1) The person's name, address, date of birth, and airman certificate number;
   (2) The type of violation that resulted in the conviction or the administrative action;
   (3) The date of the conviction or administrative action;
   (4) The State that holds the record of conviction or administrative action; and
   (5) A statement of whether the motor vehicle action resulted from the same incident or arose out of the same factual circumstances related to a previously reported motor vehicle action.
(f) Failure to comply with paragraph (e) of this section is grounds for:
   (1) Denial of an application for any certificate, rating, or authorization issued under this part for a period of up to 1 year after the date of the motor vehicle action; or
   (2) Suspension or revocation of any certificate, rating, or authorization issued under this part.

EXPLANATION

The FAA may take action under 61.15(a) and (b) even though there was no use of an airman certificate and/or an aircraft.

The reporting requirement of 61.15(c) is separate from, and in addition to, the requirement that a person fully and completely answer all questions related to traffic and other convictions on the application for a medical certificate.

Multiple "motor vehicle actions" resulting from the same driving incident or factual circumstances will be considered as one "motor vehicle action," but each action must be reported. When reporting each action, the airman should note that the action is part of a single set of factual circumstances and should reference any prior actions arising from the same facts.

If you are represented by an attorney in actions taken by local or state law enforcement as a result of a "motor vehicle action," always advise the attorney that you hold an airman certificate and refer the attorney to 61.15. This may affect the way the attorney proceeds on the local matter.

An airman may request to review and provide written comments on any information received by the FAA from the National Driver Register. (See 67.3).

Drug Convictions Which Do Not Involve Falsification (Cases Under Sections 61.15 and/or 609(c).
1.   For single conviction for simple possession, suspension of any pilot or flight instructor certificates for 120 days.
2.   For more than simple possession, except in extraordinary circumstances, revocation of any pilot or flight instructor certificates.
3.   For two or more convictions, except in extraordinary circumstances, revocation of any pilot or flight instructor certificates.

Recent National Transportation Safety Board (NTSB) decisions have held that although an airman may report a motor vehicle action on an airman medical application, this does not constitute the report to Civil Aviation Security that is required by FAR §61.15(e).

CROSS REFERENCES

63.12, Offenses Involving Alcohol or Drugs; 63.12(a), Refusal to Submit to an Alcohol Test or Furnish Results; 65.12, Offenses Involving Alcohol or Drugs; 67.7, Access to the National Driver Register; 67.107, Mental (1st Class - Talks About Substance Abuse) 67.207, Mental (2nd Class), and 67.307, Mental (3rd Class); 67.403, Applications, Certificates, Logbooks, Reports, and Records: Falsification, Reproduction, or Alteration - Incorrect Statements; 91.17(a), Alcohol or Drugs; 91.19(a), Carriage of Narcotic Drugs, Marijuana, and Depression or Stimulant Drugs or Substances; 609(c) of the Federal Aviation Act of 1958, as amended (49 U.S.C. App. 1429(c)), Transportation, Distribution, and Other Activities Related to Controlled Substances.

CASES

An agreement, whereby a respondent agreed to plead guilty to a drug related charge and cooperated with the U.S. Attorney, contained a provision that the U.S. Attorney would seek no further prosecutions of the respondent for any acts relating to the incident which gave rise to the charge, but made no reference to the airman certificates held by respondent. On the basis of the absence of any reference to the airman certificates the FAA was free to take certificate action on the basis of the incident. *Administrator v. Devrow*, EA-3590 (1992).

Whether respondent was involved in aircraft operations as part of the illegal activity is not material to whether he violated FAR §61.15(a). *Administrator v. Pinney*, EA-3545 (1992).

The Board did not allow respondent credit for the time (10 months) his airman certificate was in the possession of the state court as a condition of bond being allowed. The running of the sanction period, whether it be revocation or suspension, does not begin until the affected certificate is actually surrendered to the Administrator. *Administrator v. Pope*, 5 NTSB 538 (1985).

The Board found no merit to respondent's contention that the Administrator lacked authority to revoke his airman certificate because the revocation order was issued more than a year after his drug conviction. *Administrator v. Anderson*, 5 NTSB 564 (1985).

In a case where a pilot knowingly flew drugs, §609(c) of the Federal Aviation Act of 1958, as amended (49 U.S.C. App. 1429(c)) does not authorize a sanction less than revocation and limits the Board's review authority to affirming or reversing the Administrator's order. *Administrator v. Rawlins*, 5 NTSB 2036 (1987).

The severity of a drug offense may justify revocation of a pilot certificate, even if the pilot did not use an aircraft himself in the operation. The revocation of the pilot certificate of the leader of a very large drug-trafficking operation was warranted by the severity of his crimes. *Administrator v. Kolek*, 5 NTSB 1437 (1986), affirmed in *Kolek v. Engen*, 869 F.2d 1281 (1989) and cited by the NTSB in *Administrator v. Correa*, EA-3815 (1993); for related cases see Administrator v. Johnson, EA-3929 (1993) and *Administrator v. Serra*, EA-3938 (1993).

While revocation may be appropriate sanction for a violation of 61.15 where an aircraft is not involved, summary judgment is not an appropriate resolution of the case. Circumstances surrounding the case must be evaluated to determine if the violation is so egregious as to demonstrate a lack of qualification to hold an airman certificate. *Administrator v. Butchkosky*, EA-4229 (1994).

A pilot's airman certificate was revoked after he was convicted for conspiracy to knowingly and intentionally possess marijuana aboard a U.S. aircraft with intent to distribute it. The fact that the revocation was based on a criminal conviction did not result in double jeopardy, because the double jeopardy clause only prohibits punishing twice criminally for the same offense and the certificate action was civil in nature. *Administrator v. Davis*, EA-3740 (1992).

A pilot called his local Flight Standards District Office (FSDO) for advice within a few days after his arrest for DWI. The FSDO simply told the pilot to report the conviction on his next medical application, without mentioning the notice requirement of §61.15. The Board ruled that a suspension of the pilot's certificate was not warranted by the technical violation. *Administrator v. Smith*, EA-4088 (1994).

Under Federal law, anyone convicted of trafficking or distributing drugs will have their certificate revoked. *Administrator v. Sage*, EA-4016 (1993).

The Board granted the appeal of the Administrator to increase a pilot's six month suspension to a revocation of all airman certificates. The pilot involved in three motor vehicle actions and failed to report two of them. The Board felt that this demonstrated an attitude of noncompliance, which in and of itself is basis for revocation. *Administrator v. Bennett*, EA-4762 (1999).

FAA CHIEF COUNSEL OPINIONS

Where there is a suspension of a driver's license for failure to submit to a chemical test, when an airman is arrested for driving while under the influence of alcohol and/or drug of abuse, and the airman subsequently pleads guilty to "reckless operation" and has his license suspended for refusal to take the test, the airman does not have to report the "reckless operation" conviction under 61.15(c)(1), but must, under 61.15(c)(2) report the license suspension. (6-5-91).

If an airman refused to submit to the request for an alcohol test and his or her driver's license is suspended for such refusal, even if the airman is subsequently acquitted on the underlying criminal charge for alcohol- or drug-related operation of a motor vehicle, the administrative license suspension or revocation would be considered a "motor vehicle action" and must be reported under 61.15. (11-21-90).

61.16 REFUSAL TO SUBMIT TO AN ALCOHOL TEST OR TO FURNISH TEST RESULTS

A refusal to submit to a test to indicate the percentage by weight of alcohol in the blood, when requested by a law enforcement officer in accordance with §91.17(c) of this chapter, or a refusal to furnish or authorize the release of the test results requested by the Administrator in accordance with §91.17(c) or (d) of this chapter, is grounds for:

(a) Denial of an application for any certificate, rating, or authorization issued under this part for a period of up to 1 year after the date of that refusal; or

(b) Suspension or revocation of any certificate, rating, or authorization issued under this part.

EXPLANATION

This rule merely requires the crewmember to cooperate with an otherwise lawful investigation by a law enforcement officer. The conducting or obtaining of the test is based on local or state authority, not federal.

While the regulation does not mandate denial of an application for certificate or rating for one year or the revocation of a certificate held, the FAA anticipates that, generally, it will order revocation of a certificate held or denial of an application for a certificate or rating up to 1 year. The certificate holder or applicant are provided with procedural safeguards under §§602, 609 and 901 of the Federal Aviation Act of 1958 as amended (49 U.S.C. App. 1422, 1429 and 1471).

Whether a law enforcement officer must give the Miranda warning will be a matter of state or local law, not an FAA matter, since such warnings are not required in connection with FAA civil administrative proceedings.

The request must be made by a law enforcement officer who is authorized under state or local law governing the same or substantially similar conduct as is prohibited by the FAA alcohol rules. The officer will not be enforcing FAA rules, however, the test results may be used by the FAA in an enforcement proceeding against a crewmember. There must be a reasonable basis to believe that a crewmember may have unlawfully used alcohol in connection with his or her duties.

CROSS REFERENCES

61.15, Offenses Involving Alcohol or Drugs; 63.12, Offenses Involving Alcohol or Drugs; 63.12(a), Refusal to Submit to an Alcohol Test or Furnish Results; 65.12, Offenses Involving Alcohol or Drugs; 67.7, Access to the National Driver Register; 67.107, Mental (1st Class - Talks About Substance Abuse) 67.207, Mental (2nd Class), and 67.307, Mental (3rd Class); 67.403, Applications, Certificates, Logbooks, Reports, and Records: Falsification, Reproduction, or Alteration; Incorrect Statements; 91.17(a), Alcohol or Drugs; 91.19(a), Carriage of Narcotic Drugs, Marijuana, and Depression or Stimulant Drugs or Substances; 609(c) of the Federal Aviation Act of 1958, as amended (49 U.S.C. App. 1429(c)), Transportation, Distribution, and Other Activities Related to Controlled Substances.

61.17 TEMPORARY CERTIFICATE

(a) A temporary pilot, flight instructor, or ground instructor certificate or rating is issued for up to 120 days, at which time a permanent certificate will be issued to a person whom the Administrator finds qualified under this part.

(b) A temporary pilot, flight instructor, or ground instructor certificate or rating expires:
    (1) On the expiration date shown on the certificate;
    (2) Upon receipt of the permanent certificate; or
    (3) Upon receipt of a notice that the certificate or rating sought is denied or revoked.

EXPLANATION

An airman should be aware of the expiration date of any temporary certificate or rating. If for some reason the FAA does not issue a permanent certificate or rating or deny the issuance of the certificate or rating prior to the expiration date of the temporary certificate or rating, the FAA does not automatically extend the time the temporary certificate or rating. The airman must obtain another temporary certificate or rating or the renewal of the existing one.

CROSS REFERENCES

61.3, Requirement for Certificates, Ratings and Authorizations.

ADVISORY CIRCULARS

AC 61-65D *Certification: Pilots and Flight and Ground Instructors* (1999).

61.19 DURATION OF PILOT AND INSTRUCTOR CERTIFICATES

(a) *General.* The holder of a certificate with an expiration date may not, after that date, exercise the privileges of that certificate.

(b) *Student pilot certificate.* A student pilot certificate expires 24 calendar months from the month in which it is issued.

(c) *Other pilot certificates.* A pilot certificate (other than a student pilot certificate) issued under this part is issued without a specific expiration date. The holder of a pilot certificate issued on the basis of a foreign pilot license may exercise the privileges of that certificate only while that person's foreign pilot license is effective.

(d) *Flight instructor certificate.* A flight instructor certificate:
    (1) Is effective only while the holder has a current pilot certificate; and
    (2) Except as specified in §61.197(b) of this part, expires 24 calendar months from the month in which it was issued or renewed.

(e) *Ground instructor certificate.* A ground instructor certificate issued under this part is issued without a specific expiration date.

(f) *Surrender, suspension, or revocation.* Any certificate issued under this part ceases to be effective if it is surrendered, suspended, or revoked.

(g) *Return of certificates.* The holder of any certificate issued under this part that has been suspended or revoked must return that certificate to the FAA when requested to do so by the Administrator.

EXPLANATION

Failure to surrender a suspended or revoked certificate after being requested to do so by the FAA can subject the concerned airman to a civil penalty not to exceed $1,000 for every day until the certificate is surrendered to the FAA.

In the event an airman certificate is lost or destroyed the submission of a properly executed and notarized affidavit attesting to the loss or destruction will meet the requirements of 61.19(g) when the FAA demands the return of a certificate.

CROSS REFERENCES

61.3(a), Requirement for Certificates, Ratings, and Authorizations; 61.29, Replacement of Lost or Destroyed Airman or Medial Certificate or Knowledge Test Report; Part 13, Investigative and Enforcement Procedures; 901, Federal Aviation Act of 1958 as amended (40 U.S.C. App. 1471).

ADVISORY CIRCULARS

AC 61-65D *Certification: Pilots and Flight and Ground Instructors* (1999).

CASES

Failure of a respondent to find out the results of a NTSB hearing, which he did not attend, at which his airman certificate was suspended, did not excuse him for flying when his certificate was under suspension and the Board upheld a revocation of his airman certificate. *Administrator v. Morse*, EA-3659 (1992).

The following was included in the Board's decision: "For the purposes of this order, respondent must physically surrender his certificate to an appropriate representative of the Federal Aviation Administration, pursuant to 61.19(f), FAR." Also, the Administrator's order, which was affirmed by the Board, directed the respondent to surrender the certificate to "the Regional Counsel for the Great Lakes Region of the Federal Aviation Administrator." There was no need for any further "request" from the FAA. *Administrator v. Garber*, 4 NTSB 75, 77 (1983).

FAA CHIEF COUNSEL OPINIONS

If the regulation states "24 calendar months after or from," you have until the end of the 24th month after the month in which the time began to run. For example, if you obtain a student pilot certificate on January 2, 2000, it expires on January 31, 2002. (2-24-00).

61.21 DURATION OF A CATEGORY II AND A CATEGORY III PILOT AUTHORIZATION (FOR OTHER THAN PART 121 AND PART 135 USE)

(a) A Category II pilot authorization or a Category III pilot authorization expires at the end of the sixth calendar month after the month in which it was issued or renewed.

(b) Upon passing a practical test for a Category II or Category III pilot authorization, the authorization may be renewed for each type of aircraft for which the authorization is held.

(c) A Category II or Category III pilot authorization for a specific type aircraft for which an authorization is held will not be renewed beyond 12 calendar months from the month the practical test was accomplished in that type aircraft.

(d) If the holder of a Category II or Category III pilot authorization passes the practical test for a renewal in the month before the authorization expires, the holder is considered to have passed it during the month the authorization expired.

CROSS REFERENCES

61.3, Requirement for Certificates, Ratings, and Authorizations; 61.67, Category II Pilot Authorization Requirements; 61.68, Category III Pilot Authorization Requirements.

ADVISORY CIRCULARS

AC 91-16 *Category II Operations - General Aviation Airplanes* (1967).

61.23 MEDICAL CERTIFICATES: REQUIREMENT AND DURATION

(a) *Operations requiring a medical certificate.* Except as provided in paragraph (b) of this section, a person:
    (1) Must hold a first-class medical certificate when exercising the privileges of an airline transport pilot certificate;
    (2) Must hold at least a second-class medical certificate when exercising the privileges of a commercial pilot certificate; or
    (3) Must hold at least a third-class medical certificate—
        (i) When exercising the privileges of a private pilot certificate;
        (ii) When exercising the privileges of a recreational pilot certificate;
        (iii) Except as specified in paragraph (b)(3) of this section, when exercising the privileges of a student pilot certificate;
        (iv) When exercising the privileges of a flight instructor certificate, except for a flight instructor certificate with a glider category rating, if the person is acting as the pilot in command or is serving as a required pilot flight crewmember; or
        (v) Except for a glider category rating or a balloon class rating, prior to taking a practical test that is performed in an aircraft for a certificate or rating at the recreational, private, commercial, or airline transport pilot certificate level.

(b) *Operations not requiring a medical certificate.* A person is not required to hold a medical certificate:
    (1) When exercising the privileges of a pilot certificate with a glider category rating;
    (2) When exercising the privileges of a pilot certificate with a balloon class rating;

(3)   When exercising the privileges of a student pilot certificate while seeking a pilot certificate with a glider category rating or balloon class rating;

(4)   When exercising the privileges of a flight instructor certificate with a glider category rating;

(5)   When exercising the privileges of a flight instructor certificate if the person is not acting as pilot in command or serving as a required pilot flight crewmember;

(6)   When exercising the privileges of a ground instructor certificate;

(7)   When serving as an examiner or check airman during the administration of a test or check for a certificate, rating, or authorization conducted in a flight simulator or flight training device; or

(8)   When taking a test or check for a certificate, rating, or authorization conducted in a flight simulator or flight training device.

(c)   *Duration of a medical certificate.*

(1)   A first-class medical certificate expires at the end of the last day of—

(i)   The sixth month after the month of the date of examination shown on the certificate for operations requiring an airline transport pilot certificate;

(ii)   The 12th month after the month of the date of examination shown on the certificate for operations requiring a commercial pilot certificate or an air traffic control tower operator certificate; and

(iii) The period specified in paragraph (c)(3) of this section for operations requiring a recreational pilot certificate, a private pilot certificate, a flight instructor certificate (when acting as pilot in command or a required pilot flight crewmember in operations other than glider or balloon), or a student pilot certificate.

(2)   A second-class medical certificate expires at the end of the last day of—

(i)   The 12th month after the month of the date of examination shown on the certificate for operations requiring a commercial pilot certificate or an air traffic control tower operator certificate; and

(ii)   The period specified in paragraph (c)(3) of this section for operations requiring a recreational pilot certificate, a private pilot certificate, a flight instructor certificate (when acting as pilot in command or a required pilot flight crewmember in operations other than glider or balloon), or a student pilot certificate.

(3)   A third-class medical certificate for operations requiring a recreational pilot certificate, a private pilot certificate, a flight instructor certificate (when acting as pilot in command or a required pilot flight crewmember in operations other than glider or balloon), or a student pilot certificate issued—

(i)   Before September 16, 1996, expires at the end of the 24th month after the month of the date of examination shown on the certificate; or

(ii)   On or after September 16, 1996, expires at the end of:

(A)   The 36th month after the month of the date of the examination shown on the certificate if the person has not reached his or her 40th birthday on or before the date of examination; or

(B)   The 24th month after the month of the date of the examination shown on the certificate if the person has reached his or her 40th birthday on or before the date of the examination.

EXPLANATION

For flight operations requiring an airline transport pilot certificate, you must hold at least a first class medical certificate.

For flight operations requiring a commercial pilot certificate, you must hold at least a second class medical certificate.

Except as provided in the next paragraph, a third class medical certificate is required—
    a)   for recreational, private, or student pilot flight operations;
    b)   when performing the duties of a flight instructor; or
    c)   prior to taking a practical test for a recreation, private, commercial, or airline transport pilot certificate. However, to perform the privileges of the specific rating, you must have the appropriate medical certificate.

You do not need to hold a medical certificate when exercising the privileges of a—
    a)   student pilot certificate if you are seeking pilot certificate with a glider category or balloon class rating;
    b)   pilot certificate with a glider category rating or balloon class rating;
    c)   flight instructor certificate with a glider category rating; or
    d)   flight instructor certificate where the instructor is not the pilot in command or serving as a required pilot flight crewmember.

PREAMBLE

In the final rule, the title was changed to "Medical Certificates: Requirement and Duration," and the section was further reformatted and edited. The FAA reviewed AOPA's concerns regarding the ability of flight instructors to act as safety pilots without medical certificates. The FAA has determined that safety requires all required crewmembers, including safety pilots, to possess valid medical certificates.

The FAA agrees with the concerns of GAMA, NATA, HAI, and AOPA regarding problems in the proposed language for the duration of medical certificates and has modified the final rule to restore the provisions of the existing rule. The FAA has also retained its proposal to require that an applicant for a private, commercial, or ATP certificate possess only a third-class medical certificate; but after further review, has determined that the medical certificate requirements that were proposed to be contained in the eligibility requirements listed under each pilot certificate subpart should be placed in §61.23. The purpose of this change is to reflect the FAA's position that a medical certificate applies to the type of pilot operation being conducted.

Most commenters support the FAA's proposal, which provides that applicants would only need a third-class medical certificate to be eligible to apply for a private, commercial, airline transport pilot, or flight instructor certificate. This change also was made in §61.39, but is discussed here. These commenters feel that the proposal would encourage pilots to seek advanced training, even if they did not intend to exercise the privileges of the higher certificate. AOPA, GAMA, and NAFI support permitting applicants for a commercial or ATP certificate to hold only a third-class medical certificate. Like the other commenters, these associations felt that the proposal would encourage training toward advanced certificates and would improve safety.

With respect to the holding of medical certificates by a flight instructor, the FAA has determined that the compensation a certificated flight instructor receives for flight instruction is not compensation for piloting the aircraft, but rather is compensation for the instruction. A certificated flight instructor who is acting as pilot in command or as a required flight crewmember and is receiving compensation for his or her flight instruction is only exercising the privileges of a private pilot. A certificated flight instructor who is acting as pilot in command or as a required flight crewmember and receiving compensation for his or her flight instruction is not carrying passengers or property for compensation or hire, nor is he or she, for compensation or hire, acting as pilot in command of an aircraft. Therefore, because a certificated flight instructor who is acting as pilot in command or as a required flight crewmember and is receiving compensation for his or her flight instruction is exercising the privileges of a private pilot, he or she only needs to hold a third-class medical certificate. In this same regard, the FAA has determined that a certificated flight instructor on board an aircraft for the purpose of providing flight instruction, who does not act as pilot in command or function as a required flight crewmember, is not performing or exercising pilot privileges that would require him or her to possess a valid medical certificate under the FARs.

The changes implemented by the FAA still require a person who is involved in pilot operations requiring an ATP certificate (i.e., part 121 air carrier operations) to hold a first-class medical certificate. In addition, a person who is involved in pilot operations requiring a commercial pilot certificate (i.e., part 135 on-demand operators) will be required to hold a second-class medical certificate.

As a result of a legal interpretation that permits applicants and check airmen, under parts 121 and 135, to perform the practical tests for a type rating in a flight simulator without either person holding a medical certificate, the FAA has modified §61.23 to permit applicants, examiners, and check airmen to perform a practical test or check without being required to hold a medical certificate, provided that the test or check is only being conducted in a flight simulator or a flight training device. (62 FR 16242).

CROSS REFERENCES

61.3, Requirement for Certificates, Ratings, and Authorizations; Part 67, Medical Standards and Certification; 61.39(a)(4), Prerequisites for Practical Tests.

FAA CHIEF COUNSEL OPINIONS

A flight instructor who does not hold a current medical certificate, and is not acting as a PIC or as a required flight crewmember, may give creditable flight instruction to a pilot who is fully qualified and currently rated to act as PIC for the aircraft. A nonmedically current certificated flight instructor is not permitted to give flight instruction to a student pilot; to a pilot whose BFR has lapsed, or who is otherwise not qualified, rated, and current in the aircraft; to a noninstrument-rated pilot in IMC or on an instrument flight plan; or to a pilot practicing instrument flight under a hood (which requires the presence of a safety pilot). (9-13-89), (10-5-78), (5-5-77). This FAA position is also stated in FAA Order No. 8700.1, Vol. II, Chapter 11.

An ASI, when acting as a required pilot flight crewmember, whether he or she is providing pilot examinations or evaluations, or is receiving training as part of his or her job, is exercising the privileges of a commercial pilot certificate and needs to hold at least a second-class medical certificate. (4-26-99).

61.25 CHANGE OF NAME

(a) An application to change the name on a certificate issued under this part must be accompanied by the applicant's:
   (1) Current airman certificate; and
   (2) A copy of the marriage license, court order, or other document verifying the name change.
(b) The documents in paragraph (a) of this section will be returned to the applicant after inspection.

EXPLANATION

If the name change is not related to marriage or formal court action, it may be necessary for the airman to cite the specific state law that authorizes such change and to show that other licenses, etc. have been changed, i.e., driver's license, social security account.

61.27 VOLUNTARY SURRENDER OR EXCHANGE OF CERTIFICATE

(a) The holder of a certificate issued under this part may voluntarily surrender it for:
   (1) Cancellation;
   (2) Issuance of a lower grade certificate; or
   (3) Another certificate with specific ratings deleted.
(b) Any request made under paragraph (a) of this section must include the following signed statement or its equivalent: "This request is made for my own reasons, with full knowledge that my (insert name of certificate or rating, as appropriate) may not be reissued to me unless I again pass the tests prescribed for its issuance."

EXPLANATION

If an airman receives notice from the FAA that, pursuant to 49 U.S.C. §44709, the airman is to appear for a reexamination relating to a specific rating and the airman does not feel prepared nor will the airman be prepared for some time, the provisions of this section can be utilized. However, remember the reexamination may only relate to one phase related to the rating while reapplication at a later date will require passage of all requirements set forth in Part 61 related to the issuance of the rating.

CASES

After the FAA order of revocation had been issued and the respondent had appealed to the NTSB, but before the hearing set by the Administrative Law Judge, the respondent surrendered his certificate to the FAA for cancellation pursuant to 61.27. The respondent then filed a motion to dismiss the complaint as moot since the certificate which was the subject of the order was no longer in existence. The Board held that the surrender and cancellation of the certificate did not affect the validity of the order of revocation and that the Board would retain jurisdiction. If the respondent's motion were granted, it would mean (in theory at least) that a pilot could violate the Federal Aviation Regulations without ever acquiring a violation history. *Administrator v. Christopherson*, 5 NTSB 205 (1985).

61.29 REPLACEMENT OF A LOST OR DESTROYED AIRMAN OR MEDICAL CERTIFICATE OR KNOWLEDGE TEST REPORT

(a)   A request for the replacement of a lost or destroyed airman certificate issued under this part must be made by letter to the Department of Transportation, FAA, Airman Certification Branch, P.O. Box 25082, Oklahoma City, OK 73125, and must be accompanied by a check or money order for the appropriate fee payable to the FAA.

(b)   A request for the replacement of a lost or destroyed medical certificate must be made by letter to the Department of Transportation, FAA, Aeromedical Certification Branch, P.O. Box 25082, Oklahoma City, OK 73125, and must be accompanied by a check or money order for the appropriate fee payable to the FAA.

(c)   A request for the replacement of a lost or destroyed knowledge test report must be made by letter to the Department of Transportation, FAA, Airman Certification Branch, P.O. Box 25082, Oklahoma City, OK 73125, and must be accompanied by a check or money order for the appropriate fee payable to the FAA.

(d)   The letter requesting replacement of a lost or destroyed airman certificate, medical certificate, or knowledge test report must state:

(1)   The namc of tho person;

(2)   The permanent mailing address (including ZIP code), or if the permanent mailing address includes a post office box number, then the person's current residential address;

(3)   The social security number;

(4)   The date and place of birth of the certificate holder; and

(5)   Any available information regarding the—

(i)   Grade, number, and date of issuance of the certificate, and the ratings, if applicable;

(ii)   Date of the medical examination, if applicable; and

(iii)   Date the knowledge test was taken, if applicable.

(e)   A person who has lost an airman certificate, medical certificate, or knowledge test report may obtain a facsimile from the FAA Aeromedical Certification Branch or the Airman Certification Branch, as appropriate, confirming that it was issued and the:

(1)   Facsimile may be carried as an airman certificate, medical certificate, or knowledge test report, as appropriate, for up to 60 days pending the person's receipt of a duplicate under paragraph (a), (b), or (c) of this section, unless the person has been notified that the certificate has been suspended or revoked.

(2)   Request for such a facsimile must include the date on which a duplicate certificate or knowledge test report was previously requested.

EXPLANATION

In a situation where time is critical, an airman should contact the nearest Flight Standards District Office or Flight Standards Division Office in the Regional Office for assistance. They may be able to assist the airman, after verifying all necessary information, by the issuance of a temporary certificate. This may require that the airman appear in person at the Flight Standards office.

To receive a temporary airman certificate by fax, call (405) 954-3261 (AFS-760).
To receive a temporary medical certificate by fax, call (405) 954-4821.
Prepaid telegram service is no longer available from Western Union.

PREAMBLE

61.29(a), (b), and (c): The cost for replacement of a lost or destroyed airman certificate, medical certificate, or knowledge test report is contained in 14 CFR part 187. In response to commenters' concerns, the FAA notes that any changes to part 187 would be subject to public comment. The FAA will accept a facsimile of the letter requesting replacement of these certificates or reports in urgent cases. (62 FR 16243).

61.31 TYPE RATING REQUIREMENTS, ADDITIONAL TRAINING, AND AUTHORIZATION REQUIREMENTS

(a) *Type ratings required.* A person who acts as a pilot in command of any of the following aircraft must hold a type rating for that aircraft:
   (1) Large aircraft (except lighter-than-air).
   (2) Turbojet-powered airplanes.
   (3) Other aircraft specified by the Administrator through aircraft type certificate procedures.
(b) *Authorization in lieu of a type rating.* A person may be authorized to operate without a type rating for up to 60 days an aircraft requiring a type rating, provided—
   (1) The Administrator has authorized the flight or series of flights;
   (2) The Administrator has determined that an equivalent level of safety can be achieved through the operating limitations on the authorization;
   (3) The person shows that compliance with paragraph (a) of this section is impracticable for the flight or series of flights; and
   (4) The flight—
      (i) Involves only a ferry flight, training flight, test flight, or practical test for a pilot certificate or rating;
      (ii) Is within the United States;
      (iii) Does not involve operations for compensation or hire unless the compensation or hire involves payment for the use of the aircraft for training or taking a practical test; and
      (iv) Involves only the carriage of flight crewmembers considered essential for the flight.
   (5) If the flight or series of flights cannot be accomplished within the time limit of the authorization, the Administrator may authorize an additional period of up to 60 days to accomplish the flight or series of flights.
(c) *Aircraft category, class, and type ratings: Limitations on the carriage of persons, or operating for compensation or hire.* Unless a person holds a category, class, and type rating (if a class and type rating is required) that applies to the aircraft, that person may not act as pilot in command of an aircraft that is carrying another person, or is operated for compensation or hire. That person also may not act as pilot in command of that aircraft for compensation or hire.
(d) *Aircraft category, class, and type ratings: Limitations on operating an aircraft as the pilot in command.* To serve as the pilot in command of an aircraft, a person must—
   (1) Hold the appropriate category, class, and type rating (if a class rating and type rating are required) for the aircraft to be flown;
   (2) Be receiving training for the purpose of obtaining an additional pilot certificate and rating that are appropriate to that aircraft, and be under the supervision of an authorized instructor; or
   (3) Have received training required by this part that is appropriate to the aircraft category, class, and type rating (if a class or type rating is required) for the aircraft to be flown, and have received the required endorsements from an instructor who is authorized to provide the required endorsements for solo flight in that aircraft.

(e)   *Additional training required for operating complex airplanes.*
  (1)   Except as provided in paragraph (e)(2) of this section, no person may act as pilot in command of a complex airplane (an airplane that has a retractable landing gear, flaps, and a controllable pitch propeller; or, in the case of a seaplane, flaps and a controllable pitch propeller), unless the person has—
        (i)   Received and logged ground and flight training from an authorized instructor in a complex airplane, or in a flight simulator or flight training device that is representative of a complex airplane, and has been found proficient in the operation and systems of the airplane; and
        (ii)   Received a one-time endorsement in the pilot's logbook from an authorized instructor who certifies the person is proficient to operate a complex airplane.
  (2)   The training and endorsement required by paragraph (e)(1) of this section is not required if the person has logged flight time as pilot in command of a complex airplane, or in a flight simulator or flight training device that is representative of a complex airplane prior to August 4, 1997.

(f)   *Additional training required for operating high-performance airplanes.*
  (1)   Except as provided in paragraph (f)(2) of this section, no person may act as pilot in command of a high-performance airplane (an airplane with an engine of more than 200 horsepower), unless the person has—
        (i)   Received and logged ground and flight training from an authorized instructor in a high-performance airplane, or in a flight simulator or flight training device that is representative of a high-performance airplane, and has been found proficient in the operation and systems of the airplane; and
        (ii)   Received a one-time endorsement in the pilot's logbook from an authorized instructor who certifies the person is proficient to operate a high-performance airplane.
  (2)   The training and endorsement required by paragraph (f)(1) of this section is not required if the person has logged flight time as pilot in command of a high-performance airplane, or in a flight simulator or flight training device that is representative of a high-performance airplane prior to August 4, 1997.

(g)   *Additional training required for operating pressurized aircraft capable of operating at high altitudes.*
  (1)   Except as provided in paragraph (g)(3) of this section, no person may act as pilot in command of a pressurized aircraft (an aircraft that has a service ceiling or maximum operating altitude, whichever is lower, above 25,000 feet MSL), unless that person has received and logged ground training from an authorized instructor and obtained an endorsement in the person's logbook or training record from an authorized instructor who certifies the person has satisfactorily accomplished the ground training. The ground training must include at least the following subjects:
        (i)   High-altitude aerodynamics and meteorology;
        (ii)   Respiration;
        (iii) Effects, symptoms, and causes of hypoxia and any other high-altitude sickness;
        (iv)   Duration of consciousness without supplemental oxygen;
        (v)   Effects of prolonged usage of supplemental oxygen;
        (vi)   Causes and effects of gas expansion and gas bubble formation;
        (vii) Preventive measures for eliminating gas expansion, gas bubble formation, and high-altitude sickness;
        (viii) Physical phenomena and incidents of decompression; and
        (ix)   Any other physiological aspects of high-altitude flight.

(2) Except as provided in paragraph (g)(3) of this section, no person may act as pilot in command of a pressurized aircraft unless that person has received and logged training from an authorized instructor in a pressurized aircraft, or in a flight simulator or flight training device that is representative of a pressurized aircraft, and obtained an endorsement in the person's logbook or training record from an authorized instructor who found the person proficient in the operation of a pressurized aircraft. The flight training must include at least the following subjects:
(i)   Normal cruise flight operations while operating above 25,000 feet MSL;
(ii) Proper emergency procedures for simulated rapid decompression without actually depressurizing the aircraft; and
(iii) Emergency descent procedures.
(3) The training and endorsement required by paragraphs (g)(1) and (g)(2) of this section are not required if that person can document satisfactory accomplishment of any of the following in a pressurized aircraft, or in a flight simulator or flight training device that is representative of a pressurized aircraft:
(i)   Serving as pilot in command before April 15, 1991;
(ii) Completing a pilot proficiency check for a pilot certificate or rating before April 15, 1991;
(iii) Completing an official pilot-in-command check conducted by the military services of the United States; or
(iv) Completing a pilot-in-command proficiency check under part 121, 125, or 135 of this chapter conducted by the Administrator or by an approved pilot check airman.
(h) *Additional aircraft type-specific training.* No person may serve as pilot in command of an aircraft that the Administrator has determined requires aircraft type-specific training unless that person has—
(1) Received and logged type-specific training in the aircraft, or in a flight simulator or flight training device that is representative of that type of aircraft; and
(2) Received a logbook endorsement from an authorized instructor who has found the person proficient in the operation of the aircraft and its systems.
(i) *Additional training required for operating tailwheel airplanes.*
(1) Except as provided in paragraph (i)(2) of this section, no person may act as pilot in command of a tailwheel airplane unless that person has received and logged flight training from an authorized instructor in a tailwheel airplane and received an endorsement in the person's logbook from an authorized instructor who found the person proficient in the operation of a tailwheel airplane. The flight training must include at least the following maneuvers and procedures:
(i)   Normal and crosswind takeoffs and landings;
(ii) Wheel landings (unless the manufacturer has recommended against such landings); and
(iii) Go-around procedures.
(2) The training and endorsement required by paragraph (i)(1) of this section is not required if the person logged pilot-in-command time in a tailwheel airplane before April 15, 1991.

(j) *Additional training required for operating a glider.*
  (1) No person may act as pilot in command of a glider—
      (i) Using ground-tow procedures, unless that person has satisfactorily accomplished ground and flight training on ground-tow procedures and operations, and has received an endorsement from an authorized instructor who certifies in that pilot's logbook that the pilot has been found proficient in ground-tow procedures and operations;
      (ii) Using aerotow procedures, unless that person has satisfactorily accomplished ground and flight training on aerotow procedures and operations, and has received an endorsement from an authorized instructor who certifies in that pilot's logbook that the pilot has been found proficient in aerotow procedures and operations; or
      (iii) Using self-launch procedures, unless that person has satisfactorily accomplished ground and flight training on self-launch procedures and operations, and has received an endorsement from an authorized instructor who certifies in that pilot's logbook that the pilot has been found proficient in self-launch procedures and operations.
  (2) The holder of a glider rating issued prior to August 4, 1997 is considered to be in compliance with the training and logbook endorsement requirements of this paragraph for the specific operating privilege for which the holder is already qualified.
(k) *Exceptions.*
  (1) This section does not require a category and class rating for aircraft not type certificated as airplanes, rotorcraft, or lighter-than-air aircraft, or a class rating for gliders or powered-lifts.
  (2) The rating limitations of this section do not apply to—
      (i) An applicant when taking a practical test given by an examiner;
      (ii) The holder of a student pilot certificate;
      (iii) The holder of a pilot certificate when operating an aircraft under the authority of an experimental or provisional aircraft type certificate;
      (iv) The holder of a pilot certificate with a lighter-than-air category rating when operating a balloon; or
      (v) The holder of a recreational pilot certificate operating under the provisions of §61.101(h).

EXPLANATION

61.31(e) and (f): The NPRM had proposed to require additional training and a logbook endorsement for PIC's to operate airplanes having 200 or more horsepower and those PIC's operating complex airplanes. In response to the commenters and after further review of the costs vs. benefits, the FAA has withdrawn the proposal for the additional training and endorsement for operating an airplane of 200 horsepower or more and retained the existing additional training and endorsement requirements that only requires those airplanes of "more" than 200 horsepower. However the proposal to require separate additional training and endorsements for a PIC operating a complex airplane and a PIC operating a high performance airplane is going forward.

61.31(h) provides the FAA a means where they can require additional training and an instructor endorsement for unique or other complex aircraft. The FAA has stated that they may require "type-rating" type training for aircraft such as the Piper Malibu.

61.31(j): Although the proposal for establishing class ratings within the glider category has been withdrawn, the FAA has revised the procedures for pilot certification for the launch/tow procedure for gliders. The new revision will permit issuance of pilot certificates with the glider ratings without the existing requirements for placing launch /tow limitations on the pilot certificate. This new procedure will require glider pilots to receive additional training and a logbook endorsement from a flight instructor on the specific kind of launch/tow procedure for which that pilot desires operating privileges.

PREAMBLE

The FAA has made various clarifying changes to these sections and modified terminology because of changes implemented elsewhere in the rule. The commenter's proposal for an additional requirement for amphibious airplane pilots is outside the scope of Notice No. 95-11 and cannot be included in the rule without comment under the standard regulatory process. In addition, the FAA has added a paragraph describing additional training required for operating a glider.

61.31(d): After considering AOPA's and NAFI's comments, the FAA has decided to change the references from "enrolled in a course of training" to "receiving training", which is more generic and avoids the implication that a pilot must receive training in an FAA-certificated school.

61.31(e) and (f): The FAA believes the operating characteristics of complex aircraft and high-performance aircraft are so different as to justify separate endorsements. There are now turbine-powered aircraft that are high-performance aircraft but that are not considered complex aircraft. Also, training in one type of aircraft does not necessarily transfer to training in another type of aircraft. However, the FAA finds persuasive the commenters' objections to the proposed change in the requirement of "200 horsepower or more." Therefore, the rule will only require a separate endorsement for airplanes with "more than 200 horsepower."

61.31(g): After considering AsMA's comments, the FAA has retained the phrase "and any other physiological aspects of high altitude flight" in the final rule. However, GAMA's comment addresses a clause that was not modified in Notice No. 95-11 and is beyond the scope of this rulemaking. The proposal is adopted as modified.

61.31(h): It is the FAA's position that granting the Administrator the authority to require type-specific training, on any aircraft that the Administrator deems appropriate, provides the Administrator with the minimum means necessary to rapidly address safety concerns without the delay incurred by rulemaking. The intent of the rule is for the Administrator to only exercise this power in limited circumstances. Flight characteristics of certain aircraft may necessitate the rapid implementation of additional training. Recent Piper Malibu and Robinson R-22 accidents demonstrate the need for this requirement. When the Flight Standards Board (FSB) meets, a notice to the public is published in the Federal Register, and the opportunity for public comment is provided. The FAA believes that this will permit the FAA to be more responsive to patterns of accidents in the future, and the proposal is adopted with minor editorial changes. (62 FR 16243 - 16245).

CROSS REFERENCES

61.63, Additional Aircraft Ratings (Other than Airline Transport Pilot); 61.101, Recreational Pilot Privileges and Limitations; 121.407, Training Program: Approval of Airplane Simulators and Other Training Devices.

ADVISORY CIRCULARS

AC 61-65D Certification: Pilots and Flight and Ground Instructors (1999).

AC 61-89D *Pilot Certificates: Aircraft Type Ratings* (1991).

AC 61-98A *Currency and Additional Qualification Requirements for Certificated Pilots* (1991).

AC 61-107 *Operations of Aircraft at Altitudes Above 25,000 Feet MSL and/or MACH Numbers (Mmo) Greater Than .75* (1991).

AC 120-45A *Airplane Training Device Qualification* (1992).

CASES

The NTSB has no jurisdiction to review a denial by the FAA of "authorization in lieu of a type rating." *Administrator v. Thornton*, EA-4238 (1994).

FAA CHIEF COUNSEL OPINIONS

A private pilot may log pilot-in-command time, in a complex or high performance airplane, for those portions of the flight when he or she is the sole manipulator of the controls because the aircraft being operated is single-engine land and the private pilot holds a single-engine land rating. However, while the private pilot may log this time as pilot-in-command time, he or she may not act as the pilot-in-command unless he or she has the appropriate endorsement as required under 14 CFR section 61.31. (6-3-99).

61.33 TESTS: GENERAL PROCEDURE

Tests prescribed by or under this part are given at times and places, and by persons designated by the Administrator.

61.35 KNOWLEDGE TEST: PREREQUISITES AND PASSING GRADES

(a) An applicant for a knowledge test must have:
   (1) Received an endorsement, if required by this part, from an authorized instructor certifying that the applicant accomplished the appropriate ground-training or a home-study course required by this part for the certificate or rating sought and is prepared for the knowledge test; and
   (2) Proper identification at the time of application that contains the applicant's—
      (i)   Photograph;
      (ii) Signature;
      (iii) Date of birth, which shows the applicant meets or will meet the age requirements of this part for the certificate sought before the expiration date of the airman knowledge test report; and
      (iv) Actual residential address, if different from the applicant's mailing address.
(b) The Administrator shall specify the minimum passing grade for the knowledge test.

EXPLANATION

The latest change refers to "knowledge test," instead of "written test" in order to include computer testing and be consistent with FAA policy. This rule was amended in 1998 to show that an instructor endorsement is not a prerequisite for all knowledge tests. Refer to the cross references to see which tests require an endorsement (Recreational Pilot does, ATP does not).

PREAMBLE

In the general discussion of the preamble, the FAA inadvertently stated that a "logbook" endorsement was required for a knowledge test. The rule, however, did not include this provision and it was not the FAA's intent to require a "logbook" endorsement. The FAA notes the commenters' objections to the requirement for an endorsement as a prerequisite to the knowledge test. However, the current rule requires an applicant to show satisfactory completion of the required ground instructor or home study course. This is accomplished through the use of an endorsement. The FAA has repeatedly held that this requirement is necessary to ensure a high quality of training, and the final rule is adopted as proposed with minor editorial changes. (62 FR 16246).

CROSS REFERENCES

61.96, Recreational Pilots: Applicability and Eligibility Requirements: General; 61.103, Private Pilots: Eligibility Requirements: General; 61.123, Commercial Pilots: Eligibility Requirements: General; Subpart G, Airline Transport Pilots.

ADVISORY CIRCULARS

AC 60-25E - *Reference Materials and Subject Matter Knowledge Codes for Airman Knowledge Testing* (2001).

AC 60-26B – *Announcement of Availability: Flight Standards Service Airman Training and Testing Information* (2000).

FAA-G-8082-7, *Flight and Ground Instructor Knowledge Test Guide* (1999).

FAA-G-8082-1, *Airline Transport Pilot, Aircraft Dispatcher and Flight Navigator Knowledge Test Guide* (1999).

FAA-G-8082-5, *Commercial Pilot Knowledge Test Guide* (1999).

FAA-G-8082-17, *Recreational Pilot and Private Pilot Knowledge Test Guide* (1999).

FAA-G-8082-13, *Instrument Rating Knowledge Test Guide* (1999).

61.37 KNOWLEDGE TESTS: CHEATING OR OTHER UNAUTHORIZED CONDUCT

(a) An applicant for a knowledge test may not:
  (1) Copy or intentionally remove any knowledge test;
  (2) Give to another applicant or receive from another applicant any part or copy of a knowledge test;
  (3) Give assistance on, or receive assistance on, a knowledge test during the period that test is being given;
  (4) Take any part of a knowledge test on behalf of another person;
  (5) Be represented by, or represent, another person for a knowledge test;
  (6) Use any material or aid during the period that the test is being given, unless specifically authorized to do so by the Administrator; and
  (7) Intentionally cause, assist, or participate in any act prohibited by this paragraph.
(b) An applicant who the Administrator finds has committed an act prohibited by paragraph (a) of this section is prohibited, for 1 year after the date of committing that act, from:
  (1) Applying for any certificate, rating, or authorization issued under this chapter; and
  (2) Applying for and taking any test under this chapter.
(c) Any certificate or rating held by an applicant may be suspended or revoked if the Administrator finds that person has committed an act prohibited by paragraph (a) of this section.

EXPLANATION

Remember that any of the actions described in 61.37(a) can result in suspension or revocation of all airman certificates held.

Always ensure that any aid used while taking a written test for any airman certificate is one that is allowed by the FAA. Always check before the test begins.

If an airman is found to have unauthorized material, the chances of convincing the FAA or NTSB that he or she wasn't using it are very slim. Don't take any unauthorized material into the room.

ADVISORY CIRCULARS

AC 60-11C *Test Aids and Materials That May Be Used by Airman Knowledge Testing Applicants* (1999).

CASES

The Board upheld the revocation of the commercial pilot's certificate of a person who had unauthorized materials (written notes) and who appeared to use them while taking the written test for an airline transport pilot certificate. *Administrator v. Mignano*, EA-3435 (1991).

The Board upheld the revocation of the private pilot certificate of a person who was observed by the test examiner to be using a "cheat sheet" while taking the Instrument Rating-Airplane written test. *Administrator v. Beaudorn*, EA-3515 (1992).

A pilot who was taking a written examination was caught cheating by the test examiner. His private certificate was revoked. *Administrator v. Thompson,* EA-3854 (1993).

61.39 PREREQUISITES FOR PRACTICAL TESTS

(a) Except as provided in paragraphs (b) and (c) of this section, to be eligible for a practical test for a certificate or rating issued under this part, an applicant must:

  (1) Pass the required knowledge test within the 24-calendar-month period preceding the month the applicant completes the practical test, if a knowledge test is required;

  (2) Present the knowledge test report at the time of application for the practical test, if a knowledge test is required;

  (3) Have satisfactorily accomplished the required training and obtained the aeronautical experience prescribed by this part for the certificate or rating sought;

  (4) Hold at least a current third-class medical certificate, if a medical certificate is required;

  (5) Meet the prescribed age requirement of this part for the issuance of the certificate or rating sought;

  (6) Have an endorsement, if required by this part, in the applicant's logbook or training record that has been signed by an authorized instructor who certifies that the applicant—

    (i) Has received and logged training time within 60 days preceding the date of application in preparation for the practical test;

    (ii) Is prepared for the required practical test; and

    (iii) Has demonstrated satisfactory knowledge of the subject areas in which the applicant was deficient on the airman knowledge test; and

  (7) Have a completed and signed application form.

(b) Notwithstanding the provisions of paragraphs (a)(1) and (2) of this section, an applicant for an airline transport pilot certificate or an additional rating to an airline transport certificate may take the practical test for that certificate or rating with an expired knowledge test report, provided that the applicant:

  (1) Is employed as a flight crewmember by a certificate holder under part 121, 125, or 135 of this chapter at the time of the practical test and has satisfactorily accomplished that operator's approved—

    (i) Pilot in command aircraft qualification training program that is appropriate to the certificate and rating sought; and

    (ii) Qualification training requirements appropriate to the certificate and rating sought; or

  (2) Is employed as a flight crewmember in scheduled U.S. military air transport operations at the time of the practical test, and has accomplished the pilot in command aircraft qualification training program that is appropriate to the certificate and rating sought.

(c) A person is not required to comply with the provisions of paragraph (a)(6) of this section if that person:

  (1) Holds a foreign-pilot license issued by a contracting State to the Convention on International Civil Aviation that authorizes at least the pilot privileges of the airman certificate sought;

  (2) Is applying for a type rating only, or a class rating with an associated type rating; or

  (3) Is applying for an airline transport pilot certificate or an additional rating to an airline transport pilot certificate in an aircraft that does not require an aircraft type rating practical test.

(d) If all increments of the practical test for a certificate or rating are not completed on one date, all remaining increments of the test must be satisfactorily completed not more than 60 calendar days after the date on which the applicant began the test.

(e) If all increments of the practical test for a certificate or a rating are not satisfactorily completed within 60 calendar days after the date on which the applicant began the test, the applicant must retake the entire practical test, including those increments satisfactorily completed.

EXPLANATION

In the event the entire practical test (i.e. oral increment, flight simulator increment, and flight increment) is not satisfactorily completed with the prescribed 60 calendar days, the applicant is required to retake the entire practical test, including those increments satisfactorily completed more than 60 calendar days previously. This rule was amended in 1998 to show that an instructor endorsement is not a prerequisite for all practical tests. Refer to the cross references below to see which tests require an endorsement.

61.39(a)(4) permits those applicants applying for pilot and instructor certificates, including the commercial, ATP, and flight instructor certificates to only hold a 3rd class medical certificate.

CROSS REFERENCES

61.23(c), Duration of Medical Certificates; 61.96, Recreational Pilots: Applicability and Eligibility Requirements: General; 61.103, Private Pilots: Eligibility Requirements: General; 61.123, Commercial Pilots: Eligibility Requirements: General; Subpart G, Airline Transport Pilots.

ADVISORY CIRCULARS

AC 60-26B –*Announcement of Availability: Flight Standards Service Airman Training and Testing Information* (2000)

AC 61-65D *Certification: Pilots and Flight Instructors* (1999)

FAA CHIEF COUNSEL OPINIONS

A person took and passed ATP examination in March of 1969 and since that time has been continuously employed as a pilot for a Part 121 air carrier. In 1985 he considered taking a leave of absence for about 2 years. He wanted to know whether, after the leave, his written exam would still be valid.

> Assuming that, at the end of the leave, he returns to the Part 121 air carrier and satisfies the appropriate training requirement prior to applying for the flight test, the written exam will still be valid. (6-13-85).

Pursuant to [61.109], a person seeking a private pilot certificate is required to log at least 3 hours of flight instruction, at the earliest, within two months prior to his 17th birthday or written two months prior to his 16th birthday for a private pilot certificate with free balloon or glider rating. There is no minimum age necessary for the remaining 17 hours of flight instruction required to be logged in order to be eligible for a private pilot certificate. (4-3-78).

61.41 FLIGHT TRAINING RECEIVED FROM FLIGHT INSTRUCTORS NOT CERTIFICATED BY THE FAA

(a) A person may credit flight training toward the requirements of a pilot certificate or rating issued under this part, if that person received the training from:
  (1) A flight instructor of an Armed Force in a program for training military pilots of either—
    (i) The United States; or
    (ii) A foreign contracting State to the Convention on International Civil Aviation.
  (2) A flight instructor who is authorized to give such training by the licensing authority of a foreign contracting State to the Convention on International Civil Aviation, and the flight training is given outside the United States.
(b) A flight instructor described in paragraph (a) of this section is only authorized to give endorsements to show training given.

FAA CHIEF COUNSEL OPINIONS

The credit must be allowed regardless of the citizenship of the applicant or the instructor and regardless of the country of registry of the aircraft provided the instruction was given outside the United States by persons licensed by an ICAO state. However, 61.41 does not authorize an ICAO flight instructor to make endorsements specified in §61.3 or elsewhere in Part 61, or to provide the written statement required in §61.39. §61.41 must be interpreted to allow ICAO flight instructors to make the endorsements specified in §61.3 since they are the customary means of evidencing that the permitted instruction was given. (7-21-86).

Only flight instruction received in a military training program can be credited as such for the purposes of Part 61. Flight instruction given by an Armed Forces instructor who is not a CFI outside of one of these programs may not be used on an FAA application for the issuance of a pilot certificate or rating. (4-9-1997).

61.43 PRACTICAL TESTS: GENERAL PROCEDURES

(a) Except as provided in paragraph (b) of this section, the ability of an applicant for a certificate or rating issued under this part to perform the required tasks on the practical test is based on that applicant's ability to safely:
  (1) Perform the tasks specified in the areas of operation for the certificate or rating sought within the approved standards;
  (2) Demonstrate mastery of the aircraft with the successful outcome of each task performed never seriously in doubt;
  (3) Demonstrate satisfactory proficiency and competency within the approved standards;
  (4) Demonstrate sound judgment; and
  (5) Demonstrate single-pilot competence if the aircraft is type certificated for single-pilot operations.

(b)   If an applicant does not demonstrate single pilot proficiency, as required in paragraph (a)(5) of this section, a limitation of "Second in Command Required" will be placed on the applicant's airman certificate. The limitation may be removed if the applicant passes the appropriate practical test by demonstrating single-pilot competency in the aircraft in which single-pilot privileges are sought.

(c)   If an applicant fails any area of operation, that applicant fails the practical test.

(d)   An applicant is not eligible for a certificate or rating sought until all the areas of operation are passed.

(e)   The examiner or the applicant may discontinue a practical test at any time:

    (1)   When the applicant fails one or more of the areas of operation; or

    (2)   Due to inclement weather conditions, aircraft airworthiness, or any other safety-of-flight concern.

(f)   If a practical test is discontinued, the applicant is entitled credit for those areas of operation that were passed, but only if the applicant:

    (1)   Passes the remainder of the practical test within the 60-day period after the date the practical test was discontinued;

    (2)   Presents to the examiner for the retest the original notice of disapproval form or the letter of discontinuance form, as appropriate;

    (3)   Satisfactorily accomplishes any additional training needed and obtains the appropriate instructor endorsements, if additional training is required; and

    (4)   Presents to the examiner for the retest a properly completed and signed application.

EXPLANATION

61.43(f): If an applicant fails a flight test, and he or she retakes the test within 60 days, the examiner is not required to give the entire test over again. The examiner has the discretion to test only operations which the applicant failed on the previous test. If the applicant retakes the test more than 60 days later, the examiner may not give credit for operations which the applicant performed successfully on the first test.

ADVISORY CIRCULARS

AC 60-26B *Announcement of Availability: Flight Standards Service Airman Training and Testing Information* (2000).

AC 61-65D *Certification: Pilots and Flight and Ground Instructors* (1999).

FAA-H-8083-9 *Aviation Instructor's Handbook* (1999).

FAA CHIEF COUNSEL OPINIONS

The student may not receive credit for operations that have not been successfully completed during the test. It does not convey an absolute right to credit for operations that were completed successfully. The inspector or examiner, while probably not routinely finding it necessary to reexamine an applicant on pilot operations already successfully performed, does have the prerogative to re-examine on these operations if he or she has reason to question the applicant's qualifications. Such a situation may exist when an extended period of time has elapsed since the test was discontinued, even though the applicant may have acquired additional flight time in the interim. (4-23-80).

61.45 PRACTICAL TESTS: REQUIRED AIRCRAFT AND EQUIPMENT

(a)   *General.* Except as provided in paragraph (a)(2) of this section or when permitted to accomplish the entire flight increment of the practical test in a flight simulator or a flight training device, an applicant for a certificate or rating issued under this part must furnish:
      (1)   An aircraft of U.S. registry for each required test that—
            (i)   Is of the category, class, and type, if applicable, for which the applicant is applying for a certificate or rating; and
            (ii)   Has a current standard, limited, or primary airworthiness certificate.
      (2)   At the discretion of the examiner who administers the practical test, the applicant may furnish—
            (i)   An aircraft that has a current airworthiness certificate other than standard, limited, or primary, but that otherwise meets the requirement of paragraph (a)(1) of this section;
            (ii)   An aircraft of the same category, class, and type, if applicable, of foreign registry that is properly certificated by the country of registry; or
            (iii) A military aircraft of the same category, class, and type, if applicable, for which the applicant is applying for a certificate or rating.
(b)   *Required equipment (other than controls).*
      (1)   Except as provided in paragraph (b)(2) of this section an aircraft used for a practical test must have—
            (i)   The equipment for each area of operation required for the practical test;
            (ii)   No prescribed operating limitations that prohibit its use in any of the areas of operation required for the practical test;
            (iii) Except as provided in paragraph (e) of this section, at least two pilot stations with adequate visibility for each person to operate the aircraft safely; and
            (iv)   Cockpit and outside visibility adequate to evaluate the performance of the applicant when an additional jump seat is provided for the examiner.
      (2)   An applicant for a certificate or rating may use an aircraft with operating characteristics that preclude the applicant from performing all of the tasks required for the practical test. However, the applicant's certificate or rating, as appropriate, will be issued with an appropriate limitation.
(c)   *Required controls.* An aircraft (other than a lighter-than-air aircraft) used for a practical test must have engine power controls and flight controls that are easily reached and operable in a conventional manner by both pilots, unless the examiner determines that the practical test can be conducted safely in the aircraft without the controls being easily reached.
(d)   *Simulated instrument flight equipment.* An applicant for a practical test that involves maneuvering an aircraft solely by reference to instruments must furnish:
      (1)   Equipment on board the aircraft that permits the applicant to pass the areas of operation that apply to the rating sought; and
      (2)   A device that prevents the applicant from having visual reference outside the aircraft, but does not prevent the examiner from having visual reference outside the aircraft, and is otherwise acceptable to the Administrator.
(e)   *Aircraft with single controls.* A practical test may be conducted in an aircraft having a single set of controls, provided the:
      (1)   Examiner agrees to conduct the test;
      (2)   Test does not involve a demonstration of instrument skills; and
      (3)   Proficiency of the applicant can be observed by an examiner who is in a position to observe the applicant.

EXPLANATION

Although the regulation authorizes use of simulation for tasks of a practical test, simulation can not be used for these tasks until the simulation medium has been developed, evaluated, and qualified by the FAA to evaluate such tasks.

It is an accepted practice of evaluators and FAA inspectors to conduct the practical test from the jump seat or some other location than a pilot's seat, when necessary.

The applicant is the one responsible for providing the equipment that excludes the applicant's visual reference to objects outside the aircraft.

The FAA amended this rule in 1998 to allow centerline-thrust (Cessna Skymaster) and other aircraft that cannot perform all of the requirements of the practical test standards. If an applicant takes a multi-engine practical test in a Cessna Skymaster, the airman certificate will be issued with a centerline-thrust limitation.

PREAMBLE

After discussions with many of the manufacturers of gyroplanes, the FAA believes that there are an adequate number of two-place gyroplanes available to permit the FAA to require that a practical test in a gyroplane be taken in a two-place aircraft. The FAA notes the concerns of EAA, NAFI, and AOPA. The FAA believes the importance of the practical test makes it extremely necessary that examiners be able to observe applicants during the practical test. In addition, the FAA replaced the words "pilot seats" with "pilot stations". Balloons have pilot stations, and, therefore, this change eliminates the need for an exception to be specifically stated in the rule. Except for these changes and other editorial changes to include provisions relating to the use of approved flight simulators and approved flight training devices, the final rule is adopted as proposed. (62 FR 16247).

CROSS REFERENCES

91.7, Civil Aircraft Airworthiness; 91.203, Civil Aircraft: Certifications Required; 91.205, Powered Civil Aircraft with Standard Category U.S. Airworthiness Certificate: Instrument and Equipment Requirements; 91.213, Inoperative Instruments and Equipment.

ADVISORY CIRCULARS

FAA-H-8083-19, *Plane Sense* (1999).

AC 120-40B *Airplane Simulator Qualification* (1993).

61.47 STATUS OF AN EXAMINER WHO IS AUTHORIZED BY THE ADMINISTRATOR TO CONDUCT PRACTICAL TESTS

(a)   An examiner represents the Administrator for the purpose of conducting practical tests for certificates and ratings issued under this part and to observe an applicant's ability to perform the areas of operation on the practical test.

(b)   The examiner is not the pilot in command of the aircraft during the practical test unless the examiner agrees to act in that capacity for the flight or for a portion of the flight by prior arrangement with:
   (1)   The applicant; or
   (2)   A person who would otherwise act as pilot in command of the flight or for a portion of the flight.

(c)   Notwithstanding the type of aircraft used during the practical test, the applicant and the examiner (and any other occupants authorized to be on board by the examiner) are not subject to the requirements or limitations for the carriage of passengers that are specified in this chapter.

EXPLANATION

Prior to a flight test, if the inspector or examiner does not explain under what circumstances he or she will take over control of the aircraft and who will be pilot in command under those circumstances, the person taking the flight test should ask that this matter be resolved prior to the flight.

CROSS REFERENCES

1.1, General Definitions, "Pilot In Command"; 91.3, Responsibility and Authority of the Pilot In Command.

ADVISORY CIRCULARS

FAA-H-8083-9 *Aviation Instructor's Handbook* (1999).

61.49 RETESTING AFTER FAILURE

(a)   An applicant for a knowledge or practical test who fails that test may reapply for the test only after the applicant has received:
   (1)   The necessary training from an authorized instructor who has determined that the applicant is proficient to pass the test; and
   (2)   An endorsement from an authorized instructor who gave the applicant the additional training.

(b)   An applicant for a flight instructor certificate with an airplane category rating or, for a flight instructor certificate with a glider category rating, who has failed the practical test due to deficiencies in instructional proficiency on stall awareness, spin entry, spins, or spin recovery must:

(1)   Comply with the requirements of paragraph (a) of this section before being retested;

(2)   Bring an aircraft to the retest that is of the appropriate aircraft category for the rating sought and is certificated for spins; and

(3)   Demonstrate satisfactory instructional proficiency on stall awareness, spin entry, spins, and spin recovery to an examiner during the retest.

EXPLANATION

In the case of the initial practical test for a flight instructor certificate, a logbook endorsement from an appropriately rated flight instructor relating to spin entry, spin, and spin recovery training may be accepted without the applicant having to actually demonstrate the maneuvers. However, if a retest is required, because the applicant showed a lack of understanding of spins, there must be an actual demonstration of the maneuvers.

Failure for any reason "uses up" an endorsement, so an applicant must get a new endorsement prior to retesting.

CROSS REFERENCES

61.183, Flight Instructors: Eligibility Requirements.

ADVISORY CIRCULARS

AC 61-65D *Certification: Pilots and Flight and Ground Instructors* (1999).

AC 61-67C *Stall and Spin Awareness Training* (2000).

61.51 PILOT LOGBOOKS

(a)   *Training time and aeronautical experience.* Each person must document and record the following time in a manner acceptable to the Administrator:

(1)   Training and aeronautical experience used to meet the requirements for a certificate, rating, or flight review of this part.

(2)   The aeronautical experience required for meeting the recent flight experience requirements of this part.

(b) *Logbook entries.* For the purposes of meeting the requirements of paragraph (a) of this section, each person must enter the following information for each flight or lesson logged:
  (1) General—
    (i)   Date.
    (ii)   Total flight time or lesson time.
    (iii) Location where the aircraft departed and arrived, or for lessons in a flight simulator or flight training device, the location where the lesson occurred.
    (iv)   Type and identification of aircraft, flight simulator, or flight training device, as appropriate.
    (v)   The name of a safety pilot, if required by §91.109(b) of this chapter.
  (2) Type of pilot experience or training—
    (i)   Solo.
    (ii)   Pilot in command.
    (iii) Second in command.
    (iv)   Flight and ground training received from an authorized instructor.
    (v)   Training received in a flight simulator or flight training device from an authorized instructor.
  (3) Conditions of flight—
    (i)   Day or night.
    (ii)   Actual instrument.
    (iii) Simulated instrument conditions in flight, a flight simulator, or a flight training device.
(c) *Logging of pilot time.* The pilot time described in this section may be used to:
  (1) Apply for a certificate or rating issued under this part; or
  (2) Satisfy the recent flight experience requirements of this part.
(d) *Logging of solo flight time.* Except for a student pilot performing the duties of pilot in command of an airship requiring more than one pilot flight crewmember, a pilot may log as solo flight time only that flight time when the pilot is the sole occupant of the aircraft.
(e) *Logging pilot-in-command flight time.*
  (1) A recreational, private, or commercial pilot may log pilot-in-command time only for that flight time during which that person—
    (i)   Is the sole manipulator of the controls of an aircraft for which the pilot is rated; or
    (ii)   Is the sole occupant of the aircraft; or
    (iii) Except for a recreational pilot, is acting as pilot in command of an aircraft on which more than one pilot is required under the type certification of the aircraft or the regulations under which the flight is conducted.
  (2) An airline transport pilot may log as pilot-in-command time all of the flight time while acting as pilot-in-command of an operation requiring an airline transport pilot certificate.
  (3) An authorized instructor may log as pilot-in-command time all flight time while acting as an authorized instructor.
  (4) A student pilot may log pilot-in-command time only when the student pilot—
    (i)   Is the sole occupant of the aircraft or is performing the duties of pilot in command of an airship requiring more than one pilot flight crewmember;
    (ii)   Has a current solo flight endorsement as required under §61.87 of this part; and
    (iii) Is undergoing training for a pilot certificate or rating.

(f) *Logging second-in-command flight time.* A person may log second-in-command time only for that flight time during which that person:

   (1) Is qualified in accordance with the second-in-command requirements of §61.55 of this part, and occupies a crewmember station in an aircraft that requires more than one pilot by the aircraft's type certificate; or

   (2) Holds the appropriate category, class, and instrument rating (if an instrument rating is required for the flight) for the aircraft being flown, and more than one pilot is required under the type certification of the aircraft or the regulations under which the flight is being conducted.

(g) *Logging instrument flight time.*

   (1) A person may log instrument time only for that flight time when the person operates the aircraft solely by reference to instruments under actual or simulated instrument flight conditions.

   (2) An authorized instructor may log instrument time when conducting instrument flight instruction in actual instrument flight conditions.

   (3) For the purposes of logging instrument time to meet the recent instrument experience requirements of §61.57(c) of this part, the following information must be recorded in the person's logbook—

      (i) The location and type of each instrument approach accomplished; and

      (ii) The name of the safety pilot, if required.

   (4) A flight simulator or flight training device may be used by a person to log instrument time, provided an authorized instructor is present during the simulated flight.

(h) *Logging training time.*

   (1) A person may log training time when that person receives training from an authorized instructor in an aircraft, flight simulator, or flight training device.

   (2) The training time must be logged in a logbook and must:

      (i) Be endorsed in a legible manner by the authorized instructor; and

      (ii) Include a description of the training given, the length of the training lesson, and the authorized instructor's signature, certificate number, and certificate expiration date.

(i) *Presentation of required documents.*

   (1) Persons must present their pilot certificate, medical certificate, logbook, or any other record required by this part for inspection upon a reasonable request by—

      (i) The Administrator;

      (ii) An authorized representative from the National Transportation Safety Board; or

      (iii) Any Federal, State, or local law enforcement officer.

   (2) A student pilot must carry the following items in the aircraft on all solo cross-country flights as evidence of the required authorized instructor clearances and endorsements—

      (i) Pilot logbook;

      (ii) Student pilot certificate; and

      (iii) Any other record required by this section.

   (3) A recreational pilot must carry his or her logbook with the required authorized instructor endorsements on all solo flights—

      (i) That exceed 50 nautical miles from the airport at which training was received;

      (ii) Within airspace that requires communication with air traffic control;

      (iii) Conducted between sunset and sunrise; or

      (iv) In an aircraft for which the pilot does not hold an appropriate category or class rating.

EXPLANATION

Type of Operation and (Pilot Designation)	Type of Flight Time that can be Logged	Additional Requirements and Comments
Sole Occupant of the Aircraft (Student Pilot)	Solo and PIC	PIC – current endorsement under §61.87 – must be undergoing training for pilot certificate or rating
Sole Occupant of the Aircraft (Recreational Pilot)	Solo and PIC	Solo – Cannot be performing duties of PIC of an airship requiring more than one pilot flight crewmember
Sole Occupant of the Aircraft (Private and Commercial Pilot)	Solo and PIC	
Sole Manipulator of the Controls of the Aircraft, not receiving flight instruction (Recreational, Private, and Commercial Pilot)	PIC	Must be rated for the aircraft, which includes category, class, and type if applicable.
Acting as Pilot in Command, not being the sole manipulator of the controls (Private Pilot and Commercial Pilot)	PIC	The aircraft's type certificate must require more than one pilot. OR, the regulations under which the flight is being conducting must require more than one pilot. Must be rated for the aircraft, which includes category, class, and type if applicable.
Acting as Pilot in Command, including all flight time when the operation requires an airline transport pilot certificate (Airline Transport Pilot)	PIC	An ATP may log all flight time as sole occupant, sole manipulator of the controls, or acting PIC when the operation requires an ATP as PIC flight time.

Type of Operation and (Pilot Designation)	Type of Flight Time that can be Logged	Additional Requirements and Comments
Acting as Second in Command, in accordance with the requirements of §61.55 including operations that require an ATP (Private Pilot and Commercial Pilot)	PIC and SIC	PIC and SIC – The aircraft's type certificate must require more than one pilot. OR, the regulations under which the flight is being conducting must require more than one pilot. The pilot must hold the appropriate category, class, and instrument rating if applicable and be occupying a crewmember station. PIC – Only for the time while he or she is the sole manipulator of the controls as long as he or she is rated in that aircraft.
Acting as Safety Pilot under §91.109 (Private Pilot and Commercial Pilot)	PIC and SIC	PIC and SIC – The pilot must be rated for the aircraft, which includes category, class, and type if applicable. SIC – Only while the acting PIC is manipulating the flight controls under simulated instrument conditions. PIC – If the two pilots agree prior to initiating the flight that the safety pilot will be the acting PIC as defined in §1.1 then he or she may log all of the time as PIC flight time. However, in this case the pilot manipulating the controls under simulated instrument conditions may only log PIC flight time for the time spent under the hood and may not log any other time on the flight.

Type of Operation and (Pilot Designation)	Type of Flight Time that can be Logged	Additional Requirements and Comments
Flying under Simulated Instrument Conditions with a Safety Pilot (Private and Commercial Pilots)	PIC and Simulated Instrument	PIC - Unless otherwise agreed upon before the flight (see PIC Requirements for Safety Pilots) the pilot may log the entire flight as PIC provided they meet the qualifications for logging PIC time above. Simulated Instrument - The pilot may also log simulated instrument time for the flight time where they operate the aircraft solely by reference to instruments under simulated conditions (i.e. wearing a view limiting device). The pilot must record both the location and type of each instrument approach, and the name of the safety pilot in their logbook.
Flying under Simulated Instrument Conditions to meet the Requirements of §61.109(a)(3), (b)(3), or (e)(3) (Student Pilots)	Training Received* and Simulated Instrument	Simulated Instrument Time – To log this time as Instrument time that counts towards higher certificates or an instrument rating the instructor giving the training must be a CFII.
Flying under Simulated or Actual Instrument Conditions (Private and Commercial Pilots with Instrument Ratings)	PIC and Instrument – Actual or Simulated	Simulated Instrument Time – The pilot must log the name of the safety pilot.
Flights Conducted in a Simulator or Flight Training Device (Private and Commercial Pilots)	Simulated Instrument	An authorized instructor must be present during the flight
Receiving Flight Instruction (Student Pilots)	Training Received*	Instructor must include all information required under §61.51 and endorse the student's logbook.

Type of Operation and (Pilot Designation)	Type of Flight Time that can be Logged	Additional Requirements and Comments
Receiving Flight Instruction, including training for high performance, complex, and tail wheel aircraft (Recreational, Private, and Commercial Pilots)	PIC and Training Received*	PIC – The pilot receiving the instruction may log PIC time if he or she is the sole manipulator of the controls. They are not required to have the endorsement required by §61.31 unless they wish to act as pilot in command of a high performance, complex, or tail wheel aircraft.
Receiving Flight Instruction under Actual or Simulated Instrument Conditions (Private and Commercial Pilots)	PIC, Training Received*, and Instrument – Actual or Simulated	PIC – The pilot receiving instruction must be the sole manipulator of the controls.
Giving Flight Instruction in VMC (Certified Flight Instructors)	PIC and Training Given*	PIC – CFI's may log this time as PIC for the purpose of building total time, but the time and any landings may not be used to meet the recency requirements of §61.57.
Giving Flight Instruction in IMC (Certified Flight Instructor – Instrument)	PIC, Training Given*, and Actual Instrument	PIC – CFI's may log this time as PIC for the purpose of building total time, but the time and any landings may not be used to meet the recency requirements of §61.57.

* §61.51(h) Training Given or Received time in most logbooks is called Dual Given or Received.

PREAMBLE

61.51(a): The FAA notes the concern of EAA and NAFI, but feels that the existing phrase was redundant, and that its deletion does not impose costs or burdens on pilots. The rule was revised to clarify what flight time is required to be logged. Other flight time can be logged at the pilot's option, but it is not required. The final rule is adopted as proposed.

61.51(b): As discussed in the analysis of §61.1, the FAA has decided to retain "solo time" in this paragraph of the final rule. The FAA notes AOPA's concern, and has decided to use the less ambiguous term "flight time" in the final rule instead of the phrase "total time of flight". The final rule also deletes the language "and the certificate number of the safety pilot", as explained in the analysis of §61.51(g), and includes language pertaining to logbook entries for flights conducted in approved flight simulators and approved flight training devices.

61.51(d): The FAA notes the concerns of AOPA, HAI, and other commenters, and is not adopting the new term "supervised pilot-in-command time" in the final rule. Accordingly, the final rule adds §61.51(d), "Logging of solo flight time," which reiterates the provision of existing §61.51(c).

61.51(e): After further review, the FAA has decided not to adopt the proposal to change the provisions for the logging of pilot-in-command time. The FAA has determined that the increased regulatory and economic burden resulting from this proposal is not sufficiently supported by a safety justification based on operational requirements and accident/incident data. However, the FAA would like to take this opportunity to clarify the proper logging of pilot-in-command time for recreational, private, and commercial pilots. The FAA acknowledges there has been confusion in the past regarding the logging of pilot-in-command time by these pilots and that inconsistent policy opinions have been issued by the FAA. The FAA has determined that clarity is necessary to preserve the value of pilot-in-command time. In light of the inconsistent policy opinions issued by the FAA, however, this clarification is meant to be prospective and not to require pilots to "revisit" past logging. The FAA's position regarding the proper logging of pilot-in-command time for a recreational, private, or commercial pilot applicable after the effective date of this final rule is set forth in this response.

There are only three ways for a recreational, private, or commercial pilot to properly log pilot-in-command time in accordance with section §61.51. These pilots may properly log pilot-in-command time: (1) When the pilot is the sole manipulator of the controls of an aircraft for which the pilot is rated; (2) when the pilot is the sole occupant of the aircraft; or (3) except for recreational pilots, when the pilot is acting as pilot in command of an aircraft for which more than one pilot is required under the type certification of the aircraft or the regulations under which the flight is conducted.

As noted in Notice No. 95-11[FR], there has been a distinction between acting as pilot in command and logging of pilot-in-command time. "Pilot in command," as defined in part 1, "means the pilot responsible for the operation and safety of an aircraft during flight time." Section 61.51 is a flight-time logging regulation under which: (1) pilot-in-command time may be logged by someone who is not actually the pilot in command as defined in part 1 (e.g., when the pilot is the sole manipulator of the controls of an aircraft for which the pilot is rated but is not the pilot in command as defined in part 1); and (2) pilot-in-command time may not be logged by someone who is the actual pilot in command as defined in part 1 (e.g., when the pilot acting as pilot in command of an aircraft on which more than one pilot is not required under the type certification of the aircraft or the regulations under which the flight is conducted is not the sole manipulator of the controls of the aircraft, and the pilot who is the sole manipulator of the controls is logging that time as pilot-in-command time).

Two recreational, private, or commercial pilots may not simultaneously log pilot in command flight time when one pilot is acting as pilot in command as defined in part 1, and the other pilot is the sole manipulator of the controls, unless the aircraft type certification or the regulations under which the flight is conducted require more than one pilot. In contrast, an ATP may log all flight time as pilot-in-command time when that pilot is acting as the pilot in command as defined in part 1 during an operation requiring an ATP certificate regardless of who is manipulating the controls of the aircraft. This distinction between the concept of acting as pilot in command and the logging of pilot-in-command time will continue in this final rule.

The FAA also notes the concern of AOPA and NBAA regarding the wording "actual flight conditions" in proposed §61.51(d), redesignated as §61.51(e) in the final rule, and has deleted the objectionable language. The FAA notes that the Amendment No. 61-100 did not include a provision to permit a student pilot to log pilot-in-command time when that student is the sole occupant of the aircraft. Section 61.51(e)(4) includes such a provision.

61.51(f): The FAA addressed concerns to this rule by modifying proposed §61.55 in the final rule, as discussed below, and therefore no major changes were necessary to this paragraph. The FAA has added the phrase "the regulations under which the flight has been conducted" in paragraph (f)(2) to permit, for example, safety pilots complying with §91.109 to be allowed to log second in command time.

61.51(g): The FAA notes the privacy concerns of individual commenters and has therefore deleted the proposed language "and pilot certificate number" from the final rule. The final rule also includes language relating to the use of approved flight simulators and approved flight training devices.

61.51(h): The FAA notes the concerns of AOPA and HAI, and therefore has deleted the proposed language "for the purpose of obtaining a certificate, rating, or recency of experience requirements, of this part" from the final rule. AOPA's concern regarding the confusion between "flight time" and "actual flight" was addressed through the elimination of the wording "actual flight" elsewhere in paragraph (b) of this section, as previously discussed.

61.51(i): The proposal inadvertently deleted the word "reasonable" before "request." In the final rule, the phrase "reasonable request" has been retained. The FAA has noted HAI's concern, but is not persuaded that student pilots should be exempt from carrying logbooks on all flights. However, in partial response to HAI's concern, as well as that of individual commenters, the FAA has decided to delete the proposed logbook-carrying requirements for recreational pilots, except for flights of more than 50 nautical miles from the point of departure. In addition, the FAA has changed the heading of this paragraph for clarity, because a student is required to present more than a logbook. The FAA notes that this requirement is contained in the existing rule. Except for these changes, the final rule is adopted as proposed.

Safety Pilot Time: The FAA did not intend to prevent safety pilots from logging second in command time or to require them to comply with the requirements of proposed §61.55. The FAA has noted the concerns of AOPA and others, and has modified §61.51(f)(2) of the final rule to permit safety pilots to log second in command time. (62 FR 16249 – 16251).

CROSS REFERENCES

61.3, Requirement for Certificates, Ratings and Authorizations; 61.45, Practical Tests: Required Aircraft and Equipment; 61.57, Recent Flight Experience: Pilot In Command; 61.59, Falsification, Reproduction or Alteration of Applications, Certificates, Logbooks, Reports, or Records; 18 U.S.C. 1001, Fraud and False Statements, Statements or Entries Generally [Federal Crimes].

CASES

If a request by an Administrator to view a pilot's logbook is not a burden or inconvenience, denial is not excused by the assertion of 5th Amendment rights. *Administrator v. Jones*. EA-3876 (1993).

Following an accident, the FAA examined the logbooks of two pilots. The FAA found 200 identical PIC entries, and it was unclear when, whether, and what type of flight instruction was given. The pilots later revised the logbooks, but the NTSB affirmed the FAA's revocation of both pilot's commercial and flight instructor certificates. *Administrator v. Crow & Pearson*, EA-4008 (1993).

A pilot's position, in refusing to allow FAA inspectors to view his pilot logbook, was that he did not keep them up-to-date and, accordingly, no purpose would be served in showing them to the inspectors, was not accepted by the Board. In sustaining a violation of [§61.51(i)], the Board held that an airman, upon reasonable request, does not have the liberty to decide whether to comply with the inspector's request to see his personal logbook. *Administrator v. Chaffin*, 5 NTSB 1341 (1986).

FAA CHIEF COUNSEL OPINIONS

Pilot In Command (PIC)

If the pilot is the sole manipulator of the controls and he or she is receiving instruction, that pilot may log the same flight time as both pilot-in-command (PIC) time and training time. However, the time may only count once towards total time. (5-17-01).

A pilot may log pilot-in-command flight time while they are the sole manipulator of the controls of an aircraft for which they are rated, the sole occupant of the aircraft, acting as PIC on an aircraft on which more than one pilot is required under the type certificate or the regulations governing the flight, or while acting as pilot in command of an operation requiring an ATP certificate (ATP certificate holders only). (8-21-00).

If more than one pilot is required under the type certificate of the aircraft or the regulations governing the flight then the acting pilot in command may log PIC flight time for the entire flight even though he or she may not manipulate the flight controls, and the second in command may log PIC flight time for all of the flight time while he or she is the sole manipulator of the controls. In addition, if the regulations require the pilot in command to hold an ATP for that operation, even if more than one pilot is not required under the type certificate of the aircraft or the governing regulations, then the acting pilot in command may log PIC flight time for the entire flight and the second in command may log PIC flight time for all of the time while he or she is the sole manipulator of the controls. (8-21-00).

A private pilot may log pilot-in-command time, in a complex or high performance airplane, for those portions of the flight when he or she is the sole manipulator of the controls because the aircraft being operated is single-engine land and the private pilot holds a single-engine land rating. However, while the private pilot may log this time as pilot-in-command time, he or she may not act as the pilot-in-command unless he or she has the appropriate endorsement as required under 14 CFR section 61.31. (6-3-99).

Are there any circumstances when, during a normal flight, two Private Pilots may simultaneously act as (and therefore log the time as) Pilot In Command?

> The answer is two private pilots may not simultaneously act as PIC but they may, under certain circumstances, simultaneously log PIC time. There is a difference between serving as PIC and logging PIC time. PIC, as defined in FAR 1.1, means the pilot responsible for the operation and safety of an aircraft during flight time. 61.51 deals with logging PIC flight time, and it provides that a private or commercial pilot may log as PIC time only that flight time during which he is the sole manipulator of the controls of an aircraft for which he is rated, or when he is the sole occupant of the aircraft, or when he acts as PIC of an aircraft on which more than one pilot is required under the type certification of the aircraft, or the regulations under which the flight is conducted. It is important to note that 61.51 only regulates the recording of PIC time used to meet the requirements toward a higher certificate, higher rating, or for recent flight experience. Therefore, while it is not possible for two pilots to act as PIC simultaneously, it is possible for two pilots to log PIC flight time simultaneously. PIC flight time may be logged by both the PIC responsible for the operation and safety of the aircraft during flight time in accordance with FAR 1.1, and by the pilot who acts as the sole manipulator of the controls of the aircraft for which the pilot is rated under 61.51. (10-30-92).

Your question concerning 61.51 centers on the sentence "for which the pilot is rated." You ask "If the airplane in question requires a type rating (for example, KC-135 or B-707), does a pilot have to possess the type rating for that aircraft before he can log PIC time during that portion of the flight during which he is the sole manipulator of the controls? Or, to the contrary, are possession of a private pilot certificate and merely being the sole manipulator of the controls sufficient to log PIC time in that aircraft?"

> Under 61.51, a private or commercial pilot may log as PIC time only that flight time during which he is the sole manipulator of the controls of an aircraft for which that pilot is rated. "Rated", as used under 61.51, refers to the category, class, and type as appropriate. Therefore, pilots must be appropriately rated for the aircraft, as the term is defined above, before they may log PIC time under Part 61. The possession of a private pilot certificate and merely being the sole manipulator of the controls of an aircraft is not necessarily sufficient to log PIC time. (7-30-92).

Under 61.51, concerning the logging of PIC time, the sentence "when acting as pilot-in-command of an aircraft on which more than one pilot is required under the type certification..." does not mean that a pilot, not in possession of the type certificate for that aircraft, can nonetheless act as PIC during the portion of the flight that he is the sole manipulator of the controls and therefore log PIC time for that portion of the flight. (7-30-92).

The second in command, who is the sole manipulator of the controls of an aircraft for which he is rated may log that time as PIC flight time under 61.51, in order to use that experience to meet the requirements for a certificate or rating or recent flight experience requirements of Part 61. Also, if the pilot is acting as second in command of an aircraft on which more than one pilot is required by the FAR, he may also log that time as second-in-command time under 61.51. Of course, one hour logged under both PIC and SIC time adds up to only one hour total flight time. It should be recognized that some time may be logged as PIC time for some purposes, but not for others. For example, the 100 hours of PIC time included in 135.225(d) refers to time when the pilot actually served as PIC, not when he was the SIC manipulating the controls. (12-5-84).A noninstrument-rated pilot who is taking instrument instruction in IFR conditions may log the time he actually manipulates the controls as PIC time, but may not actually serve as the PIC. The other pilot must be the PIC, and not merely a "watch pilot." (4-6-83).

Second In Command (SIC)

A certificate holder's operations specifications may be considered regulatory if they impose a requirement on the certificate holder. If the operations specifications merely allow (not require) the certificate holder to do something that it is already allowed to do under the Federal Aviation Regulations, then the operations specifications would not be considered regulatory. In the case where a certificate holder's operations specifications require the designation of a SIC during certain conditions then that SIC may log the flight time accordingly under §61.51(f). (3-9-00).

A person may log second-in-command time only if more than one pilot is required under the type certificate of the aircraft or the regulations under which the flight is being conducted require an additional pilot. Operating under the provisions §91.109 (requiring a safety pilot during simulated instrument flight) the sole manipulator of the controls may log pilot in command time and the safety pilot may log second in command time. (10-19-99).

If more than one pilot is not required, by either the type certificate of the aircraft or the regulations under which the flight occurred, then a second commercial pilot acting as SIC may not log SIC flight time, and may only log PIC flight time for the time during which he was the sole manipulator of the controls. Also, because the time when he is not the sole manipulator of the controls cannot be logged it cannot be used to meet the aeronautical expertise requirements for an ATP certificate. (11-20-97).

Flight time logged as a copilot during the course of a military career must meet the requirements of §61.51(c)(3) to be logged as SIC time. (4-9-97).

Instrument

If the simulated instrument time that a student pilot receives in order to qualify for the Private Pilot Certificate in accordance with §§61.109(a)(3), (b)(3), and (e)(3) is given by a CFI without the authorization to give instrument instruction then that time may only be logged as instruction received time and it cannot be used to fulfill the requirements of another higher certificate or an instrument rating. A CFI without instrument authorization may give the flight training required in §§61.109(a)(3), (b)(3), and (e)(3) is not considered "instrument instruction." (8-7-97).

May a non-instrument-rated private pilot working towards an instrument rating log as pilot-in-command, flight time in which he/she is flying with a CFII on a flight which is conducted on an instrument flight plan, in controlled airspace, with an IFR clearance from ATC, and in instrument meteorological weather conditions? Does 61.3 prohibit logging such time as PIC?

> 61.51 provides, in part, that a private pilot may log as pilot-in-command time that flight time when he is the sole manipulator of the controls of an aircraft for which the pilot is rated. 61.3 provides, in part, that no person may act as pilot-in-command of a civil aircraft under instrument flight rules, or in weather conditions less than VFR minimums, unless that person holds an instrument rating. Therefore, a non-instrument rated private pilot who is taking instrument instruction from a CFII in IFR conditions may log the flight time in which he is the sole manipulator of the controls as pilot-in-command time, if he is rated in the aircraft, but may not actually serve as the pilot in command. (6-12-92).

An instrument student, who holds at least a private pilot certificate and who is rated for the aircraft flown, may log as pilot-in-command flight time under 61.51 the time spent as sole manipulator of the controls regardless of the meteorological conditions of the flight. In situations where actual IFR meteorological conditions exist, the safety pilot or flight instructor, as the case may be, must be pilot in command, as the term is defined under 1.1 of the FAR. (9-13-89).

Actual instrument conditions may occur during a flight on a moonless night over the ocean with no discernible horizon, if use of the instruments is necessary to maintain adequate control over the aircraft. The determination of whether such a flight could be logged under 61.51 is subjective and based in part on the sound judgment of the pilot. The log should include the reasons for determining the flight was under actual instrument conditions in the event the entry is challenged. (11-7-84).

Safety Pilots

How shall two Private Pilots log their flight time when one pilot is under the hood for simulated instrument time and the other pilot acts as safety pilot?

> The answer is the pilot who is under the hood may log PIC time for that flight time in which he is the sole manipulator of the controls of the aircraft, provided he is rated for that aircraft. The appropriately rated safety pilot may concurrently log as second in command (SIC) that time during which he is acting as safety pilot. The two pilots may, however, agree prior to initiating the flight that the safety pilot will be the PIC responsible for the operation and safety of the aircraft during the flight. If this is done, then the safety pilot may log all the flight time as PIC time in accordance with FAR 1.1 and the pilot under the hood may log, concurrently, all of the flight time during which he is the sole manipulator of the controls as PIC time in accordance with 61.51. (10-30-92).

Flight Instruction

Can a CFI log landings day or night if the manipulations of the flight controls are shared by both student and instructor?

> 61.51 states that a CFI may log as PIC time all flight time during which he acts as a flight instructor. For recent flight experience, however, under 61.57, to log PIC time one must be the "sole manipulator of the flight controls." In the scenario you presented, where the "flight controls are shared by both student and instructor," the CFI can log that as PIC flight time under 61.51 but the CFI cannot log this as PIC flight time towards recent flight experience under 61.57. (12-9-92).

Can a CFI log landings day or night if the manipulations of the flight controls are shared by both student and instructor?

> 61.51 states that a CFI may log as PIC time all flight time during which he acts as a flight instructor. For recent flight experience, however, under 61.57, to log PIC time one must be the "sole manipulator of the flight controls." In the scenario you presented, where the "flight controls are shared by both student and instructor," the CFI can log that as PIC flight time under 61.51 but the CFI cannot log this as PIC flight time towards recent flight experience under 61.57. (12-9-92). [Editor's Note: we have not found any NTSB cases which supports this interpretation.]

135 Operations

The letter presents the following scenario: a Part 135 certificate holder conducts operations in multi-engine airplanes under instrument flight rules (IFR). The operator has approval to conduct operations without an SIC using an approved autopilot under the provisions of 135.105. The operator has assigned a fully qualified pilot, who has had a Part 135 competency check, to act as SIC in an aircraft that does not require two pilots under its type certification. Although 135.101 requires an SIC for Part 135 operations in IFR conditions, the autopilot approval is an exception to that requirement.

While the SIC is flying the airplane, he can log PIC time in accordance with 61.51 because he is appropriately rated and current, and is the sole manipulator of the controls. Additionally, he has passed the competency checks required for Part 135 operations, at least as SIC.

The letter then asks two questions. The first asks whether the pilot designated as PIC by the employer, as required by 135.109, can log PIC time while the SIC is actually flying the airplane.

> There are two ways to log pilot-in-command flight time that are pertinent to this question. The first is as the pilot responsible for the safety and operation of an aircraft during flight time. If a pilot is designated as PIC for a flight by the certificate holder, as required by 135.109, that person is pilot in command for the entire flight, no matter who is actually manipulating the controls of the aircraft, because that pilot is responsible for the safety and operation of the aircraft. The second way to log PIC flight time that is pertinent to this question is to be the sole manipulator of the controls of an aircraft for which the pilot is rated. Thus, a multi-engine airplane flown under Part 135 by two pilots can have both pilots logging time as pilot in command when the appropriately rated second in command is manipulating the controls. We stress, however, that here we are discussing logging of flight time for purposes of FAR 61.51, where you are keeping a record to show recent flight experience or to show that you meet the requirements for a higher rating. Your question does not say if the second pilot in your example is fully qualified as a PIC, or only as an SIC. This is important, because even though an SIC can log PIC time, that pilot has not qualified to serve as a PIC under Part 135. An example of this difference is 135.225(d), which raises IFR landing minimums for pilots in command of turbine powered airplanes flown under Part 135 who have not served at least 100 hours as PIC in that type of airplane. Served and logged are not the same in this context, and no matter how the SIC logs his time, he has not served as a PIC until he has completed the training and check rides necessary for certification as a Part 135 PIC. Approval for single pilot operations with use of an operative approved autopilot system under 135.105 gives an operator an additional option in the conduct of operations. It does not mandate that all future flights be conducted in that manner. The operator can elect to fly trips with two pilots, as is otherwise required for flight in IFR conditions under 135.101, using the second in command instead of the autopilot. (3-26-92).

The second question asks if, under the circumstances given above, the SIC can log time as SIC when the designated pilot in command is flying the aircraft.

> The answer is yes, as long as the certificate holder is using the SIC as a crewmember instead of exercising the autopilot authorization. In other words, the certificate holder elects not to conduct an IFR flight using the single pilot with a functioning autopilot option, but rather conducts an IFR flight using two qualified pilots. The two pilots are then "required by the regulations under which the flight is conducted", 61.51, and the assumption is that the second pilot (SIC) will function as a required crewmember, and SIC time may validly be logged. However, if for some reason another qualified pilot "rides along" and does not function as a crewmember, then second-in-command time may not be validly logged. (3-26-92).

General

If an aircraft, operated by the U.S. Forest Service as a public aircraft, is not properly certificated, the pilot of that aircraft cannot log any time for the purposes of 14 CFR part 61. (10-19-99).

A pilot may log their flight time in any way they see fit, however the specific flight time used to meet a part 61 certification or experience requirements must be logged in accordance with Section 61.51. (4-9-97).

Improper logging of flight time and the subsequent use of that flight time on FAA applications may constitute a violation of §61.59 depending on the knowledge and intent of the individual when making such entries and whether such entries are material and actually relied upon by the FAA. (4-9-97).

61.53 PROHIBITION ON OPERATIONS DURING MEDICAL DEFICIENCY

(a)   *Operations that require a medical certificate.* Except as provided for in paragraph (b) of this section, a person who holds a current medical certificate issued under part 67 of this chapter shall not act as pilot in command, or in any other capacity as a required pilot flight crewmember, while that person:
   (1)   Knows or has reason to know of any medical condition that would make the person unable to meet the requirements for the medical certificate necessary for the pilot operation; or
   (2)   Is taking medication or receiving other treatment for a medical condition that results in the person being unable to meet the requirements for the medical certificate necessary for the pilot operation.
(b)   *Operations that do not require a medical certificate.* For operations provided for in §61.23(b) of this part, a person shall not act as pilot in command, or in any other capacity as a required pilot flight crewmember, while that person knows or has reason to know of any medical condition that would make the person unable to operate the aircraft in a safe manner.

EXPLANATION

Any change in a pilot's medical condition since his or her last airman physical under Part 67 should alert that person to the possibility that he or she is no longer medically qualified under Part 67. As a matter of self-interest the question of their medical qualifications should be resolved immediately rather than waiting until the next exam for renewal of the medical certificate.

Any change in type or amount of medication may cause a person to be not medically qualified.

If the FAA issues a letter requesting the return of a medical certificate, examine it carefully to see if it is an "order." If it is not, it is not compulsory, and you cannot appeal the issuance of such a letter to the NTSB, even if you turn in your medical certificate in response to the letter.

PREAMBLE

After consideration of the comments, the FAA has determined that the disputed language, "knows or has reason to know" is necessary to ensure that pilots seriously evaluate their health prior to operating an aircraft. The FAA does not believe that the disputed language imposes an additional burden on pilots because §61.53 already requires pilots to evaluate their health prior to each flight. The proposed language merely clarifies this existing requirement. The FAA acknowledges that the language is subjective and is relying on pilots to use reasonable judgment. After further review, the FAA has determined that for operations that do not require a medical certificate, the language referring to medication or treatment would effectively establish standards for self-evaluation. Therefore, this language has been deleted for operations that do not require a medical certificate. The FAA has decided to retain the two-paragraph format of the proposed rule because it clarifies a pilot's responsibilities for medical self evaluation, regardless of whether or not a pilot is required to hold a medical certificate.

The proposal is adopted with minor editorial changes and the changes noted above. (62 FR 16251).

CROSS REFERENCES

Part 67, Medical Standards and Certification.

CASES

A letter given to a pilot by an FAA doctor urging the pilot to surrender his medical certificate because of a medical history that might disqualify the pilot is not an order but an "invitation." Because it is not an order, the pilot cannot appeal the issuance of the letter to the NTSB. The NTSB only has jurisdiction over appeals from an "order." *Administrator v. Schart*, EA-3718 (1992).

FAA CHIEF COUNSEL OPINIONS

While there is no specific regulation requiring a pilot to report a change in his medial condition, as a matter of policy the FAA encourages reporting any changes in medical status that might render pilot unable to meet the requirements of his current medical certificate. Also, a person who violates §61.53 is subject to suspension or revocation of his/her airman certificate or a civil penalty. (11-21-80).

§61.23 governs the duration of an airman medical certificate. It is not terminated before its usual expiration date when an airman refrains from using the certificate because of and during a physical deficiency in accordance with §61.53. Should the deficiency become cured, the airman medical certificate is still valid provided it has not reached the expiration date set forth in §61.23. While not a legal requirement, it is suggested that even if the airman medical certificate is still valid at the time the medical deficiency is cured, the airman submit medical information to the Regional Flight Surgeon so his qualification to hold the certificate can be determined. Alternatively, at the end of the medical deficiency, the airman could apply for a new airman medical certificate providing information regarding the medical deficiency. (4-10-79).

61.55 SECOND-IN-COMMAND QUALIFICATIONS

(a) Except as provided in paragraph (d) of this section, no person may serve as a second in command of an aircraft type certificated for more than one required pilot flight crewmember or in operations requiring a second in command unless that person holds:
    (1) At least a current private pilot certificate with the appropriate category and class rating; and
    (2) An instrument rating that applies to the aircraft being flown if the flight is under IFR.

(b) Except as provided in paragraph (d) of this section, no person may serve as a second in command of an aircraft type certificated for more than one required pilot flight crewmember or in operations requiring a second in command unless that person has within the previous 12 calendar months:
    (1) Become familiar with the following information for the specific type aircraft for which second-in-command privileges are requested—
        (i) Operational procedures applicable to the powerplant, equipment, and systems.
        (ii) Performance specifications and limitations.
        (iii) Normal, abnormal, and emergency operating procedures.
        (iv) Flight manual.
        (v) Placards and markings.
    (2) Except as provided in paragraph (e) of this section, performed and logged pilot time in the type of aircraft or in a flight simulator that represents the type of aircraft for which second-in-command privileges are requested, which includes—
        (i) Three takeoffs and three landings to a full stop as the sole manipulator of the flight controls;
        (ii) Engine-out procedures and maneuvering with an engine out while executing the duties of pilot in command; and
        (iii) Crew resource management training.

(c) If a person complies with the requirements in paragraph (b) of this section in the calendar month before or the calendar month after the month in which compliance with this section is required, then that person is considered to have accomplished the training and practice in the month it is due.

(d) This section does not apply to a person who is:
    (1) Designated and qualified as a pilot in command under part 121, 125, or 135 of this chapter in that specific type of aircraft;
    (2) Designated as the second in command under part 121, 125, or 135 of this chapter, in that specific type of aircraft;
    (3) Designated as the second in command in that specific type of aircraft for the purpose of receiving flight training required by this section, and no passengers or cargo are carried on the aircraft; or
    (4) Designated as a safety pilot for purposes required by §91.109(b) of this chapter.

(e) The holder of a commercial or airline transport pilot certificate with the appropriate category and class rating is not required to meet the requirements of paragraph (b)(2) of this section, provided the pilot:
    (1) Is conducting a ferry flight, aircraft flight test, or evaluation flight of an aircraft's equipment; and
    (2) Is not carrying any person or property on board the aircraft, other than necessary for conduct of the flight.

(f)   For the purpose of meeting the requirements of paragraph (b) of this section, a person may
      serve as second in command in that specific type aircraft, provided:
      (1)   The flight is conducted under day VFR or day IFR; and
      (2)   No person or property is carried on board the aircraft, other than necessary for conduct of
            the flight.
(g)   Except as provided in paragraph (h) of this section, the requirements of paragraph (b) of this
      section may be accomplished in a flight simulator that is used in accordance with an approved
      course conducted by a training center certificated under part 142 of this chapter.
(h)   An applicant for an initial second-in-command qualification for a particular type of aircraft who is
      qualifying under the terms of paragraph (g) of this section must satisfactorily complete a
      minimum of one takeoff and one landing in an aircraft of the same type for which the
      qualification is sought.

EXPLANATION

The requirement to complete only one takeoff and one landing in an actual aircraft applies only to
persons who complete the rest of the requirements of 61.55 in an approved course at a training
center certificated under Part 142.

PREAMBLE

After consideration of the comments, the FAA has determined that the proposed second in command
training requirements should be adopted with the addition of paragraph (d)(4) to except a person
designated as a safety pilot as required by §91.109(b). The final rule also incorporates other editorial
changes and provisions permitting the use of approved flight simulators and approved flight training
devices to meet the requirements of this section. (62 FR 16252)

CROSS REFERENCES

61.51, Pilot Logbooks; 91.109, Flight Instruction: Simulated Instrument Flight and Certain Flight
Tests.

61.56 FLIGHT REVIEW

(a)   Except as provided in paragraphs (b) and (f) of this section, a flight review consists of a
      minimum of 1 hour of flight training and 1 hour of ground training. The review must include:
      (1)   A review of the current general operating and flight rules of part 91 of this chapter; and
      (2)   A review of those maneuvers and procedures that, at the discretion of the person giving
            the review, are necessary for the pilot to demonstrate the safe exercise of the privileges of
            the pilot certificate.
(b)   Glider pilots may substitute a minimum of three instructional flights in a glider, each of which
      includes a flight to traffic pattern altitude, in lieu of the 1 hour of flight training required in
      paragraph (a) of this section.

(c)   Except as provided in paragraphs (d), (e) and (g) of this section, no person may act as pilot in command of an aircraft unless, since the beginning of the 24th calendar month before the month in which that pilot acts as pilot in command, that person has:

    (1)   Accomplished a flight review given in an aircraft for which that pilot is rated by an authorized instructor; and

    (2)   A logbook endorsed from an authorized instructor who gave the review certifying that the person has satisfactorily completed the review.

(d)   A person who has, within the period specified in paragraph (c) of this section, passed a pilot proficiency check conducted by an examiner, an approved pilot check airman, or a U.S. Armed Force, for a pilot certificate, rating, or operating privilege need not accomplish the flight review required by this section.

(e)   A person who has, within the period specified in paragraph (c) of this section, satisfactorily accomplished one or more phases of an FAA-sponsored pilot proficiency award program need not accomplish the flight review required by this section.

(f)   A person who holds a current flight instructor certificate who has, within the period specified in paragraph (c) of this section, satisfactorily completed a renewal of a flight instructor certificate under the provisions in §61.197 need not accomplish the 1 hour of ground training specified in paragraph (a) of this section.

(g)   A student pilot need not accomplish the flight review required by this section provided the student pilot is undergoing training for a certificate and has a current solo flight endorsement as required under §61.87 of this part.

(h)   The requirements of this section may be accomplished in combination with the requirements of §61.57 and other applicable recent experience requirements at the discretion of the authorized instructor conducting the flight review.

(i)   A flight simulator or flight training device may be used to meet the flight review requirements of this section subject to the following conditions:

    (1)   The flight simulator or flight training device must be used in accordance with an approved course conducted by a training center certificated under part 142 of this chapter.

    (2)   Unless the flight review is undertaken in a flight simulator that is approved for landings, the applicant must meet the takeoff and landing requirements of §61.57(a) or §61.57(b) of this part.

    (3)   The flight simulator or flight training device used must represent an aircraft, or set of aircraft, for which the pilot is rated.

EXPLANATION

While a flight review may be accomplished using flight simulators or flight training devices, the simulator or device must be approved by the FAA for that purpose and the flight review must be accomplished in an approved course at a Part 142 training center.

Completion of one or more phases of an FAA-sponsored Pilot Proficiency Awards Program in an aircraft constitutes completion of the flight review requirements of this rule.

The FAA clarified this rule in 1998 to exclude student pilots from the Flight Review requirements.

An instructor who holds a certificate issued by an entity other than the United States may give training, but can NOT endorse a person for satisfactory completion of a §61.56 Flight Review.

A pilot may elect to combine required flight reviews and checks. For example, a pilot who satisfactorily demonstrates competency in an aircraft requiring more than one pilot (FAR 61.58) may also use this demonstration to meet the biennial flight review requirement of FAR 61.56. For the purposes of the biennial flight review, a single showing of competency in any aircraft shall suffice for all other categories or classes of aircraft for which the pilot is rated. Demonstrations of competency may also be associated with proficiency checks required by FAR Part 121 or 135 or when applying for an additional category or class of pilot certificate or for a type rating.

PREAMBLE

As adopted in Amendment No. 61-100, this section includes provisions for the use of approved flight simulators and approved flight training devices. The FAA notes that Amendment No. 61-100 omitted the provision permitting a pilot to complete a phase of an FAA-sponsored pilot proficiency award program (i.e., Wings Program) in lieu of accomplishing a flight review. Such a provision is included in paragraph (e).

In response to the comment concerning the performance of 360-degree turns, the FAA has modified the language in paragraph (b) to permit three instructional flights in a glider, each of which requires flight to traffic pattern altitude, in lieu of the 1 hour of flight training required in paragraph (a). This modification should provide instructors with greater flexibility during the conduct of a flight review for glider pilots. The FAA expects that each instructional flight to traffic pattern altitude will consist of a launch, climb, level off, turns, descent, and landing to ensure that the pilot can demonstrate proficiency in each phase of flight. (62 FR 16252).

CROSS REFERENCES

61.57, Recent Flight Experience: Pilot In Command; 61.197, Renewal of Flight Instructor Certificates; Part 91, General Operating and Flight Rules.

ADVISORY CIRCULARS

AC 61-91H *Pilot Proficiency Award Program* (1996).

AC 61-98A *Currency and Additional Qualification Requirements for Certificated Pilots* (1991).

AC 120-40B *Airplane Simulator Qualification* (1993).

AC 120-45A *Airplane Flight Training Device Qualification* (1992).

FAA CHIEF COUNSEL OPINIONS

61.56 clearly states that no pilot may act as pilot in command unless the pilot has completed a flight review within the past 24 months. Thus, if the biennial has expired, the pilot may not act as pilot in command during the flight review. (2-3-81).

61.57 RECENT FLIGHT EXPERIENCE: PILOT IN COMMAND

(a) *General experience.*
  (1) Except as provided in paragraph (e) of this section, no person may act as a pilot in command of an aircraft carrying passengers or of an aircraft certificated for more than one pilot flight crewmember unless that person has made at least three takeoffs and three landings within the preceding 90 days, and—
    (i) The person acted as the sole manipulator of the flight controls; and
    (ii) The required takeoffs and landings were performed in an aircraft of the same category, class, and type (if a type rating is required), and, if the aircraft to be flown is an airplane with a tailwheel, the takeoffs and landings must have been made to a full stop in an airplane with a tailwheel.
  (2) For the purpose of meeting the requirements of paragraph (a)(1) of this section, a person may act as a pilot in command of an aircraft under day VFR or day IFR, provided no persons or property are carried on board the aircraft, other than those necessary for the conduct of the flight.
  (3) The takeoffs and landings required by paragraph (a)(1) of this section may be accomplished in a flight simulator or flight training device that is—
    (i) Approved by the Administrator for landings; and
    (ii) Used in accordance with an approved course conducted by a training center certificated under part 142 of this chapter.
(b) *Night takeoff and landing experience.*
  (1) Except as provided in paragraph (e) of this section, no person may act as pilot in command of an aircraft carrying passengers during the period beginning 1 hour after sunset and ending 1 hour before sunrise, unless within the preceding 90 days that person has made at least three takeoffs and three landings to a full stop during the period beginning 1 hour after sunset and ending 1 hour before sunrise, and—
    (i) That person acted as sole manipulator of the flight controls; and
    (ii) The required takeoffs and landings were performed in an aircrft of the same category, class, and type (if a type rating is required).
  (2) The takeoffs and landings required by paragraph (b)(1) of this section may be accomplished in a flight simulator that is—
    (i) Approved by the Administrator for takeoffs and landings, if the visual system is adjusted to represent the period described in paragraph (b)(1) of this section; and
    (ii) Used in accordance with an approved course conducted by a training center certificated under part 142 of this chapter.
(c) *Instrument experience.* Except as provided in paragraph (e) of this section, no person may act as pilot in command under IFR or in weather conditions less than the minimums prescribed for VFR, unless within the preceding 6 calendar months, that person has:
  (1) For the purpose of obtaining instrument experience in an aircraft (other than a glider), performed and logged under actual or simulated instrument conditions, either in flight in the appropriate category of aircraft for the instrument privileges sought or in a flight simulator or flight training device that is representative of the aircraft category for the instrument privileges sought—
    (i) At least six instrument approaches;
    (ii) Holding procedures; and
    (iii) Intercepting and tracking courses through the use of navigation systems.

(2)   For the purpose of obtaining instrument experience In a glider, performed and logged under actual or simulated instrument conditions—
- (i)   At least 3 hours of instrument time in flight, of which 1-1/2 hours may be acquired in an airplane or a glider if no passengers are to be carried; or
- (ii)   3 hours of instrument time in flight in a glider if a passenger is to be carried.

(d)   *Instrument proficiency check.* Except as provided in paragraph (e) of this section, a person who does not meet the instrument experience requirements of paragraph (c) of this section within the prescribed time, or within 6 calendar months after the prescribed time, may not serve as pilot in command under IFR or in weather conditions less than the minimums prescribed for VFR until that person passes an instrument proficiency check consisting of a representative number of tasks required by the instrument rating practical test.

(1)   The instrument proficiency check must be—
- (i)   In an aircraft that is appropriate to the aircraft category;
- (ii)   For other than a glider, in a flight simulator or flight training device that is representative of the aircraft category; or
- (iii)   For a glider, in a single-engine airplane or a glider.

(2)   The instrument proficiency check must be given by—
- (i)   An examiner;
- (ii)   A person authorized by the U.S. Armed Forces to conduct instrument flight tests, provided the person being tested is a member of the U.S. Armed Forces;
- (iii)   A company check pilot who is authorized to conduct instrument flight tests under part 121, 125, or 135 of this chapter, and provided that both the check pilot and the pilot being tested are employees of that operator;
- (iv)   An authorized instructor; or
- (v)   A person approved by the Administrator to conduct instrument practical tests.

(e)   *Exceptions.*
(1)   Paragraphs (a) and (b) of this section do not apply to a pilot in command who is employed by a certificate holder under part 125 and engaged in a flight operation for that certificate holder if the pilot is in compliance with §§125.281 and 125.285 of this chapter.

(2)   This section does not apply to a pilot in command who is employed by an air carrier certificated under part 121 or 135 and is engaged in a flight operation under part 91, 121, or 135 for that air carrier if the pilot is in compliance with §§121.437 and 121.439, or §§135.243 and 135.247 of this chapter, as appropriate.

(3)   Paragraph (b) of this section does not apply to a pilot in command who operates more than one type of an airplane that is type certificated for more than one pilot flight crewmember, provided the pilot—
- (i)   Holds at least a valid commercial pilot certificate with the appropriate type rating for each airplane that the pilot seeks to operate under this alternative;
- (ii)   Has logged at least 1500 hours total time as a pilot;
- (iii)   Has accomplished at least 15 hours of flight time in the type of airplane that the pilot seeks to operate under this alternative within the preceding 90 days prior to the operation of that airplane; and

    (iv) Has accomplished—

        (A) At least three takeoffs and three landings to a full stop, during the period beginning 1 hour after sunset and ending 1 hour before sunrise as the sole manipulator of the flight controls in at least one of the types of airplanes that the pilot seeks to operate under this alternative, within the preceding 90 days prior to the operation of any of the types of airplanes that the pilot seeks to operate under this alternative; or

        (B) Completion of an approved training program under part 142 of this chapter within the preceding 12 calendar months prior to the month of the flight, which requires the performance of at least 6 takeoffs and 6 landings to a full stop as the sole manipulator of the controls in a flight simulator that is representative of at least one of the types of airplanes that the pilot seeks to operate under this alternative, and the flight simulator's visual system was adjusted to represent the period beginning 1 hour after sunset and ending 1 hour before sunrise.

EXPLANATION

While a pilot is not required to log all flight time, it is important that the time to be used to establish compliance with regulatory requirements, such as §61.57, be logged in a timely manner. Trying to recall dates and times at later dates may result in entries that are not accurate and this can lead to problems with the FAA.

This section establishes the recent flight experience for persons acting as pilot in command of an aircraft carrying passengers or for an aircraft that is certificated for more than one required pilot flight crewmember. If the aircraft is not carrying passengers and/or requires one pilot, this section does not apply.

61.57(a): Keep in mind that "category" refers to a broad classification of aircraft, such as airplane, rotorcraft or glider. In this instance, "category" does not refer to transport, normal, utility, acrobatic, etc. "Class" refers to single-engine, multi-engine, land, water, gyroplane, helicopter, airship, and free balloon. Therefore, three touch and goes in a Cessna 172 do not qualify a pilot to carry passengers in a Beech Baron, and vice versa.

61.57(b): Note that night currency requires stop and goes or full stop landings rather than touch and goes. Also note that there is no mention of tailwheel airplanes under this subsection. Therefore, if you have done three day stop and goes in a Cub in the preceding ninety days, and three night stop and goes in a Cessna 172 in the same period, you may legally carry a passenger in your Cub at night.

61.57(c) revises the instrument currency requirements by eliminating the previous 6-6-6 rule (six approaches and six hours within the preceding six months) in favor of six approaches and a holding procedure within the preceding six months. The requirement to intercept and track a course is redundant.

The term "a person authorized by the Administrator" includes an FAA inspector, a member of an armed force of the United States authorized to conduct flight tests, an FAA-approved check pilot, a certified instrument flight instructor, an evaluator for a Part 142 training centers, a designated examiner, a pilot proficiency examiner and a simulator-only instructor.

The three takeoffs and landings required in 61.57(e)(3)(iv)(A) to qualify for the exception to the night experience requirement may be accomplished in different airplanes. This still meets the intent of "... in at least one of the types of airplanes that the pilot seeks to operate under this alternative, within the preceding 90 days prior to the operation of any of the types of airplanes that the pilot seeks to operate under this alternative. . . ." In other words, all three takeoffs and landings to a full stop do not have to be performed in just one of the types, but may be spread out amongst the airplanes that the pilot seeks to operate under this night takeoff and landing currency alternative of §61.57(e)(3)

PREAMBLE

The FAA has decided to retain the existing requirement that recent instrument experience be performed in actual or simulated conditions, and withdraw the proposed requirements for recovery from unusual flight attitudes, and the intercepting and tracking of VOR radials and NDB bearings. In lieu of the latter requirement, §61.57(c)(1)(iii) is modified to require a pilot to intercept and track courses through the use of navigation systems. The FAA modified §61.57(c)(1) to require instrument experience "under actual or simulated instrument conditions either in flight appropriate to the category of aircraft for the instrument privileges sought or in an approved flight simulator or flight training device that is representative of the aircraft category for the instrument privileges sought." The FAA notes that GAMA's comment would impose an additional economic burden on pilots, and would therefore continue to require that flight time used to satisfy instrument recency experience be in the category but not the class of aircraft for which instrument privileges are sought. The FAA believes that the removal of the proposed requirement to perform and log recovery from unusual attitudes should relieve the concern expressed by NBAA since compliance with the remaining requirements should be achievable in normal flight operations. In consideration of AOPA's comment, the FAA has clarified the language of paragraph (c)(2) in the final rule. The FAA also included in paragraph (c)(2) the requirement that the instrument experience be performed and logged under actual or simulated instrument conditions.

61.57(d): After consideration of the comments, the FAA has determined that the requirement to perform a representative number of tasks required by the instrument rating practical test will promote safety, and that a required "check" every 6 months, as proposed by one commenter, would impose an unwarranted economic burden on pilots seeking to retain instrument privileges. To maintain consistency in terminology throughout the rule, the proposal to change the term "instrument competency check" to "instrument proficiency check" is also adopted. In addition, the FAA has modified the language in paragraph (d) to reflect that an instrument proficiency check need only be accomplished in the category of aircraft for which instrument privileges are sought. Amendment No. 61-100 inadvertently required that this check be accomplished in the class of aircraft for which privileges are sought. (62 FR 16252).

61.57(e)(3): SUMMARY: This final rule establishes an alternative means of compliance for the pilot-in-command (PIC) night takeoff and landing recent flight experience requirements. A pilot who operates more than one type of airplane, certificated for more than one pilot flight crewmember, can meet the PIC night takeoff and landing recent flight experience requirements in one of the types of airplanes he/she operates. The pilot would then be considered qualified to perform night flights in the other types of airplanes he/she operates as PIC. In addition, this new alternative means of compliance establishes certain qualifications, aeronautical experience, and additional training.

This action is needed to accommodate pilots employed by corporate operators and airplane manufacturers who operate diverse fleets of airplanes that are type certificated for more than one pilot flight crewmember. These operators and manufacturers require their pilots to meet a high level of aeronautical experience and training for qualification as a PIC. This final rule is intended to provide an additional means of compliance with the recent night flight experience requirements while maintaining an equivalent level of safety. (64 FR 23526)

CROSS REFERENCES

61.51, Pilot Logbooks; 61.56, Flight Review; 91.5, Pilot In Command of Aircraft Requiring more than One Required Pilot.

ADVISORY CIRCULARS

AC 61-98A *Currency and Additional Qualification Requirements for Certificated Pilots* (1991).

FAA CHIEF COUNSEL OPINIONS

The "grace month" provision of §135.301(a) does not apply to an instrument competency check required by §61.57. (5-10-89).

§61.57 contains the recent night flight experience requirements applicable to persons who act as pilot in command of an aircraft carrying passengers. This definition of "night" should be used only for the purposes of this section. (See definition of "night", §1.1) (6-4-87).

Can a CFI log landings day or night if the manipulations of the flight controls are shared by both student and instructor?

§61.51 states that a CFI may log as PIC time all flight time during which he acts as a flight instructor. For recent flight experience, however, under §61.57, to log PIC time one must be the "sole manipulator of the flight controls." In the scenario you presented, where the "flight controls are shared by both student and instructor," the CFI can log that as PIC flight time under §61.51 but the CFI cannot count this as PIC flight time towards recent flight experience under §61.57. (12-9-92).

Your letter asks whether the last sentence of §135.245(a) means that a second in command (SIC) must meet the requirements of §61.57 for recent IFR experience or an instrument competency check, or whether it means that the SIC must simply hold an instrument rating without meeting the recent experience requirements. You mention that §61.57 might tend to be confusing because it speaks to a pilot in command, while §135.245(a) pertains to a SIC.

§135.245 clearly requires recent instrument experience, not merely an instrument rating. It is also important to note that the 6 month instrument currency requirement of Part 61 is in addition to the SIC annual competency check required in §135.293(b). (6-18-91).

61.58 PILOT-IN-COMMAND PROFICIENCY CHECK: OPERATION OF AIRCRAFT REQUIRING MORE THAN ONE PILOT FLIGHT CREWMEMBER

(a)   Except as otherwise provided in this section, to serve as pilot in command of an aircraft that is type certificated for more than one required pilot flight crewmember, a person must—
   (1)   Within the preceding 12 calendar months, complete a pilot-in-command proficiency check in an aircraft that is type certificated for more than one required pilot flight crewmember; and
   (2)   Within the preceding 24 calendar months, complete a pilot-in-command proficiency check in the particular type of aircraft in which that person will serve as pilot in command.

(b)   This section does not apply to persons conducting operations under part 121, 125, 133, 135, or 137 of this chapter, or persons maintaining continuing qualification under an Advanced Qualification Program approved under SFAR 58.

(c)   The pilot-in-command proficiency check given in accordance with the provisions of part 121, 125, or 135 of this chapter may be used to satisfy the requirements of this section.

(d)   The pilot-in-command proficiency check required by paragraph (a) of this section may be accomplished by satisfactory completion of one of the following:
   (1)   A pilot-in-command proficiency check conducted by a person authorized by the Administrator, consisting of the maneuvers and procedures required for a type rating, in an aircraft type certificated for more than one required pilot flight crewmember;
   (2)   The practical test required for a type rating, in an aircraft type certificated for more than one required pilot flight crewmember;
   (3)   The initial or periodic practical test required for the issuance of a pilot examiner or check airman designation, in an aircraft type certificated for more than one required pilot flight crewmember; or
   (4)   A military flight check required for a pilot in command with instrument privileges, in an aircraft that the military requires to be operated by more than one pilot flight crewmember.

(e)   A check or test described in paragraphs (d)(1) through (d)(4) of this section may be accomplished in a flight simulator under part 142 of this chapter, subject to the following:
   (1)   Except as provided for in paragraphs (e)(2) and (e)(3) of this section, if an otherwise qualified and approved flight simulator used for a pilot-in-command proficiency check is not qualified and approved for a specific required maneuver—
      (i)   The training center must annotate, in the applicant's training record, the maneuver or maneuvers omitted; and
      (ii)   Prior to acting as pilot in command, the pilot must demonstrate proficiency in each omitted maneuver in an aircraft or flight simulator qualified and approved for each omitted maneuver.
   (2)   If the flight simulator used pursuant to paragraph (e) of this section is not qualified and approved for circling approaches—
      (i)   The applicant's record must include the statement, "Proficiency in circling approaches not demonstrated"; and
      (ii)   The applicant may not perform circling approaches as pilot in command when weather conditions are less than the basic VFR conditions described in §91.155 of this chapter, until proficiency in circling approaches has been successfully demonstrated in a flight simulator qualified and approved for circling approaches or in an aircraft to a person authorized by the Administrator to conduct the check required by this section.

(3)   If the flight simulator used pursuant to paragraph (e) of this section is not qualified and approved for landings, the applicant must—
    (i)   Hold a type rating in the airplane represented by the simulator; and
    (ii) Have completed within the preceding 90 days at least three takeoffs and three landings (one to a full stop) as the sole manipulator of the flight controls in the type airplane for which the pilot-in-command proficiency check is sought.

(f)   For the purpose of meeting the pilot-in-command proficiency check requirements of paragraph (a) of this section, a person may act as pilot in command of a flight under day VFR conditions or day IFR conditions if no person or property is carried, other than as necessary to demonstrate compliance with this part.

(g)   If a pilot takes the pilot-in-command proficiency check required by this section in the calendar month before or the calendar month after the month in which it is due, the pilot is considered to have taken it in the month in which it was due for the purpose of computing when the next pilot-in-command proficiency check is due.

EXPLANATION

A pilot may elect to combine required flight reviews and checks. For example, a pilot who satisfactorily demonstrates competency in an aircraft requiring more than one pilot (FAR 61.58) may also use this demonstration to meet the biennial flight review requirement of FAR 61.56. For the purposes of the biennial flight review, a single showing of competency in any aircraft shall suffice for all other categories or classes of aircraft for which the pilot is rated. Demonstrations of competency may also be associated with proficiency checks required by FAR Part 121 or 135 or when applying for an additional category or class of pilot certificate or for a type rating.

CROSS REFERENCES

91.155, Basic VFR Weather Minimums; Appendix F, Part 121, Proficiency Check Requirements; Special Federal Aviation Regulation 58, Advanced Qualification Program.

ADVISORY CIRCULARS

AC 120-45A *Airplane Flight Training Device Qualification* (1992).

FAA CHIEF COUNSEL OPINIONS

For those checks that must have been made "since the beginning of the 12th calendar month before the month in which the person acts as pilot in command," the date is always the first day of the month insofar as when the "currency" will lapse. For example: On October 15, 1984, a pilot wants to act as pilot in command of an aircraft which is type certificated for more than one required pilot crewmember. The pilot must have completed an appropriate check or test sometime between October 1, 1983 and October 15, 1984. (10-7-84).

The FAA interprets §61.58(g), as it interprets similar provisions in Parts 121 and 135, to permit a crewmember to serve in his position for up to one month following the month a check comes due. Accordingly, a pilot, whose check came due in December 1977 and who intended, but was unable, to take the check in January 1978, was qualified to act as pilot in command during January. (4-24-79).

61.59 FALSIFICATION, REPRODUCTION, OR ALTERATION OF APPLICATIONS, CERTIFICATES, LOGBOOKS, REPORTS, OR RECORDS

(a) No person may make or cause to be made:
  (1) Any fraudulent or intentionally false statement on any application for a certificate, rating, authorization, or duplicate thereof, issued under this part;
  (2) Any fraudulent or intentionally false entry in any logbook, record, or report that is required to be kept, made, or used to show compliance with any requirement for the issuance or exercise of the privileges of any certificate, rating, or authorization under this part;
  (3) Any reproduction for fraudulent purpose of any certificate, rating, or authorization, under this part; or
  (4) Any alteration of any certificate, rating, or authorization under this part.
(b) The commission of an act prohibited under paragraph (a) of this section is a basis for suspending or revoking any airman certificate, rating, or authorization held by that person.

EXPLANATION

The elements necessary to establish that a statement was "fraudulent" are: (1) a false representation, (2) in reference to a material fact, (3) made with knowledge of its falsity, (4) with intent to deceive, and (5) action taken in reliance upon the representation. The elements in the case of an "intentionally false statement" are (1) a false representation, (2) in reference to a material fact and (3) made with knowledge of its falsity (scienter). *Hart v. McLucas*, 535 F.2d 516 (1976).

If in doubt about a question on an application or whether flight time can be credited in a certain way, always ask the appropriate person before answering the question or making the entry.

CROSS REFERENCES

18 United States Code §1001, Fraud and False Statements, Statements or Entries Generally [Federal Crimes].

CASES

A designated pilot examiner for the FAA intentionally falsified airman records by failing three airman who had not yet taken the test. The examiner's ATP and flight instructor certificates were revoked. *Administrator v. Grillo*, EA-3994 (1993).

A pilot's certificate was revoked after his logbook and airline records showed a major difference in hours logged. He had recorded false entries to show eligibility to apply for an ATP certificate. *Administrator v. Pohl*, EA-3913 (1993).

Wholly apart from respondent's violation history consisting of a prior falsification, intentional falsification is a serious offense which in virtually all cases the Administrator imposes and the Board affirms revocation. *Administrator v. Rea*, EA-3467 (1991).

It is not the tendering of false or fraudulent information that the regulation 61.59 prohibits, but, rather, its placement in a "logbook, record, or report" that might be tendered to show compliance with specific requirements. *Administrator v. Schlagenhauf*, EA-3611 (1992).

A pilot who made 22 entries in her pilot logbook indicating she had acted as pilot in command of the aircraft on the entire flight when she knew and admitted she was not operating the controls during the entirety of each flight was found by the Board to be in violation of 61.59 and upheld the revocation of her commercial pilot certificate. *Administrator v. Runung*, EA-3629 (1992).

The Board held that, where the facts support a finding that an airline transport pilot, who will have been through the licensing procedure several times before attaining the certificate, has undertaken to purchase from an inspector a rating without passing the appropriate tests, he may be held to know that the records or documentation that must be processed by the inspector in connection with the issuance of the bogus rating will necessarily contain inaccurate information respecting such tests. Accordingly, such a pilot may reasonably be held to have knowingly caused the inspector to make those falsifications in violation of 61.59. The Board sustained the revocation of the pilot's airline transport, flight instructor, ground instructor, flight engineer and mechanic certificates. *Administrator v. Chirino*, 5 NTSB 1661 (1987).

The Board, in revoking a pilot's commercial pilot certificate for violation of 61.59, did not accept the pilot's position that, in applying for an ATP certificate, the logbook he presented contained a sufficient number of accurate entries to establish that he did indeed have the requisite 1500 hours of pilot flight time and that the false entries are mere surplusage. *Administrator v. Cassis*, 4 NTSB 555 (1982).

In the case where an Airline Transport Pilot who was not instrument rated signed an instructor's endorsement for his coworkers on their applications to test for a type rating the Board affirmed that the allegation of intentional falsification was not justified. The pilot had given his coworkers informal training and was led to believe that he had the authority to recommend them by the Designated Pilot Examiner who had conducted the training and also wanted to conduct the testing. *Administrator v. Richards*, EA-4813 (2000).

The Board found that completion of instructor's recommendation block on an airman application form by an Airline Transport Pilot who was not a certificated instructor did not constitute intentional falsification. He was instructed to complete the recommendation by a Designated Pilot Examiner and had no knowledge that he did not have the authority to do so *Administrator v. Vecchie*, EA-4816 (2000). Related cases are *Administrator v. Holland*, EA-4817 (2000); *Administrator v. Richardson*, EA-4820 (2000); *Administrator v. Luginbuhl*, EA-4821 (2000).

The Director of Operations for a 121 carrier was found to have made it a policy to enter a time not exceeding 8 hours in the operations logbooks for a certain route regardless of the actual time flown. When one of the company's pilots was asked to present his logbook (the only central place where his flight time for the company was logged) he admitted to not keeping correct and accurate time entries in his logbook. Upon inspection of it by a FAA inspector the logbook was found to have numerous white-out spots where corrections all having the exact same time and flown on the same route were entered. The pilot admitted that most of the entries he certified as being true and correct were actually "guesses" and were never meant to be a true and correct record of his time. The Board upheld the revocation of his and the Director of Operation's ATP certificates. *Administrator v. Branum and Alford*, EA-4849 (2000).

The Board affirmed the initial decision of the law judge not to revoke the ATP certificates of four pilots whose training records showed dates and times of training that did not match the availability of the aircraft and/or the instructor. The Director of Operations in charge of keeping the training records up to date testified that he had fallen behind in this aspect and had not been able to reconstruct some of the records correctly. The Administrator could offer no more evidence proving the falsification. *Administrator v. Fuller, Schwab, Knapp, and Gehres*, EA-4887 (2001).

Administrator v. Jones, EA-4888, (2001) arose from the same incident (Payne Stewart crash) and the Board applied the same judgment as in the case above.

In a case where a FAA Designated Pilot Examiner (DPE) allegedly reviewed the documents and logbooks for fifteen pilots seeking a type rating and provided seven of them with endorsed applications bearing the signature of an instructor who was never involved with the pilots' training, the Board upheld the decision of the law judge to revoke the DPE's pilot certificates. The endorsements on the blank forms were not required for this application and were therefore not considered material. However, the DPE, by signing the applications attesting that he had reviewed the applicants' logbooks and records for all required instructor endorsements, when he had not, constituted intentional falsification. *Administrator v. Carey*, EA-4912 (2001).

FAA CHIEF COUNSEL OPINIONS

Improper logging of flight time and the subsequent use of that flight time on FAA applications may constitute a violation of §61.59 depending on the knowledge and intent of the individual when making such entries and whether such entries are material and actually relied upon by the FAA. (4-9-97).

Flight time entered incorrectly on an FAA application, by someone other than the applicant, such as a flight instructor or flight school clerk, if endorsed as correct by the true applicant may constitute a violation of §61.59. This will depend on the knowledge and intent of the individual and whether or not the entries are material. However, the fact that someone else entered the information may be a mitigating factor in determining the sanction if an enforcement action is pursued. (4-9-97).

61.60 CHANGE OF ADDRESS

The holder of a pilot, flight instructor, or ground instructor certificate who has made a change in permanent mailing address may not, after 30 days from that date, exercise the privileges of the certificate unless the holder has notified in writing the FAA, Airman Certification Branch, P.O. Box 25082, Oklahoma City, OK 73125, of the new permanent mailing address, or if the permanent mailing address includes a post office box number, then the holder's current residential address.

EXPLANATION

Failure to notify the FAA of a change of address may result in an airman not receiving official communications from the FAA that affect the airman's certificates. Under these circumstances, the airman's argument that he or she was unaware of the action, having never received notification, will not be accepted.

Flight Standards District Offices (FSDOs) have change of address forms available (AC Form 8060-55).

The FAA will not send a new certificate after they are notified of a change of address. If you want a new certificate showing the new address, send a check for $2.00, made out to "Treasury of the United States." Allow 4-6 weeks for delivery.

INTENTIONALLY

LEFT

BLANK

INTENTIONALLY

LEFT

BLANK

SUBPART B — AIRCRAFT RATINGS AND PILOT AUTHORIZATIONS

61.61 APPLICABILITY

This subpart prescribes the requirements for the issuance of additional aircraft ratings after a pilot certificate is issued, and the requirements for and limitations of pilot authorizations issued by the Administrator.

61.63 ADDITIONAL AIRCRAFT RATINGS (OTHER THAN ON AN AIRLINE TRANSPORT PILOT CERTIFICATE)

(a) *General.* To be eligible for an additional aircraft rating to a pilot certificate, for other than an airline transport pilot certificate, an applicant must meet the appropriate requirements of this section for the additional aircraft rating sought.

(b) *Additional category rating.* An applicant who holds a pilot certificate and applies to add a category rating to that pilot certificate:

    (1) Must have received the required training and possess the aeronautical experience prescribed by this part that applies to the pilot certificate for the aircraft category and, if applicable, class rating sought;

    (2) Must have an endorsement in his or her logbook or training record from an authorized instructor, and that endorsement must attest that the applicant has been found competent in the aeronautical knowledge areas appropriate to the pilot certificate for the aircraft category and, if applicable, class rating sought;

    (3) Must have an endorsement in his or her logbook or training record from an authorized instructor, and that endorsement must attest that the applicant has been found proficient on the areas of operation that are appropriate to the pilot certificate for the aircraft category and, if applicable, class rating sought;

    (4) Must pass the required practical test that is appropriate to the pilot certificate for the aircraft category and, if applicable, class rating sought; and

    (5) Need not take an additional knowledge test, provided the applicant holds an airplane, rotorcraft, powered-lift, or airship rating at that pilot certificate level.

(c) *Additional class rating.* Any person who applies for an additional class rating to be added on a pilot certificate:

    (1) Must have an endorsement in his or her logbook or training record from an authorized instructor and that endorsement must attest that the applicant has been found competent in the aeronautical knowledge areas appropriate to the pilot certificate for the aircraft class rating sought;

    (2) Must have an endorsement in his or her logbook or training record from an authorized instructor, and that endorsement must attest that the applicant has been found proficient in the areas of operation appropriate to the pilot certificate for the aircraft class rating sought;

    (3) Must pass the required practical test that is appropriate to the pilot certificate for the aircraft class rating sought;

    (4) Need not meet the specified training time requirements prescribed by this part that apply to the pilot certificate for the aircraft class rating sought unless the person holds a lighter-than-air category rating with a balloon class rating and is seeking an airship class rating; and

    (5) Need not take an additional knowledge test, provided the applicant holds an airplane, rotorcraft, powered-lift, or airship rating at that pilot certificate level.

(d) *Additional type rating.* Except as specified in paragraph (d)(7) of this section, a person who applies for an additional aircraft type rating to be added on a pilot certificate, or the addition of an aircraft type rating that is accomplished concurrently with an additional aircraft category or class rating:

(1)   Must hold or concurrently obtain an instrument rating that is appropriate to the aircraft category, class, or type rating sought;

(2)   Must have an endorsement in his or her logbook or training record from an authorized instructor, and that endorsement must attest that the applicant has been found competent in the aeronautical knowledge areas appropriate to the pilot certificate for the aircraft category, class, or type rating sought;

(3)   Must have an endorsement in his or her logbook, or training record from an authorized instructor, and that endorsement must attest that the applicant has been found proficient in the areas of operation required for the issuance of an airline transport pilot certificate for the aircraft category, class, and type rating sought;

(4)   Must pass the required practical test appropriate to the airline transport pilot certificate for the aircraft category, class, and type rating sought;

(5)   Must perform the practical test in actual or simulated instrument conditions, unless the aircraft's type certificate makes the aircraft incapable of operating under instrument flight rules. If the practical test cannot be accomplished for this reason, the person may obtain a type rating limited to "VFR only." The "VFR only" limitation may be removed for that aircraft type when the person passes the practical test in actual or simulated instrument conditions. When an instrument rating is issued to a person who holds one or more type ratings, the type ratings on the amended pilot certificate shall bear the "VFR only" limitation for each aircraft type rating for which the person has not demonstrated instrument competency;

(6)   Need not take an additional knowledge test, provided the applicant holds an airplane, rotorcraft, powered-lift, or airship rating on their pilot certificate; and

(7)   In the case of a pilot employee of a part 121 or a part 135 certificate holder, must have—

   (i)   Met the appropriate requirements of paragraphs (d)(1), (d)(4), and (d)(5) of this section for the aircraft type rating sought; and

   (ii)   Received an endorsement in his or her flight training record from the certificate holder attesting that the applicant has completed the certificate holder's approved ground and flight training program appropriate to the aircraft type rating sought.

(e) *Use of a flight simulator or flight training device for an additional rating in an airplane.* The areas of operation required to be performed by paragraphs (b), (c), and (d) of this section shall be performed as follows:

(1)   Except as provided in paragraph (e)(2) of this section, the areas of operation must be performed in an airplane of the same category, class, and type, if applicable, as the airplane for which the additional rating is sought.

(2)   Subject to the limitations of paragraph (e)(3) through (e)(12) of this section, the areas of operation may be performed in a flight simulator or flight training device that represents the airplane for which the additional rating is sought.

(3)   The use of a flight simulator or flight training device permitted by paragraph (e)(2) of this section shall be conducted in accordance with an approved course at a training center certificated under part 142 of this chapter.

(4)   To complete all training and testing (except preflight inspection) for an additional airplane rating without limitations when using a flight simulator—

   (i)   The flight simulator must be qualified and approved as Level C or Level D; and

(ii) The applicant must meet at least one of the following:
  (A) Hold a type rating for a turbojet airplane of the same class of airplane for which the type rating is sought, or have been appointed by a military service as a pilot in command of an airplane of the same class of airplane for which the type rating is sought, if a type rating in a turbojet airplane is sought.
  (B) Hold a type rating for a turbopropeller airplane of the same class of airplane for which the type rating is sought, or have been designated by a military service as a pilot in command of an airplane of the same class of airplane for which the type rating is sought, if a type rating in a turbopropeller airplane is sought.
  (C) Have at least 2,000 hours of flight time, of which 500 hours is in turbine-powered airplanes of the same class of airplane for which the type rating is sought.
  (D) Have at least 500 hours of flight time in the same type airplane as the airplane for which the rating is sought.
  (E) Have at least 1,000 hours of flight time in at least two different airplanes requiring a type rating.

(5) Subject to the limitation of paragraph (e)(6) of this section, an applicant who does not meet the requirements of paragraph (e)(4) of this section may complete all training and testing (except for preflight inspection) for an additional rating when using a flight simulator if—
  (i) The flight simulator is qualified and approved as a Level C or Level D; and
  (ii) The applicant meets at least one of the following:
    (A) Holds a type rating in a propeller-driven airplane if a type rating in a turbojet airplane is sought, or holds a type rating in a turbojet airplane if a type rating in a propeller-driven airplane is sought; or
    (B) Since the beginning of the 12th calendar month before the month in which the applicant completes the practical test for an additional airplane rating, has logged:
      (1) At least 100 hours of flight time in airplanes of the same class for which the type rating is sought and which requires a type rating; and
      (2) At least 25 hours of flight time in airplanes of the same type for which the rating is sought.

(6) An applicant meeting only the requirements of paragraph (e)(5) of this section will be issued an additional rating with a limitation.

(7) The limitation on a certificate issued under the provisions of paragraph (e)(6) of this section shall state, "This certificate is subject to pilot-in-command limitations for the additional rating."

(8) An applicant who has been issued a pilot certificate with the limitation specified in paragraph (e)(7) of this section—
  (i) May not act as pilot in command of that airplane for which the additional rating was obtained under the provisions of this section until the limitation is removed from the pilot certificate; and
  (ii) May have the limitation removed by accomplishing 15 hours of supervised operating experience as pilot in command under the supervision of a qualified and current pilot in command, in the seat normally occupied by the pilot in command, in the same type of airplane to which the limitation applies.

(9) An applicant who does not meet the requirements of paragraph (e)(4) or paragraph (e)(5) of this section may be issued an additional rating after successful completion of one of the following requirements:

    (i) Compliance with paragraphs (e)(2) and (e)(3) of this section and the following tasks, which must be successfully completed on a static airplane or in flight, as appropriate:

        (A) Preflight inspection;

        (B) Normal takeoff;

        (C) Normal ILS approach;

        (D) Missed approach; and

        (E) Normal landing.

    (ii) Compliance with paragraphs (e)(2), (e)(3), and (e)(10) through (e)(12) of this section.

(10) An applicant meeting only the requirements of paragraph (e)(9)(ii) of this section will be issued an additional rating with a limitation.

(11) The limitation on a certificate issued under the provisions of paragraph (e)(10) of this section shall state, "This certificate is subject to pilot-in-command limitations for the additional rating."

(12) An applicant who has been issued a pilot certificate with the limitation specified in paragraph (e)(11) of this section—

    (i) May not act as pilot in command of that airplane for which the additional rating was obtained under the provisions of this section until the limitation is removed from the pilot certificate; and

    (ii) May have the limitation removed by accomplishing 25 hours of supervised operating experience as pilot in command under the supervision of a qualified and current pilot in command, in the seat normally occupied by the pilot in command, in that airplane of the same type to which the limitation applies.

(f) *Use of a flight simulator or flight training device for an additional rating in a helicopter.* The areas of operation required to be performed by paragraphs (b), (c), and (d) of this section shall be performed as follows:

(1) Except as provided in paragraph (f)(2) of this section, the areas of operation must be performed in a helicopter of the same type for the additional rating sought.

(2) Subject to the limitations of paragraph (f)(3) through (f)(12) of this section, the areas of operation may be performed in a flight simulator or flight training device that represents that helicopter for the additional rating sought.

(3) The use of a flight simulator or flight training device permitted by paragraph (f)(2) of this section shall be conducted in accordance with an approved course at a training center certificated under part 142 of this chapter.

(4) To complete all training and testing (except preflight inspection) for an additional helicopter rating without limitations when using a flight simulator—

    (i) The flight simulator must be qualified and approved as Level C or Level D; and

    (ii) The applicant must meet at least one of the following if a type rating is sought in a turbine-powered helicopter:

        (A) Hold a type rating in a turbine-powered helicopter or have been appointed by a military service as a pilot in command of a turbine-powered helicopter.

        (B) Have at least 2,000 hours of flight time that includes at least 500 hours in turbine-powered helicopters.

        (C) Have at least 500 hours of flight time in turbine-powered helicopters.

        (D) Have at least 1,000 hours of flight time in at least two different turbine-powered helicopters.

(5)   Subject to the limitation of paragraph (f)(6) of this section, an applicant who does not meet the requirements of paragraph (f)(4) of this section may complete all training and testing (except for preflight inspection) for an additional rating when using a flight simulator if—
       (i)   The flight simulator is qualified and approved as Level C or Level D; and
       (ii)   The applicant meets at least one of the following:
              (A)   Holds a type rating in a turbine-powered helicopter if a type rating in a turbine-powered helicopter is sought; or
              (B)   Since the beginning of the 12th calendar month before the month in which the applicant completes the practical test for an additional helicopter rating, has logged at least 25 hours of flight time in helicopters of the same type for which the rating is sought.
(6)   An applicant meeting only the requirements of paragraph (f)(5) of this section will be issued an additional rating with a limitation.
(7)   The limitation on a certificate issued under the provisions of paragraph (f)(6) of this section shall state, "This certificate is subject to pilot-in-command limitations for the additional rating."
(8)   An applicant who is issued a pilot certificate with the limitation specified in paragraph (f)(7) of this section—
       (i)   May not act as pilot in command of that helicopter for which the additional rating was obtained under the provisions of this section until the limitation is removed from the pilot certificate; and
       (ii)   May have the limitation removed by accomplishing 15 hours of supervised operating experience as pilot in command under the supervision of a qualified and current pilot in command, in the seat normally occupied by the pilot in command, in the same type of helicopter to which the limitation applies.
(9)   An applicant who does not meet the requirements of paragraph (f)(4) or paragraph (f)(5) of this section may be issued an additional rating after successful completion of one of the following requirements:
       (i)   Compliance with paragraphs (f)(2) and (f)(3) of this section and the following tasks, which must be successfully completed on a static helicopter or in flight, as appropriate:
              (A)   Preflight inspection;
              (B)   Normal takeoff;
              (C)   Normal ILS approach;
              (D)   Missed approach; and
              (E)   Normal landing.
       (ii)   Compliance with paragraphs (f)(2), (f)(3), and (f)(10) through (f)(12) of this section.
(10)   An applicant meeting only the requirements of paragraph (f)(9)(ii) of this section will be issued an additional rating with a limitation.
(11)   The limitation on a certificate issued under the provisions of paragraph (f)(10) of this section shall state, "This certificate is subject to pilot-in-command limitations for the additional rating."
(12)   An applicant who has been issued a pilot certificate with the limitation specified in paragraph (f)(11) of this section—
       (i)   May not act as pilot in command of that helicopter for which the additional rating was obtained under the provisions of this section until the limitation is removed from the pilot certificate; and
       (ii)   May have the limitation removed by accomplishing 25 hours of supervised operating experience as pilot in command under the supervision of a qualified and current pilot in command, in the seat normally occupied by the pilot in command, in that helicopter of the same type as to which the limitation applies.

(g) *Use of a flight simulator or flight training device for an additional rating in a powered-lift.* The areas of operation required to be performed by paragraphs (b), (c), and (d) of this section shall be performed as follows:

(1) Except as provided in paragraph (g)(2) of this section, the areas of operation must be performed in a powered-lift of the same type for the additional rating sought.

(2) Subject to the limitations of paragraphs (g)(3) through (g)(12) of this section, the areas of operation may be performed in a flight simulator or flight training device that represents that powered-lift for the additional rating sought.

(3) The use of a flight simulator or flight training device permitted by paragraph (g)(2) of this section shall be conducted in accordance with an approved course at a training center certificated under part 142 of this chapter.

(4) To complete all training and testing (except preflight inspection) for an additional powered-lift rating without limitations when using a flight simulator—

(i) The flight simulator must be qualified and approved as Level C or Level D; and

(ii) The applicant must meet at least one of the following if a type rating is sought in a turbine powered-lift:

(A) Hold a type rating in a turbine powered-lift or have been appointed by a military service as a pilot in command of a turbine powered-lift.

(B) Have at least 2,000 hours of flight time that includes at least 500 hours in turbine powered-lifts.

(C) Have at least 500 hours of flight time in turbine powered-lifts.

(D) Have at least 1,000 hours of flight time in at least two different turbine powered-lifts.

(5) Subject to the limitation of paragraph (g)(6) of this section, an applicant who does not meet the requirements of paragraph (g)(4) of this section may complete all training and testing (except for preflight inspection) for an additional rating when using a flight simulator if—

(i) The flight simulator is qualified and approved as Level C or Level D; and

(ii) The applicant meets at least one of the following:

(A) Holds a type rating in a turbine powered-lift if a type rating in a turbine powered-lift is sought; or

(B) Since the beginni1ng of the 12th calendar month before the month in which the applicant completes the practical test for an additional powered-lift rating, has logged at least 25 hours of flight time in powered-lifts of the same type for which the rating is sought.

(6) An applicant meeting only the requirements of paragraph (g)(5) of this section will be issued an additional rating with a limitation.

(7) The limitation on a certificate issued under the provisions of paragraph (g)(6) of this section shall state, "This certificate is subject to pilot-in-command limitations for the additional rating."

(8) An applicant who is issued a pilot certificate with the limitation specified in paragraph (g)(7) of this section—

(i) May not act as pilot in command of that powered-lift for which the additional rating was obtained under the provisions of this section until the limitation is removed from the pilot certificate; and

(ii) May have the limitation removed by accomplishing 15 hours of supervised operating experience as pilot in command under the supervision of a qualified and current pilot in command, in the seat normally occupied by the pilot in command, in the same type of powered-lift to which the limitation applies.

(9) An applicant who does not meet the requirements of paragraph (g)(4) or paragraph (g)(5) of this section may be issued an additional rating after successful completion of one of the following requirements:
  (i) Compliance with paragraphs (g)(2) and (g)(3) of this section and the following tasks, which must be successfully completed on a static powered-lift or in flight, as appropriate:
     (A) Preflight inspection;
     (B) Normal takeoff;
     (C) Normal ILS approach;
     (D) Missed approach; and
     (E) Normal landing.
  (ii) Compliance with paragraphs (g)(2), (g)(3), and (g)(10) through (g)(12) of this section.
(10) An applicant meeting only the requirements of paragraph (g)(9)(ii) of this section will be issued an additional rating with a limitation.
(11) The limitation on a certificate issued under the provisions of paragraph (g)(10) of this section shall state, "This certificate is subject to pilot-in-command limitations for the additional rating."
(12) An applicant who has been issued a pilot certificate with the limitation specified in paragraph (g)(11) of this section—
  (i) May not act as pilot in command of that powered-lift for which the additional rating was obtained under the provisions of this section until the limitation is removed from the pilot certificate; and
  (ii) May have the limitation removed by accomplishing 25 hours of supervised operating experience as pilot in command under the supervision of a qualified and current pilot in command, in the seat normally occupied by the pilot in command, in that powered-lift of the same type as to which the limitation applies.
(h) *Aircraft not capable of instrument maneuvers and procedures.* An applicant for a type rating who provides an aircraft not capable of the instrument maneuvers and procedures required by the appropriate requirements contained in §61.157 of this part for the practical test may—
  (1) Obtain a type rating limited to "VFR only"; and
  (2) Remove the "VFR only" limitation for each aircraft type in which the applicant demonstrates compliance with the appropriate instrument requirements contained in §61.157 or §61.73 of this part.
(i) *Multiengine, single-pilot station airplane.* An applicant for a type rating in a multiengine, single-pilot station airplane may meet the requirements of this part in a multiseat version of that multiengine airplane.
(j) *Single-engine, single-pilot station airplane.* An applicant for a type rating in a single-engine, single-pilot station airplane may meet the requirements of this part in a multiseat version of that single-engine airplane.
(k) *Waivers.* Unless the Administrator requires certain or all tasks to be performed, the examiner who conducts the practical test may waive any of the tasks for which the Administrator approves waiver authority.

EXPLANATION

This rule requires a logbook endorsement from an instructor for eligibility to take a knowledge test. This eliminates the FSDOs from having to allocate time to review an applicant's home study programs.

61.63(b) and (c) clarifies the required aeronautical experience requirements for applicants for additional category and class ratings.

For an applicant applying for a type rating only, the Instructor's Recommendation section of FAA Form 8710-1, Airman Certificate and/or Rating Application, need not be signed.

(1)   If the applicant is applying for a type rating to be added to an ATP certificate or for the original issuance of an ATP certificate in an airplane requiring a type rating, the applicant must have an endorsement in the applicant's logbook or training records from an authorized instructor certifying satisfactory completion of the training required by §61.157(f).

(2)   If the applicant is applying for a type rating to be placed on a private or commercial pilot certificate, the airman must have an endorsement in the airman's logbook or training records from an authorized instructor certifying satisfactory completion of the training required by §61.63(d)(6).

CROSS REFERENCES

61.73, Military Pilots or Former Military Pilots: Special Rules; 61.157, Airline Transport Pilots: Flight Proficiency.

ADVISORY CIRCULARS

AC 61-65D *Certification: Pilots and Flight Instructors* (1999).

AC 61-89E *Pilot Certificates: Aircraft Type Ratings* (2000).

FAA CHIEF COUNSEL OPINIONS

Flight time accumulated under the supervision of an appropriately rated pilot in an Aero Commander 500S does not meet the requirements of 61.63. The time does not qualify because none of the hours were logged while flying the aircraft under the supervision of an authorized flight instructor. (7-10-79).

CASES

In a case where a FAA Designated Pilot Examiner (DPE) allegedly reviewed the documents and logbooks for fifteen pilots seeking a type rating and provided seven of them with endorsed applications bearing the signature of an instructor who was never involved with the pilots' training, the Board upheld the decision of the law judge to revoke the DPE's pilot certificates. The endorsements on the blank forms were not required for this application, and were therefore, not considered material. However, the DPE, by signing the applications attesting that he had reviewed the applicants' logbooks and records for all required instructor endorsements, when he had not, constituted intentional falsification. *Administrator v.Carey*, EA-4912 (2001).

61.65 INSTRUMENT RATING REQUIREMENTS

(a) *General.* A person who applies for an instrument rating must:
   (1) Hold at least a current private pilot certificate with an airplane, helicopter, or powered-lift rating appropriate to the instrument rating sought;
   (2) Be able to read, speak, write, and understand the English language. If the applicant is unable to meet any of these requirements due to a medical condition, the Administrator may place such operating limitations on the applicant's pilot certificate as are necessary for the safe operation of the aircraft;
   (3) Receive and log ground training from an authorized instructor or accomplish a home-study course of training on the aeronautical knowledge areas of paragraph (b) of this section that apply to the instrument rating sought;
   (4) Receive a logbook or training record endorsement from an authorized instructor certifying that the person is prepared to take the required knowledge test;
   (5) Receive and log training on the areas of operation of paragraph (c) of this section from an authorized instructor in an aircraft, flight simulator, or flight training device that represents an airplane, helicopter, or powered-lift appropriate to the instrument rating sought;
   (6) Receive a logbook or training record endorsement from an authorized instructor certifying that the person is prepared to take the required practical test;
   (7) Pass the required knowledge test on the aeronautical knowledge areas of paragraph (b) of this section; however, an applicant is not required to take another knowledge test when that person already holds an instrument rating; and
   (8) Pass the required practical test on the areas of operation in paragraph (c) of this section in—
      (i) An airplane, helicopter, or powered-lift appropriate to the rating sought; or
      (ii) A flight simulator or a flight training device appropriate to the rating sought and approved for the specific maneuver or procedure performed. If a flight training device is used for the practical test, the instrument approach procedures conducted in that flight training device are limited to one precision and one nonprecision approach, provided the flight training device is approved for the procedure performed.

(b) *Aeronautical knowledge.* A person who applies for an instrument rating must have received and logged ground training from an authorized instructor or accomplished a home-study course on the following aeronautical knowledge areas that apply to the instrument rating sought:
   (1) Federal Aviation Regulations of this chapter that apply to flight operations under IFR;
   (2) Appropriate information that applies to flight operations under IFR in the "Aeronautical Information Manual;"
   (3) Air traffic control system and procedures for instrument flight operations;
   (4) IFR navigation and approaches by use of navigation systems;
   (5) Use of IFR en route and instrument approach procedure charts;
   (6) Procurement and use of aviation weather reports and forecasts and the elements of forecasting weather trends based on that information and personal observation of weather conditions;
   (7) Safe and efficient operation of aircraft under instrument flight rules and conditions;
   (8) Recognition of critical weather situations and windshear avoidance;
   (9) Aeronautical decision making and judgment; and
   (10) Crew resource management, including crew communication and coordination.

(c) *Flight proficiency.* A person who applies for an instrument rating must receive and log training from an authorized instructor in an aircraft, or in a flight simulator or flight training device, in accordance with paragraph (e) of this section, that includes the following areas of operation:
   (1) Preflight preparation;
   (2) Preflight procedures;
   (3) Air traffic control clearances and procedures;
   (4) Flight by reference to instruments;
   (5) Navigation systems;
   (6) Instrument approach procedures;
   (7) Emergency operations; and
   (8) Postflight procedures.

(d) *Aeronautical experience.* A person who applies for an instrument rating must have logged the following:
   (1) At least 50 hours of cross-country flight time as pilot in command, of which at least 10 hours must be in airplanes for an instrument—airplane rating; and
   (2) A total of 40 hours of actual or simulated instrument time on the areas of operation of this section, to include—
      (i) At least 15 hours of instrument flight training from an authorized instructor in the aircraft category for which the instrument rating is sought;
      (ii) At least 3 hours of instrument training that is appropriate to the instrument rating sought from an authorized instructor in preparation for the practical test within the 60 days preceding the date of the test;
      (iii) For an instrument—airplane rating, instrument training on cross-country flight procedures specific to airplanes that includes at least one cross-country flight in an airplane that is performed under IFR, and consists of—
         (A) A distance of at least 250 nautical miles along airways or ATC-directed routing;
         (B) An instrument approach at each airport; and
         (C) Three different kinds of approaches with the use of navigation systems;
      (iv) For an instrument—helicopter rating, instrument training specific to helicopters on cross-country flight procedures that includes at least one cross-country flight in a helicopter that is performed under IFR, and consists of—
         (A) A distance of at least 100 nautical miles along airways or ATC-directed routing;
         (B) An instrument approach at each airport; and
         (C) Three different kinds of approaches with the use of navigation systems; and
      (v) For an instrument—powered-lift rating, instrument training specific to a powered-lift on cross-country flight procedures that includes at least one cross-country flight in a powered-lift that is performed under IFR and consists of—
         (A) A distance of at least 250 nautical miles along airways or ATC-directed routing;
         (B) An instrument approach at each airport; and
         (C) Three different kinds of approaches with the use of navigation systems.

(e) *Use of flight simulators or flight training devices.* If the instrument training was provided by an authorized instructor in a flight simulator or flight training device—
   (1) A maximum of 30 hours may be performed in that flight simulator or flight training device if the training was accomplished in accordance with part 142 of this chapter; or
   (2) A maximum of 20 hours may be performed in that flight simulator or flight training device if the training was not accomplished in accordance with part 142 of this chapter.

EXPLANATION

This rule requires a logbook endorsement from an instructor for eligibility to take a knowledge test. This eliminates the FSDO's from having to allocate time to review an applicant's home study programs.

The 1997 amendment requires knowledge of windshear avoidance procedures, aeronautical decision making, judgment training, and cockpit resource management for the instrument rating.

The 1997 amendment also revised the eligibility for instrument rating to parallel ICAO requirements, and requires only a private pilot certificate. The revision eliminates the 125 total hours of aeronautical experience and only requires that the applicant hold a private pilot certificate and retains the 50 hours of PIC cross-country aeronautical experience, although the 50 hours now may include student pilot cross-country time.

PREAMBLE

The FAA acknowledges HAI's concern regarding the language "the instructor who gave that person the training" and therefore has deleted the objectionable language. The FAA has changed the language in the recreational and private pilot aeronautical knowledge area requirements so that it now refers to delays rather than specifically to ATC delays. ATC delays concerning instrument rated pilots are addressed in §61.65(b)(3), which provides for training in the air traffic control system and procedures for instrument flight operations. The FAA notes HAI's objection to proposed §61.65(d)(1). The change resulted in an inadvertent increase in the amount of instrument time that must be obtained from a CFII. The FAA has noted this error and corrected it in the final rule. The FAA is adopting in the final rule the proposal to eliminate the existing 125-hour total time requirement, but is not eliminating the 50-hour pilot in command cross-country time requirement.

In response to NATA's concerns regarding class-specific aircraft requirements within the proposed rule, the FAA has withdrawn the proposed class-specific instrument rating, with the exception of the powered-lift instrument rating. NATA's other objection regarding the elimination of the requirements for specific types of approaches, including precision approaches, is addressed in §61.65(c)(6). The requirement for specific types of approaches was deleted from the aeronautical experience requirements in §61.65; precision approaches are still covered in the PTS. The objections of AOPA and NAFI to the 100-mile leg requirement are noted, and the FAA has decided to withdraw the proposal and return to current requirements. The FAA's intent was to clarify the regulation but, based on the comments submitted, the provision resulted in greater confusion and did not provide the flexibility for pilots to plan their cross-country flights according to individual situations. In addition, based on the above, the FAA has decided to remove from the final rule the 50-mile leg requirement for helicopters.

In response to AOPA's and HAI's comment regarding the use of the term "IFR," it is the FAA's intent to require a person to file an instrument flight plan and perform a flight under IFR, although not necessarily under IMC. Therefore, the FAA is going forward with the proposal. The objections raised by commenters regarding the need for instrument training in actual or simulated conditions are not valid because the definition of instrument training includes a requirement for actual or simulated conditions.

Addressing concerns raised throughout the proposed regulations, the final rule modifications to this section also include the insertion of language restoring the ability of the Administrator to place operating limitations on an applicant unable to meet the English language requirements; and deletion of provisions for the proposed instrument airship rating, because that rating was not adopted.

Similarly, the FAA is not adopting the proposal to separate the instrument rating into single and multiengine classes, the proposed paragraph giving single-engine instrument privileges to applicants who pass the instrument rating practical test in multiengine practical test is redundant and therefore deleted.

The use of ground training devices was addressed in Amendment No. 61-100. These provisions are included in the final rule.

Additionally, the final rule corrects several errors noted in paragraph (g) of the existing rule as adopted in Amendment No. 61-100. Existing paragraph (g)(1) erroneously contains the word "any" prior to the phrase "category, class, and type aircraft that is certificated for flight in instrument conditions." This incorrectly allows the use of any category, class, and type of aircraft during the practical test; e.g., the use of a helicopter for an airplane instrument rating practical test. Also, that same paragraph in the existing rule contains the phrase "that is certificated for flight in instrument conditions." That language unintentionally precludes practical testing in some aircraft that may not be certificated for flight into instrument meteorological conditions, but which may be operated under instrument flight rules, provided the flight is conducted in weather conditions that meet the requirements for flight under visual flight rules.

In response to a comment received regarding Amendment No. 61-100, requesting clarification on the use of a flight simulator or flight training device during the practical test, the FAA has revised paragraph (a)(8) of the final rule to provide for the use of a flight simulator or a flight training device for the conduct of a practical test if that flight simulator or flight training device is approved for the procedure performed. The final rule also limits the procedures which may be performed in an approved flight training device to one precision and one nonprecision approach provided the flight training device is approved.

The format of the final rule was further changed to accommodate the included modifications. (62 FR 16255 – 16256)

CROSS REFERENCES

61.51, Pilot Logbooks; 61.63, Additional Aircraft Ratings (Other Than On Airline Transport Pilot Certificate).

ADVISORY CIRCULARS

AC 61-65D *Certification: Pilots and Flight Instructors* (1999).

FAA CHIEF COUNSEL OPINIONS

The highly variable nature of aircraft operations requires that straight line distances be used in defining cross-country flights (and cross-country flight time) to insure consistent application of §61.65, as well as §§61.93, 61.109, and 61.129. (4-16-93).

Each cross-country flight used to meet the aeronautical experience requirements under §61.65(d) must include one leg that has a point of landing that is at least a straight-line distance of more than 50 nautical miles from the original point of departure. (4-17-98).

Because 61.65(d)(2) refers to "instrument instruction" by an authorized instructor, the instructor must have an instrument instructor rating. (6-20-79).

61.67 CATEGORY II PILOT AUTHORIZATION REQUIREMENTS

(a) *General.* A person who applies for a Category II pilot authorization must hold:
    (1) At least a private or commercial pilot certificate with an instrument rating or an airline transport pilot certificate;
    (2) A type rating for the aircraft for which the authorization is sought if that aircraft requires a type rating; and
    (3) A category and class rating for the aircraft for which the authorization is sought.
(b) *Experience requirements.* An applicant for a Category II pilot authorization must have at least—
    (1) 50 hours of night flight time as pilot in command.
    (2) 75 hours of instrument time under actual or simulated instrument conditions that may include not more than—
        (i) A combination of 25 hours of simulated instrument flight time in a flight simulator or flight training device; or
        (ii) 40 hours of simulated instrument flight time if accomplished in an approved course conducted by an appropriately rated training center certificated under part 142 of this chapter.
    (3) 250 hours of cross-country flight time as pilot in command.
(c) *Practical test requirements.*
    (1) A practical test must be passed by a person who applies for—
        (i) Issuance or renewal of a Category II pilot authorization; and
        (ii) The addition of another type aircraft to the applicant's Category II pilot authorization.
    (2) To be eligible for the practical test for an authorization under this section, an applicant must—
        (i) Meet the requirements of paragraphs (a) and (b) of this section; and
        (ii) If the applicant has not passed a practical test for this authorization during the 12 calendar months preceding the month of the test, then that person must—
            (A) Meet the requirements of §61.57(c) and
            (B) Have performed at least six ILS approaches during the 6 calendar months preceding the month of the test, of which at least three of the approaches must have been conducted without the use of an approach coupler.
    (3) The approaches specified in paragraph (c)(ii)(B) of this section—
        (i) Must be conducted under actual or simulated instrument flight conditions;
        (ii) Must be conducted to the decision height for the ILS approach in the type aircraft in which the practical test is to be conducted;
        (iii) Need not be conducted to the decision height authorized for Category II operations;
        (iv) Must be conducted to the decision height authorized for Category II operations only if conducted in a flight simulator or flight training device; and
        (v) Must be accomplished in an aircraft of the same category and class, and type, as applicable, as the aircraft in which the practical test is to be conducted or in a flight simulator that—
            (A) Represents an aircraft of the same category and class, and type, as applicable, as the aircraft in which the authorization is sought; and
            (B) Is used in accordance with an approved course conducted by a training center certificated under part 142 of this chapter.
    (4) The flight time acquired in meeting the requirements of paragraph (c)(2)(ii)(B) of this section may be used to meet the requirements of paragraph (c)(2)(ii)(A) of this section.

(d)   *Practical test procedures.* The practical test consists of an oral increment and a flight increment.

    (1)   *Oral increment.* In the oral increment of the practical test an applicant must demonstrate knowledge of the following:

        (i)   Required landing distance;

        (ii)   Recognition of the decision height;

        (iii) Missed approach procedures and techniques using computed or fixed attitude guidance displays;

        (iv) Use and limitations of RVR;

        (v)   Use of visual clues, their availability or limitations, and altitude at which they are normally discernible at reduced RVR readings;

        (vi) Procedures and techniques related to transition from nonvisual to visual flight during a final approach under reduced RVR;

        (vii) Effects of vertical and horizontal windshear;

        (viii) Characteristics and limitations of the ILS and runway lighting system;

        (ix) Characteristics and limitations of the flight director system, auto approach coupler (including split axis type if equipped), auto throttle system (if equipped), and other required Category II equipment;

        (x)   Assigned duties of the second in command during Category II approaches, unless the aircraft for which authorization is sought does not require a second in command; and

        (xi) Instrument and equipment failure warning systems.

    (2)   *Flight increment.* The following requirements apply to the flight increment of the practical test:

        (i)   The flight increment must be conducted in an aircraft of the same category, class, and type, as applicable, as the aircraft in which the authorization is sought or in a flight simulator that—

           (A) Represents an aircraft of the same category and class, and type, as applicable, as the aircraft in which the authorization is sought; and

           (B) Is used in accordance with an approved course conducted by a training center certificated under part 142 of this chapter.

        (ii)   The flight increment must consist of at least two ILS approaches to 100 feet AGL including at least one landing and one missed approach.

        (iii) All approaches performed during the flight increment must be made with the use of an approved flight control guidance system, except if an approved auto approach coupler is installed, at least one approach must be hand flown using flight director commands.

        (iv) If a multiengine airplane with the performance capability to execute a missed approach with one engine inoperative is used for the practical test, the flight increment must include the performance of one missed approach with an engine, which shall be the most critical engine, if applicable, set at idle or zero thrust before reaching the middle marker.

        (v)   If a multiengine flight simulator or multiengine flight training device is used for the practical test, the applicant must execute a missed approach with the most critical engine, if applicable, failed.

        (vi) For an authorization for an aircraft that requires a type rating, the practical test must be performed in coordination with a second in command who holds a type rating in the aircraft in which the authorization is sought.

        (vii) Oral questioning may be conducted at any time during a practical test.

EXPLANATION

Permitting oral questioning at any time during the flight increment provides an opportunity to determine if any applicant is capable of recognizing and responding to outside questions, statements, or directions while conducting the landing. Examples of such outside distractions would be verbal warning from ATC or another crewmember, report of windshear, traffic, or other hazard to landing

CROSS REFERENCES

1.1, General Definitions: "Category II Operations," "Category III," "Decision Height"; 1.2, Abbreviations And Symbols: "CAT II," "CAT III," "DH," "RVR"; 61.3, Requirements For Certificates, Ratings and Authorizations, (f) Category II Pilot Authorization, (g) Category III Pilot Authorization; 61.57, Recent Flight Experience Pilot In Command: Instrument; Part 97, Standard Instrument Approach Procedures.

ADVISORY CIRCULARS

AC 91-16 *Category II Operations — General Aviation Airplanes* (1967).

61.68 CATEGORY III PILOT AUTHORIZATION REQUIREMENTS

(a) *General.* A person who applies for a Category III pilot authorization must hold:
  (1) At least a private pilot certificate or commercial pilot certificate with an instrument rating or an airline transport pilot certificate;
  (2) A type rating for the aircraft for which the authorization is sought if that aircraft requires a type rating; and
  (3) A category and class rating for the aircraft for which the authorization is sought.
(b) *Experience requirements.* An applicant for a Category III pilot authorization must have at least—
  (1) 50 hours of night flight time as pilot in command.
  (2) 75 hours of instrument flight time during actual or simulated instrument conditions that may include not more than—
    (i) A combination of 25 hours of simulated instrument flight time in a flight simulator or flight training device; or
    (ii) 40 hours of simulated instrument flight time if accomplished in an approved course conducted by an appropriately rated training center certificated under part 142 of this chapter.
  (3) 250 hours of cross-country flight time as pilot in command.
(c) *Practical test requirements.*
  (1) A practical test must be passed by a person who applies for—
    (i) Issuance or renewal of a Category III pilot authorization; and
    (ii) The addition of another type of aircraft to the applicant's Category III pilot authorization.

(2)   To be eligible for the practical test for an authorization under this section, an applicant
      must—
      (i)   Meet the requirements of paragraphs (a) and (b) of this section; and
      (ii)   If the applicant has not passed a practical test for this authorization during the 12
             calendar months preceding the month of the test, then that person must—
             (A)   Meet the requirements of §61.57(c); and
             (B)   Have performed at least six ILS approaches during the 6 calendar months
                   preceding the month of the test, of which at least three of the approaches must
                   have been conducted without the use of an approach coupler.
(3)   The approaches specified in paragraph (c)(2)(ii)(B) of this section—
      (i)   Must be conducted under actual or simulated instrument flight conditions;
      (ii)   Must be conducted to the alert height or decision height for the ILS approach in the
             type aircraft in which the practical test is to be conducted;
      (iii) Need not be conducted to the decision height authorized for Category III operations;
      (iv)   Must be conducted to the alert height or decision height, as applicable, authorized for
             Category III operations only if conducted in a flight simulator or flight training device;
             and
      (v)   Must be accomplished in an aircraft of the same category and class, and type, as
             applicable, as the aircraft in which the practical test is to be conducted or in a flight
             simulator that—
             (A)   Represents an aircraft of the same category and class, and type, as applicable,
                   as the aircraft for which the authorization is sought; and
             (B)   Is used in accordance with an approved course conducted by a training center
                   certificated under part 142 of this chapter.
(4)   The flight time acquired in meeting the requirements of paragraph (c)(2)(ii)(B) of this
      section may be used to meet the requirements of paragraph (c)(2)(ii)(A) of this section.

(d)   *Practical test procedures.* The practical test consists of an oral increment and a flight increment.
      (1)   *Oral increment.* In the oral increment of the practical test an applicant must demonstrate
            knowledge of the following:
            (i)   Required landing distance;
            (ii)   Determination and recognition of the alert height or decision height, as applicable,
                   including use of a radar altimeter;
            (iii) Recognition of and proper reaction to significant failures encountered prior to and
                   after reaching the alert height or decision height, as applicable;
            (iv)   Missed approach procedures and techniques using computed or fixed attitude
                   guidance displays and expected height loss as they relate to manual go-around or
                   automatic go-around, and initiation altitude, as applicable;
            (v)   Use and limitations of RVR, including determination of controlling RVR and required
                   transmissometers;
            (vi)   Use, availability, or limitations of visual cues and the altitude at which they are
                   normally discernible at reduced RVR readings including—
                   (A)   Unexpected deterioration of conditions to less than minimum RVR during
                         approach, flare, and rollout;
                   (B)   Demonstration of expected visual references with weather at minimum
                         conditions;
                   (C)   The expected sequence of visual cues during an approach in which visibility is
                         at or above landing minima; and
                   (D)   Procedures and techniques for making a transition from instrument reference
                         flight to visual flight during a final approach under reduced RVR.

(vii)   Effects of vertical and horizontal windshear;

(viii) Characteristics and limitations of the ILS and runway lighting system;

(ix)   Characteristics and limitations of the flight director system auto approach coupler (including split axis type if equipped), auto throttle system (if equipped), and other Category III equipment;

(x)   Assigned duties of the second in command during Category III operations, unless the aircraft for which authorization is sought does not require a second in command;

(xi)   Recognition of the limits of acceptable aircraft position and flight path tracking during approach, flare, and, if applicable, rollout; and

(xii)   Recognition of, and reaction to, airborne or ground system faults or abnormalities, particularly after passing alert height or decision height, as applicable.

(2)   *Flight increment.* The following requirements apply to the flight increment of the practical test—

   (i)   The flight increment may be conducted in an aircraft of the same category and class, and type, as applicable, as the aircraft for which the authorization is sought, or in a flight simulator that—

      (A)   Represents an aircraft of the same category and class, and type, as applicable, as the aircraft in which the authorization is sought, and

      (B)   Is used in accordance with an approved course conducted by a training center certificated under part 142 of this chapter.

   (ii)   The flight increment must consist of at least two ILS approaches to 100 feet AGL, including one landing and one missed approach initiated from a very low altitude that may result in a touchdown during the go-around maneuver;

   (iii) All approaches performed during the flight increment must be made with the approved automatic landing system or an equivalent landing system approved by the Administrator;

   (iv)   If a multiengine aircraft with the performance capability to execute a missed approach with one engine inoperative is used for the practical test, the flight increment must include the performance of one missed approach with the most critical engine, if applicable, set at idle or zero thrust before reaching the middle or outer marker;

   (v)   If a multiengine flight simulator or multiengine flight training device is used, a missed approach must be executed with an engine, which shall be the most critical engine, if applicable, failed;

   (vi)   For an authorization for an aircraft that requires a type rating, the practical test must be performed in coordination with a second in command who holds a type rating in the aircraft in which the authorization is sought;

   (vii) Oral questioning may be conducted at any time during the practical test;

   (viii) Subject to the limitations of this paragraph, for Category IIIb operations predicated on the use of a fail-passive rollout control system, at least one manual rollout using visual reference or a combination of visual and instrument references must be executed. The maneuver required by this paragraph shall be initiated by a fail-passive disconnect of the rollout control system—

      (A)   After main gear touchdown;

      (B)   Prior to nose gear touchdown;

      (C)   In conditions representative of the most adverse lateral touchdown displacement allowing a safe landing on the runway; and

      (D)   In weather conditions anticipated in Category IIIb operations.

EXPLANATION

Permitting oral questioning at any time during the flight increment provides an opportunity to determine if any applicant is capable of recognizing and responding to outside questions, statements, or directions while conducting the landing. Examples of such outside distractions would be verbal warning from ATC or another crewmember, report of windshear, traffic, or other hazards to landing.

CROSS REFERENCE

61.57, Recent Flight Experience: Pilot In Command.

ADVISORY CIRCULARS

AC 120-28D *Criteria for Approval of Category III Weather Minima for Takeoff, Landing, and Rollout* (1999).

61.69 GLIDER TOWING: EXPERIENCE AND TRAINING REQUIREMENTS

(a)   No person may act as pilot in command for towing a glider unless that person:
   (1)   Holds at least a private pilot certificate with a category rating for powered aircraft;
   (2)   Has logged at least 100 hours of pilot-in-command time in the aircraft category, class, and type, if required, that the pilot is using to tow a glider;
   (3)   Has a logbook endorsement from an authorized instructor who certifies that the person has received ground and flight training in gliders and is proficient in—
      (i)   The techniques and procedures essential to the safe towing of gliders, including airspeed limitations;
      (ii)   Emergency procedures;
      (iii)   Signals used; and
      (iv)   Maximum angles of bank.
   (4)   Except as provided in paragraph (b) of this section, has logged at least three flights as the sole manipulator of the controls of an aircraft towing a glider or simulating glider-towing flight procedures while accompanied by a pilot who meets the requirements of paragraphs (c) and (d) of this section;
   (5)   Except as provided in paragraph (b) of this section, has received a logbook endorsement from the pilot, described in paragraph (a)(4) of this section, certifying that the person has accomplished at least 3 flights in an aircraft while towing a glider, or while simulating glider-towing flight procedures; and
   (6)   Within the preceding 12 months has—
      (i)   Made at least three actual or simulated glider tows while accompanied by a qualified pilot who meets the requirements of this section; or
      (ii)   Made at least three flights as pilot in command of a glider towed by an aircraft.
(b)   Any person who before May 17, 1967, has made and logged 10 or more flights as pilot in command of an aircraft towing a glider in accordance with a certificate of waiver need not comply with paragraphs (a)(4) and (a)(5) of this section.
(c)   The pilot, described in paragraph (a)(4) of this section, who endorses the logbook of a person seeking glider-towing privileges must have:
   (1)   Met the requirements of this section prior to endorsing the logbook of the person seeking glider-towing privileges; and
   (2)   Logged at least 10 flights as pilot in command of an aircraft while towing a glider.

(d)   If the pilot described in paragraph (a)(4) of this section holds only a private pilot certificate, then that pilot must have:

(1)   Logged at least 100 hours of pilot-in-command time in airplanes, or 200 hours of pilot-in-command time in a combination of powered and other-than-powered aircraft; and

(2)   Performed and logged at least three flights within the 12 calendar months preceding the month that pilot accompanies or endorses the logbook of a person seeking glider-towing privileges—

(i)   In an aircraft while towing a glider accompanied by another pilot who meets the requirements of this section; or

(ii)   As pilot in command of a glider being towed by an aircraft.

EXPLANATION

This rule permits private pilot to log PIC time for towing gliders. The previous rule had been an unnecessary burden and this rule eliminates that burden.

PREAMBLE

The FAA considered the comments of AOPA, EAA, NAFI, and SSA, which oppose the elimination of the existing rule's method for tow endorsement (simulated tow). After further review of the proposal, the FAA has concluded that operational requirements and accident/incident data do not establish a safety justification sufficient for the increased regulatory and economic burden. Therefore, the existing method has been reinstated.

Addressing AOPA's concern that the proposal's use of the term "single-engine airplane" was too specific, the FAA has replaced that term in the final rule. The final rule requires the towing pilot to be certificated in a powered aircraft. The final rule revises the proposed 100-hour pilot-in-command time requirement to specify "category, class, and type, if required" rather than the proposed "single-engine airplanes." Other references to "single-engine airplane" were replaced by "aircraft." The final rule also restores the recency of experience requirements for glider towing. The proposed rule inadvertently deleted recency of experience requirements for glider towing, although it did include the requirements for the pilots accompanying glider towing trainees. These requirements have been included in the final rule. (62 FR 16256).

CROSS REFERENCES

91.309, Towing: Gliders.

61.71 GRADUATES OF AN APPROVED TRAINING PROGRAM OTHER THAN UNDER THIS PART: SPECIAL RULES

(a) A person who graduates from an approved training program under part 141 or part 142 of this chapter is considered to have met the applicable aeronautical experience, aeronautical knowledge, and areas of operation requirements of this part if that person presents the graduation certificate and passes the required practical test within the 60-day period after the date of graduation.

(b) A person may apply for an airline transport pilot certificate, type rating, or both under this part, and will be considered to have met the applicable requirements under §61.157 of this part for that certificate and rating, if that person has:

  (1) Satisfactorily accomplished an approved training program and the pilot-in-command proficiency check for that airplane type, in accordance with the pilot-in- command requirements under subparts N and O of part 121 of this chapter; and

  (2) Applied for the airline transport pilot certificate, type rating, or both within the 60-day period from the date the person satisfactorily accomplished the approved training program and pilot-in-command proficiency check for that airplane type.

EXPLANATION

Prior to enrolling in a Part 141 pilot school, always ensure that it meets your needs. You can do this by checking with the local FAA Flight Standards District Office or the Flight Standards Division in the Regional Office.

Watch the time limits set by regulation: For example, for aeronautical experience credit, you must apply within 60 days of graduation. You must apply within 60 days of graduation to obtain credit for aeronautical knowledge and skill requirements.

CROSS REFERENCES

61.65, Instrument Rating Requirements; 61.123, Eligibility Requirements: General; 61.183, Flight Instructors: Eligibility Requirements; Part 141, Pilot Schools.

61.73 MILITARY PILOTS OR FORMER MILITARY PILOTS: SPECIAL RULES

(a) *General.* Except for a rated military pilot or former rated military pilot who has been removed from flying status for lack of proficiency, or because of disciplinary action involving aircraft operations, a rated military pilot or former rated military pilot who meets the applicable requirements of this section may apply, on the basis of his or her military training, for:

  (1) A commercial pilot certificate;

  (2) An aircraft rating in the category and class of aircraft for which that military pilot is qualified;

  (3) An instrument rating with the appropriate aircraft rating for which that military pilot is qualified; or

  (4) A type rating, if appropriate.

(b) *Military pilots on active flying status within the past 12 months.* A rated military pilot or former rated military pilot who has been on active flying status within the 12 months before applying must:
   (1) Pass a knowledge test on the appropriate parts of this chapter that apply to pilot privileges and limitations, air traffic and general operating rules, and accident reporting rules;
   (2) Present documentation showing compliance with the requirements of paragraph (d) of this section for at least one aircraft category rating; and
   (3) Present documentation showing that the applicant is or was, at any time during the 12 calendar months before the month of application—
       (i) A rated military pilot on active flying status in an armed force of the United States; or
       (ii) A rated military pilot of an armed force of a foreign contracting State to the Convention on International Civil Aviation, assigned to pilot duties (other than flight training) with an armed force of the United States and holds, at the time of application, a current civil pilot license issued by that contracting State authorizing at least the privileges of the pilot certificate sought.

(c) *Military pilots not on active flying status during the 12 calendar months before the month of application.* A rated military pilot or former rated military pilot who has not been on active flying status within the 12 calendar months before the month of application must:
   (1) Pass the appropriate knowledge and practical tests prescribed in this part for the certificate or rating sought; and
   (2) Present documentation showing that the applicant was, before the beginning of the 12th calendar month before the month of application, a rated military pilot as prescribed by paragraph (b)(3)(i) or paragraph (b)(3)(ii) of this section.

(d) *Aircraft category, class, and type ratings.* A rated military pilot or former rated military pilot who applies for an aircraft category, class, or type rating, if applicable, is issued that rating at the commercial pilot certificate level if the pilot presents documentary evidence that shows satisfactory accomplishment of:
   (1) An official U.S. military pilot check and instrument proficiency check in that aircraft category, class, or type, if applicable, as pilot in command during the 12 calendar months before the month of application;
   (2) At least 10 hours of pilot-in-command time in that aircraft category, class, or type, if applicable, during the 12 calendar months before the month of application; or
   (3) An FAA practical test in that aircraft after—
       (i) Meeting the requirements of paragraphs (b)(1) and (b)(2) of this section; and
       (ii) Having received an endorsement from an authorized instructor who certifies that the pilot is proficient to take the required practical test, and that endorsement is made within the 60-day period preceding the date of the practical test.

(e) *Instrument rating.* A rated military pilot or former rated military pilot who applies for an airplane instrument rating, a helicopter instrument rating, or a powered-lift instrument rating to be added to his or her commercial pilot certificate may apply for an instrument rating if the pilot has, within the 12 calendar months preceding the month of application:
   (1) Passed an instrument proficiency check by a U.S. Armed Force in the aircraft category for the instrument rating sought; and
   (2) Received authorization from a U.S. Armed Force to conduct IFR flights on Federal airways in that aircraft category and class for the instrument rating sought.

(f) *Aircraft type rating.* An aircraft type rating is issued only for aircraft types that the Administrator has certificated for civil operations.

(g) *Aircraft type rating placed on an airline transport pilot certificate.* A rated military pilot or former rated military pilot who holds an airline transport pilot certificate and who requests an aircraft type rating to be placed on that person's airline transport pilot certificate may be issued that aircraft type rating at the airline transport pilot certificate level, provided that person:

    (1)   Holds a category and class rating for that type of aircraft at the airline transport pilot certificate level; and

    (2)   Passed an official U.S. military pilot check and instrument proficiency check in that type of aircraft as pilot in command during the 12 calendar months before the month of application.

(h) *Evidentiary documents.* The following documents are satisfactory evidence for the purposes indicated:

    (1)   An official identification card issued to the pilot by an armed force may be used to demonstrate membership in the armed forces.

    (2)   An original or a copy of a certificate of discharge or release may be used to demonstrate discharge or release from an armed force or former membership in an armed force.

    (3)   Current or previous status as a rated military pilot with a U.S. Armed Force may be demonstrated by—

        (i)   An official U.S. Armed Force order to flight status as a military pilot;

        (ii)   An official U.S. Armed Force form or logbook showing military pilot status; or

        (iii)   An official order showing that the rated military pilot graduated from a U.S. military pilot school and received a rating as a military pilot.

    (4)   A certified U.S. Armed Force logbook or an appropriate official U.S. Armed Force form or summary may be used to demonstrate flight time in military aircraft as a member of a U.S. Armed Force.

    (5)   An official U.S. Armed Force record of a military checkout as pilot in command may be used to demonstrate pilot in command status.

    (6)   A current instrument grade slip that is issued by a U.S. Armed Force, or an official record of satisfactory accomplishment of an instrument proficiency check during the 12 calendar months preceding the month of the application may be used to demonstrate instrument pilot qualification.

ADVISORY CIRCULAR

AC 61-65D *Certification: Pilots and Flight Instructors* (1999).

FAA CHIEF COUNSEL OPINIONS

The language of the rule explicitly requires that prior to application and prior to taking the written test an applicant must be a rated military pilot. (8-28-86).

61.75 PRIVATE PILOT CERTIFICATE ISSUED ON THE BASIS OF A FOREIGN PILOT LICENSE

(a)   *General.* A person who holds a current foreign pilot license issued by a contracting State to the Convention on International Civil Aviation may apply for and be issued a private pilot certificate with the appropriate ratings when the application is based on the foreign pilot license that meets the requirements of this section.

(b)   *Certificate issued.* A U.S. private pilot certificate that is issued under this section shall specify the person's foreign license number and country of issuance. A person who holds a current foreign pilot license issued by a contracting State to the Convention on International Civil Aviation may be issued a private pilot certificate based on the foreign pilot license without any further showing of proficiency, provided the applicant:

(1)   Meets the requirements of this section;

(2)   Holds a foreign pilot license that—

(i)   Is not under an order of revocation or suspension by the foreign country that issued the foreign pilot license; and

(ii) Does not contain an endorsement stating that the applicant has not met all of the standards of ICAO for that license;

(3)   Does not currently hold a U.S. pilot certificate;

(4)   Holds a current medical certificate issued under part 67 of this chapter or a current medical certificate issued by the country that issued the person's foreign pilot license; and

(5)   Is able to read, speak, write, and understand the English language. If the applicant is unable to meet one of these requirements due to medical reasons, then the Administrator may place such operating limitations on that applicant's pilot certificate as are necessary for the safe operation of the aircraft.

(c)   *Aircraft ratings issued.* Aircraft ratings listed on a person's foreign pilot license, in addition to any issued after testing under the provisions of this part, may be placed on that person's U.S. pilot certificate.

(d)   *Instrument ratings issued.* A person who holds an instrument rating on the foreign pilot license issued by a contracting State to the Convention on International Civil Aviation may be issued an instrument rating on a U.S. private pilot certificate provided:

(1)   The person's foreign pilot license authorizes instrument privileges;

(2)   Within 24 months preceding the month in which the person applies for the instrument rating, the person passes the appropriate knowledge test; and

(3)   The person is able to read, speak, write, and understand the English language. If the applicant is unable to meet one of these requirements due to medical reasons, then the Administrator may place such operating limitations on that applicant's pilot certificate as are necessary for the safe operation of the aircraft.

(e)   *Operating privileges and limitations.* A person who receives a U.S. private pilot certificate that has been issued under the provisions of this section:

(1)   May act as a pilot of a civil aircraft of U.S. registry in accordance with the private pilot privileges authorized by this part;

(2)   Is limited to the privileges placed on the certificate by the Administrator;

(3)   Is subject to the limitations and restrictions on the person's U.S. certificate and foreign pilot license when exercising the privileges of that U.S. pilot certificate in an aircraft of U.S. registry operating within or outside the United States; and

(4)   Shall not exercise the privileges of that U.S. private pilot certificate when the person's foreign pilot license has been revoked or suspended.

(f) *Limitation on licenses used as the basis for a U.S. certificate.* Only one foreign pilot license may be used as a basis for issuing a U.S. private pilot certificate. The foreign pilot license and medical certification used as a basis for issuing a U.S. private pilot certificate under this section must be in the English language or accompanied by an English language transcription that has been signed by an official or representative of the foreign aviation authority that issued the foreign pilot license.

(g) *Limitation placed on a U.S. private pilot certificate.* A U.S. private pilot certificate issued under this section is valid only when the holder has the foreign pilot license upon which the issuance of the U.S. private pilot certificate was based in the holder's personal possession or readily accessible in the aircraft.

EXPLANATION

This rule restricts holders of foreign pilot certificates to apply for and may only be issued a U.S. private pilot certificate (commercial certificates were previously available) with the appropriate ratings when the application is based on the foreign pilot certificate.

61.75(b)(5) deletes the exceptions for persons who are unable to read, speak, write and understand English. However the rules still provide an exception for persons with medical impairments only (i.e. hearing impaired).

CROSS REFERENCES

Part 67, Medical Standards and Certification; 61.77, Special Purpose Pilot Authorization: Operation of U.S.-Registered Civil Aircraft Leased By a Person Who Is Not a U.S. Citizen.

61.77 SPECIAL PURPOSE PILOT AUTHORIZATION: OPERATION OF U.S.-REGISTERED CIVIL AIRCRAFT LEASED BY A PERSON WHO IS NOT A U.S. CITIZEN

(a) *General.* A holder of a foreign pilot license issued by a contracting State to the Convention on International Civil Aviation who meets the requirements of this section may be issued a special purpose pilot authorization by the Administrator for the purpose of performing pilot duties:

(1) On a civil aircraft of U.S. registry that is leased to a person who is not a citizen of the United States; and

(2) For carrying persons or property for compensation or hire on that aircraft.

(b) *Eligibility.* To be eligible for the issuance or renewal of a special purpose pilot authorization, an applicant must present the following to an FAA Flight Standards District Office:

(1) A current foreign pilot license that has been issued by the aeronautical authority of a contracting State to the Convention on International Civil Aviation from which the person holds citizenship or resident status and that contains the appropriate aircraft category, class, instrument rating, and type rating, if appropriate, for the aircraft to be flown;

(2) A current certification by the lessee of the aircraft—
   (i)   Stating that the applicant is employed by the lessee;
   (ii) Specifying the aircraft type on which the applicant will perform pilot duties; and
   (iii) Stating that the applicant has received ground and flight instruction that qualifies the applicant to perform the duties to be assigned on the aircraft.
(3) Documentation showing when the applicant will reach the age of 60 years (an official copy of the applicant's birth certificate or other official documentation);
(4) Documentation that the applicant meets the medical standards for the issuance of the foreign pilot license from the aeronautical authority of the contracting State to the Convention on International Civil Aviation where the applicant holds citizenship or resident status;
(5) Documentation that the applicant meets the recent flight experience requirements of this part (a logbook or flight record); and
(6) A statement that the applicant does not already hold a special purpose pilot authorization; however, if the applicant already holds a special purpose pilot authorization, then that special purpose pilot authorization must be surrendered to either the FAA Flight Standards District Office that issued it, or the FAA Flight Standards District Office processing the application for the authorization, prior to being issued another special purpose pilot authorization.

(c) *Privileges.* A person issued a special purpose pilot authorization under this section—
   (1) May exercise the privileges prescribed on the special purpose pilot authorization; and
   (2) Must comply with the limitations specified in this section and any additional limitations specified on the special purpose pilot authorization.

(d) *General limitations.* A special purpose pilot authorization is valid only—
   (1) For flights between foreign countries or for flights in foreign air commerce within the time period allotted on the authorization;
   (2) If the foreign pilot license required by paragraph (b)(1) of this section, the medical documentation required by paragraph (b)(4) of this section, and the special purpose pilot authorization issued under this section are in the holder's physical possession or immediately accessible in the aircraft;
   (3) While the holder is employed by the person to whom the aircraft described in the certification required by paragraph (b)(2) of this section is leased;
   (4) While the holder is performing pilot duties on the U.S.-registered aircraft described in the certification required by paragraph (b)(2) of this section; and
   (5) If the holder has only one special purpose pilot authorization as provided in paragraph (b)(6) of this section.

(e) *Age limitation.* Except as provided in paragraph (g) of this section, no person who holds a special purpose pilot authorization issued under this part, and no person who holds a special purpose pilot certificate issued under this part before August 4, 1997, shall serve as a pilot on a civil airplane of U.S. registry if the person has reached his or her 60th birthday, in the following operations:
   (1) Scheduled international air services carrying passengers in turbojet-powered airplanes;
   (2) Scheduled international air services carrying passengers in airplanes having a passenger-seat configuration of more than nine passenger seats, excluding each crewmember seat;
   (3) Nonscheduled international air transportation for compensation or hire in airplanes having a passenger-seat configuration of more than 30 passenger seats, excluding each crewmember seat; or
   (4) Scheduled international air services, or nonscheduled international air transportation for compensation or hire, in airplanes having a payload capacity of more than 7,500 pounds.

(f) *Definitions.*
  (1) "International air service," as used in paragraph (e) of this section, means scheduled air service performed in airplanes for the public transport of passengers, mail, or cargo, in which the service passes through the air space over the territory of more than one country.
  (2) "International air transportation," as used in paragraph (e) of this section, means air transportation performed in airplanes for the public transport of passengers, mail, or cargo, in which service passes through the air space over the territory of more than one country.
(g) *Delayed pilot age limitations for certain operations.* Until December 20, 1999, a person may serve as a pilot in the operations specified in paragraph (e) of this section after that person has reached his or her 60th birthday, if, on March 20, 1997, that person was employed as a pilot in any of the following operations:
  (1) Scheduled international air services carrying passengers in nontransport category turbopropeller-powered airplanes type certificated after December 31, 1964, that have a passenger seat configuration of 10 to 19 seats;
  (2) Scheduled international air services carrying passengers in transport category turbopropeller-powered airplanes that have a passenger seat configuration of 20 to 30 seats; or
  (3) Scheduled international air services carrying passengers in turbojet-powered airplanes having a passenger seat configuration of 1 to 30 seats.
(h) *Expiration date.* Each special purpose pilot authorization issued under this section expires—
  (1) 60 calendar months from the month it was issued, unless sooner suspended or revoked;
  (2) When the lease agreement for the aircraft expires or the lessee terminates the employment of the person who holds the special purpose pilot authorization;
  (3) Whenever the person's foreign pilot license has been suspended, revoked, or is no longer valid; or
  (4) When the person no longer meets the medical standards for the issuance of the foreign pilot license.
(i) *Renewal.* A person exercising the privileges of a special purpose pilot authorization may apply for a 60-calendar-month extension of that authorization, provided the person—
  (1) Continues to meet the requirements of this section; and
  (2) Surrenders the expired special purpose pilot authorization upon receipt of the new authorization.
(j) *Surrender.* The holder of a special purpose pilot authorization must surrender the authorization to the Administrator within 7 days after the date the authorization terminates.

EXPLANATION

This rule replaces the special purpose flight certificate for foreign pilots of U.S.-registered aircraft with a special purpose flight authorization that will be issued by a FSDO. This will lower administrative costs for the FAA and simplify the procedures for foreign pilots seeking special purpose flight authorizations.

PREAMBLE

Notice No. 95-11 proposed to align the age 60 rule with similar provisions in part 121. As previously discussed in the analysis of §61.3, part 121 was revised to include certain commuter operations previously addressed in part 135. Accordingly, the FAA is amending the applicability of the age limitation in §61.77 to be consistent with current part 121, as well as with §61.3(j). The FAA invites comments on the inclusion of additional aircraft operations under the age 60 limitation as set forth in §61.77.

In the past, §61.77 has applied only to aircraft engaged in part 121 operations; therefore, the age 60 limitation applied to all holders of certificates issued under §61.77. Because the applicability of §61.77 is now expanded to all civil aircraft, the age 60 limitation will not apply to all special purpose pilot authorizations, and reaching the age of 60 will not result in the expiration of the authorization. (62 FR 16257).

CROSS REFERENCES

61.55, Second-in-Command Qualifications; 61.57, Recent Flight Experience: Pilot In Command; 61.58, Pilot-in-Command Proficiency Check: Operation of Aircraft Requiring More Than One Required Pilot Flight Crewmember.

ADVISORY CIRCULARS

AC 61-65D *Certification: Pilots and Flight Instructors* (1999).

CASES

The FAA's position of "one certificate, one lease" was upheld by the Board. *Petition of Raul Quintana*, EA-3737 (1992).

INTENTIONALLY

LEFT

BLANK

SUBPART C — STUDENT PILOTS

61.81 APPLICABILITY

This subpart prescribes the requirements for the issuance of student pilot certificates, the conditions under which those certificates are necessary, and the general operating rules and limitations for the holders of those certificates.

61.83 ELIGIBILITY REQUIREMENTS FOR STUDENT PILOTS

To be eligible for a student pilot certificate, an applicant must:
(a) Be at least 16 years of age for other than the operation of a glider or balloon.
(b) Be at least 14 years of age for the operation of a glider or balloon.
(c) Be able to read, speak, write, and understand the English language. If the applicant is unable to meet one of these requirements due to medical reasons, then the Administrator may place such operating limitations on that applicant's pilot certificate as are necessary for the safe operation of the aircraft.

EXPLANATION

All applicants must now be able to read, speak, write and understand English. However the rules still provide an exception for persons with medical impairments only (i.e. hearing impaired).

PREAMBLE

Upon reviewing the concerns of AOPA, IDPA, and other commentaries, the FAA has restored language permitting an operating limitation for medical conditions. (62 FR 16258).

CROSS REFERENCES

61.23, Medical Certificates: Requirement and Duration.

ADVISORY CIRCULARS

AC 61-65D *Certification: Pilots and Flight and Ground Instructors* (1999).

FAA-H-8083-27 *Student Pilot Guide* (1999).

FAA CHIEF COUNSEL OPINIONS

The task of establishing the minimum age at which all individuals applying for a particular type of airman certificate can be expected to have reached the proper level of maturity and responsibility is a difficult one. The FAA believes that the ages now prescribed for student pilot (16) and private pilot (17) certificates are necessary to ensure this level of maturity and responsibility for all applicants. (1-18-78).

61.85 APPLICATION

An application for a student pilot certificate is made on a form and in a manner provided by the Administrator and is submitted to:
(a)   A designated aviation medical examiner if applying for an FAA medical certificate under part 67 of this chapter;
(b)   An examiner; or
(c)   A Flight Standards District Office.

CROSS REFERENCES

61.19(b), Duration of Pilot and Instructor Certificates: Student Pilot Certificate; Part 67, Medical Standards and Certification.

ADVISORY CIRCULARS

FAA-H-8083-27 Student Pilot Guide (1999).

61.87 SOLO REQUIREMENTS FOR STUDENT PILOTS

(a)   *General.* A student pilot may not operate an aircraft in solo flight unless that student has met the requirements of this section. The term "solo flight," as used in this subpart, means that flight time during which a student pilot is the sole occupant of the aircraft, or that flight time during which the student performs the duties of a pilot in command of a gas balloon or an airship requiring more than one pilot flight crewmember.
(b)   *Aeronautical knowledge.* A student pilot must demonstrate satisfactory aeronautical knowledge on a knowledge test that meets the requirements of this paragraph:
  (1)   The test must address the student pilot's knowledge of—
    (i)   Applicable sections of parts 61 and 91 of this chapter;
    (ii)   Airspace rules and procedures for the airport where the solo flight will be performed; and
    (iii) Flight characteristics and operational limitations for the make and model of aircraft to be flown.
  (2)   The student's authorized instructor must—
    (i)   Administer the test; and
    (ii)   At the conclusion of the test, review all incorrect answers with the student before authorizing that student to conduct a solo flight.
(c)   *Pre-solo flight training.* Prior to conducting a solo flight, a student pilot must have:
  (1)   Received and logged flight training for the maneuvers and procedures of this section that are appropriate to the make and model of aircraft to be flown; and
  (2)   Demonstrated satisfactory proficiency and safety, as judged by an authorized instructor, on the maneuvers and procedures required by this section in the make and model of aircraft or similar make and model of aircraft to be flown.

(d) *Maneuvers and procedures for pre-solo flight training in a single-engine airplane.* A student pilot who is receiving training for a single-engine airplane rating must receive and log flight training for the following maneuvers and procedures:
  (1) Proper flight preparation procedures, including preflight planning and preparation, powerplant operation, and aircraft systems;
  (2) Taxiing or surface operations, including runups;
  (3) Takeoffs and landings, including normal and crosswind;
  (4) Straight and level flight, and turns in both directions;
  (5) Climbs and climbing turns;
  (6) Airport traffic patterns, including entry and departure procedures;
  (7) Collision avoidance, windshear avoidance, and wake turbulence avoidance;
  (8) Descents, with and without turns, using high and low drag configurations;
  (9) Flight at various airspeeds from cruise to slow flight;
  (10) Stall entries from various flight attitudes and power combinations with recovery initiated at the first indication of a stall, and recovery from a full stall;
  (11) Emergency procedures and equipment malfunctions;
  (12) Ground reference maneuvers;
  (13) Approaches to a landing area with simulated engine malfunctions,
  (14) Slips to a landing; and
  (15) Go-arounds.
(e) *Maneuvers and procedures for pre-solo flight training in a multiengine airplane.* A student pilot who is receiving training for a multiengine airplane rating must receive and log flight training for the following maneuvers and procedures:
  (1) Proper flight preparation procedures, including preflight planning and preparation, powerplant operation, and aircraft systems;
  (2) Taxiing or surface operations, including runups;
  (3) Takeoffs and landings, including normal and crosswind;
  (4) Straight and level flight, and turns in both directions;
  (5) Climbs and climbing turns;
  (6) Airport traffic patterns, including entry and departure procedures;
  (7) Collision avoidance, windshear avoidance, and wake turbulence avoidance;
  (8) Descents, with and without turns, using high and low drag configurations;
  (9) Flight at various airspeeds from cruise to slow flight;
  (10) Stall entries from various flight attitudes and power combinations with recovery initiated at the first indication of a stall, and recovery from a full stall;
  (11) Emergency procedures and equipment malfunctions;
  (12) Ground reference maneuvers;
  (13) Approaches to a landing area with simulated engine malfunctions; and
  (14) Go-arounds.
(f) *Maneuvers and procedures for pre-solo flight training in a helicopter.* A student pilot who is receiving training for a helicopter rating must receive and log flight training for the following maneuvers and procedures:
  (1) Proper flight preparation procedures, including preflight planning and preparation, powerplant operation, and aircraft systems;
  (2) Taxiing or surface operations, including runups;
  (3) Takeoffs and landings, including normal and crosswind;
  (4) Straight and level flight, and turns in both directions;

(5)   Climbs and climbing turns;
(6)   Airport traffic patterns, including entry and departure procedures;
(7)   Collision avoidance, windshear avoidance, and wake turbulence avoidance;
(8)   Descents with and without turns;
(9)   Flight at various airspeeds;
(10) Emergency procedures and equipment malfunctions;
(11) Ground reference maneuvers;
(12) Approaches to the landing area;
(13) Hovering and hovering turns;
(14) Go-arounds;
(15) Simulated emergency procedures, including autorotational descents with a power recovery and power recovery to a hover;
(16) Rapid decelerations; and
(17) Simulated one-engine-inoperative approaches and landings for multiengine helicopters.

(g)   *Maneuvers and procedures for pre-solo flight training in a gyroplane.* A student pilot who is receiving training for a gyroplane rating must receive and log flight training for the following maneuvers and procedures:
(1)   Proper flight preparation procedures, including preflight planning and preparation, powerplant operation, and aircraft systems;
(2)   Taxiing or surface operations, including runups;
(3)   Takeoffs and landings, including normal and crosswind;
(4)   Straight and level flight, and turns in both directions;
(5)   Climbs and climbing turns;
(6)   Airport traffic patterns, including entry and departure procedures;
(7)   Collision avoidance, windshear avoidance, and wake turbulence avoidance;
(8)   Descents with and without turns;
(9)   Flight at various airspeeds;
(10) Emergency procedures and equipment malfunctions;
(11) Ground reference maneuvers;
(12) Approaches to the landing area;
(13) High rates of descent with power on and with simulated power off, and recovery from those flight configurations;
(14) Go-arounds; and
(15) Simulated emergency procedures, including simulated power-off landings and simulated power failure during departures.

(h)   *Maneuvers and procedures for pre-solo flight training in a powered-lift.* A student pilot who is receiving training for a powered-lift rating must receive and log flight training in the following maneuvers and procedures:
(1)   Proper flight preparation procedures, including preflight planning and preparation, powerplant operation, and aircraft systems;
(2)   Taxiing or surface operations, including runups;
(3)   Takeoffs and landings, including normal and crosswind;
(4)   Straight and level flight, and turns in both directions;
(5)   Climbs and climbing turns;
(6)   Airport traffic patterns, including entry and departure procedures;
(7)   Collision avoidance, windshear avoidance, and wake turbulence avoidance;

(8) Descents with and without turns;
(9) Flight at various airspeeds from cruise to slow flight;
(10) Stall entries from various flight attitudes and power combinations with recovery initiated at the first indication of a stall, and recovery from a full stall;
(11) Emergency procedures and equipment malfunctions;
(12) Ground reference maneuvers;
(13) Approaches to a landing with simulated engine malfunctions;
(14) Go-arounds;
(15) Approaches to the landing area;
(16) Hovering and hovering turns; and
(17) For multiengine powered-lifts, simulated one-engine-inoperative approaches and landings.

(i) *Maneuvers and procedures for pre-solo flight training in a glider.* A student pilot who is receiving training for a glider rating must receive and log flight training for the following maneuvers and procedures:
(1) Proper flight preparation procedures, including preflight planning, preparation, aircraft systems, and, if appropriate, powerplant operations;
(2) Taxiing or surface operations, including runups, if applicable;
(3) Launches, including normal and crosswind;
(4) Straight and level flight, and turns in both directions, if applicable;
(5) Airport traffic patterns, including entry procedures;
(6) Collision avoidance, windshear avoidance, and wake turbulence avoidance;
(7) Descents with and without turns using high and low drag configurations;
(8) Flight at various airspeeds;
(9) Emergency procedures and equipment malfunctions;
(10) Ground reference maneuvers, if applicable;
(11) Inspection of towline rigging and review of signals and release procedures, if applicable;
(12) Aerotow, ground tow, or self-launch procedures;
(13) Procedures for disassembly and assembly of the glider;
(14) Stall entry, stall, and stall recovery;
(15) Straight glides, turns, and spirals;
(16) Landings, including normal and crosswind;
(17) Slips to a landing;
(18) Procedures and techniques for thermalling; and
(19) Emergency operations, including towline break procedures.

(j) *Maneuvers and procedures for pre-solo flight training in an airship.* A student pilot who is receiving training for an airship rating must receive and log flight training for the following maneuvers and procedures:
(1) Proper flight preparation procedures, including preflight planning and preparation, powerplant operation, and aircraft systems;
(2) Taxiing or surface operations, including runups;
(3) Takeoffs and landings, including normal and crosswind;
(4) Straight and level flight, and turns in both directions;
(5) Climbs and climbing turns;
(6) Airport traffic patterns, including entry and departure procedures;
(7) Collision avoidance, windshear avoidance, and wake turbulence avoidance;
(8) Descents with and without turns;
(9) Flight at various airspeeds from cruise to slow flight;
(10) Emergency procedures and equipment malfunctions;
(11) Ground reference maneuvers;
(12) Rigging, ballasting, and controlling pressure in the ballonets, and superheating; and
(13) Landings with positive and with negative static trim.

(k) *Maneuvers and procedures for pre-solo flight training in a balloon.* A student pilot who is receiving training in a balloon must receive and log flight training for the following maneuvers and procedures:

(1) Layout and assembly procedures;

(2) Proper flight preparation procedures, including preflight planning and preparation, and aircraft systems;

(3) Ascents and descents;

(4) Landing and recovery procedures;

(5) Emergency procedures and equipment malfunctions;

(6) Operation of hot air or gas source, ballast, valves, vents, and rip panels, as appropriate;

(7) Use of deflation valves or rip panels for simulating an emergency;

(8) The effects of wind on climb and approach angles; and

(9) Obstruction detection and avoidance techniques.

(l) *Limitations on student pilots operating an aircraft in solo flight.* A student pilot may not operate an aircraft in solo flight unless that student pilot has received:

(1) An endorsement from an authorized instructor on his or her student pilot certificate for the specific make and model aircraft to be flown; and

(2) An endorsement in the student's logbook for the specific make and model aircraft to be flown by an authorized instructor, who gave the training within the 90 days preceding the date of the flight.

(m) *Limitations on student pilots operating an aircraft in solo flight at night.* A student pilot may not operate an aircraft in solo flight at night unless that student pilot has received:

(1) Flight training at night on night flying procedures that includes takeoffs, approaches, landings, and go-arounds at night at the airport where the solo flight will be conducted;

(2) Navigation training at night in the vicinity of the airport where the solo flight will be conducted; and

(3) An endorsement in the student's logbook for the specific make and model aircraft to be flown for night solo flight by an authorized instructor who gave the training within the 90-day period preceding the date of the flight.

(n) *Limitations on flight instructors authorizing solo flight.*

(1) No instructor may authorize a student pilot to perform a solo flight unless that instructor has—

(i) Given that student pilot training in the make and model of aircraft or a similar make and model of aircraft in which the solo flight is to be flown;

(ii) Determined the student pilot is proficient in the maneuvers and procedures prescribed in this section;

(iii) Determined the student pilot is proficient in the make and model of aircraft to be flown;

(iv) Ensured that the student pilot's certificate has been endorsed by an instructor authorized to provide flight training for the specific make and model aircraft to be flown; and

(v) Endorsed the student pilot's logbook for the specific make and model aircraft to be flown, and that endorsement remains current for solo flight privileges, provided an authorized instructor updates the student's logbook every 90 days thereafter.

(2) The flight training required by this section must be given by an instructor authorized to provide flight training who is appropriately rated and current.

EXPLANATION

The responsibilities of the student pilot and the flight instructor regarding required endorsements are separate and distinct. Therefore, a student pilot should be familiar with the endorsements required for solo flight and ensure that they have been made before a solo flight is conducted.

A separate solo flight endorsement is required for each make and model of aircraft prior to the first solo flight in that aircraft.

An endorsement for solo flight is not an authorization for cross-country flights. A separate endorsement is required for cross-country flights.

Prior to any solo flight, a student pilot must have an endorsement dated within the 90 days prior to the flight.

PREAMBLE

61.87(a) and (b): A definition of "solo flight" similar to that of the existing rule has been added to paragraph (a) of the final rule. In this new definition, the phrase "an airship" has been replaced by "a gas balloon or an airship". In paragraph (b), the first proposed reference to the word "test" has been replaced with "knowledge test", for consistency with new FAA usage. Regarding the existence of the test requirement itself, the FAA notes the concerns of AOPA and NAFI, but points out that the requirement merely reflects the existing rule. Therefore, this final rule is adopted with the changes discussed above.

61.87(c): The FAA has modified §61.87(c)(2) to permit a student pilot to demonstrate flight proficiency in a similar make and model of aircraft to that in which the student pilot will conduct solo flight. The FAA notes that similar make and model aircraft should be of a similar design, with similar operating, performance, flight, and handling characteristics. The revision made by the FAA to the proposal made in Notice No. 95-11 will apply to all categories and classes of aircraft. As examples, the proposed revision will permit a student pilot to receive flight training in a Schweizer 2-33 and solo a Schweizer 1-26, or receive flight training in a two-place gyroplane but solo in a single-place version of that same gyroplane, even though the single-place version has a slightly smaller powerplant. The FAA also notes that a flight instructor must endorse a student pilot for solo flight in the actual make and model aircraft in which the student pilot will conduct flight operations. Except for this change the final rule is adopted as proposed.

61.87(d): The existing requirement for training on stall entries and recoveries was inadvertently omitted from the proposal. A requirement for "stall entries from various flight attitudes and power combinations with recovery initiated at the first indication of a stall, and recovery from a full stall" has been inserted into paragraphs (d) and (e) of the final rule. AOPA's concerns regarding the deletion of flight at minimum controllable airspeed were reviewed, but the change of terminology to "slow flight" was made to provide the FAA with flexibility in determining which specific tasks should be performed in the area of operation. This is issue discussed in section IV, H. Moreover, the FAA has determined that the stall training requirement of the final rule ensures that the student obtains the necessary practice in stall recognition and handling characteristics. HAI's concerns also are noted; however, this section's requirements are explicitly listed as pre-solo training, therefore, these maneuvers would be conducted with an authorized instructor. Except for these changes, the final rule is adopted as proposed.

61.87(l): The FAA agrees with part of HAI's concern over possible misinterpretation of the requirement that training be conducted in a specific aircraft, therefore, the language in the final rule for the paragraph has been changed from "in the aircraft" to "in the make and model of aircraft". Additionally, in accordance with the revision made to §61.87(c)(2) to permit a student pilot to demonstrate flight proficiency in a make and model of aircraft similar to that in which the student pilot will conduct solo flight, the FAA has revised §61.87(n)(1)(i) to permit an instructor to authorize a student pilot to perform a solo flight if the instructor has given the student pilot training in either "the make and model of aircraft or a similar make and model of aircraft in which the solo flight is to be flown".

The FAA also concurs with AOPA's objection to the requirement that certificates be endorsed every 90 days. The final rule has therefore been revised to only require additional 90-day solo endorsements to be recorded in the logbook. (62 FR 16258 – 16260).

CROSS REFERENCES

61.23, Medical Certificates: Requirements and Duration; 61.89, Student Pilots: General Limitations; 61.93, Solo Cross-country Flight Requirements; 61.95, Operations in Class B Airspace and at Airports Located Within Class B Airspace.

ADVISORY CIRCULARS

FAA-H-8083-9 *Aviation Instructor's Handbook* (1999).

FAA-H-8083-27 *Student Pilot Guide* (1999).

AERONAUTICAL INFORMATION MANUAL

Aircraft Call Signs: Student Pilots Radio Identification, Para. 4-2-4.

CASES

The NTSB has emphasized that accurate record keeping is critical to the FAA's safety enforcement program and, therefore, required by the public interest and safety in air commerce. The NTSB will not dismiss an action against a pilot under this regulation simply because no harm was done. *Administrator v. Reno*, EA-3622 (1992).

Even if the student/instructor relationship were comparable to that of the first officer/pilot in command, the cases make it clear that the respondent (student pilot) may not rely on the instructor's obligation if only because the responsibility was not solely that of the instructor. The two regulations (§61.87 and §61.93) impose on respondent (student pilot) an independent duty to obtain the necessary endorsements prior to flight. *Administrator v. Reno*, EA-3622 (1992).

A flight instructor received a 10 day suspension for endorsing a student's logbook simply "OK to solo," rather than the more comprehensive endorsement required by the regulation. *Administrator v. Couillard*, EA-4634 (1998).

61.89 GENERAL LIMITATIONS

(a) A student pilot may not act as pilot in command of an aircraft:
   (1) That is carrying a passenger;
   (2) That is carrying property for compensation or hire;
   (3) For compensation or hire;
   (4) In furtherance of a business;
   (5) On an international flight, except that a student pilot may make solo training flights from Haines, Gustavus, or Juneau, Alaska, to White Horse, Yukon, Canada, and return over the province of British Columbia;
   (6) With a flight or surface visibility of less than 3 statute miles during daylight hours or 5 statute miles at night;
   (7) When the flight cannot be made with visual reference to the surface; or
   (8) In a manner contrary to any limitations placed in the pilot's logbook by an authorized instructor.
(b) A student pilot may not act as a required pilot flight crewmember on any aircraft for which more than one pilot is required by the type certificate of the aircraft or regulations under which the flight is conducted, except when receiving flight training from an authorized instructor on board an airship, and no person other than a required flight crewmember is carried on the aircraft.

EXPLANATION

If a student pilot is found to have acted as pilot-in-command of an aircraft carrying a passenger, the sanction is generally revocation.

If a person who is charged with carrying a passenger while only the holder of a student pilot certificate, obtains a private pilot certificate prior to a hearing on the matter, the sanction is generally reduced to a substandard suspension, i.e., six to nine months.

To establish that a particular flight was for compensation or hire, the FAA does not have to show that the concerned pilot and/or operator made a profit. It is sufficient to show that the flight resulted in an economic advantage to the pilot and/or operator. Such economic advantage can be established even if there was a financial loss as a result of the flight, i.e. retention of goodwill.

Even if flights are incidental to the student pilot's business and not required by the nature of the business, such flights are prohibited.

The requirement that the flight or surface visibility be at least 3 statute miles during daylight hours or 5 statute miles at night applies in both controlled and uncontrolled airspace for flights conducted by student pilots.

Whenever a student pilot undertakes a flight with someone other than a flight instructor who is giving flight instruction, who holds a certificate higher than a student pilot certificate, the student pilot should ensure that the other pilot understands that he/she is the pilot-in-command and agrees to serve as such. The fact that a student pilot has on board an aircraft a person who holds a certificate higher than a student pilot certificate does not automatically make that pilot the PIC.

ADVISORY CIRCULARS

FAA-H-8083-27 *Student Pilot Guide* (1999).

CASES

When the Administrator learned that respondent had, after the incident of carrying a passenger while holding only a student pilot certificate, obtained a private pilot certificate, he amended his emergency order to provide for a 180-day suspension, a reduction that was also consistent with Board policy and precedent. *Administrator v. Bennett*, EA-3429 (1991). Other NTSB cases which followed this policy: *Administrator v. Winfree*, 3 NTSB 2278 (1980); *Administrator v. Dye*, 1 NTSB 1588 (1976).

A student pilot who carried a passenger in violation of §61.89, but received his commercial pilot certificate before the enforcement proceeding was completed, received a 30-day suspension. *Administrator v. Prins*, 3 NTSB 1154 (1978).

Student pilots are expected to be aware of the prohibition in §61.89 against carrying passengers, especially since this is printed on student pilot certificates. *Administrator v. Prins*, 3 NTSB 1154 (1978).

By admitting that, because he, as a (private) pilot, outranked the respondent (a student pilot), he would have taken over command and control of the aircraft in the event they encountered an emergency situation, he (the private pilot) was the pilot in command, for it establishes that, while the respondent may have been the pilot in charge of the physical management of the aircraft, the private pilot was the person who possessed the ultimate responsibility for the safety of the operation. His conceded service in that role made him the PIC, as that term is defined in the FAR. *Administrator v. Rajaratnman*, EA-3497 (1992).

61.93 SOLO CROSS-COUNTRY FLIGHT REQUIREMENTS

(a)   *General.*
  (1)   Except as provided in paragraph (b) of this section, a student pilot must meet the requirements of this section before—
    (i)   Conducting a solo cross-country flight, or any flight greater than 25 nautical miles from the airport from where the flight originated.
    (ii)   Making a solo flight and landing at any location other than the airport of origination.
  (2)   Except as provided in paragraph (b) of this section, a student pilot who seeks solo cross-country flight privileges must:
    (i)   Have received flight training from an instructor authorized to provide flight training on the maneuvers and procedures of this section that are appropriate to the make and model of aircraft for which solo cross-country privileges are sought;
    (ii)   Have demonstrated cross-country proficiency on the appropriate maneuvers and procedures of this section to an authorized instructor;
    (iii)   Have satisfactorily accomplished the pre-solo flight maneuvers and procedures required by §61.87 of this part in the make and model of aircraft or similar make and model of aircraft for which solo cross-country privileges are sought; and
    (iv)   Comply with any limitations included in the authorized instructor's endorsement that are required by paragraph (c) of this section.

(3)   A student pilot who seeks solo cross-country flight privileges must have received ground and flight training from an authorized instructor on the cross-country maneuvers and procedures listed in this section that are appropriate to the aircraft to be flown.

(b)   *Authorization to perform certain solo flights and cross-country flights.* A student pilot must obtain an endorsement from an authorized instructor to make solo flights from the airport where the student pilot normally receives training to another location. A student pilot who receives this endorsement must comply with the requirements of this paragraph.

(1)   Solo flights may be made to another airport that is within 25 nautical miles from the airport where the student pilot normally receives training, provided—

(i)   An authorized instructor has given the student pilot flight training at the other airport, and that training includes flight in both directions over the route, entering and exiting the traffic pattern, and takeoffs and landings at the other airport;

(ii)   The authorized instructor who gave the training endorses the student pilot's logbook authorizing the flight;

(iii)   The student pilot has current solo flight endorsements in accordance with §61.87 of this part;

(iv)   The authorized instructor has determined that the student pilot is proficient to make the flight; and

(v)   The purpose of the flight is to practice takeoffs and landings at that other airport.

(2)   Repeated specific solo cross-country flights may be made to another airport that is within 50 nautical miles of the airport from which the flight originated, provided—

(i)   The authorized instructor has given the student flight training in both directions over the route, including entering and exiting the traffic patterns, takeoffs, and landings at the airports to be used;

(ii)   The authorized instructor who gave the training has endorsed the student's logbook certifying that the student is proficient to make such flights;

(iii)   The student has current solo flight endorsements in accordance with §61.87 of this part; and

(iv)   The student has current solo cross-country flight endorsements in accordance with paragraph (c) of this section; however, for repeated solo cross-country flights to another airport within 50 nautical miles from which the flight originated, separate endorsements are not required to be made for each flight.

(c)   *Endorsements for solo cross-country flights.* Except as specified in paragraph (b)(2) of this section, a student pilot must have the endorsements prescribed in this paragraph for each cross-country flight:

(1)   Student *pilot certificate endorsement.* A student pilot must have a solo cross-country endorsement from the authorized instructor who conducted the training, and that endorsement must be placed on that person's student pilot certificate for the specific category of aircraft to be flown.

(2)   Logbook *endorsement.*

(i)   A student pilot must have a solo cross-country endorsement from an authorized instructor that is placed in the student pilot's logbook for the specific make and model of aircraft to be flown.

(ii)   For each cross-country flight, the authorized instructor who reviews the cross-country planning must make an endorsement in the person's logbook after reviewing that person's cross-country planning, as specified in paragraph (d) of this section. The endorsement must—

(A)   Specify the make and model of aircraft to be flown;

(B)   State that the student's preflight planning and preparation is correct and that the student is prepared to make the flight safely under the known conditions; and

(C)   State that any limitations required by the student's authorized instructor are met.

(d) *Limitations on authorized instructors to permit solo cross-country flights.* An authorized instructor may not permit a student pilot to conduct a solo cross-country flight unless that instructor has:
- (1) Determined that the student's cross-country planning is correct for the flight;
- (2) Reviewed the current and forecast weather conditions and has determined that the flight can be completed under VFR;
- (3) Determined that the student is proficient to conduct the flight safely;
- (4) Determined that the student has the appropriate solo cross-country endorsement for the make and model of aircraft to be flown; and
- (5) Determined that the student's solo flight endorsement is current for the make and model aircraft to be flown.

(e) *Maneuvers and procedures for cross-country flight training in a single-engine airplane.* A student pilot who is receiving training for cross-country flight in a single-engine airplane must receive and log flight training in the following maneuvers and procedures:
- (1) Use of aeronautical charts for VFR navigation using pilotage and dead reckoning with the aid of a magnetic compass;
- (2) Use of aircraft performance charts pertaining to cross-country flight;
- (3) Procurement and analysis of aeronautical weather reports and forecasts, including recognition of critical weather situations and estimating visibility while in flight;
- (4) Emergency procedures;
- (5) Traffic pattern procedures that include area departure, area arrival, entry into the traffic pattern, and approach;
- (6) Procedures and operating practices for collision avoidance, wake turbulence precautions, and windshear avoidance;
- (7) Recognition, avoidance, and operational restrictions of hazardous terrain features in the geographical area where the cross-country flight will be flown;
- (8) Procedures for operating the instruments and equipment installed in the aircraft to be flown, including recognition and use of the proper operational procedures and indications;
- (9) Use of radios for VFR navigation and two-way communications;
- (10) Takeoff, approach, and landing procedures, including short-field, soft-field, and crosswind takeoffs, approaches, and landings;
- (11) Climbs at best angle and best rate; and
- (12) Control and maneuvering solely by reference to flight instruments, including straight and level flight, turns, descents, climbs, use of radio aids, and ATC directives.

(f) *Maneuvers and procedures for cross-country flight training in a multiengine airplane.* A student pilot who is receiving training for cross-country flight in a multiengine airplane must receive and log flight training in the following maneuvers and procedures:
- (1) Use of aeronautical charts for VFR navigation using pilotage and dead reckoning with the aid of a magnetic compass;
- (2) Use of aircraft performance charts pertaining to cross-country flight;
- (3) Procurement and analysis of aeronautical weather reports and forecasts, including recognition of critical weather situations and estimating visibility while in flight;
- (4) Emergency procedures;
- (5) Traffic pattern procedures that include area departure, area arrival, entry into the traffic pattern, and approach;
- (6) Procedures and operating practices for collision avoidance, wake turbulence precautions, and windshear avoidance;

(7)   Recognition, avoidance, and operational restrictions of hazardous terrain features in the geographical area where the cross-country flight will be flown;

(8)   Procedures for operating the instruments and equipment installed in the aircraft to be flown, including recognition and use of the proper operational procedures and indications;

(9)   Use of radios for VFR navigation and two-way communications;

(10) Takeoff, approach, and landing procedures, including short-field, soft-field, and crosswind takeoffs, approaches, and landings;

(11) Climbs at best angle and best rate; and

(12) Control and maneuvering solely by reference to flight instruments, including straight and level flight, turns, descents, climbs, use of radio aids, and ATC directives.

(g) *Maneuvers and procedures for cross-country flight training in a helicopter.* A student pilot who is receiving training for cross-country flight in a helicopter must receive and log flight training for the following maneuvers and procedures:

(1)   Use of aeronautical charts for VFR navigation using pilotage and dead reckoning with the aid of a magnetic compass;

(2)   Use of aircraft performance charts pertaining to cross-country flight;

(3)   Procurement and analysis of aeronautical weather reports and forecasts, including recognition of critical weather situations and estimating visibility while in flight;

(4)   Emergency procedures;

(5)   Traffic pattern procedures that include area departure, area arrival, entry into the traffic pattern, and approach;

(6)   Procedures and operating practices for collision avoidance, wake turbulence precautions, and windshear avoidance;

(7)   Recognition, avoidance, and operational restrictions of hazardous terrain features in the geographical area where the cross-country flight will be flown;

(8)   Procedures for operating the instruments and equipment installed in the aircraft to be flown, including recognition and use of the proper operational procedures and indications;

(9)   Use of radios for VFR navigation and two-way communications; and

(10) Takeoff, approach, and landing procedures.

(h) *Maneuvers and procedures for cross-country flight training in a gyroplane.* A student pilot who is receiving training for cross-country flight in a gyroplane must receive and log flight training in the following maneuvers and procedures:

(1)   Use of aeronautical charts for VFR navigation using pilotage and dead reckoning with the aid of a magnetic compass;

(2)   Use of aircraft performance charts pertaining to cross-country flight;

(3)   Procurement and analysis of aeronautical weather reports and forecasts, including recognition of critical weather situations and estimating visibility while in flight;

(4)   Emergency procedures;

(5)   Traffic pattern procedures that include area departure, area arrival, entry into the traffic pattern, and approach;

(6)   Procedures and operating practices for collision avoidance, wake turbulence precautions, and windshear avoidance;

(7)   Recognition, avoidance, and operational restrictions of hazardous terrain features in the geographical area where the cross-country flight will be flown;

(8)   Procedures for operating the instruments and equipment installed in the aircraft to be flown, including recognition and use of the proper operational procedures and indications;

(9)   Use of radios for VFR navigation and two-way communications; and

(10) Takeoff, approach, and landing procedures, including short-field and soft-field takeoffs, approaches, and landings.

(i)   *Maneuvers and procedures for cross-country flight training in a powered-lift.* A student pilot who is receiving training for cross-country flight training in a powered-lift must receive and log flight training in the following maneuvers and procedures:
      (1)   Use of aeronautical charts for VFR navigation using pilotage and dead reckoning with the aid of a magnetic compass;
      (2)   Use of aircraft performance charts pertaining to cross-country flight;
      (3)   Procurement and analysis of aeronautical weather reports and forecasts, including recognition of critical weather situations and estimating visibility while in flight;
      (4)   Emergency procedures;
      (5)   Traffic pattern procedures that include area departure, area arrival, entry into the traffic pattern, and approach;
      (6)   Procedures and operating practices for collision avoidance, wake turbulence precautions, and windshear avoidance;
      (7)   Recognition, avoidance, and operational restrictions of hazardous terrain features in the geographical area where the cross-country flight will be flown;
      (8)   Procedures for operating the instruments and equipment installed in the aircraft to be flown, including recognition and use of the proper operational procedures and indications;
      (9)   Use of radios for VFR navigation and two-way communications;
      (10) Takeoff, approach, and landing procedures that include high-altitude, steep, and shallow takeoffs, approaches, and landings; and
      (11) Control and maneuvering solely by reference to flight instruments, including straight and level flight, turns, descents, climbs, use of radio aids, and ATC directives.

(j)   *Maneuvers and procedures for cross-country flight training in a glider.* A student pilot who is receiving training for cross-country flight in a glider must receive and log flight training in the following maneuvers and procedures:
      (1)   Use of aeronautical charts for VFR navigation using pilotage and dead reckoning with the aid of a magnetic compass;
      (2)   Use of aircraft performance charts pertaining to cross-country flight;
      (3)   Procurement and analysis of aeronautical weather reports and forecasts, including recognition of critical weather situations and estimating visibility while in flight;
      (4)   Emergency procedures;
      (5)   Traffic pattern procedures that include area departure, area arrival, entry into the traffic pattern, and approach;
      (6)   Procedures and operating practices for collision avoidance, wake turbulence precautions, and windshear avoidance;
      (7)   Recognition, avoidance, and operational restrictions of hazardous terrain features in the geographical area where the cross-country flight will be flown;
      (8)   Procedures for operating the instruments and equipment installed in the aircraft to be flown, including recognition and use of the proper operational procedures and indications;
      (9)   Landings accomplished without the use of the altimeter from at least 2,000 feet above the surface; and
      (10) Recognition of weather and upper air conditions favorable for cross-country soaring, ascending and descending flight, and altitude control.

(k)   *Maneuvers and procedures for cross-country flight training in an airship.* A student pilot who is receiving training for cross-country flight in an airship must receive and log flight training for the following maneuvers and procedures:

(1)   Use of aeronautical charts for VFR navigation using pilotage and dead reckoning with the aid of a magnetic compass;

(2)   Use of aircraft performance charts pertaining to cross-country flight;

(3)   Procurement and analysis of aeronautical weather reports and forecasts, including recognition of critical weather situations and estimating visibility while in flight;

(4)   Emergency procedures;

(5)   Traffic pattern procedures that include area departure, area arrival, entry into the traffic pattern, and approach;

(6)   Procedures and operating practices for collision avoidance, wake turbulence precautions, and windshear avoidance;

(7)   Recognition, avoidance, and operational restrictions of hazardous terrain features in the geographical area where the cross-country flight will be flown;

(8)   Procedures for operating the instruments and equipment installed in the aircraft to be flown, including recognition and use of the proper operational procedures and indications;

(9)   Use of radios for VFR navigation and two-way communications;

(10) Control of air pressure with regard to ascending and descending flight and altitude control;

(11) Control of the airship solely by reference to flight instruments; and

(12) Recognition of weather and upper air conditions conducive for the direction of cross-country flight.

EXPLANATION

An endorsement to solo is not an authorization to conduct solo cross-country flights. Such flights require a specific endorsement.

Even if an airport is within 25 nautical miles of the takeoff airport, a student pilot cannot land at that airport, except in an emergency, unless he/she has met the requirements of 61.93.

A student pilot has a separate and distinct responsibility to ensure that his/her student pilot certificate and logbook have the necessary endorsements prior to any solo cross-country flight.

PREAMBLE

As discussed in the analysis of §61.1, the FAA has decided not to adopt the term "supervised pilot in command." Regarding the comment on the possible terminology problem in paragraph (a) with respect to balloons, the FAA points out that it has decided to delete solo cross-country requirements for balloons in the final rule as discussed in the analysis of §61.107. Upon reviewing the comments of AOPA, HAI, and individuals regarding cross-country endorsements, the FAA has decided to replace the words "make and model" with "category" in paragraph (c)(1) of the final rule, while retaining them for logbooks in paragraph (c)(2). The intent of the change to the existing rule is to clarify that a student must be properly authorized to conduct not just all solo flights, but also all solo cross-country flights, in a specific make and model.

For reasons similar to those discussed in the section-by-section analysis of §61.87, the FAA also has modified §61.93(a)(2)(iii) to permit the pre-solo flight maneuvers and procedures required by §61.87 to be accomplished in either the make and model of aircraft or a similar make and model of aircraft for which solo cross-country flight privileges are sought. Except for these changes, the final rule is adopted as proposed. (62 FR 16260).

CROSS REFERENCES

61.87, *Solo Requirements for Student Pilots.*

ADVISORY CIRCULARS

FAA-H-8083-27 *Student Pilot Guide* (1999).

AC 61-65D *Certification: Pilots and Flight and Ground Instructors* (1999).

AERONAUTICAL INFORMATION MANUAL

Aircraft Call Signs: Student Pilot Radio Identification, Para. 4-2-4.

CASES

Violation of §61.93 may by itself justify revocation of a student pilot certificate. *Administrator v. Noll*, 3 NTSB 3877 (1981). See the discussion of *Administrator v. Reno*, EA-3622 (1992) under §61.87.

61.95 OPERATIONS IN CLASS B AIRSPACE AND AT AIRPORTS LOCATED WITHIN CLASS B AIRSPACE

(a)   A student pilot may not operate an aircraft on a solo flight in Class B airspace unless:
   (1)   The student pilot has received both ground and flight training from an authorized instructor on that Class B airspace area, and the flight training was received in the specific Class B airspace area for which solo flight is authorized;
   (2)   The logbook of that student pilot has been endorsed by the authorized instructor who gave the student pilot flight training, and the endorsement is dated within the 90-day period preceding the date of the flight in that Class B airspace area; and
   (3)   The logbook endorsement specifies that the student pilot has received the required ground and flight training, and has been found proficient to conduct solo flight in that specific Class B airspace area.
(b)   A student pilot may not operate an aircraft on a solo flight to, from, or at an airport located within Class B airspace pursuant to §91.131(b) of this chapter unless:
   (1)   The student pilot has received both ground and flight training from an instructor authorized to provide training to operate at that airport, and the flight and ground training has been received at the specific airport for which the solo flight is authorized;
   (2)   The logbook of that student pilot has been endorsed by an authorized instructor who gave the student pilot flight training, and the endorsement is dated within the 90-day period preceding the date of the flight at that airport; and
   (3)   The logbook endorsement specifies that the student pilot has received the required ground and flight training, and has been found proficient to conduct solo flight operations at that specific airport.

EXPLANATION

Class B airspace which became effective on September 16, 1993, was previously referred to as Terminal Control Area (TCA).

Solo student pilot activity is still prohibited in certain Class B airspace. A list of those areas can be found in Part 91, Appendix D, Section 4.

Student operation in Class B airspace on and after September 16, 1993, requires a specific logbook endorsement by an authorized instructor.
The endorsements made under this section are effective for 90 days.

Operation to, from, or at an airport located within Class B airspace also requires a specific endorsement in the student pilot logbook.

CROSS REFERENCES

91.131(b), Operations in Class B Airspace - Pilot Requirements.

AERONAUTICAL INFORMATION MANUAL

Class B Airspace, Para. 3-2-3.

INTENTIONALLY

LEFT

BLANK

SUBPART D — RECREATIONAL PILOTS

61.96 APPLICABILITY AND ELIGIBILITY REQUIREMENTS: GENERAL

(a) This subpart prescribes the requirement for the issuance of recreational pilot certificates and ratings, the conditions under which those certificates and ratings are necessary, and the general operating rules for persons who hold those certificates and ratings.

(b) To be eligible for a recreational pilot certificate, a person who applies for that certificate must:

    (1) Be at least 17 years of age;

    (2) Be able to read, speak, write, and understand the English language. If the applicant is unable to meet one of these requirements due to medical reasons, then the Administrator may place such operating limitations on that applicant's pilot certificate as are necessary for the safe operation of the aircraft;

    (3) Receive a logbook endorsement from an authorized instructor who—

        (i) Conducted the training or reviewed the applicant's home study on the aeronautical knowledge areas listed in §61.97(b) of this part that apply to the aircraft category and class rating sought; and

        (ii) Certified that the applicant is prepared for the required knowledge test.

    (4) Pass the required knowledge test on the aeronautical knowledge areas listed in §61.97(b) of this part;

    (5) Receive flight training and a logbook endorsement from an authorized instructor who—

        (i) Conducted the training on the areas of operation listed in §61.98(b) of this part that apply to the aircraft category and class rating sought; and

        (ii) Certified that the applicant is prepared for the required practical test.

    (6) Meet the aeronautical experience requirements of §61.99 of this part that apply to the aircraft category and class rating sought before applying for the practical test;

    (7) Pass the required practical test on the areas of operation listed in §61.98(b) of this part that apply to the aircraft category and class rating sought; and

    (8) Comply with the sections of this part that apply to the aircraft category and class rating sought.

EXPLANATION

This rule requires a logbook endorsement from an instructor for eligibility to take the knowledge test. This eliminates the FSDO's from having to allocate time to review an applicant's home study programs. It also deletes the exceptions for persons who are unable to read, speak, write and understand English. However the rule still provides an exception for persons with medical impairments only (i.e. hearing impaired).

PREAMBLE

The FAA has modified the final rule to address the commenters' concerns regarding the unintended effect in the proposed rule change that would prevent deaf pilots and pilots with other medical conditions that have a command of the English language from obtaining a recreational pilot certificate. Although the FAA notes the positive response to the proposal regarding medical self-evaluation by persons exercising recreational pilot privileges, the FAA has decided not to adopt the proposal. (62 FR 16261).

CROSS REFERENCES

61.97, Aeronautical Knowledge; 61.98, Flight Proficiency; 61.99, Aeronautical Experience; 61.101, Recreational Pilot Privileges and Limitations.

ADVISORY CIRCULARS

FAA-H-8083-27 *Student Pilot Guide* (1999).

61.97 AERONAUTICAL KNOWLEDGE

(a) *General.* A person who applies for a recreational pilot certificate must receive and log ground training from an authorized instructor or complete a home-study course on the aeronautical knowledge areas of paragraph (b) of this section that apply to the aircraft category and class rating sought.

(b) *Aeronautical knowledge areas.*

   (1) Applicable Federal Aviation Regulations of this chapter that relate to recreational pilot privileges, limitations, and flight operations;

   (2) Accident reporting requirements of the National Transportation Safety Board;

   (3) Use of the applicable portions of the "Aeronautical Information Manual" and FAA advisory circulars;

   (4) Use of aeronautical charts for VFR navigation using pilotage with the aid of a magnetic compass;

   (5) Recognition of critical weather situations from the ground and in flight, windshear avoidance, and the procurement and use of aeronautical weather reports and forecasts;

   (6) Safe and efficient operation of aircraft, including collision avoidance, and recognition and avoidance of wake turbulence;

   (7) Effects of density altitude on takeoff and climb performance;

   (8) Weight and balance computations;

   (9) Principles of aerodynamics, powerplants, and aircraft systems;

  (10) Stall awareness, spin entry, spins, and spin recovery techniques, if applying for an airplane single-engine rating;

  (11) Aeronautical decision making and judgment; and

  (12) Preflight action that includes—

    (i) How to obtain information on runway lengths at airports of intended use, data on takeoff and landing distances, weather reports and forecasts, and fuel requirements; and

    (ii) How to plan for alternatives if the planned flight cannot be completed or delays are encountered.

EXPLANATION

Recreational Pilots are now required to have knowledge of windshear avoidance procedures, aeronautical decision making, judgment training, and cockpit resource management.

PREAMBLE

The FAA agrees with commenters who state that recreational pilots are unlikely to encounter air traffic delays, and has modified the requirement for training in traffic delay planning to a more general reference to possible delays. Other terminology and changes were implemented in the final rule as well, including revising the reference to the "Airman's Information Manual," which is now titled the "Aeronautical Information Manual."

The FAA strongly believes that training in human factors and aeronautical decision making should be required. Approximately 80 percent of all accidents are related to pilot error. Training in human factors, and aeronautical decision making and judgment may decrease the number of accidents attributable to pilot error, because implementation of similar training in air carrier operations has decreased accident rates. Regarding AOPA's concern on the need for guidance material on aeronautical decision making, the FAA points out that AC No. 60-22, "Aeronautical Decision Making," contains such guidance. (62 FR 16261).

CROSS REFERENCES

61.96, Application and Eligibility Requirements: General; 61.98, Flight Proficiency; 61.100, Pilots based on Small Islands; 61.101, Recreational Pilot Privileges and Limitations.

ADVISORY CIRCULARS

FAA-G-8082-17 *Recreational Pilot and Private Pilot Knowledge Test Guide* (1999).

61.98 FLIGHT PROFICIENCY

(a) *General.* A person who applies for a recreational pilot certificate must receive and log ground and flight training from an authorized instructor on the areas of operation of this section that apply to the aircraft category and class rating sought.

(b) *Areas of operation.*
    (1) For a single-engine airplane rating:
        (i) Preflight preparation;
        (ii) Preflight procedures;
        (iii) Airport operations;
        (iv) Takeoffs, landings, and go-arounds;
        (v) Performance maneuvers;
        (vi) Ground reference maneuvers;
        (vii) Navigation;
        (viii) Slow flight and stalls;
        (ix) Emergency operations; and
        (x) Postflight procedures.

    (2)   *For a helicopter rating:*
        (i)   Preflight preparation;
        (ii)   Preflight procedures;
        (iii)   Airport and heliport operations;
        (iv)   Hovering maneuvers;
        (v)   Takeoffs, landings, and go-arounds;
        (vi)   Performance maneuvers;
        (vii) Ground reference maneuvers;
        (viii) Navigation;
        (ix)   Emergency operations; and
        (x)   Postflight procedures.
    (3)   *For a gyroplane rating:*
        (i)   Preflight preparation;
        (ii)   Preflight procedures;
        (iii)   Airport operations;
        (iv)   Takeoffs, landings, and go-arounds;
        (v)   Performance maneuvers;
        (vi)   Ground reference maneuvers;
        (vii) Navigation;
        (viii) Flight at slow airspeeds;
        (ix)   Emergency operations; and
        (x)   Postflight procedures.

CROSS REFERENCES

61.96, Application and Eligibility Requirements: General; 61.97, Aeronautical Knowledge; 61.100, Pilots based on Small Islands; 61.101, Recreational Pilot Privileges and Limitations.

ADVISORY CIRCULARS

FAA-H-8083-27 *Student Pilot Guide* (1999).

AC 61-67C *Stall and Spin Awareness Training.*

61.99 AERONAUTICAL EXPERIENCE

A person who applies for a recreational pilot certificate must receive and log at least 30 hours of flight training time that includes at least:
(a)   15 hours of flight training from an authorized instructor on the areas of operation listed in §61.98 of this part that consists of at least:
    (1)   Except as provided in §61.100 of this part, 2 hours of flight training en route to an airport that is located more than 25 nautical miles from the airport where the applicant normally trains, which includes at least three takeoffs and three landings at the airport located more than 25 nautical miles from the airport where the applicant normally trains; and
    (2)   3 hours of flight training in the aircraft for the rating sought in preparation for the practical test within the 60 days preceding the date of the practical test.
(b)   3 hours of solo flying in the aircraft for the rating sought, on the areas of operation listed in §61.98 of this part that apply to the aircraft category and class rating sought.

EXPLANATION

This rule modifies the solo flight time (hours) required for the recreational pilot certificates so that it permits the student and the flight instructor to tailor the training time toward the student's needs and capabilities.

PREAMBLE

The FAA believes the change in the dual and solo time requirements provides instructors with flexibility in determining the amount of solo and dual training required for each student. This change should not compromise safety, because the total number of hours remains unchanged and should encourage increased training and help reduce overall costs. It appears that some commenters misunderstood the proposal, because their concerns implied that the total number of hours would be reduced, which is not the case. Therefore, this section is implemented in the final rule as proposed, with the exception of the changes noted and minor editorial changes. (62 FR 16262)

CROSS REFERENCES

61.96, Applicability and Eligibility: General; 61.97, Aeronautical Knowledge; 61.98, Flight Proficiency; 61.101, Recreational Pilot Privileges and Limitations.

ADVISORY CIRCULARS

FAA-H-8083-27 *Student Pilot Guide* (1999).

61.100 PILOTS BASED ON SMALL ISLANDS

(a) An applicant located on an island from which the flight training required in §61.99(a)(1) of this part cannot be accomplished without flying over water for more than 10 nautical miles from the nearest shoreline need not comply with the requirements of that section. However, if other airports that permit civil operations are available to which a flight may be made without flying over water for more than 10 nautical miles from the nearest shoreline, the applicant must show completion of a dual flight between two airports, which must include three landings at the other airport.

(b) An applicant who complies with paragraph (a) of this section and meets all requirements for the issuance of a recreational pilot certificate, except the requirements of §61.99(a)(1) of this part, will be issued a pilot certificate with an endorsement containing the following limitation, "Passenger carrying prohibited on flights more than 10 nautical miles from (the appropriate island)." The limitation may be subsequently amended to include another island if the applicant complies with the requirements of paragraph (a) of this section for another island.

(c) Upon meeting the requirements of §61.99(a)(1) of this part, the applicant may have the limitation(s) in paragraph (b) of this section removed.

61.101 RECREATIONAL PILOT PRIVILEGES AND LIMITATIONS

(a)   A person who holds a recreational pilot certificate may:
   (1)   Carry no more than one passenger; and
   (2)   Not pay less than the pro rata share of the operating expenses of a flight with a passenger, provided the expenses involve only fuel, oil, airport expenses, or aircraft rental fees.

(b)   A person who holds a recreational pilot certificate may act as pilot in command of an aircraft on a flight that is within 50 nautical miles from the departure airport, provided that person has:
   (1)   Received ground and flight training for takeoff, departure, arrival, and landing procedures at the departure airport;
   (2)   Received ground and flight training for the area, terrain, and aids to navigation that are in the vicinity of the departure airport;
   (3)   Been found proficient to operate the aircraft at the departure airport and the area within 50 nautical miles from that airport; and
   (4)   Received from an authorized instructor a logbook endorsement, which is carried in the person's possession in the aircraft, that permits flight within 50 nautical miles from the departure airport.

(c)   A person who holds a recreational pilot certificate may act as pilot in command of an aircraft on a flight that exceeds 50 nautical miles from the departure airport, provided that person has:
   (1)   Received ground and flight training from an authorized instructor on the cross-country training requirements of subpart E of this part that apply to the aircraft rating held;
   (2)   Been found proficient in cross-country flying; and
   (3)   Received from an authorized instructor a logbook endorsement, which is carried on the person's possession in the aircraft, that certifies the person has received and been found proficient in the cross-country training requirements of subpart E of this part that apply to the aircraft rating held.

(d)   Except as provided in paragraph (h) of this section, a recreational pilot may not act as pilot in command of an aircraft:
   (1)   That is certificated for more than four occupants, with more than one powerplant, with a powerplant of more than 180 horsepower, or with retractable landing gear.
   (2)   That is classified as a multiengine airplane, powered-lift, glider, airship, or balloon;
   (3)   That is carrying a passenger or property for compensation or hire;
   (4)   For compensation or hire;
   (5)   In furtherance of a business;
   (6)   Between sunset and sunrise;
   (7)   In airspace in which communication with air traffic control is required;
   (8)   At an altitude of more than 10,000 feet MSL or 2,000 feet AGL, whichever is higher;
   (9)   When the flight or surface visibility is less than 3 statute miles;
   (10) Without visual reference to the surface;
   (11) On a flight outside the United States;
   (12) To demonstrate that aircraft in flight to a prospective buyer;
   (13) That is used in a passenger-carrying airlift and sponsored by a charitable organization; and
   (14) That is towing any object.

(e)   A recreational pilot may not act as a pilot flight crewmember on any aircraft for which more than one pilot is required by the type certificate of the aircraft or the regulations under which the flight is conducted, except when:
   (1)   Receiving flight training from a person authorized to provide flight training on board an airship; and
   (2)   No person other than a required flight crewmember is carried on the aircraft.

(f)   A person who holds a recreational pilot certificate, has logged fewer than 400 flight hours, and has not logged pilot-in-command time in an aircraft within the 180 days preceding the flight shall not act as pilot in command of an aircraft until the pilot receives flight training and a logbook endorsement from an authorized instructor, and the instructor certifies that the person is proficient to act as pilot in command of the aircraft. This requirement can be met in combination with the requirements of §§61.56 and 61.57 of this part, at the discretion of the authorized instructor.

(g)   A recreational pilot certificate issued under this subpart carries the notation, "Holder does not meet ICAO requirements."

(h)   For the purpose of obtaining additional certificates or ratings while under the supervision of an authorized instructor, a recreational pilot may fly as the sole occupant of an aircraft:
      (1)   For which the pilot does not hold an appropriate category or class rating;
      (2)   Within airspace that requires communication with air traffic control; or
      (3)   Between sunset and sunrise, provided the flight or surface visibility is at least 5 statute miles.

(i)   In order to fly solo as provided in paragraph (h) of this section, the recreational pilot must meet the appropriate aeronautical knowledge and flight training requirements of §61.87 for that aircraft. When operating an aircraft under the conditions specified in paragraph (h) of this section, the recreational pilot shall carry the logbook that has been endorsed for each flight by an authorized instructor who:
      (1)   Has given the recreational pilot training in the make and model of aircraft in which the solo flight is to be made;
      (2)   Has found that the recreational pilot has met the applicable requirements of §61.87; and
      (3)   Has found that the recreational pilot is competent to make solo flights in accordance with the logbook endorsement.

EXPLANATION

This rule permits recreational pilots to operate aircraft in cross country flight that is more than 50 nm from their base of training provided those recreational pilots receive the cross country training given to a private pilot.

PREAMBLE

The FAA inadvertently omitted "aircraft rental fees" from the list of expenses that private and recreational pilots may share. This is current FAA policy. Therefore, §61.101(a) is appropriately modified in the final rule. In response to those commenters who want additional operating costs shared, only direct operating and rental expenses may be shared. To avoid a pilot receiving compensation for a flight, indirect operating costs, such as maintenance expenses, are not permitted to be shared. In response to the comment regarding the equal sharing of expenses, the FAA has determined that a pilot may not pay less than the pro rata share of operating expenses. The rationale is that if pilots pay less, they would not just be sharing expenses but would actually be flying for compensation or hire. The rule has been modified accordingly. (62 FR 16263).

CROSS REFERENCES

61.109, Private Pilots: Aeronautical Experience.

ADVISORY CIRCULARS

FAA-H-8083-27 *Student Pilot Guide* (1999).

INTENTIONALLY

LEFT

BLANK

SUBPART E — PRIVATE PILOTS

61.102 APPLICABILITY

This subpart prescribes the requirements for the issuance of private pilot certificates and ratings, the conditions under which those certificates and ratings are necessary, and the general operating rules for persons who hold those certificates and ratings.

61.103 ELIGIBILITY REQUIREMENTS: GENERAL

To be eligible for a private pilot certificate, a person must:
(a) Be at least 17 years of age for a rating in other than a glider or balloon.
(b) Be at least 16 years of age for a rating in a glider or balloon.
(c) Be able to read, speak, write, and understand the English language. If the applicant is unable to meet one of these requirements due to medical reasons, then the Administrator may place such operating limitations on that applicant's pilot certificate as are necessary for the safe operation of the aircraft.
(d) Receive a logbook endorsement from an authorized instructor who:
　　(1) Conducted the training or reviewed the person's home study on the aeronautical knowledge areas listed in §61.105(b) of this part that apply to the aircraft rating sought; and
　　(2) Certified that the person is prepared for the required knowledge test.
(e) Pass the required knowledge test on the aeronautical knowledge areas listed in §61.105(b) of this part.
(f) Receive flight training and a logbook endorsement from an authorized instructor who:
　　(1) Conducted the training in the areas of operation listed in §61.107(b) of this part that apply to the aircraft rating sought; and
　　(2) Certified that the person is prepared for the required practical test.
(g) Meet the aeronautical experience requirements of this part that apply to the aircraft rating sought before applying for the practical test.
(h) Pass a practical test on the areas of operation listed in §61.107(b) of this part that apply to the aircraft rating sought.
(I) Comply with the appropriate sections of this part that apply to the aircraft category and class rating sought.

EXPLANATION

To be eligible to take the knowledge test, you must have a logbook endorsement from an authorized instructor. This eliminates the FSDO's from having to allocate time to review an applicant's home study programs. You must also be able to read, speak, write and understand English. However the rules still provide an exception for persons with medical impairments only (i.e. hearing impaired).

PREAMBLE

The final rule includes language restoring the option for the Administrator to place an operating limitation on an applicant's pilot certificate, waiving the applicant's English language requirements on medical grounds. In addition, the language on medical requirements for private pilots is deleted from this section and placed in §61.23. This topic is discussed in the analysis of §61.23. The FAA also made other minor editorial and formatting changes to this section of the final rule. (62 FR 16263).

CROSS REFERENCES

61.105, Aeronautical Knowledge; 61.107, Flight Proficiency; 61.109, Aeronautical Experiences; 61.110, Night Flying Exceptions; 61.111, Cross-country flights: Pilots based on small islands; 61.113, Private Pilot Privileges and Limitations: Pilot in Command; 61.115, Balloon Rating: Limitations; 61.117, Private Pilot Privileges and Limitations: Second in Command of Aircraft Requiring More than One Pilot.

ADVISORY CIRCULARS

AC 61-65D *Certification: Pilots and Flight and Ground Instructors* (1999).

FAA CHIEF COUNSEL OPINIONS

The task of establishing the minimum age at which all individuals applying for a particular type of airman certificate can be expected to have reached the proper level of maturity and responsibility is a difficult one. The FAA believes that the ages now prescribed for student pilot and private pilot certificates are necessary to ensure this level of maturity and responsibility for all applicants. (1-18-78).

61.105 AERONAUTICAL KNOWLEDGE

(a) *General.* A person who is applying for a private pilot certificate must receive and log ground training from an authorized instructor or complete a home-study course on the aeronautical knowledge areas of paragraph (b) of this section that apply to the aircraft category and class rating sought.

(b) *Aeronautical knowledge areas.*

   (1) Applicable Federal Aviation Regulations of this chapter that relate to private pilot privileges, limitations, and flight operations;

   (2) Accident reporting requirements of the National Transportation Safety Board;

   (3) Use of the applicable portions of the "Aeronautical Information Manual" and FAA advisory circulars;

   (4) Use of aeronautical charts for VFR navigation using pilotage, dead reckoning, and navigation systems;

   (5) Radio communication procedures;

   (6) Recognition of critical weather situations from the ground and in flight, windshear avoidance, and the procurement and use of aeronautical weather reports and forecasts;

(7)   Safe and efficient operation of aircraft, including collision avoidance, and recognition and avoidance of wake turbulence;
(8)   Effects of density altitude on takeoff and climb performance;
(9)   Weight and balance computations;
(10) Principles of aerodynamics, powerplants, and aircraft systems;
(11) Stall awareness, spin entry, spins, and spin recovery techniques for the airplane and glider category ratings;
(12) Aeronautical decision making and judgment; and
(13) Preflight action that includes—
      (I)   How to obtain information on runway lengths at airports of intended use, data on takeoff and landing distances, weather reports and forecasts, and fuel requirements; and
      (ii) How to plan for alternatives if the planned flight cannot be completed or delays are encountered.

EXPLANATION

Private pilots are now required to have knowledge of windshear avoidance procedures, aeronautical decision making, judgment training, and cockpit resource management.

PREAMBLE

The FAA agrees with commenters who state that private pilots are less likely to encounter air traffic delays, and has modified the requirement for training in traffic delay planning to a more general reference to possible delays.

The FAA strongly believes that training in human factors and aeronautical decision making should be required. Approximately 80 percent of all accidents are related to pilot error, and training in human factors, and aeronautical decision making and judgment may decrease the number of accidents attributable to pilot error, because implementation of similar training in air carrier operations has decreased accident rates. Regarding AOPA's concern on the need for guidance material on aeronautical decision making, the FAA points out that AC 60-22, "*Aeronautical Decision Making*," contains such guidance. (62 FR 16263).

CROSS REFERENCES

61.103, Eligibility Requirements: General; 61.107, Flight Proficiency; 61.109, Aeronautical Experiences; 61.110, Night Flying Exceptions; 61.111, Cross-country flights: Pilots based on small islands; 61.113, Private Pilot Privileges and Limitations: Pilot in Command; 61.115, Balloon Rating: Limitations; 61.117, Private Pilot Privileges and Limitations: Second in Command of Aircraft requiring more than one Pilot.

ADVISORY CIRCULARS

AC 00-2.x *Advisory Circular Checklist (and Status of Other FAA Publications)* **Editor's Note**: This AC is updated annually.

AC 00-6A *Aviation Weather* (1975).

AC 00-24B *Thunderstorms* (1983).

AC 00-30B *Atmospheric Turbulence Avoidance* (1997).

AC 00-45E *Aviation Weather Services* (1999).

AC 00-54 *Pilot's Windshear Guide* (1988).

AC 60-4A *Pilot's Spatial Disorientation* (1983).

AC 60-22 *Aeronautical Decision Making* (1991).

AC 61-23C *Pilot's Handbook of Aeronautical Knowledge* (1997).

AC 61-65D *Certification: Pilots and Flight and Ground Instructors* (1999).

AC 61-67C *Stall and Spin Awareness Training* (2000).

AC 90-42F *Traffic Advisory Practices at Airports Without Operating Control Towers* (1990).

AC 90-48C *Pilots' Role in Collision Avoidance* (1983).

AC 90-87 *Helicopter Dynamic Rollover* (1986).

AC 91-13C *Cold Weather Operation of Aircraft* (1979).

AC 91-32B *Safety in and Around Helicopters* (1997).

AC 91-42D *Hazards of Rotating Propeller and Helicopter Rotor Blades* (1983).

AC 91-67 *Minimum Equipment Requirement for General Aviation Operations Under Part 91* (1991).

FAA-H-8083-1 *Aircraft Weight and Balance Handbook* (1999).

FAA-H-8083-3 *Airplane Flying Handbook* (1999).

FAA-H-8083-21 *Rotorcraft Flying Handbook* (2000).

FAA-H-8083-27 *Student Pilot Guide* (1999).

61.107 FLIGHT PROFICIENCY

(a) *General.* A person who applies for a private pilot certificate must receive and log ground and flight training from an authorized instructor on the areas of operation of this section that apply to the aircraft category and class rating sought.

(b) *Areas of operation.*

    (1) For an airplane category rating with a single-engine class rating:
        (I) Preflight preparation;
        (ii) Preflight procedures;
        (iii) Airport and seaplane base operations;
        (iv) Takeoffs, landings, and go-arounds;
        (v) Performance maneuvers;
        (vi) Ground reference maneuvers;
        (vii) Navigation;
        (viii) Slow flight and stalls;
        (ix) Basic instrument maneuvers;
        (x) Emergency operations;
        (xi) Night operations, except as provided in §61.110 of this part; and
        (xii) Postflight procedures.

    (2) *For an airplane category rating with a multiengine class rating:*
        (I) Preflight preparation;
        (ii) Preflight procedures;
        (iii) Airport and seaplane base operations;
        (iv) Takeoffs, landings, and go-arounds;
        (v) Performance maneuvers;
        (vi) Ground reference maneuvers;
        (vii) Navigation;
        (viii) Slow flight and stalls;
        (ix) Basic instrument maneuvers;
        (x) Emergency operations;
        (xi) Multiengine operations;
        (xii) Night operations, except as provided in §61.110 of this part; and
        (xiii) Postflight procedures.

    (3) *For a rotorcraft category* rating *with a helicopter class rating:*
        (I) Preflight preparation;
        (ii) Preflight procedures;
        (iii) Airport and heliport operations;
        (iv) Hovering maneuvers;
        (v) Takeoffs, landings, and go-arounds;
        (vi) Performance maneuvers;
        (vii) Navigation;
        (viii) Emergency operations;
        (ix) Night operations, except as provided in §61.110 of this part; and
        (x) Postflight procedures.

(4) *For a rotorcraft category* rating *with a gyroplane class rating:*
   (I)   Preflight preparation;
   (ii)   Preflight procedures;
   (iii) Airport operations;
   (v)   Takeoffs, landings, and go-arounds;
   (v)   Performance maneuvers;
   (vi)   Ground reference maneuvers;
   (vii) Navigation;
   (viii) Flight at slow airspeeds;
   (ix)   Emergency operations;
   (x)   Night operations, except as provided in §61.110 of this part; and
   (xi)   Postflight procedures.
(5) *For a powered-lift category rating:*
   (I)   Preflight preparation;
   (ii)   Preflight procedures;
   (iii) Airport and heliport operations;
   (iv)   Hovering maneuvers;
   (v)   Takeoffs, landings, and go-arounds;
   (vi)   Performance maneuvers;
   (vii) Ground reference maneuvers;
   (viii) Navigation;
   (ix)   Slow flight and stalls;
   (x)   Basic instrument maneuvers;
   (xi)   Emergency operations;
   (xii) Night operations, except as provided in §61.110 of this part; and
   (xiii) Postflight procedures.
(6) *For a glider* category *rating:*
   (I)   Preflight preparation;
   (ii)   Preflight procedures;
   (iii) Airport and gliderport operations;
   (iv)   Launches and landings;
   (v)   Performance speeds;
   (vi)   Soaring techniques;
   (vii) Performance maneuvers;
   (viii) Navigation;
   (ix)   Slow flight and stalls;
   (x)   Emergency operations; and
   (xi)   Postflight procedures.
(7) *For a lighter-than-air category rating with an airship class rating:*
   (I)   Preflight preparation;
   (ii)   Preflight procedures;
   (iii) Airport operations;
   (iv)   Takeoffs, landings, and go-arounds;
   (v)   Performance maneuvers;
   (vi)   Ground reference maneuvers;
   (vii) Navigation;
   (viii) Emergency operations; and
   (ix)   Postflight procedures.

(8) *For a lighter-than-air category rating with a balloon class rating:*
   (I)   Preflight preparation
   (ii)   Preflight procedures
   (iii) Airport operations
   (iv)   Launches and landings
   (v)   Performance maneuvers
   (vi)   Navigation
   (vii) Emergency operations; and
   (viii) Postflight procedures.

EXPLANATION

An applicant should be aware of the requirement of 61.107 and ensure that the flight instructor provides adequate instruction in each area. Always be sure you understand each area and what is expected of you.

In-flight spin training is not required for any pilot certificate other than flight instructor in airplanes or gliders. However, a flight instructor may give spin training to any student.

PREAMBLE

In response to commenter concerns, the term "balloonport" was replaced with the term "airport", and the term "lift offs" was replaced with the term "launches". The FAA also is not proposing separate flight proficiency requirements for powered and nonpowered gliders. (62 FR 16264).

CROSS REFERENCES

61.103, Eligibility Requirements: General; 61.105, Aeronautical Knowledge; 61.107, Flight Proficiency; 61.109, Aeronautical Experiences; 61.110, Night Flying Exceptions; 61.111, Cross-country flights: Pilots based on small islands; 61.113, Private Pilot Privileges and Limitations: Pilot in Command; 61.115, Balloon Rating: Limitations; 61.117, Private Pilot Privileges and Limitations: Second in Command of Aircraft Requiring More than One Pilot.

ADVISORY CIRCULARS

AC 61-65D *Certification: Pilots and Flight and Ground Instructors* (1999).

AC 61-67C *Stall and Spin Awareness Training* (2000).

AC 61-84B *Role of Preflight Preparation* (1985).

AC 90-48C *Pilot's Role in Collision Avoidance.* (1983).

AC 91-67 *Minimum Equipment Requirements for General Aviation Operations Under Part 91* (1991).

FAA-H-8083-1 *Aircraft Weight and Balance Handbook* (1999).

FAA-H-8083-3 *Airplane Flying Handbook* (1999).

FAA-H-8083-27 *Student Pilot Guide* (1999).

FAA CHIEF COUNSEL OPINIONS

§61.107 refers to "instruction from an authorized flight instructor" and to "control and maneuvering an airplane solely by reference to instruments" rather than to "instrument instruction;" therefore, any certificated flight instructor (CFI) may give the type of instruction described in §61.107. (6-20-79).

61.109 AERONAUTICAL EXPERIENCE

(a) *For an airplane single-engine rating.* Except as provided in paragraph (i) of this section, a person who applies for a private pilot certificate with an airplane category and single-engine class rating must log at least 40 hours of flight time that includes at least 20 hours of flight training from an authorized instructor and 10 hours of solo flight training in the areas of operation listed in §61.107(b)(1) of this part, and the training must include at least—
  (1) 3 hours of cross-country flight training in a single-engine airplane;
  (2) Except as provided in §61.110 of this part, 3 hours of night flight training in a single-engine airplane that includes—
    (i)   One cross-country flight of over 100 nautical miles total distance; and
    (ii) 10 takeoffs and 10 landings to a full stop (with each landing involving a flight in the traffic pattern) at an airport.
  (3) 3 hours of instrument flight training in a single-engine airplane on the control and maneuvering of an airplane solely by reference to instruments, including straight and level flight, constant airspeed climbs and descents, turns to a heading, recovery from unusual flight attitudes, radio communications, and the use of navigation systems/facilities and radar services appropriate to instrument flight;
  (4) 3 hours of flight training in preparation for the practical test in a single-engine airplane, which must have been performed within 60 days preceding the date of the test; and
  (5) 10 hours of solo flight time in a single-engine airplane, consisting of at least—
    (i)   5 hours of solo cross-country time;
    (ii) One solo cross-country flight of at least 150 nautical miles total distance, with full-stop landings at a minimum of three points, and one segment of the flight consisting of a straight-line distance of at least 50 nautical miles between the takeoff and landing locations; and
    (iii) Three takeoffs and three landings to a full stop (with each landing involving a flight in the traffic pattern) at an airport with an operating control tower.
(b) *For an airplane multiengine rating.* Except as provided in paragraph (i) of this section, a person who applies for a private pilot certificate with an airplane category and multiengine class rating must log at least 40 hours of flight time that includes at least 20 hours of flight training from an authorized instructor and 10 hours of solo flight training in the areas of operation listed in §61.107(b)(2) of this part, and the training must include at least—
  (1) 3 hours of cross-country flight training in a multiengine airplane;
  (2) Except as provided in §61.110 of this part, 3 hours of night flight training in a multiengine airplane that includes—
    (i)   One cross-country flight of over 100 nautical miles total distance; and
    (ii) 10 takeoffs and 10 landings to a full stop (with each landing involving a flight in the traffic pattern) at an airport.

(3)   3 hours of flight training in a multiengine airplane on the control and maneuvering of an airplane solely by reference to instruments, including straight and level flight, constant airspeed climbs and descents, turns to a heading, recovery from unusual flight attitudes, radio communications, and the use of navigation systems/facilities and radar services appropriate to instrument flight;

(4)   3 hours of flight training in preparation for the practical test in a multiengine airplane, which must have been performed within the 60-day period preceding the date of the test; and

(5)   10 hours of solo flight time in an airplane consisting of at least—
    (i)   5 hours of solo cross-country time;
    (ii)   One solo cross-country flight of at least 150 nautical miles total distance, with full-stop landings at a minimum of three points, and one segment of the flight consisting of a straight-line distance of at least 50 nautical miles between the takeoff and landing locations; and
    (iii) Three takeoffs and three landings to a full stop (with each landing involving a flight in the traffic pattern) at an airport with an operating control tower.

(c)   *For a helicopter rating.* Except as provided in paragraph (i) of this section, a person who applies for a private pilot certificate with rotorcraft category and helicopter class rating must log at least 40 hours of flight time that includes at least 20 hours of flight training from an authorized instructor and 10 hours of solo flight training in the areas of operation listed in §61.107(b)(3) of this part, and the training must include at least—

(1)   3 hours of cross-country flight training in a helicopter;

(2)   Except as provided in §61.110 of this part, 3 hours of night flight training in a helicopter that includes—
    (i)   One cross-country flight of over 50 nautical miles total distance; and
    (ii)   10 takeoffs and 10 landings to a full stop (with each landing involving a flight in the traffic pattern) at an airport.

(3)   3 hours of flight training in preparation for the practical test in a helicopter, which must have been performed within 60 days preceding the date of the test; and

(4)   10 hours of solo flight time in a helicopter, consisting of at least—
    (i)   3 hours cross-country time;
    (ii)   One solo cross-country flight of at least 75 nautical miles total distance, with landings at a minimum of three points, and one segment of the flight being a straight-line distance of at least 25 nautical miles between the takeoff and landing locations; and
    (iii) Three takeoffs and three landings to a full stop (with each landing involving a flight in the traffic pattern) at an airport with an operating control tower.

(d)   *For a gyroplane rating.* Except as provided in paragraph (i) of this section, a person who applies for a private pilot certificate with rotorcraft category and gyroplane class rating must log at least 40 hours of flight time that includes at least 20 hours of flight training from an authorized instructor and 10 hours of solo flight training in the areas of operation listed in §61.107(b)(4) of this part, and the training must include at least—

(1)   3 hours of cross-country flight training in a gyroplane;

(2)   Except as provided in §61.110 of this part, 3 hours of night flight training in a gyroplane that includes—
    (i)   One cross-country flight of over 50 nautical miles total distance; and
    (ii)   10 takeoffs and 10 landings to a full stop (with each landing involving a flight in the traffic pattern) at an airport.

(3)   3 hours of flight training in preparation for the practical test in a gyroplane, which must have been performed within the 60-day period preceding the date of the test; and

    (4)   10 hours of solo flight time in a gyroplane, consisting of at least—
        (i)   3 hours of cross-country time;
        (ii)   One solo cross-country flight of over 75 nautical miles total distance, with landings at a minimum of three points, and one segment of the flight being a straight-line distance of at least 25 nautical miles between the takeoff and landing locations; and
        (iii) Three takeoffs and three landings to a full stop (with each landing involving a flight in the traffic pattern) at an airport with an operating control tower.

(e) *For a powered-lift rating.* Except as provided in paragraph (i) of this section, a person who applies for a private pilot certificate with a powered-lift category rating must log at least 40 hours of flight time that includes at least 20 hours of flight training from an authorized instructor and 10 hours of solo flight training in the areas of operation listed in §61.107(b)(5) of this part, and the training must include at least—

    (1)   3 hours of cross-country flight training in a powered-lift;
    (2)   Except as provided in §61.110 of this part, 3 hours of night flight training in a powered-lift that includes—
        (i)   One cross-country flight of over 100 nautical miles total distance; and
        (ii)   10 takeoffs and 10 landings to a full stop (with each landing involving a flight in the traffic pattern) at an airport.
    (3)   3 hours of flight training in a powered-lift on the control and maneuvering of a powered-lift solely by reference to instruments, including straight and level flight, constant airspeed climbs and descents, turns to a heading, recovery from unusual flight attitudes, radio communications, and the use of navigation systems/facilities and radar services appropriate to instrument flight;
    (4)   3 hours of flight training in preparation for the practical test in a powered-lift, which must have been performed within the 60-day period preceding the date of the test; and
    (5)   10 hours of solo flight time in an airplane or powered-lift consisting of at least—
        (i)   5 hours cross-country time;
        (ii)   One cross-country flight of at least 150 nautical miles total distance, with landings at a minimum of three points, and one segment of the flight being a straight-line distance of at least 50 nautical miles between the takeoff and landing locations; and
        (iii) Three takeoffs and three landings to a full stop (with each landing involving a flight in the traffic pattern) at an airport with an operating control tower.

(f) *For a glider category rating.*

    (1)   If the applicant for a private pilot certificate with a glider category rating has not logged at least 40 hours of flight time as a pilot in a heavier-than-air aircraft, the applicant must log at least 10 hours of flight time in a glider in the areas of operation listed in §61.107(b)(6) of this part, and that flight time must include at least—
        (i)   20 flights in a glider in the areas of operations listed in §61.107(b)(6) of this part, including at least 3 training flights in a glider with an authorized instructor in preparation for the practical test that must have been performed within the 60-day period preceding the date of the test; and
        (ii)   2 hours of solo flight time in a glider in the areas of operation listed in §61.107(b)(6) of this part, with not less than 10 launches and landings being performed; and

(2)   If the applicant has logged at least 40 hours of flight time in heavier-than-air aircraft, the applicant must log at least 3 hours of flight time in a glider in the areas of operation listed in §61.107(b)(6) of this part, and that flight time must include at least—

    (i)   10 solo flights in a glider in the areas of operation listed in §61.107(b)(6) of this part; and

    (ii)   3 training flights in a glider with an authorized instructor in preparation for the practical test that must have been performed within the 60-day period preceding the date of the test.

(g)   *For an airship rating.* A person who applies for a private pilot certificate with a lighter-than-air category and airship class rating must log at least—:

(1)   25 hours of flight training in airships on the areas of operation listed in §61.107(b)(7) of this part, which consists of at least:

    (i)   3 hours of cross-country flight training in an airship;

    (ii)   Except as provided in §61.110 of this part, 3 hours of night flight training in an airship that includes:

        (A)   A cross-country flight of over 25 nautical miles total distance; and

        (B)   Five takeoffs and five landings to a full stop (with each landing involving a flight in the traffic pattern) at an airport.

(2)   3 hours of flight training in an airship on the control and maneuvering of an airship solely by reference to instruments, including straight and level flight, constant airspeed climbs and descents, turns to a heading, recovery form unusual flight attitudes, radio communications, and the use of navigation systems/facilities and radar services appropriate to instrument flight;

(3)   3 hours of flight training in an airship in preparation for the practical test within the 60 days preceding the date of the test; and

(4)   5 hours performing the duties of pilot in command in an airship and with an authorized instructor.

(h)   *For a balloon rating.* A person who applies for a private pilot certificate with a lighter-than-air category and balloon class rating must log at least 10 hours of flight training that includes at least six training flights with an authorized instructor in the areas of operation listed in §61.107(b)(8) of this part, that includes—

(1)   *Gas balloon.* If the training is being performed in a gas balloon, at least two flights of 2 hours each that consists of—

    (i)   At least one training flight with an authorized instructor within 60 days prior to application for the rating on the areas of operation for a gas balloon;

    (ii)   At least one flight performing the duties of pilot in command in a gas balloon with an authorized instructor; and

    (iii)   At least one flight involving a controlled ascent to 3,000 feet above the launch site.

(2)   *Balloon with an airborne heater.* If the training is being performed in a balloon with an airborne heater, at least—

    (i)   Two flights of 1 hour each within 60 days prior to application for the rating on the areas of operation appropriate to a balloon with an airborne heater;

    (ii)   One solo flight in a balloon with an airborne heater; and

    (iii)   At least one flight involving a controlled ascent to 2,000 feet above the launch site.

(i)   *Permitted credit for use of a flight simulator or flight training device.*
   (1)   Except as provided in paragraphs (i)(2) of this section, a maximum of 2.5 hours of training in a flight simulator or flight training device representing the category, class, and type, if applicable, of aircraft appropriate to the rating sought, may be credited toward the flight training time required by this section, if received from an authorized instructor.
   (2)   A maximum of 5 hours of training in a flight simulator or flight training device representing the category, class, and type, if applicable, of aircraft appropriate to the rating sought, may be credited toward the flight training time required by this section if the training is accomplished in a course conducted by a training center certificated under part 142 of this chapter.
   (3)   Except when fewer hours are approved by the Administrator, an applicant for a private pilot certificate with an airplane, rotorcraft, or powered-lift rating, who has satisfactorily completed an approved private pilot course conducted by a training center certificated under part 142 of this chapter need only have a total of 35 hours of aeronautical experience to meet the requirements of this section.

EXPLANATION

The 1997 amendment to 61.109 modifies the solo flight time (hours) required for the private pilot certificate so that it permits the student and the flight instructor to tailor the training time toward the student's needs and capabilities. It also establishes a dual training requirement by aircraft class for night cross country at the private and commercial pilot certificate levels for powered aircraft. Also added are two new dual cross-country training flight requirements. One is for a day-VFR and one is for a night-VFR. Both must be in the class of aircraft for which the rating is sought.

The 1998 amendment to 61.109 delineates which aeronautical experience requirements need to be accomplished with an instructor for glider, airship and balloon category ratings.

PREAMBLE

The FAA believes the change in the composition of dual and solo time, within the total number of hours required for each certificate, provides instructors with flexibility in determining the amount of dual and solo training required for each student. The FAA has decided not to adopt the concept of supervised pilot in command as set forth in Notice No. 95-11, and has therefore replaced references to "supervised pilot in command" time with "solo" time.

The proposal does not compromise safety because the total number of hours required for the issuance of a private pilot certificate remains unchanged. The rule should encourage increased training and help reduce overall costs. It appears that some commenters misunderstood the proposal, because their concerns implied that the total number of hours would be reduced, which is not the case. The FAA has, however, increased solo flight time requirements and solo cross-country flight distance requirements in the final rule in order to meet the minimum requirements under Annex 1 to the Convention on International Civil Aviation.

The FAA believes that night cross-country training should be required for private pilot applicants because a private pilot may later be placed in circumstances where the pilot may inadvertently fly at night, without appropriate night training. This issue was identified as an area of concern in the FAA's Job Task Analysis. Increased night flight training will reduce the issuance of certificates with a night flying limitation, as well the associated administrative costs to the FAA in reissuing such certificates when the limitation is removed. In response to AOPA's request, the FAA has clarified the cross-country requirements in this section by replacing the word "duration" with the term "total distance."

Regarding the proposal for required solo flight in multiengine aircraft for pilots seeking that rating, the FAA is convinced by the commenters' arguments and has modified the final rule to require that an applicant accomplish solo flight in an airplane. This would allow an applicant for a multiengine rating to accomplish solo flight time requirements in a single-engine airplane.

The FAA believes that a similar problem to that presented by the commenters could arise for powered-lifts, and has made a similar modification to the regulations applicable to those aircraft requiring that solo flight time be accomplished in an airplane or powered-lift. The FAA recognizes HAI's concern regarding an inconsistency with the definition of "cross country," and has revised the cross-country requirements for rotorcraft accordingly.

Currently the FAA requires training within 60 days of application for a practical test in a balloon. The FAA, in order to clarify what is meant by "training," is requiring a minimum of two flights within 60 days of application. The FAA considers this requirement reasonable to ensure proper preparation for the practical test.

The FAA disagrees with NAFI regarding night flight requirements for airships, and finds that the majority of airships do have sufficient electrical power to operate at night. The FAA believes that night flight training should be required for airships as these aircraft currently operate at night in the NAS. Therefore, the FAA will require night training in airships.

To address commenters' arguments against required instrument training in airships that may not be equipped for instrument flight, the FAA has modified the requirements to state only that instrument training is required, without referring specifically to airships.

The FAA also has modified the proposed requirements for the issuance of a glider rating to be consistent with the decision not to establish separate class ratings for powered and nonpowered gliders. Additionally, the FAA has included provisions as set forth in Amendment No. 61-100, which permit credit to be given for the use of an approved flight simulator or approved flight training device. (62 FR 16265 – 16266)

CROSS REFERENCES

61.103, Eligibility Requirements: General; 61.105, Aeronautical Knowledge; 61.107, Flight Proficiency; 61.109, Aeronautical Experience; 61.110, Night Flying Exceptions; 61.111, Cross-country flights: Pilots based on small islands; 61.113, Private Pilot Privileges and Limitations: Pilot in Command; 61.115, Balloon Rating: Limitations; 61.117, Private Pilot Privileges and Limitations: Second in Command of Aircraft requiring more than one Pilot.

ADVISORY CIRCULARS

AC 61-65D Certification: *Pilots and Flight and Ground Instructors* (1999).

AC 61-84B *Role of Preflight Preparation* (1985).

FAA-H-8083-3 *Airplane Flying Handbook* (1999).

FAA-S-8081-14 *Private Pilot Practical Test Standards for Airplane (SEL, MEL, SES, MES).*

FAA CHIEF COUNSEL OPINIONS

A minimum age requirement exists for logging solo flight time since a person must hold a student pilot certificate with appropriate endorsements in order to fly solo. The minimum age therefore is 16, or 14 for a student pilot certificate limited to glider or free balloon operations. (4-3-78).

61.110 NIGHT FLYING EXCEPTIONS

(a)   Subject to the limitations of paragraph (b) of this section, a person is not required to comply with the night flight training requirements of this subpart if the person receives flight training in and resides in the State of Alaska.

(b)   A person who receives flight training in and resides in the State of Alaska but does not meet the night flight training requirements of this section:

(1)   May be issued a pilot certificate with a limitation "Night flying prohibited"; and

(2)   Must comply with the appropriate night flight training requirements of this subpart within the 12-calendar-month period after the issuance of the pilot certificate. At the end of that period, the certificate will become invalid for use until the person complies with the appropriate night training requirements of this subpart. The person may have the "Night flying prohibited" limitation removed if the person—

(i)   Accomplishes the appropriate night flight training requirements of this subpart; and

(ii)   Presents to an examiner a logbook or training record endorsement from an authorized instructor that verifies accomplishment of the appropriate night flight training requirements of this subpart.

EXPLANATION

The 1997 amendment to 61.110 eliminates the night flying and aeronautical experience exception at the private and commercial certificate level, except for those persons who receive their training in Alaska and in those cases a person will be given one year to obtain the required night flying aeronautical experience. This means that all private and commercial pilot applicants will be required to receive the night flying training that is specified in Part 61.

PREAMBLE

The FAA points out that a change in the proposed and final rules to §61.109 will disqualify all applicants from being issued certificates without meeting night flying requirements, unless they qualify for an exception under §61.110. Therefore, the 12-month limit of §61.110 does not discriminate against Alaskan airmen, but rather allows them a special privilege.

In the final rule, the 12-month limitation remains, but the FAA has deleted language referring to the issuance of a 12-month temporary certificate, because existing FAA temporary certificates are valid for 120 days. The FAA has also added a provision that a person seeking to obtain this exception must both receive the flight training for the certificate and reside in the State of Alaska.

By deleting the exception for pilots who have night flying restrictions due to medical conditions, these pilots will now be required to have 3 hours of night flight training. However, the certificates of such pilots will be issued with an operating limitation prohibiting night flying. The FAA has determined that safety will be enhanced because this requirement will reduce the likelihood of pilots later being placed in circumstances where they may be required to engage in flight at night without appropriate night training. (16 FR 16266).

CROSS REFERENCE

61.131, Exceptions to the Night Flying Requirements.

61.111 CROSS-COUNTRY FLIGHTS: PILOTS BASED ON SMALL ISLANDS

(a) Except as provided in paragraph (b) of this section, an applicant located on an island from which the cross-country flight training required in §61.109 of this part cannot be accomplished without flying over water for more than 10 nautical miles from the nearest shoreline need not comply with the requirements of that section.
(b) If other airports that permit civil operations are available to which a flight may be made without flying over water for more than 10 nautical miles from the nearest shoreline, the applicant must show completion of two round-trip solo flights between those two airports that are farthest apart, including a landing at each airport on both flights.
(c) An applicant who complies with paragraph (b) of this section, and meets all requirements for the issuance of a private pilot certificate, except the cross-country training requirements of §61.109 of this part, will be issued a pilot certificate with an endorsement containing the following limitation, "Passenger carrying prohibited on flights more than 10 nautical miles from (the appropriate island)." The limitation may be subsequently amended to include another island if the applicant complies with the requirements of paragraph (b) of this section for another island.
(d) Upon meeting the cross-country training requirements of §61.109 of this part, the applicant may have the limitation in paragraph (c) of this section removed.

CROSS REFERENCES

61.109, Airplane Rating: Aeronautical Experience.

61.113 PRIVATE PILOT PRIVILEGES AND LIMITATIONS: PILOT IN COMMAND

(a) Except as provided in paragraphs (b) through (g) of this section, no person who holds a private pilot certificate may act as pilot in command of an aircraft that is carrying passengers or property for compensation or hire; nor may that person, for compensation or hire, act as pilot in command of an aircraft.

(b) A private pilot may, for compensation or hire, act as pilot in command of an aircraft in connection with any business or employment if:

    (1) The flight is only incidental to that business or employment; and

    (2) The aircraft does not carry passengers or property for compensation or hire.

(c) A private pilot may not pay less than the pro rata share of the operating expenses of a flight with passengers, provided the expenses involve only fuel, oil, airport expenditures, or rental fees.

(d) A private pilot may act as pilot in command of an aircraft used in a passenger-carrying airlift sponsored by a charitable organization described in paragraph (d)(7) of this section, and for which the passengers make a donation to the organization, when the following requirements are met:

    (1) The sponsor of the airlift notifies the FAA Flight Standards District Office with jurisdiction over the area concerned at least 7 days before the event and furnishes—

        (i) A signed letter from the sponsor that shows the name of the sponsor, the purpose of the charitable event, the date and time of the event, and the location of the event; and

        (ii) A photocopy of each pilot in command's pilot certificate, medical certificate, and logbook entries that show the pilot is current in accordance with §§61.56 and 61.57 of this part and has logged at least 200 hours of flight time.

    (2) The flight is conducted from a public airport that is adequate for the aircraft to be used, or from another airport that has been approved by the FAA for the operation.

    (3) No aerobatic or formation flights are conducted.

    (4) Each aircraft used for the charitable event holds a standard airworthiness certificate.

    (5) Each aircraft used for the charitable event is airworthy and complies with the applicable requirements of subpart E of part 91 of this chapter.

    (6) Each flight for the charitable event is made during day VFR conditions.

    (7) The charitable organization is an organization identified as such by the U.S. Department of Treasury.

(e) A private pilot may be reimbursed for aircraft operating expenses that are directly related to search and location operations, provided the expenses involve only fuel, oil, airport expenditures, or rental fees, and the operation is sanctioned and under the direction and control of:

    (1) A local, State, or Federal agency; or

    (2) An organization that conducts search and location operations.

(f) A private pilot who is an aircraft salesman and who has at least 200 hours of logged flight time may demonstrate an aircraft in flight to a prospective buyer.

(g) A private pilot who meets the requirements of §61.69 of this part may act as pilot in command of an aircraft towing a glider.

EXPLANATION

The 1997 amendment permits private pilots to perform search and location operations for law enforcement agencies and organizations such as CAP and to be reimbursed for certain expenses without conflicting with limitations of the private pilot's privileges forbidding private pilots from receiving compensation or hire. For years this privilege has been accommodated through the exemption process and now petitioners and the FAA will no longer be required to submit and process exemptions on this issue.

If a pilot gains any economic advantage, not just the receipt of money, from the operation of an aircraft, the FAA may take the position that he is acting as pilot in command of an aircraft for compensation or hire. An example would be the ferrying of aircraft for no charge to build up flight hours.

If you are in doubt about any particular type of operation, you should check your insurance coverage to ensure that they do not consider what you are doing as flying for compensation or hire and, as a result, might deny coverage in the event of an accident.

A flight where there is a sharing of expenses by the pilot and the passengers might be construed as a flight carrying passengers for compensation or hire under the terms of an insurance policy. The same might be true for a passenger carrying charitable airlift. Before such flights make sure you insurance covers such operations. Some policies have specific provisions that "exclude any use for which a charge is made."

If your position with the company requires that you hold a pilot certificate, your operation of an aircraft, as pilot in command, might not be considered incidental to your employment depending on the percentage of your work that involves flying.

If you are in the aerial photography business your operation of an aircraft is not "only incidental" to your business.

If you provide a "package" trip, like a fishing trip to Canada, that involves you as a private pilot, flying persons to the fishing camp, your operation of the aircraft cannot be considered as "only incidental" to your business.

PREAMBLE

In response to objections to the language of proposed §61.101(a) as well as §61.113(c), the FAA has decided to add "rental fees" to this list of allowable shared expenses in both those sections, as discussed in the analysis for §61.101(a). This language is therefore added to §61.113(e) in the final rule. The CAP's concerns regarding types of agencies that conduct search and location missions were noted, and the term "law enforcement" has therefore been deleted from paragraph (e)(1) in the final rule.

In response to CAP's comments regarding the omission of any provisions permitting a private pilot to be reimbursed for maintenance costs, the proposed rule did not specifically provide for reimbursement of maintenance costs, and neither does the final rule. Any reimbursement for compensation of maintenance costs will be handled on a case-by-case basis through the exemption process. In addition, CAP commented that the rule be modified to account for agencies other than law enforcement agencies for which it operates. In Notice No. 95-11, the FAA proposed to allow pilots under the direction and control of an "organization that conducts search and location operations" to be reimbursed. The FAA has determined that this addresses CAP's concerns and is adopting the final rule as proposed.

In response to HAI's comment that search and location operations should remain under the exemption process, since the early 1980's the FAA has permitted private pilots to perform search and location operations, and has continually reissued those exemptions without any known problems. Provided that pilots comply with the requirements in this final rule, which are identical to the exemption's conditions and limitations, the FAA has codified those conditions and limitations in this final rule.

After further review, the FAA has decided to reinstate the provision allowing a private pilot who is an aircraft salesman and who has at least 200 hours of logged flight time to demonstrate an aircraft in flight to a prospective buyer. The FAA has concluded that these operations would not be "incidental to business," and therefore is reinstating this provision into the final rule. (16 FR 16267).

CROSS REFERENCES

Previous Designation, 61.118; 61.133, Commercial Pilot Privileges and Limitations; 61.167, Airline Transport Pilot: Privileges.

CASES

A private pilot who flew a friend's sick father to the hospital, and was later compensated for the flight, received a 30 days suspension of his airman certificate, although the FAA had sought an emergency revocation. The Board found that, although the pilot and his sick friend had no "common purpose" in flying to the hospital, the pilot had not held himself out as available for flights for compensation. *Administrator v. Carter*, EA-3730 (1992).

Private pilot certificate was suspended for 120 days when, on six flights, the pilot flew passengers to fishing site and charged them $35.00 for a "package" of an ice shanty and round trip air transportation. *Administrator v. Scherf*, EA-3456. (1991).

The Board, in affirming a violation where the operator claimed the flight was one where the expenses were shared as allowed by [§61.113] of the Federal Aviation Regulations and therefore not one for compensation or hire, agreed with the Administrative Law Judge on what constituted a true "shared expense" flight. The amounts shared are nominal and include actual operating expenses such as fuel, oil, and parking fees. Such amounts do not include such costs as the capital costs of purchasing the aircraft, interest on financing, insurance and maintenance. *Administrator v. Richard*, 4 NTSB 99 (1982).

In finding a flight to be one for compensation or hire, the Board held that the $48.00 per passenger was not based on the out-of-pocket costs for a single flight, which appears to be the type of cost-sharing contemplated by [§61.113]. Rather, it was based on the costs for the entire year, including fuel, oil, maintenance and insurance. It went on to say that it had previously held that "a sharing of expenses" applies more logically to a situation where the pilot is making the trip for his own purposes and others accompany him and share with him the costs of the transportation. *Administrator v. Henderson*, 3 NTSB 4029 (1981).

In finding a private pilot in violation of [§61.113] for carrying parachute jumpers on four flights for which he received a total of $700, the Board held that the "sharing of expenses" exception has been restricted to apply to a situation "where the pilot is making the trip for his own purposes and others accompany him and share with the costs of the transportation." In this case there was no common purpose. The purpose of the passengers was to sky dive while the pilot's purpose was to gain flight time under an arrangement where the costs of operation would be at least partially borne by others. *Administrator v. Reimer*, 3 NTSB 2306 (1980).

A private pilot, who flew skydivers for free, received a 45 day suspension. The skydivers paid the skydiving club for instruction, and therefore, the FAA and the NTSB found that the flights were for compensation or hire, and that the pilot's ability to log the time can be viewed as compensation. The NTSB specifically rejected the pilot's argument that his free flight time could be excused as "sharing expenses." *Administrator v. Rawlins*, EA-4583 (1997).

FAA CHIEF COUNSEL OPINIONS

Private pilots making volunteer air flights involving the carriage of persons or property are in violation of [§61.113] if they receive any reimbursement of expenses or take any tax deductions for those flights. (3-8-93).

A private pilot, acting as pilot in command of an aircraft towing gliders, is not operating an aircraft that is "carrying passengers or property." Therefore, the first prong of [61.113] is not at issue. However, if the private pilot is logging the time spent as pilot in command while towing gliders, he is building flight time and would be considered to be operating the aircraft for compensation or hire. One way to avoid this would be for the pilot not to log this time. (10-30-90).

On charitable airlift flights, conducted by private pilots, the pilots may be paid for, or supplied, the fuel and oil consumed during the flights. (12-7-90).

The FAA has interpreted [61.113] so that the only allowable share-the-cost operations are those which are bona fide, i.e., joint ventures for a common purpose with expenses being defrayed by all passengers and the pilot. (12-26-85).

Assuming that no economic benefits from the carriage of passengers flow to the owner or to the pilot, such as may be the case if the passengers were, for instance, induced to enter into a beneficial economic relationship with the owner based in part on the balloon ride, a private pilot could act as pilot in command of a balloon designed with the balloon owner's logo on a voluntary, noncompensated basis, and the passengers are not charged a fee. (8-6-84).

When a pilot charges his passengers more than an equal share of the operating expenses for the flight, it indicates that he is not "sharing" the expenses. In the case of a glider carrying a passenger, the pilot could ask the passenger to pay any amount up to 50% of the flight's operating costs, without being in violation of [§61.113]. (2-11-78) (4-7-78).

Under [§61.113] a private pilot who wants to build up time toward a commercial pilot certificate is not permitted to carry expense sharing passengers or cargo to a destination at which he, the pilot, has no particular business. (4-7-78).

Advertising in any form, including the use of a college bulletin board, raises a question of whether, in light of all the circumstances involved, the pilot is holding himself or herself out as available to provide transportation to the public. If the evidence indicated that common carriage is, in fact, involved, the pilot would be in violation of Part 135. (4-7-78).

In the case of a balloon gathering where the organizer or sponsor of the event (which is not a charitable airlift operation) pays the $25 entry fee for the Sanctioned Task Score Sheet for the Balloon Federation of America and for the propane used by the balloons, acceptance of the foregoing by private pilots would be in violation of [61.113]. (9-8-77).

Where a balloon organizer provides housing and/or food for the pilots and crew, whether the pilot flies or not, these items would not be considered to be compensation. (9-8-77).

Where the pilot is receiving compensation for participation in the (balloon) race is determined by what, if anything, he receives, not by what he is requested to do in order to participate in the race. Moreover, even if another person, e.g., a paint company, were to pay the organizer to require an advertising banner on each balloon, the display of the banner would not be considered to be the carrying property for compensation or hire within the meaning of [61.113]. (9-8-77).

In your letter you present the following situation: a commercially rated pilot offers to provide pilot service to various entities. He also suggests that they rent an aircraft from the local fixed base operator and hire him to fly the rental aircraft. This plan is being marketed as more cost effective than chartering an aircraft. The commercial pilot is not certificated as a Part 135 air carrier.

In your first question you ask whether such a plan would be violative of FAR Part 135 as an unlicensed air charter operation. Please understand that with the meager facts you have presented we are unable to give more than a very general answer. It would be important to know the purpose of the entities' flights, and whether they are carrying passengers for compensation or hire.

> If, in the situation you describe, the pilot is perceived as actually arranging the entire flight, and the entity who rents the aircraft acts as the agent of the pilot, it would amount to an impermissible avoidance of the certification requirements of §135.5 and §135.25. It is important, however, to distinguish the situation where there is a simple provision of pilot services, and the pilot has no part in the renting of the aircraft, where it is clear that the renter hires the pilot and has operational control over the airplane. The pilot must be the servant of the entity renting the aircraft, and the fewer the ties between the pilot and the FBO who rents the airplane the clearer the line between pilot service and an operation conducted for hire. The pilot must be paid by the entity renting the aircraft, and should not be involved in any way in the renting process. An enterprising businessman may realize that he can save money over charter rates by renting an aircraft and hiring a qualified local pilot to fly the trip for him, and we are not criticizing such an arrangement. (4-8-91).

In your letter you state that you are considering starting a hunting and fishing business on the eastern shore of Maryland in a remote location 123 miles from National Airport or BWI. As part of the hunting or fishing package the customer will be flown from one of those airports to a grass strip airfield located on the property. Customers will not be specifically charged for the flight, and you state that the aviation aspect is only an incidental part of the business. You hold a private pilot license, and you ask if it will be necessary for you to obtain a commercial pilot license in order for you to carry out your plan. You cite [§61.113] of the Federal Aviation Regulations (FAR) in the hope that you may be exempt from the requirement for a commercial license, since you believe that the flying is only incidental to the operation of the business.

It will not only be necessary for you to obtain a commercial pilot license, you will also need an instrument rating, and you will need to have your operation certificated under Part 135 of the FAR and obtain an Air Taxi/Commercial Operator (ATCO) certificate.

Your letter quotes FAR [61.113], which reads: A private pilot may, for compensation or hire, act as pilot in command of an aircraft in connection with any business or employment if the flight is only incidental to that business or employment and the aircraft does not carry passengers or property for compensation or hire. The threshold question is whether the passenger carrying flights you propose are conducted for compensation or hire.

An operation is conducted for compensation or hire when the operator furthers his economic interests by transporting persons or property by air. It is not necessary that there be a charge for the flight or that there be an actual profit to constitute compensation or hire. *Administrator v. Motley*, 2 NTSB 178, 180 (1973). In the example you cite, there can be no doubt that you would be furthering your economic interests by providing air transportation, whether or not you are directly reimbursed, or whether the cost is factored into the cost of the hunting package or the cost of the business.

Since you will be carrying passengers for compensation or hire under the definition cited above, it is not necessary to consider whether or not the flights are incidental to the business.

This classification places you in the category of flying which is regulated by Part 135 of the FAR, assuming you will be using a small aircraft. Operations under Part 135 require a commercial pilot license and an instrument rating. While §135.243 does contain an exemption to the instrument rating requirement for operations in isolated areas, the eastern shore of Maryland and operations in and out of the high density airports you mention would not qualify for that exemption.

There are two Federal court cases that bear upon your fact situation. In *Las Vegas Hacienda v. Civil Aeronautics Board*, 298 F.2d 430 (9th Cir. 1962), a resort hotel sold package tours from the Los Angeles area which included a "free" airplane ride to and from Las Vegas. In an action for a cease and desist order, the court agreed with the Civil Aeronautics Board that the hotel was actually a "common carrier for compensation or hire" and required to be certificated as such.

In *United States v. Carribean Ventures, Ltd.*, 387 F.Supp. 1256 (1974), the Civil Aeronautics Board sought to enjoin the activities of casino hotel operators who offered package tours including air transportation, even though the advertisements included a disclaimer of costs for air transportation. The court relied on the *Hacienda* case in finding that the government would likely prevail in proving the Defendants to be "common carriers for compensation or hire." (4-9-91).

In determining what is considered compensation, it has been the FAA's longstanding policy to define compensation in very broad terms. For example, any reimbursement of expenses (fuel, oil, transportation, lodging, meals, etc.), if conditioned upon the pilot operating the aircraft, would constitute compensation. In addition, the building up of flight time may be compensatory in nature if the pilot does not have to pay the costs of operating the aircraft. While it could be argued that the accumulation of flight time is not always of value to the pilot involved, the FAA does not consider it appropriated to enter into a case-by-case analysis to determine whether the logging of time is of value to a particular pilot, or what the pilot's motives or intentions are on each flight. (10-23-97).

A police officer, holding a private pilot certificate, who works in the Air Support Unit of the Phoenix Police Department that operates its aircraft under Part 91, is not considered to be flying incidental to his or her employment while conducting a surveillance mission. To properly conduct this mission the pilot must hold at least a commercial pilot certificate in order to act as the pilot-in-command of the aircraft. (3-5-98).

61.115 BALLOON RATING: LIMITATIONS

(a)   If a person who applies for a private pilot certificate with a balloon rating takes a practical test in a balloon with an airborne heater:
    (1)   The pilot certificate will contain a limitation restricting the exercise of the privileges of that certificate to a balloon with an airborne heater; and
    (2)   The limitation may be removed when the person obtains the required aeronautical experience in a gas balloon and receives a logbook endorsement from an authorized instructor who attests to the person's accomplishment of the required aeronautical experience and ability to satisfactorily operate a gas balloon.
(b)   If a person who applies for a private pilot certificate with a balloon rating takes a practical test in a gas balloon:
    (1)   The pilot certificate will contain a limitation restricting the exercise of the privilege of that certificate to a gas balloon; and
    (2)   The limitation may be removed when the person obtains the required aeronautical experience in a balloon with an airborne heater and receives a logbook endorsement from an authorized instructor who attests to the person's accomplishment of the required aeronautical experience and ability to satisfactorily operate a balloon with an airborne heater.

ADVISORY CIRCULARS

AC 61-65D *Certification: Pilots and Flight and Ground Instructors* (1999).

61.117 PRIVATE PILOT PRIVILEGES AND LIMITATIONS: SECOND IN COMMAND OF AIRCRAFT REQUIRING MORE THAN ONE PILOT

Except as provided in §61.113 of this part, no private pilot may, for compensation or hire, act as second in command of an aircraft that is type certificated for more than one pilot, nor may that pilot act as second in command of such an aircraft that is carrying passengers or property for compensation or hire.

CROSS REFERENCES

61.55, Second-In-Command Qualifications; 61.113, Private Pilot Privileges and Limitations: Pilot In Command.

CASES

See 61.113.

FAA CHIEF COUNSEL OPINIONS

See 61.113.

Section 61.117 sets forth the privileges and limitations of the holder of a private pilot certificate: second in command. That section provides, in pertinent part, that a person who holds a private pilot certificate may not, for compensation or hire, act as second in command of an aircraft that is type certificated for more than one pilot, nor may that pilot act as second in command of such an aircraft that is carrying passengers or property for compensation or hire. Section 61.117 does provide for the exceptions to the above (incidental business activity, expense sharing, charitable airlifts, search and location missions). (4-26-99).

INTENTIONALLY

LEFT

BLANK

SUBPART F — COMMERCIAL PILOTS

61.121 APPLICABILITY

This subpart prescribes the requirements for the issuance of commercial pilot certificates and ratings, the conditions under which those certificates and ratings are necessary, and the general operating rules for persons who hold those certificates and ratings.

ADVISORY CIRCULARS

AC 00-2x *Advisory Circular Checklist (and Status of Other FAA Publications)*
Editor's Note: This AC is updated annually.

AC 60-22 *Aeronautical Decision Making* (1991).

AC 61-65D *Certification: Pilots and Flight and Ground Instructors* (1999).

61.123 ELIGIBILITY REQUIREMENTS: GENERAL

To be eligible for a commercial pilot certificate, a person must:
(a)   Be at least 18 years of age;
(b)   Be able to read, speak, write, and understand the English language. If the applicant is unable to meet one of these requirements due to medical reasons, then the Administrator may place such operating limitations on that applicant's pilot certificate as are necessary for the safe operation of the aircraft.
(c)   Receive a logbook endorsement from an authorized instructor who:
  (1)   Conducted the required ground training or reviewed the person's home study on the aeronautical knowledge areas listed in §61.125 of this part that apply to the aircraft category and class rating sought; and
  (2)   Certified that the person is prepared for the required knowledge test that applies to the aircraft category and class rating sought.
(d)   Pass the required knowledge test on the aeronautical knowledge areas listed in §61.125 of this part;
(e)   Receive the required training and a logbook endorsement from an authorized instructor who:
  (1)   Conducted the training on the areas of operation listed in §61.127(b) of this part that apply to the aircraft category and class rating sought; and
  (2)   Certified that the person is prepared for the required practical test.
(f)   Meet the aeronautical experience requirements of this subpart that apply to the aircraft category and class rating sought before applying for the practical test;
(g)   Pass the required practical test on the areas of operation listed in §61.127(b) of this part that apply to the aircraft category and class rating sought;
(h)   Hold at least a private pilot certificate issued under this part or meet the requirements of §61.73; and
(i)   Comply with the sections of this part that apply to the aircraft category and class rating sought.

EXPLANATION

An applicant for a commercial pilot certificate can take the knowledge test at such time as he/she is at least 16 years of age.

An applicant must present a birth certificate or other appropriate official document as evidence that he/she meets age requirements.

An applicant should be prepared to provide identification that includes a photograph of the applicant, the applicant's signature, and the applicant's actual residential address.

A satisfactory completed knowledge test expires at the end of the last day of the 24th month after the month in which the test is taken.

PREAMBLE

The final rule inserts language restoring the option for the Administrator to place an operating limitation on an applicant's pilot certificate, waiving the applicant's English language requirements based on medical reasons. As discussed in the analysis of §61.23, the rule has placed all medical requirements into that section.

In response to AOPA's comment, the existing rule requires that persons seeking a commercial certificate in airplanes must either hold a private pilot certificate or meet the requirements for holding a private pilot certificate. A commercial pilot applicant is therefore required to have completed the ground and flight training for a private pilot certificate, and have passed the required knowledge and practical tests before making an application for a commercial pilot certificate. Private pilot applicants are tested on a number of tasks that commercial pilot applicants are not tested on. The FAA wants to ensure that all commercial pilots possess the aeronautical knowledge and flight proficiency that must be mastered by all private pilots. The FAA has determined that the requirement will not be an additional regulatory burden or economic burden because experience has shown that nearly all persons seeking commercial pilot certificates already possess at least a private pilot certificate. In the final rule, other minor editorial and formatting changes to the proposed rule were also made. Except for these changes, the final rule is adopted as proposed. (62 FR 16268).

CROSS REFERENCES

61.125, Aeronautical Knowledge; 61.127, Flight Proficiency; 61.129, Commercial Pilots: Aeronautical Experience; 61.131, Exceptions to the Night Flying Requirements; 61.133, Commercial Pilot Privileges and Limitations; 49 Code of Federal Regulations Part 830, Rules Pertaining to the Notification and reporting of Aircraft Accidents or Incidents and Overdue Aircraft, and Preservation of Aircraft Wreckage, Mail, Cargo and Records (NTSB).

61.125 AERONAUTICAL KNOWLEDGE

(a) *General.* A person who applies for a commercial pilot certificate must receive and log ground training from an authorized instructor, or complete a home-study course, on the aeronautical knowledge areas of paragraph (b) of this section that apply to the aircraft category and class rating sought.

(b) *Aeronautical knowledge areas.*
   (1) Applicable Federal Aviation Regulations of this chapter that relate to commercial pilot privileges, limitations, and flight operations;
   (2) Accident reporting requirements of the National Transportation Safety Board;
   (3) Basic aerodynamics and the principles of flight;
   (4) Meteorology to include recognition of critical weather situations, windshear recognition and avoidance, and the use of aeronautical weather reports and forecasts;
   (5) Safe and efficient operation of aircraft;
   (6) Weight and balance computations;
   (7) Use of performance charts;
   (8) Significance and effects of exceeding aircraft performance limitations;
   (9) Use of aeronautical charts and a magnetic compass for pilotage and dead reckoning;
   (10) Use of air navigation facilities;
   (11) Aeronautical decision making and judgment;
   (12) Principles and functions of aircraft systems;
   (13) Maneuvers, procedures, and emergency operations appropriate to the aircraft;
   (14) Night and high-altitude operations;
   (15) Procedures for operating within the National Airspace System; and
   (16) Procedures for flight and ground training for lighter-than-air ratings.

EXPLANATION

Commercial pilots are now required to have knowledge of windshear avoidance procedures, aeronautical decision making, judgment training, and cockpit resource management.

PREAMBLE

In response to GAMA's concern regarding the exclusion of training in wake turbulence recognition and avoidance, the FAA notes that this training is required to be provided to all private pilots as specified in §61.105(b)(7). The rule also requires that all applicants for a commercial pilot certificate possess a private pilot certificate, thereby ensuring that such training has been received. Regarding AOPA's concern on the need for guidance material regarding aeronautical decision making, the FAA points out that AC 60-22, "*Aeronautical Decision Making*," contains such guidance. (62 FR 16268).

CROSS REFERENCES

61.123, Eligibility Requirements: General; 61.127, Flight Proficiency; 61.129, Aeronautical Experience; 61.131, Exceptions to the Night Flying Requirements; 61.133, Commercial Pilot Privileges and Limitations; 49 Code of Federal Regulations Part 830, Rules Pertaining to the Notification and reporting of Aircraft Accidents or Incidents and Overdue Aircraft, and Preservation of Aircraft Wreckage, Mail, Cargo and Records (NTSB).

ADVISORY CIRCULARS

AC 00-6A *Aviation Weather* (1975).

AC 00-24B *Thunderstorms* (1983).

AC 00-45E *Aviation Weather Services* (1999).

AC 20-34D *Prevention of Retractable Landing Gear Failures* (1980).

AC 60-22 *Aeronautical Decision Making* (1991).

AC 61-23C *Pilot's Handbook of Aeronautical Knowledge* (1997).

AC 61-65D *Certification: Pilots and Flight and Ground Instructors* (1999).

AC 61-67C *Stall and Spin Awareness Training* (2000).

AC 91-32B *Safety in and Around Helicopters* (1997).

AC 91-42D *Hazards of Rotating Propellers and Helicopter Rotor Blades* (1983).

FAA-H-8083-1 *Aircraft Weight and Balance Handbook* (1999).

FAA-H-8083-21 *Rotorcraft Flying Handbook* (2000).

61.127 FLIGHT PROFICIENCY

(a) *General.* A person who applies for a commercial pilot certificate must receive and log ground and flight training from an authorized instructor on the areas of operation of this section that apply to the aircraft category and class rating sought.

(b) *Areas of operation.*
  (1) *For an airplane category rating with a single-engine class rating:*
    (i)   Preflight preparation;
    (ii)   Preflight procedures;
    (iii) Airport and seaplane base operations;
    (iv)   Takeoffs, landings, and go-arounds;
    (v)   Performance maneuvers;
    (vi)   Ground reference maneuvers;
    (vii) Navigation;
    (viii) Slow flight and stalls;
    (ix)   Emergency operations;
    (x)   High-altitude operations; and
    (xi)   Postflight procedures.

(2) For *an airplane category rating with a multiengine class rating:*
    (i)   Preflight preparation;
    (ii)   Preflight procedures;
    (iii) Airport and seaplane base operations;
    (iv) Takeoffs, landings, and go-arounds;
    (v)   Performance maneuvers;
    (vi) Navigation;
    (vii) Slow flight and stalls;
    (viii) Emergency operations;
    (ix) Multiengine operations;
    (x)   High-altitude operations; and
    (xi) Postflight procedures.

(3) For *a* rotorcraft *category rating with a helicopter class rating:*
    (i)   Preflight preparation;
    (ii)   Preflight procedures;
    (iii) Airport and heliport operations;
    (iv) Hovering maneuvers;
    (v)   Takeoffs, landings, and go-arounds,
    (vi) Performance maneuvers;
    (vii) Navigation;
    (viii) Emergency operations;
    (ix) Special operations; and
    (x)   Postflight procedures.

(4) For *a* rotorcraft *category rating with a gyroplane class rating:*
    (i)   Preflight preparation;
    (ii)   Preflight procedures;
    (iii) Airport operations;
    (iv) Takeoffs, landings, and go-arounds;
    (v)   Performance maneuvers;
    (vi) Navigation;
    (vii) Flight at slow airspeeds;
    (viii) Emergency operations; and
    (ix) Postflight procedures.

(5) For *a powered*-lift *category rating:*
    (i)   Preflight preparation;
    (ii)   Preflight procedures;
    (iii) Airport and heliport operations;
    (iv) Hovering maneuvers;
    (v)   Takeoffs, landings, and go-arounds;
    (vi) Performance maneuvers;
    (vii) Ground reference maneuvers;
    (viii) Navigation;
    (ix) Slow flight and stalls;
    (x)   Emergency operations;
    (xi) High-altitude operations;
    (xii) Special operations; and
    (xiii) Postflight procedures.

(6)   *For a glider category rating:*
    (i)   Preflight preparation;
    (ii)   Preflight procedures;
    (iii)   Airport and gliderport operations;
    (iv)   Launches and landings;
    (v)   Performance speeds;
    (vi)   Soaring techniques;
    (vii   Performance maneuvers;
    (viii) Navigation;
    (ix)   Slow flight and stalls;
    (x)   Emergency operations; and
    (xi)   Postflight procedures.

(7)   *For a lighter-than-air category rating with an airship class rating:*
    (i)   Fundamentals of instructing;
    (ii)   Technical subjects;
    (iii)   Preflight preparation;
    (iv)   Preflight lesson on a maneuver to be performed in flight;
    (v)   Preflight procedures;
    (vi)   Airport operations;
    (vii)   Takeoffs, landings, and go-arounds;
    (viii) Performance maneuvers;
    (ix)   Navigation;
    (x)   Emergency operations; and
    (xi)   Postflight procedures.

(8)   *For a lighter-than-air category rating with a balloon class rating:*
    (i)   Fundamentals of instructing;
    (ii)   Technical subjects;
    (iii)   Preflight preparation;
    (iv)   Preflight lesson on a maneuver to be performed in flight;
    (v)   Preflight procedures;
    (vi)   Airport operations;
    (vii)   Launches and landings;
    (viii) Performance maneuvers;
    (ix)   Navigation;
    (x)   Emergency operations; and
    (xi)   Postflight procedures.

EXPLANATION

Commercial pilot "students" should not depend on their instructors to be aware of the requirements of §61.127. If you are preparing for the commercial pilot checkride, and you doubt your ability in any particular area, ask for more instruction.

In-flight spin training is not required for a commercial pilot certificate. However, an instructor may give spin instruction to any student, regardless of their experience.

For helicopters, an applicant must demonstrate the ability to recognize and recover from imminent entry into settling the power, rather than actually entering the flight regime from which it may be difficult to recover.

PREAMBLE

In the final rule, the proposed "ground reference maneuvers" were deleted from the areas of operation for the gyroplane rating, because it is not a task that is required to be tested in gyroplanes and was inadvertently included in the proposal. As a result of the FAA's decision not to adopt flight instructor certificates for the lighter-than-air category, the areas of operation associated with flight instruction have been added to the required areas of operation for airship and balloon ratings. The FAA also is not adopting separate flight proficiency requirements for powered and nonpowered gliders. (62 FR 16268)

CROSS REFERENCES

61.123, Eligibility Requirements: General; 61.125, Aeronautical Knowledge; 61.129, Aeronautical Experience; 61.131, Exceptions to the Night Flying Requirements; 61.133, Commercial Pilot Privileges and Limitations; 49 Code of Federal Regulations Part 830, Rules Pertaining to the Notification and reporting of Aircraft Accidents or Incidents and Overdue Aircraft, and Preservation of Aircraft Wreckage, Mail, Cargo and Records (NTSB).

ADVISORY CIRCULARS

AC 43-9C *Maintenance Records* (1998).

AC 60-22 *Aeronautical Decision Making* (1991).

AC 61-65D *Certification: Pilots and Flight and Ground Instructors* (1999).

AC 61-67C *Stall and Spin Awareness Training* (2000).

AC 61-84B *Role of Preflight Preparation* (1985).

AC 90-42F *Traffic Advisory Practices at Airports Without Operating Control Towers* (1985).

AC 90-48C *Pilot's Role in Collision Avoidance* (1983).

AC 90-87 *Helicopter Dynamic Rollover* (1986).

AC 91-32B *Safety in and Around Helicopters* (1997).

FAA-H-8083-1 *Aircraft Weight and Balance Handbook* (1999).

FAA-H-8083-21 *Rotorcraft Flying Handbook* (2000).

FAA CHIEF COUNSEL OPINIONS

The instrument instruction required by FAR 61.129 must be given by a certificated flight instructor with an instrument instruction rating. Other noninstrument instruction required by FAR 61.127 may be given by any CFI. (6-20-79).

61.129 AERONAUTICAL EXPERIENCE

(a) *For an airplane single-engine rating.* Except as provided in paragraph (i) of this section, a person who applies for a commercial pilot certificate with an airplane category and single-engine class rating must log at least 250 hours of flight time as a pilot that consists of at least:

(1) 100 hours in powered aircraft, of which 50 hours must be in airplanes.

(2) 100 hours of pilot-in-command flight time, which includes at least—

    (i) 50 hours in airplanes; and

    (ii) 50 hours in cross-country flight of which at least 10 hours must be in airplanes.

(3) 20 hours of training on the areas of operation listed in §61.127(b)(1) of this part that includes at least—

    (i) 10 hours of instrument training of which at least 5 hours must be in a single-engine airplane;

    (ii) 10 hours of training in an airplane that has a retractable landing gear, flaps, and a controllable pitch propeller, or is turbine-powered, or for an applicant seeking a single-engine seaplane rating, 10 hours of training in a seaplane that has flaps and a controllable pitch propeller;

    (iii) One cross-country flight of at least 2 hours in a single-engine airplane in day VFR conditions, consisting of a total straight-line distance of more than 100 nautical miles from the original point of departure;

    (iv) One cross-country flight of at least 2 hours in a single-engine airplane in night VFR conditions, consisting of a total straight-line distance of more than 100 nautical miles from the original point of departure; and

    (v) 3 hours in a single-engine airplane in preparation for the practical test within the 60-day period preceding the date of the test.

(4) 10 hours of solo flight in a single-engine airplane on the areas of operation listed in §61.127(b)(1) of this part, which includes at least—

    (i) One cross-country flight of not less than 300 nautical miles total distance, with landings at a minimum of three points, one of which is a straight-line distance of at least 250 nautical miles from the original departure point. However, if this requirement is being met in Hawaii, the longest segment need only have a straight-line distance of at least 150 nautical miles; and

    (ii) 5 hours in night VFR conditions with 10 takeoffs and 10 landings (with each landing involving a flight in the traffic pattern) at an airport with an operating control tower.

(b) *For an airplane multiengine rating.* Except as provided in paragraph (i) of this section, a person who applies for a commercial pilot certificate with an airplane category and multiengine class rating must log at least 250 hours of flight time as a pilot that consists of at least:

(1) 100 hours in powered aircraft, of which 50 hours must be in airplanes.

(2) 100 hours of pilot-in-command flight time, which includes at least—

    (i) 50 hours in airplanes; and

    (ii) 50 hours in cross-country flight of which at least 10 hours must be in airplanes.

(3) 20 hours of training on the areas of operation listed in §61.127(b)(2) of this part that includes at least—

    (i) 10 hours of instrument training of which at least 5 hours must be in a multiengine airplane;

    (ii) 10 hours of training in a multiengine airplane that has a retractable landing gear, flaps, and controllable pitch propellers, or is turbine-powered, or for an applicant seeking a multiengine seaplane rating, 10 hours of training in a multiengine seaplane that has flaps and a controllable pitch propeller;

    (iii) One cross-country flight of at least 2 hours in a multiengine airplane in day VFR conditions, consisting of a total straight-line distance of more than 100 nautical miles from the original point of departure;

    (iv) One cross-country flight of at least 2 hours in a multiengine airplane in night VFR conditions, consisting of a total straight-line distance of more than 100 nautical miles from the original point of departure; and

    (v) 3 hours in a multiengine airplane in preparation for the practical test within the 60-day period preceding the date of the test.

(4) 10 hours of solo flight time in a multiengine airplane or 10 hours of flight time performing the duties of pilot in command in a multiengine airplane with an authorized instructor (either of which may be credited towards the flight time requirement in paragraph (b)(2) of the section), on the areas of operation listed in §61.127(b)(2) of this part that includes at least—

    (i) One cross-country flight of not less than 300 nautical miles total distance with landings at a minimum of three points, one of which is a straight-line distance of at least 250 nautical miles from the original departure point. However, if this requirement is being met in Hawaii, the longest segment need only have a straight-line distance of at least 150 nautical miles; and

    (ii) 5 hours in night VFR conditions with 10 takeoffs and 10 landings (with each landing involving a flight with a traffic pattern) at an airport with an operating control tower.

(c) *For a helicopter rating.* Except as provided in paragraph (i) of this section, a person who applies for a commercial pilot certificate with a rotorcraft category and helicopter class rating must log at least 150 hours of flight time as a pilot that consists of at least:

(1) 100 hours in powered aircraft, of which 50 hours must be in helicopters.

(2) 100 hours of pilot-in-command flight time, which includes at least—

    (i) 35 hours in helicopters; and

    (ii) 10 hours in cross-country flight in helicopters.

(3) 20 hours of training on the areas of operation listed in §61.127(b)(3) of this part that includes at least—

    (i) 10 hours of instrument training in an aircraft;

    (ii) One cross-country flight of at least 2 hours in a helicopter in day VFR conditions, consisting of a total straight-line distance of more than 50 nautical miles from the original point of departure;

    (iii) One cross-country flight of at least 2 hours in a helicopter in night VFR conditions, consisting of a total straight-line distance of more than 50 nautical miles from the original point of departure; and

    (iv) 3 hours in a helicopter in preparation for the practical test within the 60-day period preceding the date of the test.

(4) 10 hours of solo flight in a helicopter on the areas of operation listed in §61.127(b)(3) of this part, which includes at least—

   (i)   One cross-country flight with landings at a minimum of three points, with one segment consisting of a straight-line distance of at least 50 nautical miles from the original point of departure; and

   (ii) 5 hours in night VFR conditions with 10 takeoffs and 10 landings (with each landing involving a flight in the traffic pattern).

(d) *For a gyroplane rating.* A person who applies for a commercial pilot certificate with a rotorcraft category and gyroplane class rating must log at least 150 hours of flight time as a pilot (of which 5 hours may have been accomplished in a flight simulator or flight training device that is representative of a gyroplane) that consists of at least:

(1) 100 hours in powered aircraft, of which 25 hours must be in gyroplanes.

(2) 100 hours of pilot-in-command flight time, which includes at least—

   (i)   10 hours in gyroplanes; and

   (ii) 3 hours in cross-country flight in gyroplanes.

(3) 20 hours of training on the areas of operation listed in §61.127(b)(4) of this part that includes at least—

   (i)   5 hours of instrument training in an aircraft;

   (ii) One cross-country flight of at least 2 hours in a gyroplane in day VFR conditions, consisting of a total straight-line distance of more than 50 nautical miles from the original point of departure;

   (iii) One cross-country flight of at least 2 hours in a gyroplane in night VFR conditions, consisting of a total straight-line distance of more than 50 nautical miles from the original point of departure; and

   (iv) 3 hours in a gyroplane in preparation for the practical test within the 60-day period preceding the date of the test.

(4) 10 hours of solo flight in a gyroplane on the areas of operation listed in §61.127(b)(4) of this part, which includes at least—

   (i)   One cross-country flight with landings at a minimum of three points, with one segment consisting of a straight-line distance of at least 50 nautical miles from the original point of departure; and

   (ii) 5 hours in night VFR conditions with 10 takeoffs and 10 landings (with each landing involving a flight in the traffic pattern).

(e) *For a powered-lift rating.* Except as provided in paragraph (i) of this section, a person who applies for a commercial pilot certificate with a powered-lift category rating must log at least 250 hours of flight time as a pilot that consists of at least:

(1) 100 hours in powered aircraft, of which 50 hours must be in a powered-lift.

(2) 100 hours of pilot-in-command flight time, which includes at least—

   (i)   50 hours in a powered-lift; and

   (ii) 50 hours in cross-country flight of which at least 10 hours must be in a powered-lift.

(3) 20 hours of training on the areas of operation listed in §61.127(b)(5) of this part that includes at least—

   (i)   10 hours of instrument training, of which at least 5 hours must be in a powered-lift;

   (ii) One cross-country flight of at least 2 hours in a powered-lift in day VFR conditions, consisting of a total straight-line distance of more than 100 nautical miles from the original point of departure;

   (iii) One cross-country flight of at least 2 hours in a powered-lift in night VFR conditions, consisting of a total straight-line distance of more than 100 nautical miles from the original point of departure; and

   (iv) 3 hours in a powered-lift in preparation for the practical test within the 60-day period preceding the date of the test.

(4)   10 hours of solo flight in a powered-lift on the areas of operation listed in §61.127(b)(5) of this part, which includes at least—
    (i)   One cross-country flight of not less than 300 nautical miles total distance with landings at a minimum of three points, one of which is a straight-line distance of at least 250 nautical miles from the original departure point. However, if this requirement is being met in Hawaii the longest segment need only have a straight-line distance of at least 150 nautical miles; and
    (ii)   5 hours in night VFR conditions with 10 takeoffs and 10 landings (with each landing involving a flight in the traffic pattern) at an airport with an operating control tower.

(f)   *For a glider rating.* A person who applies for a commercial pilot certificate with a glider category rating must log at least:
(1)   25 hours of flight time as a pilot in command in a glider and that flight time must include at least 100 flights in a glider as pilot in command, including at least—
    (i)   3 hours of flight training in a glider or 10 training flights in a glider with an authorized instructor on the areas of operation listed in §61.127(b)(6) of this part, including at least 3 training flights in a glider with an authorized instructor in preparation for the practical test within the 60-day period preceding the date of the test; and ;
    (ii)   2 hours of solo flight that include not less than 10 solo flights in a glider on the areas of operation listed in §61.127(b)(6) of this part; or
(2)   200 hours of flight time as a pilot in heavier-than-air aircraft, and at least 20 flights in a glider as pilot in command, including at least—
    (i)   3 hours of flight training in a glider or 10 training flights in a glider with an authorized instructor on the areas of operation listed in §61.127(b)(6) of this part, including at least 3 training flights in a glider with an authorized instructor in preparation for the practical test within the 60-day period preceding the date of the test; and
    (ii)   5 solo flights in a glider on the areas of operation listed in §61.127(b)(6) of this part.

(g)   *For an airship rating.* A person who applies for a commercial pilot certificate with a lighter-than-air category and airship class rating must log at least 200 hours of flight time as a pilot, which includes at least the following hours:
(1)   50 hours in airships.
(2)   30 hours of pilot-in-command time in airships, which consists of at least—
    (i)   10 hours of cross-country flight time in airships; and
    (ii)   10 hours of night flight time in airships.
(3)   40 hours of instrument time, which consists of at least 20 hours in flight, of which 10 hours must be in flight in airships.
(4)   20 hours of flight training in airships on the areas of operation listed in §61.127(b)(7) of this part, which includes at least—
    (i)   3 hours in an airship in preparation for the practical test within the 60-day period preceding the date of the test;
    (ii)   One cross-country flight of at least 1 hour in duration in an airship in day VFR conditions, consisting of a total straight-line distance of more than 25 nautical miles from the original point of departure; and
    (iii)   One cross-country flight of at least 1 hour in duration in an airship in night VFR conditions, consisting of a total straight-line distance of more than 25 nautical miles from the original point of departure.

(5) 10 hours of flight training performing the duties of pilot in command with an authorized instructor on the areas of operation listed in §61.127(b)(7) of this part, which includes at least—

    (i) One cross-country flight with landings at a minimum of three points, with one segment consisting of a straight-line distance of at least 25 nautical miles from the original point of departure; and

    (ii) 5 hours in night VFR conditions with 10 takeoffs and 10 landings (with each landing involving a flight in the traffic pattern).

(h) *For a balloon rating.* A person who applies for a commercial pilot certificate with a lighter-than-air category and a balloon class rating must log at least 35 hours of flight time as a pilot, which includes at least the following requirements:

(1) 20 hours in balloons;

(2) 10 flights in balloons;

(3) Two flights in balloons as the pilot in command; and

(4) 10 hours of flight training that includes at least 10 training flights with an authorized instructor in balloons on the areas of operation listed in §61.127(b)(8) of this part, which consists of at least—

    (i) For a gas balloon—

        (A) 2 training flights of 2 hours each with an authorized instructor in a gas balloon on the areas of operation appropriate to a gas balloon within 60 days prior to application for the rating;

        (B) 2 flights performing the duties of pilot in command in a gas balloon with an authorized instructor on the appropriate areas of operation; and

        (C) One flight involving a controlled ascent to 5,000 feet above the launch site.

    (ii) For a balloon with an airborne heater—

        (A) 2 training flights of 1 hour each with an authorized instructor in a balloon with an airborne heater on the areas of operation appropriate to a balloon with an airborne heater within 60 days prior to application for the rating;

        (B) 2 solo flights in a balloon with an airborne heater on the appropriate areas of operation; and

        (C) One flight involving a controlled ascent to 3,000 feet above the launch site.

(i) *Permitted credit for use of a flight simulator or flight training device.*

(1) Except as provided in paragraph (i)(2) of this section, an applicant who has not accomplished the training required by this section in a course conducted by a training center certificated under part 142 of this chapter may:

    (i) Credit a maximum of 50 hours toward the total aeronautical experience requirements for an airplane or powered-lift rating, provided the aeronautical experience was obtained from an authorized instructor in a flight simulator or flight training device that represents that class of airplane or powered-lift category and type, if applicable, appropriate to the rating sought; and

    (ii) Credit a maximum of 25 hours toward the total aeronautical experience requirements of this section for a helicopter rating, provided the aeronautical experience was obtained from an authorized instructor in a flight simulator or flight training device that represents a helicopter and type, if applicable, appropriate to the rating sought.

(2)   An applicant who has accomplished the training required by this section in a course
      conducted by a training center certificated under part 142 of this chapter may:
      (i)   Credit a maximum of 100 hours toward the total aeronautical experience
             requirements of this section for an airplane and powered-lift rating, provided the
             aeronautical experience was obtained from an authorized instructor in a flight
             simulator or flight training device that represents that class of airplane or powered-lift
             category and type, if applicable, appropriate to the rating sought; and
      (ii)   Credit a maximum of 50 hours toward the total aeronautical experience requirements
             of this section for a helicopter rating, provided the aeronautical experience was
             obtained from an authorized instructor in a flight simulator or flight training device that
             represents a helicopter and type, if applicable, appropriate to the rating sought.
(3)   Except when fewer hours are approved by the Administrator, an applicant for a commercial
      pilot certificate with an airplane or a powered-lift rating who has satisfactorily completed an
      approved commercial pilot course conducted by a training center certificated under part
      142 of this chapter need only have 190 hours of total aeronautical experience to meet the
      requirements of this section.

EXPLANATION

The 1997 amendment to §61.129 establishes a dual training requirement by aircraft class for night
cross country at the private and commercial pilot certificate levels for powered aircraft. It also permits
turbojet flight training in lieu of the previous requirement of flight training in an airplane with
retractable landing gear, flaps, and a controllable pitch propeller. The previous rules prevented the
use of a turbojet airplane to substitute for a complex airplane. The 1997 change added two new dual
cross-country training flight requirements. One is for a day-VFR and one is for a night-VFR. Both must
be in the class of aircraft for which the rating is sought.

The 1998 amendment to §61.129(b)(4) adds "solo flight time" to the time that can be counted towards
the 10 hour requirement described in that section. The 1998 amendments also clarified when an
instructor must be used for the glider and balloon ratings.

Now, where the FARs specifically permit it, time in a flight simulator or flight training device can be
credited in lieu of the required flight time towards meeting the total aeronautical experience or recency
of experience; but it CANNOT be logged as flight time.

PREAMBLE

The FAA has retained the requirements for class-specific training, however the final rule is revised to
permit certain requirements such as the solo flight requirements for the multiengine airplane rating, to
be met in any class of aircraft within an aircraft category. In response to HAI's comment regarding the
performance of emergency maneuvers without an instructor on board the aircraft, the FAA notes that
other training maneuvers such as stalls and slow flight, that are routinely performed in solo flight by
pilot applicants may, when improperly performed, result in situations that adversely affect the safety of
a flight. The FAA contends that these maneuvers when properly performed pose no adverse risk to
the safety of the flight. Flight instructors should ensure that emergency maneuvers, like other
maneuvers, only be performed in solo flight after an instructor determines that such maneuvers may
be safely performed by the applicant, and under any restrictions that may be established by the
instructor to ensure the safety of the flight.

The FAA acknowledges AOPA's argument that solo time in multiengine airplanes may be impractical due to liability and insurance concerns, and is therefore replacing the term "supervised pilot in command flying" with "flight time performing the duties of pilot in command with an authorized instructor" for multiengine airplanes. The FAA has therefore deleted any requirement for solo flight time in a multiengine aircraft.

In response to the concerns of HAI and others regarding the hazards of increased night training, the FAA reiterates its view that safety will be enhanced because it increased night training requirements, which will reduce the likelihood of pilots later being placed in circumstances where they may be required to engage in flight at night without appropriate experience.

The FAA concurs with the comments of HAI and others that instrument training may be impractical in helicopters and gyroplanes and has accordingly removed category and class-specific references to the instrument training requirements in §61.129 for helicopters and gyroplanes. Similarly, in response to AOPA and other commenters, the FAA has modified the instrument requirements for airships.

Upon reviewing SSA's comments, and as a result of the FAA's decision not to adopt the proposed separation of the glider category into powered and nonpowered classes in the final rule, the requirements for gliders are clarified and consolidated under one paragraph.

The FAA has also included provisions set forth in Amendment No. 61-100, which permit credit to be given for the use of an approved flight simulator or approved flight training device. The FAA notes that Amendment No. 61-100 inadvertently omitted the requirement for an applicant for a commercial pilot certificate with an airplane rating to log at least 100 hours of flight time in powered aircraft, at least 50 hours of which must be in airplanes. This requirement has been reinstated in this final rule.

In addition, the FAA has added language to the existing solo cross-country requirements to ensure pilots meet minimum standards specified under Annex 1 to the Convention on International Civil Aviation. The additional language requires that an applicant for a commercial pilot certificate complete a solo cross-country flight of a total of not less than 300 nautical miles. The existing rule states that a cross-country flight must have landings at a minimum of three points, one of which is at least a straight line distance of 250 nautical miles from the original point of departure. All commercial pilot applicants with a private pilot certificate currently meet the total 300-nautical-mile requirement; however, private pilots certificated after the effective date of this rule will not, due to the decrease in the solo cross-country flight requirements for private pilots set forth in this rule. The FAA wants to ensure that the requirements under Annex 1 to the Convention on International Civil Aviation are specifically met, to facilitate the acceptance of U.S. pilot certificates internationally.

Additionally, because the FAA has withdrawn the proposal to establish a separate airship instrument rating, the FAA is reinstating the instrument aeronautical experience requirements found in existing §61.135(c) into paragraph (g)(3) of the final rule. An applicant seeking a commercial pilot certificate with an airship rating must have 40 hours of instrument time, of which at least 20 hours must be in flight, with 10 hours of that flight time in airships. (62 FR 16269).

CROSS REFERENCES

61.123, Eligibility Requirements: General; 61.125, Aeronautical Knowledge; 61.127, Flight Proficiency; 61.131, Exceptions to the Night Flying Requirements; 61.133, Commercial Pilot Privileges and Limitations; 49 Code of Federal Regulations Part 830, Rules Pertaining to the Notification and reporting of Aircraft Accidents or Incidents and Overdue Aircraft, and Preservation of Aircraft Wreckage, Mail, Cargo and Records (NTSB).

ADVISORY CIRCULARS

AC 61-23C *Pilot's Handbook of Aeronautical Knowledge* (1997).

FAA-H-8083-3 *Airplane Flying Handbook* (1999).

FAA-H-8083-15 *Instrument Flying Handbook* (1999).

61.131 EXCEPTIONS TO THE NIGHT FLYING REQUIREMENTS

(a)   Subject to the limitations of paragraph (b) of this section, a person is not required to comply with the night flight training requirements of this subpart if the person receives flight training in and resides in the State of Alaska.

(b)   A person who receives flight training in and resides in the State of Alaska but does not meet the night flight training requirements of this section:

(1)   May be issued a pilot certificate with the limitation "night flying prohibited."

(2)   Must comply with the appropriate night flight training requirements of this subpart within the 12-calendar-month period after the issuance of the pilot certificate. At the end of that period, the certificate will become invalid for use until the person complies with the appropriate night flight training requirements of this subpart. The person may have the "night flying prohibited" limitation removed if the person—

(i)   Accomplishes the appropriate night flight training requirements of this subpart; and

(ii)   Presents to an examiner a logbook or training record endorsement from an authorized instructor that verifies accomplishment of the appropriate night flight training requirements of this subpart.

EXPLANATION

The 1997 amendment eliminates the night flying aeronautical experience exception at the commercial certificate level, except for those persons who receive their training in Alaska and in those cases a person will be given one year to obtain the required night flying aeronautical experience. This means that all commercial pilot applicants are required to receive the night flying training that is specified in Part 61.

A takeoff and landing separated by an enroute phase of flight can be comprised of a takeoff, a short flight in the vicinity of the takeoff point and a landing at the same place as the takeoff. An example would be a flight around the landing pattern.

The basis for not requiring any instrument training for rotorcraft ratings is that encountering IFR conditions in a rotorcraft is not analogous to the same situation in an airplane, where suitable landing sites are far less numerous and altitude restrictions may be greater.

PREAMBLE

AOPA's objection is noted and addressed in the FAA's response to AOPA's comment in §61.110. As in that section, the FAA has eliminated the reference to a 12-month temporary certificate from §61.131 in the final rule, because current FAA temporary certificates are valid for 120 days. In addition, by deleting the exception for pilots who have night flying restrictions due to medical conditions, these pilots will now be required to have 3 hours of night flight training. However, the certificates of such pilots will be issued with an operating limitation prohibiting night flying. The FAA has determined that safety will be enhanced because this requirement will reduce the likelihood of pilots later being placed in circumstances where they may be required to engage in flight at night without appropriate night training. (62 FR 16269)

CROSS REFERENCES

61.110, Night Flying Exceptions.

61.133 COMMERCIAL PILOT PRIVILEGES AND LIMITATIONS

(a) *Privileges.*
   (1) *General.* A person who holds a commercial pilot certificate may act as pilot in command of an aircraft—
      (i) Carrying persons or property for compensation or hire, provided the person is qualified in accordance with this part and with the applicable parts of this chapter that apply to the operation; and
      (ii) For compensation or hire, provided the person is qualified in accordance with this part and with the applicable parts of this chapter that apply to the operation.
   (2) *Commercial pilots with lighter-than-air category ratings.* A person with a commercial pilot certificate with a lighter-than-air category rating may—
      (i) *For an airship—*
         (A) Give flight and ground training in an airship for the issuance of a certificate or rating;
         (B) Give an endorsement for a pilot certificate with an airship rating;
         (C) Endorse a student pilot certificate or logbook for solo operating privileges in an airship;
         (D) Act as pilot in command of an airship under IFR or in weather conditions less than the minimum prescribed for VFR flight; and
         (E) Give flight and ground training and endorsements that are required for a flight review, an operating privilege, or recency-of-experience requirements of this part.
      (ii) *For a balloon—*
         (A) Give flight and ground training in a balloon for the issuance of a certificate or rating;
         (B) Give an endorsement for a pilot certificate with a balloon rating;
         (C) Endorse a student pilot certificate or logbook for solo operating privileges in a balloon; and
         (D) Give ground and flight training and endorsements that are required for a flight review, an operating privilege, or recency-of-experience requirements of this part.

(b) *Limitations.*
(1) A person who applies for a commercial pilot certificate with an airplane category or powered-lift category rating and does not hold an instrument rating in the same category and class will be issued a commercial pilot certificate that contains the limitation, "The carriage of passengers for hire in (airplanes) (powered-lifts) on cross-country flights in excess of 50 nautical miles or at night is prohibited." The limitation may be removed when the person satisfactorily accomplishes the requirements listed in §61.65 of this part for an instrument rating in the same category and class of aircraft listed on the person's commercial pilot certificate.
(2) If a person who applies for a commercial pilot certificate with a balloon rating takes a practical test in a balloon with an airborne heater—
(i)   The pilot certificate will contain a limitation restricting the exercise of the privileges of that certificate to a balloon with an airborne heater.
(ii) The limitation specified in paragraph (b)(2)(i) of this section may be removed when the person obtains the required aeronautical experience in a gas balloon and receives a logbook endorsement from an authorized instructor who attests to the person's accomplishment of the required aeronautical experience and ability to satisfactorily operate a gas balloon.
(3) If a person who applies for a commercial pilot certificate with a balloon rating takes a practical test in a gas balloon—
(i)   The pilot certificate will contain a limitation restricting the exercise of the privileges of that certificate to a gas balloon.
(ii) The limitation specified in paragraph (b)(3)(i) of this section may be removed when the person obtains the required aeronautical experience in a balloon with an airborne heater and receives a logbook endorsement from an authorized instructor who attests to the person's accomplishment of the required aeronautical experience and ability to satisfactorily operate a balloon with an airborne heater.

EXPLANATION

Simply obtaining a commercial pilot certificate does not allow you to buy an airplane and offer charter services to the public. Offering both airplane and pilot services together for compensation generally requires additional qualifications under Parts 119, 121, 125, or 135.

§119.1(e) lists several specific operations, such as student instruction and certain sightseeing flights, which are not governed by Parts 119, 121, 125, or 135. This list shows what a commercial pilot can do "for hire" without flying for a Part 121, 125 or 135 operation.

CROSS REFERENCES

Previous Designation: 61.139; 61.113, Private Pilot Privileges and Limitations: Pilot in Command.

CASES

On its face, §61.139(a) does not require a commercial pilot to satisfy any further requirements before exercising the privilege of carrying persons or property for compensation or hire. However, Part 61 must be construed in conjunction with Part 135. §135.1 [Now Part 119] states that Part 135 covers

"The carrying in air commerce by any person, other than as an air carrier, of persons or property for compensation or hire. . ." The NTSB did not accept the argument of a commercial pilot that he was "sharing expenses" and/or he was qualified to fly an essentially charter flight simply because he was a commercial pilot. *Administrator v. Sabar*, 3 NTSB 3119 (1980).

Can a commercially certificated pilot fly a friend for full compensation or hire under Part 91?

The answer is that there are some limited circumstances when it is permissible. From the standpoint of Part 61, the holder of a commercial pilot certificate is permitted to accept compensation for piloting. There is a question, however, whether the operation can be conducted under Part 91 as opposed to Part 135. A pilot flying under Part 91 may not carry persons or property in air commerce for compensation or hire. This means that the aircraft owner may only transport passengers and property that pertain to the owner or the owner's business, as long as that business is not air transportation (See §91.501).

One example of this Part 91 operation is the corporate pilot flying a company airplane carrying company property and passengers. The corporate pilot is paid for his work, and therefore must have a commercial pilot certificate. Another example is pilot service, where a commercial pilot is paid by an airplane owner to fly the airplane for the owner. As long as there is no "carriage in air commerce of persons or property for compensation or hire", the commercial pilot can operate under Part 91 and be paid for his services.

We stress that §135.1, §135.5, and §135.7 [Now Part 119] make it clear that the "carriage in air commerce of persons or property for compensation or hire" requires an air taxi/commercial operator operating certificate. (12-9-92).

INTENTIONALLY

LEFT

BLANK

INTENTIONALLY

LEFT

BLANK

SUBPART G — AIRLINE TRANSPORT PILOTS

61.151 APPLICABILITY

This subpart prescribes the requirements for the issuance of airline transport pilot certificates and ratings, the conditions under which those certificates and ratings are necessary, and the general operating rules for persons who hold those certificates and ratings.

EXPLANATION

The airline transport pilot certificate is the only certificate that has "good moral character" as a requirement for the issuance of the certificate. This requirement is enforced by the FAA. When a person's airline transport pilot certificate is revoked on the basis that the holder lacks good moral character, that action does not affect any other certificate held by that person.

An applicant, upon reaching 21 years of age, may take the knowledge test, provided the applicant has the aeronautical experience required by §61.159, §61.161, or §61.163.

When applying for an ATP certificate without the benefit of a high school diploma, an applicant should prepare a very detailed account of occupational and aeronautical experience before presenting a request to the FAA for waiver of the high school diploma requirement.

61.153 ELIGIBILITY REQUIREMENTS: GENERAL

To be eligible for an airline transport pilot certificate, a person must:
(a)   Be at least 23 years of age;
(b)   Be able to read, speak, write, and understand the English language. If the applicant is unable to meet one of these requirements due to medical reasons, then the Administrator may place such operating limitations on that applicant's pilot certificate as are necessary for the safe operation of the aircraft;
(c)   Be of good moral character;
(d)   Meet at least one of the following requirements:
    (1)   Hold at least a commercial pilot certificate and an instrument rating;
    (2)   Meet the military experience requirements under §61.73 of this part to qualify for a commercial pilot certificate, and an instrument rating if the person is a rated military pilot or former rated military pilot of an Armed Force of the United States; or
    (3)   Hold either a foreign airline transport pilot or foreign commercial pilot license and an instrument rating, without limitations, issued by a contracting State to the Convention on International Civil Aviation.
(e)   Meet the aeronautical experience requirements of this subpart that apply to the aircraft category and class rating sought before applying for the practical test;
(f)   Pass a knowledge test on the aeronautical knowledge areas of §61.155(c) of this part that apply to the aircraft category and class rating sought;
(g)   Pass the practical test on the areas of operation listed in §61.157(e) of this part that apply to the aircraft category and class rating sought; and
(h)   Comply with the sections of this part that apply to the aircraft category and class rating sought.

EXPLANATION

The 1997 amendment deletes the exceptions for persons who are unable to read, speak, write and understand English. However the rules still provide an exception for persons with medical impairments (i.e. hearing impaired). It also requires an applicant for an ATP certificate to hold a commercial pilot certificate with an instrument rating. This is a minor revision as in most cases applicants already hold a commercial pilot certificate with an instrument rating. However, the rule retains certain exceptions (i.e. military pilots and foreign pilots).

PREAMBLE

In response to comments regarding the proposed English language requirements the provisions regarding English language proficiency have been standardized throughout Part 61. The stated requirement for an applicant for an ATP certificate to possess only a third-class medical certificate has also been placed in §61.23 as have similar requirements for other pilot certificates. A first class medical certificate however is still required to exercise the privileges of the ATP certificate. The FAA also contends that all ATP applicants should possess the knowledge, skill, and experience required of a holder of a commercial pilot certificate with an instrument rating. This level of initial proficiency in an ATP applicant can only be ensured by requiring an applicant to meet the objective evaluation criteria for the issuance of the commercial pilot certificate with an instrument rating. Regarding ALPA's and NATA's comments on the elimination in this section of the requirement for a high school diploma, the FAA's experience is that ATP certificate applicants typically achieve a higher level of education, which makes the existing requirement obsolete. (62 FR 16271).

CROSS REFERENCE

Previous Designation: 61.151; 61.1, Applicability and Definitions; 61.73, Military Pilots or former Military Pilots: Special Rules; 61.155, Aeronautical Knowledge.

CASES

To establish a charge of "lack of good moral character," the FAA must establish by a preponderance of the evidence that the pilot had a pattern of conduct which departs from ordinary pattern of morality and shows that the pilot is capable of acting without inhibition in an unstable manner and without regard to the rights of others. In this case, a pilot had been convicted of indecent exposure. The FAA did not offer any evidence of a "pattern of conduct"; they thought the mere fact of the conviction would be enough to revoke the pilot's ATP certificate. It was not. The NTSB stated that the mere fact of the conviction alone did not meet the burden necessary to establish lack of good moral character. *Administrator v. Saunders*, EA-3672 (1992).

A conviction of failure to pay Federal income tax, file tax returns or properly fill out a W-4 form does not constitute a lack of moral character. *Administrator v. Neff*, EA-3920 (1993).

Drug smuggling is an example of a "pattern of conduct" which shows a "lack of good moral character." *Administrator v. Johnson*, 5 NTSB 279 (1985).

Generally, a pilot charged with intentional falsification will be found to lack the good moral character required by [§61.153]. However, mitigating circumstances may be found which do not require the revocation of the pilot's ATP certificate. In this case, an ATP pilot who was also a CFI falsified some of the information on applications for airman certifications. It was clear to the NTSB from the record that the pilot was not attempting to present unqualified pilots to the FAA for ratings which they had not adequately trained for. The NTSB decided to revoke his instructor certificate, but not his ATP. *Administrator v. Crawford* 5 NTSB 343 (1985).

A conviction of drug smuggling using an aircraft warranted the revocation of a pilot's ATP certificate for lack of good moral character. *Administrator v. Daughenbaugh*, 4 NTSB 767 (1983).

The Director of Operations for a 121 carrier was found to have made it a policy to enter a time not exceeding 8 hours in the operations logbooks for a certain route regardless of the actual time flown. When one of the company's pilots was asked to present his logbook (the only central place where his flight time for the company was logged) he admitted to not keeping correct and accurate time entries in his logbook. Upon inspection of it by a FAA inspector the logbook was found to have numerous white-out spots where corrections all having the exact same time and flown on the same route were entered. The pilot admitted that most of the entries he certified as being true and correct were actually "guesses" and were never meant to be a true and correct record of his time. The Board upheld the revocation of his and the Director of Operation's ATP certificates. *Administrator v. Branum and Alford*, EA-4849 (2000).

The Board ruled that a conviction of interstate travel with the intent to engage in a sexual act with a minor proved that a pilot lacked the good moral character to hold an ATP. *Administrator v. Tucker*, EA-4872 (2001).

FAA CHIEF COUNSEL OPINIONS

Any felony conviction may affect an individual's ability to obtain an airline transport pilot certificate because the holder of an ATP certificate is required to be of good moral character. (2-17-98).

61.155 AERONAUTICAL KNOWLEDGE

(a) *General.* The knowledge test for an airline transport pilot certificate is based on the aeronautical knowledge areas listed in paragraph (c) of this section that are appropriate to the aircraft category and class rating sought.

(b) *Aircraft type rating.* A person who is applying for an additional aircraft type rating to be added to an airline transport pilot certificate is not required to pass a knowledge test if that person's airline transport pilot certificate lists the aircraft category and class rating that is appropriate to the type rating sought.

(c) *Aeronautical knowledge areas.*
    (1) Applicable Federal Aviation Regulations of this chapter that relate to airline transport pilot privileges, limitations, and flight operations;
    (2) Meteorology, including knowledge of and effects of fronts, frontal characteristics, cloud formations, icing, and upper-air data;
    (3) General system of weather and NOTAM collection, dissemination, interpretation, and use;
    (4) Interpretation and use of weather charts, maps, forecasts, sequence reports, abbreviations, and symbols;
    (5) National Weather Service functions as they pertain to operations in the National Airspace System;
    (6) Windshear and microburst awareness, identification, and avoidance;
    (7) Principles of air navigation under instrument meteorological conditions in the National Airspace System;
    (8) Air traffic control procedures and pilot responsibilities as they relate to en route operations, terminal area and radar operations, and instrument departure and approach procedures;
    (9) Aircraft loading, weight and balance, use of charts, graphs, tables, formulas, and computations, and their effect on aircraft performance;
    (10) Aerodynamics relating to an aircraft's flight characteristics and performance in normal and abnormal flight regimes;
    (11) Human factors;
    (12) Aeronautical decision making and judgment; and
    (13) Crew resource management to include crew communication and coordination.

EXPLANATION

Airline Transport pilots are now required to have knowledge of windshear avoidance procedures, aeronautical decision making, judgment training, and cockpit resource management.

PREAMBLE

The FAA purposely deleted the recognition and avoidance of wake turbulence as an aeronautical knowledge area for the ATP certificate. This training was deleted because it is provided at lower certificate levels (student and private) and requiring it in §61.155 would be duplicative of these requirements. The FAA, through this regulatory review, has made an effort to eliminate repetitive requirements, and conform with the "step-by-step building block" concept of pilot certification. Also, the FAA has replaced the term "flight crewmember physiological factors" with "human factors" because the latter term encompasses the former, and is more commonly recognized and understood in the aviation community. As stated in the FAA's previous discussion of this issue, the FAA believes that training in human factors and aeronautical decision making may decrease the number of accidents attributable to pilot error, because the implementation of similar training in air carrier operations has decreased accident rates. In response to ALPA's comment, the FAA provides pilots and instructors with guidance materials regarding human factors and aeronautical decision making in: AC 67-2, "Medical Handbook for Pilots"; AC 61-107, "Operations of Aircraft at Altitudes Above 25,000 feet MSL and/or MACH numbers (Mmo) Greater Than .75"; and in the Airline Transport Pilot, Aircraft Dispatcher, and Flight Navigator Knowledge Test Guide. (62 FR 16271).

CROSS REFERENCES

61.157, Airline Transport Pilot: Flight Proficiency.

61.157 FLIGHT PROFICIENCY

(a) *General.*
   (1) The practical test for an airline transport pilot certificate is given for—
      (i) An airplane category and single-engine class rating;
      (ii) An airplane category and multiengine class rating;
      (iii) A rotorcraft category and helicopter class rating;
      (iv) A powered-lift category rating; and
      (v) An aircraft type rating for the category and class ratings listed in paragraphs (a)(1)(i) through (a)(1)(iv) of this section.
   (2) A person who is applying for an airline transport pilot practical test must meet—
      (i) The eligibility requirements of §61.153 of this part; and
      (ii) The aeronautical knowledge and aeronautical experience requirements of this subpart that apply to the aircraft category and class rating sought.
(b) *Aircraft type rating.* Except as provided in paragraph (c) of this section, a person who is applying for an aircraft type rating to be added to an airline transport pilot certificate:
   (1) Must receive and log ground and flight training from an authorized instructor on the areas of operation in this section that apply to the aircraft type rating sought;
   (2) Must receive a logbook endorsement from an authorized instructor certifying that the applicant completed the training on the areas of operation listed in paragraph (e) of this section that apply to the aircraft type rating sought; and
   (3) Must perform the practical test in actual or simulated instrument conditions, unless the aircraft's type certificate makes the aircraft incapable of operating under instrument flight rules. If the practical test cannot be accomplished for this reason, the person may obtain a type rating limited to "VFR only." The "VFR only" limitation may be removed for that aircraft type when the person passes the practical test in actual or simulated instrument conditions.
(c) *Exceptions.* A person who is applying for an aircraft type rating to be added to an airline transport pilot certificate or an aircraft type rating concurrently with an airline transport pilot certificate, and who is an employee of a certificate holder operating under part 121 or part 135 of this chapter, need not comply with the requirements of paragraph (b) of this section if the applicant presents a training record that shows satisfactory completion of that certificate holder's approved pilot-in-command training program for the aircraft type rating sought.
(d) *Upgrading type ratings.* Any type rating(s) on the pilot certificate of an applicant who successfully completes an airline transport pilot practical test shall be included on the airline transport pilot certificate with the privileges and limitations of the airline transport pilot certificate, provided the applicant passes the practical test in the same category and class of aircraft for which the applicant holds the type rating(s). However, if a type rating for that category and class of aircraft on the superseded pilot certificate is limited to VFR, that limitation shall be carried forward to the person's airline transport pilot certificate level.

(e) *Areas of operation.*
  (1) *For an airplane category—single-engine class rating:*
      (i) Preflight preparation;
      (ii) Preflight procedures;
      (iii) Takeoff and departure phase;
      (iv) In-flight maneuvers;
      (v) Instrument procedures;
      (vi) Landings and approaches to landings;
      (vii) Normal and abnormal procedures;
      (viii) Emergency procedures; and
      (ix) Postflight procedures.
  (2) *For an airplane category—multiengine class rating:*
      (i) Preflight preparation;
      (ii) Preflight procedures;
      (iii) Takeoff and departure phase;
      (iv) In-flight maneuvers;
      (v) Instrument procedures;
      (vi) Landings and approaches to landings;
      (vii) Normal and abnormal procedures;
      (viii) Emergency procedures; and
      (ix) Postflight procedures.
  (3) *For a powered-lift category rating:*
      (i) Preflight preparation;
      (ii) Preflight procedures;
      (iii) Takeoff and departure phase;
      (iv) In-flight maneuvers;
      (v) Instrument procedures;
      (vi) Landings and approaches to landings;
      (vii) Normal and abnormal procedures;
      (viii) Emergency procedures; and
      (ix) Postflight procedures.
  (4) *For a rotorcraft category—helicopter class rating:*
      (i) Preflight preparation;
      (ii) Preflight procedures;
      (iii) Takeoff and departure phase;
      (iv) In-flight maneuvers;
      (v) Instrument procedures;
      (vi) Landings and approaches to landings;
      (vii) Normal and abnormal procedures;
      (viii) Emergency procedures; and
      (ix) Postflight procedures.
(f) *Proficiency and competency checks conducted under part 121 or part 135.*
  (1) Successful completion of a pilot-in-command proficiency check under §121.441 of this chapter or successful completion of both a competency check, under §135.293 of this chapter, and a pilot-in-command instrument proficiency check, under §135.297 of this chapter, satisfies the requirements of this section for the appropriate aircraft rating.
  (2) The checks specified in paragraph (f)(1) of this section must be conducted by an authorized designated pilot examiner or FAA aviation safety inspector.

(g) *Use of a flight simulator or flight* training *device for an airplane rating.* If a flight simulator or flight training device is used for accomplishing all of the training and the required practical test for an airline transport pilot certificate with an airplane category, class, and type rating, if applicable, the applicant, flight simulator, and flight training device are subject to the following requirements:

(1) The flight simulator and flight training device must represent that airplane type if the rating involves a type rating in an airplane, or is representative of an airplane if the applicant is only seeking an airplane class rating and does not require a type rating.

(2) The flight simulator and flight training device must be used in accordance with an approved course at a training center certificated under part 142 of this chapter.

(3) All training and testing (except preflight inspection) must be accomplished by the applicant to receive an airplane class rating and type rating, if applicable, without limitations and—

   (i)   The flight simulator must be qualified and approved as Level C or Level D; and

   (ii) The applicant must meet the aeronautical experience requirements of §61.159 of this part and at least one of the following—

      (A) Hold a type rating for a turbojet airplane of the same class of airplane for which the type rating is sought, or have been designated by a military service as a pilot in command of an airplane of the same class of airplane for which the type rating is sought, if a turbojet type rating is sought;

      (B) Hold a type rating for a turbopropeller airplane of the same class as the airplane for which the type rating is sought, or have been appointed by a military service as a pilot in command of an airplane of the same class of airplane for which the type rating is sought, if a turbopropeller airplane type rating is sought;

      (C) Have at least 2,000 hours of flight time, of which 500 hours must be in turbine-powered airplanes of the same class as the airplane for which the type rating is sought;

      (D) Have at least 500 hours of flight time in the same type of airplane as the airplane for which the type rating is sought; or

      (E) Have at least 1,000 hours of flight time in at least two different airplanes requiring a type rating.

(4) Subject to the limitation of paragraph (g)(5) of this section, an applicant who does not meet the requirements of paragraph (g)(3) of this section may complete all training and testing (except for preflight inspection) for an additional rating if—

   (i)   The flight simulator is qualified and approved as Level C or Level D; and

   (ii) The applicant meets the aeronautical experience requirements of §61.159 of this part and at least one of the following—

      (A) Holds a type rating in a propeller-driven airplane if a type rating in a turbojet airplane is sought, or holds a type rating in a turbojet airplane if a type rating in a propeller-driven airplane is sought;

      (B) Since the beginning of the 12th calendar month before the month in which the applicant completes the practical test for the additional rating, has logged—

         (1) At least 100 hours of flight time in airplanes in the same class as the airplane for which the type rating is sought and which requires a type rating; and

         (2) At least 25 hours of flight time in airplanes of the same type for which the type rating is sought.

(5) An applicant meeting only the requirements of paragraph (g)(4)(ii)(A) and (B) of this section will be issued an additional rating, or an airline transport pilot certificate with an added rating, as applicable, with a limitation. The limitation shall state: "This certificate is subject to pilot-in-command limitations for the additional rating."

(6)   An applicant who has been issued a certificate with the limitation specified in paragraph
      (g)(5) of this section—
      (i)   May not act as pilot in command of the aircraft for which an additional rating was
             obtained under the provisions of this section until the limitation is removed from the
             certificate; and
      (ii)   May have the limitation removed by accomplishing 15 hours of supervised operating
             experience as pilot in command under the supervision of a qualified and current pilot
             in command, in the seat normally occupied by the pilot in command, in an airplane of
             the same type for which the limitation applies.
(7)   An applicant who does not meet the requirements of paragraph (g)(3)(ii)(A) through (E) or
      (g)(4)(ii)(A) and (B) of this section may be issued an airline transport pilot certificate or an
      additional rating to that pilot certificate after successful completion of one of the following
      requirements—
      (i)   An approved course at a part 142 training center that includes all training and testing
             for that certificate or rating, followed by training and testing on the following tasks,
             which must be successfully completed on a static airplane or in flight, as
             appropriate—
             (A)   Preflight inspection;
             (B)   Normal takeoff;
             (C)   Normal ILS approach;
             (D)   Missed approach; and
             (E)   Normal landing.
      (ii)   An approved course at a part 142 training center that complies with paragraphs (g)(8)
             and (g)(9) of this section and includes all training and testing for a certificate or rating.
(8)   An applicant meeting only the requirements of paragraph (g)(7)(ii) of this section will be
      issued an additional rating or an airline transport pilot certificate with an additional rating,
      as applicable, with a limitation. The limitation shall state: "This certificate is subject to pilot-
      in-command limitations for the additional rating."
(9)   An applicant issued a pilot certificate with the limitation specified in paragraph (g)(8) of this
      section—
      (i)   May not act as pilot in command of the aircraft for which an additional rating was
             obtained under the provisions of this section until the limitation is removed from the
             certificate; and
      (ii)   May have the limitation removed by accomplishing 25 hours of supervised operating
             experience as pilot in command under the supervision of a qualified and current pilot
             in command, in the seat normally occupied by the pilot in command, in an airplane of
             the same type for which the limitation applies.

(h)   *Use of a flight simulator or flight training device for a helicopter rating.* If a flight simulator or
      flight training device is used for accomplishing all of the training and the required practical test
      for an airline transport pilot certificate with a helicopter class rating and type rating, if applicable,
      the applicant, flight simulator, and flight training device are subject to the following requirements:
      (1)   The flight simulator and flight training device must represent that helicopter type if the
            rating involves a type rating in a helicopter, or is representative of a helicopter if the
            applicant is only seeking a helicopter class rating and does not require a type rating.
      (2)   The flight simulator and flight training device must be used in accordance with an approved
            course at a training center certificated under part 142 of this chapter.

(3)   All training and testing requirements (except preflight inspection) must be accomplished by the applicant to receive a helicopter class rating and type rating, if applicable, without limitations and—

   (i)   The flight simulator must be qualified and approved as a Level C or Level D; and

   (ii)   The applicant must meet the aeronautical experience requirements of §61.161 of this part and at least one of the following—

      (A)   Hold a type rating for a turbine-powered helicopter, or have been designated by a military service as a pilot in command of a turbine-powered helicopter, if a turbine-powered helicopter type rating is sought;

      (B)   Have at least 1,200 hours of flight time, of which 500 hours must be in turbine-powered helicopters;

      (C)   Have at least 500 hours of flight time in the same type helicopter as the helicopter for which the type rating is sought; or

      (D)   Have at least 1,000 hours of flight time in at least two different helicopters requiring a type rating.

(4)   Subject to the limitation of paragraph (h)(5) of this section, an applicant who does not meet the requirements of paragraph (h)(3) of this section may complete all training and testing (except for preflight inspection) for an additional rating if—

   (i)   The flight simulator is qualified and approved as Level C or Level D; and

   (ii)   The applicant meets the aeronautical experience requirements of §61.161 of this part and, since the beginning of the 12th calendar month before the month in which the applicant completes the practical test for the additional rating, has logged—

      (A)   At least 100 hours of flight time in helicopters; and

      (B)   At least 15 hours of flight time in helicopters of the same type of helicopter for which the type rating is sought.

(5)   An applicant meeting only the requirements of paragraph (h)(4)(ii) (A) and (B) of this section will be issued an additional rating or an airline transport pilot certificate with a limitation. The limitation shall state: "This certificate is subject to pilot-in-command limitations for the additional rating."

(6)   An applicant who has been issued a certificate with the limitation specified in paragraph (h)(5) of this section—

   (i)   May not act as pilot in command of the helicopter for which an additional rating was obtained under the provisions of this section until the limitation is removed from the certificate; and

   (ii)   May have the limitation removed by accomplishing 15 hours of supervised operating experience as pilot in command under the supervision of a qualified and current pilot in command, in the seat normally occupied by the pilot in command, in a helicopter of the same type for which the limitation applies.

(7)   An applicant who does not meet the requirements of paragraph (h)(3)(ii) (A) through (D), or (h)(4)(ii) (A) and (B) of this section may be issued an airline transport pilot certificate or an additional rating to that pilot certificate after successful completion of one of the following requirements—

   (i)   An approved course at a part 142 training center that includes ll training and testing for that certificate or rating, followed by training and testing on the following tasks, which must be successfully completed on a static aircraft or in flight, as appropriate—

      (A)   Preflight inspection;

      (B)   Normal takeoff from a hover;

      (C)   Manually flown precision approach; and

      (D)   Steep approach and landing to an off-airport heliport; or

   (ii)   An approved course at a training center that includes all training and testing for that certificate or rating and compliance with paragraphs (h)(8) and (h)(9) of this section.

(8)   An applicant meeting only the requirements of paragraph (h)(7)(ii) of this section will be issued an additional rating or an airline transport pilot certificate with an additional rating, as applicable, with a limitation. The limitation shall state: "This certificate is subject to pilot-in-command limitations for the additional rating."

(9)   An applicant issued a certificate with the limitation specified in paragraph (h)(8) of this section—

     (i)   May not act as pilot in command of the aircraft for which an additional rating was obtained under the provisions of this section until the limitation is removed from the certificate; and

     (ii)   May have the limitation removed by accomplishing 25 hours of supervised operating experience as pilot in command under the supervision of a qualified and current pilot in command, in the seat normally occupied by the pilot in command, in an aircraft of the same type for which the limitation applies.

(i)   *Use of a flight simulator or flight training device for a powered-lift rating.* If a flight simulator or flight training device is used for accomplishing all of the training and the required practical test for an airline transport pilot certificate with a powered-lift category rating and type rating, if applicable, the applicant, flight simulator, and flight training device are subject to the following requirements:

(1)   The flight simulator and flight training device must represent that powered-lift type, if the rating involves a type rating in a powered-lift, or is representative of a powered-lift if the applicant is only seeking a powered-lift category rating and does not require a type rating.

(2)   The flight simulator and flight training device must be used in accordance with an approved course at a training center certificated under part 142 of this chapter.

(3)   All training and testing requirements (except preflight inspection) must be accomplished by the applicant to receive a powered-lift category rating and type rating, if applicable, without limitations; and—

     (i)   The flight simulator must be qualified and approved as Level C or Level D; and

     (ii)   The applicant must meet the aeronautical experience requirements of §61.163 of this part and at least one of the following—

         (A)   Hold a type rating for a turbine-powered powered-lift, or have been designated by a military service as a pilot in command of a turbine-powered powered-lift, if a turbine-powered powered-lift type rating is sought;

         (B)   Have at least 1,200 hours of flight time, of which 500 hours must be in turbine-powered powered-lifts;

         (C)   Have at least 500 hours of flight time in the same type of powered-lift for which the type rating is sought; or

         (D)   Have at least 1,000 hours of flight time in at least two different powered-lifts requiring a type rating.

(4)   Subject to the limitation of paragraph (i)(5) of this section, an applicant who does not meet the requirements of paragraph (i)(3) of this section may complete all training and testing (except for preflight inspection) for an additional rating if—

     (i)   The flight simulator is qualified and approved as Level C or Level D; and

     (ii)   The applicant meets the aeronautical experience requirements of §61.163 of this part and, since the beginning of the 12th calendar month before the month in which the applicant completes the practical test for the additional rating, has logged—

         (A)   At least 100 hours of flight time in powered-lifts; and

         (B)   At least 15 hours of flight time in powered-lifts of the same type of powered-lift for the type rating sought.

(5)	An applicant meeting only the requirements of paragraph (i)(4)(ii) (A) and (B) of this section will be issued an additional rating or an airline transport pilot certificate with a limitation. The limitation shall state: "This certificate is subject to pilot-in-command limitations for the additional rating."

(6)	An applicant who has been issued a certificate with the limitation specified in paragraph (i)(5) of this section—

(i)	May not act as pilot in command of the powered-lift for which an additional rating was obtained under the provisions of this section until the limitation is removed from the certificate; and

(ii)	May have the limitation removed by accomplishing 15 hours of supervised operating experience as pilot in command under the supervision of a qualified and current pilot in command, in the seat normally occupied by the pilot in command, in a powered-lift of the same type for which the limitation applies.

(7)	An applicant who does not meet the requirements of paragraph (i)(3)(ii) (A) through (D) or (i)(4)(ii) (A) and (B) of this section may be issued an airline transport pilot certificate or an additional rating to that pilot certificate after successful completion of one of the following requirements—

(i)	An approved course at a part 142 training center that includes all training and testing for that certificate or rating, followed by training and testing on the following tasks, which must be successfully completed on a static aircraft or in flight, as appropriate—

(A)	Preflight inspection;

(B)	Normal takeoff from a hover;

(C)	Manually flown precision approach; and

(D)	Steep approach and landing to an off-airport site; or

(ii)	An approved course at a training center that includes all training and testing for that certificate or rating and is in compliance with paragraphs (i)(8) and (i)(9) of this section.

(8)	An applicant meeting only the requirements of paragraph (i)(7)(ii) of this section will be issued an additional rating or an airline transport pilot certificate with an additional rating, as applicable, with a limitation. The limitation shall state: "This certificate is subject to pilot-in-command limitations for the additional rating."

(9)	An applicant issued a pilot certificate with the limitation specified in paragraph (i)(8) of this section—

(i)	May not act as pilot in command of the aircraft for which an additional rating was obtained under the provisions of this section until the limitation is removed from the certificate; and

(ii)	May have the limitation removed by accomplishing 25 hours of supervised operating experience as pilot in command under the supervision of a qualified and current pilot in command, in the seat normally occupied by the pilot in command, in a powered-lift of the same type for which the limitation applies.

(j)	*Waiver authority.* Unless the Administrator requires certain or all tasks to be performed, the examiner who conducts the practical test for an airline transport pilot certificate may waive any of the tasks for which the Administrator approves waiver authority.

EXPLANATION

In giving the practical test, the FAA inspector or designated examiner is given wide discretion.

A sample curriculum is outlined in to AC 61-89D to AC 61-89E *Pilot Certificates: Aircraft Type Ratings* (2000) to assist in complying with §61.157.

Time in a flight simulator or flight training device can be credited in lieu of the required flight time towards meeting the total aeronautical experience or recency of experience, but it CANNOT be logged as flight time.

For an applicant applying for a type rating only, the Instructor's Recommendation section of FAA Form 8710-1, Airman Certificate and/or Rating Application, need not be signed.

(1)   If the applicant is applying for a type rating to be added to an ATP certificate or for the original issuance of an ATP certificate in an airplane requiring a type rating, the applicant must have an endorsement in the applicant's logbook or training records from an authorized instructor certifying satisfactory completion of the training required by §61.157(f).

(2)   If the applicant is applying for a type rating to be placed on a private or commercial pilot certificate, the airman must have an endorsement in the airman's logbook or training records from an authorized instructor certifying satisfactory completion of the training required by §61.63(d)(6).

The addition of a type rating is accomplished under §61.157 by a practical test for which no medical certificate is required.

CROSS REFERENCE

61.98, Flight Proficiency, Recreational Pilots; 61.107, Flight Proficiency, Private Pilots; 61.127, Flight Proficiency, Commercial Pilots; 61.153, Airline Transport Pilot: Eligibility and Requirements; 61.159, Aeronautical Experience: Airplane Category Rating; 61.187, Flight Proficiency, Flight Instructor.

ADVISORY CIRCULARS

AC 61-89E *Pilot Certificates: Aircraft Type Ratings* (2000).

61.159 AERONAUTICAL EXPERIENCE: AIRPLANE CATEGORY RATING

(a)   Except as provided in paragraphs (b), (c), and (d) of this section, a person who is applying for an airline transport pilot certificate with an airplane category and class rating must have at least 1,500 hours of total time as a pilot that includes at least:
(1)   500 hours of cross-country flight time.
(2)   100 hours of night flight time.
(3)   75 hours of instrument flight time, in actual or simulated instrument conditions, subject to the following:
(i)   Except as provided in paragraph (a)(3)(ii) of this section, an applicant may not receive credit for more than a total of 25 hours of simulated instrument time in a flight simulator or flight training device.

(ii) A maximum of 50 hours of training in a flight simulator or flight training device may be credited toward the instrument flight time requirements of paragraph (a)(3) of this section if the training was accomplished in a course conducted by a training center certificated under part 142 of this chapter.

(iii) Training in a flight simulator or flight training device must be accomplished in a flight simulator or flight training device, representing an airplane.

(4) 250 hours of flight time in an airplane as a pilot in command, or as second in command performing the duties of pilot in command while under the supervision of a pilot in command or any combination thereof, which includes at least—

(i) 100 hours of cross-country flight time; and

(ii) 25 hours of night flight time.

(5) Not more than 100 hours of the total aeronautical experience requirements of paragraph (a) of this section may be obtained in a flight simulator or flight training device that represents an airplane, provided the aeronautical experience was obtained in an approved course conducted by a training center certificated under part 142 of this chapter.

(b) A person who has performed at least 20 night takeoffs and landings to a full stop may substitute each additional night takeoff and landing to a full stop for 1 hour of night flight time to satisfy the requirements of paragraph (a)(2) of this section; however, not more than 25 hours of night flight time may be credited in this manner.

(c) A commercial pilot may credit the following second-in-command flight time or flight-engineer flight time toward the 1,500 hours of total time as a pilot required by paragraph (a) of this section:

(1) Second-in-command time, provided the time is acquired in an airplane—

(i) Required to have more than one pilot flight crewmember by the airplane's flight manual, type certificate, or the regulations under which the flight is being conducted;

(ii) Engaged in operations under part 121 or part 135 of this chapter for which a second in command is required; or

(iii) That is required by the operating rules of this chapter to have more than one pilot flight crewmember.

(2) Flight-engineer time, provided the time—

(i) Is acquired in an airplane required to have a flight engineer by the airplane's flight manual or type certificate;

(ii) Is acquired while engaged in operations under part 121 of this chapter for which a flight engineer is required;

(iii) Is acquired while the person is participating in a pilot training program approved under part 121 of this chapter; and

(iv) Does not exceed more than 1 hour for each 3 hours of flight engineer flight time for a total credited time of no more than 500 hours.

(d) An applicant may be issued an airline transport pilot certificate with the endorsement, "Holder does not meet the pilot in command aeronautical experience requirements of ICAO," as prescribed by Article 39 of the Convention on International Civil Aviation, if the applicant:

(1) Credits second-in-command or flight-engineer time under paragraph (c) this section toward the 1,500 hours total flight time requirement of paragraph (a) of this section;

(2) Does not have at least 1,200 hours of flight time as a pilot, including no more than 50 percent of his or her second-in-command time and none of his or her flight-engineer time; and

(3) Otherwise meets the requirements of paragraph (a) of this section.

(e)   When the applicant specified in paragraph (d) of this section presents satisfactory evidence of the accumulation of 1,200 hours of flight time as a pilot including no more than 50 percent of his or her second-in-command flight time and none of his or her flight-engineer time, the applicant is entitled to an airline transport pilot certificate without the endorsement prescribed in that paragraph.

EXPLANATION

Time in a flight simulator or flight training device can be credited in lieu of the required flight time towards meeting the total aeronautical experience or recency of experience, but it CANNOT be logged as flight time.

According to the *Frequently Asked Questions for 14 CFR Part 61*: As for what §61.159(d)(2) means where it states "Does not have at least 1,200 hours of flight time as a pilot, including no more than 50 percent of his or her second-in-command time and none of his or her flight-engineer time," the provision is no longer valid. It applies to an old ICAO ATP aeroplane aeronautical experience rule that changed in 1974. If §61.159(d) were written correctly, it should read as follows:

(d)   An applicant may be issued an airline transport pilot certificate with the endorsement, "Holder does not meet the pilot in command aeronautical experience requirements of ICAO," as prescribed by Article 39 of the Convention on International Civil Aviation, if an applicant does not meet the ICAO requirements contained in Annex 1 "Personnel Licensing" to the Convention on International Civil Aviation, but otherwise meets the aeronautical experience requirements of this section.

And if §61.159(e) were written correctly, it should read as follows:

(e)   An applicant is entitled to an airline transport pilot certificate without the ICAO endorsement specified in paragraph (d) of this section when that applicant presents satisfactory evidence of having met the ICAO requirements referred to in paragraph (d) of this section, and otherwise meets the aeronautical experience requirements of this section.

Therefore, §61.159(d) and (e) must be changed so that the FAA's ATP-airplane category aeronautical experience rule (i.e., §61.159) reflect the existing ICAO's ATP-aeroplane category requirements (i.e., paragraphs 2.5.1.3 and 2.1.9.2 of the Personnel Licensing, Annex 1, to the Convention on International Civil Aviation).

The FAA has initiated a direct final rulemaking project to correct this mistake in §61.159(d) and (e).

PREAMBLE

The FAA agrees with AOPA's arguments regarding the confusion produced by the phrase "in actual flight" and has deleted the word "actual." An incorrect reference to part 119 certificate holders was also eliminated. The FAA also agrees with AOPA's comment regarding safety pilots logging second in command time, and has added §61.159(c)(1)(iii), which permits a safety pilot to credit second in command time toward the total flight time requirements for an ATP certificate. In addition, the provisions of proposed §61.167(b) and (c) were placed in §61.159(d) and (e) in the final rule. Provisions for the use of flight simulators and flight training devices were also included as set forth in the final rule, Amendment No. 61-100. (62 FR 16272).

CROSS REFERENCES

61.51(f), Pilot Logbooks: Logging Second-In-Command Flight Time; 61.73, Military Pilots or Former Military Pilots: Special Rules.

ADVISORY CIRCULARS

AC 61-65D *Certification: Pilots and Flight and Ground Instructors* (1999).

61.161 AERONAUTICAL EXPERIENCE: ROTORCRAFT CATEGORY AND HELICOPTER CLASS RATING

(a) A person who is applying for an airline transport pilot certificate with a rotorcraft category and helicopter class rating, must have at least 1,200 hours of total time as a pilot that includes at least:

(1) 500 hours of cross-country flight time;

(2) 100 hours of night flight time, of which 15 hours are in helicopters;

(3) 200 hours of flight time in helicopters, which includes at least 75 hours as a pilot in command, or as second in command performing the duties of a pilot in command under the supervision of a pilot in command, or any combination thereof; and

(4) 75 hours of instrument flight time in actual or simulated instrument meteorological conditions, of which at least 50 hours are obtained in flight with at least 25 hours in helicopters as a pilot in command, or as second in command performing the duties of a pilot in command under the supervision of a pilot in command, or any combination thereof.

(b) Training in a flight simulator or flight training device may be credited toward the instrument flight time requirements of paragraph (a)(4) of this section, subject to the following:

(1) Training in a flight simulator or a flight training device must be accomplished in a flight simulator or flight training device that represents a rotorcraft.

(2) Except as provided in paragraph (b)(3) of this section, an applicant may receive credit for not more than a total of 25 hours of simulated instrument time in a flight simulator and flight training device.

(3) A maximum of 50 hours of training in a flight simulator or flight training device may be credited toward the instrument flight time requirements of paragraph (a)(4) of this section if the aeronautical experience is accomplished in an approved course conducted by a training center certificated under part 142 of this chapter.

CROSS REFERENCES

61.73, Military Pilots or Former Military Pilots: Special Rules.

ADVISORY CIRCULARS

AC 61-65D *Certification: Pilots and Flight and Ground Instructors* (1999).

FAA-H-8083-15 *Instrument Flying Handbook* (2001).

61.163 AERONAUTICAL EXPERIENCE: POWERED-LIFT CATEGORY RATING

(a) A person who is applying for an airline transport pilot certificate with a powered-lift category rating must have at least 1,500 hours of total time as a pilot that includes at least:

(1) 500 hours of cross-country flight time;

(2) 100 hours of night flight time;

(3) 250 hours in a powered-lift as a pilot in command, or as a second in command performing the duties of a pilot in command under the supervision of a pilot in command, or any combination thereof, which includes at least:

(i) 100 hours of cross-country flight time; and

(ii) 25 hours of night flight time.

(4) 75 hours of instrument flight time in actual or simulated instrument conditions, subject to the following:

(i) Except as provided in paragraph (a)(4)(ii) of this section, an applicant may not receive credit for more than a total of 25 hours of simulated instrument time in a flight simulator or flight training device.

(ii) A maximum of 50 hours of training in a flight simulator or flight training device may be credited toward the instrument flight time requirements of paragraph (a)(4) of this section if the training was accomplished in a course conducted by a training center certificated under part 142 of this chapter.

(iii) Training in a flight simulator or flight training device must be accomplished in a flight simulator or flight training device that represents a powered-lift.

(b) Not more than 100 hours of the total aeronautical experience requirements of paragraph (a) of this section may be obtained in a flight simulator or flight training device that represents a powered-lift, provided the aeronautical experience was obtained in an approved course conducted by a training center certificated under part 142 of this chapter.

EXPLANATION

This rule establishes the minimum experience requirements for the powered-lift ATP certificate tailored after the airplane ATP certificate.

PREAMBLE

In the final rule, the FAA removed the reference to "actual" flight and changed the section to include provisions for the use of approved flight simulators and flight training devices. (62 FR 16272).

61.165 ADDITIONAL AIRCRAFT CATEGORY AND CLASS RATINGS

(a) *Rotorcraft category and helicopter class rating.* A person applying for an airline transport certificate with a rotorcraft category and helicopter class rating who holds an airline transport pilot certificate with another aircraft category rating must:
- (1) Meet the eligibility requirements of §61.153 of this part;
- (2) Pass a knowledge test on the aeronautical knowledge areas of §61.155(c) of this part;
- (3) Comply with the requirements in §61.157(b) of this part, if appropriate;
- (4) Meet the applicable aeronautical experience requirements of §61.161 of this part; and
- (5) Pass the practical test on the areas of operation of §61.157(e)(4) of this part.

(b) *Airplane category rating with a single-engine class rating.* A person applying for an airline transport certificate with an airplane category and single-engine class rating who holds an airline transport pilot certificate with another aircraft category rating must:
- (1) Meet the eligibility requirements of §61.153 of this part;
- (2) Pass a knowledge test on the aeronautical knowledge areas of §61.155(c) of this part;
- (3) Comply with the requirements in §61.157(b) of this part, if appropriate;
- (4) Meet the applicable aeronautical experience requirements of §61.159 of this part; and
- (5) Pass the practical test on the areas of operation of §61.157(e)(1) of this part.

(c) *Airplane category rating with a multiengine class rating.* A person applying for an airline transport certificate with an airplane category and multiengine class rating who holds an airline transport certificate with another aircraft category rating must:
- (1) Meet the eligibility requirements of §61.153 of this part;
- (2) Pass a knowledge test on the aeronautical knowledge areas of §61.155(c) of this part;
- (3) Comply with the requirements in §61.157(b) of this part, if appropriate;
- (4) Meet the applicable aeronautical experience requirements of §61.159 of this part; and
- (5) Pass the practical test on the areas of operation of §61.157(e)(2) of this part.

(d) *Powered-lift category.* A person applying for an airline transport pilot certificate with a powered-lift category rating who holds an airline transport certificate with another aircraft category rating must:
- (1) Meet the eligibility requirements of §61.153 of this part;
- (2) Pass a required knowledge test on the aeronautical knowledge areas of §61.155(c) of this part;
- (3) Comply with the requirements in §61.157(b) of this part, if appropriate;
- (4) Meet the applicable aeronautical experience requirements of §61.163 of this part; and
- (5) Pass the required practical test on the areas of operation of §61.157(e)(3) of this part.

(e) *Additional class rating within the same aircraft category.* A person applying for an airline transport certificate with an additional class rating who holds an airline transport certificate in the same aircraft category must—
- (1) Meet the eligibility requirements of §61.153, except paragraph (f) of that section;
- (2) Comply with the requirements in §61.157(b) of this part, if applicable;
- (3) Meet the applicable aeronautical experience requirements of subpart C of this part; and
- (4) Pass a practical test on the areas of operation of §61.157(e) appropriate to the aircraft rating sought.

CROSS REFERENCES

61.51, Pilot Logbooks; 61.159 Aeronautical experience: Airplane category rating. 61.161 Aeronautical experience: Rotorcraft category and helicopter class rating; 61.163, Aeronautical Experience: Powered-lift Category Rating.

ADVISORY CIRCULARS

AC 61-65D *Certification: Pilots and Flight and Ground Instructors* (1999).

61.167 PRIVILEGES

(a) A person who holds an airline transport pilot certificate is entitled to the same privileges as those afforded a person who holds a commercial pilot certificate with an instrument rating.

(b) An airline transport pilot may instruct—

   (1) Other pilots in air transportation service in aircraft of the category, class, and type, as applicable, for which the airline transport pilot is rated and endorse the logbook or other training record of the person to whom training has been given;

   (2) In flight simulators, and flight training devices representing the aircraft referenced in paragraph (b)(1) of this section, when instructing under the provisions of this section and endorse the logbook or other training record of the person to whom training has been given;

   (3) Only as provided in this section, unless the airline transport pilot also holds a flight instructor certificate, in which case the holder may exercise the instructor privileges of subpart H of part 61 for which he or she is rated; and

   (4) In an aircraft, only if the aircraft has functioning dual controls, when instructing under the provisions of this section.

(c) Excluding briefings and debriefings, an airline transport pilot may not instruct in aircraft, flight simulators, and flight training devices under this section—

   (1) For more than 8 hours in any 24-consecutive-hour period; or

   (2) For more than 36 hours in any 7-consecutive-day period.

(d) An airline transport pilot may not instruct in Category II or Category III operations unless he or she has been trained and successfully tested under Category II or Category III operations, as applicable.

CROSS REFERENCES

61.133, Commercial Pilot Privileges and Limitations: General.

ADVISORY CIRCULARS

AC 61-65D *Certification: Pilots and Flight and Ground Instructors* (1999).

CASES

The provisions of 61.157(b)(1) and (2) allow an airline transport pilot to instruct in limited situations and to endorse the logbook or other training record of the person receiving the instruction. These are the only types of flight training endorsements an ATP can make. See the Cases under §61.59.

FAA CHIEF COUNSEL OPINIONS

An ATP who flies for a Part 121 air carrier may not give flight instruction under contract to individuals who are enrolled in a Part 141 pilot school, unless he/she is a CFI. The authorization to instruct is limited to instructing other pilots in air transportation service. Individuals who are enrolled in a Part 141 pilot school would not fall within that class. This opinion would be the same even if the school were a Part 141/121 school. (5-15-79).

INTENTIONALLY

LEFT

BLANK

SUBPART H — FLIGHT INSTRUCTORS

61.181 APPLICABILITY

This subpart prescribes the requirements for the issuance of flight instructor certificates and ratings, the conditions under which those certificates and ratings are necessary, and the limitations on those certificates and ratings.

CASES

In a situation where the flight instructor did not hold a medical certificate and therefore could not act as pilot in command, he was nevertheless held to be the pilot in command by the NTSB, and held in violation of §91.13, Careless or Reckless Operation. The instructor grabbed the yoke (too late), trying to avoid the crash. The NTSB held that grabbing the yoke was enough to make the CFI PIC. *Administrator v. Ridpath*, EA-3736 (1992).

61.183 ELIGIBILITY REQUIREMENTS

To be eligible for a flight instructor certificate or rating a person must:
(a) Be at least 18 years of age;
(b) Be able to read, speak, write, and understand the English language. If the applicant is unable to meet one of these requirements due to medical reasons, then the Administrator may place such operating limitations on that applicant's flight instructor certificate as are necessary;
(c) Hold either a commercial pilot certificate or airline transport pilot certificate with:
    (1) An aircraft category and class rating that is appropriate to the flight instructor rating sought; and
    (2) An instrument rating or privileges on that person's pilot certificate that are appropriate to the flight instructor rating sought, if applying for—
        (i) A flight instructor certificate with an airplane category and single-engine class rating;
        (ii) A flight instructor certificate with an airplane category and multiengine class rating;
        (iii) A flight instructor certificate with a powered-lift rating; or
        (iv) A flight instructor certificate with an instrument rating.
(d) Receive a logbook endorsement from an authorized instructor on the fundamentals of instructing listed in §61.185(a)(1) of this part appropriate to the required knowledge test;
(e) Pass a knowledge test on the areas listed in §61.185(a)(1) of this part, unless the applicant:
    (1) Holds a flight instructor certificate or ground instructor certificate issued under this part;
    (2) Holds a current teacher's certificate issued by a State, county, city, or municipality that authorizes the person to teach at an educational level of the 7th grade or higher; or
    (3) Is employed as a teacher at an accredited college or university.

(f) Pass a knowledge test on the aeronautical knowledge areas listed In §61.185(a)(2) and (a)(3) of this part that are appropriate to the flight instructor rating sought;

(g) Receive a logbook endorsement from an authorized instructor on the areas of operation listed in §61.187(b) of this part, appropriate to the flight instructor rating sought;

(h) Pass the required practical test that is appropriate to the flight instructor rating sought in an:

   (1) Aircraft that is representative of the category and class of aircraft for the aircraft rating sought; or

   (2) Flight simulator or flight training device that is representative of the category and class of aircraft for the rating sought, and used in accordance with an approved course at a training center certificated under part 142 of this chapter.

(i) Accomplish the following for a flight instructor certificate with an airplane or a glider rating:

   (1) Receive a logbook endorsement from an authorized instructor indicating that the applicant is competent and possesses instructional proficiency in stall awareness, spin entry, spins, and spin recovery procedures after providing the applicant with flight training in those training areas in an airplane or glider, as appropriate, that is certificated for spins; and

   (2) Demonstrate instructional proficiency in stall awareness, spin entry, spins, and spin recovery procedures. However, upon presentation of the endorsement specified in paragraph (i)(1) of this section an examiner may accept that endorsement as satisfactory evidence of instructional proficiency in stall awareness, spin entry, spins, and spin recovery procedures for the practical test, provided that the practical test is not a retest as a result of the applicant failing the previous test for deficiencies in the knowledge or skill of stall awareness, spin entry, spins, or spin recovery instructional procedures. If the retest is a result of deficiencies in the ability of an applicant to demonstrate knowledge or skill of stall awareness, spin entry, spins, or spin recovery instructional procedures, the examiner must test the person on stall awareness, spin entry, spins, and spin recovery instructional procedures in an airplane or glider, as appropriate, that is certificated for spins;

(j) Log at least 15 hours as pilot in command in the category and class of aircraft that is appropriate to the flight instructor rating sought; and

(k) Comply with the appropriate sections of this part that apply to the flight instructor rating sought.

EXPLANATION

If an applicant requires a retest on spin entry, spin, and spin recovery maneuvers after failing either the oral or flight portion of the practical test, merely obtaining additional training and a new logbook endorsement is not acceptable. The applicant must, on the retest, demonstrate spin entry, spin, and spin recovery maneuvers on the flight portion of the practical test.

The knowledge test may be taken when the applicant reaches the age of 16.

The requirements of §61.185 must be met prior to the taking of the knowledge test required by §61.183.

Except for medical reasons, there is no exception to the requirement that the applicant must be able to read, speak, write, and understand English.

PREAMBLE

The FAA concurs with the views of AOPA, HAI, and NAFI that requiring an applicant for a flight instructor certificate with a helicopter possess an instrument rating is unnecessary and burdensome. The FAA is therefore deleting this proposed requirement from the final rule. As the FAA has decided not to establish a flight instructor rating for airships, the proposed requirement that an applicant for a flight instructor rating for an airship possess an instrument rating has also been withdrawn. However, the FAA has decided that the proposal remains valid for powered-lift and instrument ratings. In response to SSA's comment regarding 15 hours of pilot-in-command experience in category and class for an additional flight instructor rating, the FAA notes that this is an existing requirement as found in §61.191(b). Additionally, the FAA revised the rule to permit an applicant to forego taking the knowledge test specified in §61.185(a) if certain equivalent conditions are met by the applicant. The FAA did not propose to change this requirement. Except for these changes and other editorial changes to include the use of flight simulators and flight training devices, the final rule is adopted as proposed. (62 FR 16273).

CROSS REFERENCES

61.185, Flight Instructors: Aeronautical Knowledge; 61.187, Flight Instructors: Flight Proficiency.

ADVISORY CIRCULARS

AC 61-67C *Stall and Spin Awareness Training* (2000).

CASES

Revocation of any flight instructor certificate is not necessary to preclude its use. Flight instructor certificates may not be used when a pilot certificate is under suspension, as flight instruction requires a valid pilot certificate. *Administrator v. Morse*, EA-3659 (1992).

61.185 AERONAUTICAL KNOWLEDGE

(a)   A person who is applying for a flight instructor certificate must receive and log ground training from an authorized instructor on:
    (1)   Except as provided in paragraph (b) of this section, the fundamentals of instructing, including:
        (i)   The learning process;
        (ii)   Elements of effective teaching;
        (iii)   Student evaluation and testing;
        (iv)   Course development;
        (v)   Lesson planning; and
        (vi)   Classroom training techniques.
    (2)   The aeronautical knowledge areas for a recreational, private, and commercial pilot certificate applicable to the aircraft category for which flight instructor privileges are sought; and
    (3)   The aeronautical knowledge areas for the instrument rating applicable to the category for which instrument flight instructor privileges are sought.

(b)   The following applicants do not need to comply with paragraph (a)(1) of this section:
   (1)   The holder of a flight instructor certificate or ground instructor certificate issued under this part;
   (2)   The holder of a current teacher's certificate issued by a State, county, city, or municipality that authorizes the person to teach at an educational level of the 7th grade or higher; or
   (3)   A person employed as a teacher at an accredited college or university.

PREAMBLE

The FAA agrees with NAFI's comment and has incorporated language in this section that excepts certain individuals, including certificated teachers, from meeting the requirements of paragraph (a) of this section. (62 FR 16273).

ADVISORY CIRCULARS

AC 61-23C *Pilot's Handbook of Aeronautical Knowledge* (1997).

AC 61-65D *Certification: Pilots and Flight and Ground Instructors* (1999).

FAA-H-8083-9 *Aviation Instructor's Handbook* (1999).

FAA-H-8083-15 *Instrument Flying Handbook* (2001).

61.187 FLIGHT PROFICIENCY

(a)   *General.* A person who is applying for a flight instructor certificate must receive and log flight and ground training from an authorized instructor on the areas of operation listed in this section that apply to the flight instructor rating sought. The applicant's logbook must contain an endorsement from an authorized instructor certifying that the person is proficient to pass a practical test on those areas of operation.
(b)   *Areas of operation.*
   (1)   *For an airplane category rating with a single-engine class rating:*
      (i)   Fundamentals of instructing;
      (ii)   Technical subject areas;
      (iii)   Preflight preparation;
      (iv)   Preflight lesson on a maneuver to be performed in flight;
      (v)   Preflight procedures;
      (vi)   Airport and seaplane base operations;
      (vii)   Takeoffs, landings, and go-arounds;
      (viii) Fundamentals of flight;
      (ix)   Performance maneuvers;
      (x)   Ground reference maneuvers;
      (xi)   Slow flight, stalls, and spins;
      (xii)   Basic instrument maneuvers;
      (xiii) Emergency operations; and
      (xiv)   Postflight procedures.

(2)   *For an airplane category rating with a multiengine class rating:*
   (i)   Fundamentals of instructing;
   (ii)   Technical subject areas;
   (iii) Preflight preparation;
   (iv) Preflight lesson on a maneuver to be performed in flight;
   (v)   Preflight procedures;
   (vi) Airport and seaplane base operations;
   (vii) Takeoffs, landings, and go-arounds;
   (viii) Fundamentals of flight;
   (ix) Performance maneuvers;
   (x)   Ground reference maneuvers;
   (xi) Slow flight and stalls;
   (xii) Basic instrument maneuvers;
   (xiii) Emergency operations;
   (xiv) Multiengine operations; and
   (xv) Postflight procedures.

(3)   For *a rotorcraft category rating with a helicopter class rating:*
   (i)   Fundamentals of instructing;
   (ii)   Technical subject areas;
   (iii) Preflight preparation;
   (iv) Preflight lesson on a maneuver to be performed in flight;
   (v)   Preflight procedures;
   (vi) Airport and heliport operations;
   (vii) Hovering maneuvers;
   (viii) Takeoffs, landings, and go-arounds;
   (ix) Fundamentals of flight;
   (x)   Performance maneuvers;
   (xi) Emergency operations;
   (xii) Special operations; and
   (xiii) Postflight procedures.

(4)   *For a* rotorcraft *category rating with a gyroplane class rating:*
   (i)   Fundamentals of instructing;
   (ii)   Technical subject areas;
   (iii) Preflight preparation;
   (iv) Preflight lesson on a maneuver to be performed in flight;
   (v)   Preflight procedures;
   (vi) Airport operations;
   (vii) Takeoffs, landings, and go-arounds;
   (viii) Fundamentals of flight;
   (ix) Performance maneuvers;
   (x)   Flight at slow airspeeds;
   (xi) Ground reference maneuvers;
   (xii) Emergency operations; and
   (xiii) Postflight procedures.

   (5)   *For a* powered-*lift category rating:*
      (i)   Fundamentals of instructing;
      (ii)   Technical subject areas;
      (iii) Preflight preparation;
      (iv) Preflight lesson on a maneuver to be performed in flight;
      (v)   Preflight procedures;
      (vi) Airport and heliport operations;
      (vii) Hovering maneuvers;
      (viii) Takeoffs, landings, and go-arounds;
      (ix) Fundamentals of flight;
      (x)   Performance maneuvers;
      (xi) Ground reference maneuvers;
      (xii) Slow flight and stalls;
      (xiii) Basic instrument maneuvers;
      (xiv) Emergency operations;
      (xv) Special operations; and
      (xvi) Postflight procedures.
   (6)   *For a glider category rating:*
      (i)   Fundamentals of instructing;
      (ii)   Technical subject areas;
      (iii) Preflight preparation;
      (iv) Preflight lesson on a maneuver to be performed in flight;
      (v)   Preflight procedures;
      (vi) Airport and gliderport operations;
      (vii) Launches, landings, and go-arounds;
      (viii) Fundamentals of flight;
      (ix) Performance speeds;
      (x)   Soaring techniques;
      (xi) Performance maneuvers;
      (xii) Slow flight, stalls, and spins;
      (xiii) Emergency operations; and
      (xiv) Postflight procedures.
   (7)   *For an* instrument *rating with the appropriate aircraft category and class rating:*
      (i)   Fundamentals of instructing;
      (ii)   Technical subject areas;
      (iii) Preflight preparation;
      (iv) Preflight lesson on a maneuver to be performed in flight;
      (v)   Air traffic control clearances and procedures;
      (vi) Flight by reference to instruments;
      (vii) Navigation aids;
      (viii) Instrument approach procedures;
      (ix) Emergency operations; and
      (x)   Postflight procedures.
(c)   The flight training required by this section may be accomplished:
   (1)   In an aircraft that is representative of the category and class of aircraft for the rating sought; or
   (2)   In a flight simulator or flight training device representative of the category and class of aircraft for the rating sought, and used in accordance with an approved course at a training center certificated under part 142 of this chapter.

EXPLANATION

While newly certificated flight instructors can provide the instruction required for additional flight instructor ratings, such a flight instructor could not provide instruction to a person seeking initial flight instructor certification.

The flight instructor providing the instruction under this section need not have held the flight instructor certificate continuously during the preceding 24 months, but must have held it sometime during that period.

Time in a flight simulator or flight training device can be credited in lieu of the required flight time towards meeting the total aeronautical experience or recency of experience, but it CANNOT be logged as flight time.

PREAMBLE

The FAA replaced existing flight proficiency requirements for certificates and ratings with general areas of operation. The FAA has decided not to adopt the proposal for separate powered and nonpowered glider class ratings, and therefore the final rule consolidates proposed glider areas of operation within one category. The final rule does not adopt the proposal for flight instructor certificates in the lighter-than-air category, therefore, the associated areas of operation have been deleted. Except for these changes, and other editorial changes to include the use of flight simulators and flight training devices, the final rule is adopted as proposed. (62 FR 16273 - 16274).

ADVISORY CIRCULARS

AC 61-67C *Stall and Spin Awareness Training* (2000).

61.189 FLIGHT INSTRUCTOR RECORDS

(a)   A flight instructor must sign the logbook of each person to whom that instructor has given flight training or ground training.
(b)   A flight instructor must maintain a record in a logbook or a separate document that contains the following:
    (1)   The name of each person whose logbook or student pilot certificate that instructor has endorsed for solo flight privileges, and the date of the endorsement; and
    (2)   The name of each person that instructor has endorsed for a knowledge test or practical test, and the record shall also indicate the kind of test, the date, and the results.
(c)   Each flight instructor must retain the records required by this section for at least 3 years.

EXPLANATION

Complete records are the best evidence of what you did and didn't do. In enforcement actions and lawsuits, good records can often win your case for you.

Always make sure that entries in the pilot's logbook and in your logbook clearly describe what instruction and/or endorsement was given.

PREAMBLE

The FAA acknowledges the concerns of AOPA regarding logbook entry requirements and the retention of test results, but points out that these are existing requirements. The FAA has withdrawn the proposal for flight instructors to follow a written syllabus; therefore, the record keeping requirements of this section pertaining to syllabuses have been eliminated. Apart from these and minor editorial changes, the final rule has been adopted as proposed. (62 FR 16274)

CROSS REFERENCES

61.51, Pilot Logbooks; 61.59, Falsification, Reproduction or Alteration of Applications, Certificates, Logbooks, Reports, or Records.

ADVISORY CIRCULARS

AC 61-65D *Certification: Pilots and Flight and Ground Instructors* (1999).

AC 61-98A *Currency and Additional Qualification Requirements for Certificated Pilots* (1991).

CASES

An instructor would have had to disregard the clear regulatory intent of §61.189 in signing for logged instruction which he had not personally provided. *Administrator v. Damsky*, 3 NTSB 543 (1977).

61.191 ADDITIONAL FLIGHT INSTRUCTOR RATINGS

(a) A person who applies for an additional flight instructor rating on a flight instructor certificate must meet the eligibility requirements listed in §61.183 of this part that apply to the flight instructor rating sought.

(b) A person who applies for an additional rating on a flight instructor certificate is not required to pass the knowledge test on the areas listed in §61.185(a)(1) of this part.

PREAMBLE

SSA's concerns are addressed in the FAA comments to proposed §61.183. With respect to HAI's concern, the FAA points out that the knowledge test requirements are incorporated into §61.183, and that §61.183(f) requires a flight instructor applicant to pass a knowledge test on the aeronautical knowledge areas listed in §61.185 (b) and (c) that are appropriate to the rating on the flight instructor certificate sought. The final rule is adopted as proposed. (62 FR 16274)

CROSS REFERENCES

61.63, Additional Aircraft Ratings (Other Than on an Airline Transport Pilot Certificate); 61.183, Flight Instructors: Eligibility Requirements.

ADVISORY CIRCULARS

AC 61-65D *Certification: Pilots and Flight and Ground Instructors* (1999).

AC 61-98A *Currency and Additional Qualification Requirements for Certificated Pilots* (1991).

61.193 FLIGHT INSTRUCTOR PRIVILEGES

A person who holds a flight instructor certificate is authorized within the limitations of that person's flight instructor certificate and ratings to give training and endorsements that are required for, and relate to:
(a)   A student pilot certificate;
(b)   A pilot certificate;
(c)   A flight instructor certificate;
(d)   A ground instructor certificate;
(e)   An aircraft rating;
(f)   An instrument rating;
(g)   A flight review, operating privilege, or recency of experience requirement of this part;
(h)   A practical test; and
(i)   A knowledge test.

61.195 FLIGHT INSTRUCTOR LIMITATIONS AND QUALIFICATIONS.

A person who holds a flight instructor certificate is subject to the following limitations:
(a)   *Hours of training.* In any 24-consecutive-hour period, a flight instructor may not conduct more than 8 hours of flight training.
(b)   *Aircraft ratings.* A flight instructor may not conduct flight training in any aircraft for which the flight instructor does not hold:
(1)   A pilot certificate and flight instructor certificate with the applicable category and class rating; and
(2)   If appropriate, a type rating.
(c)   *Instrument Rating.* A flight instructor who provides instrument flight training for the issuance of an instrument rating or a type rating not limited to VFR must hold an instrument rating on his or her flight instructor certificate and pilot certificate that is appropriate to the category and class of aircraft in which instrument training is being provided.
(d)   *Limitations on endorsements.* A flight instructor may not endorse a:
(1)   Student pilot's certificate or logbook for solo flight privileges, unless that flight instructor has—
(i)   Given that student the flight training required for solo flight privileges required by this part; and
(ii)   Determined that the student is prepared to conduct the flight safely under known circumstances, subject to any limitations listed in the student's logbook that the instructor considers necessary for the safety of the flight.
(2)   Student pilot's certificate and logbook for a solo cross-country flight, unless that flight instructor has determined the student's flight preparation, planning, equipment, and proposed procedures are adequate for the proposed flight under the existing conditions and within any limitations listed in the logbook that the instructor considers necessary for the safety of the flight;

    (3)   Student pilot's certificate and logbook for solo flight in a Class B airspace area or at an airport within Class B airspace unless that flight instructor has—

        (i)   Given that student ground and flight training in that Class B airspace or at that airport; and

        (ii)   Determined that the student is proficient to operate the aircraft safely.

    (4)   Logbook of a recreational pilot, unless that flight instructor has—

        (i)   Given that pilot the ground and flight training required by this part; and

        (ii)   Determined that the recreational pilot is proficient to operate the aircraft safely.

        (5)   Logbook of a pilot for a flight review, unless that instructor has conducted a review of that pilot in accordance with the requirements of §61.56(a) of this part; or

        (6)   Logbook of a pilot for an instrument proficiency check, unless that instructor has tested that pilot in accordance with the requirements of §61.57(d) of this part.

(e)   *Training in an aircraft that requires a type rating.* A flight instructor may not give flight training in an aircraft that requires the pilot in command to hold a type rating unless the flight instructor holds a type rating for that aircraft on his or her pilot certificate.

(f)   *Training received in a multiengine airplane, a helicopter, or a powered-lift.* A flight instructor may not give training required for the issuance of a certificate or rating in a multiengine airplane, a helicopter, or a powered-lift unless that flight instructor has at least 5 flight hours of pilot-in-command time in the specific make and model of multiengine airplane, helicopter, or powered-lift, as appropriate.

(g)   *Position in aircraft and required pilot stations for providing flight training.*

    (1)   A flight instructor must perform all training from in an aircraft that complies with the requirements of §91.109 of this chapter.

    (2)   A flight instructor who provides flight training for a pilot certificate or rating issued under this part must provide that flight training in an aircraft that meets the following requirements—

        (i)   The aircraft must have at least two pilot stations and be of the same category, class, and type, if appropriate, that applies to the pilot certificate or rating sought.

        (ii)   For single-place aircraft, the pre-solo flight training must have been provided in an aircraft that has two pilot stations and is of the same category, class, and type, if appropriate.

(h)   *Qualifications of the flight instructor for training first-time flight instructor applicants.*

    (1)   The ground training provided to an initial applicant for a flight instructor certificate must be given by an authorized instructor who—

        (i)   Holds a current ground or flight instructor certificate with the appropriate rating, has held that certificate for at least 24 months, and has given at least 40 hours of ground training; or

        (ii)   Holds a current ground or flight instructor certificate with the appropriate rating, and has given at least 100 hours of ground training in an FAA-approved course.

    (2)   Except for an instructor who meets the requirements of paragraph (h)(3)(ii) of this section, a flight instructor who provides training to an initial applicant for a flight instructor certificate must—

        (i)   Meet the eligibility requirements prescribed in §61.183 of this part;

        (ii)   Hold the appropriate flight instructor certificate and rating;

        (iii)   Have held a flight instructor certificate for at least 24 months;

        (iv)   For training in preparation for an airplane, rotorcraft, or powered-lift rating, have given at least 200 hours of flight training as a flight instructor; and

        (v)   For training in preparation for a glider rating, have given at least 80 hours of flight training as a flight instructor.

(3)   A flight instructor who serves as a flight instructor in an FAA-approved course for the issuance of a flight instructor rating must hold a current flight instructor certificate with the appropriate rating and pass the required initial and recurrent flight instructor proficiency tests, in accordance with the requirements of the part under which the FAA-approved course is conducted, and must—

     (i)   Meet the requirements of paragraph (h)(2) of this section; or

     (ii) Have trained and endorsed at least five applicants for a practical test for a pilot certificate, flight instructor certificate, ground instructor certificate, or an additional rating, and at least 80 percent of those applicants passed that test on their first attempt; and

        (A) Given at least 400 hours of flight training as a flight instructor for training in an airplane, a rotorcraft, or for a powered-lift rating; or

        (B) Given at least 100 hours of flight training as a flight instructor, for training in a glider rating.

(i)   *Prohibition against self-endorsements.* A flight instructor shall not make any self-endorsement for a certificate, rating, flight review, authorization, operating privilege, practical test, or knowledge test that is required by this part.

(j)   *Additional qualifications required to give training in Category II or Category III operations.* A flight instructor may not give training in Category II or Category III operations unless the flight instructor has been trained and tested in Category II or Category III operations, pursuant to §61.67 or §61.68 of this part, as applicable.

EXPLANATION

61.195(h) added another method for qualifying flight instructors who give training to initial CFI applicants in FAA-approved courses. This proposal will be relieving because the previous rule required CFI's to hold their certificates for 24 months **and** have given at least 200 hours of instruction. Under the new rule, if an instructor is instructing in a Part 141 school, and has given at least 400 hours (for powered aircraft and lower hour requirements for airships, gliders, and balloons) and that instructor will not have to wait for the entire 24 months to expire.

PREAMBLE

The objections of AOPA and HAI to the proposed flight instructor duty time limitations were reviewed. The FAA agrees, and has decided to delete the proposed wording "or any combination of commercial flying and flight training" in the final rule. The FAA acknowledges the objections of AOPA and NAFI to the existing and proposed 200-hour, 24-month experience requirements for instructors who train first time instructor applicants. The FAA did not propose changes to the provisions to the existing rule; therefore, AOPA and NAFI's recommendations are beyond the scope of this rulemaking.

Regarding SPA's comment to require 5 hours of experience as pilot in command in a seaplane or gyroplane for instructors providing flight training in these aircraft, the FAA did not propose this change in Notice No. 95-11; therefore, the recommended change is beyond the scope of this rulemaking. With respect to objections to the proposed dual control requirements, the FAA points out that throwover yokes are permitted for instrument instruction. The requirement for instruction in an aircraft with dual flight controls is an existing requirement in §91.109, and this rule merely incorporates that requirement into the provisions of this section. The FAA agrees with the commenter regarding the proposed rule's provisions that require all training to be given from a control seat. Therefore, the FAA has eliminated provisions from the rule that required a flight instructor to occupy a control seat when providing flight training. The FAA has concluded that operational requirements and accident/incident data do not establish a sufficient safety justification for this increased regulatory and economic burden. Regarding AOPA's comment on the proposal to require the use of aircraft with similar flight characteristics when providing presolo training to a pilot seeking solo flight privileges in a single-place aircraft, the FAA has determined that the proposed language is vague and has removed it in the final rule. In addition, the FAA replaced the phrase "pilot seats" with "pilot stations". The FAA made this change to accommodate balloon category aircraft, which do not have seats, and therefore make applicable all categories and classes of aircraft. In response to AOPA and GAMA, with respect to separate single-engine and multiengine flight instructor instrument ratings, the FAA has withdrawn the proposal. References to all flight instructor certificates that were proposed, but not adopted, have also been deleted. Additionally, paragraph (j) was added in accordance with provisions set forth in Amendment No. 61-100. Except for these changes, and various formatting and editing changes, the final rule is adopted as proposed. (62 FR 16275 - 16276)

CROSS REFERENCES

61.87, Solo Flight Requirements For Student Pilots: 61.93 Solo Cross-country Flight Requirements; 61.95, Operations in Class B Airspace and at Airports Located Within Class B Airspace; 61.101, Recreational Pilot Privileges and Limitations.

ADVISORY CIRCULARS

AC 61-65D *Certification: Pilots and Flight and Ground Instructors* (1999).

AC 61-98A *Currency and Additional Qualification Requirements for Certificated Pilots* (1991).

FAA CHIEF COUNSEL OPINIONS

If the simulated instrument time that a student pilot receives in order to qualify for the Private Pilot Certificate in accordance with §§61.109(a)(3), (b)(3), and (e)(3) is given by a CFI without the authorization to give instrument instruction, then that time may only be logged as instruction received time and it cannot be used to fulfill the requirements of another higher certificate or an instrument rating. A CFI, without instrument authorization, may give the flight training required in §§61.109(a)(3), (b)(3), and (e)(3) is not considered "instrument instruction." (8-7-97).

61.197 RENEWAL OF FLIGHT INSTRUCTOR CERTIFICATES

(a) A person who holds a flight instructor certificate that has not expired may renew that certificate by—
  (1) Passing a practical test for—
    (i) One of the ratings listed on the current flight instructor certificate; or
    (ii) An additional flight instructor rating; or
  (2) Presenting to an authorized FAA Flight Standards Inspector—
    (i) A record of training students showing that, during the preceding 24 calendar months, the flight instructor has endorsed at least five students for a practical test for a certificate or rating, and at least 80 percent of those students passed that test on the first attempt;
    (ii) A record showing that, within the preceding 24 calendar months, the flight instructor has served as a company check pilot, chief flight instructor, company check airman, or flight instructor in a Part 121 or Part 135 operation, or in a position involving the regular evaluation of pilots; or
    (iii) A graduation certificate showing that, within the preceding 3 calendar months, the person has successfully completed an approved flight instructor refresher course consisting of ground training or flight training, or a combination of both.
(b) The expiration month of a renewed flight instructor certificate shall be 24 calendar months from—
  (1) The month the renewal requirements of paragraph (a) of this section are accomplished; or
  (2) The month of expiration of the current flight instructor certificate provided—
    (i) The renewal requirements of paragraph (a) of this section are accomplished within the 3 calendar months preceding the expiration month of the current flight instructor certificate; and
    (ii) If the renewal is accomplished under paragraph (a)(2)(iii) of this section, the approved flight instructor refresher course must be completed within the 3 calendar months preceding the expiration month of the current flight instructor certificate.
(c) The practical test required by paragraph (a)(1) of this section may be accomplished in a flight simulator or flight training device if the test is accomplished pursuant to an approved course conducted by a training center certificated under part 142 of this chapter.

EXPLANATION

This regulation applies only to unexpired flight instructor certificates. Reinstatement of expired flight instructor certificates is regulated by §61.199.

According to the *Frequently Asked Questions for 14 CFR Part 61*: "An additional clarification change to §61.197 is coming in an upcoming final rule correction. In response to FAA management's desires, I have been directed to change §61.197 back to permitting a person to complete an approved flight instructor refresher clinic (FIRC) to renew their certificate, even if it was not completed within the "90 day window" but the new rule will still require that the flight instructor certificate to not have expired. As an example, the clarification change will permit a person who wants to attend a FIRC once a year, once a month, or once a week will be permitted to do so and be given a new expiration date."

PREAMBLE

The FAA points out that completion of a flight instructor refresher clinic will continue to remain a valid renewal option under this final rule, and that its completion may be used for any number of successive renewals. In response to AOPA and NAFI's objection to the removal of provisions that allow flight instructors to renew by demonstrating competence to the local FSDO, the FAA notes that it did not remove these provisions, and that they have been included in §61.197(a)(2). This paragraph lists what must be contained in an individual's record of instruction and establishes specific criteria upon which certificate renewal will be based. In response to the elimination of the term "pilot in command" from the proposed rule, the FAA notes that deletion of the term "comparable position" from proposed paragraph (b)(2) would continue to permit a pilot other than a "check airman" who is involved in the regular evaluation of pilots to renew a flight instructor certificate under that paragraph's provisions. (62 FR 16276).

1998 Preamble: Section 61.197 Renewal of flight instructor certificates. Section 61.197(a) permits a person to renew a current flight instructor certificate by passing a practical test or by presenting certain documentation to a FAA Flight Standards Inspector. A person may renew a current flight instructor certificate at any time with one exception. As adopted in the final rule, a person may renew a current flight instructor certificate through presentation of a graduation certificate from an approved flight instructor refresher course (FIRC) only if the FIRC was completed within the 90 days preceding the expiration of the current flight instructor certificate.

The FAA has revised paragraph (a)(2)(iii) to permit the renewal of a current flight instructor certificate at any time by presenting a graduation certificate demonstrating that the applicant has successfully completed an approved FIRC. The FAA notes, however, that if a flight instructor renews his or her flight instructor certificate more than 3 calendar months before the expiration of that certificate by presenting a graduation certificate from an FIRC, that course must have been completed within the 3 calendar months preceding the date of presentation of the graduation certificate to the Flight Standards Inspector. The FAA has replaced the "90 day" language with the phrase "3 calendar months" throughout §61.197 to facilitate the calculation of the relevant time periods. Section 61.197(b)(2) will provide that if renewal is sought within the 3 calendar months preceding the expiration month of the current flight instructor certificate through the presentation of an FIRC graduation certificate, the FIRC must have been completed within the 3 calendar months preceding the expiration month of the certificate.

In addition to the correction discussed above, the FAA has made other minor revisions to §61.197 to clarify the provisions of that section. The following discussion is provided to explain the provisions of §61.197 as adopted in this final rule.

Paragraph (a)(1)(i) has been revised to state that a person may renew a current flight instructor certificate by passing a practical test "for one of the ratings listed on the current flight instructor certificate." For example, if a flight instructor holds a current flight instructor certificate with single-engine airplane and multiengine airplane ratings, that instructor would be required to pass a practical test for only one of those ratings to be issued a new flight instructor certificate with both ratings. The previous language, which required the applicant to take a practical test "for renewal of the flight instructor certificate," may have given the impression that an applicant had to take a practical test for each of the ratings listed on the applicant's flight instructor certificate. This has never been the policy of the FAA and it was not the intention of the FAA to impose such a requirement when the final rule language was adopted.

Paragraph (a)(2)(ii) permits a person to renew their flight instructor certificate without accomplishing a practical test by presenting to an authorized FAA Flight Standards Inspector a record that shows that within the preceding 24 calendar months the flight instructor has served in a position involving the regular evaluation of pilots. The FAA offers the following examples of "a position involving the regular evaluation of pilots." A person who regularly determines whether pilots may use a fixed base operator's aircraft may be in a position involving the regular evaluation of pilots. A captain for a certificate holder operating under part 121 or part 135 may be in a position involving the regular evaluation of pilots. These individuals may renew their flight instructor's certificate under paragraph (a)(2)(ii) if the authorized FAA Flight Standards Inspector is acquainted with the duties and responsibilities of the applicant's position and the applicant has satisfactory knowledge of current pilot training, certification, and standards.

Paragraph (b)(1) has been revised to state the general rule that a current flight instructor certificate will be renewed for an additional 24 months from the month the person accomplishes any of the renewal requirements of paragraph (a). This provision allows a flight instructor to renew his or her flight instructor certificate at any time. The FAA notes that if renewal is accomplished through the presentation of a graduation certificate from an FIRC under paragraph (a)(2)(iii), the new expiration date will be calculated from the date the graduation certificate is presented to the Flight Standards Inspector rather than the date the FIRC is completed.

Paragraph (b)(2) allows a person who accomplishes any of the renewal requirements of paragraph (a) in the 3 calendar months preceding the expiration month of the person's current flight instructor certificate to renew their certificate for an additional 24 months from the month of expiration of the current flight instructor certificate. However, as previously noted, if renewal is accomplished under paragraph (b)(2) through the presentation of a graduation certificate from an FIRC, that course must have been completed within the 3 calendar months preceding the expiration month of the current flight instructor certificate. For example, if a person whose current flight instructor certificate expires on May 31, 1998, seeks to renew his or her certificate through presentation of a graduation certificate from an FIRC and obtain a new expiration date of May 31, 2000, that person must complete the FIRC and present the graduation certificate to the Flight Standards Inspector on or after February 1, 1998. The 3-calendar-month window is computed from the first day of the expiration month rather than the last day of the expiration month of the current flight instructor certificate. Therefore, if a person's flight instructor certificate expires on May 31, 1998, the 3-calendar-month window is computed from May 1, 1998. (63 FR 20282).

CROSS REFERENCES

61.19, Duration of Pilot and Flight Instructor Certificates; 61.199, Expired Flight Instructor Certificates and Ratings; 141.79, Flight Training.

ADVISORY CIRCULARS

AC 61-65D *Certification: Pilots and Flight and Ground Instructors* (1999).

AC 61-98A *Currency and Additional Qualification Requirements for Certificated Pilots* (1991).

CASES

The Board upheld the suspension of a pilot's flight instructor certificate pending a successful reexamination of her qualifications. As justification for denying the respondent's appeal the Board stated that the Administrator has the authority to question an instructor's qualifications if any one of their students fail a test they were endorsed to take by that instructor. It is therefore not unreasonable to ask an instructor, who trained only 57 percent of her students adequately enough for them to pass the particular test on the first attempt, to submit to a reexamination. *Administrator v. Maitland*, EA-4878 (2001)

61.199 EXPIRED FLIGHT INSTRUCTOR CERTIFICATES AND RATINGS

(a) *Flight instructor certificates.* The holder of an expired flight instructor certificate may exchange that certificate for a new certificate with the same ratings by passing a practical test prescribed in §61.183(h) of this part for one of the ratings listed on the expired flight instructor certificate.
(b) *Flight instructor ratings.*
    (1) A flight instructor rating or a limited flight instructor rating on a pilot certificate is no longer valid and may not be exchanged for a similar rating or a flight instructor certificate.
    (2) The holder of a flight instructor rating or a limited flight instructor rating on a pilot certificate may be issued a flight instructor certificate with the current ratings, but only if the person passes the required knowledge and practical test prescribed in this subpart for the issuance of the current flight instructor certificate and rating.

EXPLANATION

This regulation applies to expired flight instructor certificates, while §61.197 applies to flight instructor certificates which have not yet expired.

PREAMBLE

1998 revision: The FAA has revised §61.199 to clarify that a flight instructor who holds an expired flight instructor certificate may exchange that certificate for a new flight instructor certificate with the same ratings by passing a practical test as required in §61.183(h) for only one of the ratings listed on the expired certificate. Section 61.199 previously did not require a flight instructor who held an expired flight instructor certificate to pass a practical test for each rating listed on that certificate and the FAA did not intend to impose such a requirement when it revised that section [in 1997]. (63 FR 20282).

CROSS REFERENCES

61.19, Duration of Pilot and Flight Instructor Certificates; 61.183, Eligibility Requirements; 61.185, Aeronautical Knowledge; 61.187, Flight Proficiency; 61.197, Renewal of Flight Instructor Certificates.

ADVISORY CIRCULARS

AC 61-65D *Certification: Pilots and Flight and Ground Instructors* (1999).

AC 61-98A *Currency and Additional Qualification Requirements for Certificated Pilots* (1991).

INTENTIONALLY

LEFT

BLANK

INTENTIONALLY

LEFT

BLANK

SUBPART I — GROUND INSTRUCTORS

61.211 APPLICABILITY

This subpart prescribes the requirements for the issuance of ground instructor certificates and ratings, the conditions under which those certificates and ratings are necessary, and the limitations upon those certificates and ratings.

61.213 ELIGIBILITY REQUIREMENTS

(a) To be eligible for a ground instructor certificate or rating a person must:
   (1) Be at least 18 years of age;
   (2) Be able to read, write, speak, and understand the English language. If the applicant is unable to meet one of these requirements due to medical reasons, then the Administrator may place such operating limitations on that applicant's ground instructor certificate as are necessary,
   (3) Except as provided in paragraph (b) of this section, pass a knowledge test on the fundamentals of instructing to include—
      (i) The learning process;
      (ii) Elements of effective teaching;
      (iii) Student evaluation and testing;
      (iv) Course development;
      (v) Lesson planning; and
      (vi) Classroom training techniques.
   (4) Pass a knowledge test on the aeronautical knowledge areas in—
      (i) For a basic ground instructor rating, §§61.97 and 61.105;
      (ii) For an advanced ground instructor rating, §§61.97, 61.105, 61.125, and 61.155; and
      (iii) For an instrument ground instructor rating, §61.65.
(b) The knowledge test specified in paragraph (a)(3) of this section is not required if the applicant:
   (1) Holds a ground instructor certificate or flight instructor certificate issued under this part;
   (2) Holds a current teacher's certificate issued by a State, county, city, or municipality that authorizes the person to teach at an educational level of the 7th grade or higher; or
   (3) Is employed as a teacher at an accredited college or university.

EXPLANATION

The 1997 amendment removes FAR Part 143-Ground Instructors. Ground instructor certification has been incorporated into Part 61, in the new Subpart I-Ground Instructors.

PREAMBLE

The FAA is adopting the proposal to move the ground instructor requirements to part 61. However, the FAA is not adopting the category-specific ground instructor certificates as discussed in the analysis of §61.5(d). Therefore, this subpart has been rewritten to restore the existing basic, advanced, and instrument ground instructor ratings. The proposed sections on aeronautical knowledge, ground instructor proficiency, ground instructor records, additional ground instructor ratings, ground instructor endorsements and authorizations, recency of experience for the holder of a ground instructor certificate, and conversion to current system of ground instructor ratings are not adopted in the final rule. Therefore, a section-by-section analysis of those proposals is not included.

In response to commenters' concerns regarding the English language requirements, the FAA has added language to §61.213(a)(2) providing that if an applicant is unable to meet one of the English language proficiency requirements for medical reasons, the Administrator may place operating limitations on the applicant's pilot certificate that are necessary for the safe operation of the aircraft.

This subpart reflects existing requirements with editorial and format changes to clarify the privileges and limitations of the ground instructor ratings, and to permit a seamless integration of part 143 into part 61. (62 FR 16277)

61.215 GROUND INSTRUCTOR PRIVILEGES

(a)   A person who holds a basic ground instructor rating is authorized to provide:
  (1)   Ground training in the aeronautical knowledge areas required for the issuance of a recreational pilot certificate, private pilot certificate, or associated ratings under this part;
  (2)   Ground training required for a recreational pilot and private pilot flight review; and
  (3)   A recommendation for a knowledge test required for the issuance of a recreational pilot certificate or private pilot certificate under this part.
(b)   A person who holds an advanced ground instructor rating is authorized to provide:
  (1)   Ground training in the aeronautical knowledge areas required for the issuance of any certificate or rating under this part;
  (2)   Ground training required for any flight review; and
  (3)   A recommendation for a knowledge test required for the issuance of any certificate under this part.
(c)   A person who holds an instrument ground instructor rating is authorized to provide:
  (1)   Ground training in the aeronautical knowledge areas required for the issuance of an instrument rating under this part;
  (2)   Ground training required for an instrument proficiency check; and
  (3)   A recommendation for a knowledge test required for the issuance of an instrument rating under this part.
(d)   A person who holds a ground instructor certificate is authorized, within the limitations of the ratings on the ground instructor certificate, to endorse the logbook or other training record of a person to whom the holder has provided the training or recommendation specified in paragraphs (a) through (c) this section.

EXPLANATION

According to the *Frequently Asked Questions for 14 CFR Part 61*: "The knowledge test for the Advanced Ground Instructor rating does not adequately cover the areas for Instrument privileges. However, 61.215(b)(1) states that an Advanced Ground Instructor may provide training 'required for the issuance of any certificate or rating under this part.' This was a mistake in the wording of the final rule, but there is a draft NPRM under review that revises back the privileges for the Advanced Ground Instructor rating that will only allow ground instructors with the Advanced rating to provide ground training that exclude the training required for an instrument rating."

CROSS REFERENCE

61.193, Flight Instructor Privileges.

61.217 RECENT EXPERIENCE REQUIREMENTS

The holder of a ground instructor certificate may not perform the duties of a ground instructor unless, within the preceding 12 months:

(a)   The person has served for at least 3 months as a ground instructor; or

(b)   The person has received an endorsement from an authorized ground or flight instructor certifying that the person has demonstrated satisfactory proficiency in the subject areas prescribed in §61.213(a)(3) and (a)(4), as applicable.

INTENTIONALLY

LEFT

BLANK

FEDERAL AVIATION REGULATIONS

PART 91 GENERAL OPERATING AND FLIGHT RULES

TABLE OF CONTENTS

SUBPART A — GENERAL

SUBPART B — FLIGHT RULES
GENERAL

TABLE OF CONTENTS

SUBPART B — FLIGHT RULES (Continued)

VISUAL FLIGHT RULES

INSTRUMENT FLIGHT RULES

TABLE OF CONTENTS

SUBPART B — INSTRUMENT FLIGHT RULES (Continued)

SUBPART C — EQUIPMENT, INSTRUMENT, AND CERTIFICATE REQUIREMENTS

TABLE OF CONTENTS

SUBPART D — SPECIAL FLIGHT OPERATIONS

SUBPART E — MAINTENANCE, PREVENTIVE MAINTENANCE, AND ALTERATIONS

TABLE OF CONTENTS

SUBPART F — LARGE AND TURBINE-POWERED MULTIENGINE AIRPLANES

SUBPART G — ADDITIONAL EQUIPMENT AND OPERATING REQUIREMENTS FOR LARGE AND TRANSPORT CATEGORY AIRCRAFT

TABLE OF CONTENTS

SUBPART H — FOREIGN AIRCRAFT OPERATIONS AND OPERATIONS OF U.S.-REGISTERED CIVIL AIRCRAFT OUTSIDE OF THE UNITED STATES

SUBPART I — OPERATING NOISE LIMITS

TABLE OF CONTENTS

SUBPART I — OPERATING NOISE LIMITS (Continued)

SUBPART J — WAIVERS

INTENTIONALLY

LEFT

BLANK

SUBPART A — GENERAL

91.1 APPLICABILITY

(a)   Except as provided in paragraph (b) and (c) of this section and §§91.701 and 91.703, this part prescribes rules governing the operation of aircraft (other than moored balloons, kites, unmanned rockets, and unmanned free balloons, which are governed by part 101 of this chapter, and ultralight vehicles operated in accordance with part 103 of this chapter) within the United States, including the waters within 3 nautical miles of the U.S. coast.

(b)   Each person operating an aircraft in the airspace overlying the waters between 3 and 12 nautical miles from the coast of the United States shall comply with §§91.1 through 91.21; §§91.101 through 91.143; §§91.151 through 91.159; §§91.167 through 91.193; §§91.203; §91.205; §§91.209 through 91.217; §91.221; §§91.303 through 91.319; §91.323; §91.605; §91.609; §§91.703 through 91.715; and 91.903.

(c)   This part applies to each person on board an aircraft being operated under this part, unless otherwise specified.

91.3 RESPONSIBILITY AND AUTHORITY OF THE PILOT IN COMMAND

(a)   The pilot in command of an aircraft is directly responsible for, and is the final authority as to, the operation of that aircraft.

(b)   In an in-flight emergency requiring immediate action, the pilot in command may deviate from any rule of this part to the extent required to meet that emergency.

(c)   Each pilot in command who deviates from a rule under paragraph (b) of this section shall, upon the request of the Administrator, send a written report of that deviation to the Administrator.

EXPLANATION

91.3(a): This subsection must be read in conjunction with the following "emergency authority" subsection of 91.3. A pilot may not exercise his or her "final authority" over the aircraft to deviate from a regulation or controller's instruction unless there is a pressing safety related reason for doing so. This subsection is the basis for the FAA taking action against the pilot in command in the event there is a violation of the FARs relating to the operation of the aircraft. CAUTION: when flying with another pilot, always agree on who will be the pilot in command before the flight begins.

91.3(b): The AIM succinctly points out that "pilots who become apprehensive for their safety for **any** reason should **request assistance immediately** . . . . Delay has caused accidents and cost lives" (AIM Para. 6-1-2). Although the NTSB has routinely found that pilots may not be excused for violating the regulations in an emergency of their own making, pilots should worry about the possible legal consequences of admitting a mistake **after** they have safely landed. If the emergency authority of FAR 91.3(b) is used to deviate from the provisions of an ATC clearance, the pilot in command must notify ATC as soon as possible and obtain an amended clearance (AIM Para. 6-1-1). Unless deviation is necessary under the emergency authority of FAR 91.3, pilots of IFR flights experiencing two-way radio communications failure are expected to adhere to the procedures prescribed under FAR 91.185 (AIM Para. 6-1-1).

91.3(c): If the FAA requests a written report, the pilot will be advised what information is required and to whom it should be sent.

CROSS REFERENCES

Previous designation: 91.3. See 1.1 for definition of "pilot in command."

ADVISORY CIRCULARS

AC 61-23C *Pilot's Handbook of Aeronautical Knowledge* (1997), "Emergency Procedures."

AERONAUTICAL INFORMATION MANUAL

Clearance, Para. 4-4-1;
Pilot/Controller Roles and Responsibilities: General, Para. 5-5-1;
References to "emergency procedures", Para. 6-1-1 through 6-4-3.

CASES

91.3(a): This provision is general in nature and must give way to the specific requirements of [91.123 Compliance with ATC clearances and instructions] and [91.129 Operation at Airports with Operating Control Towers]. *Administrator v. Hayes*, 3 NTSB 236 (1977).

91.3(b): Deviating from an ATC clearance to avoid a collision constitutes emergency action under 91.3(b). *Administrator v. Owen*, 3 NTSB 854 (1977).

The exculpatory effect of 91.3(b) comes into play only when the IFR weather conditions in which a VFR pilot finds himself were unforeseeable and not avoidable by the exercise of sound judgment before and during the flight. *Administrator v. Hollis*, 2 NTSB 43 (1973).

An example of unforeseen IFR conditions which were not avoidable by the exercise of sound judgment before and during the flight. *Administrator v. Spradlin*, 7 NTSB 268 (1990).

A pilot is not excused under 91.3(b) because of a passenger's need for immediate medical attention. *Administrator v. Chritten*, Jr., 5 NTSB 2444 (1987).

When a pilot reacts to a passenger who is in sudden pain (passenger spilled coffee on self and the pilot's attention is diverted so that he exceeds his assigned altitude, he should not be held accountable under the regulations. *Administrator v. Mew*, 6 NTSB 980 (1989).

The fact that a pilot does not formally declare an emergency on his radio does not preclude reliance on 91.3(b) as a defense. *Administrator v. Clark*, 2 NTSB 2015 (1973).

FAA CHIEF COUNSEL OPINIONS

While the type of emergency contemplated by this section generally relates to safety of flight of the aircraft involved, it has, in a few instances, also been used where life or death situations existed outside the aircraft, e.g. in a rescue mission. (10-29-79).

When a pilot, who is also a CFI, flies with another appropriately rated pilot who has been designated or agrees to act as pilot in command for that flight, only the pilot actually acting as PIC has the responsibility specified in §91.3. The fact that a pilot is a CFI does not automatically impose this responsibility on him. (8-30-77).

The pilot in command of an aircraft has the authority to reject an ATC clearance or instruction that would compromise the safe operation of that aircraft. A pilot unable to comply with an ATC clearance may have been encountering icing, turbulence, or equipment problems, and is not expected to comply until he or she states that they are able by accepting the clearance.

A clearance is legally amended when after being verbally issued by ATC, it is replied to by the pilot. The pilot alone holds the responsibility to determine if he or she is able to accept the amended clearance. If the pilot expresses his or her inability to comply, the controller would await further communications from the pilot indicating the ability to execute the clearance. (7-28-99).

91.5 PILOT IN COMMAND OF AIRCRAFT REQUIRING MORE THAN ONE REQUIRED PILOT

No person may operate an aircraft that is type certificated for more than one required pilot flight crewmember unless the pilot in command meets the requirements of §61.58 of this chapter.

EXPLANATION

Self explanatory, but it fails to note the requirement for co-pilot training found in 61.55.

CROSS REFERENCES

Previous designation: 91.4. 61.58 Pilot-In-Command Proficiency Check: Operation of Aircraft Requiring More Than One Required Pilot; 61.55 Second-In-Command Qualifications. See 1.1 for definitions of "Operate" and "pilot in command."

91.7 CIVIL AIRCRAFT AIRWORTHINESS

(a) No person may operate a civil aircraft unless it is in an airworthy condition.
(b) The pilot in command of a civil aircraft is responsible for determining whether that aircraft is in condition for safe flight. The pilot in command shall discontinue the flight when unairworthy mechanical, electrical, or structural conditions occur.

EXPLANATION

91.7(a): The terms "person" and "operate" give the FAA the power to sanction not only the pilot of an unairworthy aircraft, but also the business or individual who authorizes the use of an unairworthy aircraft.

91.7(b): This subsection **does not** give the pilot in command the authority to overrule a mechanic's determination that an aircraft is unairworthy. Flyability should not be equated with airworthiness. The term "airworthy" comprises two different concepts, both requisite to the airworthiness of an aircraft. These are (1) that the aircraft conforms to a type design approved under a type certificate or supplemental type certificate and to applicable Airworthiness Directives; and (2) that the aircraft must be in condition for safe operation. Discretion is the better part of valor: check with a mechanic anytime you discover damage to an aircraft.

CROSS REFERENCES

Previous designation: 91.29. 91.9 Civil Aircraft Flight Manual, Marking, and Placard Requirements; Part 39 Airworthiness Directives; Part 43 Maintenance, Preventive Maintenance, Rebuilding, and Alteration; FAR 91 Subpart E Maintenance, Preventive Maintenance, and Alterations; 91.205 Powered Civil Aircraft with Standard Category U.S. Airworthiness Certificates: Instrument and Equipment Requirements; 91.213 Inoperative Instruments and Equipment; 91.403(a) General; 91.405 Maintenance Required; See 1.1 for definitions of "pilot in command," "operate," and "person."

ADVISORY CIRCULARS

AC 91-67 *Minimum Equipment Requirements For General Aviation Operations Under FAR Part 91* (1991).

CASES

A pilot believed that a STC for autogas issued to the EAA permitted the use of autogas in his airplane. The STC lists engine models, including the engine installed in his airplane. However, the STC also provides that the aircraft model must be approved by the FAA to ensure that the fuel system is compatible with autogas. The pilot received a five day certificate suspension. *Administrator v. Patenaude*, EA-4098 (1994).

While taxiing aircraft to parking area, a propeller blade hit a cable and was damaged. Even though the pilot was advised not to fly the aircraft, he did so and the flight was accomplished without incident. The court, in sustaining the finding by the NTSB of violations of Section 135.65(b) and 91.29(a) (now 91.7(a)), held that the statutory requirement of airworthiness (49 U.S.C. App. §1423) does not mean flyability. *Copsey v. NTSB*, 993 F.2d 736 (10th Cir. 1993).

To establish a violation of 91.7(a), it must be shown that the airman operated an aircraft he knew or reasonably should have known was not airworthy. *Administrator v. Bernstein*, EA-4112 (1994).

The Board affirmed the revocation of an air carrier's operating certificate, and the ATP of it's president for violations of §91.7 (among others) due to fraudulent recordkeeping which resulted in the operation of unairworthy aircraft. *Administrator v. Air San Juan*, EA-3567 (1992).

A helicopter pilot's ATP certificate was revoked after he took off in a twin engine helicopter with one engine shut down. *Administrator v. Robinson*, EA-4052 (1993).

Although the pilot in command is ultimately responsible for determining whether an aircraft is safe for flight, the pilot is not in a position to override the opinion of an expert in aircraft maintenance who specifically states that "this engine is not airworthy." *Administrator v. Yarsley*, 6 NTSB 524 (1988).

Flyability should not be equated with airworthiness. *Administrator v. Bakeeff*, 3 NTSB 2765 (1980).

The statement in the regulation that the pilot shall discontinue the flight is mandatory; while it does not mean that the flight must plummet out of the air and land at the nearest grass strip, the flight should be discontinued at the first available point consistent with the safe operation of the aircraft. *Administrator v. Genereaux*, 4 NTSB 1245 (1984).

Because airworthiness decisions may require judgmental ability based on a level of mechanical expertise not ordinarily demanded of pilots, the standard for accountability under the regulation is whether a reasonable and prudent pilot would have concluded that a specific condition rendered a craft unairworthy, not whether an aviation mechanic would have so concluded. *Administrator v. Parker*, 3 NTSB 3005 (1980).

A pilot can **always** avoid liability for a violation [of 91.7] by obtaining a qualified opinion on airworthiness before an operation. *Administrator v. Parker*, 3 NTSB 3005 (1980).

The term "airworthy" comprises two different concepts, both requisite to the airworthiness of an aircraft. These are (1) that the aircraft conforms to a type design approved under a type certificate or supplemental type certificate and to applicable Airworthiness Directives; and (2) that the aircraft must be in condition for safe operation. *Administrator v. Doppes*, 5 NTSB 50 (1985).
An aircraft is unairworthy when an applicable Airworthiness Directive (AD) has not been accomplished. *Administrator v. Muscatine Flying Service, Inc. & Loel K. Letts*, 5 NTSB 1785 (1987).

A pilot who failed to notice duct tape over pitot tubes and static ports on preflight violated [91.7]. *Administrator v. Bell*, 5 NTSB 501 (1985).

A pilot who began to land gear-up on a short gravel runway decided to continue on to an airport 43 miles away in order to have longer runways and emergency services available, despite the fact that he had damaged the airplanes propellers and flaps. The NTSB upheld the FAA's charge that the pilot violated 91.13(a), but dismissed the FAA's charge that the decision to continue the flight violated 91.7(b). *Administrator v. Gordon*, EA-4329 (1995).

The NTSB dismissed a complaint against a pilot under FAR 91.7. Among other things, the FAA alleged that an aircraft is not airworthy if its flight manual does not contain a permanent revision control page. *Administrator v. Frost*, EA-4680 (1998).

The Board upheld the finding against two separate first officers who failed to notice during their preflight inspection that all of the screws securing the lower forward portion of the cowling were missing. *Administrator v. Crissey and Pittet*, EA-4749 (1999).

In the case where a check airman failed to report that engine temperatures were exceeded during a stall recovery and subsequently flew the aircraft on to several other destinations, the Board reinstated the order of revocation sought by the Administrator. The unintended stall occurred during an airline flight with (screaming) passengers aboard. *Administrator v. Carter*, EA-4765 (1999).

If a special flight permit (SFP) is issued with the restriction that only "essential flight crew" can be aboard, a certificated mechanic cannot ride along even if the reasoning behind the SFP is to get the aircraft to a maintenance base for work to be done. *Administrator v. Barrie*, EA-4801 (1999).

A 30-day suspension was imposed on a pilot's airman certificates after he operated an out of service autopilot in-flight for several legs of a flight on the premise that he was functionally testing the system. *Administrator v. Shorter*, EA-4805 (1999).

A pilot's ATP certificate was revoked when he decided to continue a flight to its destination at an altitude which required emergency oxygen for passengers in case of a depressurization after that supply of oxygen had been used when the masks deployed earlier in the flight. *Administrator v. Reese*, EA-4896 (2001). The first officer's ATP certificate was suspended for 4 months. *Administrator v. Danet*, EA-4902 (2001).

The owner/operator of a flight school was assessed a civil penalty of $750 for sending a flight instructor, who happened to be an A&P, out to inspect and fix an aircraft that had just had a propeller strike. The employee was neither qualified to perform major repairs on a propeller, nor provided with the proper tools, manuals, or other approved information to inspect or repair the aircraft. Therefore, he should not have been authorized by the owner/operator to make a decision on airworthiness that led to the decision to fly the aircraft in an unairworthy condition. *FAA v. Gatewood*, FAA Order No. 2001-1 (5-16-2001).

Allowing an aircraft to be repeatedly operated with open discrepancies that could have easily been corrected by following the manufacturer's service bulletin and using the provided kit resulted in the operator being fined $7,500. Because one of the discrepancies listed that the left fuel gauge was "stuck" the operator was also in violation of §91.205(a) and (b)(9). *FAA v. General Aviation, Inc.*, FAA Order No. 98-18 (10-9-1998).

A Part 135 certificate holder operated a helicopter 400 hours beyond the mandatory replacement time for a life-limited part. The law judge held that the certificate holder was responsible for the actions of its employees who certified that the aircraft was airworthy after the replacement time had been passed. The certificate holder was fined $7,000. *FAA v. Pacific Aviation International, Inc.*, FAA Order No. 97-8 (2-20-1997).

A $3,000 penalty was imposed on an aircraft owner whose maintenance records failed to reveal that he had complied with an applicable Airworthiness Directive that required visual inspections of the aircraft's cabin heater shroud. *FAA v. Northwest Aircraft Rental*, FAA Order No. 94-4 (3-10-1994).

On appeal the law judge upheld a penalty of $6,000 for violations of §§91.7, 91.405, and 91.407 (formerly §§91.29, 91.167, and 91.165) where a pilot, who had been advised by an FAA Inspector that his aircraft was in a dangerous condition, flew the aircraft after a gear up landing. The law judge rejected the pilot's claim of financial hardship. *FAA v. Costello*, FAA Order No. 93-10 (3-25-1993).

A Part 135 certificate holder operated an aircraft 46 times after the time for conducting a radiographic inspection, required by an Airworthiness Directive, had passed. On appeal the original $3,000 penalty was increased only to $10,000 instead of the $25,000 penalty sought by the FAA. The law judge ruled that $3,000 was too low for such a violation, but in light of the fact that the operator was relying on a certificated maintenance facility to keep its aircraft in an airworthy condition the $25,000 penalty was excessive. *FAA v. Flight Unlimited, Inc.*, FAA Order No. 92-10 (2-6-1992).

A civil penalty of $1,400 was imposed on an operator who allowed an aircraft to be flown when it had exceeded certain time intervals where maintenance was required that had not been performed. Operators must select and adhere to a method of determining the time in operation in order to comply with maintenance requirements. If the operator has been using tachometer time for this purpose, it cannot later assert as a defense for not complying with maintenance requirements that it was not required to perform certain maintenance because its tachometer was inaccurate. *FAA v. Watts Agricultural Aviation, Inc.*, FAA Order No. 91-8 (4-11-1991).

FAA CHIEF COUNSEL OPINIONS

There is no inconsistency between [91.7(b)] and [91.403(a)], which makes the owner or operator primarily responsible for maintaining an aircraft in an airworthy condition. (6-10-77).

91.9 CIVIL AIRCRAFT FLIGHT MANUAL, MARKING, AND PLACARD REQUIREMENTS

(a)   Except as provided in paragraph (d) of this section, no person may operate a civil aircraft without complying with the operating limitations specified in the approved Airplane or Rotorcraft Flight Manual, markings, and placards, or as otherwise prescribed by the certificating authority of the country of registry.

(b)   No person may operate a U.S. registered civil aircraft —

    (1)   For which an Airplane or Rotorcraft Flight Manual is required by §21.5 of this chapter unless there is available in the aircraft a current, approved Airplane or Rotorcraft Flight Manual or the manual provided for in §121.141(b); and

    (2)   For which an Airplane or Rotorcraft Flight Manual is not required by §21.5 of this chapter, unless there is available in the aircraft a current approved Airplane or Rotorcraft Flight Manual, approved manual material, markings, and placards, or any combination thereof.

(c)   No person may operate a U.S. registered civil aircraft unless that aircraft is identified in accordance with part 45 of this chapter.

(d)   Any person taking off or landing a helicopter certificated under part 29 of this chapter at a heliport constructed over water may make such momentary flight as is necessary for takeoff or landing through the prohibited range of the limiting height-speed envelope established for that helicopter if that flight through the prohibited range takes place over water on which a safe ditching can be accomplished and if the helicopter is amphibious or is equipped with floats or other emergency flotation gear adequate to accomplish a safe emergency ditching on open water.

EXPLANATION

91.9(a): Accidents often result from a pilot's failure to observe an aircraft's operating limitations. Exceeding an aircraft's weight and balance limitations is a common violation of 91.9, and it can be a fatal one.

91.9(b): Airplane Flight Manuals (AFMs) are required for all airplanes certificated in the transport category. No provision exists for approval of an AFM for airplanes type certificated in the normal or acrobatic categories under Civil Air Regulations (CAR) 04 or 4a.

AFMs are also required for airplanes type certificated under CAR 3 and FAR Part 23 at gross weights over 6,000 pounds, however, all aircraft that were manufactured after March 1, 1979, must have an AFM. The required information for airplanes, type certificated at gross weights of 6,000 pounds or under, which are not required to have an AFM, may be furnished in an airplane flight manual or in any combination of approved manual material, markings, and placards.

AFMs may be required for certain other airplane types which have been issued supplementary type certificates changing the original type certification requirements.

§21.5 of the FAR provides that for each airplane that was not type certificated with an AFM and that has had no flight prior to March 1, 1979, the holder of the Type Certificate (including a Supplemental Type Certificate or the licensee of a Type Certificate) shall make available to the owner at the time of delivery of the airplane a current approved AFM. The AFM must contain operating limitations and information required to be furnished in an AFM or manual material, markings, and placards, by the applicable regulations under which the airplane was certificated. The maximum ambient atmospheric temperature for which engine cooling was demonstrated must be in the AFM performance section, if not required to be in the operating limitations section.

Specific placards and markings are prescribed by airworthiness standards in addition to required AFMs or approved manual materials.

Supplemental operating and performance information which has not been specifically or formally approved by the FAA is usually provided by the manufacturer for a particular type airplane. This information generally appears in an "Owner's Handbook," an "Owner's Manual," or as supplemental pages in an AFM.

The required AFM, placards, and manuals are identified in the FAA Type Certificate Data Sheet or Aircraft Specification issued for each airplane eligible for an airworthiness certificate. This information may be obtained from the FAA or from an aircraft mechanic with a reference library of Type Certificate Data Sheets.

91.9(c): Part 45 refers not only to the registration number painted on an aircraft, but also to the identification information (data plates) on engines and propellers.

In an October 8, 1998, legal interpretation the Assistant Chief Counsel, Regulations Division, AGC-200, affirmed the long held belief and wrote as follows: "Section 91.9(a) provides that no person may operate a civil aircraft without complying with the operating limitations specified in the approved Airplane or Rotorcraft Flight Manual," and further, "it is clear that those parts of the AFM/RFM that are not "operating limitations" are not imposed on the operator as a section 91.9(a) operating requirement." [Author's Note: The referenced interpretation was not published.]

CROSS REFERENCES

Previous designation: 91.31. 45.13 Part 39 Airworthiness Directives; Part 43 Maintenance, Preventive Maintenance, Rebuilding, and Alteration; FAR 91 Subpart E Maintenance, Preventive Maintenance, and Alterations; 91.205 Powered Civil Aircraft with Standard Category U.S. Airworthiness Certificates: Instrument and Equipment Requirements; 91.213 Inoperative Instruments and Equipment; 91.403(a) General; 91.405 Maintenance Required; See 1.1 for definitions of "pilot in command," "operate," and "person."

ADVISORY CIRCULARS

AC 60-6B *Airplane Flight Manuals (AFM), Approved Manual Materials, Markings and Placards - Airplanes* (1980).

CASES

A pilot's airman certificate was revoked for rolling a BAE-3201 Jetstream (not authorized for aerobatics). The pilot's claim that he rolled the airplane to avoid a collision was not supported by the copilot or passengers. *Administrator v. Stricklen*, EA-3814 (1993).

A pilot believed that a STC for autogas issued to the EAA permitted the use of autogas in his airplane. The STC lists engine models, including the engine installed in his airplane. However, the STC also provides that the aircraft model must be approved by the FAA to ensure that the fuel system is compatible with autogas. The pilot received a five day certificate suspension. *Administrator v. Patenaude*, EA-4098 (1994).

Even if the center of gravity limits are exceeded only slightly, the safety implications are obvious and significant. *Administrator v. Southeast Air, Inc.*, 5 NTSB 705 (1985).

An airplane was not "identified" as required by [91.9(c)] after the pilot/mechanic involved fraudulently removed the data plate and installed one from a different airplane. The FAA revoked his pilot certificate and his mechanic certificate. *Administrator v. Lott*, 5 NTSB 2394 (1987).

A pilot violated [91.9(c)] by painting a new registration number on his airplane without authorization from the FAA. *Administrator v. Chaffin*, 5 NTSB 1341 (1986).

A pilot, flew into "known icing conditions" in violation of [§91.9] when his airplane's flight manual prohibited such flight. "Known icing conditions" means that icing conditions are being reported or forecast. In this instance, a SIGMET warned against "occasional" icing, and 3 or 4 PIREPS reported no icing. The NTSB stated that the pilot could not pick and choose between the SIGMET and the PIREPs. The forecast of icing was sufficient to sustain the violation. *Administrator v. Groszer*, EA-3770 (1993).

If a special flight permit (SFP) is issued with the restriction that only "essential flight crew" can be aboard, a certificated mechanic cannot ride along even if the reasoning behind the SFP is to get the aircraft to a maintenance base for work to be done. *Administrator v. Barrie*, EA-4801 (1999).

FAA CHIEF COUNSEL OPINIONS

Hypothetically, if a pilot landed a Boeing 767 at a weight below the Landing Field Length Weight and its Maximum Climb Limit Landing Weight, but above the Maximum Structural Landing Weight specified in its flight manual, the pilot would be in violation of §§91.9 and 91.605. (11-8-93).

91.11 PROHIBITION ON INTERFERENCE WITH CREWMEMBERS

No person may assault, threaten, intimidate, or interfere with a crewmember in the performance of the crewmember's duties aboard an aircraft being operated.

EXPLANATION

Self explanatory.

CROSS REFERENCES

Previous designation: 91.8. See 1.1 for definitions of "crewmember," "person," and "operate."

ADVISORY CIRCULARS

AC 120-65 *Interference with Crewmembers in the Performance of their Duties* (1996).

CASES

This regulation has not been used successfully as a defense to a charge under 91.13, Careless or Reckless Operation. A helicopter pilot who took off with someone standing on the skid claimed that the person was "interfering," but the NTSB held that, under the circumstances, the pilot overreacted. *Administrator v. York*, 4 NTSB 1275 (1984).

An American Airlines passenger caused a scene at the gate when she was not allowed to board without picture identification. The flight was delayed and she was able to produce this identification and was then allowed to board. While boarding she bumped into a flight attendant shoving her into an open closet. During the flight she would not comply with the flight attendants' requests to clear the aisle until the seat belt sign had been illuminated. At one point the captain left the cockpit to have a word with the passenger. His conversation did not change her behavior and later a flight attendant had to physically move the passenger's legs off of the seat across the aisle in order to get by. Although the passenger's behavior was offensive the Law Judge found that it did not constitute a violation of §91.11. The basis for this decision was that the scene at the gate was before the passenger boarded, the passenger did not assault the flight attendant by bumping into her, the captain's decision to speak with the passenger was prudent, but not necessary, and that blocking the aisle was a minimal interference and did not have a significant bearing on the actions of the flight attendant. *FAA v. Dorfman*, FAA Order No. 99-16 (12-22-99).

The law judge held that gripping the flight attendant's shoulder and then tightening his grip when she told him to remove his hand constituted an assault, even though the event lasted only a few seconds. The respondent was assessed a civil penalty of $500. *FAA v. Gotbetter*, FAA Order No. 2000-17 (8-11-2000).

A passenger interfered with the captain's and flight attendant's duties by refusing to buckle his seat belt, thus requiring the captain and flight attendant to interrupt their activities in order to persuade him to comply with the seat belt regulation. Whether or not the passenger had buckled his seat belt by the time the crewmembers made it back to him is immaterial. *FAA v. Stout*, FAA Order No. 98-12 (6-16-1998).

A passenger, who was upset that the flight attendant had stained his pants by "throwing" a sandwich in his lap, sought revenge by putting the sandwich down the flight attendant's blouse. The law judge found that because he provoked the initial event by placing his sandwich back on the cart twice, contrary to the attendant's express instructions, his act constituted an assault, and clearly interfered with the crewmember's duties in serving meals and beverages to the other passengers on the plane. He was fined $1,500. *FAA v. Mayer*, FAA Order No. 97-12 (2-20-1997).

A passenger was fined $1,750 for two separate violations of §91.11. The passenger yelled violently at the flight attendant and tried to push her beverage cart out of his way. When this did not work he grabbed her by the shoulders to step around her and the cart, pushing her back and stepping hard on her foot. This constituted an interference with a crewmember and assault. *FAA v. Ignatov*, FAA Order No. 96-6 (2-13-1996).

A $1,000 civil penalty was assessed to a passenger, assigned to a non-smoking seat, who refused to put out his cigarette and return to his seat eventually requiring, at different points, both the captain and first officer to leave the cockpit and try to resolve the situation. *FAA v. Park*, FAA Order No. 92-3 (1-9-1992).

FAA CHIEF COUNSEL OPINIONS

Assault on a crewmember performing duties during aircraft boarding is covered by [91.11]. The aircraft does not have to be in flight or in motion. (5-4-79).

Within the meaning of [91.11], "crewmember" includes flight attendants and their supervisors. (9-3-79).

91.13 CARELESS OR RECKLESS OPERATION

(a) *Aircraft operations for the purpose of air navigation.* No person may operate an aircraft in a careless or reckless manner so as to endanger the life or property of another.

(b) *Aircraft operations other than for the purpose of air navigation.* No person may operate an aircraft, other than for the purpose of air navigation, on any part of the surface of an airport used by aircraft for air commerce (including areas used by those aircraft for receiving or discharging persons or cargo), in a careless or reckless manner so as to endanger the life or property of another.

EXPLANATION

(a) The NTSB broadened the scope of this regulation by ruling that the FAA need only prove "potential" rather than "actual" endangerment. Note that the FAA can establish a violation by proving careless **OR** reckless operation. Careless operation is usually inadvertent conduct, while reckless is generally deliberate or heedless conduct.

(b) This covers not only pilots, but mechanics taxiing aircraft to refuel, park, or to run-up an engine after maintenance.

CROSS REFERENCES

Previous designation: 91.9 and 91.10. See 1.1 for definitions of "person" and "operate."

CASES

A pilot failed to discover an improperly installed fuel cap during preflight inspection and received a 15 day suspension. *Administrator v. Stimble*, EA-4177 (1994).

An airline flight crew failed to check fuel before takeoff, and did not notice that the airplane had not been refueled until they reached FL330. The crew then lied to ATC, claiming engine failure. Suspensions were ordered, but waived under the Aviation Safety Reporting Program. *Administrator v. Wieland & Perry*, EA-4190 (1994).

A flight instructor and student flew at less than 100' AGL above a freeway where two police officers observed that the airplane continued the low pass for at least a quarter of a mile. The flight instructor claimed that they were practicing emergency procedures. The instructor received a 90 day suspension. The suspension was not waived under the Aviation Safety Reporting Program (ASRP) because it was not considered inadvertent. *Administrator v. Traub*, EA-4188 (1994).

A pilot's failure to tie down the tail securely and to have a qualified pilot in the cockpit when hand propping an engine resulted in an accident and a 90 day suspension. *Administrator v. Kapton*, EA-4046 (1993).

Flying under IFR without an instrument rating is careless (if not reckless) and creates potential endangerment within the scope of [91.13]. *Administrator v. Feldman*, EA-2913 (1989).

The fact that damage was minor and not reportable to the FAA or the NTSB does not mean that a violation of [91.13] did not occur. *Administrator v. Barwa*, EA-2840 (1988).

Landing at the wrong airport is careless within the meaning of [91.13]. *Administrator v. Holter*, et.al., 5 NTSB 826 (1985).

A pilot's failure to take minimum precautions by chocking the wheels, tying the airplane down, and having a qualified person at the controls while hand-proping the aircraft was careless. *Administrator v. Pauley*, 2 NTSB 1369 (1975).

A gear-up landing may be careless in violation of [91.13], absent a showing of a malfunction in the landing gear systems. *Administrator v. Jennings*, 2 NTSB 715 (1974).

The inadvertent operation of the wrong switches is not reckless, but merely careless. *Administrator v. Gilfoil*, EA-2937 (1989).

Landing on a road may be careless unless proper precautions are taken. *Administrator v. Carter*, 2 NTSB 853 (1974).

In order to establish a violation of [91.13], it is sufficient to show potential, as opposed to actual, endangerment. *Administrator v. Haines*, 1 NTSB 769 (1970); aff'd 449 F.2d 1073 (D.C.Cir. 1971).

Where a landing by a pilot involved a final approach path under a bridge, and the approach was both unnecessary and inappropriate, the operation within 500 feet of structures was not excused by the prefatory clause in [91.119] ("Except when necessary for takeoff or landing . . ."). *Administrator v. Bellows*, 3 NTSB 3844 (1981).

Switching a fuel selector to "off" was careless, and a violation of [91.13], even though the pilot landed safely. *Administrator v. Jakobsson*, 3 NTSB 4133 (1981).

The standard procedure set forth in the FAA Flight Training Handbook is a factor that can be considered in determining whether there has been a violation of [91.13]. Factors beyond the face of the regulation, such as custom and practice and standard operating procedures, may be considered. *Administrator v. Pascarella*, 4 NTSB 1083 (1983).

Regardless of whether or not an employer authorizes a pilot to leave an aircraft idling with the parking brake set and no chocks, it still constitutes reckless behavior that potentially endangers the life and property of others. *Administrator v. Miller*, EA-4738 (1999).

In the case where a check airman failed to report that engine temperatures were exceeded during a stall recovery and subsequently flew the aircraft on to several other destinations, the Board reinstated the order of revocation sought by the Administrator. The stall occurred during an airline flight with (screaming) passengers aboard. *Administrator v. Carter*, EA-4765 (1999).

Announcing to ATC the loss of sight of the lead aircraft by the pilot in the wing aircraft is the reasonable course of action in controlled airspace. Trying to reacquire the lead aircraft visually while the transponder is in standby mode creates the possibility for a collision hazard. In this case, the Board found that the pilot of the wing Cessna Citation violated §91.111 and §91.13. However, sanction was waved due to the proper filing of an Aviation Safety Reporting Program report. *Administrator v. Magnusson*, EA-4780 (1999).

During taxi on a day when the visibility was poor and the taxiway was partially scooped off leaving mounds of snow on the edges, the pilots of an aircraft inadvertently missed the left turn to intercept the taxiway and ended up in the unpaved area beyond the ramp. Due to the conditions, and the fact that the respondents were taxiing slowly and looking for the taxiway lights, the Board found that there was insufficient evidence to indicate that the respondents failed to exercise due care. *Administrator v. Sklenka and Ophir*, EA-4783 (1999).

Use of the emergency defense is not justification for an unqualified pilot to manipulate the controls of an aircraft, or for the PIC to allow him to do so. *Administrator v.Basco and Koch*, EA-4788 (1999).

A pilot, not knowing exactly how much fuel was on board before fueling the aircraft, but not filling the tanks, used her estimation of the fuel on board to calculate her reserve which proved not to be enough for the flight in question, leading to fuel starvation. The Board considered this to be a careless action. *Administrator v. Holmgaard*, EA-4799 (1999).

The following case eventually resulted in caselaw, which states that a pilot is *not* protected from a violation by a "readback" of the clearance as understood by the pilot. The initial ruling of the Board was to reverse the suspension of the non-flying pilot-in-command's certificate whose incorrect readback was not heard, and then whose aircraft subsequently ascended to an altitude that resulted in the loss of the standard safety separation with another transport category aircraft. *Administrator v. Merrell*, EA-4530 (1997).

The FAA filed a petition for reconsideration stating that the Board was substituting its interpretation for that of the Administrator, and that the Board's policy on this issue threatened aviation safety. The Board denied the petition replying that the FAA failed to offer any written policy guidance on this issue and that the policy to dismiss certificate action against a pilot for failing to follow the clearance that the pilot clearly misunderstood did not threaten aviation safety. In fact, they stated the policy fostered aviation safety by placing the burden of accurate communication on both the pilot and the controller. *Administrator v. Merrell*, EA-4670 (1998).

The FAA appealed the case to the United States Court of Appeals, District of Columbia Circuit, which overturned the Board's finding of no violation. On September 21, 1999, the court ruled that FAR 91.123 states that a pilot must follow ATC directions unless there is an emergency, and does not suggest that he may rely on readback procedures to absolve himself of responsibility. *FAA v. Merrell*, 190 F.3rd 571 (C.A.D.C. 1999).

As a result of the district court's ruling the Board vacated the previous two orders and affirmed the initial decision of the law judge. The Board stated that "under the Administrator's interpretation of the relevant regulations...an error of perception does not constitute a reasonable explanation for a deviation from a clearly transmitted clearance or instruction. Rather, inattentiveness or carelessness is presumed from the occurrence of a deviation unless, as we understand it, the misperception or mistake concerning the clearance was attributable to some factor for which the airman was not responsible, such as an equipment failure." *Administrator v. Merrell*, EA-4814 (2000).

By diverting to airports that had marginal or below minimum weather conditions instead of proceeding to an alternate set forth in the dispatch release that had favorable weather conditions, the pilots operated the aircraft in a careless and reckless manner so as to endanger the lives and property of others. *Administrator v. Morris and Wallace*, EA-4866 (2000).

A pilot's ATP certificate was revoked when he decided to continue a flight to its destination at an altitude which required emergency oxygen for passengers in case of a depressurization after that supply of oxygen had been used when the masks deployed earlier in the flight. *Administrator v. Reese*, EA-4896 (2001). The first officer's ATP certificate was suspended for 4 months. *Administrator v. Danet*, EA-4902 (2001).

If the landing site is inappropriate under the circumstances, then the low flight cannot be excused under the regulation as necessary for landing. *Administrator v. Christ*, EA-4922 (2001).

A company that provided banner towing services to local merchants was fined $1,100 for violating §91.119 and §91.13 by operating the aircraft at altitudes of only 600-800 feet above congested areas. *FAA v. High Exposure*, FAA Order No. 2001-2 (5-16-2001).

A pilot flying a rented aircraft at night ran out of fuel nine or ten miles short of his destination. In addition to not ensuring that the fuel tanks were full before the flight the pilot, in planning the flight, used a fuel burn rate he obtained from a flight manual for a different model of aircraft, which was lower than the actual rate for the aircraft he operated. He was fined $3,000. *FAA v. Hereth*, FAA Order No. 95-26 (12-19-1995).

The respondent's petition for reconsideration of the Administrator's decision that he had violated §§91.9, 91.111, and 91.113 was denied, and the civil penalty of $2,500 was upheld. The respondent caused the in-flight collision by following another aircraft too closely, which he knew to be in the vicinity, and by not continuing to maintain his awareness by moving his head to eliminated blind spots and/or make radio contact with the other aircraft. The pilot did not testify that he turned or tried to contact the other aircraft and failed to present any evidence that he filed an ASRP report with NASA. *FAA v. Sweeney*, FAA Order No. 94-21 (6-22-1994).

A $2,000 penalty was imposed on an air carrier for careless and reckless taxi operations with five aircraft. On three of the five occasions, the mechanics taxing the aircraft taxied onto runways without ATC clearance. On appeal the law judge held that the mechanics were acting within the scope of their employment and upheld the penalty. *FAA v. Westair Commuter Airlines, Inc.*, FAA Order No. 93-18 (6-10-1993).

The pilot in command of a helicopter was assessed a civil penalty of $2,000 for hovering only 30 to 40 feet above persons in a swimming hole three times. Although only one of the three hovering incidents was proven, the law judge held, on appeal, that because each incident violated both §§91.119 and 91.13 (formerly 91.79 and 91.9) each of which carried a maximum fine of $1,000, the assessed penalty of $2,000 was not excessive. *FAA v. Metcalf*, FAA Order No. 93-17 (6-10-1993).

Upon hearing a loud noise during the pushback operation, the aircraft's captain had a duty to investigate before proceeding to taxi and take off, and should not have relied on the pushback operator's response that everything was "okay." *FAA v. USAir, Inc.,* FAA Order No. 92-70 (12-21-1992).

A violation of §91.123 (formerly 91.75) for the pilot in command and of §91.13 (formerly 91.9) for both the PIC and the flying pilot occurred when they deviated from their "maintain flight level one eight zero" clearance and descended below 18,000 feet without an amended clearance. Although both pilots testified that they did not hear "maintain," there was no evidence on the air traffic control tapes that the clearance was garbled, muffled, or unclear. *FAA v. Richardson*, FAA Order No. 92-49 (7-22-1992).

A pilot was fined $1,000 for coming within 50 to 80 feet of several fishing boats while landing his float plane on a river. The law judge affirmed the initial decision in part that this was a violation of §91.119 (formerly 91.79) and reversed the initial finding in part by ruling that it was also a violation of §91.13 (formerly 91.9). *FAA v. Cornwall*, FAA Order No. 92-47 (7-22-1992).

The initial decision of the law judge in finding that the respondent was in violation of §91.13 (formerly 91.9) and §91.123 (formerly 91.75) when while taxing on a runway he mistakenly taxied across an intersecting runway, was reversed. The absence of the usual cues present on a taxiway enabling a pilot to identify an intersecting runway combined with confusing instructions from air traffic control, would make a finding of violation unjust. *FAA v. Wendt*, FAA Order No. 92-40 (6-15-1992).

A civil penalty of $2,000 was not excessive in the case where a pilot taxied his aircraft onto the wrong runway. The instructions from the ground controllers were clear, and the fact that weather conditions did not allow controllers to see the aircraft and that the taxiways were similar were not mitigating circumstances warranting a reduction. *FAA v. Watkins*, FAA Order No. 92-8 (1-31-1992).

A pilot in command and first officer of a Piedmont Airlines flight misinterpreted a clearance for a Cessna ahead of them to takeoff and then moved onto the runway in preparation for takeoff. This action constituted a violation of §§91.13, 91.123, and 91.129 (formerly 91.9, 91.75, and 91.87), however because they both filed ASRP reports with NASA, no penalty was assessed. *FAA v. Terry*, FAA Order No. 91-12 (4-12-1991).

FAA CHIEF COUNSEL OPINIONS

Someone directing a taxiing airplane cannot be sanctioned under §91.13 because of a collision. The person's actions outside the airplane do not amount to an "operation" of the airplane. The FAA could take action against the air carrier that employs the ground handler. (1-19-93), (3-13-93).

Definition of "operate" found in 1.1 applies to [91.13]. (1979).

Definition of "operate" found in Amendment 91-43 (32 F.R. 9640; July 4, 1967), states that the term "operate" as used in [91.13] applies to "those acts which impart some physical movement to the aircraft, or involve the manipulation of the controls of the aircraft such as starting or running an aircraft engine." (1979).

If a certificate holder authorizes a flight crewmember to operate an aircraft when it knows, or should know, that because of total duty time, the crewmember was fatigued or lacked proper rest, and that condition caused the flight crewmember to operate the aircraft in a careless or reckless manner so as to endanger the lives or property of others, then the certificate holder would be in violation of §91.13. (8-30-93).

Although Part 121 prescribes crew duty and rest requirements for certificate holders to follow, the FAA may bring an enforcement action against a pilot who accepts, at the request of the air carrier, an assignment to duty without having been given a required rest period. (8-30-93).

91.15 DROPPING OBJECTS

No pilot in command of a civil aircraft may allow any object to be dropped from that aircraft in flight that creates a hazard to persons or property. However, this section does not prohibit the dropping of any object if reasonable precautions are taken to avoid injury or damage to persons or property.

EXPLANATION

There is no official guidance from the FAA on what constitutes "reasonable precautions," but it can be inferred from NTSB caselaw that dropping objects over congested areas or highways could pose a danger to persons or property.

CROSS REFERENCES

Previous designation: 91.13. See 1.1 for definitions of "pilot in command" and "civil aircraft."

CASES

A pilot who dropped a 25 foot by 25 foot banner from a balloon at an altitude of 200 to 500 feet over a congested area did not take "reasonable precautions" by merely surveying the scene from the balloon before releasing the banner. Although the banner did not in fact cause any damage or injury, the potential danger was sufficient to constitute a violation of the regulation. *Administrator v. DiGiovanni*, 3 NTSB 1048 (1978).

FAA CHIEF COUNSEL OPINIONS

Firing model rockets from an aircraft over unpopulated areas under visual conditions: the expended rockets would not pose a hazard to persons or property on the ground. (7-23-76).

91.17 ALCOHOL OR DRUGS

(a)   No person may act or attempt to act as a crewmember of a civil aircraft —
    (1)   Within 8 hours after the consumption of any alcoholic beverage;
    (2)   While under the influence of alcohol;
    (3)   While using any drug that affects the person's faculties in any way contrary to safety; or
    (4)   While having .04 percent by weight or more alcohol in the blood.
(b)   Except in an emergency, no pilot of a civil aircraft may allow a person who appears to be intoxicated or who demonstrates by manner or physical indications that the individual is under the influence of drugs (except a medical patient under proper care) to be carried in that aircraft.
(c)   A crewmember shall do the following:
    (1)   On request of a law enforcement officer, submit to a test to indicate the percentage by weight of alcohol in the blood, when —
        (I)   The law enforcement officer is authorized under State or local law to conduct the test or to have the test conducted; and
        (ii)   The law enforcement officer is requesting submission to the test to investigate a suspected violation of State or local law governing the same or substantially similar conduct prohibited by paragraph (a)(1), (a)(2), or (a)(4) of this section.

(2) Whenever the Administrator has a reasonable basis to believe that a person may have violated paragraph (a)(1), (a)(2), or (a)(4) of this section, that person shall, upon request by the Administrator, furnish the Administrator, or authorize any clinic, hospital, doctor, or other person to release to the Administrator, the results of each test taken within 4 hours after acting or attempting to act as a crewmember that indicates percentage by weight of alcohol in the blood.

(d) Whenever the Administrator has a reasonable basis to believe that a person may have violated paragraph (a)(3) of this section, that person shall, upon request by the Administrator, furnish the Administrator, or authorize any clinic, hospital, doctor, or other person to release to the Administrator, the results of each test taken within 4 hours after acting or attempting to act as a crew- member that indicates the presence of any drugs in the body.

(e) Any test information obtained by the Administrator under paragraph (c) or (d) of this section may be evaluated in determining a person's qualifications for any airman certificate or possible violations of this chapter and may be used as evidence in any legal proceeding under section 602, 609, or 901 of the Federal Aviation Act of 1958.

EXPLANATION

91.17(a): Note that (1) through (4) provide four distinct methods for the FAA to prove a violation of 91.17(a). If the FAA can prove that a pilot violated the eight hour "bottle to throttle" rule, it does not have to prove that the pilot was "under the influence" on the flight, and vice versa.

91.17(b): Self-explanatory.

91.17(c) - (e): An action by the FAA to revoke or suspend an airman's certificate is not a criminal proceeding, so the FAA is not required to give the "Miranda" warning ("You have the right to remain silent. . .") before obtaining evidence from a pilot to be used in an administrative proceeding.

CROSS REFERENCES

Previous designation: 91.11. 61.15 Offenses Involving Alcohol or Drugs. §§602(b)(2) and 609(c) of the Federal Aviation Act of 1958, as amended by 49 U.S.C. App. §§1422(b)(2) and1429(c). See 1.1 for definitions of "operate" and "person."

ADVISORY CIRCULARS

AC 91.11-1 *Guide To Drug Hazards In Aviation Medicine* (1963).

AERONAUTICAL INFORMATION MANUAL

References to "medical facts for pilots," including the effects of medication and alcohol: Para. 8-1-1.

CASES

A pilot's ATP certificate was revoked for flying within eight hours of drinking alcohol. *Administrator v. Lindsay*, EA-4095 (1994).

A pilot's lack of consent to a blood test does not require exclusion of the test results. *Administrator v. Kremer*, EA-4050 (1993).

The degree of alcoholic influence is not critical to the violation of [91.17(a)(2)] or to the residual violation of [91.13]. The operation of an aircraft while under the influence of alcohol is inherently reckless and dangerous. *Administrator v. McGee*, 3 NTSB 4074 (1981).

An alphabet recital test administered at an airport to determine if a pilot was intoxicated was properly admitted into evidence at administrative hearings, despite the fact that the pilot had never received the "Miranda" warning. A "Miranda" warning is not required if the pilot is not detained or questioned in a "coercive environment" and no criminal charges were contemplated. Eyewitness accounts are sufficient evidence to prove a charge under [91.17(a)(1) or (2)], blood or breath tests are not required. *Sorenson v. NTSB*, 684 F.2d 683 (10th Cir. 1982), affirming *Administrator v. Sorenson*, 3 NTSB 3456 (1981).

The statutory requirements to support a criminal conviction may be entirely different from those necessary to support a violation of [91.17(a)(2)]. *Administrator v. Butner*, 2 NTSB 2289 (1976).

The NTSB was not persuaded by the testimony of a pilot that his long friendship with his passengers caused him to make a judgment that they were not intoxicated enough to be a threat to safety. The pilot called other witnesses who testified that these passengers conduct themselves in a "hurly-burly, raucous manner, even when sober." Witnesses for the FAA testified that the passengers were shouting, making hostile comments and obscene remarks. The carriage of passengers who are obviously under the influence is a potential threat to safety, especially in a small aircraft (a Cessna 210). *Administrator v. Walsh*, 5 NTSB 305 (1985).

91.19 CARRIAGE OF NARCOTIC DRUGS, MARIHUANA, AND DEPRESSANT OR STIMULANT DRUGS OR SUBSTANCES

(a)   Except as provided in paragraph (b) of this section, no person may operate a civil aircraft within the United States with knowledge that narcotic drugs, marihuana, and depressant or stimulant drugs or substances as defined in Federal or State statutes are carried in the aircraft.

(b)   Paragraph (a) of this section does not apply to any carriage of narcotic drugs, marihuana, and depressant or stimulant drugs or substances authorized by or under any Federal or State statute or by any Federal or State agency.

EXPLANATION

It may seem unnecessary for the FARs to prohibit drug smuggling in aircraft when there are other laws which impose harsher sanctions than the loss of a pilot certificate or the imposition of a civil penalty. However, in a criminal case, the prosecutor must prove the allegations "beyond the shadow of a doubt," while in administrative cases, the FAA only needs to prove the violations by a "preponderance of the evidence." Thus, a pilot might be found not guilty of a criminal charge of drug smuggling, or the pilot might be allowed to plead guilty to a lesser offense, such as drug possession rather than distribution. The fact that a pilot avoids conviction on a criminal charge of drug smuggling does not prevent the FAA from imposing administrative sanctions if the violations can be proved under the lesser burden of proof.

CROSS REFERENCES

Previous designation: 91.12. 61.15 Offenses Involving Alcohol or Drugs. §§602(b)(2) and 609(c) of the Federal Aviation Act of 1958, as amended by 49 U.S.C. App. §§1422(b)(2) and 1429(c). See 1.1 for definitions of "operate" and "person."

CASES

Evidence obtained by the Drug Enforcement Administration (DEA) (a federal agency) in violation of a pilot's constitutional rights may not be offered by the FAA to establish a violation under 91.19 ("exclusionary rule" applied). *Administrator v. Danielson*, 3 NTSB 161 (1977).

The exclusionary rule does not apply when the evidence was improperly obtained by state officials. The NTSB followed the U.S. Supreme Court's decision in U.S. v. Janis, 96 S.Ct. 3021 (1976), which held that evidence unconstitutionally seized by a state officer was admissible in a civil proceeding brought by the Federal Government. The purpose of the exclusionary rule is to deter the "sovereign" (state or federal) which had performed the search. *Administrator v. Franklin*, 3 NTSB 978 (1978).

Circumstantial evidence (no one directly observed the accused pilot at the controls of the aircraft) is sufficient to carry the FAA's burden of proof if the pilot cannot offer contradictory evidence. FAR 61.15(b) does not impose any time limitation on the FAA's power to revoke an airman's certificate under [91.19]. *Administrator v. King*, 4 NTSB 1311 (1984).

If a pilot is convicted of, or the FAA determines that a pilot knowingly engaged in, an activity punishable by death or imprisonment for a term exceeding one year under state or federal law relating to a controlled substance, other than simple possession, and the FAA determines that an aircraft was used to carry out or facilitate the activity, and the person served as a crewmember, or was on board the aircraft, then the FAA shall take action to revoke that person's airman certificates. If, after all appeals, the FAA is upheld, that person will never be allowed to obtain another airman certificate. §609(c)(1) and (2) and §602(b)(2) of the Federal Aviation Act of 1958, as amended by 49 U.S.C. App. §§1422(b)(2) and 1429(c).

FAA CHIEF COUNSEL OPINIONS

FAR 61.15 and [91.19] only apply to airman certificates. The FAA is limited to taking suspension or revocation actions against mechanics or other certificate holders under Part 43 where a specific FAR is violated. A reputation for drunkenness would not, by itself, subject a mechanic to enforcement action. (8-16-77).

91.21 PORTABLE ELECTRONIC DEVICES

(a) Except as provided in paragraph (b) of this section, no person may operate, nor may any operator or pilot in command of an aircraft allow the operation of, any portable electronic device on any of the following U.S.—registered civil aircraft:
    (1) Aircraft operated by a holder of an air carrier operating certificate or an operating certificate; or
    (2) Any other aircraft while it is operated under IFR.
(b) Paragraph (a) of this section does not apply to —
    (1) Portable voice recorders;
    (2) Hearing aids;
    (3) Heart pacemakers;
    (4) Electric shavers; or
    (5) Any other portable electronic device that the operator of the aircraft has determined will not cause interference with the navigation or communication system of the aircraft on which it is to be used.
(c) In the case of an aircraft operated by a holder of an air carrier operating certificate or an operating certificate, the determination required by paragraph (b) (5) of this section shall be made by that operator of the aircraft on which the particular device is to be used. In the case of other aircraft, the determination may be made by the pilot in command or other operator of the aircraft.

EXPLANATION

Note that this regulation does not restrict the use of portable electronic devices on Part 91 flights **unless** the flights are conducted under IFR. This regulation preceded the popularity of cellular phones, and the FAA has not yet published any information to pilots regarding the effect, if any, of cellular phones on communication and navigation systems. However, the Federal Communication Commission (FCC) has prohibited the use of cellular phones in aircraft while airborne. See FCC Regulation 22.911. The FAA has indicated to its own personnel that cellular phones may be operated in aircraft on the ground in accordance with 91.21(b)(5). Letter of Thomas C. Accordi to all Flight Standards District Offices, February 4, 1992.

Portable GPS units which are attached by Velcro tape or hard yoke mount that require an antenna (internally or externally mounted) are considered to be portable electronic devices and are subject to the provisions of FAR 91.21.

CROSS REFERENCES

Previous designation: 91.19. See 1.1 for definitions of "operate" and "person."

ADVISORY CIRCULARS

AC 91.21-1A *Use of Portable Electronic Devices Aboard Aircraft* (2000).

91.23 TRUTH–IN–LEASING CLAUSE REQUIREMENT IN LEASES AND CONDITIONAL SALES CONTRACTS

(a) Except as provided in paragraph (b) of this section, the parties to a lease or contract of conditional sale involving a U.S.-registered large civil aircraft and entered into after January 2, 1973, shall execute a written lease or contract and include therein a written truth-in-leasing clause as a concluding paragraph in large print, immediately preceding the space for the signature of the parties, which contains the following with respect to each such aircraft:

    (1) Identification of the Federal Aviation Regulations under which the aircraft has been maintained and inspected during the 12 months preceding the execution of the lease or contract of conditional sale, and certification by the parties thereto regarding the aircraft's status of compliance with applicable maintenance and inspection requirements in this part for the operation to be conducted under the lease or contract of conditional sale.

    (2) The name and address (printed or typed) and the signature of the person responsible for operational control of the aircraft under the lease or contract of conditional sale, and certification that each person understands that person's responsibilities for compliance with applicable Federal Aviation Regulations.

    (3) A statement that an explanation of factors bearing on operational control and pertinent Federal Aviation Regulations can be obtained from the nearest FAA Flight Standards district office.

(b) The requirements of paragraph (a) of this section do not apply —

    (1) To a lease or contract of conditional sale when —

        (i) The party to whom the aircraft is furnished is a foreign air carrier or certificate holder under part 121, 125, 135, or 141 of this chapter, or

        (ii) The party furnishing the aircraft is a foreign air carrier or a person operating under Part 121, 125, and 141 of this chapter, or a person operating under part 135 of this chapter having authority to engage in on demand operations with large aircraft.

    (2) To a contract of conditional sale, when the aircraft involved has not been registered anywhere prior to the execution of the contract, except as a new aircraft under a dealer's aircraft registration certificate issued in accordance with §47.61 of this chapter.

    (c) No person may operate a large civil aircraft of U.S. registry that is subject to a lease or contract of conditional sale to which paragraph (a) of this section applies, unless —

    (1) The lessee or conditional buyer, or the registered owner if the lessee is not a citizen of the United States, has mailed a copy of the lease or contract that complies with the requirements of paragraph (a) of this section, within 24 hours of its execution, to the Aircraft Registration Branch, Attn: Technical Section, P.O. Box 25724, Oklahoma City, Oklahoma 73125;

    (2) A copy of the lease or contract that complies with the requirements of paragraph (a) of this section is carried in the aircraft. The copy of the lease or contract shall be made available for review upon request by the Administrator; and

    (3) The lessee or conditional buyer, or the registered owner if the lessee is not a citizen of the United States, has notified by telephone or in person, the FAA Flight Standards district office nearest the airport where the flight will originate. Unless otherwise authorized by that office, the notification shall be given at least 48 hours before takeoff in the case of the first flight of that aircraft under that lease or contract and inform the FAA of —

        (I) The location of the airport of departure;

        (ii) The departure time; and

        (iii) The registration number of the aircraft involved.

(d) The copy of the lease or contract furnished to the FAA under paragraph (c) of this section is commercial or financial information obtained from a person. It is, therefore, privileged and confidential and will not be made available by the FAA for public inspection or copying under 5 U.S.C. 552(b)(4), unless recorded with the FAA under part 49 of this chapter.

(e) For the purpose of this section, a lease means any agreement by a person to furnish an aircraft to another person for compensation or hire, whether with or without flight crewmembers, other than an agreement for the sale of an aircraft and a contract of conditional sale under section 101 of the Federal Aviation Act of 1958. The person furnishing the aircraft is referred to as the lessor, and the person to whom it is furnished is the lessee.

EXPLANATION

New 6 (b)(1)(i) revised April 27, 2001, effective April 27, 2001, removed references to Part 127.

This regulation is often overlooked when persons enter into aircraft lease agreements pursuant to FAR 91.501. Anyone interested in leasing arrangements involving large civil airplanes (more than 12,500 pounds) should obtain the advisory circular discussed below. Parties entering into leases which are not required to comply with this regulation because the aircraft involved does not meet the definition of "large civil aircraft" would be well advised to comply with the regulation in order to clarify the responsibilities of the parties. The parties to any lease agreement should also review AC 120-12A to ensure that the proposed arrangement does not violate the provisions of FAR Part 121 or 135.

§101 of the Federal Aviation Act of 1958 defines a "contract of conditional sale" as:

(a) any contract for the sale of an aircraft, aircraft engine, propeller, appliance, or spare part under which possession is delivered to the buyer and the property is to vest in the buyer at a subsequent time, upon the payment of part or all of the price, or upon the performance of any other condition or the happening of any contingency; or

(b) any contract for the bailment or leasing of an aircraft, aircraft engine, propeller, appliance, or spare part, by which the bailee or lessee contracts to pay as compensation a sum substantially equivalent to the value thereof, and by which it is agreed that the bailee or lessee is bound to become, or has the option of becoming, the owner thereof upon full compliance with the terms of the contract. The buyer, bailee, or lessee shall be deemed to be the person by whom any such contract is made or given.

CROSS REFERENCES

Previous designation: 91.54. See Part 91 Subpart F-Large and Turbine-Powered Multi-engine Airplanes, 91.501 Applicability. See 1.1 for definitions of "operate," "person," "large aircraft," "civil aircraft."

ADVISORY CIRCULARS

AC 91-37A *Truth in Leasing* (1978).

AC 120-12A *Private Carriage Versus Common Carriage of Persons or Property* (1986).

FAA CHIEF COUNSEL OPINIONS

§[91.23(c)(3)] requires the lessee or conditional buyer to provide notification to the FAA at least 48 hours prior to the first flight of an aircraft under that lease or contract. Since the agency recognized that notification 48 hours prior to takeoff might cause a hardship, the rule does allow the Administrator to authorize receipt of the notification in less than 48 hours. This means, for example, that a district office representative is authorized to allow the operation of a large aircraft subject to the provisions of §[91.23], even if he has only been given notification two hours prior to takeoff of the first flight. Of course, if the district office representative determines inspection is necessary and needs more time to conduct it, he can insist that the aircraft not be operated until such inspection and has up to 48 hours after notification to complete the inspection. It must be emphasized that the purpose of the 48 hour notification is to provide for sufficient advance notice to facilitate any surveillance and preflight inspections that may be considered appropriate. If it is decided that surveillance is not necessary, then there is no need to adhere to the 48 hour requirement. (1-19-78).

91.25 AVIATION SAFETY REPORTING PROGRAM: PROHIBITION AGAINST USE OF REPORTS FOR ENFORCEMENT PURPOSES

The Administrator of the FAA will not use reports submitted to the National Aeronautics and Space Administration under the Aviation Safety Reporting Program (or information derived therefrom) in any enforcement action, except information concerning accidents or criminal offenses which are wholly excluded from the program.

EXPLANATION

Most pilots are afraid to bare their souls to the FAA following a possible violation of the FARs, fearing the enforcement action which the FAA might take upon learning of the violation. The FAA recognized this safety problem and initiated the Aviation Safety Reporting Program (ASRP) to gather information on problems and dangers in aviation operations. The ASRP offers anonymity and a form of "immunity" to pilots who promptly fill out a "NASA Form" describing the circumstances surrounding a potentially dangerous situation. To ensure anonymity, NASA, rather than the FAA, collects and processes the information. Those who wish to file a report should obtain NASA ARC Form 277 ("NASA Form") from the NASA ASRP address listed below. NASA Forms may also be obtained from Flight Service Stations, Flight Standards District Offices, and the Aircraft Owners and Pilots Association. Copies of the form are accepted. Pick up NASA Forms now, don't wait until an "event" occurs.

A NASA Form will provide a form of immunity to the reporter if the four following conditions are met:

1. The violation was inadvertent and not deliberate.
2. The violation did not involve a criminal offense, accident, or action which "discloses a lack of qualifications." The FAA alleges a "lack of qualifications" when it seeks to revoke a pilot's certificate. The ASRP was designed to give immunity to pilots in suspension or civil penalty cases, not cases in which the FAA would seek to revoke a pilot's certificate.

WARNING! If a NASA Form reveals a criminal offense or an accident, NASA will send the information, with the reporter's identification, to the FAA, to the NTSB and the Department of Justice, as appropriate. NASA follows the definition of "accident" found in NTSB Regulations Part 830.

3.	The reporter has not been found in any prior FAA enforcement action to have committed a violation of the Federal Aviation Act, or of any FAR in the last five years.

4.	The reporter proves that, within ten days after the event, he or she filled out and sent the NASA Form to:

NASA ASRP Office
P.O.Box 189
Moffet Field, CA 94035

Since timely filing is critical, it is recommended, though not required, that the NASA Form be sent certified mail, return receipt requested.

The FAA may chose to process a violation despite the filing of a NASA Form, so a pilot may chose to appeal the FAA's proposed certificate or civil penalty action. If the FAA succeeds in prosecuting the violation, the pilot's record will reflect the violation, but the pilot will not be required to serve the suspension or pay the penalty, if the four preceding requirements are satisfied.

CROSS REFERENCES

Previous designation: 91.57.

ADVISORY CIRCULARS

AC 00-46D *Aviation Safety Reporting Program* (1997).

AERONAUTICAL INFORMATION MANUAL

Para. 7-6-1 *Aviation Safety Reporting Program,* gives a brief description of the program.

CASES

A flight instructor and student flew at less than 100' AGL above a freeway where two police officers observed that the airplane continued the low pass for at least a quarter of a mile. The flight instructor claimed they were practicing emergency procedures. The instructor received a 90 day suspension. The suspension was not waived under the Aviation Safety Reporting Program (ASRP) because it was not considered inadvertent. *Administrator v. Traub*, EA-4188 (1994).

A pilot's decision to fly an aircraft with a damaged propeller was deliberate and not inadvertent, and he was not entitled to a waiver of sanction under the Aviation Safety Reporting Program. *Harry G. Copsey v. NTSB*, 993 F.2d 736 (10th Cir. 1993).

An airline flight crew failed to check fuel before takeoff, and did not notice that the airplane had not been refueled until they reached FL330. The crew then lied to ATC, claiming engine failure. Suspensions were ordered, but waived under the Aviation Safety Reporting Program. *Administrator v. Wieland & Perry*, EA-4190 (1994).

Low passes over a congested residential area cannot be found to be inadvertent, and therefore a pilot cannot have his certificate suspension waived under the ASRP. *Administrator v. Wood*, EA-2633 (1987).

The filing of a NASA form would not, of itself, preclude all discovery by the FAA. The FAA would still be allowed to take the reporter's deposition. *Administrator v. Smith*, 4 NTSB 978, 979 (1983).

The ASRP does not apply to a refusal to allow an FAA inspector into a cockpit. *Administrator v. Crim*, 3 NTSB 2471 (1980).

The NTSB has ruled that its administrative law judges should not reduce the suspension period sought by the FAA for violations found proved when the FAA has waived service of any suspension due to the pilot's timely filing of a NASA form. *Administrator v. Andreolas*, EA-3446 (1991).

INTENTIONALLY

LEFT

BLANK

INTENTIONALLY

LEFT

BLANK

SUBPART B — FLIGHT RULES

GENERAL

91.101 APPLICABILITY

This subpart prescribes flight rules governing the operation of aircraft within the United States and within 12 nautical miles from the coast of the United States.

EXPLANATION

This rule controls the operation of domestic and foreign aircraft. Also, insofar as "public aircraft" are concerned there must be compliance with all sections that are not specifically limited to "civil aircraft." The FAA can issue certificates of waiver that allow deviation from some of the rules in this part under certain conditions (see 91.903-91.905).

CROSS REFERENCES

Previous designation: 91.61. 91.703 Operation of Civil Aircraft of U.S. Registry Outside of the United States; 91.707 Flights Between Mexico or Canada and the United States; 91.903 and 91.905 Waivers.

ADVISORY CIRCULARS

AC 20-132 *Public Aircraft* (1988).

AC 91-5C *Waivers of Subpart B, Part 91 of the Federal Aviation Regulations* (1982).

FAA CHIEF COUNSEL OPINIONS

The FARs are generally applicable only to civil aircraft. However, there are a number of operating rules in FAR Part 91 that apply to all aircraft, whether civil or public. These can be identified by the lack of limiting references to civil aircraft. (6-22-77).

91.103 PREFLIGHT ACTION

Each pilot in command shall, before beginning a flight, become familiar with all available information concerning that flight. This information must include —

(a)   For a flight under IFR or a flight not in the vicinity of an airport, weather reports and forecasts, fuel requirements, alternatives available if the planned flight cannot be completed, and any known traffic delays of which the pilot in command has been advised by ATC;

(b)   For any flight, runway lengths at airports of intended use, and the following takeoff and landing distance information:

   (1)   For civil aircraft for which an approved Airplane or Rotorcraft Flight Manual containing takeoff and landing distance data is required, the takeoff and landing distance data contained therein; and

   (2)   For civil aircraft other than those specified in paragraph (b)(1) of this section, other reliable information appropriate to the aircraft, relating to aircraft performance under expected values of airport elevation and runway slope, aircraft gross weight, and wind and temperature.

EXPLANATION

This section places a very heavy burden on the pilot in command when it provides that the pilot must become familiar with **all** available information concerning the proposed flight. The information in 91.103(a) and (b) indicates specifically some of the information that must be covered. Other types of information would include all NOTAMs relating to the route of flight, configuration and boundaries of Class B or Class C airspace that may be along the route of flight, weather reporting facilities with appropriate frequencies and any restricted or prohibited areas along the route. Fuel exhaustion cases will generally result in a charge of violation under 91.103. A violation of this section may also result from a violation of 91.155. The FAA may allege that nearly any violation was contributed to by a failure to take all necessary preflight action in accordance with 91.103.

CROSS REFERENCES

Previous designation: 91.5. 91.151 Fuel Requirements for Flight in VFR Conditions; 91.155 Basic VFR Weather Minimums; 91.167 Fuel Requirements for Flight in IFR Conditions; 91.503 Flying Equipment and Operating Information (Large and Turbine-Powered Multi-engine Airplanes).

ADVISORY CIRCULARS

AC 00-6A *Aviation Weather* (1975).

AC 00-30B *Atmospheric Turbulence Avoidance* (1997).

AC 00-24B *Thunderstorms* (1983).

AC 00-45E *Aviation Weather Services* (1999).

AC 20-43C *Aircraft Fuel Control* (1976).

AC 61-84B *Role of Preflight Preparation* (1985).

FAA-H-8083-1 *Aircraft Weight and Balance Handbook* (1999).

AERONAUTICAL INFORMATION MANUAL

Airspace Para. 3-1-1 through 3-5-7;
Services Available to Pilots, Para. 4-1-1 through 4-1-22;
Preflight, Para. 5-1-1 through 5-1-13;
Meteorology, Para. 7-1-1 through 7-1-31;
Fitness For Flight, Para. 8-1-1 through 8-1-8;
Types of Charts Available, Para. 9-1-1 through 9-1-5.

CASES

[91.103] requires that pilots familiarize themselves with all available information concerning the flight which would include [Class B] boundaries. *Administrator v. Smith*, EA-3558 (1992).

A visual estimate of the runway length at night does not satisfy the requirements of [91.103(b)]. *Administrator v. Holter*, 5 NTSB 826 (1985).

A violation of [91.103(a)] was found when a pilot who was aware that his fuel gauges overestimated the helicopter's true fuel status, ignored this fact and took off when the gauges indicated one eighth capacity. (The flight ended in a crash landing due to fuel exhaustion). *Administrator v. Shippee*, 5 NTSB 1367 (1986).

A pilot in command is no more obligated under [91.103] to supervise or vouch for the fueling of an aircraft as to grade and quantity than he is to monitor or warrant the correctness or adequacy of any other servicing or maintenance procedure the aircraft may require. However, the pilot in command has an obligation, during preflight of the aircraft, to check to see that the proper quantity and grade of fuel have been loaded. *Administrator v. Doty*, 5 NTSB 1529 (1986).

A pilot flying a rented aircraft at night ran out of fuel nine or ten miles short of his destination. In addition to not ensuring that the fuel tanks were full before the flight the pilot, in planning the flight, used a fuel burn rate he obtained from a flight manual for a different model of aircraft, which was lower than the actual rate for the aircraft he operated. He was fined $3,000. *FAA v. Hereth*, FAA Order No. 95-26 (12-19-1995).

FAA CHIEF COUNSEL OPINIONS

To determine the "standard of care" in a given case, documents such as the *Aeronautical Information Manual* and FAA Advisory Circulars are sometimes admitted into evidence. (3-31-78).

Someone questioned the meaning of the phrase, "...in the vicinity of an airport.", as specified in FAR §91.103(a) The FAA has no specific, fixed definition of "vicinity," but instead, interprets its meaning on a case-by-case basis. (1-28-92).

91.105 FLIGHT CREWMEMBERS AT STATIONS

(a) During takeoff and landing, and while enroute, each required flight crewmember shall —
  (1) Be at the crewmember station unless the absence is necessary to perform duties in connection with the operation of the aircraft or in connection with physiological needs; and
  (2) Keep the safety belt fastened while at the crewmember station.
(b) Each required flight crewmember of a U.S.-registered civil aircraft shall, during takeoff and landing, keep his or her shoulder harness fastened while at his or her assigned duty station. This paragraph does not apply if—
  (1) The seat at the crewmember's station is not equipped with a shoulder harness; or
  (2) The crewmember would be unable to perform required duties with the shoulder harness fastened.

EXPLANATION

This section is based primarily on the fact that each flight crewmember has specific duties that must be performed as the occasion arises. Accordingly, they must be in a position to perform these duties, especially those of an emergency nature, without delay. The requirement for use of a seatbelts and shoulder harnesses (when available) is to ensure that a sudden, unanticipated movement by the aircraft does not place the crewmember in a position where he or she can not properly react to the situation. Absences for physiological needs must be specifically for that purpose and reasonable in length. Any other absence from the station must be related solely to the safe operation of the aircraft. The requirement for use of seatbelts and shoulder harnesses (when available) applies to rotorcraft as well. A pilot may unfasten his seatbelt and harness in order to moor or launch a seaplane or a float equipped rotorcraft.

CROSS REFERENCES

Previous designation: 91.7. 91.107 Use of Safety Belts.

CASES

The Board stated that a review of the regulatory history of [91.105(b)] reveals that there is a sound safety basis for the requirement that a shoulder harness be employed by all specified crewmembers. *Administrator v. Hoyle*, 4 NTSB 1448 (1984).

FAA CHIEF COUNSEL OPINIONS

If the operation of the aircraft requires two pilots, cabin service or serving food and drinks in flight is not considered to be necessary in connection with the safe operation of the aircraft and the required pilot who left his station to perform such service would be considered to be in violation of [91.105(a)(1)].

"Physiological needs" means using the restroom, stretching one's limbs briefly during a long flight, and other such physiological requirements. The length of the absence depends on what is reasonable under all of the circumstances of a given situation. (6-5-90).

91.107 USE OF SAFETY BELTS, SHOULDER HARNESSES, AND CHILD RESTRAINT SYSTEMS

(a)   Unless otherwise authorized by the Administrator —
   (1)   No pilot may take off a U.S.-registered civil aircraft (except a free balloon that incorporates a basket or gondola, or an airship type certificated before November 2, 1987) unless the pilot in command of that aircraft ensures that each person on board is briefed on how to fasten and unfasten that person's safety belt and, if installed, shoulder harness.
   (2)   No pilot may cause to be moved on the surface, take off, or land a U.S.-registered civil aircraft (except a free balloon that incorporates a basket or gondola, or an airship type certificated before November 2, 1987) unless the pilot in command of that aircraft ensures that each person on board has been notified to fasten his or her safety belt and, if installed, his or her shoulder harness.
   (3)   Except as provided in this paragraph, each person on board a U.S.-registered civil aircraft (except a free balloon that incorporates a basket or gondola or an airship type certificated before November 2, 1987) must occupy an approved seat or berth with a safety belt and, if installed, shoulder harness, properly secured about him or her during movement on the surface, takeoff, and landing. For seaplane and float equipped rotorcraft operations during movement on the surface, the person pushing off the seaplane or rotorcraft from the dock and the person mooring the seaplane or rotorcraft at the dock are excepted from the preceding seating and safety belt requirements. Notwithstanding the preceding requirements of this paragraph, a person may:
      (I)   Be held by an adult who is occupying an approved seat or berth, provided that the person being held has not reached his or her second birthday and does not occupy or use any restraining device;
      (ii)   Use the floor of the aircraft as a seat, provided that the person is on board for the purpose of engaging in sport parachuting; or
      (iii) Notwithstanding any other requirement of this chapter, occupy an approved child restraint system furnished by the operator or one of the persons described in paragraph (a)(3)(iii)(A) of this section provided that:
         (A)   The child is accompanied by a parent, guardian, or attendant designated by the child's parent or guardian to attend to the safety of the child during the flight;
         (B)   Except as provided in paragraph (a)(3)(iii)(B)(4) of this section, the approved child restraint system bears one or more labels as follows:
            (1)   Seats manufactured to U.S. standards between January 1, 1981, and February 25, 1985, must bear the label: "This child restraint system conforms to all applicable Federal motor vehicle safety standards.";
            (2)   Seats manufactured to U.S. standards on or after February 26, 1985, must bear two labels:
               (i)   "This child restraint system conforms to all applicable Federal motor vehicle safety standards"; and
               (ii)   "THIS RESTRAINT IS CERTIFIED FOR USE IN MOTOR VEHICLES AND AIRCRAFT" in red lettering;
            (3)   Seats that do not qualify under paragraphs (a)(3)(iii)(B)(1) and (a)(3)(iii)(B)(2) of this section must bear either a label showing approval of a foreign government or a label showing that the seat was manufactured under the standards of the United Nations;
            (4)   Notwithstanding any other provision of this section, booster-type child restraint systems (as defined in Federal Motor Vehicle Safety Standard No. 213 (49 CFR 571.213)), vest -and harness-type child restraint systems, and lap held child restraints are not approved for use in aircraft; and

    (C)   The operator complies with the following requirements:

        (1)   The restraint system must be properly secured to an approved forward-facing seat or berth;

        (2)   The child must be properly secured in the restraint system and must not exceed the specified weight limit for the restraint system; and

        (3)   The restraint system must bear the appropriate label(s).

(b)   Unless otherwise stated, this section does not apply to operations conducted under Part 121, 125, or 135 of this chapter. Paragraph (a)(3) of this section does not apply to persons subject to §91.105.

EXPLANATION

The requirements of this regulation must be met before any movement of the aircraft on the surface. The responsibility of the pilot in command under §91.107 is first to ensure that each person on board is briefed on how to fasten and unfasten the seat belt, and, if installed, the shoulder harness and secondly, to ensure that all have been notified to fasten the seat belt and harness before takeoff or landing. The pilot in command does not have to personally conduct the briefing, but he or she must ensure that the briefing is accomplished. In the case of airships or balloons, no seat belts are required. Except for children under the age of two, who may be held by an adult, and persons on board an aircraft for parachuting, each person must occupy an approved seat or berth with a seat belt and harness (if installed) secured. Children under the age of two should not share a seatbelt with an adult. §91.107 was recently amended to approve, but not require the use of child seats, and to establish standards for their use. Parachutists may sit on the floor of an aircraft, but they still must have a seat belt available and fastened. A person pushing off or mooring a seaplane or float equipped rotorcraft is excepted from the seating and seat belt requirements. This section does not apply to public aircraft.

Special Federal Aviation Regulation (SFAR) No. 71 requires that, prior to takeoff, each pilot-in-command of an air tour flight, using an airplane or helicopter, of Hawaii with a flight segment beyond the ocean shore of any island shall ensure that each passenger has been briefed on the following in addition to requirements set forth in Section 91.107: (a) Water ditching procedures; (b) Use of required flotation equipment; and (c) Emergency egress from the aircraft in event of a water landing. This emergency action has been taken as a result of an escalation of air tour accidents. SFAR No. 71 is effective October 26, 1994 and expires October 26, 1997. 59 F.R. 4913 (1994).

CROSS REFERENCES

Previous designation: 91.14. 91.105, Flight Crewmembers at Stations; 91.903-91.905, Waivers.

ADVISORY CIRCULARS

AC 91-62A *Use of Child/Infant Seats in Aircraft* (1992).

AC 91-65 *Use of Shoulder Harness in Passenger Seats* (1986).

CASES

A pilot violated [91.107(b)] when he allowed a ninth passenger to sit on the floor or on a wooden luggage box at the rear of an aircraft which had a capacity limited to one pilot and seven passengers. *Administrator v. Nowak*, 4 N I SB 1709 (1984).

FAA CHIEF COUNSEL OPINIONS

There is no requirement for separate seats for each person in Part 91 operations, unlike operations under Part 121 and 127. As long as approved safety belts are carried aboard the aircraft for all occupants, and the structural strength requirements for the seats are not exceeded, two persons may be seated under one safety belt on the same seat, if their combined weight is less than 170 pounds and the belt can be properly secured. (6-5-90).

91.109 FLIGHT INSTRUCTION: SIMULATED INSTRUMENT FLIGHT AND CERTAIN FLIGHT TESTS

(a)   No person may operate a civil aircraft (except a manned free balloon) that is being used for flight instruction unless that aircraft has fully functioning dual controls. However, instrument flight instruction may be given in a single-engine airplane equipped with a single, functioning throwover control wheel in place of fixed, dual controls of the elevator and ailerons, when —
        (1)   The instructor has determined that the flight can be conducted safely; and
        (2)   The person manipulating the controls has at least a private pilot certificate with appropriate category and class ratings.

(b)   No person may operate a civil aircraft in simulated instrument flight unless —
        (1)   The other control seat is occupied by a safety pilot who possesses at least a private pilot certificate with category and class ratings appropriate to the aircraft being flown.
        (2)   The safety pilot has adequate vision forward and to each side of the aircraft, or a competent observer in the aircraft adequately supplements the vision of the safety pilot; and
        (3)   Except in the case of lighter-than-air aircraft, that aircraft is equipped with fully functioning dual controls. However, simulated instrument flight may be conducted in a single-engine airplane, equipped with a single, functioning, throwover control wheel, in place of fixed, dual controls of the elevator and ailerons, when —
            (I)   The safety pilot has determined that the flight can be conducted safely; and
            (ii)   The person manipulating the controls has at least a private pilot certificate with appropriate category and class ratings.

(c)   No person may operate a civil aircraft that is being used for a flight test for an airline transport pilot certificate or a class or type rating on that certificate, or for a part 121 proficiency flight test, unless the pilot seated at the controls, other than the pilot being checked, is fully qualified to act as pilot in command of the aircraft.

EXPLANATION

91.109(b): This section sets forth the requirements for simulated instrument flight in regard to the qualifications of the safety pilot, his/her ability to scan for traffic, and the aircraft requirements, which are the same as 91.109(a). Note that the safety pilot must have appropriate category (airplane/rotorcraft/glider etc.) and class (single-engine/multi-engine/land/water etc.). A safety pilot is a "required crewmember," and may log the time as "second in command."

CROSS REFERENCES

Previous designation: 91.21. 61.57 Recent Flight Experience: Pilot in Command.

ADVISORY CIRCULARS

AC 61-98A *Currency and Additional Qualification Requirements for Certified Pilots* (1991).

FAA-H-8083-3 *Airplane Flying Handbook* (1999).

FAA-H-8083-9 *Aviation Instructor's Handbook* (1999).

FAA-H-8083-15 *Instrument Flying Handbook* (2001).

AERONAUTICAL INFORMATION MANUAL

Follow IFR Procedures Even When Operating VFR, Para. 5-1-2.

FAA CHIEF COUNSEL OPINIONS

Since the safety pilot must be appropriately rated and is assigned to perform certain duties under [91.109], it follows that the safety pilot is a required crewmember and must hold a current and appropriate medical certificate. (6-17-85); (10-5-77).

During the test described in [91.109(c)] both the pilot being tested and the other required pilot would be crewmembers. If there are no persons in the aircraft other than crewmembers, the pilot in command need not comply with the recent experience requirements of [61.57(a)]. (9-20-77).

Does an appropriately rated safety pilot have to have a high performance sign-off prior to acting as second in command (safety pilot) in a high-performance airplane? (For example: a Piper Arrow or a Cessna Cutlass).

> The safety pilot would need only a private pilot certificate with an airplane category and single engine land class rating.

While our opinion is that there is no regulatory requirement that a safety pilot have a high performance endorsement to act as safety pilot, we are advised by the General Aviation & Commercial Division of the Flight Standards Service that they have always encouraged those pilots who act as safety pilots to be thoroughly familiar and current in the aircraft that is used. We are also advised by the General Aviation and Commercial Division that the FAA is currently in the process of reviewing the appropriate parts of the FAR to determine, among other things, if a safety pilot should be required to have a high performance endorsement. (6-24-91).

The term "dual controls" under 14 CFR section 91.109(a) means that the operating controls accessible to the right seat of the aircraft must be capable of performing the same function as the operating controls accessible to the left seat of the aircraft. It does not mean that the operating controls must be identical. (7-29-99).

A person may log second-in-command time only if more than one pilot is required under the type certificate of the aircraft or the regulations under which the flight is being conducted require an additional pilot. Operating under the provisions §91.109 (requiring a safety pilot during simulated instrument flight), the sole manipulator of the controls may log pilot in command time and the safety pilot may log second-in-command time. (10-19-99).

The term "dual controls" under §91.109(a) refers to flight controls (e.g. pitch, yaw, and roll controls). These flight controls are the only required dual controls for the purposes of §91.109(a). (4-4-00).

91.111 OPERATING NEAR OTHER AIRCRAFT

(a)   No person may operate an aircraft so close to another aircraft as to create a collision hazard.
(b)   No person may operate an aircraft in formation flight except by arrangement with the pilot in command of each aircraft in the formation.
(c)   No person may operate an aircraft, carrying passengers for hire, in formation flight.

CROSS REFERENCES

Previous designation: 91.65. 91.103-91.105 Waivers.

ADVISORY CIRCULARS

AC 90-48C *Pilot's Role in Collision Avoidance* (1983).

AC 90-23E *Aircraft Wake Turbulence* (1991).

AERONAUTICAL INFORMATION MANUAL

Emergency Airborne Inspection of Other Aircraft, Para. 7-5-9;
Vision in Flight, Para. 8-1-6;
Judgment Aspects of Collision Avoidance, Para. 8-1-8;
Pilot/Controller Glossary, "formation flight."

CASES

A helicopter pilot crossed over an active runway and began hovering after an airplane began its takeoff roll. The airplane collided with the helicopter. The airplane pilot died, the helicopter pilot received a 180 days suspension. *Administrator v. Blanc*, EA-4112 (1994).

The pilot of an aerobatic biplane received a suspension because he executed an aileron roll at 500'-800' AGL and other maneuvers within a mile of an airport, then made a high speed pass with a steep dive then climbed above a runway after cutting off a C172 on short final. *Administrator v. Swift*, EA-4122 (1994).

A captain relied on his first officer's report that ATC cleared them for a right turn which put them in a potential collision hazard. The pilot has duty to see and avoid traffic and should have challenged clearance. *Administrator v. Bennett*, EA-4124 (1994).

Where two aircraft, carrying passengers for hire, were being operated about 3000 feet apart with one aircraft handling all the radio communications with ATC and both aircraft landed on the same runway, it was held that they were engaged in formation flight. *Administrator v. Rickes*, 5 NTSB 299 (1985).

Where aircraft passed above and slightly to side of aircraft on runway while landing, pilot was held to have violated [91.111(a)]. The Board held that the pilot had no basis to assume that the aircraft would exit the runway and should have gone around. Further, when he realized it was not exiting, a go-around was the safer course of action. This is not a right of way situation, since the aircraft did not taxi onto the runway while the pilot was on final approach, but was on the runway when the pilot turned final. *Administrator v. Streeter*, 5 NTSB 394 (1985).

A pilot flew a Cherokee so close to a helicopter that the helicopter pilot had to descend quickly to avoid a collision. The airplane pilot argued that he never saw the helicopter, but the NTSB stated that the fact that the pilot did not see the helicopter by no means negated the violation of [91.111(a)]. *Administrator v. Cox*, 5 NTSB 430 (1985).

At an uncontrolled airport, a pilot taxied onto the active runway and took off, while there was an aircraft turning final for an approach to that runway. The Board held that the pilot who took off violated [91.111(a)]. *Administrator v. Mannix*, 4 NTSB 1193 (1984).

Where a pilot operated an aircraft dangerously close to another aircraft in order to obtain its registration numbers because he felt it was operating too low, the Board recognized that such action was precipitated by "provocation," but held that his actions were not justified, and a violation of [91.111(a)] was sustained. *Administrator v. Stone*, 4 NTSB 1685 (1984).

Announcing to ATC the loss of sight of the lead aircraft by the pilot in the wing aircraft is the reasonable course of action in controlled airspace. Trying to reacquire the lead aircraft visually while the transponder is in standby mode creates the possibility for a collision hazard. In this case the Board found that the pilot of the wing Cessna Citation violated §91.111 and §91.13. However, sanction was waved due to the proper filing of an Aviation Safety Reporting Program report. *Administrator v. Magnusson*, EA-4780 (1999).

When a balloon drifted over to the area where an aerobatic demonstration was still in progress the pilot chose to drop down towards the crowd instead of climbing into Class B airspace in order to avoid the other aircraft. A NOTAM was filed and extended informing pilots that an airshow was in progress. The Board felt that the balloon pilot should have recognized the potential hazard and avoided the area. They affirmed a 90-day suspension of his airman certificates. *Administrator v. Blose*, EA-4759 (1999).

The respondent's petition for reconsideration of the Administrator's decision that he had violated §§91.9, 91.111, and 91.113 was denied, and the civil penalty of $2,500 was upheld. The respondent caused the in-flight collision by following another aircraft to closely, which he knew to be in the vicinity, and by not continuing to maintain his awareness by moving his head to eliminated blind spots and/or make radio contact with the other aircraft. The pilot did not testify that he turned or tried to contact the other aircraft and failed to present any evidence that he filed an ASRP report with NASA. *FAA v. Sweeney*, FAA Order No. 94-21 (6-22-1994).

FAA CHIEF COUNSEL OPINIONS

Without further action by the agency, §91.111(c) should not be viewed as prohibiting formation flight carrying parachutists on the basis of a conclusion that they are passengers. (7-31-92).

There are no regulations which prohibit formation flights from conducting instrument approaches and/or landings during Instrument Meteorological Conditions. (2-12-97).

91.113 RIGHT-OF-WAY RULES: EXCEPT WATER OPERATIONS

(a)   *Inapplicability.* This section does not apply to the operation of an aircraft on water.

(b)   *General.* When weather conditions permit, regardless of whether an operation is conducted under instrument flight rules or visual flight rules, vigilance shall be maintained by each person operating an aircraft so as to see and avoid other aircraft. When a rule of this section gives another aircraft the right-of-way, the pilot shall give way to that aircraft and may not pass over, under, or ahead of it unless well clear.

(c)   *In distress.* An aircraft in distress has the right-of-way over all other air traffic.

(d)   *Converging.* When aircraft of the same category are converging at approximately the same altitude (except head-on, or nearly so) the aircraft to the other's right has the right-of-way. If the aircraft are of different categories —

    (1)   A balloon has the right-of-way over any other category of aircraft;

    (2)   A glider has the right-of-way over an airship, airplane or rotorcraft; and

    (3)   An airship has the right-of-way over an airplane or rotorcraft.

    However, an aircraft towing or refueling other aircraft has the right-of-way over all other engine-driven aircraft.

(e)   *Approaching head-on.* When aircraft are approaching each other head-on, or nearly so, each pilot of each aircraft shall alter course to the right.

(f)   *Overtaking.* Each aircraft that is being overtaken has the right-of-way and each pilot of an overtaking aircraft shall alter course to the right to pass well clear.

(g) *Landing.* Aircraft, while on final approach to land or while landing, have the right-of-way over other aircraft in flight or operating on the surface, except that they shall not take advantage of this rule to force an aircraft off the runway surface which has already landed and is attempting to make way for an aircraft on final approach. When two or more aircraft are approaching an airport for the purpose of landing, the aircraft at the lower altitude has the right-of-way, but it shall not take advantage of this rule to cut in front of another which is on final approach to land or to overtake that aircraft.

EXPLANATION

The purpose of this section is to establish rules which each pilot will adhere to when faced with a particular situation. The importance of knowing and complying with these rules is that the other pilot's action will normally be based on his or her belief and hope that you will comply.

CROSS REFERENCES

Previous designation: 91.67. 91.903-91.905 Waivers; 91.115 Right-of-way Rules: Water Operations.

ADVISORY CIRCULARS

AC 90-42F *Traffic Advisory Practices at Airports Without Operating Control Towers* (1990).

AC 90-48C *Pilot's Role in Collision Avoidance* (1983).

AC 90-66A *Recommended Standard Traffic Patterns and Practices for Aeronautical Operations at Airports without Operating Control Towers* (1993).

AERONAUTICAL INFORMATION MANUAL

Airport Operations, Para. 4-3-1 through Para. 4-3-26;
Accident Cause Factors: Giving Way, Para. 7-5-1(d).

CASES

The Board affirmed a 180 day suspension of a pilot's private pilot's certificate for violations of [91.113(b)] and [91.13(a)] following a mid-air collision between two aircraft on approach to landing. It held that where a pilot failed to fly a base leg and instead made essentially a continuous turn from downwind to final, he reduced his opportunity to see other traffic in the pattern, such as the Citabria that had the right-of-way because it was ahead of him on the final approach and, also, reduced his opportunity to be seen. *Administrator v. Kohorst*, EA-3799 (1993).

The respondent's petition for reconsideration of the Administrator's decision that he had violated §§91.9, 91.111, and 91.113 was denied, and the civil penalty of $2,500 was upheld. The respondent caused the in-flight collision by following another aircraft to closely, which he knew to be in the vicinity, and by not continuing to maintain his awareness by moving his head to eliminated blind spots and/or make radio contact with the other aircraft. The pilot did not testify that he turned or tried to contact the other aircraft and failed to present any evidence that he filed an ASRP report with NASA. *FAA v. Sweeney*, FAA Order No. 94-21 (6-22-1994).

FAA CHIEF COUNSEL OPINIONS

Under §91.113(b), when weather conditions permit, a pilot must operate his aircraft so as to see and avoid other aircraft regardless of whether the flight is conducted under VFR or under IFR. However, under Part 91, a pilot generally is not required to adhere to a published IFR departure procedure. Under IMC, a pilot should, but is not required to, follow an IFR departure procedure. When outside of radar coverage, however, a pilot remains responsible for terrain and obstacle clearance. (11-30-93).

If a helicopter is approaching an uncontrolled airport for landing, a fixed-wing aircraft must give way to the helicopter for landing. (7-3-89).

At an uncontrolled airport, once an aircraft has landed and slowed to a speed such that the pilot can stop the aircraft through the application of normal braking, the pilot no longer has the right of way as a "landing aircraft." (1-7-81).

[91.113(d)] applies only to aircraft in flight since the reference is made to altitude and there is no reference to operations on the surface. (1-7-81).

91.115 RIGHT-OF-WAY RULES: WATER OPERATIONS

(a) *General.* Each person operating an aircraft on the water shall, insofar as possible, keep clear of all vessels and avoid impeding their navigation, and shall give way to any vessel or other aircraft that is given the right-of-way by any rule of this section.

(b) *Crossing.* When aircraft, or an aircraft and a vessel, are on crossing courses, the aircraft or vessel to the other's right has the right-of-way.

(c) *Approaching head-on.* When aircraft, or an aircraft and a vessel, are approaching head-on, or nearly so, each shall alter its course to the right to keep well clear.

(d) *Overtaking.* Each aircraft or vessel that is being overtaken has the right-of-way, and the one overtaking shall alter course to keep well clear.

(e) *Special circumstances.* When aircraft, or an aircraft and a vessel, approach so as to involve risk of collision, each aircraft or vessel shall proceed with careful regard to existing circumstances, including the limitations of the respective craft.

CROSS REFERENCES

Previous designation: 91.69. 91.903-91.905 Waivers.

ADVISORY CIRCULARS

AC 91-69A *Seaplane Safety for 14 CFR Part 91 Operators* (1999).

FAA-H-8083-3 *Airplane Flying Handbook* (1999), Chapter 16 — Transition to Seaplanes.

AERONAUTICAL INFORMATION MANUAL

Seaplane Safety, Para. 7-5-7;
Pilot/Controller Glossary, "Sea Lane.".

91.117 AIRCRAFT SPEED

(a) Unless otherwise authorized by the Administrator, no person may operate an aircraft below 10,000 feet MSL at an indicated airspeed of more than 250 knots (288 m.p.h.).

(b) Unless otherwise authorized or required by ATC, no person may operate an aircraft at or below 2,500 feet above the surface within 4 nautical miles of the primary airport of a Class C or Class D airspace area at an indicated airspeed of more than 200 knots (230 mph.). This paragraph (b) does not apply to any operations within a Class B airspace area. Such operations shall comply with paragraph (a) of this section.

(c) No person may operate an aircraft in the airspace underlying a Class B airspace area designated for an airport or in a VFR corridor designated through such a Class B airspace area, at an indicated airspeed of more than 200 knots (230 mph.).

(d) If the minimum safe airspeed for any particular operation is greater than the maximum speed prescribed in this section, the aircraft may be operated at that minimum speed.

EXPLANATION

The maximum allowable speed is governed by the altitude at which the aircraft is operating and/or the designation of the airspace in which the operation is conducted. As part of the overall handling of traffic in an orderly manner, ATC depends on adherence to the stated indicated airspeeds. The lower altitudes can become more crowded than the flight levels, therefore speed restrictions become necessary so that high speed aircraft can respond to course changes quickly and without using excessive airspace. This regulation does provide an exception, in the interest of safety, where the minimum safe airspeed for a particular operation is greater than the maximum prescribed by this section, the aircraft may be operated at that minimum. While not specifically required, if it is necessary to exceed the maximum, ATC should be advised. If ATC issues a clearance or instruction calling for speeds in excess of 250 knots below 10,000 feet or 200 knots in the airspace below a Class B airspace or in a VFR corridor, confirm the speed with ATC.

CROSS REFERENCES

Previous designation: 91.70. 91.902-91.905, Waivers; 91.131 Operations in Class B Airspace.

ADVISORY CIRCULARS

AC 91-43 *Unreliable Airspeed Indicators* (1975).

AERONAUTICAL INFORMATION MANUAL

Speed Adjustments, Para. 4-4-11 and 5-5-9;
Local Flow Traffic Management Program, Para. 5-4-2;
Instrument Approach Procedures, Para. 5-4-7.

FAA CHIEF COUNSEL OPINIONS

It is now clear that aircraft may exceed 250 knots above 10,000 feet MSL in Class B airspace. (10-7-93).

The speed restrictions prescribed in [91.117] do not distinguish between IFR operations and those conducted under VFR. Their application is based on the flight altitude or the designation of the airspace in which the operation occurs. (5-17-78).

91.119 MINIMUM SAFE ALTITUDES: GENERAL

Except when necessary for takeoff or landing, no person may operate an aircraft below the following altitudes:

(a) *Anywhere.* An altitude allowing, if a power unit fails, an emergency landing without undue hazard to persons or property on the surface.

(b) *Over congested areas.* Over any congested area of a city, town, or settlement, or over any open air assembly of persons, an altitude of 1,000 feet above the highest obstacle within a horizontal radius of 2,000 feet of the aircraft.

(c) *Over other than congested areas.* An altitude of 500 feet above the surface, except over open water or sparsely populated areas. In those cases, the aircraft may not be operated closer than 500 feet to any person, vessel, vehicle, or structure.

(d) *Helicopters.* Helicopters may be operated at less than the minimums prescribed in paragraph (b) or (c) of this section if the operation is conducted without hazard to persons or property on the surface. In addition, each person operating a helicopter shall comply with any routes or altitudes specifically prescribed for helicopters by the Administrator.

EXPLANATION

This section can cause many problems, because it uses terms that do not have a specific definition or objective standards, i.e. "when necessary for take off or landing," "undue hazard," "congested areas," "other than congested areas," "sparsely populated areas," and "hazard." The definitions of these terms have been developed through FAA Chief Counsel opinions and NTSB caselaw.

The fact that you are taking off or landing does not, in and of itself, allow you to operate below the prescribed altitudes. The site of the takeoff or landing must be an "appropriate site." All landing, except emergency landings, are prohibited in inappropriate locations. These emergency landings do not come under the exception "where necessary," but are related to the emergency provisions of 91.3(b). Most cases before the NTSB regarding 91.119 are resolved on the credibility of the pilot's testimony, i.e. does the judge believe that the action was appropriate.

91.119(a): This speaks to being at an altitude which would allow, in the event of the failure of an engine, or airborne heater, in the case of a balloon, an emergency landing to be made without undue hazard to persons or property on the surface. The use of the word "undue" means that there must be more than a simple hazard.

91.119(b): This subsection establishes the minimum altitude over "congested areas" of a city, town or settlement and any open air assembly of persons. Ten houses and a school and a university campus have been held to be congested areas. When in doubt, treat the area as a congested area. Note that this subsection does not simply require that a pilot remain 1,000 feet above ground level over congested areas: pilots must also clear towers, and other obstacles by 2,000 feet horizontally **or** 1,000 feet vertically.

91.119(c): This subsection relates to "other than congested areas." This means areas that are not congested, but are more than "sparsely populated areas." Use good judgment in deciding how "populated" an area appears to be.

91.119(d): In the case of helicopters, the standards become even more ambiguous. This subsection allows helicopter pilots to ignore subsections (b) and (c) (but not (a)) if the operation is conducted without hazard to persons or property on the surface. The word used here is "hazard" not "undue hazard." To establish a violation of this subsection it must be shown that an actual hazard was created. If the FAA can only show a "potential hazard," then a violation of 91.119(d) cannot be established, **but** a violation of 91.13(a) may be found.

CROSS REFERENCES

Previous designation: 91.79. 91.13 Careless or Reckless Operation; 91.103-91.905 Waivers; FAR Part 137 Agricultural Aircraft Operations.

AERONAUTICAL INFORMATION MANUAL

Pilot/Controller Glossary, "Minimum Safe Altitude."

CASES

A flight instructor and student flew at less than 100' AGL above a freeway where two police officers observed that the airplane continued the low pass for at least a quarter of a mile. The flight instructor claimed they were practicing emergency procedures. The instructor received a 90 day suspension. The suspension was not waived under the Aviation Safety Reporting Program (ASRP) because it was not considered inadvertent. *Administrator v. Traub*, EA-4188 (1994).

A pilot caught buzzing a nude beach received a 120 day suspension. *Administrator v. Paradowski*, EA-3962 (1993).

In the case of [91.119(d)], to establish a violation there must be evidence sufficient to show that the flight produced an actual hazard as opposed to a potential hazard. *Administrator v. Wolf* EA-3450 (1991); *Administrator v. Michelson*, 3 NTSB 3111 (1980); and *Administrator v. Reynolds*, 4 NTSB 240 (1982).

The appropriateness of the landing site, at least in terms of the necessity for a landing there, could fairly be weighted in the overall context of the choices available to the pilot. *Administrator v. Rees*, 4 NTSB 1323 (1984); *Administrator v. Pringle*, EA-3428 (1991).

Operation of a helicopter over a fire scene at such a low altitude that the noise hampered the firefighters ability to communicate and its downdraft moved the smoke about so as to affect the visibility, constituted an actual hazard. *Administrator v. Tur*, EA-3458 (1991).

To establish a violation of [91.119(d)], it must be shown that an actual hazard was created. However, to do this, it is not required that there have been actual injury to persons or property. *Administrator v. Tur*, EA-3490 (1992).

Whatever else "undue hazard" may mean, it embraces a situation where a pilot's cruising altitude would not likely permit the aircraft to land without striking or passing dangerously close to people and property on the surface. To prove a violation of [91.119(a)], it is not necessary that it be shown that is would have been made, in the event of an engine failure, it is sufficient to show that an emergency landing from the pilot's altitude presented and unreasonable risk of such harm. *Administrator v. Michelson*, 3 NTSB 3111 (1980); *Administrator v. Oeming*, EA-3542 (1992).

Landing a helicopter on a sand and gravel parking lot in front of a restaurant and two gas stations was a violation of [91.119(d)]. This was based on the fact that the landing area was not secured from traffic that could have entered the area and from vehicles and persons at the gas station and the pilot's failure to evaluate the surface of the area insofar as the potential for blowing debris. Violations have also been found where a helicopter landed on a parking lot-delivery area behind a shopping center open to the public and in a residential area without securing the area prior to landing. *Administrator v. Lewis*, 5 NTSB 879 (1986).

The Board has stated that the prefatory language of [91.119] allows a pilot to fly his airplane below minimum altitude requirements not just when necessary for the actual landing or takeoff, but also for other approved purposes, such as touch and goes, practice missed approaches, and practice instrument approaches, that are conducted to improve a pilot's capabilities in those areas. *Administrator v. Kunkel*, 5 NTSB 1400 (1986).

[Editor's Note: The appropriateness of the landing site may still be taken into consideration.]

The Board traditionally has held that, when other suitable takeoff paths are available, a takeoff path that causes an aircraft to be in violation of [91.119] is not to be construed as "necessary for takeoff." *Administrator v. Stone*, 4 NTSB 1685 (1984).

The term "structure" includes objects such as electrical or telephone wires as well as the poles they hang from. *Administrator v. Scollam*, 2 NTSB 538 (1973).

When a balloon drifted over to the area where an aerobatic demonstration was still in progress the pilot chose to drop down towards the crowd instead of climbing into Class B airspace in order to avoid the other aircraft. A NOTAM was filed and extended informing pilots that an airshow was in progress. The Board felt that the balloon pilot should have recognized the potential hazard and avoided the area. They affirmed a 90-day suspension of his airman certificates. *Administrator v. Blose*, EA-4759 (1999).

The Board overturned the ruling that the respondent's action of step-taxiing his floatplane within 100 feet of a dwelling on the bank of a lake was not necessary for his landing and constituted an unacceptable risk of loss of control. Their basis for this decision was that the Administrator's complaint revolved around the respondents actions in-flight, prior to landing and therefore the ALJ could not rule on unalleged grounds. *Administrator v. Lepping*, EA-4874 (2001).

A company that provided banner towing services to local merchants was fined $1,100 for violating §91.119 and §91.13 by operating the aircraft at altitudes of only 600-800 feet above congested areas. *FAA v. High Exposure*, FAA Order No. 2001-2 (5-16-2001).

The pilot in command of a helicopter was assessed a civil penalty of $2,000 for hovering only 30 to 40 feet above persons in a swimming hole three times. Although only one of the three hovering incidents was proven, the law judge held, on appeal, that because each incident violated both §§91.119 and 91.13 (formerly §§91.79 and 91.9) each of which carried a maximum fine of $1,000, the assessed penalty of $2,000 was not excessive. *FAA v. Metcalf*, FAA Order No. 93-17 (6-10-1993).

A pilot was fined $1,000 for coming within 50 to 80 feet of several fishing boats while landing his float plane on a river. The law judge affirmed the initial decision in part that this was a violation of §91.119 (formerly 91.79) and reversed the initial finding in part by ruling that it was also a violation of §91.13 (formerly 91.9). *FAA v. Cornwall*, FAA Order No. 92-47 (7-22-1992).

FAA CHIEF COUNSEL OPINIONS

"Congested area" is determined on a case by case basis. Examples of what was determined by the Civil Aeronautics Board [now the NTSB] are 1) an area consisting of 10 houses and a school; 2) a university campus; 3) a beach area along a highway; 4) over a boy's camp where there were numerous people on the dock and children playing on the shore. The presence of people is important to the determination of whether a particular area is "congested." The term "congested area" has been interpreted to apply to flights that cut the corners of large, heavily congested residential areas. The congested area must be an area of a city, town or settlement. (10-3-79), (1-5-78), (9-13-76).

Use of the emergency defense of 91.3(b) in a situation where the aircraft is operated contrary to [91.119] is normally available where the emergency relates to safety of flight. It has in a few instances been used where life and death situations existed outside the aircraft, such as on a rescue mission. (10-29-79).

The term "sparsely populated area" is not expressly defined. A subdivision of at least 40 occupied residential homes on adjacent one acre lots is not considered a "sparsely populated area." (10-3-79).

[91.119(a)] requires an operator to select an altitude which, in the event of a power unit failure, will permit an emergency landing to be made without excessive or unwarranted hazard to persons or property on the surface. (3-28-77).

The word "undue" in [91.119(a)] modifies the word "hazard," so that the requirement is based upon more than a simple hazard. (4-1-77).

To determine whether flight below a §91.119 minimum safe altitude is permissible, one must determine whether that portion of the flight is **necessary** to permit the pilot to transition between the surface and the enroute or pattern altitude in connection with a takeoff or a landing. (10-30-97).

## 91.121	ALTIMETER SETTINGS

(a)	Each person operating an aircraft shall maintain the cruising altitude or flight level of that aircraft, as the case may be, by reference to an altimeter that is set, when operating —
   (1)	Below 18,000 feet MSL, to —
       (I)	The current reported altimeter setting of a station along the route and within 100 nautical miles of the aircraft;
       (ii)	If there is no station within the area prescribed in paragraph (a)(1)(I) of this section, the current reported altimeter setting of an appropriate available station; or
       (iii)	In the case of an aircraft not equipped with a radio, the elevation of the departure airport or an appropriate altimeter setting available before departure; or
   (2)	At or above 18,000 feet MSL, to 29.92" Hg.
(b)	The lowest usable flight level is determined by the atmospheric pressure in the area of operation, as shown in the following table:

Current altimeter setting	Lowest usable flight level
29.92 (or higher)	180
29.91 through 29.42	185
29.41 through 28.92	190
28.91 through 28.42	195
28.41 through 27.92	200
27.91 through 27.42	205
27.41 through 26.92	210

(c)	To convert minimum altitude prescribed under §§91.119 and 91.177 to the minimum flight level, the pilot shall take the flight level equivalent of the minimum altitude in feet and add the appropriate number of feet specified below, according to the current reported altimeter setting:

Current altimeter setting	Adjustable factor level
29.92 (or higher)	None
29.91 through 29.42	500
29.41 through 28.92	1,000
28.91 through 28.42	1,500
28.41 through 27.92	2,000
27.91 through 27.42	2,500
27.41 through 26.92	3,000

EXPLANATION

This section is crucial to safety. As stated in the *Aeronautical Information Manual*, an inch of error on an altimeter setting equals 1,000 feet of altitude. During the flight, a pilot should obtain the current altimeter setting frequently along the route. During preflight and the flight itself, a pilot should pay attention to the weather systems, especially when a flightpath leads from a high pressure system to a low pressure system. ("High to low, look out below.")

91.121(a)(1): This subsection provides the altimeter procedures when flying below 18,000 feet M.S.L. When it is necessary to utilize the procedure described in (a)(1)(iii), extreme caution should be exercised, because, in the event of frontal passage during the flight, the original reading may be substantially different from the actual altitude.

91.121(a)(2): When operating at or above 18,000 feet M.S.L., set the altimeter to 29.92" Hg.

91.121(b): This table allows a determination of the lowest usable flight level for the various altimeter settings.

91.121(c): This table converts the minimum altitude set forth in 91.119 and 91.177 to the minimum flight level using the current altimeter setting.

CROSS REFERENCES

Previous designation: 91.81. 91.119 Minimum Safe Altitudes, General; 91.177, Minimum Altitudes for IFR Operations; 91.903-91.905 Waivers.

ADVISORY CIRCULARS

AC 91-14D *Altimeter Setting Sources* (1979).

AERONAUTICAL INFORMATION MANUAL

Altimeter Setting Procedures, Para. 7-2-1 through 7-2-5;
Weather Observing Programs, Para. 7-1-12.

91.123 COMPLIANCE WITH ATC CLEARANCES AND INSTRUCTIONS

(a)   When an ATC clearance has been obtained, no pilot in command may deviate from that clearance unless an amended clearance is obtained, an emergency exists, or the deviation is in response to a traffic alert and collision avoidance system resolution advisory. However, except in Class A airspace, a pilot may cancel an IFR flight plan if the operation is being conducted in VFR weather conditions. When a pilot is uncertain of an ATC clearance, that pilot shall immediately request clarification from ATC.

(b)   Except in an emergency, no person may operate an aircraft contrary to an ATC instruction in an area in which air traffic control is exercised.

(c)   Each pilot in command who, in an emergency, or in response to a traffic alert and collision avoidance system resolution advisory, deviates from an ATC clearance or instruction shall notify ATC of that deviation as soon as possible.

(d)   Each pilot in command who (though not deviating from a rule of this subpart) is given priority by ATC in an emergency, shall submit a detailed report of that emergency within 48 hours to the manager of that ATC facility, if requested by ATC.

(e)   Unless otherwise authorized by ATC, no person operating an aircraft may operate that aircraft according to any clearance or instruction that has been issued to the pilot of another aircraft for radar air traffic control purposes.

EXPLANATION

The NTSB has stated the importance of 91.123 when it stated that the efficiency of the ATC system is predicated on prompt and strict adherence to instructions and clearances issued by controllers, who alone are in a position to be fully aware of all the traffic within a given area and to take the appropriate steps to assure that adequate separation will be maintained between such traffic.

Read back a clearance or instruction when acknowledging it. This helps both pilots and controllers avoid misunderstandings.

A pilot can request a different clearance or instruction, but, until an amended clearance or new instruction is given, the pilot should comply with the original one unless to do so would endanger the flight, or if it is beyond the aircraft's performance to do so.

When in doubt about a clearance or instruction, always ask for clarification, never assume what you are unsure of.

In aircraft requiring two pilots always ensure that there is a clear definition of the responsibilities of the flying and non-flying pilots insofar as communication with ATC. Each pilot should be double checking the other to ensure compliance. The pilot in command always has the primary responsibility for the conduct of the flight.

91.123(a): This subsection deals with ATC clearances. Note that the first two sentences apply specifically to the pilot in command. If the co-pilot is found to have contributed to the "deviation," the co-pilot will be charged under 91.13(a), not 91.123(a). Either pilot may seek clarification of a clearance. In accordance with 91.3, deviation is allowed in emergency situations.

91.123(b): This section deals with instructions and applies to both the pilot in command and any other required pilot crewmember on board. It also allows operation contrary to an ATC instruction in an emergency.

91.123(c): Where there is a deviation from an ATC clearance or instruction on the basis of an emergency, the pilot in command must notify ATC as soon as possible.

91.123(d): In cases where an aircraft is given priority in an emergency, if requested by ATC the pilot in command is required to submit a detailed report to the manager of the ATC facility within 48 hours. This must be done, even if the pilot did not deviate from any rule under Part 91.

91.123(e): Unless authorized by ATC, a pilot may not operate pursuant to a clearance or instruction issued to the pilot of another aircraft for radar or traffic control purposes. Carefully reading back clearances may prevent violations of this subsection.

1995 changes to §91.123:
> This rule accomplishes two things. First, it authorizes deviations from an ATC clearance when responding to a Traffic alert and collision avoidance system resolution advisory (TCAS RA). Secondly, it requires pilots to notify ATC as soon as possible if they deviate from a clearance in response to a TCAS RA. This action codifies existing policies and practices that were initiated during the TCAS implementation period.
>
> TCAS is airborne equipment that interrogates ATC transponders of other aircraft nearby. By computer analysis of the replies, TCAS equipment determines which transponder-equipped aircraft are potential collision hazards and provides appropriate advisory information to the flight crew. If a TCAS-equipped airplane interrogates an aircraft that is equipped with a transponder without altitude reporting capability (Mode A), range and azimuth information will be provided to the TCAS-equipped aircraft. If the interrogated aircraft is equipped with an altitude encoding transponder (Mode C or Mode S), then relative altitude information will be provided in addition to range and azimuth. TCAS equipment cannot detect the presence of an aircraft that is not equipped with a transponder.
>
> TCAS equipment performs proximity tests on each detected target. If the path of a target is projected to pass within certain horizontal and vertical distance criteria, then that target is declared an intruder. An intruder that is determined to pose an even greater risk of collision is declared a threat. When a threat is declared, TCAS equipment determines the appropriate direction that the TCAS-equipped aircraft must move (climb or descend) and the vertical rate that must be maintained to achieve separation from the threat.
>
> There are two classes of advisories provided by TCAS equipment. The first class, the "traffic advisory" (TA), provides supplemental information to the pilot that aids in visual detection of other aircraft. TA's include the range, bearing, and if the intruder has altitude-reporting equipment, the altitude of intruding aircraft relative to the TCAS equipped aircraft. TA's without altitude information may also be provided from non-altitude reporting transponder-equipped intruders. TCAS I equipment provides TA's that only assist the pilot in visually detecting an intruder aircraft. The second class of advisory, the "resolution advisory" (RA), indicates the vertical direction and rate that must be achieved by an aircraft in order to prevent insufficient separation. When an RA occurs, the pilot flying should respond by direct attention to RA displays and should maneuver as indicated unless doing so would jeopardize the safe operation of the flight or unless the flight crew has definitive visual acquisition of the aircraft causing the RA. TCAS II equipment provides both traffic and resolution advisories only in the vertical plane.

The decisions made under the certificate action against Richard Lee Merrell (see Cases) marked an important change in policy for handling radio communication misunderstandings. In the past, when a controller failed to correct a pilot's readback which subsequently led to that pilot violating §91.123, the pilot would usually receive a suspension of his or her airman certificates from the FAA. When the pilot appealed the suspension to the NTSB, the Board had the option to dismiss any certificate action against the pilot for failing to follow the clearance that he or she clearly misunderstood.

As a result of the FAA's timely publication of a legal interpretation (see FAA Chief Counsel Opinions) on this matter, the U.S. District Court of Appeals ruled that a pilot must follow ATC directions unless there is an emergency, and that §91.123 does not suggest that he may rely on readback procedures to absolve himself of responsibility.

CROSS REFERENCES

Previous designation: 91.75. 91.3 Responsibility and Authority of Pilot In Command; 91.125 ATC Light Signals; 91.903-905 Waivers; 121.542 Flight Crewmember Duties; 135.100, Flight Crewmember Duties.

ADVISORY CIRCULARS

AC 91-70 *Oceanic Operations, an Authorization Guide to Oceanic Operations* (1994.)

AC 99-1C *Security Control of Air Traffic* (1989).

AERONAUTICAL INFORMATION MANUAL

Radio Communication Phraseology and Techniques, Para. 4-2-1 through 4-2-14; ATC Clearances/Separations, Para. 4-4-1 through 4-4-15; Closing VFR/DVFR Flight Plans, Para. 5-1-12 Pilot/Controller Roles and Responsibilities, Para. 5-5-1 through 5-5-15.

CASES

A pilot and co-pilot who knew that they would not be able to meet ATC's altitude restriction should have told ATC before the deviation occurred. The fact that ATC knew other aircraft could not reach that altitude requirement or that standard separation was not lost does not negate the deviation. *Administrator v. Cannon & Winter,* EA-4056 (1994).

To prove that a landing gear problem justified operating contrary to an ATC clearance, it must be shown that it required the immediate, exclusive attention of either or both pilots, such that the aircraft altimeters could not be monitored while the problem was being investigated and corrected, or that disregarding the altitude clearance or gaining additional altitude was necessary in order to remedy the problem. *Administrator v. Black,* 5 NTSB 902 (1986).

Where the crew was having difficulty in determining how close they were to the intersection, the proper course of action would have been to stop the plane and confirm position with ATC, especially when the operation occurred at night and the visual cues to the intersection, while adequate, were not optimal. *Administrator v. Liddell,* 5 NTSB 1957 (1987).

Where a duty imposed on FAA employees and instituted, at least in part, for the benefit of the pilots, i.e. immediate notification of the pilot by ATC of a possible altitude deviation, is not complied with, if violations of [91.123(a) and 91.13(a)] are found, no sanction will be imposed. *Administrator v. Brasher,* 5 NTSB 2116 (1987).

When a pilot elects to acknowledge a clearance or instruction without a readback, he violated a safe operating practice and can not complain that he did not understand it or hear it at all. *Administrator v. Drawdy,* EA-2994 (1989).

Adherence to a controller's clearance is imperative if the safe and orderly flow of traffic in and around an airport is to be maintained. *Administrator v. Frownfelter*, 2 NTSB 993 (1974).

Pilots can request different instructions or clearance when they believe them to be warranted or desirable. However, where the controller does not grant a change, a pilot would need a safety related reason for not complying with the instruction or clearance. *Administrator v. Brandy*, 3 NTSB 2957 (1980).

In a case where a controller issued a clearance to an aircraft using "Citation One Zero Eight" to identify the aircraft, and an acknowledgment was received from a pilot identifying himself as "Cessna One Zero Echo," the NTSB reversed a suspension of the Cessna pilot's certificate, stating that it is the controller's responsibility to listen to the acknowledgment and assure its consistency with his instruction. *Administrator v. Holstein*, EA-2782 (1988).

In a case where a pilot's incorrect readback was not heard by ATC, the United States Court of Appeals, District of Columbia Circuit, overturned the NTSB's finding of no violation. The court ruled that FAR 91.123 states that a pilot must follow ATC directions unless there is an emergency, and does not suggest that he may rely on readback procedures to absolve himself of responsibility. *Administrator v. NTSB*, 190 F.3d 571, (D.C. Cir. 1999).

The following case eventually resulted in caselaw which states that a pilot is **not** protected from a violation by a "readback" of the clearance as understood by the pilot. The initial ruling of the Board was to reverse the suspension of the non-flying pilot-in-command's certificate whose incorrect readback was not heard, and then whose aircraft subsequently ascended to an altitude that resulted in the loss of the standard safety separation with another transport category aircraft. *Administrator v. Merrell*, EA-4530 (1997).

The FAA filed a petition for reconsideration stating that the Board was substituting its interpretation for that of the Administrator, and that the Board's policy on this issue threatened aviation safety. The Board denied the petition replying that the FAA failed to offer any written policy guidance on this issue, and that the policy to dismiss certificate action against a pilot for failing to follow the clearance that the pilot clearly misunderstood did not threaten aviation safety. In fact, they stated, the policy fostered aviation safety by placing the burden of accurate communication on both the pilot and the controller. *Administrator v. Merrell*, EA-4670 (1998).

The FAA appealed the case to the United States Court of Appeals, District of Columbia Circuit, which overturned the Board's finding of no violation. On September 21, 1999, the court ruled that FAR 91.123 states that a pilot must follow ATC directions unless there is an emergency, and does not suggest that he may rely on readback procedures to absolve himself of responsibility. *FAA v. Merrell*, 190 F.3rd 571 (C.A.D.C. 1999).

As a result of the district court's ruling the Board vacated the previous two orders and affirmed the initial decision of the law judge. The Board stated that "under the Administrator's interpretation of the relevant regulations…an error of perception does not constitute a reasonable explanation for a deviation from a clearly transmitted clearance or instruction. Rather, inattentiveness or carelessness is presumed from the occurrence of a deviation unless, as we understand it, the misperception or mistake concerning the clearance was attributable to some factor for which the airman was not responsible, such as an equipment failure." *Administrator v. Merrell*, EA-4814 (2000).

After being given clearance to land on the active runway, a pilot landed the aircraft on the active taxiway. The Board upheld the violation of 91.123. *Administrator v. Grant*, EA-4827 (2000).

A pilot in command did not initiate the required turn at the required location for the Standard Instrument Departure due to an interruption by the first officer who was questioning the interpretation of the SID regarding this turn. The Board agreed that the first officer's misinterpretation and resulting interruption constituted an emergency which the PIC handled sufficiently, and which he did not create, thereby voiding the violation of 91.123. *Administrator v. Moore*, EA-4929 (2001).

A violation of §91.123 (formerly 91.75) for the pilot in command and of §91.13 (formerly 91.9) for both the PIC and the flying pilot occurred when they deviated from their "maintain flight level one eight zero" clearance and descended below 18,000 feet without an amended clearance. Although both pilots testified that they did not hear "maintain," there was no evidence on the air traffic control tapes that the clearance was garbled, muffled, or unclear. *FAA v. Richardson*, FAA Order No. 92-49 (7-22-1992).

The initial decision of the law judge in finding that the respondent was in violation of §91.13 (formerly 91.9) and §91.123 (formerly 91.75) when, while taxing on a runway, he mistakenly taxied across an intersecting runway, was reversed. The absence of the usual cues present on a taxiway enabling a pilot to identify an intersecting runway combined with confusing instructions from air traffic control, would make a finding of violation unjust. *FAA v. Wendt*, FAA Order No. 92-40 (6-15-1992).

A civil penalty of $2,000 was not excessive in the case where a pilot taxied his aircraft onto the wrong runway. The instructions from the ground controllers were clear, and the fact that weather conditions did not allow controllers to see the aircraft and that the taxiways were similar were not mitigating circumstances warranting a reduction. *FAA v. Watkins*, FAA Order No. 92-8 (1-31-1992).

A pilot in command and first officer of a Piedmont Airlines flight misinterpreted a clearance for a Cessna ahead of them to takeoff and then moved onto the runway in preparation for takeoff. This action constituted a violation of §§91.13, 91.123, and 91.129 (formerly 91.9, 91.75, and 91.87), however because they both filed ASRP reports with NASA no penalty was assessed. *FAA v. Terry*, FAA Order No. 91-12 (4-12-1991).

FAA CHIEF COUNSEL OPINIONS

If a pilot is uncertain whether the IFR approach procedure for which he obtained ATC clearance requires or only permits a procedure turn, he is required under [91.123(a)] to immediately request clarification from ATC. (7-25-77).

Giving a full readback of an air traffic control transmission could result in the mitigation of sanctions for a regulatory violation when the air traffic controller, under the circumstances, reasonably should correct the pilot's error but fails to do so. Accordingly, the FAA may take this factor into consideration in setting the amount of sanction in FAA enforcement orders. However, the simple act of giving a readback does not shift full responsibility to air traffic control and cannot insulate pilots from their primary responsibility under 14 CFR 91.123 and related regulations to listen attentively, to hear accurately, and to construe reasonably in the first instance. (April 1, 1999).

Full and complete readbacks can benefit safety when the overall volume of radio communications is relatively light; however, they can be detrimental during periods of concentrated communications. However, the simple act of giving a readback does not shift full responsibility to air traffic control and cannot insulate pilots from their primary responsibility under 14 CFR 91.123 and related regulations to listen attentively, to hear accurately, and to construe reasonably in the first instance. (4-1-99).

When air traffic control (ATC) issued a clearance to "descend and maintain 7000 feet," and the pilot replied, "unable," the pilot's notice of inability was presumed to be based on one of the exceptions for deviation in §91.123, and clearance was therefore amended. The exceptions include emergencies or responses to a traffic alert and collision avoidance system resolution. (7-28-99).

The pilot in command of an aircraft has the authority to reject an ATC clearance or instruction that would compromise the safe operation of that aircraft. A pilot unable to comply with an ATC clearance may have been encountering icing, turbulence, or equipment problems, and is not expected to comply until he or she states that they are able by accepting the clearance. (7-28-99).

A clearance is legally amended when after being verbally issued by ATC, it is replied to by the pilot. The pilot alone holds the responsibility to determine if he or she is **able** to accept the amended clearance. If the pilot expresses his or her inability to comply, the controller would await further communications from the pilot indicating the ability to execute the clearance. (7-28-99).

Replying "stand by" to an ATC request is not a violation of §91.123. The pilot is not accepting or rejecting the pending ATC clearance. This response merely indicates his immediate inability to execute the clearance, and because ATC cannot know why the pilot has made this request, the pilot will not be expected to comply until he communicates with ATC again. However, when a pilot requests a clearance and ATC replies "stand by" the clearance has not legally been amended and the pilot must comply with the previous clearance until ATC approves or denies the request. (7-28-99).

While controllers may use the hemispherical rule to manage aircraft operation within controlled airspace, they are not required to do so. Other factors such as ATC procedures, airspace sectorization, and the volume of air traffic may require the use of other altitudes. Therefore, the rule in controlled airspace is that ATC assigns each pilot an altitude to be flown, which ensures separation from other known traffic. The pilot must comply with that assignment. (7-28-99).

91.125   ATC LIGHT SIGNALS

ATC light signals have the meaning shown in the following table.

Color and type of signal	Meaning with respect to aircraft on the surface	Meaning with respect to aircraft in flight
Steady green......	Cleared for takeoff	Clear to land.
Flashing green.....	Cleared to taxi.....	Return for landing (to be followed by steady green at proper time).
Steady red......	Stop......	Give way to other aircraft and continue circling.
Flashing red......	Taxi clear of runway in use.	Airport unsafe — do not land.
Flashing white......	Return to starting point on airport.	Not applicable.
Alternating red and green	Exercise extreme caution.	Exercise extreme caution.

EXPLANATION

In the event you are operating an aircraft that does not have a radio, and you have obtained a waiver to operate into an airport with an operating control tower, or you lose your radios in flight, ATC clearances will be communicated with light signals. The signals given by ATC with a light gun have the same force and effect as those given by radio. It is recommended that pilots keep a copy of this table accessible in the cockpit at all times.

CROSS REFERENCES

Previous designation: 91.77. 91.123 Compliance with ATC Clearances and Instructions; 91.127 Operating On and In the Vicinity of an Airport: General Rules; 91.129 Operation at Airports with Operating Control Towers; 91.903-91.905 Waivers.

ADVISORY CIRCULARS

AC 90-67B *Light Gun Signals from the Control Tower for Ground Vehicles, Equipment, and Personnel* (1994).

AERONAUTICAL INFORMATION MANUAL

Visual Indicators at Airports without an Operating Control Tower, Para. 4-3-13.

91.126 OPERATING ON OR IN THE VICINITY OF AN AIRPORT IN CLASS G AIRSPACE

(a) *General.* Unless otherwise authorized or required, each person operating an aircraft on or in the vicinity of an airport in a Class G airspace area must comply with the requirements of this section.

(b) *Direction* of *turns.* When approaching to land at an airport without an operating control tower in Class G airspace —

  (1) Each pilot of an airplane must make all turns of that airplane to the left unless the airport displays approved light signals or visual markings indicating that turns should be made to the right, in which case the pilot must make all turns to the right; and

  (2) Each pilot of a helicopter must avoid the flow of fixed-wing aircraft.

(c) *Flap settings.* Except when necessary for training or certification, the pilot in command of a civil turbojet-powered aircraft must use, as a final flap setting, the minimum certificated landing flap setting set forth in the approved performance information in the Airplane Flight Manual for the applicable conditions. However, each pilot in command has the final authority and responsibility for the safe operation of the pilot's airplane, and may use a different flap setting for that airplane if the pilot determines that it is necessary in the interest of safety.

(d) *Communications with control towers.* Unless otherwise authorized or required by ATC, no person may operate an aircraft to, from, through, or on an airport having an operational control tower unless two-way radio communications are maintained between that aircraft and the control tower. Communications must be established prior to 4 nautical miles from the airport, up to and including 2,500 feet AGL. However, if the aircraft radio fails in flight, the pilot in command may operate that aircraft and land if weather conditions are at or above basic VFR weather minimums, visual contact with the tower is maintained, and a clearance to land is received. If the aircraft radio fails while in flight under IFR, the pilot must comply with §91.185.

EXPLANATION

91.126(b): When approaching to land at an airport without an operating control tower, all turns should be made to the left, unless airport markings indicate that turns should be made to the right in one or more of the traffic patterns. When a flight includes landings at unfamiliar airports, the Airport/Facility Directory should be consulted for nonstandard traffic pattern procedures. When approaching the airport, check for a segmented circle with "L" shaped extensions indicating the direction of turns in the pattern. Helicopters approaching to land are to stay clear of fixed-wing traffic flow. If the airport has departure procedures set forth in Part 93, they must be complied with on takeoff.

91.126(c): This subsection prescribes the final landing flap setting for civil turbojet-powered aircraft with certain exceptions.

CROSS REFERENCES

Previous designations: 91.127, 91.85 and 91.89. 91.103 Preflight Action; 91.127, Operating on or in the Vicinity of an Airport in Class E Airspace; 91.129, Operations in Class D Airspace; 91.155, Basic VFR Weather Minimums; Part 93 Special Air Traffic Rules and Airport Traffic Patterns; 91.903-91.905 Waivers.

ADVISORY CIRCULARS

AC 90-42F *Traffic Advisory Practices at Airports Without Operating Control Towers* (1990).

AC 90-66A *Recommended Standard Traffic Patterns and Practices for Aeronautical Operations at Airports without Operating Control Towers* (1993).

AERONAUTICAL INFORMATION MANUAL

Class G Airspace, Para. 3-3-1 through 3-3-3;
Airport Advisory Area, Para. 3-5-1;
Visual Indicators at Airports without an Operating Control Tower, Para. 4-3-3;
Traffic Patterns, Para. 4-3-4;
Pilot/Controller Glossary:
    Straight-In Approach-IFR
    Straight-In Approach-VFR
    Traffic Pattern

CASES

The Board has stated that, in its opinion, a Boeing 737 making a 90 degree turn to achieve alignment with a runway as close as 4 miles from its threshold cannot be deemed to have made a straight-in approach. *Administrator v. Rivard*, EA-3413 (1991).

FAA CHIEF COUNSEL OPINIONS

A helicopter may not enter the pattern in front of a fixed-wing aircraft. Provided there are no fixed-wing aircraft entering the traffic pattern for the purpose of landing, a helicopter can enter the traffic pattern behind a fixed-wing aircraft. (7-3-89).

91.127 OPERATING ON OR IN THE VICINITY OF AN AIRPORT IN CLASS E AIRSPACE

(a)   Unless otherwise required by part 93 of this chapter or unless otherwise authorized or required by the ATC facility having jurisdiction over the Class E airspace area, each person operating an aircraft on or in the vicinity of an airport in a Class E airspace area must comply with the requirements of §91.126.

(b)   *Departures.* Each pilot of an aircraft must comply with any traffic patterns established for that airport in part 93 of this chapter.

(c)   *Communications with control towers.* Unless otherwise authorized or required by ATC, no person may operate an aircraft to, from, through, or on an airport having an operational control tower unless two-way radio communications are maintained between that aircraft and the control tower. Communications must be established prior to 4 nautical miles from the airport, up to and including 2,500 feet AGL. However, if the aircraft radio fails in flight, the pilot in command may operate that aircraft and land if weather conditions are at or above basic VFR weather minimums, visual contact with the tower is maintained, and a clearance to land is received. If the aircraft radio fails while in flight under IFR, the pilot must comply with §91.185.

EXPLANATION

91.127(a): When approaching to land at an airport without an operating control tower, all turns should be made to the left, unless airport markings indicate that turns should be made to the right in one or more of the traffic patterns. When a flight includes landings at unfamiliar airports, the Airport/Facility Directory should be consulted for nonstandard traffic pattern procedures. When approaching the airport, check for a segmented circle with "L" shaped extensions indicating the direction of turns in the pattern.

CROSS REFERENCES

Previous designations: 91.85 and 91.89. 91.103 Preflight Action; 91.126, Operating on or in the Vicinity of an Airport in Class G Airspace; 91.129, Operations In Class D Airspace; 91.155, Basic VFR Weather Minimums; 91.157, Special VFR Weather Minimums; Part 93 Special Air Traffic Rules and Airport Traffic Patterns; 91.903-91.905 Waivers.

ADVISORY CIRCULARS

AC 90-42F *Traffic Advisory Practices at Airports Without Operating Control Towers* (1990).

AC 90-66A *Recommended Standard Traffic Patterns and Practices for Aeronautical Operations at Airports without Operating Control Towers* (1993).

AERONAUTICAL INFORMATION MANUAL

Class E Airspace, Para. 3-2-6;
Airport Advisory Area, Para. 3-5-1;
Visual Indicators at Airports without an Operating Control Tower, Para. 4-3-3;
Traffic Patterns, Para. 4-3-4;
Pilot/Controller Glossary:
    Straight-In Approach-IFR
    Straight-In Approach-VFR
    Traffic Pattern

CASES

The Board has stated that, in its opinion, a Boeing 737 making a 90 degree turn to achieve alignment with a runway as close as 4 miles from its threshold cannot be deemed to have made a straight-in approach. *Administrator v. Rivard*, EA-3413 (1991).

FAA CHIEF COUNSEL OPINIONS

A helicopter may not enter the pattern in front of a fixed-wing aircraft. Provided there are no fixed-wing aircraft entering the traffic pattern for the purpose of landing, a helicopter can enter the traffic pattern behind a fixed-wing aircraft. (7-3-89).

91.129 OPERATIONS IN CLASS D AIRSPACE

(a) *General.* Unless otherwise authorized or required by the ATC having jurisdiction over the Class D airspace area, each person operating an aircraft in Class D airspace must comply with the applicable provisions of this section. In addition, each person must comply with §§91.126 and 91.127. For the purpose of this section, the primary airport is the airport for which the Class D airspace area is designated. A satellite airport is any other airport within the Class D airspace area.

(b) *Deviations.* An operator may deviate from any provision of this section under the provisions of an ATC authorization issued by the ATC facility having jurisdiction over the airspace concerned. ATC may authorize a deviation on a continuing basis or for an individual flight, as appropriate.

(c) *Communications.* Each person operating an aircraft in Class D airspace must meet the following two-way radio communications requirements:

    (1) *Arrival or through flight.* Each person must establish two-way radio communications with the ATC facility (including foreign ATC in the case of foreign airspace designated in the United States) providing air traffic services prior to entering that airspace and thereafter maintain those communications while within that airspace.

    (2) *Departing flight.* Each person —

        (i) From the primary airport or satellite airport with an operating control tower must establish and maintain two-way radio communications with the control tower, and thereafter as instructed by ATC while operating in the Class D airspace area; or

        (ii) From a satellite airport without an operating control tower, must establish and maintain two-way radio communications with the ATC facility having jurisdiction over the Class D airspace area as soon as practicable after departing.

(d) *Communications failure.* Each person who operates an aircraft in a Class D airspace area must maintain two-way radio communications with the ATC facility having jurisdiction over that area.

    (1) If the aircraft radio fails in flight under IFR, the pilot must comply with §91.185 of the part.

    (2) If the aircraft radio fails in flight under VFR, the pilot in command may operate that aircraft and land if —

        (i) Weather conditions are at or above basic VFR weather minimums;

        (ii) Visual contact with the tower is maintained; and

        (iii) A clearance to land is received.

(e) *Minimum altitudes.* Each pilot of a large or turbine-powered airplane must —

    (1) Unless otherwise required by the applicable distance from cloud criteria, enter the traffic pattern at an altitude of at least 1,500 feet above the elevation of the airport and maintain at least 1,500 feet until further descent is required for a safe landing;

    (2) When approaching to land on a runway served by an instrument landing system (ILS), if the airplane is ILS-equipped, fly that airplane at an altitude at or above the glide slope between the outer marker (or point of interception of glide slope, if compliance with the applicable distance from clouds criteria requires interception closer in) and the middle marker; and

    (3) When operating an airplane approaching to land on a runway served by a visual approach slope indicator, maintain an altitude at or above the glide slope until a lower altitude is necessary for safe landing. Paragraphs (e)(2) and (e)(3) of this section do not prohibit normal bracketing maneuvers above or below the glide slope that are conducted for the purpose of remaining on the glide slope.

(f)   *Approaches.* Except when conducting a circling approach under Part 97 of this chapter or
        unless otherwise required by ATC, each pilot must —
        (1)   Circle the airport to the left, if operating an airplane; or
        (2)   Avoid the flow of fixed-wing aircraft, if operating a helicopter.
(g)   *Departures.* No person may operate an aircraft departing from an airport except in compliance
        with the following:
        (1)   Each pilot must comply with any departure procedures established for that airport by the
               FAA.
        (2)   Unless otherwise required by the prescribed departure for that airport or the applicable
               distance from clouds criteria, each pilot of a turbine-powered airplane and each pilot of a
               large airplane must climb to an altitude of 1,500 feet above the surface as rapidly as
               practicable.
(h)   *Noise abatement.* Where a formal runway use program has been established by the FAA, each
        pilot of a large or turbine-powered airplane assigned a noise abatement runway by ATC must
        use that runway. However, consistent with the final authority of the pilot in command concerning
        the safe operation of the aircraft as prescribed in §91.3(a). ATC may assign a different runway if
        requested by the pilot in the interest of safety.
(I)   *Takeoff, landing, taxi clearance.* No person may, at any airport with an operating control tower,
        operate an aircraft on a runway or taxiway, or take off or land an aircraft, unless an appropriate
        clearance is received from ATC. A clearance to "taxi to" the takeoff runway assigned to the
        aircraft is not a clearance to cross that assigned takeoff runway, or to taxi on that runway at any
        point, but is a clearance to cross other runways that intersect the taxi route to that assigned
        takeoff runway. A clearance to "taxi to" any point other than an assigned takeoff runway is
        clearance to cross all runways that intersect the taxi route to that point.

EXPLANATION

91.129(c): "Radio contact" is established when a controller acknowledges a transmission.

91.129(e)(1): As a noise abatement measure, this subsection requires turbine-powered or large
aircraft, unless otherwise required in order to comply with 91.155, to enter airport traffic areas at 1500
feet above the surface and to maintain that altitude even in the traffic pattern until descent is required
for a safe landing.

91.129(I): On an airport, with an operating control tower, a clearance from ATC is necessary before
an aircraft can be operated on a taxiway or runway or before it can takeoff or land. When cleared to
"taxi to" the takeoff runway a pilot is authorized to cross all other runways that intersect the taxi route,
but may not cross or taxi onto the assigned takeoff runway. A clearance to "taxi to" any other point on
the airport other than the takeoff runway is a clearance to cross all runways that intersect the taxi
route. If not given a specific taxi route a pilot should consider asking for "progressive taxi instructions,"
especially at an unfamiliar airport.

CROSS REFERENCES

Previous designation: 91.187. 91.103, Preflight Action; 91.125, ATC Light Signals; 91.126, Operating
on or in the Vicinity of an Airport in Class G Airspace; 91.127, Operating on or in the Vicinity of an
Airport in Class E Airspace; 91.155, Basic VFR Weather Minimums; 91.157, Special VFR Weather
Minimums; 91.903-91.905 Waivers.

ADVISORY CIRCULARS

AC 90-42F *Traffic Advisory Practices at Airports Without Operating Control Towers* (1990).

AC 90-66A *Recommended Standard Traffic Patterns and Practices for Aeronautical Operations at Airports without Operating Control Towers* (1993).

AERONAUTICAL INFORMATION MANUAL

Class D Airspace, Para. 3-2-5;
Airport Advisory Area, Para. 3-5-1;
Airport Operations, Para. 4-3-1 through 4-3-26;
Airports with an Operating Control Tower, Para. 4-3-2;
Traffic Patterns, Para. 4-3-4.

CASES

A pilot has the responsibility to request clearances before entering a taxiway and a runway. A controller's silence after an airplane taxied onto a taxiway and then a runway did not in any way relieve the pilot of his responsibility. *Administrator v. Gerrion*, 5 NTSB 1011 (1986).

A civil penalty of $2,000 was not excessive in the case where a pilot taxied his aircraft onto the wrong runway. The instructions from the ground controllers were clear, and the fact that weather conditions did not allow controllers to see the aircraft, and that the taxiways were similar, were not mitigating circumstances warranting a reduction. *FAA v. Watkins*, FAA Order No. 92-8 (1-31-1992).

A pilot in command and first officer of a Piedmont Airlines flight misinterpreted a clearance for a Cessna ahead of them to takeoff and then moved onto the runway in preparation for takeoff. This action constituted a violation of §§91.13, 91.123, and 91.129 (formerly 91.9, 91.75, and 91.87), however because they both filed ASRP reports with NASA no penalty was assessed. *FAA v. Terry*, FAA Order No. 91-12 (4-12-1991).

FAA CHIEF COUNSEL OPINIONS

The term "normal bracketing maneuvers," as it appears in [91.129], involves maneuvers conducted for the purpose of remaining within the higher and lower limits of the glideslope scale as displayed on the pilot's flight instruments, i.e. within 150 microamperes of the center or null position of the glideslope. A pilot who remains within these limits, which constitute the glideslope "envelope," is not in violation of [91.129(d)]. (2-18-75).

§60.18(h)(6)(ii) of the Civil Air Regulations from which [91.129] was recodified in 1983, with no substantive change intended, provided that a fixed-wing aircraft approaching to land on a runway with a visual glideslope device shall be flown so as to remain at or above the glideslope until arrival at the runway threshold. This change of wording, "until a lower altitude is necessary for a safe landing," was not intended to alter substantially that location. (8-24-77).

91.130 OPERATIONS IN CLASS C AIRSPACE

(a) *General.* Each aircraft operation in Class C airspace must be conducted in compliance with this section and §91.129. For the purpose of this section, the primary airport is the airport for which the Class C airspace area is designated. A satellite airport is any other airport within the Class C airspace area.

(b) *Traffic patterns.* No person may take off or land an aircraft at a satellite airport within a Class C airspace area except in compliance with FAA arrival and departure traffic patterns.

(c) *Communications.* Each person operating an aircraft in Class C airspace must meet the following two-way radio communications requirements:

    (1) *Arrival or through flight.* Each person must establish two-way radio communications with the ATC facility (including foreign ATC in the case of foreign airspace designated in the United States) providing air traffic services prior to entering that airspace and thereafter maintain those communications while within that airspace.

    (2) *Departing flight.* Each person —

        (I) From the primary airport or satellite airport with an operating control tower must establish and maintain two-way radio communications with the control tower, and thereafter as instructed by ATC while operating in the Class C airspace area; or

        (ii) From a satellite airport without an operating control tower, must establish and maintain two-way radio communications with the ATC facility having jurisdiction over the Class C airspace area as soon as practicable after departing.

(d) *Equipment requirements.* Unless otherwise authorized by the ATC having jurisdiction over the Class C airspace area, no person may operate an aircraft within a Class C airspace area designated for an airport unless that aircraft is equipped with the applicable equipment specified in §91.215.

(e) *Deviations.* An operator may deviate from any provision of this section under the provisions of an ATC authorization issued by the ATC facility having jurisdiction over the airspace concerned. ATC may authorize a deviation on a continuing basis for an individual flight, as appropriate.

EXPLANATION

91.130(a): Class C airspace consists of controlled airspace extending upward from the surface or higher to specified altitudes, within which all aircraft are subject to the operating rules and pilot and equipment requirements set forth below. Class C airspace areas are charted on Sectional Charts, and some Terminal Area Charts.

The basic Class C airspace consists of two circles, both centered on the primary/Class C airspace area airport. The inner circle has a radius of 5 nautical miles. The outer circle has a radius of 10 nautical miles. The airspace of the inner circle extends from the surface up to 4,000 feet above the airport. The airspace area between the 5 and 10 nautical miles rings begins at a height of 1,200 feet AGL and extends to the same altitude as the inner circle.

The Outer Area surrounding a Class C airspace area has a normal radius of 20 nautical miles, with some variations based on site specific requirements. The outer area extends outward from the primary/Class C airspace area airport and extends from the lower limits of radar/radio coverage up to the ceiling of the approach control's delegated airspace, excluding the Class C airspace area and other airspace as appropriate. While pilot participation is required within the Class C airspace area, it is voluntary within the Outer Area and can be discontinued at any time at the pilot's request.

91.130(c): Radio contact must be established with the ATC facility having jurisdiction over the Class C airspace area prior to entry and thereafter as instructed by ATC. Pilots of arriving aircraft should contact the Class C airspace area facility using the frequency published on the sectional charts and in the Airport/Facility Directory. Pilots should state their position, altitude, transponder code, destination, and request Class C airspace area service. Radio contact should be initiated far enough from the Class C airspace area boundary to preclude entering the Class C airspace area before radio communications are established. If the controller responds to a radio call with, "(aircraft callsign) standby," radio communications have been established and the pilot can enter the Class C airspace area. If workload or traffic conditions prevent immediate provision of Class C airspace area services, the controller will inform the pilot to remain outside the Class C airspace area until conditions permit the services to be provided.

91.130(c)(2): The FAA has not defined "as soon as practicable," but it seems logical that an pilot should remain on the common traffic advisory frequency briefly after taking off and before switching to the Class C airspace area frequency so that he/she can communicate with traffic at the uncontrolled airport.

91.130(d): Equipment requirements: two-way radio and a Mode C transponder. The Mode C transponder is required within **and** above Class C airspace, up to 10,000 feet MSL.

CROSS REFERENCES

Previous designation: 91.88. 91.126, Operating on or in the Vicinity of an Airport in Class G Airspace; 91.127, Operating on or in the Vicinity of an Airport in Class E Airspace; 91.131, Operations in Class B Airspace; 91.129, Operations in Class D Airspace; 91.155, Basic VFR Weather Minimums; 91.157, Special VFR Weather Minimums; 91.215 ATC Transponder and Altitude Reporting Equipment and Use.

AERONAUTICAL INFORMATION MANUAL

Class C airspace, Para. 3-2-4;
Airports with an Operating Control Tower, Para. 4-3-2.

CASES

A nervous and inexperienced pilot is still held to the level of responsibility that his certificate implies, and a private pilot is expected to know how to navigate to and from [Class C airspace]. *Administrator v. Soghanalian*, SE-8359 (1988).

91.131 OPERATIONS IN CLASS B AIRSPACE

(a)   *Operating rules.* No person may operate an aircraft within a Class B airspace area except in compliance with §91.129 and the following rules:

   (1)   The operator must receive an ATC clearance from the ATC facility having jurisdiction for that area before operating an aircraft in that area.

   (2)   Unless otherwise authorized by ATC, each person operating a large turbine engine-powered airplane to or from a primary airport for which a Class B airspace area is designated must operate at or above the designated floors of the Class B airspace area while within the lateral limits of that area.

   (3)   Any person conducting pilot training operations at an airport within a Class B airspace area must comply with any procedures established by ATC for such operations in that area.

(b)   *Pilot requirements.*

   (1)   No person may take off or land a civil aircraft at an airport within a Class B airspace area or operate a civil aircraft within a Class B airspace area unless —

     (I)   The pilot in command holds at least a private pilot certificate; or

     (ii)   The aircraft is operated by a student pilot or recreational pilot who seeks private pilot certification and has met the requirements of §61.95 of this chapter.

   (2)   Notwithstanding the provisions of paragraph (b)(1)(ii) of this section, no person may take off or land a civil aircraft at those airports listed in section 4 of appendix D of this part unless the pilot in command holds at least a private pilot certificate.

(c)   *Communications and navigation equipment requirements.* Unless otherwise authorized by ATC, no person may operate an aircraft within a Class B airspace area unless that aircraft is equipped with—

   (1)   *For IFR* operation. An operable VOR or TACAN receiver; and

   (2)   *For all* operations. An operable two-way radio capable of communications with ATC on appropriate frequencies for that Class B airspace area.

(d)   Transponder *requirements.* No person may operate an aircraft in a Class B airspace area unless the aircraft is equipped with the applicable operating transponder and automatic altitude reporting equipment specified in paragraph (a) of §91.215, except as provided in paragraph (d) of that section.

EXPLANATION

91.131(a): Regardless of weather conditions, a clearance from ATC is required prior to entering Class B airspace. The proper frequency for obtaining the clearance can be found on sectional charts and terminal area charts. The AIM contains detailed information about operating procedures for both IFR and VFR operations within Class B airspace. A clearance for a visual approach to the primary airport within Class B airspace is not authorization for turbine powered airplanes to operate below the designated floors of the Class B airspace.

91.131(b): No pilot may operate within Class B airspace without at least a private pilot certificate, although student pilots may fly solo in Class B airspace if they meet the requirements of 61.95 and the Class B airspace is not listed in 91.131(b)(2).

91.131(c): No pilot may operate within Class B airspace without an operable two-way radio. Only IFR operations require an operable VOR or TACAN receiver.

91.131(d): Unless otherwise authorized, an operable radar beacon transponder with automatic altitude reporting equipment is required for flight within Class B airspace. See 91.215 for exceptions, and the AIM sections listed below. 91.215 also sets forth the transponder requirements within a 30 mile radius of Class B airspace (the "veil"). AIM Para. 3-30 sets forth exceptions to the veil rule.

CROSS REFERENCES

Previous number: 91.90. 61.95 Operations in Class B airspace and at airports located within Class B airspace; 91.126, Operating on or in the Vicinity of an Airport in Class G Airspace; 91.127, Operating on or in the Vicinity of an Airport in Class E Airspace; 91.129, Operations in Class D Airspace; 91.155, Basic VFR Weather Minimums; 91.157, Special VFR Weather Minimums; 91.215, ATC Transponder and Altitude Reporting Equipment and Use; 91.903-91.905 Waivers.

ADVISORY CIRCULARS

AC 91-50 *Importance of Transponder Operation and Altitude Reporting* (1977).

AERONAUTICAL INFORMATION MANUAL

Class B Airspace, Para. 3-2-3;
Terminal Radar Services for VFR Aircraft, Para. 4-1-17;
Transponder Operation, Para. 4-1-19.

CASES

A pilot who did not have an instrument rating flew into Class B airspace without requesting or obtaining a clearance and with his transponder turned off. The pilot then requested a clearance to "poke through some clouds," which was understood by ATC to be a request for an IFR clearance. The pilot received a 120 day suspension. *Administrator v. White*, EA-3791 (1993).

The examination of the encoder which indicated it was 600 feet in error was conducted over three months after the alleged [Class B airspace] violation and thus cannot be accepted as reliable evidence of the condition of the instrument at the earlier time. *Administrator v. Hyde*, EA-3083 (1990).

In [Class B airspace] cases the authorization requirement is strictly construed and applied. The degree of incursion without a clearance is irrelevant. *Administrator v. Wyffels*, EA-3468 (1992).

ATC's knowledge of a VFR pilot's course intentions does not relieve the pilot from the responsibility to obtain whatever clearance may be required to operate along the course. The approval by ATC for a right turn, which was completed well in advance of the [Class B airspace] boundary, was not an authorization to enter the [Class B airspace]. *Administrator v. Duke*, 4 NTSB 404 (1982).

Where a pilot was using VFR flight following, and making it clear that he intended to pass through the [Class B airspace], and ATC failed to hand him off to approach control before he entered the [Class B airspace], the Board held that the pilot did not violate [91.131]. *Administrator v. Keller*, EA-3011 (1989).

However, a pilot is not absolved of [Class B airspace] violation simply because he or she is in contact with another ATC facility when he or she enters the [Class B airspace]. In this case, the pilot was speaking with a tower controller when he entered the [Class B airspace]. *Administrator v. Meili*, EA-3340 (1991).

The Board upheld a suspension against a pilot who entered [Class B airspace] without a clearance after departing an uncontrolled airport, and while in the process of picking up his IFR clearance. *Administrator v. Bruder*, EA-3147 (1990).

91.133 RESTRICTED AND PROHIBITED AREAS

(a)   No person may operate an aircraft within a restricted area (designated in part 73) contrary to the restrictions imposed, or within a prohibited area, unless that person has the permission of the using or controlling agency, as appropriate.

(b)   Each person conducting, within a restricted area, an aircraft operation (approved by the using agency) that creates the same hazards as the operations for which the restricted area was designated may deviate from the rules of this subpart that are not compatible with his operation of the aircraft.

EXPLANATION

91.133(a): Prohibited areas are depicted on charts and flight is prohibited in these areas for security or other reasons. Permission may be granted by the controlling agency for flight in restricted areas. Prior to commencing a flight, a pilot must determine whether there are any restricted or prohibited areas on or near the intended route and make sure to avoid these areas. Remember that some of these areas are used for artillery firing, aerial gunnery, or guided missiles.

91.133(b): Aircraft cleared into a restricted area to perform a mission related to the nature of that area are not restricted by the rules of this subpart in performing that mission.

CROSS REFERENCES

Previous designation: 91.95. 91.103 Preflight Action; Part 73 Special Use Airspace.

ADVISORY CIRCULARS

210-5B *Military Flying Activities* (1990).

AERONAUTICAL INFORMATION MANUAL

Prohibited Area, Para. 3-4-2;
Restricted Area, Para. 3-4-3;
Warning Area, Para. 3-4-4;
Military Operations Area (MOA), Para. 3-4-5;
Alert Area, Para. 3-4-6;
Controlled Firing Area, Para. 3-4-7.

CASES

Incursion into restricted airspace designated for a space shuttle launch was careless and inadvertent. *Administrator v. Reid*, EA-4040 (1993).

Although the sectional chart, if considered by itself, could be misleading as to the vertical limits of the restricted area (i.e. "8000 TO BUT NOT INCL FL 180"), the Board held that the pilot, given the nature of the event, a space shuttle launch, should have directly apprised himself of the details of the NOTAM, which extended the restricted area to the surface. *Administrator v. Whilly*, 5 NTSB 1224 (1986).

Given a hot air balloon's lack of maneuverability and potential for extended exposure to danger, if winds shift or become becalmed, a balloonist should be extremely careful to avoid flights over or near restricted areas. *Administrator v. Spais*, 5 NTSB 1805 (1987).

FAA CHIEF COUNSEL OPINIONS

Who is responsible for obtaining clearance through a restricted area when an aircraft is operating on an IFR clearance, and the ATC clearance assigns, "VFR conditions on top?"

If the aircraft is operating via a route which lies within joint-use restricted airspace, and if the restricted area is not active and has been released to the controlling agency (FAA), the ATC facility will allow the aircraft to operate in the restricted airspace without issuing specific clearance for it to do so. Conversely, if the restricted area is active and has **not** been released to the controlling agency (FAA), the ATC facility will issue a clearance which will ensure the aircraft avoids the restricted airspace, unless it is on an approved altitude reservation mission or has obtained its own permission to operate in the airspace and so informs the controlling facility. If the aircraft is operating via a route which lies within nonjoint-use restricted airspace, the ATC facility will issue a clearance so the aircraft will avoid the restricted airspace, unless it is on an approved altitude reservation mission or has obtained its own permission to operate in the airspace and so informs the controlling facility. These procedures are set forth in the *Aeronautical Information Manual*, [Para. 3-43]. (1-28-92).

91.135 OPERATIONS IN CLASS A AIRSPACE

Except as provided in paragraph (d) of this section, each person operating an aircraft in Class A airspace must conduct that operation under instrument flight rules (IFR) and in compliance with the following:

(a)   *Clearance.* Operations may be conducted only under an ATC clearance received prior to entering the airspace.

(b)   *Communications.* Unless otherwise authorized by ATC, each aircraft operating in Class A airspace must be equipped with a two-way radio capable of communicating with ATC on a frequency assigned by ATC. Each pilot must maintain two-way radio communications with ATC while operating in Class A airspace.

(c)   *Transponder requirement.* Unless otherwise authorized by ATC, no person may operate an aircraft within Class A airspace unless that aircraft is equipped with the applicable equipment specified in §92.215.

(d)   *ATC authorizations.* An operator may deviate from any provision of this section under the provisions of an ATC authorization issued by the ATC facility having jurisdiction of the airspace concerned. In the case of an inoperative transponder, ATC may immediately approve an operation within a Class A airspace area allowing flight to continue, if desired, to the airport of ultimate destination, including any intermediate stops, or to proceed to a place where suitable repairs can be made, or both. Requests for deviation from any provision of this section must be submitted in writing, at least 4 days before the proposed operation. ATC may authorize a deviation on a continuing basis or for an individual flight.

EXPLANATION

Class A airspace includes what was formerly designated positive control airspace. Class A airspace is designated in 71.33. This area includes specified airspace within the conterminous U.S. from 18,000 feet to and including FL 600, excluding Santa Barbara Island, Farallon Island, and that portion south of latitude 25 degrees 04 minutes north. In Alaska, it includes the airspace over the state of Alaska from 18,000 feet to and including FL 600, but not including the airspace less than 1,500 feet above the surface of the earth and the Alaskan Peninsula west of longitude 160 degrees 00 minutes west.

91.135(c): The reference to §91.215 refers to the requirement in that regulation that an aircraft flying in Class A airspace have a Mode C transponder.

91.135(d): Deviation from the requirements of §91.135(c) **may** be authorized by ATC. Requests for this deviation must be submitted at least 48 hours in advance of the proposed operation to the ATC air route traffic control center (ARTCC) having jurisdiction over the Class A area. Such deviations may be on a one-time or on a continuing basis.

In the case of an inoperative transponder, while in flight in Class A airspace, ATC can grant an immediate deviation from this rule and allow aircraft to fly to their original destination, with intermediate stops if desired or necessary, or to a place where repairs can be accomplished, or both.

CROSS REFERENCES

Previous designation: 91.97. 91.215 ATC Transponder and Altitude Reporting Equipment and Use; 91.903-91.905 Waivers.

AERONAUTICAL INFORMATION MANUAL

Class A Airspace, Para. 3-2-2.

CASES

The fact that the pilot had good visibility or that his intrusion into [Class A airspace] lasted only a few minutes or that the closest traffic was 2500 feet vertically and 10-12 miles laterally does not excuse the violation of [91.135(a)(1)]. *Administrator v. Tuomela*, 4 NTSB 1422 (1984).

91.137 TEMPORARY FLIGHT RESTRICTIONS IN THE VICINITY OF DISASTER/HAZARD AREAS

(a)   The Administrator will issue a Notice to Airmen (NOTAM) designating an area within which temporary flight restrictions apply and specifying the hazard or condition requiring their imposition, whenever he determines it is necessary in order to —

   (1)   Protect persons and property on the surface or in the air from a hazard associated with an incident on the surface;

   (2)   Provide a safe environment for the operation of disaster relief aircraft; or

   (3)   Prevent an unsafe congestion of sightseeing and other aircraft above an incident or event which may generate a high degree of public interest. The Notice to Airmen will specify the hazard or condition that requires the imposition of temporary flight restrictions.

(b)   When a NOTAM has been issued under paragraph (a)(1) of this section, no person may operate an aircraft within the designated area unless that aircraft is participating in the hazard relief activities and is being operated under the direction of the official in charge of on scene emergency response activities.

(c)   When a NOTAM has been issued under paragraph (a)(2) of this section, no person may operate an aircraft within the designated area unless at least one of the following conditions are met:

   (1)   The aircraft is participating in hazard relief activities and is being operated under the direction of the official in charge of on scene emergency response activities.

   (2)   The aircraft is carrying law enforcement officials.

   (3)   The aircraft is operating under the ATC approved IFR flight plan.

   (4)   The operation is conducted directly to or from an airport within the area, or is necessitated by the impracticability of VFR flight above or around the area due to weather, or terrain; notification is given to the Flight Service Station (FSS) or ATC facility specified in the NOTAM to receive advisories concerning disaster relief aircraft operations; and the operation does not hamper or endanger relief activities and is not conducted for the purpose of observing the disaster.

   (5)   The aircraft is carrying properly accredited news representatives, and, prior to entering the area, a flight plan is filed with the appropriate FAA or ATC facility specified in the Notice to Airmen and the operation is conducted above the altitude used by the disaster relief aircraft, unless otherwise authorized by the official in charge of on scene emergency response activities.

(d)   When a NOTAM has been issued under paragraph (a)(3) of this section, no person may operate an aircraft within the designated area unless at least one of the following conditions is met:

   (1)   The operation is conducted directly to or from an airport within the area, or is necessitated by the impracticability of VFR flight above or around the area due to weather or terrain, and the operation is not conducted for the purpose of observing the incident or event.

   (2)   The aircraft is operating under an ATC approved IFR flight plan.

   (3)   The aircraft is carrying incident or event personnel, or law enforcement officials.

   (4)   The aircraft is carrying properly accredited news representatives and, prior to entering that area, a flight plan is filed with the appropriate FSS or ATC facility specified in the NOTAM.

(e)   Flight plans filed and notifications made with an FSS or ATC facility under this section shall include the following information:

   (1)   Aircraft identification, type and color.

   (2)   Radio communications frequencies to be used.

   (3)   Proposed times of entry of, and exit from, the designated area.

   (4)   Name of news media or organization and purpose of flight.

   (5)   Any other information requested by ATC.

EXPLANATION

91.137(a): The FAA may issue a Notice To Airmen (NOTAM) imposing temporary flight restrictions in a designated area. When this is done the NOTAM will specify the basis for its issuance which can be any or all of the following:

1. To protect persons or property on the surface or in the air from a hazard associated with an incident on the surface. Examples: toxic or flammable liquids or fumes; volcano eruptions; nuclear incidents; hijacking incidents.
2. To provide a safe environment for the operation of disaster relief aircraft. Examples: forest fires; disaster relief activities following an earthquake, flood, etc.
3. To prevent an unsafe congestion of sightseeing and other aircraft above an incident or event which may generate a high degree of public interest. Examples: some sporting events.

91.137(b): This subsection sets forth the conditions for flight in an area designated under 91.137(a)(1).

91.137(c): This subsection sets forth the conditions for flight in an area designated under 91.137(a)(2).

91.137(d): This subsection sets forth the conditions for flight in an area designated under 91.137(a)(3).

91.137(e): The information required in the notification to Flight Service Station (FSS) or other ATC facility under 91.137(c) and in the flight plans filed under 91.137(c) and (d) is set forth in this subsection.

PREAMBLE

The FAA agrees that temporary flight restrictions have been misapplied in certain instances. The current procedure is for the FAA Headquarters to provide management oversight of TFRs. Whenever Headquarters becomes aware of misapplication of TFR regulations, action is quickly taken to correct the matter. Additionally, the FAA is aggressively taking steps to educate all users (both pilots and controllers) regarding TFRs. The changing of the title of this section is one of the first steps in this education process. (66 FR 47373). (Editor's Note: "in the vicinity of disaster/hazard areas" was added to the title.

The establishment of a TFR over certain aerial demonstrations or sporting events is not aimed at regulating where aerial advertisers are allowed to operate. The FAA never surrenders control of the navigable airspace, and event promoters do not determine who can or cannot fly over an event. The sole intent of the FAA is to manage aircraft operations in an efficient and safe manner. The proposed §91.145 continues the FAA's practice of using TFRs for certain qualifying events and clarifies that the FAA will no longer use §91.137 as the authority for those TFRs because we believe §91.137 should be limited to hazard or disaster areas. (66 FR 47376).

CROSS REFERENCES

Previous designation: 91.91. 91.103 Preflight Action; 91.138 Temporary Flight Restrictions in National Disaster Areas in the State of Hawaii; 91.903-91.905 Waivers.

ADVISORY CIRCULARS

AC 61-84B *Role of Preflight Preparation* (1985).

AC 91-63B *Temporary Flight Restrictions (TFRs)* (1997).

AERONAUTICAL INFORMATION MANUAL

Temporary Flight Restrictions, Para. 3-5-3.

CASES

[91.137] can only be violated if a NOTAM is in force. The FAA is required to prove that the NOTAM was issued. *Administrator v. Latham*, EA-3506 (1992).

91.138 TEMPORARY FLIGHT RESTRICTIONS IN NATIONAL DISASTER AREAS IN THE STATE OF HAWAII

(a) When the Administrator has determined, pursuant to a request and justification provided by the Governor of the State of Hawaii, or the Governor's designee, that an inhabited area within a declared national disaster area in the State of Hawaii is in need of protection for humanitarian reasons, the Administrator will issue a Notice to Airmen (NOTAM) designating an area within which temporary flight restrictions apply. The Administrator will designate the extent and duration of the temporary flight restrictions necessary to provide for the protection of persons and property on the surface.

(b) When a NOTAM has been issued in accordance with this section, no person may operate an aircraft within the designated area unless at least one of the following conditions is met:

(1) That person has obtained authorization from the official in charge of associated emergency or disaster relief response activities, and is operating the aircraft under the conditions of that authorization.

(2) The aircraft is carrying law enforcement officials.

(3) The aircraft is carrying persons involved in an emergency or a legitimate scientific purpose.

(4) The aircraft is carrying properly accredited newspersons, and that prior to entering the area, a flight plan is filed with the appropriate FAA or ATC facility specified in the NOTAM and the operation is conducted in compliance with the conditions and restrictions established by the official in charge of on-scene emergency response activities.

(5) The aircraft is operating in accordance with an ATC clearance or instruction.

(c) A NOTAM issued under this section is effective for 90 days or until the national disaster area designation is terminated, whichever comes first, unless terminated by notice or extended by the Administrator at the request of the Governor of the State of Hawaii or the Governor's designee.

EXPLANATION

91.138(a): This regulation was adopted as a result of §9124 of the Aviation Safety and Capacity Act of 1990 which provided, in part, that the FAA would adopt regulations that would be similar to those in 91.137 that would apply specifically to declared national disaster areas in Hawaii. Unlike 91.137, this temporary flight restrictions based on 91.138 can be based on humanitarian reasons. A NOTAM is used to establish the restrictions.

91.138(b): This subsection describes the conditions that must exist for an aircraft to be operated in an area established under 91.138.

91.138(c): A NOTAM issued under 91.138(a) would be effective for 90 days or until the natural disaster designation is terminated, whichever comes first, unless terminated by notice or extended by the FAA.

PREAMBLE

In Notice No. 00-13, the FAA proposed to clarify the operating requirements detailed in §91.138 by modifying subparagraph (b) to read: "When a NOTAM has been issued in accordance with this section, no person may operate an aircraft within the designated airspace unless at least one of the following conditions is met." The language currently in §91.138(b) could be misinterpreted to mean that all of the conditions must be met before operating an aircraft within the designated airspace. (66 FR 47374)

CROSS REFERENCES

Previous designation: none (new regulation 6-19-91). 91.137, Temporary Flight Restrictions in the Vicinity of Disaster/Hazard Areas.

ADVISORY CIRCULARS

AC 61-84B *Role of Preflight Preparation* (1985).

AC 91-63B *Temporary Flight Restrictions (TFRs)* (1997).

AERONAUTICAL INFORMATION MANUAL

Temporary Flight Restrictions, Para. 3-5-3.

91.139 EMERGENCY AIR TRAFFIC RULES

(a)   This section prescribes a process for utilizing Notices to Airmen (NOTAMs) to advise of the issuance and operations under emergency air traffic rules and regulations and designates the official who is authorized to issue NOTAMs on behalf of the Administrator in certain matters under this section.

(b)   Whenever the Administrator determines that an emergency condition exists, or will exist, relating to the FAA's ability to operate the air traffic control system and during which normal flight operations under this chapter cannot be conducted consistent with the required levels of safety and efficiency —

   (1)   The Administrator issues an immediately effective air traffic rule or regulation in response to that emergency condition, and

   (2)   The Administrator or the Associate Administrator for Air Traffic may utilize the NOTAM system to provide notification of the issuance of the rule or regulation.

   Those NOTAMs communicate information concerning the rules and regulations that govern flight operations, the use of navigation facilities, and designation of that airspace in which the rules and regulations apply.

(c)   When a NOTAM has been issued under this section, no person may operate an aircraft, or other device governed by the regulation concerned, within the designated airspace except in accordance with the authorizations, terms, and conditions prescribed in the regulation covered by the NOTAM.

EXPLANATION

This regulation allows the FAA to immediately issue emergency air traffic rules through the Notices to Airmen (NOTAM) system, which is one more reason that it is important for pilots to check for NOTAM advisories as part of their preflight preparation.

CROSS REFERENCES

Previous number: 91.100. 91.137 Temporary Flight Restrictions in the Vicinity of Disaster/Hazard Areas; 91.141 Flight Restriction in the Proximity of the Presidential and other parties; 91.143 Flight Limitation in the Proximity of Space Flight Operations.

ADVISORY CIRCULARS

AC 91-63B *Temporary Flight Restrictions (TFRs)* (1997).

AERONAUTICAL INFORMATION MANUAL

Temporary Flight Restrictions, Para. 3-5-3;
Notice to Airmen (NOTAM) System, Para. 5-1-3.

91.141 FLIGHT RESTRICTIONS IN THE PROXIMITY OF THE PRESIDENTIAL AND OTHER PARTIES

No person may operate an aircraft over or in the vicinity of any area to be visited or traveled by the President, the Vice President, or other public figures contrary to the restrictions established by the Administrator and published in a Notice to Airmen (NOTAM).

CROSS REFERENCES

91.137 Temporary Flight Restrictions in the Vicinity of Disaster/Hazard Areas; 91.143 Flight Limitation in the Proximity of Space Flight Operations

ADVISORY CIRCULARS

AC 91-63B *Temporary Flight Restrictions (TFRs)* (1997).

AERONAUTICAL INFORMATION MANUAL

Temporary Flight Restrictions, Para. 3-5-3;
Notices to Airmen, Para. 5-1-3.

91.143 FLIGHT LIMITATION IN THE PROXIMITY OF SPACE FLIGHT OPERATIONS

No person may operate any aircraft of U.S. registry, or pilot any aircraft under the authority of an airman certificate issued by the Federal Aviation Administration within areas designated in a Notice to Airmen (NOTAM) for space flight operations except when authorized by ATC, or operated under the control of the Department of Defense Manager for Space Transportation System Contingency Support Operations.

EXPLANATION

This regulation provides protection from potentially hazardous situations for pilots and space flight crews and costly delays of shuttle operations.

CROSS REFERENCES

91.137 Temporary Flight Restrictions in the Vicinity of Disaster/Hazard Areas; 91.141 Flight Restriction in the Proximity of the Presidential and other parties.

ADVISORY CIRCULARS

AC 91-63B *Temporary Flight Restrictions (TFRs)* (1997).

AERONAUTICAL INFORMATION MANUAL

Temporary Flight Restrictions, Para. 3-5-3;
Notices to Airmen, Para. 5-1-3.

CASES

Incursion into restricted airspace designated for a space shuttle launch was careless and inadvertent. *Administrator v. Reid*, EA-4040 (1993).

91.144 TEMPORARY RESTRICTION ON FLIGHT OPERATIONS DURING ABNORMALLY HIGH BAROMETRIC PRESSURE CONDITIONS

(a) *Special flight restrictions.* When any information indicates that barometric pressure on the route of flight currently exceeds or will exceed 31 inches of mercury, no person may operate an aircraft or initiate a flight contrary to the requirements established by the Administrator and published in a Notice to Airmen issued under this section.

(b) *Waivers.* The Administrator is authorized to waive any restriction issued under paragraph (a) of this section to permit emergency supply, transport, or medical services to be delivered to isolated communities, where the operation can be conducted with an acceptable level of safety.

EXPLANATION

Cold, dry air masses may produce barometric pressures in excess of 31.00 inches of Mercury, and many altimeters do not have an accurate means of being adjusted for these settings. When the altimeter cannot be set to the higher pressure setting, the aircraft's actual altitude will be higher than the altimeter indicates.

ADVISORY CIRCULARS

AC 91-14D, *Altimeter Setting Sources* (1979).

AERONAUTICAL INFORMATION MANUAL

Altimeter Errors, Para 7-2-3 through 7-2-5.

91.145 MANAGEMENT OF AIRCRAFT OPERATIONS IN THE VICINITY OF AERIAL DEMONSTRATIONS AND MAJOR SPORTING EVENTS

(a) The FAA will issue a Notice to Airmen (NOTAM) designating an area of airspace in which a temporary flight restriction applies when it determines that a temporary flight restriction is necessary to protect persons or property on the surface or in the air, to maintain air safety and efficiency, or to prevent the unsafe congestion of aircraft in the vicinity of an aerial demonstration or major sporting event. These demonstrations and events may include:

(1) United States Naval Flight Demonstration Team (Blue Angels);
(2) United States Air Force Air Demonstration Squadron (Thunderbirds);
(3) United States Army Parachute Team (Golden Knights);
(4) Summer/Winter Olympic Games;
(5) Annual Tournament of Roses Football Game;
(6) World Cup Soccer;
(7) Major League Baseball All-Star Game;
(8) World Series;
(9) Kodak Albuquerque International Balloon Fiesta;
(10) Sandia Classic Hang Gliding Competition;
(11) Indianapolis 500 Mile Race;
(12) Any other aerial demonstration or sporting event the FAA determines to need a temporary flight restriction in accordance with paragraph (b) of this section.

(b)   In deciding whether a temporary flight restriction is necessary for an aerial demonstration or major sporting event not listed in paragraph (a) of this section, the FAA considers the following factors:

      (1)   Area where the event will be held.

      (2)   Effect flight restrictions will have on known aircraft operations.

      (3)   Any existing ATC airspace traffic management restrictions.

      (4)   Estimated duration of the event.

      (5)   Degree of public interest.

      (6)   Number of spectators.

      (7)   Provisions for spectator safety.

      (8)   Number and types of participating aircraft.

      (9)   Use of mixed high and low performance aircraft.

      (10) Impact on non-participating aircraft.

      (11) Weather minimums.

      (12) Emergency procedures that will be in effect.

(c)   A NOTAM issued under this section will state the name of the aerial demonstration or sporting event and specify the effective dates and times, the geographic features or coordinates, and any other restrictions or procedures governing flight operations in the designated airspace.

(d)   When a NOTAM has been issued in accordance with this section, no person may operate an aircraft or device, or engage in any activity within the designated airspace area, except in accordance with the authorizations, terms, and conditions of the temporary flight restriction published in the NOTAM, unless otherwise authorized by:

      (1)   Air traffic control; or

      (2)   A Flight Standards Certificate of Waiver or Authorization issued for the demonstration or event.

(e)   For the purpose of this section:

      (1)   Flight restricted airspace area for an aerial demonstration -- The amount of airspace needed to protect persons and property on the surface or in the air, to maintain air safety and efficiency, or to prevent the unsafe congestion of aircraft will vary depending on the aerial demonstration and the factors listed in paragraph (b) of this section. The restricted airspace area will normally be limited to a 5 nautical mile radius from the center of the demonstration and an altitude 17000 mean sea level (for high performance aircraft) or 13000 feet above the surface (for certain parachute operations), but will be no greater than the minimum airspace necessary for the management of aircraft operations in the vicinity of the specified area.

      (2)   Flight restricted area for a major sporting event--The amount of airspace needed to protect persons and property on the surface or in the air, to maintain air safety and efficiency, or to prevent the unsafe congestion of aircraft will vary depending on the size of the event and the factors listed in paragraph (b) of this section. The restricted airspace will normally be limited to a 3 nautical mile radius from the center of the event and 2500 feet above the surface but will not be greater than the minimum airspace necessary for the management of aircraft operations in the vicinity of the specified area.

(f)   A NOTAM issued under this section will be issued at least 30 days in advance of an aerial demonstration or a major sporting event, unless the FAA finds good cause for a shorter period and explains this in the NOTAM.

(g) When warranted, the FAA Administrator may exclude the following flights from the provisions of this section:
   (1) Essential military.
   (2) Medical and rescue.
   (3) Presidential and Vice Presidential.
   (4) Visiting heads of state.
   (5) Law enforcement and security.
   (6) Public health and welfare.

EXPLANATION

When a temporary flight restriction is issued, aircraft management procedures for the event will be published in a National Flight Data Center (FDC) NOTAM. The NOTAM will detail, for example, general procedures to include altitudes, times, frequency, point of contact, Air Traffic Control facility, special clearances, and any other necessary information.

PREAMBLE

The FAA agrees with AOPA and EAA in part. Whenever possible, TFR information will be published in the Airport/Facility Directory and on applicable charts provided the information is available to meet the required cutoff dates for the printing cycle. It is current policy to review NOTAMs to ensure TFRs are correctly utilized and implemented. Additionally, it is our plan to continue to work with the airspace users to further identify any additional requirements. It should be noted that while comments relating to improvements to the NOTAM system are beyond the scope of this rulemaking effort, these comments have been forwarded to the appropriate FAA Air Traffic office for action.

Notice No. 00-13 provided examples of major sporting events and aerial demonstrations where TFRs or SFARs have been used in the past. While we anticipate using §91.145 to implement TFRs for these types of events, there may be unique circumstances that eliminate the need for a TFR. In addition, there may be sporting events not listed in Notice No. 00-13 that may develop into events of such magnitude that a TFR may be necessary. §91.145 is designed to provide the FAA with the flexibility to meet future contingencies and better use its rulemaking resources, which are finite.

In addition to the examples cited in the preamble and the rule, guidance concerning the type of sporting event or aerial demonstration that may warrant a TFR will continue to be placed in FAA directives. The rule is not intended to provide TFR coverage for events at which public safety and the potential for the unsafe congestion of aircraft are not interests requiring action by the FAA.

Additionally, the FAA will review current TFR guidelines and, if appropriate, will provide more stringent guidelines for the establishment of a TFR in FAA directives. As stated in Notice No. 00-13, the amount of airspace needed to provide a safe environment for aerial demonstrations/major sporting events would vary depending on the event. The area that would be restricted would normally be limited to the minimum airspace area/altitude/time required to manage participating and non-participating aircraft in the area.

The establishment of a TFR over certain aerial demonstrations or sporting events is not aimed at regulating where aerial advertisers are allowed to operate. The FAA never surrenders control of the navigable airspace, and event promoters do not determine who can or cannot fly over an event. The sole intent of the FAA is to manage aircraft operations in an efficient and safe manner. The proposed §91.145 continues the FAA's practice of using TFRs for certain qualifying events and clarifies that the FAA will no longer use §91.137 as the authority for those TFRs because we believe §91.137 should be limited to hazard or disaster areas. This final rule provides a regulation to cover TFRs for major sporting events and aerial demonstrations. Notice No. 00-13 and final rule provides examples of events where the FAA has used TFRs, to inform the public about the type of event that may qualify for a TFR. Again, a TFR will use the minimum amount of airspace necessary, based on the activity or event, to ensure public safety and prevent the unsafe congestion of aircraft.

Many commenters believe that there is potential for abuse under the proposed rule by the FAA and event promoters/coordinators. AOPA believes that thirty days advance notification is acceptable for the establishment of TFRs, but is concerned that the good cause exception could lead to notification issues and excessive TFR usage for smaller sporting events or outdoor events. AOPA states the NPRM outlines the criteria to be used for establishing TFRs; however, many of these elements are highly subjective. Several commenters recommend promoting procedures rather than limitations, and others are of the opinion that Flight Standards District Office (FSDO) inspectors are given too much power under the proposal, and have the power to stop aerial advertising at will.

The FAA does not agree with these commenters. The intent of this rulemaking effort is to prevent the unsafe congestion of aircraft operations in the affected area, and to ensure the safety of persons and property on the ground. The list of events cited in this section are for example only, and not meant to be an all-inclusive list that will require regulatory action to establish a TFR for an event that is not included in this list. As stated previously, the FAA monitors the issuance of TFRs, to ensure that the TFR is warranted and that regulations are complied with. The FAA Airspace and Rules Division, at Washington Headquarters, will provide management oversight of TFRs issued under Section 91.145. The good cause exception tracks the language of the Administrative Procedure Act. It allows the FAA to issue a TFR in less than thirty days, if the FAA finds that good cause exists. The good cause exception does not relate to the type or size of events covered by §91.145. The FAA is currently working with the Flight Standards Service to clarify and review TFR procedures utilized by FSDO inspectors. (66 FR 47374-47376).

CROSS REFERENCES

91.137, Temporary Flight Restrictions in the Vicinity of Disaster/Hazard Areas.

ADVISORY CIRCULARS

AC 91-63B *Temporary Flight Restrictions (TFRs)* (1997).

AERONAUTICAL INFORMATION MANUAL

Temporary Flight Restrictions, Para. 3-5-3.

VISUAL FLIGHT RULES

91.151 FUEL REQUIREMENTS FOR FLIGHT IN VFR CONDITIONS

(a)   No person may begin a flight in an airplane under VFR conditions unless (considering wind and forecast weather conditions) there is enough fuel to fly to the first point of intended landing and, assuming normal cruising speed —
   (1)   During the day, to fly after that for at least 30 minutes; or
   (2)   At night, to fly after that for at least 45 minutes.
(b)   No person may begin a flight in a rotorcraft under VFR conditions unless (considering wind and forecast weather conditions) there is enough fuel to fly to the first point of intended landing and, assuming normal cruising speed, to fly after that for at least 20 minutes.

EXPLANATION

91.151(a): This subsection establishes the 30 minutes day-45 minutes night VFR fuel reserve requirements for airplanes.

91.151(b): This subsection establishes the 20 minutes VFR fuel reserve requirement for rotorcraft.

CROSS REFERENCES

Previous number: 91.22. 91.103 Preflight action; 91.167 Fuel Requirements for Flight in IFR conditions.

ADVISORY CIRCULARS

AC 61-23C *Pilot's Handbook of Aeronautical Knowledge* (1997).

AC 90-91E *North American Route Program.*

FAA-H-8083-3 *Airplane Flying Handbook* (1999).

FAA-H-8083-21 *Rotorcraft Flying Handbook* (2000).

AERONAUTICAL INFORMATION MANUAL

Minimum Fuel Advisory, Para. 5-5-15.

CASES

A helicopter pilot claimed he thought he had 20 minutes of fuel left after the "low fuel" light came on. He also claimed that he cut the power and did an autorotation to a crash landing because he believed that a fuel line had severed. The evidence did not support his story, and it was determined that he had begun the flight with insufficient fuel under §91.151(b), and that he had been careless in failing to monitor his fuel. *Administrator v. Vogt*, EA-4143 (1994).

A charge of a violation of [91.151(a)(2)] pertains solely to the **planning** stages of flight. There must be evidence of poor fuel planning in addition to the evidence of the amount of fuel which remained at the end of the flight. *Administrator v. Bailey*, 5 NTSB 1021 (1986).

Where a helicopter crashed due to fuel exhaustion, the "operator," who, with his wife, owned the business that operated the helicopter, was held to have violated [91.151(b)] although he was not piloting or even aboard the helicopter at the time of the accident. The Board held that he was at the site where the helicopter operated from and was in a position where he could and should have monitored the fuel status of the helicopter before takeoff. *Administrator v. Brown*, 5 NTSB 478 (1985).

A pilot, not knowing exactly how much fuel was on board before fueling the aircraft, but not filling the tanks, used her estimation of the fuel on board to calculate her reserve which proved not to be enough for the flight in question leading to fuel starvation. The Board considered this to be a careless action. *Administrator v. Holmgaard*, EA-4799 (1999).

A pilot flying a rented aircraft at night ran out of fuel nine or ten miles short of his destination. In addition to not ensuring that the fuel tanks were full before the flight, the pilot, in planning the flight, used a fuel burn rate he obtained from a flight manual for a different model of aircraft, which was lower than the actual rate for the aircraft he operated. He was fined $3,000. *FAA v. Hereth*, FAA Order No. 95-26 (12-19-1995).

91.153 VFR FLIGHT PLAN: INFORMATION REQUIRED

(a)   *Information Required.* Unless otherwise authorized by ATC, each person filing a VFR flight plan shall include in it the following information:
  (1)   The aircraft identification number and, if necessary, its radio call sign.
  (2)   The type of the aircraft or, in the case of a formation flight, the type of each aircraft and the number of aircraft in the formation.

(3)   The full name and address of the pilot in command or, in the case of a formation flight, the formation commander.
(4)   The point and proposed time of departure.
(5)   The proposed route, cruising altitude (or flight level), and true airspeed at that altitude.
(6)   The point of first intended landing and the estimated elapsed time until over that point.
(7)   The amount of fuel on board (in hours).
(8)   The number of persons in the aircraft, except where that information is otherwise readily available to the FAA.
(9)   Any other information the pilot in command or ATC believes is necessary for ATC purposes.
(b)   *Cancellation.* When a flight plan has been activated, the pilot in command, upon canceling or completing the flight under the flight plan, shall notify an FAA Flight Service Station or ATC facility.

EXPLANATION

As pointed out in the FAA Chief Counsel opinion discussed below, there are expensive and wasteful consequences when pilots forget to close their flight plans. Search and rescue efforts are an expensive waste of time if the pilot is sitting in a coffee shop at his or her destination. According to FAA Order No. 2150.3A, the FAA will usually take "administrative action" against a pilot for failing to close a flight plan, although they may seek a minimum civil penalty (usually a $500.00 fine).

CROSS REFERENCES

Previous designation: 91.83. 91.169 IFR Flight Plan: Information Required; 91.103 Preflight Action.

AERONAUTICAL INFORMATION MANUAL

Closing VFR/DVFR Flight Plans, Para. 5-1-12
Preflight, Para. 5-1-1 through 5-1-13.

FAA CHIEF COUNSEL OPINIONS

[91.153] has three objectives: first, to preclude the unnecessary expenditure of time and money in search and rescue efforts caused by a failure to cancel or close a flight plan; second, to preclude the needless restriction of the subsequent use of airspace by IFR traffic; and third, to provide the most timely assistance, under the circumstances involved, to pilots who may have experienced trouble during the flight. (11-30-77).

A pilot operating under an IFR flight plan must comply with all IFR regulations until such time as he/she cancels his/her flight plan which can only be done by providing the nearest FSS or ATC facility with actual notice of such cancellation. (11-30-77).

91.155 BASIC VFR WEATHER MINIMUMS

(a) Except as provided in paragraph (b) of this section and §91.157, no person may operate an aircraft under VFR when the flight visibility is less, or at a distance from clouds that is less, than that prescribed for the corresponding altitude and class of airspace in the following table:

Altitude	Flight visibility	Distance from clouds
Class A	Not applicable	Not Applicable.
Class B	3 statute miles . . .	Clear of Clouds.
Class C	3 statute miles . . .	500 feet below. 1,000 feet above. 2,000 feet horizontal.
Class D	3 statute miles . . .	500 feet below. 1,000 feet above. 2,000 feet horizontal.
Class E: Less than 10,000 feet MSL	3 statute miles . . .	500 feet below. 1,000 feet above. 2,000 feet horizontal.
At or above 10,000 feet MSL	5 statute miles . . .	1,000 feet below. 1,000 feet above. 1 statute mile horizontal.
Class G: 1,200 feet or less above the surface (regardless of MSL altitude). Day, except as provided in §91.155(b)	1 statute mile . . .	Clear of clouds.
Night, except as provided in §91.155(b)	3 statute miles . . .	500 feet below. 1,000 feet above. 2,000 feet horizontal.
More than 1,200 feet above the surface but less than 10,000 feet MSL Day	1 statute mile . . .	500 feet below. 1,000 feet above. 2,000 feet horizontal.
Night	3 statute miles . . .	500 feet below. 1,000 feet above. 2,000 feet horizontal.
More than 1,200 feet above the surface and at or above 10,000 feet MSL	5 statute miles . . .	1,000 feet below. 1,000 feet above. 1 statute mile horizontal.

(b) *Class G Airspace.* Notwithstanding the provisions of paragraph (a) of this section, the following operations may be conducted in Class G airspace below 1,200 feet above the surface:

    (1) *Helicopter.* A helicopter may be operated clear of clouds if operated at a speed that allows the pilot adequate opportunity to see any air traffic or obstruction in time to avoid a collision.

    (2) *Airplane.* When the visibility is less than 3 statute miles but not less than 1 statute mile during night hours, an airplane may be operated clear of clouds if operated in an airport traffic pattern within one-half mile of the runway.

(c) Except as provided in §91.157, no person may operate an aircraft beneath the ceiling under VFR within the lateral boundaries of controlled airspace designated to the surface for an airport when the ceiling is less than 1,000 feet.

(d) Except as provided in §91.157 of this part, no person may take off or land an aircraft, or enter the traffic pattern of an airport, under VFR, within the lateral boundaries of the surface areas of Class B, Class C, Class D, or Class E airspace designated for an airport —

    (1) Unless ground visibility at that airport is at least 3 statute miles; or

    (2) If ground visibility is not reported at that airport, unless flight visibility during landing or takeoff, or while operating in the traffic pattern is at least 3 statute miles.

(e) For the purpose of this section, an aircraft operating at the base altitude of a Class E airspace area is considered to be within the airspace directly below that area.

EXPLANATION

91.155(b): This subsection creates narrow exceptions to the visibility and cloud clearance requirements set forth in 91.155(a). 91.155(b)(2) does not specify "flight" or "ground" visibility.

91.155(c) & (d): These subsections establish the general requirement for a 1,000 feet ceiling and 3 miles visibility for VFR operation at airports in Class B, C, D or E airspace. Note the preference for "ground visibility" as opposed to "flight visibility."

CROSS REFERENCES

Previous designation: 91.105. 91.157, Special VFR weather minimums.

ADVISORY CIRCULARS

AC 00-6A *Aviation Weather* (1975).

AC 00-45E *Aviation Weather Services* (1999).

AERONAUTICAL INFORMATION MANUAL

Basic VFR Weather Minimums, 3-1-4;
Special VFR Clearances, Para. 4-4-5;
Meteorology, Para. 7-1-1 through 7-1-31.

CASES

A pilot who did not have an instrument rating flew into Class B airspace without requesting or obtaining a clearance and with his transponder turned off. The pilot then requested a clearance to "poke through some clouds," which was understood by ATC to be a request for an IFR clearance. The pilot received a 120 day suspension. *Administrator v. White*, EA-3791 (1993).

A pilot obtained weather information from his airline's computer service. He did not check current weather, but relied on his own observations that the visibility was VFR. Approximately 30 minutes before his departure, the visibility was reported at 1.5 miles. Approximately 25 minutes after departure, visibility was reported at 3 miles. The Board dismissed the FAA's claim that the pilot had taken off below VFR minimums. *Administrator v. Rolund*, EA-3991 (1993).

The potential existence of an error on a ground visibility report obtained from air traffic control facility or flight service station does not alter the fact that such information constitutes reported visibility within the purview of [91.155(d)(1)]. *Administrator v. Harris*, 5 NTSB 785 (1985).

Flight visibility, which is measured forward from the cockpit of the aircraft, cannot be used as a substitute for ground visibility. *Administrator v. Kokkonen*, 4 NTSB 881 (1983).

If a pilot landing or taking off in a control zone [now Class D airspace] does substitute his own judgment of ceiling heights based upon his airborne observation of the weather within the control zone, he is still required to comply with the provisions of [91.155(c)]. *Administrator v. Gaub*, 5 NTSB 1653 (1986).

[Editor's Note: Whether a pilot's judgment is accepted or not will be based on a credibility determination by the administrative law judge.]

FAA CHIEF COUNSEL OPINIONS

The reported ceiling at the primary airport in a control zone [now Class D airspace] governs as to whether VFR operations can be conducted within that particular control zone. The report by the weather station on the primary airport, or, if not on the airport, used by the primary airport governs notwithstanding that there are other weather stations within the control zone. (5-21-79).

If a pilot were to takeoff VFR when the reported weather at the primary airport was "indefinite ceiling, sky obscured, visibility zero, fog" there would be a violation of [91.55(c)] because the ceiling, which is defined as the height above the earth's surface of the lowest layer of clouds or obscuring phenomena, is lower than 1,000 feet above the earth's surface, the fog being the "obscuring phenomena." (10-14-80).

91.157 SPECIAL VFR WEATHER MINIMUMS

(a)   Except as provided in appendix D, section 3, of this part, special VFR operations may be conducted under the weather minimums and requirements of this section, instead of those contained in §91.155, below 10,000 feet MSL within the airspace contained by the upward extension of the lateral boundaries of the controlled airspace designated to the surface for an airport.

(b)   Special VFR operations may only be conducted—
    (1)   With an ATC clearance;
    (2)   Clear of clouds;
    (3)   Except for helicopters, when flight visibility is at least 1 statute mile; and
    (4)   Except for helicopters, between sunrise and sunset (or in Alaska, when the sun is 6 degrees or more below the horizon) unless—
        (i)   The person being granted the ATC clearance meets the applicable requirements for instrument flight under part 61 of this chapter; and
        (ii)   The aircraft is equipped as required in §91.205(d).

(c)   No person may take off or land an aircraft (other than a helicopter) under special VFR—
    (1)   Unless ground visibility is at least 1 statute mile; or
    (2)   If ground visibility is not reported, unless flight visibility is at least 1 statute mile. For The purposes of this paragraph, the term flight visibility includes the visibility from the cockpit of an aircraft in takeoff position if:
        (i)   The flight is conducted under this part 91; and
        (ii)   The airport at which the aircraft is located is a satellite airport that does not have weather reporting capabilities.

(d)   The determination of visibility by a pilot in accordance with paragraph (c)(2) of this section is not an official weather report or an official ground visibility report.

EXPLANATION

91.157(a): The reference to appendix D, section 3 refers to the fact that special VFR clearances are not available at certain airports. Airports where a special VFR clearance is not available will be indicated on sectional charts by "NO SVFR" above the airport name.

91.157(b)(2): A special VFR clearance does not allow a pilot to fly into instrument meteorology conditions (IMC).

91.157(b)(3): A special VFR clearance requires at least 1 mile "flight visibility," i.e., as judged from the cockpit, not the official weather for the airport.

91.157(b)(4): This subsection restricts the availability of special VFR clearances at night to instrument pilots in aircraft equipped for instrument flight.

91.157(c): This subsection states a preference for "ground visibility" where available for takeoffs and landings.

CROSS REFERENCES

Previous designation: 91.107. 91.205 Powered Civil Aircraft with Standard Category U.S. Airworthiness Certificates: Instrument and Equipment Requirements.

AERONAUTICAL INFORMATION MANUAL

Basic VFR Weather Minimums, 3-1-4;
Special VFR Clearance, Para. 4-4-5;
Meteorology Para. 7-1-1 through 7-1-31.

CASES

The fact that the controller, in responding to the pilot's request for a special VFR clearance, used the word "roger" did not amount to the issuance of the requested clearance but only acknowledged the controller's receipt of the pilot's request. *Administrator v. Heberer*, 5 NTSB 69 (1985).

A special VFR clearance is designed to allow a pilot to depart from an airport in a control zone [now Class D airspace] when the weather is below VFR minimums but normal VFR flight is possible once clear of the control zone. A special VFR clearance is no assurance that a safe flight can be made, however, but is given in marginal conditions and requires an exercise of judgment by the pilot in command. A prudent pilot will ascertain that his flight in the control zone and in the airspace beyond it can be accomplished with one mile visibility, clear of clouds, in the control zone and with appropriate visibility beyond. *Administrator v. Donaldson*, 4 NTSB 594 (1982).

91.159 VFR CRUISING ALTITUDE OR FLIGHT LEVEL

Except while holding in a holding pattern of 2 minutes or less, or while turning, each person operating an aircraft under VFR in level cruising flight more than 3,000 feet above the surface shall maintain the appropriate altitude or flight level prescribed below, unless otherwise authorized by ATC:
(a)   When operating below 18,000 feet MSL and —
    (1)   On a magnetic course of zero degrees through 179 degrees, any odd thousand foot MSL altitude + 500 feet (such as 3,500, 5,500, or 7,500); or
    (2)   On a magnetic course of 180 degrees through 359 degrees, any even thousand foot MSL altitude + 500 feet (such as 4,500, 6,500 or 8,500).
(b)   When operating above 18,000 feet MSL to flight level 290 (inclusive), and —
    (1)   On a magnetic course of zero degrees through 179 degrees, any odd flight level + 500 feet (such as 195, 215 or 235); or
    (2)   On a magnetic course of 180 degrees through 359 degrees, any even flight level + 500 feet (such as 185, 205, or 225).
(c)   When operating above flight level 290 and —
    (1)   On a magnetic course of zero degrees through 179 degrees, any flight level, at 4,000-foot intervals, beginning at and including flight level 300 (such as flight level 300, 340, or 380); or
    (2)   On a magnetic course of 180 degrees through 359 degrees, any flight level at 4,000 foot intervals, beginning at and including flight level 320 (such as flight level 320, 360, or 400).

EXPLANATION

Note that it refers to "magnetic course," and thus magnetic variation is accounted for.

CROSS REFERENCES

Previous designation: 91.107. 91.179 IFR Cruising Altitude or Flight Level; 91.119 Minimum Safe Altitudes: General.

AERONAUTICAL INFORMATION MANUAL

VFR Cruising Altitudes and Flight Levels, Para. 3-1-5.

INSTRUMENT FLIGHT RULES

91.167 FUEL REQUIREMENTS FOR FLIGHT IN IFR CONDITIONS

(a) No person may operate a civil aircraft in IFR conditions unless it carries enough fuel (considering weather reports and forecasts and weather conditions) to—
   (1) Complete the flight to the first airport of intended landing;
   (2) Except as provided in paragraph (b) of this section, fly from that airport to the alternate airport; and
   (3) Fly after that for 45 minutes at normal cruising speed or, for helicopters, fly after that for 30 minutes at normal cruising speed.
(b) Paragraph (a)(2) of this section does not apply if:
   (1) Part 97 of this chapter prescribes a standard instrument approach procedure to, or a special instrument approach procedure has been issued by the Administrator to the operator for, the first airport of intended landing; and
   (2) Appropriate weather reports or weather forecasts, or a combination of them, indicate the following:
      (i) *For aircraft other than helicopters.* For at least 1 hour before and for 1 hour after the estimated time of arrival, the ceiling will be at least 2,000 feet above the airport elevation and the visibility will be at least 3 statute miles.
      (ii) *For helicopters.* At the estimated time of arrival and for 1 hour after the estimated time of arrival, the ceiling will be at least 1,000 feet above the airport elevation, or at least 400 feet above the lowest applicable approach minima, whichever is higher, and the visibility will be at least 2 statute miles.

EXPLANATION

91.167(a): This regulation states the 45 minutes fuel reserve requirement for flight in IFR conditions (30 minutes helicopters). This regulation requires pilots to plan their fuel requirements based on the forecasted weather for the flight.

91.167(b): Fuel for flight to an alternate airport need not be carried if there is a published instrument approach to the destination airport, and the "1-2-3" rule (for at least **1** hour before and **1** hour after the estimated time of arrival at the airport, the forecast indicates at least a **2,000** feet ceiling and **3** miles visibility) is met. For helicopters, the time period, ceiling, and visibility are reduced. See 91.169(c) for IFR alternate airport weather minimums.

PREAMBLE

Flight planning requirements (including alternate airport weather minima) for helicopters and other aircraft are virtually identical, even though their operating characteristics are substantially different. The only distinction between the flight planning requirements for helicopters and other aircraft is addressed in 14 CFR 91.167, which specifies different requirements for the amount of fuel helicopters and other aircraft must carry after completing a flight to the first airport of intended landing. Helicopters, however, fly shorter distances at slower airspeeds than most other aircraft, and they generally remain in the air for shorter periods between landings. A helicopter is therefore less likely to fly into unanticipated, unknown, or unforecast weather. The relatively short duration of the typical helicopter flight means that the departure weather and the destination weather are likely to be within the same weather system. This final rule revises the flight planning requirements for helicopter IFR operations to take into account their unique operating characteristics. (65 FR 3539).

CROSS REFERENCES

Previous designation: 91.23. 91.103 Preflight Action; 91.169 IFR Flight Plan: Information Required.

ADVISORY CIRCULARS

AC 61-23C *Pilot's Handbook of Aeronautical Knowledge* (1997).

AC 90-91E *North American Route Program.*

FAA-H-8083-3 *Airplane Flying Handbook* (1999).

FAA-H-8083-15 *Instrument Flying Handbook* (2001).

AERONAUTICAL INFORMATION MANUAL

Minimum Fuel Advisory, Para. 5-5-15.

CASES

An airline flight crew failed to check fuel before takeoff, and did not notice that the airplane had not been refueled until they reached FL330. The crew then lied to ATC, claiming engine failure. Suspensions were ordered, but waived under the Aviation Safety Reporting Program. *Administrator v. Wieland & Perry*, EA-4190 (1994).

[91.167] is not restricted to flights conducted under an IFR flight plan. It applies to flights in IFR conditions, whether the pilot intended to enter IFR conditions or not. *Administrator v. Barnes*, 3 NTSB 2026 (1979).

91.169 IFR FLIGHT PLAN: INFORMATION REQUIRED

(a) *Information required.* Unless otherwise authorized by ATC, each person filing an IFR flight plan must include in it the following information:
  (1) Information required under §91.153(a) of this part;
  (2) Except as provided in paragraph (b) of this section, an alternate airport.
(b) Paragraph (a)(2) of this section does not apply if:
  (1) Part 97 of this chapter prescribes a standard instrument approach procedure to, or a special instrument approach procedure has been issued by the Administrator to the operator for, the first airport of intended landing; and
  (2) Appropriate weather reports or weather forecasts, or a combination of them, indicate the following:
    (i) *For aircraft other than helicopters.* For at least 1 hour before and for 1 hour after the estimated time of arrival, the ceiling will be at least 2,000 feet above the airport elevation and the visibility will be at least 3 statute miles.
    (ii) *For helicopters.* At the estimated time of arrival and for 1 hour after the estimated time of arrival, the ceiling will be at least 1,000 feet above the airport elevation, or at least 400 feet above the lowest applicable approach minima, whichever is higher, and the visibility will be at least 2 statute miles.
(c) *IFR alternate airport weather minima.* Unless otherwise authorized by the Administrator, no person may include an alternate airport in an IFR flight plan unless appropriate weather reports or weather forecasts, or a combination of them, indicate that, at the estimated time of arrival at the alternate airport, the ceiling and visibility at that airport will be at or above the following weather minima:
  (1) If an instrument approach procedure has been published in part 97 of this chapter, or a special instrument approach procedure has been issued by the Administrator to the operator, for that airport, the following minima:
    (i) *For aircraft other than helicopters:* The alternate airport minima specified in that procedure, or if none are specified the following standard approach minima:
      (A) *For a precision approach procedure.* Ceiling 600 feet and visibility 2 statute miles.
      (B) *For a nonprecision approach procedure.* Ceiling 800 feet and visibility 2 statute miles.
    (ii) *For helicopters:* Ceiling 200 feet above the minimum for the approach to be flown, and visibility at least 1 statute mile but never less than the minimum visibility for the approach to be flown, and
  (2) If no instrument approach procedure has been published in part 97 of this chapter and no special instrument approach procedure has been issued by the Administrator to the operator, for the alternate airport, the ceiling and visibility minima are those allowing descent from the MEA, approach, and landing under basic VFR.
(d) *Cancellation.* When a flight plan has been activated, the pilot in command, upon canceling or completing the flight under the flight plan, shall notify an FAA Flight Service Station or ATC facility.

EXPLANATION

91.169(a): ATC may accept an IFR flight plan with less than the required information (See "Abbreviated IFR Flight Plans," in the AIM Pilot/Controller Glossary). However, this is usually done when an airborne pilot "pops up" and requests an IFR approach into an airport. List an alternate airport and plan fuel accordingly anytime the weather forecasts indicate that the weather will be at or near the minima specified in subsection (b).

91.169(b): Fuel for flight to an alternate airport need not be carried if an alternate airport is not required.

91.169(c): Note that this subsection, which sets forth the IFR alternate airport weather minimums, does not require that the prescribed weather exist prior to or after the estimated time of arrival. The only relevant time under this subsection is estimated time of arrival.

91.169(d): An IFR flight plan may be canceled at any time the flight is operating in VFR conditions outside positive controlled airspace, although special considerations apply within Class B airspace, Class C airspace, and TRSAs. If a flight ends at an airport with an operating control tower, the flight plan will be closed automatically upon landing. If a flight ends at an airport without an operating control tower, the pilot is responsible for canceling the flight plan. If possible, a pilot should cancel IFRA while still airborne. This will not only save the time and expense of canceling by phone but will also quickly release the airspace for use by other pilots.

PREAMBLE

Prior to this rule change, §91.167 (b) stated in part that, "paragraph (a)(2) of this section does not apply if part 97 of this chapter prescribes a standard instrument approach procedure for the first airport of intended landing." Additionally, §91.169 (b) stated in part that "paragraph (a)(2) of this section does not apply if part 97 of this chapter prescribes a standard instrument approach procedure for the first airport of intended landing." That regulatory language did not provide for the use of special instrument approach procedures in determining an aircraft operator's ability to meet alternate airport requirements. This rule will permit an aircraft operator to use an authorized approach procedure in determining compliance with alternate airport requirements.

The language used in this final rule reflects current usage of the terms "weather forecasts" and "weather reports" by meteorologists and aviation industry personnel. It also includes the term "appropriate" when referring to weather reports and weather forecasts to indicate that an operator must consider current weather reports and current and valid weather forecasts when determining if a flight requires an alternate airport. Use of the term "appropriate" is consistent with references to weather reports and forecasts in other operating rules. Its inclusion should eliminate any ambiguity and ensure conformity in determining those reports and forecasts that should be considered by an operator when designating an alternate airport. Use of the term "appropriate" is also consistent with the provisions of 14 CFR 91.103, which requires each pilot in command, before beginning a flight, to become familiar with all available information concerning that flight.

With regard to the use of weather forecasts, the FAA notes that although a weather forecast may be valid for a period as long as 24 hours, only the most current and valid weather forecast is considered "appropriate." In some instances, a current weather forecast may be issued however, it may not be valid for the time period required to be considered by an operator when choosing an alternate airport. Such a report is not considered "appropriate." Any superceded weather report is not considered current and its use in determining an alternate airport is not considered appropriate.

The rule also does not include the descriptive term "prevailing" with the phrase "weather forecasts" because "prevailing" is used to refer to actual weather conditions observed at a station and not to weather forecasts. Its use in the context of the original proposal was therefore improper and has been deleted. (65 FR 3543-3544).

CROSS REFERENCES

Previous designation: 91.83. 91.153 VFR Flight Plan: Information Required; 91.167 Fuel Requirements for Flight in IFR conditions.

ADVISORY CIRCULARS

AC 61-23C *Pilot's Handbook of Aeronautical Knowledge* (1997).

AC 90-91E *North American Route Program.*

FAA-H-8083-3 *Airplane Flying Handbook* (1999).

FAA-H-8083-15 *Instrument Flying Handbook* (2001).

AERONAUTICAL INFORMATION MANUAL

IFR flight plans, Para. 5-1-7 through 5-1-13;
Pilot/Controller Glossary, "Abbreviated IFR Flight Plan."

CASES

Alternate airport information is only required to be filed when destination weather does not meet the conditions specified in [91.167(b)]. Thus, the fact that ATC issues a clearance on a flight plan that does not list an alternate cannot automatically be viewed as an authorization not to file one, for the omission may simply reflect the pilot's judgment that the listing of an alternate was unnecessary given the weather forecasts for his/her destination. However, there may be circumstances where ATC may expressly or by implication accept an abbreviated IFR flight plan without a listed alternate, even though an alternate is required by the weather conditions. *Administrator v. Gately*, 3 NTSB 3968 (1981).

[Editor's note: Abbreviated IFR flight plans are usually accepted from aircraft in flight, while the pilot in the case above was on the ground when ATC advised him that his destination airport was closed. He changed his destination to the airport he had previously listed as an alternate, without listing a new alternate.]

FAA CHIEF COUNSEL OPINIONS

Forecasts which state that weather conditions will be "occasionally," "intermittently," "briefly," or "chance of" below minimum conditions at the estimated time of arrival do not satisfy the requirements relating to the selection of an alternate airport under [91.169]. (5-18-79).

The critical time period for purposes of determining whether an airport can be listed as an alternate pursuant to [91.169] is the estimated time of arrival. That is why this regulation speaks only to "weather forecasts" as controlling operations, while other regulations speak to "weather reports and forecasts." (7-18-84).

91.171 VOR EQUIPMENT CHECK FOR IFR OPERATIONS

(a) No person may operate a civil aircraft under IFR using the VOR system of radio navigation unless the VOR equipment of that aircraft —
   (1) Is maintained, checked, and inspected under an approved procedure; or
   (2) Has been operationally checked within the preceding 30 days, and was found to be within the limits of the permissible indicated bearing error set forth in the paragraph (b) or (c) of this section.
(b) Except as provided in paragraph (c) of this section, each person conducting a VOR check under paragraph (a)(2) of this section shall —
   (1) Use, at the airport of intended departure, an FAA-operated or approved test signal or a test signal radiated by a certificated and appropriately rated radio repair station or, outside the United States, a test signal operated or approved by an appropriate authority to check the VOR equipment (the maximum permissible indicated bearing error is plus or minus 4 degrees); or
   (2) Use, at the airport of intended departure, a point on the airport surface designated as a VOR system checkpoint by the Administrator, or, outside the United States, by an appropriate authority (the maximum permissible bearing error is plus or minus 4 degrees);
   (3) If neither a test signal nor a designated checkpoint on the surface is available, use an airborne checkpoint designated by the Administrator or, outside the United States, by an appropriate authority (the maximum permissible bearing error is plus or minus 6 degrees); or
   (4) If no check signal or point is available, while in flight —
       (i) Select a VOR radial that lies along the centerline of an established VOR airway;
       (ii) Select a prominent ground point along the selected radial preferably more than 20 nautical miles from the VOR ground facility and maneuver the aircraft directly over the point at a reasonably low altitude; and
       (iii) Note the VOR bearing indicated by the receiver when over the ground point (the maximum permissible variation between the published radial and the indicated bearing is 6 degrees).
(c) If dual system VOR (units independent of each other except for the antenna) is installed in the aircraft, the person checking the equipment may check one system against the other in place of the check procedures specified in paragraph (b) of this section. Both systems shall be tuned to the same VOR ground facility and note the indicated bearings to that station. The maximum permissible variation between the two indicated bearings is 4 degrees.

(d)   Each person making the VOR operational check, as specified in paragraph (b) or (c) of this section, shall enter the date, place, bearing error, and sign the aircraft log or other record. In addition, if a test signal radiated by a repair station, as specified in paragraph (b)(1) of this section, is used, an entry must be made in the aircraft log or other record by the repair station certificate holder or the certificate holder's representative certifying to the bearing transmitted by the repair station for the check and the date of transmission.

EXPLANATION

91.171(a): The 30 day VOR check required by this regulation applies anytime an instrument flight plan is used, and not merely when instrument meteorological conditions are to be encountered.

91.171(b)(1): The FAA VOR test facility (VOT) transmits a test signal which provides users a convenient means to check the operational status of a VOR while on the ground where a VOT is located. A VOT may be used while airborne, but only as prescribed in the Airport/Facility Directory.

To use the VOT service, tune in the VOT frequency on your VOR receiver. With the Course Deviation Indicator (CDI) centered, the omni bearing selector should read 0 degrees with the TO/FROM indication showing "FROM." Should the VOR receiver operate an RMI it will indicate 180 degrees. Two means of identification are used. One is a series of dots and the other is a continuous tone. Information concerning an individual test signal can be obtained from the local FSS. The maximum permissible error for a VOT test, on the ground or airborne, is " 4 degrees.

91.171(b)(2): Ground checkpoints using nearby VOR radials as checkpoints are described in the Airport/Facility Directory and the maximum permissible error is also " 4 degrees.

91.171(b)(3): Airborne checkpoints using nearby VOR radials as checkpoints are described in the Airport/Facility Directory and the maximum permissible error is " 6 degrees.

91.171(b)(4): This subsection describes a method for checking a VOR receiver when no check point or test signal is available.

91.171(c): If an aircraft has two independent VORs, they may be tested against one another, instead of using the procedures set forth in subsection (b). The maximum permissible variation between the two is 4 degrees.

91.171(d): A record must be made of the VOR checks required by this regulation, although the record does not have to kept in the aircraft logs. Pilots who fly a variety of aircraft may wish to keep their own VOR check logs to ensure compliance with this regulation.

CROSS REFERENCES

Previous designation: 91.25.

ADVISORY CIRCULARS

FAA-H-8083-15 *Instrument Flying Handbook* (2001), VOR Receiver Accuracy Check.

AERONAUTICAL INFORMATION MANUAL

VHF Omni-Directional Range (VOR), Para. 1-1-3;
VOR Receiver Check, Para. 1-1-4;
VHF Omni-Directional Range/Tactical Air Navigation (VORTAC), Para. 1-1-6.

CASES

Failing to see whether the 30 day VOR check and 24 month altimeter and transponder checks have been performed is not excused simply because the aircraft logs are not in the airplane prior to flight. *Administrator v. Kocsis*, 3 NTSB 461 (1982).

91.173 ATC CLEARANCE AND FLIGHT PLAN REQUIRED

No person may operate an aircraft in controlled airspace under IFR unless that person has —
(a)   Filed an IFR flight plan; and
(b)   Received an appropriate ATC clearance.

EXPLANATION

It is legal to fly in uncontrolled airspace without an IFR flight plan or clearance. Thus, when receiving an IFR clearance on the ground at an uncontrolled airport, the clearance may include the phrase "upon entering controlled airspace. . . ."

CROSS REFERENCES

Previous Number: 91.115. 91.169 IFR Flight Plan: Information Required; 91.123 Compliance with ATC Clearances and Instructions; 91.177, Minimum Altitudes for IFR Operations; 91.179, IFR Cruising Altitude or Flight Level.

ADVISORY CIRCULARS

FAA-H-8083-15 *Instrument Flying Handbook* (2001).

AERONAUTICAL INFORMATION MANUAL

Pilot/Controller Glossary, "Controlled Airspace;"
IFR flight plans, Para. 5-1-7 through 5-1-13.

FAA CHIEF COUNSEL OPINIONS

Military pilots, or any pilot, flying a military aircraft could not operate in controlled airspace under IFR unless an IFR flight plan has been filed and the pilot has received an appropriate ATC clearance, as required by [91.173]. (7-9-79).

91.175 TAKEOFF AND LANDING UNDER IFR

(a) *Instrument approaches to civil airports.* Unless otherwise authorized by the Administrator, when an instrument letdown to a civil airport is necessary, each person operating an aircraft, except a military aircraft of the United States, shall use a standard instrument approach procedure prescribed for the airport in part 97 of this chapter.

(b) *Authorized DH or MDA.* For the purpose of this section, when the approach procedure being used provides for and requires the use of a DH or MDA, the authorized DH or MDA is the highest of the following:
  (1) The DH or MDA prescribed by the approach procedure.
  (2) The DH or MDA prescribed for the pilot in command.
  (3) The DH or MDA for which the aircraft is equipped.

(c) *Operation below DH or MDA.* Where a DH or MDA is applicable, no pilot may operate an aircraft, except a military aircraft of the United States, at any airport below the authorized MDA or continue an approach below the authorized DH unless —
  (1) The aircraft is continuously in a position from which a descent to a landing on the intended runway can be made at a normal rate of descent using normal maneuvers, and for operations conducted under part 121 or part 135 unless that descent rate will allow touchdown to occur within the touchdown zone of the runway of intended landing.
  (2) The flight visibility is not less than the visibility prescribed in the standard instrument approach procedure being used; and
  (3) Except for a Category II or Category III approach where any necessary visual reference requirements are specified by the Administrator, at least one of the following visual references for the intended runway is distinctly visible and identifiable to the pilot:
    (i) The approach light system, except that the pilot may not descend below 100 feet above the touchdown zone elevation using the approach lights as a reference unless the red terminating bars or the red side row bars are also distinctly visible and identifiable.
    (ii) The threshold.
    (iii) The threshold markings.
    (iv) The threshold lights.
    (v) The runway end identifier lights.
    (vi) The visual approach slope indicator.
    (vii) The touchdown zone or touchdown zone markings.
    (viii) The touchdown zone lights.
    (ix) The runway or runway markings.
    (x) The runway lights.

(d) *Landing.* No pilot operating an aircraft, except a military aircraft of the United States, may land that aircraft when the flight visibility is less than the visibility prescribed in the standard instrument approach procedure being used.

(e) *Missed approach procedures.* Each pilot operating an aircraft, except a military aircraft of the United States, shall immediately execute an appropriate missed approach procedure when either of the following conditions exist:
  (1) Whenever the requirements of paragraph (c) of this section are not met at either of the following times:
    (I) When the aircraft is being operated below MDA; or
    (ii) Upon arrival at the missed approach point, including a DH where a DH is specified and its use is required, and at any time after that until touchdown.

(2)   Whenever an identifiable part of the airport is not distinctly visible to the pilot during a circling maneuver at or above MDA, unless the inability to see an identifiable part of the airport results only from a normal bank of the aircraft during the circling approach.

(f)   *Civil airport takeoff minimums.* Unless otherwise authorized by the Administrator, no pilot operating an aircraft under parts 121, 125, 129, or 135 of this chapter may takeoff from a civil airport under IFR unless weather conditions are at or above the weather minimum for IFR takeoff prescribed for that airport under part 97 of this chapter. If takeoff minimums are not prescribed under part 97 of this chapter for a particular airport, the following minimums apply to takeoffs under IFR for aircraft operating under those parts:

(1)   For aircraft, other than helicopters, having two engines or less - 1 statute mile visibility.

(2)   For aircraft having more than two engines - 1/2 statute mile visibility.

(3)   For helicopters - 1/2 statute mile visibility.

(g)   *Military airports.* Unless otherwise prescribed by the Administrator, each person operating a civil aircraft under IFR into or out of a military airport shall comply with the instrument approach procedures and the takeoff and landing minimum prescribed by the military authority having jurisdiction of that airport.

(h)   *Comparable values of RVR and ground visibility.*

(1)   Except for Category II or Category III minimums, if RVR minimums for takeoff or landing are prescribed in an instrument approach procedure, but RVR is not reported for the runway of intended operation, the RVR minimum shall be converted to ground visibility in accordance with the table in paragraph (h)(2) of this section and shall be the visibility minimum for takeoff or landing on that runway.

(2)   RVR Table:

RVR (feet)	Visibility (statute miles)
1,600	1/4
2,400	1/2
3,200	5/8
4,000	3/4
4,500	7/8
5,000	1
6,000	1 1/4

(i)   *Operations on unpublished routes and use of radar in instrument approach procedures.* When radar is approved at certain locations for ATC purposes, it may be used not only for surveillance and precision radar approaches, as applicable, but also may be used in conjunction with instrument approach procedures predicated on other types of radio navigational aids. Radar vectors may be authorized to provide course guidance through the segments of an approach to the final course or fix. When operating on an unpublished route or while being radar vectored, the pilot, when an approach clearance is received, shall, in addition to complying with §91.177, maintain the last altitude assigned to that pilot until the aircraft is established on a segment of a published route or instrument approach procedure unless a different altitude is assigned by ATC. After the aircraft is so established, published altitudes apply to descent within each succeeding route or approach segment unless a different altitude is assigned by ATC. Upon reaching the final approach course or fix, the pilot may either complete the instrument approach in accordance with a procedure approved for the facility or continue a surveillance or precision radar approach to a landing.

(j)   *Limitation on procedure turns.* In the case of a radar vector to a final approach course or fix, a timed approach from a holding fix, or an approach for which the procedure specifies "No PT," no pilot may make a procedure turn unless cleared to do so by ATC.

(k)   *ILS components.* The basic ground components of an ILS are the localizer, glide slope, outer marker, middle marker, and, when installed for use with Category II or Category III instrument approach procedures, an inner marker. A compass locator or precision radar may be substituted for the outer or middle marker. DME, VOR, or nondirectional beacon fixes authorized in the standard instrument approach procedure or surveillance radar may be substituted for the outer marker. Applicability of, and substitution for, the inner marker for Category II or III approaches is determined by the appropriate part 97 approach procedure, letter of authorization, or operations specification pertinent to the operations.

EXPLANATION

91.175(a): Unless otherwise authorized by ATC, the **published** instrument approach must be used when an instrument approach is necessary.

91.175(b): Decision height (DH) is the limit to which a pilot can descend before having to decide to continue the approach visually or to execute a missed approach. Minimum descent altitude (MDA) is the lowest altitude to which descent is authorized on final approach or during circle-to-land maneuvering in execution of a standard instrument approach procedure where no glide slope is provided i.e. not an ILS approach. Category II and III approaches allow lower DHs or MDAs for qualified pilots in qualified aircraft.

91.175(c)(1): This subsection cannot be simplified, as nearly every word has been interpreted by the NTSB The purpose of this subsection is to prevent pilots from lingering at DH or MAP, hoping to catch a glimpse of the runway in time to chop the power and drop like a brick. It also prohibits a pilot from continuing an approach below MDA or DH if he or she loses sight of the runway environment at any time after beginning the approach.

91.175(c)(2): "Flight visibility" is not what the tower reports, and this allows pilots operating under Part 91 to take a look for themselves to see what the visibility is, but if the tower reports visibility drastically lower than that required to make the approach, then the FAA will doubt a pilot who claims that "flight visibility" was adequate to make the approach.

91.175(c)(3) lists the items which, if in sight, allow a pilot to continue the approach below DH or MDA.

91.175(d): This subsection uses the term "flight visibility" as well, and the same explanation given for (c)(2) applies.

91.175(e): If at anytime the approach is in doubt at or below MDA or DH, execute a missed approach.

91.175(f): Takeoff minimums are published in the Terminal Procedures Publications ("approach charts"), and do not apply to Part 91 flights.

91.175(l): The FAA has never **officially** defined "established." The International Civil Aviation Organization (ICAO) publishes a document on flight procedures (Doc.8768 Vol. I) which states that "established" is considered as being within half full scale deflection for the ILS and VOR, or within +/- 5 degrees of the required bearing for the NDB. This definition was quoted by the FAA in the April 1993 edition of *FAA Aviation News*, page 25. The article went on to note that the FAA's Practical Test Standards (PTS) for an instrument rating applicant are no more than three-quarter scale CDI or glide slope deflection during a VOR or ILS approach and no more than plus or minus 10 degrees deviation for an NDB approach. Stricter standards apply for ATP and type rating tests. The FAA seemed to acknowledge that a practical definition of "established" is that a pilot is established when he/she is flying within the PTS parameters.

91.175(k): This subsection allows pilots to substitute certain navigation aids when certain components of an ILS approach are unavailable.

CROSS REFERENCES

Previous designation: 91.116.

ADVISORY CIRCULARS

FAA-H-8083-15 *Instrument Flying Handbook* (2001).

AERONAUTICAL INFORMATION MANUAL

Departure Procedures, Para. 5-2-1 through 5-2-6;
En Route Procedures, Para. 5-3-1 through 5-3-7;
Arrival Procedures, Para. 5-4-1 through 5-4-24;
Pilot/Controller Roles and Responsibilities, Para. 5-5-1 through 5-5-15.

CASES

The pilots of a Learjet decided to "take a look" even though the tower reported the ground visibility to be below minimums. The pilots reported "missed approach" shortly before they scraped the landing gear off on the runway. The pilot in command was found in violation of [91.175(c)(d)(e) and 91.13]. *Administrator v. King*, EA-2960 (1989).

A pilot who made a VOR 12L approach after being cleared to fly a VOR 30R approach was found in violation of [91.175(a), 91.123(a)(b) and 91.13]. *Administrator v. Abbott*, 3 NTSB 1072 (1978).

The controlling visibility in [91.175(b) and (d)] is flight visibility, even if the standard instrument approach being used prescribes minimum visibility in terms of RVR. Where the reported RVR was 2200 feet, and the required flight visibility was 2400 feet RVR, the pilot's testimony that the flight visibility was 2 mile or 2400 feet was believable. *Administrator v. Davey*, 3 NTSB 3164 (1980).

[91.175(f)] simply uses the phrase "weather conditions," it does not state "weather conditions reported by the U.S. National Weather Service." Thus, the visibility reported at the field by ATIS or ATC does not necessarily determine whether the "weather conditions" are at or above the takeoff minimums for a Part 135 flight. In this case, RVR was reported at 1800 feet. The pilot informed the tower that visibility appeared to be better than 2 mile, and took off. The law judge believed the pilot, and the Board affirmed that a violation of [91.175(f)] was not established. *Administrator v. Thomas*, 3 NTSB 3203 (1981).

FAA CHIEF COUNSEL OPINIONS

This is a clarification of our response to your letter of August 23, 1993. In that letter you requested an interpretation of Section 91.175 of the Federal Aviation Regulations. You address the necessity of executing a complete Standard Instrument Approach Procedure (SIAP) in a non-radar environment while operating under Instrument Flight Rules (IFR). Our response assumes that each of the specific scenarios you pose speaks to a flight conducted under IFR in a non-radar environment.

Section 91.175(a) provides that unless otherwise authorized by the Administrator, when an instrument letdown to a civil airport is necessary, each person operating an aircraft, except a military aircraft of the United States, shall use a standard instrument approach procedure prescribed for the airport in Part 97.

First you ask whether an arriving aircraft must begin the SIAP at a published Initial Approach Fix (IAF). A pilot must begin a SIAP at the IAF as defined in Part 97. Descent gradients, communication, and obstruction clearance, as set forth in the U.S. Standard for Terminal Instrument Approach Procedures (TERPs), cannot be assured if the entire procedure is not flown.

You also ask whether a Distance Measuring Equipment (DME) arc initial approach segment can be substituted for a published IAF along any portion of the published arc. A DME arc cannot be substituted for a published IAF along a portion of the published arc. If a feeder route to an IAF is part of the published approach procedure, it is considered a mandatory part of the approach.

Finally, you ask whether a course reversal segment is optional "when one of the conditions of Section 91.175(j) is not present." Section 91.175(j) states that in the case of a radar vector to a final approach for which the procedure specifies "no procedure turn," no pilot may make a procedure turn unless cleared to do so by ATC.

> Section 97.3(p) defines a procedure turn, in part, as a maneuver prescribed when it is necessary to reverse direction to establish the aircraft on an intermediate or final approach course. A SIAP may or may not prescribe a procedure turn bases on the application of certain criteria contained in the TERPs. However, if a SIAP does contain a procedure turn and ATC has cleared a pilot to execute the SIAP, the pilot must make the procedure turn when one of the conditions of Section 91.175(j) is not present. (5-24-95).

[91.175(f)] applies only to Part 121, 125, 129 and 135 operations at any civil airport, but in no way abrogates the enforceability of the provisions of [91.129(f)] as to departure procedures against Part 91 operators. (2-4-75).

Under [91.175], Part 97 standard instrument approach procedures are regulatory and, unless otherwise authorized, such as by an ATC clearance to the contrary, a pilot is required to execute an IFR approach in accordance with the standard instrument approach procedure prescribed in Part 97. (7-25-77).

If the flight visibility exceeds the published minimum for the approach, then the pilot may proceed as long as the other requirements of [91.175(c)] are met, regardless of the reported RVR. The pilot's judgment of flight visibility is not necessarily conclusive if there is a question as to the actual flight visibility conditions at the time of the approach. (3-10-88).

91.177 MINIMUM ALTITUDES FOR IFR OPERATIONS

(a) *Operation of aircraft at minimum altitudes.* Except when necessary for takeoff or landing, no person may operate an aircraft under IFR below —
    (1) The applicable minimum altitudes prescribed in parts 95 and 97 of this chapter; or
    (2) If no applicable minimum altitude is prescribed in those parts —
        (i) In the case of operations over an area designated as a mountainous area in part 95, an altitude of 2,000 feet above the highest obstacle within a horizontal distance of 4 nautical miles from the course to be flown; or
        (ii) In any other case, an altitude of 1,000 feet above the highest obstacle within a horizontal distance of 4 nautical miles from the course to be flown.
        However, if both a MEA and a MOCA are prescribed for a particular route or route segment, a person may operate an aircraft below the MEA down to, but not below, the MOCA, when within 22 nautical miles of the VOR concerned (based on the pilot's reasonable estimate of that distance).
(b) *Climb.* Climb to a higher minimum IFR altitude shall begin immediately after passing the point beyond which that minimum altitude applies, except that when ground obstructions intervene, the point beyond which that higher minimum altitude applies shall be crossed at or above the applicable MCA.

EXPLANATION

91.177(a)(1): Part 95 prescribes Minimum Enroute Altitudes (MEAs), Minimum Obstruction Clearance Altitudes (MOCAs), Changeover Points (COPs), and Minimum Reception Altitudes (MRAs). Part 97 prescribes Standard Instrument Approach Procedures, and the minimum altitudes associated with approaches include Minimum Safe Altitudes (MSAs), Minimum Descent Altitudes (MDAs) and Decision Heights (DHs).

91.177(a)(2): Minimum Enroute Altitudes (MEAs) assure acceptable navigational signal coverage and meet obstacle clearance requirements between radio fixes. Minimum Obstruction Clearance Altitudes (MOCAs) meet obstacle clearance requirements but only assure acceptable navigational signal coverage within 25 statute (22 nautical) miles of a VOR.

91.177(b): Minimum Crossing Altitude (MCA) is the lowest altitude at certain fixes at which an aircraft must cross when proceeding in the direction of a higher minimum en route IFR altitude (MEA). If the MEA is higher after crossing a VOR on an airway, the pilot does not need to begin the climb from the lower MEA to the higher MEA until crossing the VOR, unless there is a MCA listed for the VOR.

CROSS REFERENCES

Previous designation: 91.119.

ADVISORY CIRCULARS

FAA-H-8083-15 *Instrument Flying Handbook* (2001).

AERONAUTICAL INFORMATION MANUAL

IFR Requirements, Para. 3-3-3;
Instrument Approach Procedure Charts, Para. 5-4-5;
Altimeter Setting Procedures, Para. 7-2-2.

FAA CHIEF COUNSEL OPINIONS

An aircraft on an IFR flight plan, but cleared by ATC to maintain VFR conditions on top, may not be operated below minimum enroute IFR altitudes. The minimum altitude rules of [91.177] are designed to ensure safe vertical separation between the aircraft and the terrain. These minimum altitude rules apply to all IFR flights, whether in IFR or VFR weather conditions, and whether assigned a specific altitude or VFR conditions on top. However, 121.657 provides for an analogous "over the top" IFR operation under certain restrictive conditions at minimum altitudes that may be below those prescribed in Part 95. (4-8-76).

91.179 IFR CRUISING ALTITUDE OR FLIGHT LEVEL

(a)   *In controlled airspace.* Each person operating an aircraft under IFR in level cruising flight in controlled airspace shall maintain the altitude or flight level assigned that aircraft by ATC. However, if the ATC clearance assigns "VFR conditions on-top," that person shall maintain an altitude or flight level as prescribed by §91.159.

(b)   *In uncontrolled airspace.* Except while holding in a holding pattern of 2 minutes or less or while turning, each person operating an aircraft under IFR in level cruising flight in uncontrolled airspace shall maintain an appropriate altitude as follows:

(1)   When operating below 18,000 feet MSL and —

(i)   On a magnetic course of zero degrees through 179 degrees, any odd thousand foot MSL altitude (such as 3,000, 5,000, or 7,000); or

(ii)   On a magnetic course of 180 degrees through 359 degrees, any even thousand foot MSL altitude (such as 2,000, 4,000, or 6,000).

(2)   When operating at or above 18,000 feet MSL but below flight level 290, and —

(i)   On a magnetic course of zero degrees through 179 degrees, any odd flight level (such as 190, 210, or 230); or

(ii)   On a magnetic course of 180 degrees through 359 degrees, any even flight level (such as 180, 200, or 220).

(3)   When operating at flight level 290 and above, and —
    (i)   On a magnetic course of zero degrees through 179 degrees, any flight level, at 4,000-foot intervals, beginning at and including flight level 290 (such as flight level 29, 330, or 370); or
    (ii)   On a magnetic course of 180 degrees through 359 degrees, any flight level, at 4,000-foot intervals, beginning at and including flight level 310 (such as flight level 310, 350, or 390).

EXPLANATION

91.179(a): Pilots flying IFR within controlled airspace must fly at an altitude/flight level assigned by ATC. When flying IFR within controlled airspace on a VFR On Top clearance, flight is to be conducted at an appropriate VFR altitude which is not below the minimum IFR altitude for the route (MEA).

91.179(b): Note that this subsection refers to magnetic course, not true course, which means that magnetic variation is taken into account.

CROSS REFERENCES

Previous designation: 91.121. 91.159 VFR Altitude or Flight Level; 91.177 Minimum for IFR Operations.

ADVISORY CIRCULARS

FAA-H-8083-15 *Instrument Flying Handbook* (2001).

AERONAUTICAL INFORMATION MANUAL

VFR Cruising Altitudes and Flight Levels, Para. 3-1-5;
IFR Altitudes and Flight Levels — Class G Airspace, Para. 3-3-3(b);
IFR Clearance VFR On Top, Para. 4-4-7.

FAA CHIEF COUNSEL OPINIONS

While controllers may use the hemispherical rule to manage aircraft operation within controlled airspace, they are not required to do so. Other factors such as ATC procedures, airspace sectorization, and the volume of air traffic may require the use of other altitudes. Therefore, the rule in controlled airspace is that ATC assigns each pilot an altitude to be flown, which ensures separation from other known traffic. The pilot must comply with that assignment.

A pilot cannot violate the "hemispherical rule" stated in 91.179(b), which designates appropriate flight altitudes, simply by filing a flight plan with flight levels that violate the rule. A violation can only occur if the pilot fails to comply with an air traffic control assigned altitude clearance or instruction. (7-28-99).

91.181 COURSE TO BE FLOWN

Unless otherwise authorized by ATC, no person may operate an aircraft within controlled airspace under IFR except as follows:
(a) On a Federal alrway, along the centerline of that airway.
(b) On any other route, along the direct course between the navigational aids or fixes defining that route.

However, this section does not prohibit maneuvering the aircraft to pass well clear of other air traffic or the maneuvering of the aircraft in VFR conditions to clear the intended flight path both before and during climb or decent.

EXPLANATION

It is permissible, and sometimes necessary to lead a turn on an airway by beginning the turn to the new course before crossing the fix. This does not violate the requirement to fly the centerline of the airway.

CROSS REFERENCES

Previous designation: 91.123.

ADVISORY CIRCULARS

FAA-H-8083-15 *Instrument Flying Handbook* (2001).

AERONAUTICAL INFORMATION MANUAL

Airways and Route Systems, Para. 5-3-4;
Airway or Route Course Changes, Para. 5-3-5;
Changeover Points (COPs), Para. 5-3-6.

91.183 IFR RADIO COMMUNICATIONS

The pilot in command of each aircraft operated under IFR in controlled airspace shall have a continuous watch maintained on the appropriate frequency and shall report by radio as soon as possible—
(a) The time and altitude of passing each designated reporting point, or the reporting points specified by ATC, except that while the aircraft is under radar control, only the passing of those reporting points specifically requested by ATC need be reported.
(b) Any unforecast weather conditions encountered; and
(c) Any other information relating to the safety of flight.

EXPLANATION

In addition to the items listed in this regulation, the AIM recommends that the following reports should be made to ATC or FSS without a specific request:

1. When vacating any previously assigned altitude or flight level for a newly assigned altitude or flight level;
2. When an altitude change will be made if operating VFR On Top;
3. When unable to climb/descend at a rate of at least 500 feet per minute;
4. When an approach has been missed;
5. Change in the average true airspeed (at cruising altitude) when it varies by 5 percent or 10 knots (whichever is greater) from that filed in the flight plan;
6. The time and altitude or flight level upon reaching a holding fix or point to which cleared;
7. When leaving any assigned holding fix or point.

CROSS REFERENCES

Previous designation: 91.125. 91.185 IFR Operations: Two-Way Radio Communications Failure. 91.187 Operation under IFR in Controlled Airspace: Malfunction Reports.

AERONAUTICAL INFORMATION MANUAL

ARTCC Communications, Para. 5-3-1;
Position Reporting, Para. 5-3-2;
Additional Reports, Para. 5-3-3.

CASES

A pilot was suspended for holding with right turns after being instructed by ATC to hold with left turns. He also did not have low altitude charts, and had to continuously ask ATC for fixes. The FAA and the NTSB did not believe the pilot's hypoxia defense. *Administrator v. Ellis*, EA-3910 (1993).

91.185 IFR OPERATIONS: TWO-WAY RADIO COMMUNICATIONS FAILURE

(a) *General.* Unless otherwise authorized by ATC, each pilot who has two-way radio communications failure when operating under IFR shall comply with the rules of this section.
(b) *VFR conditions.* If the failure occurs in VFR conditions, or if VFR conditions are encountered after the failure, each pilot shall continue the flight under VFR and land as soon as practicable.
(c) *IFR conditions.* If the failure occurs in IFR conditions, or if paragraph (b) of this section cannot be complied with, each pilot shall continue the flight according to the following:
   (1) *Route.*
      (i) By the route assigned in the last ATC clearance received;
      (ii) If being radar vectored, by the direct route from the point of radio failure to the fix, route, or airway specified in the vector clearance;
      (iii) In the absence of an assigned route, by the route that ATC has advised may be expected in a further clearance, or
      (iv) In the absence of an assigned route or a route that ATC has advised may be expected in a further clearance, by the route filed in the flight plan.

(2) *Altitude.*

At the highest of the following altitudes or flight levels for the route segment being flown:

(i) The altitude or flight level assigned in the last ATC clearance received;

(ii) The minimum altitude (converted, if appropriate, to minimum flight level as prescribed in §91.121(c)) for IFR operations; or

(iii) The altitude or flight level ATC has advised may be expected in a further clearance.

(3) *Leave clearance limit.*

(i) When clearance limit is a fix from which an approach begins, commence descent or descent and approach as close as possible to the expect-further-clearance time if one has been received, or if one has not been received, as close as possible to the estimated time of arrival as calculated from the filed or amended (with ATC) estimated time en route.

(ii) If the clearance limit is not a fix from which an approach begins, leave the clearance limit at the expect-further-clearance time if one has been received, or if none has been received, upon arrival over the clearance limit, and proceed to a fix from which an approach begins and commence descent or descent and approach as close as possible to the estimated time of arrival as calculated from the filed or amended (with ATC) estimated time en route.

EXPLANATION

Whether a radio failure constitutes an emergency such that a pilot may deviate from this rule depends on the circumstances. The purpose of this rule is to give ATC some idea of what airspace to keep clear until the aircraft with radio problems can land safely.

91.185(b): This procedure also applies when two-way radio failure occurs while operating in Class A airspace. The primary objective of this provision is to preclude extended IFR operation in the ATC system in VFR weather conditions. However, it is not intended that the requirement to "land as soon as practicable" be construed to mean "as soon as possible." The pilot retains his/her prerogative of exercising his/her best judgment and is not required to land at an unauthorized airport, at an airport unsuitable for the type of aircraft flown, or to land only minutes short of his/her destination.

91.185(c)(2): Example: A pilot loses his radios at an assigned altitude of 7,000 feet and is cleared along a direct route which will require a climb to a minimum IFR altitude of 9,000 feet. He should climb to 9,000 in accordance with 91.177(b). Later, while flying on an airway with an MEA of 5,000 feet, the pilot would descend to 7,000 feet (the last assigned altitude), because that altitude is higher than the MEA.

CROSS REFERENCES

Previous designation: 91.127. 91.3 Responsibility and Authority of Pilot in Command.

ADVISORY CIRCULARS

FAA-H-8083-15 *Instrument Flying Handbook* (2001).

AERONAUTICAL INFORMATION MANUAL

Two-Way Radio Communications Failure, Para. 6-4-1;
Transponder Operation During Two-Way Communications Failure, Para. 6-4-2;
Reestablishing Radio Contact, Para. 6-4-3.

CASES

Where a pilot continued for approximately 25 minutes after losing his radios on an IFR flight and landed at his destination, the Board found that the pilot, an ATP, did not adequately explain why he failed to land as soon as practicable, given that he passed several suitable airports in good VFR conditions. *Administrator v. Gad*, 3 NTSB 3671 (1981).

FAA CHIEF COUNSEL OPINIONS

When can a pilot leave a fix, from which an approach begins, to commence his approach, if he is operating under IFR on a tower enroute clearance and experiences two-way radio communications failure?

The procedures specified in §91.185 apply when operating under IFR on a tower en route clearance. §91.185(c)(3)(I) provides that, "When the clearance limit is a fix from which an approach begins, commence descent or descent and approach as close as possible to the expect-further-clearance time if one has been received, or if one has not been received, as close as possible to the estimated time of arrival as calculated from the filed or amended (with ATC) estimated time enroute." (1-28-92).

Someone asked at what point may a pilot begin his descent for an instrument approach if he experiences communications failure when operating under IFR.

The example assumes the clearance limit is not a fix from which an approach begins. §91.185(b) provides that, "If the failure occurs in VFR conditions, or if VFR conditions are encountered after the failure, each pilot shall continue the flight under VFR and land as soon as practicable." If the failure occurs in IFR conditions, or if §91.185(b) cannot be complied with, §91.185(c)(2) specifies that the pilot shall continue the flight at the highest of the following altitudes or flight levels for the route segment being flown: (I) The altitude or flight level assigned in the last ATC clearance received; (ii) The minimum altitude (converted, if appropriate, to minimum flight level as prescribed in §91.121(c)) for IFR operations; or (iii) The altitude or flight level ATC has advised may be expected in a further clearance. §91.185(c)(3)(ii) provides, in pertinent part, that if the clearance limit is not a fix from which an approach begins, "...proceed to a fix from which an approach begins and commence descent or descent and approach as close as possible to the estimated time of arrival as calculated from the filed or amended (with ATC) estimated time en route." In sum, if the communications failure occurs in IFR conditions, or if §91.185(b) cannot be complied with, the pilot maintains the highest of the altitudes or flight levels specified in §91.185(c)(2) for the particular route segment being flown until reaching the fix from which his approach begins. After reaching this fix, he may commence his descent as close as possible to the estimated time of arrival as calculated from the filed or amended estimated time en route. (1-28-92).

91.187 OPERATION UNDER IFR IN CONTROLLED AIRSPACE: MALFUNCTION REPORTS

(a)   The pilot in command of each aircraft operated in controlled airspace under IFR shall report as soon as practical to ATC any malfunctions of navigational, approach, or communication equipment occurring in flight;

(b)   In each report required by paragraph (a) of this section, the pilot in command shall include the—
  (1)   Aircraft identification;
  (2)   Equipment affected;
  (3)   Degree to which the capability of the pilot to operate under IFR in the ATC system is impaired; and
  (4)   Nature and extent of assistance desired from ATC.

CROSS REFERENCES

Previous designation: 91.129. 91.183 IFR Radio Communications; 91.185 IFR Operations: Two-Way Radio Communications Failure.

ADVISORY CIRCULARS

FAA-H-8083-15 *Instrument Flying Handbook* (2001).

AERONAUTICAL INFORMATION MANUAL

ARTCC Communications, Para. 5-3-1;
Position Reporting, Para. 5-3-2;
Additional Reports, Para. 5-3-3.

91.189 CATEGORY II AND III OPERATIONS: GENERAL OPERATING RULES

(a)   No person may operate a civil aircraft in a Category II or Category III operation unless:
  (1)   The flight crew of the aircraft consists of a pilot in command and a second in command who hold the appropriate authorizations and ratings prescribed in §61.3 of this chapter;
  (2)   Each flight crewmember has adequate knowledge of, and familiarity with, the aircraft and the procedures to be used; and
  (3)   The instrument panel in front of the pilot who is controlling the aircraft has appropriate instrumentation for the type of flight control guidance system that is being used.

(b)   Unless otherwise authorized by the Administrator, no person may operate a civil aircraft in a Category II or Category III operation unless each ground component required for that operation and the related airborne equipment is installed and operating.

(c)   Authorized *DH*. For the purpose of this section, when the approach procedure being used provides for and requires the use of a DH, the authorized DH is the highest of the following:
  (1)   The DH prescribed by the approach procedure.
  (2)   The DH prescribed for the pilot in command.
  (3)   The DH for which the aircraft is equipped.

(d)   Unless otherwise authorized by the Administrator, no pilot operating an aircraft in a Category II or Category III approach that provides and requires use of a DH may continue the approach below the authorized decision height unless the following conditions are met:

(1)   The aircraft is in a position from which a descent to a landing on the intended runway can be made at a normal rate of descent using normal maneuvers, and where that descent rate will allow touchdown to occur within the touchdown zone of the runway of intended landing.

(2)   At least one of the following visual references for the intended runway is distinctly visible and identifiable to the pilot:

(i)   The approach light system, except that the pilot may not descend below 100 feet above the touchdown zone elevation using the approach lights as a reference unless the red terminating bars or the red side row bars are also distinctly visible and identifiable.

(ii)   The threshold.

(iii)   The threshold markings.

(iv)   The threshold lights.

(v)   The touchdown zone or touchdown zone markings.

(vi)   The touchdown zone lights.

(e)   Unless otherwise authorized by the Administrator, each pilot operating an aircraft shall immediately execute an appropriate missed approach whenever prior to touchdown, the requirements of paragraph (d) of this section are not met.

(f)   No person operating an aircraft using a Category III approach without decision height may land that aircraft except in accordance with the provisions of the letter of authorization issued by the Administrator.

(g)   Paragraphs (a) through (f) of this section do not apply to operations conducted by the holders of certificates issued under parts 121, 125, 129, or 135 of this chapter. No person may operate a civil aircraft in a Category II or Category III operation conducted by the holder of a certificate issued under parts 121, 125, 129, or 135 of this chapter unless the operation is conducted in accordance with that certificate holder's operations specifications.

EXPLANATION

91.189(a): This subsection sets forth the crew and equipment requirements for Category II or III operations.

91.189(b): This subsection overrules 91.175(k) for Category II or III operations, in that all ground components must be working for such operations.

91.189(c): This subsection determines which decision height applies under the circumstances described.

91.189(d): This subsection sets forth the circumstances which must exist for a pilot to continue an approach below decision height.

91.189(e): This subsection requires a missed approach at any time that the pilot loses sight of the runway or runway environment as described in subsection (d).

91.189(f): The FAA may grant an operator permission to conduct Category II or III operations without a decision height. If so, the operator must adhere to all the conditions which the FAA establishes for such operation.

91.189(g): Part 121, 125, 129 and 135 operations conduct Category II or III operations pursuant to their own operations specifications.

CROSS REFERENCES

Previous designation: 91.6. 91.191 Category II Manual; 91.193 Certificate of Authorization for Certain Category II Operations; 61.3 Requirement for Certificates, Rating and Authorizations.

ADVISORY CIRCULARS

AC 91-16 *Category II Operations-General Aviation Airplanes* (1967).

AC 120-28D *Criteria for Approval of Category III Weather Minima for Takeoff, Landing, and Rollout* (1999).

FAA CHIEF COUNSEL OPINIONS

A pilot is authorized to descend below DH/MDA even if the only clearly visible external reference upon reaching that point is a segment of the approach light system. A pilot may properly rely on an automatic flight control system or flight path instrumentation for vertical guidance during descent below DH/MDA if the only clearly visible external reference is a segment of the approach light system. (1-25-78).

91.191 CATEGORY II AND CATEGORY III MANUAL

(a) Except as provided in paragraph (c) of this section, after August 4, 1997, no person may operate a U.S.-registered civil aircraft in a Category II or a Category III operation unless —
  (1) There is available in the aircraft a current, approved Category II or Category III manual, as appropriate, for that aircraft;
  (2) The operation is conducted in accordance with the procedures, instructions, and limitations in the appropriate manual; and
  (3) The instruments and equipment listed in the manual that are required for a particular Category II or Category III operation have been inspected and maintained in accordance with the maintenance program contained in the manual.
(b) Each operator must keep a current copy of each approved manual at its principal base of operations and must make each manual available for inspection upon request by the Administrator.
(c) This section does not apply to operations conducted by the holder of a certificate issued under part 121 or part 135 of this chapter.

CROSS REFERENCES

Previous designation: 91.34. 91.189 Category II and III Operations: General Operating Rules; 91.193 Certificate of Authorization for Certain Category II Operations.

ADVISORY CIRCULARS

AC 91-16 *Category II Operations-General Aviation Airplanes* (1967).

AC 120-28D *Criteria for Approval of Category III Weather Minima for Takeoff, Landing, and Rollout* (1999).

91.193 CERTIFICATE OF AUTHORIZATION FOR CERTAIN CATEGORY II OPERATIONS

The Administrator may issue a certificate of authorization authorizing deviations from the requirements of §§91.189, 91.191, and 91.205(f) for the operation of small aircraft identified as Category A aircraft in §97.3 of this chapter in Category II operations if the Administrator finds that the proposed operation can be safely conducted under the terms of the certificate. Such authorization does not permit operation of the aircraft carrying persons or property for compensation or hire.

CROSS REFERENCES

Previous designation: 91.2. 91.189 Category II and III Operations: General Operating Rules; 91.191 Category II Manual.

ADVISORY CIRCULARS

AC 91-16 *Category II Operations-General Aviation Airplanes* (1967).

INTENTIONALLY

LEFT

BLANK

INTENTIONALLY

LEFT

BLANK

SUBPART C — EQUIPMENT, INSTRUMENT, AND CERTIFICATE REQUIREMENTS

91.203 CIVIL AIRCRAFT: CERTIFICATIONS REQUIRED

(a)   Except as provided in §91.715, no person may operate a civil aircraft unless it has within it the following:

(1)   An appropriate and current airworthiness certificate. Each U.S. airworthiness certificate used to comply with this subparagraph (except a special flight permit, a copy of the applicable operations specifications issued under §21.197(c) of this chapter, appropriate sections of the air carrier manual required by Parts 121 and 135 of this chapter containing that portion of the operations specifications issued under §21.197(c), or an authorization under §91.611), must have on it the registration number assigned to the aircraft under Part 47 of this chapter. However, the airworthiness certificate need not have on it an assigned special identification number before 10 days after that number is first affixed to the aircraft. A revised airworthiness certificate having on it an assigned special identification number, that has been affixed to an aircraft, may only be obtained upon application to an FAA Flight Standards district office.

(2)   An effective U.S. registration certificate issued to its owner or, for operation within the United States, the second duplicate copy (pink) of the Aircraft Registration Application as provided for in §47.31(b), or a registration certificate issued under the laws of a foreign country.

(b)   No person may operate a civil aircraft unless the airworthiness certificate required by paragraph (a) of this section or a special flight authorization issued under §91.715 is displayed at the cabin or cockpit entrance so that it is legible to passengers or crew.

(c)   No person may operate an aircraft with a fuel tank installed within the passenger compartment or a baggage compartment unless the installation was accomplished pursuant to Part 43 of this chapter, and a copy of FAA Form 337 authorizing that installation is on board the aircraft.

(d)   No person may operate a civil airplane (domestic or foreign) into or out of an airport in the United States unless it complies with the fuel venting and exhaust emissions requirements of Part 34 of this chapter.

EXPLANATION

Prior to a flight, a pilot must ensure that the aircraft has on board both an appropriate and current airworthiness certificate and an effective U.S. registration certificate issued to its owner or a second duplicate copy (pink) of the application for aircraft registration certificate or a registration certificate issued by a foreign country. The pink copy is not good for flights outside the United States. If the aircraft is unairworthy, the airworthiness certificate is ineffective, and application may be made to the FAA for a special flight permit (ferry permit), and, if issued, the ferry permit may be substituted for the airworthiness certificate. Always read and comply with any operating limitations imposed by the FAA on the ferry permit authorization. If the aircraft has fuel tanks installed in the passenger compartment or the baggage compartment, the FAA Form 337 authorizing such an installation must be on board the aircraft. All aircraft, U.S. or foreign, operating in and out of an airport in the United States must be in compliance with Part 34 of the FAR, Fuel Venting and Exhaust Emission Requirements for Turbine Engine Powered Aircraft. The basic documents which are required to be on board may be remembered by the word "**AROW:**" **A**irworthiness certificate, **R**egistration certificate, **O**perating handbook, **W**eight and balance information. FCC Radio Station Certificates are no longer required, unless operating outside the U.S.

CROSS REFERENCES

Previous designation: 91.127. 21.197 Special Flight Permits; Part 34, Fuel Venting and Exhaust Emission Requirements for Turbine Engine Powered Aircraft; Part 39, Airworthiness Directives; Part 43, Maintenance, Preventive Maintenance, Rebuilding and Alteration; Part 47, Aircraft Registration; 91.417(d) Maintenance Records; 91.611, Authorization For Ferry Flight With One Engine Inoperative; 91.175, Special Flight Authorizations For Foreign Civil Aircraft.

ADVISORY CIRCULARS

AC 20-65 *Airworthiness Certificates and Authorizations for Operation of Domestic and Foreign Aircraft* (1969).

AC 21-12A *Application for U.S. Airworthiness Certificate, FAA Form 8130-6* (1987).

AC 39-7C *Airworthiness Directives* (1995).

AC 91-59 *Inspection and Care of General Aviation Exhaust Systems* (1982).

CASES

A pilot's ATP and mechanic certificates were suspended after he installed an unapproved fuel system and then flew the airplane with the unapproved fuel system. *Administrator v. Sorenson*, EA-4191 (1994).

A private pilot was suspended for flying an airplane after mechanics gave him a list of uncorrected discrepancies, including an Airworthiness Directive (AD). *Administrator v. Bognuda*, EA-4139 (1994).

In a situation where, upon request of an FAA inspector at the scene of the landing, a pilot could not produce a valid registration certificate, but later established the existence of a valid registration certificate and claimed that it was in his possession on the flight, the NTSB held that there was a violation. However, the Board held that the violation was technical in nature and required no sanction. *Administrator v. Wright*, 5 NTSB 931 (1986).

The Board did not accept a pilot's argument that the owner of the aircraft should be held responsible for ensuring that the registration certificate was on board. The Board held that, as pilot in command, the pilot was the operator of the aircraft and can be held accountable under [91.203(a)(2)]. *Administrator v. Poirier*, 5 NTSB 1928 (1987).

Someone who exercised operational control by hiring the pilot and directing where the aircraft flew on demonstration flights was found to have "operated" the aircraft under the definition of "operate" in FAR 1.1. At the time of the flights, the aircraft did not have on board a valid airworthiness certificate or a valid registration certificate in violation of [91.203(a)(1) and (2)]. The person exercising operational control, though not on board, was held to have violated these FARs. *Administrator v. Lott*, 5 NTSB 2394 (1987).

An auxiliary fuel tank located in the cargo compartment, but not connected to any aircraft system and properly stowed as cargo does not constitute an alteration and therefore does not require a Form 337. *FAA v. Africa Air Corp.*, FAA Order No. 99-5 (8-31-1999).

FAA CHIEF COUNSEL OPINIONS

The regulation does not require that the airworthiness certificate be legible to both passengers and to the crew. It requires that it be legible to either the passengers **or** the crew. (8-7-90).

Under 21.181, an airworthiness certificate is effective only as long as maintenance, preventive maintenance, and alterations are performed in accordance with the FARs. Since a U.S. registered aircraft operated outside the United States must have an appropriate current airworthiness certificate within it, the aircraft, while in a foreign country, must be maintained in accordance with U.S. standards. (1-28-85).

If an aircraft is type certificated for instrument flight rules, a clock is required by [91.205(d)(6)]. To maintain the validity of the airworthiness certificate without a change in the type certificate, the clock must be operating for all operations. Operating with the clock permanently inoperative would violate [91.405]. (4-23-81). [Editor's Note: 91.213 could provide relief in this situation.]

91.205 POWERED CIVIL AIRCRAFT WITH STANDARD CATEGORY U.S. AIRWORTHINESS CERTIFICATES: INSTRUMENT AND EQUIPMENT REQUIREMENTS

(a)   *General.* Except as provided in paragraphs (c)(3) and (e) of this section, no person may operate a powered civil aircraft with a standard category U.S. airworthiness certificate in any operation described in paragraphs (b) through (f) of this section unless that aircraft contains the instruments and equipment specified in those paragraphs (or FAA-approved equivalents) for that type of operation, and those instruments and items of equipment are in operable condition.

(b)   *Visual flight rules (day).* For VFR flight during the day, the following instruments and equipment are required:
   (1)   Airspeed indicator.
   (2)   Altimeter.
   (3)   Magnetic direction indicator.
   (4)   Tachometer for each engine.
   (5)   Oil pressure gauge for each engine using pressure system.
   (6)   Temperature gauge for each liquid-cooled engine.
   (7)   Oil temperature gauge for each air-cooled engine.
   (8)   Manifold pressure gauge for each altitude engine.
   (9)   Fuel gauge indicating the quantity of fuel in each tank.
   (10) Landing gear position indicator, if the aircraft has a retractable landing gear.
   (11) For small civil airplanes certificated after March 11, 1996, in accordance with Part 23 of this chapter, an approved aviation red or aviation white anticollision light system. In the event of failure of any light of the anticollision light system, operation of the aircraft may continue to a location where repairs or replacement can be made.
   (12) If the aircraft is operated for hire over water and beyond power-off gliding distance from shore, approved flotation gear readily available to each occupant, and at least one pyrotechnic signaling device. As used in this section, "shore" means that area of the land adjacent to the water which is above the high water mark and excludes land areas which are intermittently under water.

(13) An approved safety belt with an approved metal-to-metal latching device for each occupant 2 years of age or older.

(14) For small civil airplanes manufactured after July 18, 1978, an approved shoulder harness for each front seat. The shoulder harness must be designed to protect the occupant from serious head injury when the occupant experiences the ultimate inertia forces specified in §23.561(b)(2) of this chapter. Each shoulder harness installed at a flight crewmember station must permit the crewmember, when seated and with the safety belt and shoulder harness fastened, to perform all functions necessary for flight operations. For purposes of this paragraph —

    (i) The date of manufacture of an airplane is the date the inspection acceptance records reflect that the airplane is complete and meets the FAA-approved type design data; and

    (ii) A front seat is a seat located at a flight crewmember station or any seat located alongside such a seat.

(15) An emergency locator transmitter, if required by §91.207.

(16) For normal, utility, and acrobatic category airplanes with a seating configuration, excluding pilot seats, of 9 or less, manufactured after December 12, 1986, a shoulder harness for —

    (i) Each front seat that meets the requirements of §23.785(g) and (h) of this chapter in effect on December 12, 1985;

    (ii) Each additional seat that meets the requirements of §23.785(g) of this chapter in effect on December 12, 1985.

(17) For rotorcraft manufactured after September 16, 1992, a shoulder harness for each seat that meets the requirements of §27.2 or §29.2 of this chapter in effect on September 16, 1991.

(c) *Visual flight rules (night).* For VFR flight at night, the following instruments and equipment are required:

(1) Instruments and equipment specified in paragraph (b) of this section.

(2) Approved position lights.

(3) An approved aviation red or aviation white anticollision light system on all U.S.-registered civil aircraft. Anticollision light systems initially installed after August 11, 1971, on aircraft for which a type certificate was issued or applied for before August 11, 1971, must at least meet the anticollision light standards of Part 23, 25, 27, or 29, as applicable, that were in effect on August 10, 1971, except that the color may be either aviation red or aviation white. In the event of failure of any light of the anti-collision light system, operations with the aircraft may be continued to a stop where repairs or replacement can be made.

(4) If the aircraft is operated for hire, one electric landing light.

(5) An adequate source of electrical energy for all installed electrical and radio equipment.

(6) One spare set of fuses, or three spare fuses of each kind required, that are accessible to the pilot in flight.

(d) *Instrument flight rules.* For IFR flight, the following instruments and equipment are required:

(1) Instruments and equipment specified in paragraph (b) of this section, and, for night flight, instruments and equipment specified in paragraph (c) of this section.

(2) Two-way radio communications system and navigational equipment appropriate to the ground facilities to be used.

    (3)   Gyroscopic rate-of-turn indicator, except on the following aircraft:
        (i)   Airplanes with a third attitude instrument system usable through flight attitudes of 360 degrees of pitch and roll and installed in accordance with the instrument requirements prescribed in §121.305(j) of this chapter; and
        (ii)   Rotorcraft with a third attitude instrument system usable through flight attitudes of "80 degrees of pitch and "120 degrees of roll and installed in accordance with §29.1303(g) of this chapter.
    (4)   Slip-skid indicator.
    (5)   Sensitive altimeter adjustable for barometric pressure.
    (6)   A clock displaying hours, minutes, and seconds with a sweep-second pointer or digital presentation.
    (7)   Generator or alternator of adequate capacity.
    (8)   Gyroscopic pitch and bank indicator (artificial horizon).
    (9)   Gyroscopic direction indicator (directional gyro or equivalent.)
(e)   *Flight at and above 24,000 feet MSL (FL 240).* If VOR navigational equipment is required under paragraph (d)(2) of this section, no person may operate a U.S.-registered civil aircraft within the 50 states and the District of Columbia at or above FL 240 unless that aircraft is equipped with approved distance measuring equipment (DME). When DME required by this paragraph fails at and above FL 240, the pilot in command of the aircraft shall notify ATC immediately, and then may continue operations at and above FL 240 to the next airport of intended landing at which repairs or replacement of the equipment can be made.
(f)   *Category II operations.* The requirements for Category II operations are the instruments and equipment specified in—
    (1)   Paragraph (d) of this section; and
    (2)   Appendix A to this part.
(g)   *Category III operations.* The instruments and equipment required for Category III operations are specified in paragraph (d) of this section.
(h)   *Exclusions.* Paragraphs (f) and (g) of this section do not apply to operations conducted by a holder of a certificate issued under part 121 or part 135 of this chapter.

EXPLANATION

"Operable condition" means that the instruments and equipment are operating as intended by the manufacturer. This section authorizes a pilot to continue a flight to a place where repairs or replacement can be made in two situations: (1) failure of any light of the anticollision light system and (2) failure of DME required for flights at and above FL 240. The requirements for the various operations are cumulative; i.e. visual flight rules (night) requires the instruments and equipment required for visual flight rules (day) plus those required for visual flight rules (night). Instrument flight rules operation requires that, in addition to the instruments and equipment specifically required in that subsection, the requirements of visual flight rules (day) be met and, in addition, if flight is at night, visual flight rules (night) requirements be met.

This regulation uses the term "night" which is defined in FAR 1.1 as "the time between the end of evening civil twilight and the beginning of morning civil twilight, as published in the American Air Almanac, converted to local time." Twilight is the period of incomplete darkness following sunset or preceding sunrise. The darker limit of civil twilight occurs when the center of the sun is at a zenith distance of 96 degrees. Depending on the latitude and the season, this usually translates to about thirty minutes of twilight. Note that FAR 91.209 requires aircraft lights to be turned on between sunset and sunrise, while FAR 61.57(d) requires "night" takeoffs and landings to be performed within the period from one hour after sunset to one hour before sunrise.

If an aircraft meets the instrument and equipment requirements of this section, it does not mean it has met all requirements for these items. There may be additional requirements set forth in other regulations, i.e.: aircraft equipment lists, aircraft flight manuals, and airworthiness directives. For example, see 91.215 and 91.131. Another example is Airworthiness Directive 82-06-01, which requires that a Cessna 210 have two operational vacuum pumps prior to entering IFR conditions.

CROSS REFERENCES

Previous designation: 91.33. 23.561, Emergency Landing Conditions; 23.785, Seats, Berths, Litters, Safety Belts and Shoulder Harnesses; 29.2, Special Retroactive Requirements (safety belts and harnesses) Airworthiness Requirements: Transport Category Rotorcraft; 29.1303(g), Flight and Navigation Instruments (turn and bank indicator), Airworthiness Standards: Transport Category Rotorcraft; 91.207, Emergency Locator Transmitters; 121.305(j), Flight and Navigational Equipment (gyroscopic bank and pitch indicators); 135.3(a), Rules Applicable to Operations Subject to this Part; 135.141, Applicability (Aircraft and Equipment).

ADVISORY CIRCULARS

AC 20-34D *Prevention of Retractable Landing Gear Failures* (1980).

AC 20-94 *Digital Clock Installation in Aircraft* (1976).

AC 90-96 *Approval of U.S. Operators and Aircraft to Operate Under Instrument Flight Rules (IFR) in European Airspace Designated for Basic Area Navigation (BRNAV/RNP-5)* (1998).

AC 91-43 *Unreliable Airspeed Indicators* (1975).

AC 91-46 *Gyroscopic Instruments-Good Operating Practices* (1977).

AC 91-65 *Use of Shoulder Harness In Passenger Seats* (1986).

AC 91-67 *Minimum Equipment Requirements For General Aviation Operations Under Part 91* (1991).

CASES

A pilot was suspended for accepting a clearance for an instrument approach that required Distance Measuring Equipment (DME), even though he knew that his airplane did not have a DME. He claimed that he intended to cancel his IFR clearance before landing, but the evidence showed that he did in fact shoot the approach in IMC. *Administrator v. Fausak*, EA-4167 (1994).

In a case where an aircraft did not have an installed clock, a violation of §91.205(a) was sustained where the aircraft was operated on an IFR clearance in VFR weather. *Administrator v. Hammerstrand*, EA-3739 (1993).

The Board has held that although it recognizes that the utility of a magnetic compass for which there is no correction card may be open to question, it does not follow under the regulation that the lack of such a card renders the compass itself inoperative in a mechanical sense. The pilot in this case testified that there were two functioning compasses on board, one magnetic and one electric, and that by checking them against one another, he noted no deviation. *Administrator v. Hanley,* 4 NTSB 1773 (1984).

In a case in which a pilot made several flights even though he knew that the aileron trim tab switch was operating in reverse, a federal court ruled that "operable condition" means that the instruments and equipment required to comply with the airworthiness requirements under which the airplane is type-certified shall be in a condition so as to operate efficiently and in the manner intended by the manufacturer. *United States v. Newman,* 331 F.Supp. 1240 (1971).

Allowing an aircraft to be repeatedly operated with open discrepancies that could have easily been corrected by following the manufacturer's service bulletin and using the provided kit resulted in the operator being fined $7,500. Because one of the discrepancies listed that the left fuel gauge was "stuck" the operator was also in violation of §91.205(a) and (b)(9). *FAA v. General Aviation, Inc.,* FAA Order No. 98-18 (10-9-1998).

FAA CHIEF COUNSEL DECISIONS

Where a single engine aircraft, operating as an air taxi flight, operates over water for the purpose of takeoff or landing pursuant to 135.183(b), the requirements of [91.205(b)(11)] are applicable. (4-11-75).

If an aircraft is type certificated for instrument flight rules, a clock is required by [91.205(d)(6)]. To maintain the validity of the airworthiness certificate without a change in the type certificate, the clock must be operating for all operations. Operating with the clock permanently inoperative would violate [91.205]. (4-23-81). [Editor's Note: 91.213 could provide relief in this situation.]

91.207 EMERGENCY LOCATOR TRANSMITTERS

(a)   Except as provided in paragraphs (e) and (f) of this section, no person may operate a U.S.-registered civil airplane unless —

(1)   There is attached to the airplane an approved automatic type emergency locator transmitter that is in operable condition for the following operations, except that after June 21, 1995, an emergency locator transmitter that meets the requirements of TSO-C91 may not be used for new installations.

(i)   Those operations governed by the supplemental air carrier and commercial operator rules of Parts 121 and 125;

(ii)   Charter flights governed by the domestic and flag air carrier rules of Part 121 of this chapter; and

(iii)   Operations governed by Part 135 of this chapter; or

(2)   For operations other than those specified in paragraph (a)(1) of this section, there must be attached to the airplane an approved personal type or an approved automatic type emergency locator transmitter that is in operable condition, except that after June 21, 1995, an emergency locator transmitter that meets the requirements of TSO-C91 may not be used for new installations.

(b)   Each emergency locator transmitter required by paragraph (a) of this section must be attached to the airplane in such a manner that the probability of damage to the transmitter in the event of crash impact is minimized. Fixed and deployable automatic type transmitters must be attached to the airplane as far aft as practicable.

(c)   Batteries used in the emergency locator transmitters required by paragraphs (a) and (b) of this section must be replaced (or recharged, if the battery is rechargeable) —

   (1)   When the transmitter has been in use for more than 1 cumulative hour; or

   (2)   When 50 percent of their useful life (or, for rechargeable batteries, 50 percent of their useful life of charge) has expired, as established by the transmitter manufacturer under its approval. The new expiration date for replacing (or recharging) the battery must be legibly marked on the outside of the transmitter and entered in the aircraft maintenance record. Paragraph (c)(2) of this section does not apply to batteries (such as water-activated batteries) that are essentially unaffected during probable storage intervals.

(d)   Each emergency locator transmitter required by paragraph (a) of this section must be inspected within 12 calendar months after the last inspection for —

   (1)   Proper installation;

   (2)   Battery corrosion;

   (3)   Operation of the controls and crash sensor; and

   (4)   The presence of a sufficient signal radiated from its antenna.

(e)   Notwithstanding paragraph (a) of this section, a person may —

   (1)   Ferry a newly acquired airplane from the place where possession of it was taken to a place where the emergency locator transmitter is to be installed; and

   (2)   Ferry an airplane with an inoperative emergency locator transmitter from a place where repairs or replacements cannot be made to a place where they can be made. No person other than required crewmembers may be carried aboard an airplane being ferried under paragraph (e) of this section.

(f)   Paragraph (a) of this section does not apply to -

   (1)   Before January 1, 2004, turbojet-powered aircraft;

   (2)   Aircraft while engaged in scheduled flights by scheduled air carriers;

   (3)   Aircraft while engaged in training operations conducted entirely within a 50-nautical mile radius of the airport from which such local flight operations began;

   (4)   Aircraft while engaged in flight operations incident to design and testing;

   (5)   New aircraft while engaged in flight operations incident to their manufacture, preparation, and delivery;

   (6)   Aircraft while engaged in flight operations incident to the aerial application of chemicals and other substances for agricultural purposes;

   (7)   Aircraft certificated by the Administrator for research and development purposes;

   (8)   Aircraft while used for showing compliance with regulations, crew training, exhibition, air racing, or market surveys;

   (9)   Aircraft equipped to carry not more than one person.

   (10)   An aircraft during any period for which the transmitter has been temporarily removed for inspection, repair, modification, or replacement, subject to the following:

      (i)   No person may operate the aircraft unless the aircraft records contain an entry which includes the date of initial removal, the make, model, serial number, and reason for removing the transmitter, and a placard located in view of the pilot to show "ELT not installed."

      (ii)   No person may operate the aircraft more than 90 days after the ELT is initially removed from the aircraft; and

   (11)   On and after January 1, 2004, aircraft with a maximum payload capacity of more than 18,000 pounds when used in air transportation.

EXPLANATION

The term "attached to the airplane" was used to ensure that the ELT was located so as to be subject to the crush-inertia force and be automatically activated. If located on a seat or the floor or on the pilot's person, it may not activate in a crash.

To be exempt from the ELT requirement, under 91.207(e)(6), the aircraft must be engaged in flight operation incident to the spray operation. The mere fact that the aircraft was certificated or equipped for aerial application is not controlling.

A procedure should be established to ensure batteries do not pass their replacement or recharge times because this is a very common violation.

Whether a person is a required crewmember in the case of 91.207(d) is determined by whether the person is required by the type certificate or by the nature of the operations conducted.

The AIM emphasizes the need to check to see that an ELT is not accidentally activated. Also, it recommends in-flight monitoring of 121.5 MHz and/or 243.0 MHz to help in identifying emergency signals.

CROSS REFERENCES

Previous designation: 91.52. Appendix A, Part 91 - Category II Operations: Manual, Instruments, Equipment, and Maintenance; §601(d) of the Federal Aviation Act of 1958, as amended (49 United States Code Annotated 1421(d)), Emergency Locator Transmitters.

ADVISORY CIRCULARS

AC 91-44A *Operational and Maintenance Practices for Emergency Locator Transmitters and Receivers* (1980).

AERONAUTICAL INFORMATION MANUAL

Emergency Locator Transmitters, Para. 6-2-5.

FAA CHIEF COUNSEL OPINIONS

When an aircraft is used by a soaring association in a specific geographic location to launch and tow a glider to altitude for release and then returns directly to the airport of departure, the airplane is engaged in a "training" operation within the meaning of [91.207(e)(3)]. Therefore, the aircraft is excepted from the ELT requirement when the operation is conducted solely within a 50-mile radius of the airport from which the local flight operation began. (5-6-81).

91.209 AIRCRAFT LIGHTS

No person may:

(a) During the period from sunset to sunrise (or, in Alaska, during the period a prominent unlighted object cannot be seen from a distance of 3 statute miles or the sun is more than 6 degrees below the horizon) —

  (1) Operate an aircraft unless it has lighted position lights;

  (2) Park or move an aircraft in, or in dangerous proximity to, a night flight operations area of an airport unless the aircraft —

    (i) Is clearly illuminated;

    (ii) Has lighted position lights; or

    (iii) Is in an area that is marked by obstruction lights.

  (3) Anchor an aircraft unless the aircraft —

    (i) Has lighted anchor lights; or

    (ii) Is in an area where anchor lights are not required on vessels; or

(b) Operate an aircraft that is equipped with an anticollision light system, unless it has lighted anticollision lights. However, the anticollision lights need not be lighted when the pilot in command determines that, because of operating conditions, it would be in the interest of safety to turn the lights off.

EXPLANATION

This regulation uses the terms "sunset" and "sunrise" instead of "night." [See explanation of the term "night" under FAR 91.205.] The regulations do not specify an official source for time of sunset and sunrise. Flight Service Stations usually have such information.

A pilot should be aware that the use of high-intensity anti-collision lights, under certain meteorological conditions, can induce vertigo or cause spatial disorientation. §91.209(d) provides the pilot the authority to not turn on or to turn off these lights in the interest of safety.

The FAA's "Operation Lights On" encourages pilots to use anti-collision or position lights at all times to assist the "see and avoid" concept.

CROSS REFERENCES

Previous designation: 91.73. 91.903-91.905, Waivers.

ADVISORY CIRCULARS

AC 20-30B *Aircraft Position Light and Anti-Collision Light Installation* (1981).

AC 20-74 *Aircraft Position and Anti-Collision Light Measurements* (1971).

AERONAUTICAL INFORMATION MANUAL

Use of Aircraft Lights (Operation Lights On), Para. 4-3-23.

CASES

A hot air balloon pilot was suspended for flying after sunset without navigation lights. *Administrator v. Barker*, EA-3794 (1993).

FAA CHIEF COUNSEL OPINIONS

Tethered hot air balloons are subject to the lighting requirements of §91.209. (3-11-94).

To assist the "see and avoid" concept the FAA has an "Operation Lights On" safety program to encourage pilots to use their anti-collision lights or aircraft position lights anytime the aircraft engines are running. (5-27-77).

91.211 SUPPLEMENTAL OXYGEN

(a)   *General.* No person may operate a civil aircraft of U.S. registry —

    (1)   At cabin pressure altitudes above 12,500 feet (MSL) up to and including 14,000 feet (MSL) unless the required minimum flight crew is provided with and uses supplemental oxygen for that part of the flight at those altitudes that is of more than 30 minutes duration;

    (2)   At cabin pressure altitudes above 14,000 feet (MSL) unless the required minimum flight crew is provided with and uses supplemental oxygen during the entire flight time at those altitudes; and

    (3)   At cabin pressure altitudes above 15,000 feet (MSL) unless each occupant of the aircraft is provided with supplemental oxygen.

(b)   *Pressurized cabin aircraft.*

    (1)   No person may operate a civil aircraft of U.S. registry with a pressurized cabin —

        (i)   At flight altitudes above flight level 250 unless at least a 10- minute supply of supplemental oxygen, in addition to any oxygen required to satisfy paragraph (a) of this section, is available for each occupant of the aircraft for use in the event that a descent is necessitated by loss of cabin pressurization; and

        (ii)   At flight altitudes above flight level 350 unless one pilot at the controls of the airplane is wearing and using an oxygen mask that is secured and sealed and that either supplies oxygen at all times or automatically supplies oxygen whenever the cabin pressure altitude of the airplane exceeds 14,000 feet (MSL), except that the one pilot need not wear and use an oxygen mask while at or below flight level 410 if there are two pilots at the controls and each pilot has a quick-donning type of oxygen mask that can be placed on the face with one hand from the ready position within 5 seconds, supplying oxygen and properly secured and sealed.

    (2)   Notwithstanding paragraph (b)(1)(ii) of this section, if for any reason at any time it is necessary for one pilot to leave the controls of the aircraft when operating at flight altitudes above flight level 350, the remaining pilot at the controls shall put on and use an oxygen mask until the other pilot has returned to that crewmember's station.

EXPLANATION

Note the distinction between "cabin pressure altitude" and "flight altitude." A flight crew does not have to don oxygen masks in a pressurized aircraft when they pass through 14,000 feet MSL.

CROSS REFERENCES

Previous designation: 91.32. 121.327, Supplemental Oxygen: Reciprocating Engine Powered Airplanes; 121.329, Supplemental Oxygen for Sustenance, Turbine Engine Powered Airplanes; 121.331, Supplemental Oxygen Requirements for Pressurized Cabin Airplanes; Reciprocating Engine Powered Airplanes; 121.333, Supplemental Oxygen for Emergency Descent and for First Aid: Turbine Engine Powered Airplanes with Pressurized Cabins; 125.23, Rules Applicable to Operations Subject to this Part; 135.89 Pilot Requirements; Use of Oxygen; 135.157, Oxygen Equipment Requirements.

AERONAUTICAL INFORMATION MANUAL

Effects of Altitude, Para. 8-1-2.

91.213 INOPERATIVE INSTRUMENTS AND EQUIPMENT

(a) Except as provided in paragraph (d) of this section, no person may take off an aircraft with inoperative instruments or equipment installed unless the following conditions are met:
    (1) An approved Minimum Equipment List exists for that aircraft.
    (2) The aircraft has within it a letter of authorization, issued by the FAA Flight Standards district office having jurisdiction over the area in which the operator is located, authorizing operation of the aircraft under the Minimum Equipment List. The letter of authorization may be obtained by written request of the airworthiness certificate holder. The Minimum Equipment List and the letter of authorization constitute a supplemental type certificate for the aircraft.
    (3) The approved Minimum Equipment List must —
        (i) Be prepared in accordance with the limitations specified in paragraph (b) of this section; and
        (ii) Provide for the operation of the aircraft with the instruments and equipment in an inoperable condition.
    (4) The aircraft records available to the pilot must include an entry describing the inoperable instruments and equipment.
    (5) The aircraft is operated under all applicable conditions and limitations contained in the Minimum Equipment List and the letter authorizing the use of the list.
(b) The following instruments and equipment may not be included in a Minimum Equipment List:
    (1) Instruments and equipment that are either specifically or otherwise required by the airworthiness requirements under which the aircraft is type certificated and which are essential for safe operations under all operating conditions.
    (2) Instruments and equipment required by an airworthiness directive to be in operable condition unless the airworthiness directive provides otherwise.
    (3) Instruments and equipment required for specific operations by this part.

(c)   A person authorized to use an approved Minimum Equipment List issued for a specific aircraft under part 121, 125, or 135 of this chapter shall use that Minimum Equipment List in connection with operations conducted with that aircraft under this part without additional approval requirements.

(d)   Except for operations conducted in accordance with paragraphs (a) or (c) of this section, a person may takeoff an aircraft in operations conducted under this part with inoperative instruments and equipment without an approved Minimum Equipment List provided —

   (1)   The flight operation is conducted in a —

      (i)   Rotorcraft, nonturbine-powered airplane, glider, or lighter-than- air aircraft for which a master Minimum Equipment List has not been developed; or

      (ii)   Small rotorcraft, nonturbine-powered small airplane, glider, or lighter-than-air aircraft for which a Master Minimum Equipment List has been developed; and

   (2)   The inoperative instruments and equipment are not —

      (i)   Part of the VFR-day type certification instruments and equipment prescribed in the applicable airworthiness regulations under which the aircraft was type certificated;

      (ii)   Indicated as required on the aircraft's equipment list, or on the Kinds of Operations Equipment List for the kind of flight operation being conducted;

      (iii)   Required by §91.205 or any other rule of this part for the specific kind of flight operation being conducted; or

      (iv)   Required to be operational by an airworthiness directive; and

   (3)   The inoperative instruments and equipment are —

      (i)   Removed from the aircraft, the cockpit control placarded, and the maintenance recorded in accordance with §43.9 of this chapter; or

      (ii)   Deactivated and placarded "Inoperative." If deactivation of the inoperative instrument or equipment involves maintenance, it must be accomplished and recorded in accordance with part 43 of this chapter; and

   (4)   A determination is made by a pilot, who is certificated and appropriately rated under part 61 of this chapter, or by a person, who is certificated and appropriately rated to perform maintenance on the aircraft, that the inoperative instrument or equipment does not constitute a hazard to the aircraft.

     An aircraft with inoperative instruments or equipment as provided in paragraph (d) of this section is considered to be in a properly altered condition acceptable to the Administrator.

(e)   Notwithstanding any other provision of this section, an aircraft with inoperable instruments or equipment may be operated under a special flight permit issued in accordance with §§21.197 and 21.199 of this chapter.

EXPLANATION

The placarding requirement can be met by writing the word "Inoperative" on a piece of masking tape or piece of paper and attaching it to the instrument or device. The initial placarding can be accomplished by a certificated and appropriately rated pilot or by a person certificated and appropriately rated to perform maintenance on the aircraft. However, at the first and each succeeding required inspection, the placarding required by 91.405 cannot be accomplished by the pilot.

If a person has an approved MEL, he must use it and not the provisions of 91.213(d). If the provisions of 91.213(d) are used, the approved MEL and letter of authorization must be surrendered to the appropriate Flight Standards District Office.

"Deactivating" an instrument or item of equipment can be accomplished, in some cases, by pulling the circuit breaker, while other cases may require that it be accomplished by a certificated and appropriately rated maintenance person.

If the maintenance required to de-activate is preventive maintenance, as described in Appendix A, Part 43, then a certificated and appropriately rated pilot can accomplish the de-activation. In either case, appropriate entries must be made in the aircraft maintenance records and the required placarding accomplished.

CROSS REFERENCES

Previous designation: 91.30. Part 39, Airworthiness Directives; Part 43, Maintenance, Preventive Maintenance, Rebuilding and Alteration; 91.205, Powered Civil Aircraft with Standard Category U.S. Airworthiness Certificates: Instrument and Equipment Requirements; 91.405, Maintenance Required. 121.303 Airplane Instruments and Equipment; 121.627, Continuing Flight In Unsafe Conditions; 121.628, Inoperable Instruments and Equipment. 125.201, Inoperable Instruments and Equipment; 135.179, Inoperable Instruments and Equipment.

ADVISORY CIRCULARS

AC 91-67 *Minimum Equipment Requirements for General Aviation Operations Under Part 91* (1991).

FAA CHIEF COUNSEL OPINIONS

Your question is whether an approved air carrier MEL, under Part 135, may have limitations in the MEL body which address flight legs which are flown under Part 91 instead of Part 135.

§91.213(c) states: A person authorized to use an approved Minimum Equipment List issued for a specific aircraft under Part 121, 125, or 135 of this chapter shall use that Minimum Equipment List in connection with operations conducted with that aircraft under this part without additional approval requirements.

A Part 135 air carrier operating under an approved MEL, would be required to operate under that Part 135 MEL even when conducting operations under Part 91. (6-17-91)

91.215 ATC TRANSPONDER AND ALTITUDE REPORTING EQUIPMENT AND USE

(a) *All airspace*: U.S.-registered civil aircraft. For operations not conducted under part 121 or 135 of this chapter, ATC transponder equipment installed must meet the performance and environmental requirements of any class of TSO-C74b (Mode A) or any class of TSO-C74c (Mode A with altitude reporting capability) as appropriate, or the appropriate class of TSO-C112 (Mode S).

(b) *All airspace:* Unless otherwise authorized or directed by ATC, no person may operate an aircraft in the airspace described in paragraphs (b)(1) through (b)(5) of this section, unless that aircraft is equipped with an operable coded radar beacon transponder having either Mode 3/A 4096 code capability, replying to Mode 3/A interrogations with the code specified by ATC, or a Mode S capability, replying to Mode 3/A interrogations with the code specified by ATC and intermode and Mode S interrogations in accordance with the applicable provisions specified in TSO C-112, and that aircraft is equipped with automatic pressure altitude reporting equipment having a Mode C capability that automatically replies to Mode C interrogations by transmitting pressure altitude information in 100-foot increments. This requirement applies —

(1) *All aircraft.* In Class A, Class B, and Class C airspace areas;

(2) *All aircraft.* In all airspace within 30 nautical miles of an airport listed in appendix D, section 1 of this part from the surface upward to 10,000 feet MSL;

(3) Notwithstanding paragraph (b)(2) of this section, any aircraft which was not originally certificated with an engine-driven electrical system or which has not subsequently been certified with such a system installed, balloon or glider may conduct operations in the airspace within 30 nautical miles of an airport listed in appendix D, section 1 of this part provided such operations are conducted —

(i) Outside any Class A, Class B, or Class C airspace area; and

(ii) Below the altitude of the ceiling of a Class B or Class C airspace area designated for an airport or 10,000 feet MSL, whichever is lower; and

(4) All aircraft in all airspace above the ceiling and within the lateral boundaries of a Class B or Class C airspace area designated for an airport upward to 10,000 feet MSL; and

(5) All aircraft except any aircraft which was not originally certificated with an engine-driven electrical system or which has not subsequently been certified with such a system installed, balloon, or glider —

(i) In all airspace of the 48 contiguous states and the District of Columbia at and above 10,000 feet MSL, excluding the airspace at and below 2,500 feet above the surface; and

(ii) In the airspace from the surface to 10,000 feet MSL within a 10-nautical mile radius of any airport listed in appendix D, section 2 of this part, excluding the airspace below 1,200 feet outside of the lateral boundaries of the surface area of the airspace designated for that airport.

(c) *Transponder-on operation.* While in the airspace as specified in paragraph (b) of this section or in all controlled airspace, each person operating an aircraft equipped with an operable ATC transponder maintained in accordance with §91.413 of this part shall operate the transponder, including Mode C equipment if installed, and shall reply on the appropriate code or as assigned by ATC.

(d) *ATC authorized deviations.* Requests for ATC authorized deviations must be made to the ATC facility having jurisdiction over the concerned airspace within the time periods specified as follows:

(1) For operation of an aircraft with an operating transponder but without operating automatic pressure altitude reporting equipment having a Mode C capability, the request may be made at any time.

(2) For operation of an aircraft with an inoperative transponder to the airport of ultimate destination, including any intermediate stops, or to proceed to a place where suitable repairs can be made or both, the request may be made at any time.

(3) For operation of an aircraft that is not equipped with a transponder, the request must be made at least one hour before the proposed operation.

EXPLANATION

Mode S Transponders will not become a requirement for aircraft operating under Part 91 until at least 1995 at the earliest. (See NPRM dated 5-26-92, 57 F.R. 23038, 5-29-92)

Since transponder equipment, including Mode C equipment, increases the degree of the aircraft's visibility on radar, the FAA requires that each aircraft, whether in the specific airspace described in 91.215(b) or any controlled airspace, have its equipment on, provided the equipment is in compliance with 91.413.

The time requirements for asking ATC for deviations from the requirements of this section provide that for the operation of an aircraft that is not equipped with a transponder, the request must be made at least one hour before the proposed operation. All other requests can be made anytime.

CROSS REFERENCES

Previous designation: 91.24. 91.217, Data Correspondence Between Automatically Reported Pressure Altitude Data and the Pilot's Altitude Reference; 91.413, ATC Transponder Tests and Inspections; Appendix D, Part 91, Airports/Locations Where the Transponder Requirements of Section 91.215(b)(5)(ii) apply.

ADVISORY CIRCULARS

AC 43-6A *Automatic Pressure Altitude Encoding Systems and Transponders Maintenance and Inspection Practices* (1977).

AC 91-50 *Importance of Transponder Operation and Altitude Reporting* (1977).

AERONAUTICAL INFORMATION MANUAL

Transponder Operation, Para. 4-1-19;
Transponder Emergency Operation, Para. 6-2-2;
Transponder Operation During Two-Way Communications failure, Para. 6-4-2.

CASES

A pilot who did not have an instrument rating flew into Class B airspace without requesting or obtaining a clearance and with his transponder turned off. The pilot then requested a clearance to "poke through some clouds," which was understood by ATC to be a request for an IFR clearance. The pilot received a 120 day suspension. *Administrator v. White*, EA-3791 (1993).

91.217 DATA CORRESPONDENCE BETWEEN AUTOMATICALLY REPORTED PRESSURE ALTITUDE DATA AND THE PILOT'S ALTITUDE REFERENCE

No person may operate any automatic pressure altitude reporting equipment associated with a radar beacon transponder —

(a)   When deactivation of that equipment is directed by ATC;

(b)   Unless, as installed, that equipment was tested and calibrated to transmit altitude data corresponding within 125 feet (on a 95 percent probability basis) of the indicated or calibrated datum of the altimeter normally used to maintain flight altitude, with that altimeter referenced to 29.92 inches of mercury for altitudes from sea level to the maximum operating altitude of the aircraft; or

(c)   Unless the altimeters and digitizers in that equipment meet the standards in TSO-C10b and TSO-C88, respectively.

EXPLANATION

ATC will sometimes instruct a pilot to deactivate the Mode C operation of a transponder. §§23.1527, 25.1527, 27.1527 and 29.1527 describe maximum operating altitude limitations which establish the maximum operating altitude. These limitations are also set forth in the aircraft flight manual.

CROSS REFERENCES

Previous designation: 91.36. 91.215, ATC Transponder and Altitude Reporting Equipment and Use.

ADVISORY CIRCULARS

AC 91-50 *Importance of Transponder Operation and Altitude Reporting* (1977).

AERONAUTICAL INFORMATION MANUAL

Transponder Operation, Para. 4-1-19.

91.219 ALTITUDE ALERTING SYSTEM OR DEVICE: TURBOJET-POWERED CIVIL AIRPLANES

(a)   Except as provided in paragraph (d) of this section, no person may operate a turbojet-powered U.S.-registered civil airplane unless that airplane is equipped with an approved altitude alerting system or device that is in operable condition and meets the requirements of paragraph (b) of this section.

(b)   Each altitude alerting system or device required by paragraph (a) of this section must be able to —

(1)   Alert the pilot —

(i)   Upon approaching a preselected altitude in either ascent or descent, by a sequence of both aural and visual signals in sufficient time to establish level flight at that preselected altitude; or

(ii)   Upon approaching a preselected altitude in either ascent or descent, by a sequence of visual signals in sufficient time to establish level flight at that preselected altitude, and when deviating above and below that preselected altitude, by an aural signal;

(2) Provide the required signals from sea level to the highest operating altitude approved for the airplane in which it is installed;

(3) Preselect altitudes in increments that are commensurate with the altitudes at which the aircraft is operated;

(4) Be tested without special equipment to determine proper operation of the alerting signals; and

(5) Accept necessary barometric pressure settings if the system or device operates on barometric pressure.

However, for operations below 3,000 feet AGL, the system or device need only provide one signal, either visual or aural, to comply with this paragraph. A radio altimeter may be included to provide the signal if the operator has an approved procedure for its use to determine DH or MDA, as appropriate,

(c) Each operator to which this section applies must establish and assign procedures for the use of the altitude alerting system or device and each flight crewmember must comply with those procedures assigned to him.

(d) Paragraph (a) of this section does not apply to any operation of an airplane that has an experimental certificate or to the operation of any airplane for the following purposes:

(1) Ferrying a newly acquired airplane from the place where possession of it was taken to a place where the altitude alerting system or device is to be installed.

(2) Continuing a flight as originally planned, if the altitude alerting system or device becomes inoperative after the airplane has taken off; however, the flight may not depart from a place where repair or replacement can be made.

(3) Ferrying an airplane with any inoperative altitude alerting system or device from a place where repairs or replacements cannot be made to a place where it can be made.

(4) Conducting an airworthiness flight test of the airplane.

(5) Ferrying an airplane to a place outside the United States for the purpose of registering it in a foreign country.

(6) Conducting a sales demonstration of the operation of the airplane.

(7) Training foreign flight crews in the operation of the airplane before ferrying it to a place outside the United States for the purpose of registering it in a foreign country.

EXPLANATION

If the altitude alerting system becomes inoperative after initial takeoff, the flight can continue as planned except that it can not depart any place where repair or replacement can be accomplished until repair or replacement is accomplished.

All operators of turbojet powered U.S. registered aircraft must establish a procedure for the use of the system, including the assignment of duties and responsibilities to the flying and non-flying pilots, and the pilots must comply with the procedures.

CROSS REFERENCES

Previous designation: 91.51.

ADVISORY CIRCULARS

AC 91-22A *Altitude Alerting Devices/Systems* (1971).

91.221 TRAFFIC ALERT AND COLLISION AVOIDANCE SYSTEM EQUIPMENT AND USE

(a) *All airspace: U.S.-registered civil aircraft.* Any traffic alert and collision avoidance system installed in a U.S.-registered civil aircraft must be approved by the Administrator.

(b) *Traffic alert and collision avoidance system, operation required.* Each person operating an aircraft equipped with an operable traffic alert and collision avoidance system shall have that system on and operating.

EXPLANATION

If an aircraft has a TCAS system, it must be one approved by the FAA. If approved and operable, it must be on and operating.

If a pilot deviates from a clearance or instruction as the result of a resolution advisory, he must advise ATC as soon as practicable and, when the conflict is resolved, return to the current clearance.

Complete reliance on TCAS is not a good operating procedure since it does not respond to aircraft without transponders or inoperable transponders. "See and avoid" is still the best defense to a midair collision.

CROSS REFERENCES

Previous designation: 91.26. 91.3, Responsibility and Authority of the Pilot in Command; 91.123, Compliance with ATC Clearances and Instructions; 121.356, Traffic Alert and Collision Avoidance System; 125.224, Traffic Alert and Collision Avoidance System; 129.18 Traffic Alert and Collision Avoidance System; 135.180, Traffic Alert and Collision Avoidance System.

ADVISORY CIRCULARS

AC 90-48C *Pilots' Role In Collision Avoidance* (1983).

AERONAUTICAL INFORMATION MANUAL

Clearances, Para. 4-4-1;
Traffic Alert and Collision Avoidance Systems (TCAS I & II), Para. 4-4-15.

91.223 TERRAIN AWARENESS AND WARNING SYSTEM

(a) *Airplanes manufactured after March 29, 2002.* Except as provided in paragraph (d) of this section, no person may operate a turbine-powered U.S.-registered airplane configured with six or more passenger seats, excluding any pilot seat, unless that airplane is equipped with an approved terrain awareness and warning system that as a minimum meets the requirements for Class B equipment in Technical Standard Order (TSO)-C151.

(b) *Airplanes manufactured on or before March 29, 2002.* Except as provided in paragraph (d) of this section, no person may operate a turbine-powered U.S.-registered airplane configured with six or more passenger seats, excluding any pilot seat, after March 29, 2005, unless that airplane is equipped with an approved terrain awareness and warning system that as a minimum meets the requirements for Class B equipment in Technical Standard Order (TSO)-C151.

(Approved by the Office of Management and Budget under control number 2120-0631)

(c) *Airplane Flight Manual.* The Airplane Flight Manual shall contain appropriate procedures for--
    (1) The use of the terrain awareness and warning system; and
    (2) Proper flight crew reaction in response to the terrain awareness and warning system audio and visual warnings.

(d) *Exceptions.* Paragraphs (a) and (b) of this section do not apply to--
    (1) Parachuting operations when conducted entirely within a 50 nautical mile radius of the airport from which such local flight operations began.
    (2) Firefighting operations.
    (3) Flight operations when incident to the aerial application of chemicals and other substances.

EXPLANATION

Both 91.223(a) and (b) state: "airplane configured with six or more passenger seats." This exempts operators with aircraft type-certificated for six or more passenger seats, but who do not operate the aircraft with that many seats from complying.

PREAMBLE

The National Business Aviation Association (NBAA) recommends that the FAA exempt turbine-powered airplanes operated under part 91 from the rule because part 91 allows operators the flexibility "to equip their aircraft as necessary to accomplish the missions set forth by the company." The NBAA cites the safety record of corporate operations under part 91. The Aircraft Owners and Pilots Association (AOPA) recommends applying the proposed rule only to large turbojet airplanes used in commercial passenger-carrying operations. Several other part 91 operators also state that they should be exempt from the proposed rule.

The FAA disagrees with these commenters for the following reasons: (1) Two of the three NTSB recommendations discussed earlier were based on CFIT accidents involving airplanes operating under part 91. (2) The number of CFIT accidents occurring in part 91 operations is excessively high. (3) The Volpe part 91 study provides evidence that TAWS would have prevented 95 percent of the CFIT accidents studied.

The FAA disagrees with Raytheon and other commenters who oppose TAWS on turboprop airplanes and has determined that turboprop airplanes should continue to be covered. A study done for the FAA as part of the 1992 rulemaking amending part 135, requiring GPWS equipment, revealed that turboprop airplanes have just as many, if not more CFIT accidents than turbojet airplanes. In fact, the Volpe part 91 study shows that 33 of 44 CFIT accidents involved turboprop airplanes.

In response to Federal Express and others who state that passenger-carrying planes converted to cargo planes should not have to comply with the rule, the FAA partially agrees in that if the airplane (cargo carrying or not) is configured with fewer than 6 passenger seats and is operating under part 91, then TAWS is not required. However, for operations conducted under part 121 (cargo carrying or not), TAWS is required regardless of the number of passenger seats. Under existing rules, the FAA requires GPWS for part 121 regardless of the number of seats and is continuing to maintain the same safety standard. (65 FR 16738).

ADVISORY CIRCULARS

AC 23-18 *Installation of Terrain Awareness and Warning System (TAWS) Approved for Part 23 Airplanes* (2000).

AC 25-23 *Airworthiness Criteria for the Installation Approval of a Terrain Awareness and Warning System (TAWS) for Part 25 Airplanes* (2000).

INTENTIONALLY

LEFT

BLANK

SUBPART D — SPECIAL FLIGHT OPERATIONS

91.303 ACROBATIC FLIGHT

No person may operate an aircraft in acrobatic flight —
(a)   Over any congested area of a city, town, or settlement;
(b)   Over an open air assembly of persons;
(c)   Within the lateral boundaries of the surface areas of Class B, Class C, Class D, or Class E airspace designated for an airport;
(d)   Within 4 nautical miles of the center line of any Federal airway;
(e)   Below an altitude of 1,500 feet above the surface; or
(f)   When flight visibility is less than three statute miles.

For the purposes of this section, acrobatic flight means an intentional maneuver involving an abrupt change in an aircraft's attitude, an abnormal attitude, or abnormal acceleration, not necessary for normal flight.

EXPLANATION

Prior to a flight that will include aerobatic maneuvers, always check FAR 91.307 to see if parachutes are required. However, the flight parameters set forth in 91.307 do not necessarily define the limits of "normal flight."

Be familiar with the physiological aspects of aerobatic flight and factor these into the planning of the flight.

An aerobatic flight must be carefully planned. Points to consider: (l) the area where operation will be conducted to ensure avoidance of areas where acrobatics are not permitted; (2) altitude at which maneuvers must begin to ensure completion at or above 1500 feet; and (3) operating limitations of aircraft.

Training flights, including the maneuvers required for training under the regulations are, in fact, "normal flights" for the purpose of this section.

CROSS REFERENCES

Previous designation: 91.71. 91.307(c), Parachutes and Parachuting; 91.903-91.905, Waivers.

ADVISORY CIRCULARS

AC 61-67C *Stall and Spin Awareness Training* (2000).

AC 91-45C *Waivers; Aviation Events* (1990).

AC 91-48 *Aerobatics-Precision Flying With A Purpose* (1977).

AC 91-61 *A Hazard In Aerobatics: Effects Of G-Forces On Pilots* (1984).

AERONAUTICAL INFORMATION MANUAL

Emergency Locator Transmitter (ELT), Para. 6-2-5 (Aerobatic maneuvers can activate ELT. Always check by monitoring 121.5 and/or 243.0 MHz);
Aerobatic flight, Para. 8-1-7.

CASES

The pilot of an aerobatic biplane received a suspension because he executed an aileron roll at 500'-800' AGL and other maneuvers within a mile of an airport, then made a high speed pass with a steep dive then climbed above a runway after cutting off a C172 on short final. The passenger was not wearing a parachute. *Administrator v. Swift*, EA-4122 (1994).

On takeoff, a steep climb out with a left turn at about 300 feet was an aerobatic maneuver in that it was abnormal and not necessary for normal flight. *Administrator v. Steel*, 5 NTSB 239 (1985).

The Board indicated, in sustaining a violation of [91.303(b) and (d)] that pedal turns of 360 degrees by a helicopter were aerobatic within the meaning of the regulation since they involved abnormal attitude and were not necessary for normal flight. *Administrator v. Peelgrane*, 5 NTSB 2263 (1987).

The maneuver known as the Dutch roll is defined as banking the aircraft alternately from side to side. The maneuver can be performed slowly with shallow banks (not aerobatics) or it can be performed abruptly with steep banks (aerobatic). *Administrator v. Morgan*, 4 NTSB 1517 (1984).

A pilot who flew skydivers in a King Air was accused of performing aerobatic maneuvers by performing rapidly descending spirals after discharging the skydivers. The NTSB dismissed the charges against the pilot because the FAA failed to prove that this method of descent was not "normal" for skydiving operations. *Administrator v. Chandler*, EA-4717 (1998).

FAA CHIEF COUNSEL OPINIONS

Steep turns, approaches to stalls, stalls, unusual attitudes for the purpose of demonstrating recovery procedures with angles of pitch not exceeding 30 degrees and angles of bank not exceeding 60 degrees, and emergency descents with angles of pitch not to exceed 30 degrees performed during initial pilot training or pilot proficiency training are not considered aerobatics if smoothly executed and not done in a manner causing an abrupt change in attitude. The maneuvers would also not fall into any category involving "an abnormal attitude, or abnormal acceleration, not necessary for normal flight" because they are incident to and necessary for normal training flights which are, in fact, normal flights. (6-11-80).

The FAR requires that any "aerobatic flight" be fully accomplished 1500 feet or more above the surface. A stall, in and of itself, is not a prohibited maneuver since it can be an element in normal flight. The actions of a flight instructor can be considered as "intentionally" operating an aircraft in aerobatic flight if the instructor deliberately does nothing while permitting a student pilot to maneuver an aircraft in aerobatic flight contrary to the provisions of the regulation. This is based on the fact that the flight instructor is the pilot in command of all student training flights regardless of who is manipulating the controls. (3-19-81).

A certified flight instructor and his/her student are excepted from the parachute requirements only for those maneuvers that are required by the regulations for any certificate or rating (even one not presently sought by the student). Any maneuver not required by the regulations for any certificate or rating must be taught employing parachutes pursuant to [91.307(c)]. (7-28-77).

Aerobatic flight is permitted outside of Class B airspace provided that it is not conducted within the lateral boundaries of the surface areas of Class B, Class C, Class D, or Class E airspace designated for an airport as provided by section 91.303(c). Along with being conducted in accordance with regulations applicable to the airspace in which the operation is executed.

Aerobatic operations are not permitted within the surface area of controlled airspace regardless of its alpha designator, "surface area" being defined as the airspace contained in the lateral boundary of the Class B, C, D, or E airspace designated for an airport, that begins at the surface and extends upward. (7-14-99).

Pursuant to section 91.903, under certain circumstances a waiver to operate within controlled airspace may be granted. (1-19-00).

91.305 FLIGHT TEST AREAS

No person may flight test an aircraft except over open water, or sparsely populated areas, having light air traffic.

EXPLANATION

The object of the regulation is to ensure flight tests are conducted in areas where the least number of persons and property are subject to possible injury from this potentially hazardous operation.

It is recommended that the proposed areas be discussed with the appropriate Flight Standards District Office, recognizing that approval is not required.

CROSS REFERENCES

Previous designation: 91.93. 91.407, Operation After Maintenance, Preventive Maintenance, Rebuilding, Or Alteration; 91.903-91.905, Waivers.

91.307 PARACHUTES AND PARACHUTING

(a)   No pilot of a civil aircraft may allow a parachute that is available for emergency use to be carried in that aircraft unless it is an approved type and —

(1)   If a chair type (canopy in back), it has been packed by a certificated and appropriately rated parachute rigger within the preceding 120 days; or

(2)   If any other type, it has been packed by a certificated and appropriately rated parachute rigger —

(I)   Within the preceding 120 days, if its canopy, shrouds, and harness are composed exclusively of nylon, rayon, or other similar synthetic fiber or materials that are substantially resistant to damage from mold, mildew, or other fungi and other rotting agents propagated in a moist environment; or

(ii)   Within the preceding 60 days, if any part of the parachute is composed of silk, pongee, or other natural fiber, or materials not specified in paragraph (a)(2)(I) of this section.

(b)   Except in an emergency, no pilot in command may allow, and no person may conduct, a parachute operation from an aircraft within the United States except in accordance with part 105 of this chapter.

(c)   Unless each occupant of the aircraft is wearing an approved parachute, no pilot of a civil aircraft, carrying any person (other than a crewmember) may execute any intentional maneuver that exceeds —

(1)   A bank of 60 degrees relative to the horizon; or

(2)   A nose-up or nose-down attitude of 30 degrees relative to the horizon.

(d)   Paragraph (c) of this section does not apply to —

(1)   Flight tests for pilot certification or rating; or

(2)   Spins and other flight maneuvers required by the regulations for any certificate or rating when given by —

(I)   A certificated flight instructor; or

(ii)   An airline transport pilot instructing in accordance with §61.167 of this chapter.

(e)   For the purposes of this section, "approved parachute" means —

(1)   A parachute manufactured under a type certificate or a technical standard order (C-23 series); or

(2)   A personnel-carrying military parachute identified by an NAF, AAF, or AN drawing number, an AAF order number, or any other military designation or specification number.

EXPLANATION

A pilot carrying parachute jumpers must be thoroughly familiar with Part 105 of the FAR since this regulation places the responsibility to comply with Part 105 on the pilot as well as the jumper. A majority of the sections of Part 105 contain the following wording, "no person may make a parachute jump, and no pilot in command may allow a parachute jump to be made from that aircraft . ." A pilot must check each parachute to ensure that it has been packed by the appropriately rated person within the prescribed time limits.

If none of the occupants, including the pilot and any other crewmember, are wearing approved parachutes, banking of the aircraft relative to the horizon cannot exceed 60 degrees and nose-up/nose-down altitude relative to the horizon must be 30 degrees or less. FAR 1.1 defines "crewmember" as "a person assigned to perform duty in an aircraft during flight time."

A certificated flight instructor may teach spins to any student without parachutes.

CROSS REFERENCES

Previous designation: 91.15. 61.169, Instruction In Air Transportation Service; Part 149, Parachute Lofts, 91.303, Aerobatic Flight.

ADVISORY CIRCULARS

AC 61-67C *Stall and Spin Awareness Training* (2000).

AC 105-2C *Sport Parachute Jumping* (1991).

AERONAUTICAL INFORMATION MANUAL

Parachute Jump Aircraft Operations, Para. 3-5-4;
Traffic Advisory Practices At Airports Without Operating Control Towers: Recommended Traffic Advisory Practices, Para. 4-1-9(c).

CASES

The pilot of an aerobatic biplane received a suspension because he executed an aileron roll at 500'-800' AGL and other maneuvers within a mile of an airport, then made a high speed pass with a steep dive then climbed above a runway after cutting off a C172 on short final. The passenger was not wearing a parachute. *Administrator v. Swift*, EA-4122 (1994).

The fact that another pilot, with a multi-engine rating, was employed by alleged violator as an aircraft sales representative and claimed she manipulated the controls during the aerobatic maneuver of the Piper Aerostar Model 601P consisting of a 360 degree aileron roll and assisted the respondent in other ways during the flight, she was not a "crewmember" within the meaning of §[91.307(c)] and all occupants were required to be wearing approved parachutes. *Administrator v. Roach*, 4 NTSB 432 (1983).

FAA CHIEF COUNSEL OPINIONS

A certificated flight instructor (CFI) and his student are excepted from the parachute requirement for only those maneuvers which are required by the regulations for any certificate or rating (even one not presently sought by the student). Any maneuver which is not required by the regulations for any certificate or rating must be taught employing parachutes pursuant to [91.307(c)]. (7-28-77).

When a CFI is providing a recreational, private, or commercial certificate applicant with spin training, wearing parachutes is not required. This operation falls under the exceptions to the parachute requirement which are provided in instances where wearing a parachute might cause a hazard by reducing the pilot's visibility or hamper operation of controls. (6-17-98).

91.309 TOWING: GLIDERS

(a)   No person may operate a civil aircraft towing a glider unless —
   (1)   The pilot in command of the towing aircraft is qualified under §61.69 of this chapter.
   (2)   The towing aircraft is equipped with a tow-hitch of a kind, and installed in a manner, that is approved by the Administrator.
   (3)   The towline used has a breaking strength not less than 80 percent of the maximum certificated operating weight of the glider and not more than twice this operating weight. However, the towline used may have a breaking strength more than twice the maximum certificated operating weight of the glider if —
      (I)   A safety link is installed at the point of attachment of the towline to the glider with a breaking strength not less than 80 percent of the maximum certificated operating weight of the glider and not greater than twice this operating weight.
      (ii) A safety link is installed at the point of attachment of the towline to the towing aircraft with a breaking strength greater, but not more than 25 percent greater, than that of the safety link at the towed glider end of the towline and not greater than twice the maximum certificated operating weight of the glider.
   (4)   Before conducting any towing operation within the lateral boundaries of the surface areas of Class B, Class C, Class D, or Class E airspace designated for an airport, or before making each towing flight within such controlled airspace if required by ATC, the pilot in command notifies the control tower. If a control tower does not exist or is not in operation, the pilot in command must notify the FAA flight service station serving that controlled airspace before conducting any towing operations in that airspace; and
   (5)   The pilots of the towing aircraft and the glider have agreed upon a general course of action, including takeoff and release signals, airspeeds, and emergency procedures for each pilot.
(b)   No pilot of a civil aircraft may intentionally release a towline, after release of a glider, in a manner so as to endanger the life or property of another.

EXPLANATION

Compliance with §61.69 must have been accomplished before any glider tow operation is conducted by a pilot.

The pilot must ensure that the towline and/or the safety link meet the requirements of this section. Well prior to a flight the pilot should establish a method for determining that these requirements are being met.

CROSS REFERENCES

Previous designation: 91.17. 61.69, Glider Towing; Experience And Instruction Requirements; 91.311, Towing: Other Than Under 91.309.

91.311 TOWING: OTHER THAN UNDER §91.309.

No pilot of a civil aircraft may tow anything with that aircraft (other than under §91.309) except in accordance with the terms of a certificate of waiver issued by the Administrator.

EXPLANATION

For operations such as banner towing, target towing, etc., a waiver, under the provisions of §§91.903 and 91.905 must be obtained. The waiver will contain prohibitions, restrictions and/or conditions which must be complied with fully.

CROSS REFERENCES

Previous designation: 91.18. 91.309, Towing: Gliders; 91.903- 91.905, Waivers.

91.313 RESTRICTED CATEGORY CIVIL AIRCRAFT: OPERATING LIMITATIONS

(a)   No person may operate a restricted category civil aircraft —
  (1)   For other than the special purpose for which it is certificated; or
  (2)   In an operation other than one necessary to accomplish the work activity directly associated with that special purpose.
(b)   For the purpose of paragraph (a) of this section, operating a restricted category civil aircraft to provide flight crewmember training in a special purpose operation for which the aircraft is certificated is considered to be an operation for that special purpose.
(c)   No person may operate a restricted category civil aircraft carrying persons or property for compensation or hire. For the purposes of this paragraph, a special purpose operation involving the carriage of persons or material necessary to accomplish that operation, such as crop dusting, seeding, spraying, and banner towing (including the carrying of required persons or material to the location of that operation), and operation for the purpose of providing flight crewmember training in a special purpose operation, are not considered to be the carriage of persons or property for compensation or hire.
(d)   No person may be carried on a restricted category civil aircraft unless that person —
  (1)   Is a flight crewmember;
  (2)   Is a flight crewmember trainee;
  (3)   Performs an essential function in connection with a special purpose operation for which the aircraft is certificated; or
  (4)   Is necessary to accomplish the work activity directly associated with that special purpose.
(e)   Except when operating in accordance with the terms and conditions of a certificate of waiver or special operating limitations issued by the Administrator, no person may operate a restricted category civil aircraft within the United States —
  (1)   Over a densely populated area;
  (2)   In a congested airway; or
  (3)   Near a busy airport where passenger transport operations are conducted.
(f)   This section does not apply to nonpassenger-carrying civil rotorcraft external-load operations conducted under Part 133 of this chapter.

(g) No person may operate a small restricted-category civil airplane manufactured after July 18, 1978, unless an approved shoulder harness is installed for each front seat. The shoulder harness must be designed to protect each occupant from serious head injury when the occupant experiences the ultimate inertia forces specified in §23.561 (b)(2) of this chapter. The shoulder harness installation at each flight crewmember station must permit the crewmember, when seated and with his safety belt and shoulder harness fastened, to perform all functions necessary for flight operations. For purposes of this paragraph —

(1) The date of manufacture of an airplane is the date the inspection acceptance records reflect that the airplane is complete and meets the FAA-approved type design data; and

(2) A front seat is a seat located at a flight crewmember station or any seat located alongside such a seat.

EXPLANATION

The special purposes for which restricted category civil aircraft are certificated are agricultural, aerial survey, patrolling, weather control, forest and wildlife conservation, cargo carrying and aerial advertising.

In accordance with Advisory Circular 21-17, carriage of cargo is a "special purpose" for which restricted category aircraft are certificated. However, the prohibition against carrying persons or property for hire prevents this "special purpose" from becoming profitable.

Because of the special nature of the intended use of these aircraft, airworthiness certificate standards are not designed to provide the same level of safety as in the case of standard category aircraft since some standards would be inappropriate for the aircraft's special purpose.

Persons who can be carried in the aircraft would include a farmer who has contracted for crop dusting. The farmer may have to go up before or during the actual operation to point out the fields to be dusted.

CROSS REFERENCES

Previous designation: 91.39. 21.185, Issue of Airworthiness Certificates to Restricted Category Aircraft; 23.561(b)(2), Seats, seatbelts and shoulder harnesses, static inertia loads; 91.903-91.905, Waivers; Part 133, Rotorcraft External Load Operations.

ADVISORY CIRCULARS

AC 20-65 *U.S. Airworthiness Certificate and Authorization For Operation of Domestic and Foreign Aircraft* (1969).

AC 21-12A *Application for U.S. Airworthiness Certificate, FAA Form 8130-6* (1987).

AC 21-17 *Carriage of Cargo in Restricted Category Aircraft and Other Special Purpose Operations* (1982).

AC 12-21 *Use of Automobile Gasoline in Agricultural Aircraft* (1984).

AC 137-1 *Agricultural Aircraft Operations* (1965).

CASES

When seeking a waiver under [91.313(e) and 91.903(b)] to conduct operations using a restricted category aircraft, over a densely populated area, in a congested airway, or near a busy airport where passenger transport operations are conducted, a mere telephone call to an FAA office telling of the proposed operation cannot be considered as approval, tacit or otherwise, for the operation. The application for waiver must be made on the form and in the manner prescribed by the FAA. *Administrator v. Downing*, 4 NTSB 687 (1982).

91.315 LIMITED CATEGORY CIVIL AIRCRAFT: OPERATING LIMITATIONS

No person may operate a limited category civil aircraft carrying persons or property for compensation or hire.

EXPLANATION

Although it has not interpreted this particular regulation, the National Transportation Safety Board has held that an operation "for compensation or hire" need not involve profit. It is sufficient that a person's economic interests are being furthered by the operation. *Administrator v. Motley*, 2 NTSB 178 (1973).

CROSS REFERENCES

Previous designation: 91.40. 21.189, Issue of Airworthiness Certificate for Limited Category Aircraft.

91.317 PROVISIONALLY CERTIFICATED CIVIL AIRCRAFT: OPERATING LIMITATIONS

(a) No person may operate a provisionally certificated civil aircraft unless that person is eligible for a provisional airworthiness certificate under §21.213 of this chapter.

(b) No person may operate a provisionally certificated civil aircraft outside the United States unless that person has specific authority to do so from the Administrator and each foreign country involved.

(c) Unless otherwise authorized by the Director, Flight Standards Service, no person may operate a provisionally certificated civil aircraft in air transportation.

(d) Unless otherwise authorized by the Administrator, no person may operate a provisionally certificated civil aircraft except —

(1) In direct conjunction with the type or supplemental type certification of that aircraft;

(2) For training flight crews, including simulated air carrier operations;

(3) Demonstration flight by the manufacturer for prospective purchasers;

(4) Market surveys by the manufacturer;

(5) Flight checking of instruments, accessories, and equipment, that do not affect the basic airworthiness of the aircraft; or

(6) Service testing of the aircraft.

(e)   Each person operating a provisionally certificated civil aircraft shall operate within the prescribed limitations displayed in the aircraft or set forth in the provisional aircraft flight manual or other appropriate document. However, when operating in direct conjunction with the type or supplemental type certification of the aircraft, that person shall operate under the experimental aircraft limitations of §21.191 of this chapter and when flight testing, shall operate under the requirements of §91.305 of this part.

(f)   Each person operating a provisionally certificated civil aircraft shall establish approved procedures for —
    (1)   The use and guidance of flight and ground personnel in operating under this section; and
    (2)   Operating in and out of airports where takeoffs or approaches over populated areas are necessary. No person may operate that aircraft except in compliance with the approved procedures.

(g)   Each person operating a provisionally certificated civil aircraft shall ensure that each flight crewmember is properly certificated and has adequate knowledge of, and familiarity with, the aircraft and procedures to be used by that crewmember.

(h)   Each person operating a provisionally certificated civil aircraft shall maintain it as required by applicable regulations and as may be specially prescribed by the Administrator.

(i)   Whenever the manufacturer, or the Administrator, determines that a change in design, construction, or operation is necessary to ensure safe operation, no person may operate a provisionally certificated civil aircraft until that change has been made and approved. Section 21.99 of this chapter applies to operations under this section.

(j)   Each person operating a provisionally certificated civil aircraft —
    (1)   May carry in that aircraft only persons who have a proper interest in the operations allowed by this section or who are specifically authorized by both the manufacturer and the Administrator; and
    (2)   Shall advise each person carried that the aircraft is provisionally certificated.

(k)   The Administrator may prescribe additional limitations or procedures that the Administrator considers necessary, including limitations on the number of persons who may be carried in the aircraft.

EXPLANATION

Persons eligible to apply for a provisional airworthiness certificate are manufacturers, Part 121 and/or Part 127 certificate holders, and aircraft engine manufacturers that are United States citizens.

Aircraft with a provisional airworthiness certificate may have restrictions and limitations in addition to the ones set forth in this section. Accordingly, prior to operating an aircraft with this type of airworthiness certificate, a pilot should review the aircraft flight manual and other certificating documents.

CROSS REFERENCES

Previous designation: 91.41. 21.99, Required Design Changes; 21.191, Experimental Certificates; 21.213, Eligibility, Provisional Airworthiness Certificates; 91.305, Flight Test Areas.

ADVISORY CIRCULARS

AC 20-65 *U.S. Airworthiness Certificates and Authorizations for Operation of Domestic and Foreign Aircraft* (1969).

AC 21-12A *Application for U.S. Airworthiness Certificate, FAA Form 8130-6* (1987).

91.319 AIRCRAFT HAVING EXPERIMENTAL CERTIFICATES: OPERATING LIMITATIONS

(a)No person may operate an aircraft that has an experimental certificate —
  (1)For other than the purpose for which the certificate was issued; or
  (2)Carrying persons or property for compensation or hire.
(b)No person may operate an aircraft that has an experimental certificate outside of an area assigned by the Administrator until it is shown that —
  (1)The aircraft is controllable throughout its normal range of speeds and throughout all the maneuvers to be executed; and
  (2)The aircraft has no hazardous operating characteristics or design features.
(c)Unless otherwise authorized by the Administrator in special operating limitations, no person may operate an aircraft that has an experimental certificate over a densely populated area or in a congested airway. The Administrator may issue special operating limitations for particular aircraft to permit takeoffs and landings to be conducted over a densely populated area or in a congested airway, In accordance with terms and conditions specified in the authorization in the interest of safety in air commerce.
(d)Each person operating an aircraft that has an experimental certificate shall —
  (1)Advise each person carried of the experimental nature of the aircraft;
  (2)Operate under VFR, day only, unless otherwise specifically authorized by the Administrator; and
  (3)Notify the control tower of the experimental nature of the aircraft when operating the aircraft into or out of airports with operating control towers.
(e)The Administrator may prescribe additional limitations that the Administrator considers necessary, including limitations on the persons that may be carried in the aircraft.

EXPLANATION

The "purposes" for which the FAA issues experimental certificates include: research and development; showing compliance with the regulations (in preparation for issuance of a standard airworthiness certificate); crew training; exhibition; air racing; market survey; and operating amateur-built aircraft.

While the flight test areas referred to in §91.305 do not require FAA approval, the areas of operation under this regulation are assigned by the FAA.

Before you can take off or land an aircraft, with an experimental certificate, from an airport that requires the takeoff and/or landing to be over a densely populated area or in a congested airway, the FAA must have issued special operating limitations for the particular aircraft which will be included in the authorization.

Authorization to operate an experimental aircraft under IFR and/or at night may be received by requesting special operating limitations from the FAA (see AC 20-27D).

On initial contact with a control tower, immediately advise them that the aircraft is being operated pursuant to an experimental certificate.

A current listing of eligible amateur-built aircraft kits may be obtained from the FAA Office of Aviation System Standards Engineering and Manufacturing Branch, Oklahoma City, OK 73125.

The owner of an amateur-built experimental aircraft may pay a flight instructor for instruction in that aircraft, but a commercial operator may not provide such an aircraft for the purpose of giving flight instruction for hire.

CROSS REFERENCES

Previous designation: 91.42. 21.191, Experimental Certificates; 21.195, Experimental Certificates: Aircraft To Be Used For Market Surveys; Sales Demonstrations; and Customer Crew Training; 91.129, Operations At Airports With Operating Control Towers.

ADVISORY CIRCULARS

AC 20-27E *Certification and Operation of Amateur-Built Aircraft* (2001).

AC 20-65 *U.S. Airworthiness Certificates and Authorization for Operation of Domestic and Foreign Aircraft* (1969).

AC 21-12A *Application for U.S. Airworthiness Certificate, FAA Form 8130-6* (1987).

AC 20-126G *Aircraft Certification Service Field Office Listing* (1999).

AC 90-89A *Amateur-Built Aircraft & Ultralight Flight Testing Handbook* (1995).

AC 91-68 *Pilot Qualification and Operation of All Surplus Military Turbine-Powered Airplanes* (1992).

FAA CHIEF COUNSEL OPINIONS

An airship-balloon operated under an experimental certificate issued for the purpose of exhibition, pursuant to §21.193, would not be in violation of [91.319(a)(2)] if it had advertising on the side of the airship-balloon for which the operator received compensation. The subsection only prohibits the carrying of persons or property for compensation or hire. The pilot would have to hold at least a commercial pilot certificate. (1-29-81).

Agricultural application — An amateur-built aircraft issued an experimental certificate may be operated for agricultural purposes provided that:

1   All of the requirements applicable to amateur-built aircraft have been complied with;
2.   The applicable operating time in an assigned flight test area is satisfied with the dispensing equipment installed on the aircraft;
3.   The following operating limitation is prescribed: The operator of this aircraft must be certified under FAR 137 prior to any agricultural aircraft operations.

Under this policy, an amateur-builder may conduct agricultural aircraft operations over his own land or crops as provided in FAR 137.19. No commercial or for hire (compensation) operations are permitted. The operator of the aircraft must complete all certification requirements for a private agricultural aircraft operator certificate prior to such operations.

Flight training — An aircraft with an experimental certificate, amateur-built, may be used for crew training or flight instruction where no charges or reimbursement for the use of the aircraft are involved. A pilot or owner may avail themselves of the services of an instructor to take dual instruction in an experimental aircraft, however, a commercial operator may not provide such an aircraft for the purpose of giving flight instruction for hire. (5-27-82).

Media or public relation rides in experimental aircraft, given under a contract which compensates the air show performers giving the rides, constitutes carriage of persons for compensation or hire and is a violation of §91.319. (8-5-97).

91.321 CARRIAGE OF CANDIDATES IN FEDERAL ELECTIONS

(a)   An aircraft operator, other than one operating an aircraft under the rules of part 121, 125, or 135 of this chapter, may receive payment for the carriage of a candidate in a Federal election, an agent of the candidate, or a person traveling on the behalf of the candidate, if —
   (1)   That operator's primary business is not as an air carrier or commercial operator;
   (2)   The carriage is conducted under the rules of part 91; and
   (3)   The payment for the carriage is required, and does not exceed the amount required to be paid, by regulations of the Federal Election Commission (11 CFR *et seq.*).
(b)   For the purposes of this section, the terms "candidate" and "election" have the same meaning as that set forth in the regulations of the Federal Election Commission.

EXPLANATION

This section applies only to candidates in Federal elections. It does not apply to candidates in state or local elections.

If a candidate in a Federal election, his/her agent, or persons traveling on his/her behalf used aircraft owned or operated by a corporation or labor organization, the Federal Election Commission requires that the aircraft operator must be reimbursed.

The amount of the reimbursement to be made is set forth in 11 C.F.R. 114.9(e) and presently is: (1) in the case of travel to a city served by regularly scheduled commercial service, the first class airfare and, (2) in the case of travel to a city not served by regularly scheduled commercial service, the usual charter rate.

If involved in an operation governed by this section, prior to the flight, contact should be made with your insurance agent/broker to ensure that your policy will cover the flight since it is a flight for compensation or hire.

If flights are made that are subject to this section, you should contact your tax consultant regarding any liability for air transportation tax (IRS Code §4261).

The FAA was directed by Congress in Public Law 104-264 to amend this rule by extending the same requirements to the carriage of state and local candidates. This directive was made in 1996, but the FAA has yet to address this issue in a rulemaking session.

Public Law 104-264 104th Congress

SEC. 1214. CARRIAGE OF CANDIDATES IN STATE AND LOCAL ELECTIONS. The Administrator of the Federal Aviation Administration shall revise section 91.321 of the Administration's regulations (14 C.F.R. 91.321), relating to the carriage of candidates in Federal elections, to make the same or similar rules applicable to the carriage of candidates for election to public office in State and local government elections.

CROSS REFERENCES

Previous designation: 91.59. 91.501, Applicability; 11 C.F.R. Parts 100 and 114 (Federal Election Commission Regulations).

FAA CHIEF COUNSEL OPINIONS

An individual cannot accept payment for the transportation of a Federal candidate under [91.321] since the Federal Election Commission only requires payment if the aircraft used for the transportation is owned or leased by a corporation or labor organization. (10-30-80).

Insofar as the FAA is concerned there are no reporting or record keeping requirements associated with [91.321]. Contact should be made with the Federal Election Commission and/or the Internal Revenue Service regarding any requirements they may have. (11-5-80).

91.323 INCREASED MAXIMUM CERTIFICATED WEIGHTS FOR CERTAIN AIRPLANES OPERATED IN ALASKA

(a) Notwithstanding any other provision of the Federal Aviation Regulations, the Administrator will approve, as provided in this section, an increase in the maximum certificated weight of an airplane type certificated under Aeronautics Bulletin No. 7-A of the U.S. Department of Commerce dated January 1, 1931, as amended, or under the normal category of part 4a of the former Civil Air Regulations (14 CFR Part 4a, 1964 ed.), if that airplane is operated in the State of Alaska by —
   (1) A certificate holder conducting operations under part 121 or part 135 of this chapter; or
   (2) The U.S. Department of Interior in conducting its game and fish law enforcement activities or its management, fire detection, and fire suppression activities concerning public lands.

(b) The maximum certificated weight approved under this section may not exceed —
   (1) 12,500 pounds;
   (2) 115 percent of the maximum weight listed in the FAA aircraft specifications;
   (3) The weight at which the airplane meets the positive maneuvering load factor requirement for the normal category specified in §23.337 of this chapter; or
   (4) The weight at which the airplane meets the climb performance requirements under which it was type certificated.

(c) In determining the maximum certificated weight, the Administrator considers the structural soundness of the airplane and the terrain to be traversed.

(d) The maximum certificated weight determined under this section is added to the airplane's operation limitations and is identified as the maximum weight authorized for operations within the State of Alaska.

EXPLANATION

This regulation permits the FAA to approve the use of aircraft, type certificated under Aeronautics Bulletin 7A or the normal category of Part 4a, at takeoff and landing weights greater than the maximum certified weights determined during type certification. The section further provides the maximum weight that can be approved.

CROSS REFERENCES

Previous designation: 91.38. 91.9, Civil Aircraft Manual, Marking, and Placard Requirements.

ADVISORY CIRCULARS

FAA-H-8083-1, Aircraft Weight and Balance Handbook (1999).

91.325 PRIMARY CATEGORY AIRCRAFT: OPERATING LIMITATIONS

(a)   No person may operate a primary category aircraft carrying persons or property for compensation or hire.

(b)   No person may operate a primary category aircraft that is maintained by the pilot-owner under an approved special inspection and maintenance program except—
      (1)   The pilot-owner; or
      (2)   A designee of the pilot-owner, provided that the pilot-owner does not receive compensation for the use of the aircraft.

INTENTIONALLY

LEFT

BLANK

SUBPART E — MAINTENANCE, PREVENTIVE MAINTENANCE, AND ALTERATIONS

91.401 APPLICABILITY

(a) This subpart prescribes rules governing the maintenance, preventive maintenance, and alterations of U.S.-registered civil aircraft operating within or outside the United States.

(b) Sections 91.405, 91.409, 91.411, 91.417, and 91.419 of this subpart do not apply to an aircraft maintained in accordance with a continuous airworthiness maintenance program as provided in part 121, 129, or §135.411(a)(2) of this chapter.

(c) Sections 91.405 and 91.409 of this part do not apply to an airplane inspected in accordance with part 125 of this chapter.

EXPLANATION

Except as stated in 91.401(b) and (c), the regulations of this subpart apply to all U.S. registered aircraft whether operated within or outside the United States. Such action was necessary for the United States to meet its obligations under the Convention on International Civil Aviation (Chicago Convention) and §1102 of the Federal Aviation Act of 1958, as amended (49 U.S.C. App. 1502).

CROSS REFERENCES

Previous designation: 91.161. 21.181, Duration (Airworthiness Certificates); 43.17, Maintenance, Preventive Maintenance, and Alterations Performed on U.S. Aeronautical Products by Certain Canadian Pilots; 91-703, Operation of Civil Aircraft of U.S. Registry Outside the United States.

ADVISORY CIRCULARS

AC 43-10A *Mechanical Work Performed on U.S. and Canadian Registered Aircraft* (1983).

91.403 GENERAL

(a) The owner or operator of an aircraft is primarily responsible for maintaining that aircraft in an airworthy condition, including compliance with part 39 of this chapter.

(b) No person may perform maintenance, preventive maintenance, or alterations on an aircraft other than as prescribed in this subpart and other applicable regulations, including part 43 of this chapter.

(c) No person may operate an aircraft for which a manufacturer's maintenance manual or instructions for continued airworthiness has been issued that contains an airworthiness limitations section unless the mandatory replacement times, inspection intervals, and related procedures specified in that section or alternative inspection intervals and related procedures set forth in an operations specification approved by the Administrator under part 121 or 135 of this chapter or in accordance with an inspection program approved under §91.409(e) have been complied with.

EXPLANATION

This section clearly establishes that the owner or operator of the aircraft is primarily responsible for maintaining an aircraft in an airworthy condition.

Acceptable alternatives to compliance with the airworthiness limitations section in the manufacturer's maintenance manual or instructions for continued airworthiness are identified in §91.403(c).

A pilot may perform preventive maintenance on an aircraft and if the pilot holds at least a private pilot certificate, approve the aircraft for return to service. Preventive maintenance is limited to the work described in Appendix A, paragraph (c) of Part 43 of the FAR. Any preventive maintenance must be logged in the aircraft maintenance records as set forth in §43.9.

If a pilot is going to work on an aircraft, he/she must be familiar with all the requirements of Part 43 of the FAR.

With the exception of the inspections required by Part 91, Part 125, or performed after a major repair or alterations, any person may perform maintenance provided it is done under the supervision of a person authorized to perform the specific work.

Airworthiness is not defined in the Federal Aviation Act or in the FAR. Based on CAB and NTSB decisions, it is held to mean that the aircraft conforms to the type certificate for the aircraft and is in a condition for safe operation.

As owner or operator of an aircraft, it is your responsibility to ensure that persons performing maintenance on your aircraft are properly certificated.

CROSS REFERENCES

Previous designation: 91.163. 1.1 General Definitions: "Maintenance"; §21.50, Instructions for Continued Airworthiness and Manufacturers Maintenance Manuals Having Airworthiness, Limitations Sections; Part 39, Airworthiness Directives; Part 43, Maintenance, Preventive Maintenance, Rebuilding and Alterations; 91.7 Civil Aircraft Airworthiness; Appendix A, Part 91, Category II Operations: Manual, Instruments, Equipment, and Maintenance.

ADVISORY CIRCULARS

AC 20-62D *Eligibility, Quality, and Identification of Aeronautical Replacement Parts* (1996).

AC 20-77 *Use of Manufacturers' Maintenance Manuals* (1972).

AC 20-106 *Aircraft Inspections for the General Aviation Aircraft Owner* (1978).

AC 39-7C *Airworthiness Directives* (1995).

AC 43-9C *Maintenance Records* (1998).

AC 43.13-1B *Acceptable Methods, Techniques and Practices Aircraft Inspection and Repair* (2001).

AC 43.13-2A *Acceptable Methods, Techniques, and Practices-Aircraft Alterations* (1977).

AC 65-13T *FAA Inspection Authorization Directory* (1999).

AC 91-56A *Continuing Structural Integrity Program for Large Transport Category Airplanes* (1998).

CASES

A non-certificated employee of a fixed-base operator that repaired aircraft performed maintenance on an aircraft within the scope of his employment, which constituted a violation of §91.403(b) by the FBO. When the aircraft was next flown its gear would not extend resulting in a gear-up landing. The FBO was fined $4,750. *FAA v. Sanford Air, Inc.*, FAA Order No. 97-31 (10-8-1997).

A Part 135 certificate holder operated a helicopter 400 hours beyond the mandatory replacement time for a life-limited part. The law judge held that the certificate holder was responsible for the actions of its employees who certified that the aircraft was airworthy after the replacement time had been passed. The certificate holder was fined $7,000. *FAA v. Pacific Aviation International, Inc.*, FAA Order No. 97-8 (2-20-1997).

91.405 MAINTENANCE REQUIRED

Each owner or operator of an aircraft —
(a)   Shall have that aircraft inspected as prescribed in subpart E of this part and shall between required inspections, except as provided in paragraph (c) of this section, have discrepancies repaired as prescribed in part 43 of this chapter;
(b)   Shall ensure that maintenance personnel make appropriate entries in the aircraft maintenance records indicating the aircraft has been approved for return to service;

(c)   Shall have any inoperative instrument or item of equipment, permitted to be inoperative by
        §91.213(d)(2) of this part, repaired, replaced, removed, or inspected at the next required
        inspection; and

(d)   When listed discrepancies include inoperative instruments or equipment, shall ensure that a
        placard has been installed as required by §43.11 of this chapter.

EXPLANATION

Any inoperative instrument or equipment, deactivated or removed in accordance with §91.213,
Inoperative Instruments and Equipment, must be inspected at every required inspection. This is to
allow a re-evaluation of the inoperative instrument or equipment to ensure that the discrepancy will
not affect the operation of any other installed instruments or equipment. If the item is not repaired or
replaced, ensure that it has been properly placarded before flight. Whenever picking up an aircraft
after any maintenance, always ensure that an entry has been made in the aircraft records indicating
that it has been approved for return to service.

"Required inspections" are those required to be conducted by §91.409(a)(1), (b), or (d); an inspection
program selected under §91.409(e) and (f); §135.411 (a)(1); or inspections and maintenance
programs selected under the provisions of Part 125.

CROSS REFERENCES

Previous designation: 91.165. 91.401, Applicability; Part 43, Maintenance, Preventive Maintenance,
Rebuilding and Alteration; 91.213 Inoperative Instruments and Equipment; 91.409 Inspections;
91.411 Altimeter System and Altitude Reporting Equipment Tests and Inspections; 91.413 ATC
Transponder tests and Inspections.

ADVISORY CIRCULARS

AC 20-106 *Aircraft Inspection for The General Aviation Aircraft Owner* (1978).

AC 43-9C *Maintenance Records* (1998).

AC 91-67 *Minimum Equipment Requirement for General Aviation Operators under FAR Part 91.*
(1991)

CASES

An aircraft owner received a suspension for allowing his airplane to be operated without a current
annual inspection. *Administrator v. Morse*, EA-3766 (1992).

The purpose of the company's discrepancy reporting system was to have any written discrepancy corrected before the aircraft was operated again. The fact that the uncorrected component, which was written up, was not used during the ensuing flights does not make any difference. A pilot never knows when he will have to use or rely on a particular component due to an unexpected turn of events. *Administrator v. Southeast Air, Inc.*, 5 NTSB 705 (1985).

Even though there seemed to be no doubt that the work had been done, the NTSB found a violation of [91.405(b)], because the owner of the airplane failed to ensure that the maintenance personnel made the appropriate entries in the aircraft maintenance records indicating that the aircraft had been approved for return to service. *Administrator v. Reid*, 4 NTSB 934 (1983).

The Law Judge ruled that flying a helicopter with an open discrepancy on a "squawk sheet" was a violation of both §91.405(a), which directs discrepancies to be repaired unless properly deferred, and §91.405(b), which requires discrepancies to be signed off by an authorized person as approved for return to service. The certificate holder was assessed a $2,200 civil penalty. *FAA v. California Helitech*, FAA Order No. 2000-18 (8-11-2000).

The owner/operator of a flight school was assessed a civil penalty of $750 for sending a flight instructor, who happened to be an A&P, out to inspect and fix an aircraft that had just had a propeller strike. The employee was neither qualified to perform major repairs on a propeller, nor provided with the proper tools, manuals, or other approved information to inspect or repair the aircraft. Therefore, he should not have been authorized by the owner/operator to make a decision on airworthiness that led to the decision to fly the aircraft in an unairworthy condition. *FAA v. Gatewood*, FAA Order No. 2001-1 (5-16-2001).

Allowing an aircraft to be repeatedly operated with open discrepancies that could have easily been corrected by following the manufacturer's service bulletin and using the provided kit resulted in the operator being fined $7,500. Because one of the discrepancies listed that the left fuel gauge was "stuck" the operator was also in violation of §91.205(a) and (b)(9). *FAA v. General Aviation, Inc.*, FAA Order No. 98-18 (10-9-1998).

A Part 135 certificate holder's civil penalty of $20,000 was affirmed in the case where they operated an aircraft three times after welding an oil scavenge line instead of replacing it and made no entry regarding the repair or return to service of the aircraft in the logbooks. *FAA v. Larry's Flying Service, Inc.*, FAA Order No. 98-4 (3-12-1998).

On appeal the law judge upheld a penalty of $6,000 for violations of §§91.7, 91.405, and 91.407 (formerly 91.29, 91.167, and 91.165) where a pilot, who had been advised by an FAA Inspector that his aircraft was in a dangerous condition, flew the aircraft after a gear up landing. The law judge rejected the pilot's claim of financial hardship. *FAA v. Costello*, FAA Order No. 93-10 (3-25-1993).

91.407 OPERATION AFTER MAINTENANCE, PREVENTIVE MAINTENANCE, REBUILDING, OR ALTERATION

(a) No person may operate any aircraft that has undergone maintenance, preventive maintenance, rebuilding, or alteration unless —
   (1) It has been approved for return to service by a person authorized under §43.7 of this chapter; and
   (2) The maintenance record entry required by §43.9 or §43.11, as applicable, of this chapter has been made.
(b) No person may carry any person (other than crewmembers) in an aircraft that has been maintained, rebuilt, or altered in a manner that may have appreciably changed its flight characteristics or substantially affected its operation in flight until an appropriately rated pilot with at least a private pilot certificate flies the aircraft, makes an operational check of the maintenance performed or alteration made, and logs the flight in the aircraft records.
(c) The aircraft does not have to be flown as required by paragraph (b) of this section if, prior to flight, ground tests, inspections, or both show conclusively that the maintenance, preventive maintenance, rebuilding, or alteration has not appreciably changed the flight characteristics or substantially affected the flight operation of the aircraft.

EXPLANATION

This section sets forth the specific conditions that must be met after maintenance, preventive maintenance, rebuilding, or alterations have been performed and before an aircraft can be operated.

"Approval for return to service" does not involve the operation of the aircraft. The aircraft must be approved for return to service **before** any operations, including the flight tests provided for in §91.407(b).

CROSS REFERENCES

Previous designation: 91.167. 43.7 Persons Authorized to Approve Aircraft, Airframes, Aircraft Engines, Propellers, Appliances or Component Parts for Return to Service After Maintenance, Preventive Maintenance, Rebuilding and Alteration Records (Except Inspections Performed in Accordance with Part 91, Part 123, Part 125 and 135.411(a)(1) and 135.419; 43.9 Content, Form, and Disposition of Maintenance, Preventive Maintenance, Rebuilding, and Alteration Records (except inspections performed in accordance with Part 91, Part 123 {Part 123 was replaced by part 125. - Ed}, Part 125, §135.411(a)(1), and §135.419 of this chapter).

ADVISORY CIRCULARS

AC 43-9C *Maintenance Records* (1998).

AC 43-12A *Preventive Maintenance* (1983).

CASES

A pilot who did not have a medical certificate flew an aircraft powered by an auto engine without annual inspection or experimental airworthiness certificate after an FAA inspector told him he could not fly the aircraft. The Board affirmed the emergency order revoking his private pilot certificate. *Administrator v. Erickson*, EA-3735 (1992).

An experimental device, designed to control and to limit engine temperature and torque in an aircraft, was installed on an aircraft. Such action was a major alteration requiring the application for a supplemental type certificate. No application was made, no entries regarding the installation were made in the aircraft maintenance records, and there was no approval for return to service. Although required, no flight test was conducted. Subsequently, the aircraft was operated with other than crew members on board. The owner of the aircraft was found to have been responsible for the installation of the equipment. The Board found, that among other regulations, the owner had also violated [91.407(a)(1), (a) (2) and (b)]. Even though the owner did not manipulate the controls, he was held to have "operated" the aircraft since as owner of the aircraft and president of the company that leased it, he caused and/or authorized the flight. *Administrator v. Moore* 5 NTSB 655 (1985).

Neither the placement of unconnected oil lines through wing cavities or the placement of an auxiliary fuel tank properly stowed as cargo in the cargo bay constitutes an alteration for which a Form 337 and appropriate maintenance entries must be made. *FAA v. Africa Air Corp.*, FAA Order No. 99-5 (8-31-1999).

91.407(a)(1) is directed at any "person" involved with the operation of an aircraft, not an operator. Since the definition of "person" includes "an individual," this regulation clearly applies to the pilot of a flight. *Administrator v. Smith*, EA-4869 (2000).

The owner/operator of a flight school was assessed a civil penalty of $750 for sending a flight instructor, who happened to be an A&P, out to inspect and fix an aircraft that had just had a propeller strike. The employee was neither qualified to perform major repairs on a propeller, nor provided with the proper tools, manuals, or other approved information to inspect or repair the aircraft. Therefore, he should not have been authorized by the owner/operator to make a decision on airworthiness that led to the decision to fly the aircraft in an unairworthy condition. *FAA v. Gatewood*, FAA Order No. 2001-1 (5-16-2001).

A Part 135 certificate holder's civil penalty of $20,000 was affirmed in the case where they operated an aircraft three times after welding an oil scavenge line instead of replacing it and made no entry regarding the repair or return to service of the aircraft in the logbooks. *FAA v. Larry's Flying Service, Inc.*, FAA Order No. 98-4 (3-12-1998).

On appeal the law judge upheld a penalty of $6,000 for violations of §§91.7, 91.405, and 91.407 (formerly §§91.29, 91.167, and 91.165) where a pilot, who had been advised by an FAA Inspector that his aircraft was in a dangerous condition, flew the aircraft after a gear up landing. The law judge rejected the pilot's claim of financial hardship. *FAA v. Costello*, FAA Order No. 93-10 (3-25-1993).

91.409 INSPECTIONS

(a) Except as provided in paragraph (c) of this section, no person may operate an aircraft unless, within the preceding 12 calendar months, it has had —
(1) An annual inspection in accordance with part 43 of this chapter and has been approved for return to service by a person authorized by §43.7 of this chapter; or
(2) An inspection for the issuance of an airworthiness certificate in accordance with part 21 of this chapter.
No inspection performed under paragraph (b) of this section may be substituted for any inspection required by this paragraph unless it is performed by a person authorized to perform annual inspections and is entered as an "annual" inspection in the required maintenance records.
(b) Except as provided in paragraph (c) of this section, no person may operate an aircraft carrying any person (other than a crewmember) for hire, and no person may give flight instruction for hire in an aircraft which that person provides, unless within the preceding 100 hours of time in service the aircraft has received an annual or 100-hour inspection and been approved for return to service in accordance with part 43 of this chapter, or has received an inspection for the issuance of an airworthiness certificate in accordance with part 21 of this chapter. The 100-hour limitation may be exceeded by not more than 10 hours while enroute to reach a place where the inspection can be done. The excess time used to reach a place where the inspection can be done must be included in computing the next 100 hours of time in service.
(c) Paragraphs (a) and (b) of this section do not apply to—
(1) An aircraft that carries a special flight permit, a current experimental certificate, or a provisional airworthiness certificate;
(2) An aircraft inspected in accordance with an approved aircraft inspection program under part 125 or 135 of this chapter and so identified by the registration number in the operations specifications of the certificate holder having the approved inspection program;
(3) An aircraft subject to the requirements of paragraph (d) or (e) of this section; or
(4) Turbine-powered rotorcraft when the operator elects to inspect that rotorcraft in accordance with paragraph (e) of this section.
(d) *Progressive inspection.* Each registered owner or operator of an aircraft desiring to use a progressive inspection program must submit a written request to the FAA Flight Standards district office having jurisdiction over the area in which the applicant is located, and shall provide —
(1) A certificated mechanic holding an inspection authorization, a certificated airframe repair station, or the manufacturer of the aircraft to supervise or conduct the progressive inspection;
(2) A current inspection procedures manual available and readily understandable to pilot and maintenance personnel containing, in detail —
(i) An explanation of the progressive inspection, including the continuity of inspection responsibility, the making of reports, and the keeping of records and technical reference material;
(ii) An inspection schedule, specifying the intervals in hours or days when routine and detailed inspections will be performed and including instructions for exceeding an inspection interval by not more than 10 hours while enroute and for changing an inspection interval because of service experience;
(iii) Sample routine and detailed inspection forms and instructions for their use; and
(iv) Sample reports and records and instructions for their use;
(3) Enough housing and equipment for necessary disassembly and proper inspection of the aircraft; and

(4) Appropriate current technical information for the aircraft.
The frequency and detail of the progressive inspection shall provide for the complete inspection of the aircraft within each 12 calendar months and be consistent with the manufacturer's recommendations, field service experience, and the kind of operation in which the aircraft is engaged. The progressive inspection schedule must ensure that the aircraft, at all times, will be airworthy and will conform to all applicable FAA aircraft specifications, type certificate data sheets, airworthiness directives, and other approved data. If the progressive inspection is discontinued, the owner or operator shall immediately notify the local FAA Flight Standards district office, in writing, of the discontinuance. After the discontinuance, the first annual inspection under §91.409(a)(1) is due within 12 calendar months after the last complete inspection of the aircraft under the progressive inspection. The 100-hour inspection under §91.409(b) is due within 100 hours after that complete inspection. A complete inspection of the aircraft, for the purpose of determining when the annual and 100-hour inspections are due, requires a detailed inspection of the aircraft and all its components in accordance with the progressive inspection. A routine inspection of the aircraft and a detailed inspection of several components is not considered to be a complete inspection.

(e) *Large airplanes (to which part 125 is not applicable), turbojet multi-engine airplanes, turbopropeller-powered multi-engine airplanes, and turbine-powered rotorcraft.* No person may operate a large airplane, turbojet multi-engine airplane, turbopropeller-powered multi-engine airplane, or turbine-powered rotorcraft unless the replacement times for life-limited parts specified in the aircraft specifications, type data sheets, or other documents approved by the Administrator are complied with and the airplane or turbine-powered rotorcraft, including the airframe, engines, propellers, rotors, appliances, survival equipment, and emergency equipment, is inspected in accordance with an inspection program selected under the provisions of paragraph (f) of this section, except that, the owner or operator of a turbine-powered rotorcraft may elect to use the inspection provisions of §91.409(a), (b), (c), or (d) in lieu of an inspection option of §91.409(f).

(f) *Selection of inspection program under paragraph (e) of this section.* The registered owner or operator of each airplane or turbine-powered rotorcraft described in paragraph (e) of this section must select, identify in the aircraft maintenance records, and use one of the following programs for the inspection of the aircraft:

(1) A continuous airworthiness inspection program that is part of a continuous airworthiness maintenance program currently in use by a person holding an air carrier operating certificate or an operating certificate issued under part 121 or 135 of this chapter and operating that make and model aircraft under part 121 of this chapter or operating that make and model under part 135 of this chapter and maintaining it under §135.411(a)(2) of this chapter.

(2) An approved aircraft inspection program approved under §135.419 of this chapter and currently in use by a person holding an operating certificate issued under part 135 of this chapter.

(3) An current inspection program recommended by the manufacturer.

(4) Any other inspection program established by the registered owner or operator of that airplane or turbine-powered rotorcraft and approved by the Administrator under paragraph (g) of this section. However, the Administrator may require revision to this inspection program in accordance with the provisions of §91.415.
Each operator shall include in the selected program the name and address of the person responsible for scheduling the inspections required by the program and make a copy of that program available to the person performing inspections on the aircraft and, upon request, to the Administrator.

(g) *Inspection program approved under paragraph (e) of this section.* Each operator of an airplane or turbine-powered rotorcraft desiring to establish or change an approved inspection program under paragraph (f)(4) of this section must submit the program for approval to the local FAA Flight Standards district office having jurisdiction over the area in which the aircraft is based. The program must be in writing and include at least the following information:

(1) Instructions and procedures for the conduct of inspections for the particular make and model airplane or turbine-powered rotorcraft, including necessary tests and checks. The instructions and procedures must set forth in detail the parts and areas of the airframe, engines, propellers, rotors, and appliances, including survival and emergency equipment required to be inspected.

(2) A schedule for performing the inspections that must be performed under the program expressed in terms of the time in service, calendar time, number of system operations, or any combination of these.

(h) *Changes from one inspection program to another.* When an operator changes from one inspection program under paragraph (f) of this section to another, the time in service, calendar times, or cycles of operation accumulated under the previous program must be applied in determining inspection due times under the new program.

EXPLANATION

If a person provides his/her own aircraft when receiving flight instruction that is being given for hire, the aircraft is not required to have a 100-hour inspection.

Aircraft provided under rental or lease agreement without a pilot (dry lease) are not required to have a 100-hour inspection.

A person may seek reconsideration of changes, directed by the FAA, to a §91.409(f)(4) inspection program under the provisions of §91.415. A Petition for Reconsideration must be filed within 30 days after the receipt of the notice from the FAA.

The requirement for a 100-hour inspection can be satisfied by an annual inspection or one done for the purpose of issuing an airworthiness certificate under Part 21 if accomplished within the preceding 100 hours of time in service.

When receiving an aircraft back after an annual or 100 hour inspection, in addition to checking the entry approving it for return service, check the airworthiness directive list to ensure that all those that were due were accomplished and appropriate notations made.

CROSS REFERENCES

Previous designation: 91.169. 91.401 Applicability; 91.415, Changes to Aircraft Inspection Programs.

ADVISORY CIRCULARS

AC 20-106 *Aircraft Inspection for General Aviation Aircraft Owner* (1978).

AC 39-7C *Airworthiness Directives* (1995).

AC 43-9C *Maintenance Records* (1998).

AC 43.13-1B *Acceptable Methods, Techniques and Practices Aircraft Inspection and Repair* (2001).

AC 65-13T *FAA Inspection Authorization Directory* (1999).

CASES

An aircraft owner received a suspension for allowing his airplane to be operated without a current annual inspection. *Administrator v. Morse*, EA-3766 (1992).

In a case where a pilot operated an aircraft when it had not had an annual inspection within the preceding 12 calendar months, the Board upheld a finding of violation of [91.409(a)(1)] but it did not impose a sanction. The Board said that the pilot's reliance on owner's representation regarding the condition of the aircraft, and his personal experience with the plane including occasional reviews of its maintenance records that led him to assume that it was being properly maintained, did not appear so unreasonable as to warrant a sanction for the violation growing out of this reliance. The Board went further and said that the regulations did not require him to make a records check and since he was only a sporadic user of the aircraft, the direct responsibility for ensuring timely annual inspection lies with the owner of the aircraft. *Administrator v. Miller*, 5 NTSB 407 (1985). [Editor's Note: There was still a finding of violation.]

A renter pilot received a 15 day suspension for flying an airplane without a current annual inspection. The NTSB stated that it was not reasonable to presume that an aircraft held out for rental would be perfectly maintained and inspected. *Administrator v. Southworth*, EA-4742 (1999).

Section 91.409(b) is directed at any "person" involved with the operation of an aircraft, not an operator. Since the definition of "person" includes "an individual," this regulation clearly applies to the pilot of a flight. *Administrator v. Smith*, EA-4869 (2000).

Presuming that an aircraft offered for rent is perfectly maintained and inspected is not reasonable. The pilot-in-command is ultimately responsible for conducting the flight in accordance with applicable regulations, one of which prohibits the operation of an aircraft that has not received an annual inspection with the past 12 months. The expectation that an inspection had been done is not sufficient to relieve a pilot from this responsibility. *Administrator v. Southworth*, EA-4742 (1999).

FAA CHIEF COUNSEL OPINIONS

If a person merely leases or rents an aircraft to another person and does not provide the pilot, the aircraft is not required by [91.409(b)] to have a 100-hour inspection. (1984).

In the case of a tow plane towing a glider which was carrying a passenger for hire, the tow plane would not require a 100-hour inspection, but the glider would be required to have a 100-hour inspection. (1977).

When a Part 141 certificated school uses an aircraft in its school operations, it must be maintained and inspected in accordance with the requirements of Part 91 that apply to aircraft used to give flight instruction for hire, [91.409(b)]. This means that aircraft used by the school's students for solo flight must have 100-hour inspections. (1975).

The requirement for a 100-hour maintenance inspection under §91.409 applies to any aircraft used to carry any person, other than a crewmember, for hire, or to provide flight instruction for hire along with providing the aircraft, regardless of the ownership of the aircraft. Thus, flying clubs are only exempt from this required inspection if they do not carry persons for hire or provide flight instruction with the provided aircraft, or if they fall under one of the four exemptions under §91.409(c). (2-24-00).

91.410 SPECIAL MAINTENANCE PROGRAM REQUIREMENTS

(a) No person may operate an Airbus Model A300 (excluding the -600 series), British Aerospace Model BAC 1-11, Boeing Model, 707, 720, 727, 737 or 747, McDonnell Douglas Model DC-8, DC-9/MD-80 or DC-10, Fokker Model F28, or Lockheed Model L-1011 airplane beyond applicable flight cycle implementation time specified below, or May 25, 2001, whichever occurs later, unless repair assessment guidelines applicable to the fuselage pressure boundary (fuselage skin, door skin, and bulkhead webs) that have been approved by the FAA Aircraft Certification Office (ACO), or office of the Transport Airplane Directorate, having cognizance over the type certificate for the affected airplane are incorporated within its inspection program:

    (1) For the Airbus Model A300 (excluding the -600 series), the flight cycle implementation time is:

        (i)   Model B2: 36,000 flights.

        (ii) Model B4-100 (including Model B4-2C): 30,000 flights above the window line, and 36,000 flights below the window line.

        (iii) Model B4-200: 25,500 flights above the window line, and 34,000 flights below the window line.

    (2) For all models of the British Aerospace BAC 1-11, the flight cycle implementation time is 60,000 flights.

    (3) For all models of the Boeing 707, the flight cycle implementation time is 15,000 flights.

    (4) For all models of the Boeing 720, the flight cycle implementation time is 23,000 flights.

    (5) For all models of the Boeing 727, the flight cycle implementation time is 45,000 flights.

    (6) For all models of the Boeing 737, the flight cycle implementation time is 60,000 flights.

    (7) For all models of the Boeing 747, the flight cycle implementation time is 15,000 flights.

    (8) For all models of the McDonnell Douglas DC-8, the flight cycle implementation time is 30,000 flights.

    (9) For all models of the McDonnell Douglas DC-9/MD-80, the flight cycle implementation time is 60,000 flights.

    (10) For all models of the McDonnell Douglas DC-10, the flight cycle implementation time is 30,000 flights.

    (11) For all models of the Lockheed L-1011, the flight cycle implementation time is 27,000 flights.

    (12) For the Fokker F-28 Mark 1000, 2000, 3000, and 4000, the flight cycle implementation time is 60,000 flights.

(b) After June 7, 2004, no person may operate a turbine-powered transport category airplane with a type certificate issued after January 1, 1958, and either a maximum type certificated passenger capacity of 30 or more, or a maximum type certificated payload capacity of 7,500 pounds or more, unless instructions for maintenance and inspection of the fuel tank system are incorporated into its inspection program. These instructions must address the actual configuration of the fuel tank systems of each affected airplane, and must be approved by the FAA Aircraft Certification Office (ACO), or office of the Transport Airplane Directorate, having cognizance over the type certificate for the affected airplane. Operators must submit their request through the cognizant Flight Standards District Office, who may add comments and then send it to the manager of the appropriate office. Thereafter, the approved instructions can be revised only with the approval of the FAA Aircraft Certification Office (ACO), or office of the Transport Airplane Directorate, having cognizance over the type certificate for the affected airplane. Operators must submit their request for revisions through the cognizant Flight Standards District Office, who may add comments and then send it to the manager of the appropriate office.

PREAMBLE

In April 1988, a high-cycle transport airplane enroute from Hilo to Honolulu, Hawaii, suffered major structural damage to its pressurized fuselage during flight. This accident was attributed in part to the age of the airplane involved. The economic benefit of operating certain older technology airplanes has resulted in the operation of many such airplanes beyond their previously projected retirement age. Because of the problems revealed by the accident in Hawaii and the continued operation of older airplanes, both the FAA and industry generally agreed that increased attention needed to be focused on the aging fleet and on maintaining its continued operational safety.

In June 1988, the FAA sponsored a conference on aging airplanes. As a result of that conference, the FAA established a task force in August 1988 as a sub-group of the FAA's Research, Engineering, the Development Advisory Committee, representing the interests of the aircraft operators, aircraft manufacturers, regulatory authorities, and other aviation representatives. The task force, then known as the Airworthiness Assurance Task Force (AATF), set forth five major elements of a program for each airplane model in the aging transport fleet that would serve to keep the aging fleet safe:

- Select service bulletins describing modificaitons and inspections necessary to maintain structural integrity;
- Develop inspection and prevention programs to address corrosion;
- Develop generic structural maintenance program guidelines for aging airplanes;
- Review and update the Supplemental Structural Inspection Documents (SSID) which describe inspection programs to detect fatigue cracking, and
- Assess damage-tolerance of structural repairs.

By Federal Register notice, dated November 30, 1992 (57 FR 56627), the AATF was placed under the auspices of the Aviation Rulemaking Advisory Committee (ARAC) and renamed as the Airworthiness Assurance Working Group (AAWG). Structures Task Groups, sponsored by the AAWG, were assigned the task of developing the five elements into workable programs. The AAWG completed work on the first four of the elements lists above at the time Notice 97-16 was issued. Issuance of this final rule completes the fifth element.

This final rule addresses the specific task assigned to the AAWG relevant to the fifth element, which was to develop recommendations concerning whether new or revised requirements and compliance methods for structural repair assessments of existing repairs should be initiated and mandated for the following airplanes.

- Airbus Model A300 (excluding the -600 series);
- British Aerospace Model BAC 1-11;
- Boeing Models 707/720, 727, 737, and 747;
- McDonnell Douglas Models DC-8, DC-9/MD-80, and DC-10;
- Fokker Model F-28;and
- Lockheed Model L-1011.

(65 FR 24108-24109).

ADVISORY CIRCULARS

AC 120-73 *Damage Tolerance Assessment of Repairs to Pressurized Fuselages* (2000).

91.411 ALTIMETER SYSTEM AND ALTITUDE REPORTING EQUIPMENT TESTS AND INSPECTIONS

(a)   No person may operate an airplane, or helicopter, in controlled airspace under IFR unless —
  (1)   Within the preceding 24 calendar months, each static pressure system, each altimeter instrument, and each automatic pressure altitude reporting system has been tested and inspected and found to comply with Appendix E of part 43 of this chapter:
  (2)   Except for the use of system drain and alternate static pressure valves, following any opening and closing of the static pressure system, that system has been tested and inspected and found to comply with paragraph (a), Appendices E and F, of part 43 of this chapter; and
  (3)   Following installation or maintenance on the automatic pressure altitude reporting system of the ATC transponder where data correspondence error could be introduced, the integrated system has been tested, inspected, and found to comply with paragraph (c), Appendix E, of part 43 of this chapter.
(b)   The tests required by paragraph (a) of this section must be conducted by —
  (1)   The manufacturer of the airplane, or helicopter, on which the tests and inspections are to be performed;
  (2)   A certificated repair station properly equipped to perform those functions and holding —
      (i)   An instrument rating, Class I;
      (ii)   A limited instrument rating appropriate to the make and model of appliance to be tested;
      (iii) A limited rating appropriate to the test to be performed;
      (iv)   An airframe rating appropriate to the airplane, or helicopter, to be tested; or
      (v)   A limited rating for a manufacturer issued for the appliance in accordance with §145.101(b)(4) of this chapter; or
  (3)   A certificated mechanic with an airframe rating (static pressure system tests and inspections only).
(c)   Altimeter and altitude reporting equipment approved under Technical Standard Orders are considered to be tested and inspected as of the date of their manufacture.
(d)   No person may operate an airplane, or helicopter, in controlled airspace under IFR at an altitude above the maximum altitude at which all altimeters and the automatic altitude reporting system of that airplane, or helicopter, have been tested.

EXPLANATION

§91.411(b)(2)(v) removed August 6, 2001, effective April 6, 2003.

Always ensure that the person/facility that is to perform the required test or inspection is qualified to do so. §91.411(b) sets forth what is required.

Prior to a flight under IFR in controlled airspace be sure to check the altitude at which the instruments/equipment was tested so that you know what your altitude limit is for the flight.

Be aware of the two events, which, in addition to the passage of 24 months since last test and inspection, trigger the need for a test and inspection, set forth in 91.411(a)(2) and (a)(3).

PREAMBLE

FAA Response: As previously noted, the FAA is not adopting the proposed ratings and classes. However, the final rule amends §91.411 by removing paragraph (b)(2)(v), which referred to the limited rating for manufacturers.) (66 FR 41111).

CROSS REFERENCES

Previous designation: 91.171. 91.401, Applicability; Part 43, Appendix E, Altimeter System Test and Inspection; Part 43, Appendix F, ATC Transponder Tests and Inspections; 91.215, ATC Transponder and Altitude Reporting Equipment And Use; 91.217, Data Correspondence Between Automatically Reported Pressure Altitude Data and the Pilot's Altitude Reference.

ADVISORY CIRCULARS

AC 20-106 *Aircraft Inspection for the General Aviation Aircraft Owner* (1978).

AC 39-7C *Airworthiness Directives* (1995).

AC 43-203B *Altimeter and Static System Tests and Inspections* (1979).

FAA CHIEF COUNSEL OPINIONS

If the regulation mandates compliance "within the preceding 24 calendar months," you have from the beginning of the 24th calendar month before the month in which you are required to comply. So, to operate an airplane in controlled airspace under IFR on January 15, 2000, it must have, since January 1, 1998, met the requirements of §91.411(a). (2-24-00).

91.413 ATC TRANSPONDER TESTS AND INSPECTIONS

(a)   No persons may use an ATC transponder that is specified in 91.215(a), 121.345(c), or §135.143(c) of this chapter unless, within the preceding 24 calendar months, the ATC transponder has been tested and inspected and found to comply with appendix F of part 43 of this chapter; and

(b)   Following any installation or maintenance on an ATC transponder where data correspondence error could be introduced, the integrated system has been tested, inspected, and found to comply with paragraph (c), appendix E, of part 43 of this chapter.

(c)   The tests and inspections specified in this section must be conducted by —
    (1)   A certificated repair station properly equipped to perform those functions and holding —
        (i)   A radio rating, Class III;
        (ii)   A limited radio rating appropriate to the make and model transponder to be tested;
        (iii)   A limited rating appropriate to the test to be performed;
        (iv)   A limited rating for a manufacturer issued for the transponder in accordance with §145.101(b)(4) of this chapter; or
    (2) A holder of a continuous airworthiness maintenance program as provided in part 121 or §135.411(a)(2) of this chapter; or
    (3)   The manufacturer of the aircraft on which the transponder to be tested is installed, if the transponder was installed by that manufacturer.

EXPLANATION

§91.413 (c)(1)(iv) removed August 6, 2001, effective April 6, 2003.

This section describes when and by whom ATC transponders must be tested and inspected prior to being used in any operation under Parts 91, 121, 127 or 135 of the FARs.

PREAMBLE

Summary of Proposal/Issue: The proposal would have revised §91.413 to reflect the proposed ratings and classes. In addition, the FAA proposed to eliminate the provision relating to the limited rating for manufacturers.

Comments: A foreign air carrier opposed the proposed specialized service rating.

FAA Response: As previously noted, the FAA is not adopting the proposed ratings and classes. However, the final rule amends §91.413 by removing paragraph (c)(1)(iv), which referred to the limited rating for manufacturers. (66 FR 41111).

CROSS REFERENCES

Previous designation: 91.172. Part 43, Appendix F, ATC Transponder Tests and Inspections; 91.215(a), ATC Transponder and Altitude Reporting Equipment And Use; 121.345(c) Radio Equipment; 127.123(b), Radio Equipment; 135.143(c) General Requirements; 145.101(b)(4), Application and Issue, Limited Ratings For Manufacturers (Repair Station Certificates).

ADVISORY CIRCULARS

AC 20-106 *Aircraft Inspection For The General Aviation Aircraft Owner* (1978).

AC 43-6A *Automatic Pressure Altitude Encoding Systems And Transponders Maintenance And Inspection Practices* (1977).

91.415 CHANGES TO AIRCRAFT INSPECTION PROGRAMS

(a)   Whenever the Administrator finds that revisions to an approved aircraft inspection program under §91.409(f)(4) are necessary for the continued adequacy of the program, the owner or operator shall, after notification by the Administrator, make any changes in the program found to be necessary by the Administrator.

(b)   The owner or operator may petition the Administrator to reconsider the notice to make any changes in a program in accordance with paragraph (a) of this section.

(c)   The petition must be filed with the FAA Flight Standards district office which requested the change to the program within 30 days after the certificate holder receives the notice.

(d)   Except in the case of an emergency requiring immediate action in the interest of safety, the filing of the petition stays the notice pending a decision by the Administrator.

EXPLANATION

Under this section the FAA can require changes in an approved aircraft inspection program. It also sets forth the procedure for having the FAA reconsider its action, if the owner or operator does not consider the change necessary or appropriate. Caution must be taken since there is a time limit for requesting reconsideration; i.e., within 30 days of receipt of FAA notice.

CROSS REFERENCES

Previous designation: 91.170. 91.409(f)(4), Inspections.

91.417 MAINTENANCE RECORDS

(a)   Except for work performed in accordance with §§91.411 and 91.413, each registered owner or operator shall keep the following records for the periods specified in paragraph (b) of this section:

(1)   Records of the maintenance, preventive maintenance, and alteration, and records of the 100-hour, annual, progressive, and other required or approved inspections, as appropriate, for each aircraft (including the airframe) and each engine, propeller, rotor, and appliance of an aircraft. The records must include —

(i)   A description (or reference to data acceptable to the Administrator) of the work performed; and

(ii)   The date of completion of the work performed; and

(iii)   The signature and certificate number of the person approving the aircraft for return to service.

   (2)   Records containing the following information:

       (i)   The total time in service of the airframe, each engine, each propeller, and each rotor.

      (ii)   The current status of life-limited parts of each airframe, engine, propeller, rotor, and appliance.

    (iii)   The time since last overhaul of all items installed on the aircraft which are required to be overhauled on a specified time basis.

    (iv)   The current inspection status of the aircraft, including the time since the last inspection required by the inspection program under which the aircraft and its appliances are maintained.

     (v)   The current status of applicable airworthiness directives (AD) including, for each, the method of compliance, the AD number, and revision date. If the AD involves recurring action, the time and date when the next action is required.

    (vi)   Copies of the forms prescribed by §43.9(a) of this chapter for each major alteration to the airframe and currently installed engines, rotors, propellers, and appliances.

(b)   The owner or operator shall retain the following records for the periods prescribed:

   (1)   The records specified in paragraph (a)(1) of this section shall be retained until the work is repeated or superseded by other work or for 1 year after the work is performed.

   (2)   The records specified in paragraph (a)(2) of this section shall be retained and transferred with the aircraft at the time the aircraft is sold.

   (3)   A list of defects furnished to a registered owner or operator under §43.11 of this chapter shall be retained until the defects are repaired and the aircraft is approved for return to service.

(c)   The owner or operator shall make all maintenance records required to be kept by this section available for inspection by the Administrator or any authorized representative of the National Transportation Safety Board (NTSB). In addition, the owner or operator shall present Form 337 described in paragraph (d) of this section for inspection upon request of any law enforcement officer.

(d)   When a fuel tank is installed within the passenger compartment or a baggage compartment pursuant to part 43 of this chapter, a copy of FAA Form 337 shall be kept on board the modified aircraft by the owner or operator.

EXPLANATION

The FAA classifies the installation of glider wings and tail surfaces, specifically designed for quick disassembly and assembly; the installation of balloon baskets and burners, specifically designed for quick removal; and the assembly of gliders and balloons as operational functions as opposed to maintenance functions. Therefore, in the case of the above described functions no entry needs to be made in the aircraft maintenance records. However, where a balloon has been type certificated to permit use of multiple models of baskets, the FAA has determined that this component interchange constitutes preventive maintenance and the appropriate entries must be made.

The terms "life limited parts" refer to parts or components for which retirement or life limitations exist. Such limitations are those required by the FAA and set forth on the type certificate data sheet or product specification that is part of the type certificate. They also may be established in an airworthiness directive, operations specifications, FAA-approved maintenance program, including an inspection program, or in the limitation section of an Airplane Flight Manual or other manual required by an operating rule. The terms "required to be overhauled on a specific basis" means "required" by the FAA under the FAR and refers to items that must be overhauled on a specific or "hard time" in-service basis established by one of the same procedures as apply to life-limited parts.

The requirements regarding the FAA Form 337 for fuel tank installations in the passenger compartment or baggage compartments applies to all aircraft, even those operating under a special flight permit for the purpose of delivery or export. This requirement is mandated by §605(c) of the Federal Aviation Act of 1958, as amended (49 U.S.C. App. 1425(c)) as part of the U.S. war on drugs.

When reviewing the records, after an aircraft has been returned following an inspection or maintenance, an owner or operator should ensure that all required data has been updated to its current status.

While not required by the FAR, in view of the difficulty in reconstructing the maintenance records in the event they are lost or destroyed, consideration should be given to photocopying the records on a regular basis so that there is an up-to-date duplicate set of records.

CROSS REFERENCES

Previous designation: 91.173. 91.401, Applicability; Part 39, Airworthiness Directives; 43.9, Content, Form And Disposition Of Maintenance, Preventive Maintenance, Rebuilding, and Alteration Record (Except Inspections Performed in Accordance With Part 91, Part 123, Part 125 and 135. 411(a)(1) and 135.419; 91.405, Maintenance Required; 91.409, Inspections.

ADVISORY CIRCULARS

AC 20-106, *Aircraft Inspection for the General Aviation Aircraft Owner* (1978).

AC 43-9C *Maintenance Records* (1998).

AC 43-12A, *Preventive Maintenance* (1983).

CASES

A violation of [91.417(c)] was upheld where owner, who was responsible for the maintenance of the aircraft, failed to ensure that there was a reconstruction of the aircraft logbooks which had been stolen. *Administrator v. Robbins*, 5 NTSB 807 (1983).

§91.417 requires that "the current status of applicable airworthiness directives, including the date" must be kept. Each of these entries indicates the current status of the AD at the time the entry was completed, and per §13.7 these entries may be used to prove past violations where the AD was not complied within the required interval. *FAA v. Scenic Mountain Air, Inc.*, FAA Order No. 2001-5 (5-16-2001).

A civil penalty of $1,400 was imposed on an operator who allowed an aircraft to be flown when it had exceeded certain time intervals where maintenance was required that had not been performed. Operators must select and adhere to a method of determining the time in operation in order to comply with maintenance requirements. If the operator has been using tachometer time for this purpose, it cannot later assert as a defense for not complying with maintenance requirements that it was not required to perform certain maintenance because its tachometer was inaccurate. *FAA v. Watts Agricultural Aviation, Inc.*, FAA Order No. 91-8 (4-11-1991).

FAA CHIEF COUNSEL OPINIONS

[91.417(a)(2)(v)] requires the recordation of "checks" whenever and by whomever performed in compliance with an airworthiness directive requirement. The term "check" is understood to mean work in the nature of a simple inspection which, under the terms of an airworthiness directive, may be performed by a flight crewmember who is not a certificated mechanic. (1977).

FAR §§91.417(a)(2)(ii), 121.380(a)(2)(ii), and 135.439(a)(2)(ii) require owners, operators, or certificate holders to keep records containing the current status of life-limited parts of each airframe, engine, propeller, rotor, and appliance. The current status of a life-limited part always has been interpreted as the total time on the life-limited part. The area of dispute is as to how an operator must demonstrate to the FAA that the recorded total time on the life-limited part is accurate.

Under these sections, the operator needs to maintain a record keeping system that will substantiate the time that has accrued on the life-limited part. A complete audit trail to the origin is not needed for all life-limited parts. However, it is the responsibility of the operator to substantiate that its record keeping system produces sufficient and accurate data to determine how the current status was obtained. The requirement is merely to show with a sufficient degree of certainty that the time elapsed on a life-limited part is correct. An audit trail tracing a life-limited part back to its origin would be required only in those situations where the operator's records are so incomplete that an accurate determination of the time elapsed on the life-limited part could not be made. The FAA would expect a request for such records to be the exception rather than the norm. (6-1-92).

91.419 TRANSFER OF MAINTENANCE RECORDS

Any owner or operator who sells a U.S.-registered aircraft shall transfer to the purchaser, at the time of sale, the following records of that aircraft, in plain language form or in coded form at the election of the purchaser, if the coded form provides for the preservation and retrieval of information in a manner acceptable to the Administrator.

(a) The records specified in §91.417(a)(2).

(b) The records specified in §91.417(a)(1) which are not included in the records covered by paragraph (a) of this section, except that the purchaser may permit the seller to keep physical custody of such records. However, custody of records by the seller does not relieve the purchaser of the responsibility under §91.417(c), to make the records available for inspection by the Administrator or any authorized representative of the National Transportation Safety Board (NTSB).

EXPLANATION

If a problem occurs between buyer and seller and the seller refuses to transfer the maintenance records to the buyer, the matter must be resolved by agreement or in the courts. The FAA does not have the authority to demand that the seller transfer the records to the buyer. The FAA can, in the appropriate case, institute enforcement action against the seller for violation of this section.

If, under the provisions of this regulation, a buyer allows the seller to retain physical custody of some of the records, if a demand is made under §91.417(c) that these records be produced, it is the buyer who is responsible to produce them. The seller's refusal to produce them might not be a valid excuse for the buyer.

CROSS REFERENCES

Previous designation: 91.174. 91.401, Applicability; 91.417, Maintenance Records.

ADVISORY CIRCULARS

AC 43-9C *Maintenance Records* (1998).

AC 39-7C *Airworthiness Directives* (1995).

91.421 REBUILT ENGINE MAINTENANCE RECORDS

(a)   The owner or operator may use a new maintenance record, without previous operating history, for an aircraft engine rebuilt by the manufacturer or by an agency approved by the manufacturer.

(b)   Each manufacturer or agency that grants zero time to an engine rebuilt by it shall enter in the new record —
   (1)   A signed statement of the date the engine was rebuilt;
   (2)   Each change made as required by airworthiness directives; and
   (3)   Each change made in compliance with manufacturer's service bulletins, if the entry is specifically requested in that bulletin.

(c)   For the purposes of this section, a rebuilt engine is a used engine that has been completely disassembled, inspected, repaired as necessary, reassembled, tested, and approved in the same manner and to the same tolerances and limits as a new engine with either new or used parts. However, all parts used in it must conform to the production drawing tolerances and limits for new parts or be of approved oversize or undersized dimensions for a new engine.

EXPLANATION

If an engine is rebuilt by anyone other than the manufacturer, always confirm that the rebuilding agency/person has been approved to do the work by the manufacturer. Never accept someone's word on this matter.

CROSS REFERENCES

Previous designation: 91.175. 91.417, Maintenance Records.

ADVISORY CIRCULARS

AC 43-9C *Maintenance Records* (1998).

INTENTIONALLY

LEFT

BLANK

INTENTIONALLY

LEFT

BLANK

SUBPART F — LARGE AND TURBINE-POWERED MULTI-ENGINE AIRPLANES

91.501 APPLICABILITY

(a)   This subpart prescribes operating rules, in addition to those prescribed in other subparts of this part, governing the operation of large and of turbojet-powered multi-engine civil airplanes of U.S. registry. The operating rules in this subpart do not apply to those airplanes when they are required to be operated under parts 121, 125, 129, 135, and 137 of this chapter. (Section 91.409 prescribes an inspection program for large and for turbine-powered (turbojet and turboprop) multi-engine airplanes of U.S. registry when they are operated under this part or parts 129 or 137.)

(b)   Operations that may be conducted under the rules in this subpart instead of those in parts 121, 129, 135, and 137 of this chapter when common carriage is not involved, include —

(1)   Ferry or training flights;

(2)   Aerial work operations such as aerial photography or survey, or pipeline patrol, but not including fire fighting operations;

(3)   Flights for the demonstration of an airplane to prospective customers when no charge is made except for those specified in paragraph (d) of this section;

(4)   Flights conducted by the operator of an airplane for his personal transportation, or the transportation of his guests when no charge, assessment, or fee is made for the transportation;

(5)   Carriage of officials, employees, guests, and property of a company on an airplane operated by that company, or the parent or a subsidiary of the company or a subsidiary of the parent, when the carriage is within the scope of, and incidental to, the business of the company (other than transportation by air) and no charge, assessment or fee is made for the carriage in excess of the cost of owning, operating, and maintaining the airplane, except that no charge of any kind may be made for the carriage of a guest of a company, when the carriage is not within the scope of, and incidental to, the business of that company.

(6)   The carriage of company officials, employees, and guests of the company on an airplane operated under a time sharing, interchange, or joint ownership agreement as defined in paragraph (c) of this section;

(7)   The carriage of property (other than mail) on an airplane operated by a person in the furtherance of a business or employment (other than transportation by air) when the carriage is within the scope of, and incidental to, that business or employment and no charge, assessment, or fee is made for the carriage other than those specified in paragraph (d) of this section;

(8)   The carriage on an airplane of an athletic team, sports group, choral group, or similar group having a common purpose or objective when there is no charge, assessment, or fee of any kind made by any person for that carriage; and

(9)   The carriage of persons on an airplane operated by a person in the furtherance of a business other than transportation by air for the purpose of selling them land, goods, or property, including franchises or distributorships, when the carriage is within the scope of, and incidental to, that business and no charge, assessment, or fee is made for that carriage.

(c)   As used in this section —

    (1)   A "time sharing agreement" means an arrangement whereby a person leases his airplane with flight crew to another person, and no charge is made for the flights conducted under that arrangement other than those specified in paragraph (d) of this section;

    (2)   An "interchange agreement" means an arrangement whereby a person leases his airplane to another person in exchange for equal time, when needed, on the other person's airplane, and no charge, assessment, or fee is made, except that a charge may be made not to exceed the difference between the cost of owning, operating, and maintaining the two airplanes;

    (3)   A "joint ownership agreement" means an arrangement whereby one of the registered joint owners of an airplane employs and furnishes the flight crew for that airplane and each of the registered joint owners pays a share of the charge specified in the agreement.

(d)   The following may be charged, as expenses of a specific flight, for transportation as authorized by paragraphs (b)(3) and (7) and (c)(1) of this section:

    (1)   Fuel, oil, lubricants, and other additives.

    (2)   Travel expenses of the crew, including food, lodging, and ground transportation.

    (3)   Hangar and tie-down costs away from the aircraft's base of operations.

    (4)   Insurance obtained for the specific flight.

    (5)   Landing fees, airport taxes, and similar assessments.

    (6)   Customs, foreign permit, and similar fees directly related to the flight.

    (7)   In flight food and beverages.

    (8)   Passenger ground transportation.

    (9)   Flight planning and weather contract services.

    (10) An additional charge equal to 100 percent of the expenses listed in paragraph (d)(1) of this section.

EXPLANATION

91.501(a): The applicability of Subpart F is widely misunderstood. Although the title of the Subpart might suggest that this Subpart governs turboprops under 12,500 pounds, the language of 91.501(a) excludes small turboprops from coverage. 91.501(a) fails to mention that an exemption to operate a small turboprop under this subpart can be easily obtained. The procedures for seeking an exemption are set forth in Part 11 of the Federal Aviation Regulations. Such an exemption has been issued to the National Business Aircraft Association for its members. (See Exemption 1637).

The provisions of Subpart F do not apply to helicopters, unless the operator has an exemption (the NBAA exemption applies to helicopters as well).

Only U.S. registered aircraft may be operated under Subpart F.

The lease of an aircraft without crew (referred to by the FAA as a "dry" lease) is not governed by §91.501. The FAA does not regulate the pricing of dry leases.

The potential hazards involved in the leasing of aircraft include tort liability, asset forfeitures by Customs or Drug Enforcement Agency, foreign statutory liens, etc. Any lease agreement should speak to all such issues, no matter how short the term of the lease. Where an airplane is leased with flight crew to another, it is considered a "wet lease." In the case of a "wet lease" there is a presumption that operational control and safety responsibility for the airplane remains with the lessor. Accordingly, the intent of the parties should be clearly spelled out in the lease or operating agreement. Refer to §91.23 for written lease requirements.

Any operation conducted under the provisions of §91.501, where any fee or charge is made, may have tax and insurance consequences. Prior to entering into any of these arrangements, consultation with insurance and tax advisors is imperative. Some of the matters that must be considered include liability for the payment of transportation tax, IRS recognized "affiliated group" status and insurance policy exclusions for the operation of an airplane for compensation or hire.

Under §91.501(a) the rules of Subpart F, including the expense recoupment provisions, do not apply to the described airplanes if they are required to be operated under the certification rules of Parts 121, 125, 129, 135, and 137 of Subchapter G of the FAR. §91.501 is aimed primarily at the corporate airplane operator who wishes to conduct company business without following the more stringent safety and certification requirements of the FAR that apply to commercial operators responsible for transporting the public. Where a corporation is established **solely** to own and operate an airplane so as to provide transportation to a parent corporation, subsidiary corporation or other corporation, it cannot operate under the provisions of §91.501, but must obtain an appropriate operating certificate under Parts 135 or 121.

91.501(b): The four elements of "common carriage" are: (1) a holding out of a willingness to (2) transport persons or property (3) from place to place (4) for compensation. Essentially, it is a known willingness to fly anyone anywhere anytime for hire.

91.501(b)(5): The cost of owning, operating, and maintaining an airplane can be determined by reference to the costs associated with the use of the airplane as established by the accounting department in the conduct of the normal business of the company.

Note that the FAR does not prevent an airplane owner from accepting less reimbursement, it only prohibits the owner from accepting more than the cost of airplane ownership, operation, and maintenance.

91.501(b)(6): This regulation does not authorize the carriage of property under "time sharing agreements," "interchange agreements" or "joint ownership agreements".

91.501(c)(1): Lessees may enter into "time sharing agreements." There is no requirement that the operator of the aircraft be the registered owner.

91.501(c)(2): An "interchange agreement" must provide for "equal" time, not "equivalent" time. The difference in the cost of operating the airplane for equal times can be covered by the terms of the agreement provided the charge does not exceed the difference between the cost of owning, operating and maintaining the two airplanes.

91.501(c)(3): The term "joint ownership agreement" does not specifically limit the number of joint owners. In the "joint ownership agreement" arrangement all owners must appear on the registration certificate.

91.501(d): If an operator feels that it has a unique situation which would justify the allowance of an additional charge not provided for in §91.501(d), a petition for an exemption, allowing the cost to be recovered, may be filed under FAR §11.25.

91.501(d)(10): The charge permitted under §91.501(d)(10), 100% of the expenses listed in (d)(1), is to provide for recovery by the operator of an amount that would reasonably approximate expenses not incurred as a direct result of a particular flight, but appropriately attributed to it. Such expenses include salaries of flight crews employed by the airplane operator, aircraft depreciation, insurance premiums, crew training costs and maintenance cost.

PREAMBLE

For many years the term "compensation," as used in the definition of a commercial operator and the applicability provisions of Part 121, has been construed in its legal sense which does not limit that term to an element of profit, but includes any reimbursement for the expenses for the operation of the aircraft. Comments received from the corporate operators strongly urged a change in that policy. They contend that in most cases involving wet lease agreements (lease of an aircraft with flight crew) a charge is made for the operating expenses of the aircraft solely for the purpose of complying with the requirements of the U.S. Internal Revenue Service--not for the purpose of making a profit. Therefore, in response to the request for comments in regard to time sharing and interchange agreements, these commentators urged that a monetary charge be permitted under either of these arrangements, so long as there is no profit motive involved in the charges made.

> As stated in the preamble to NPRM 71-32 the decision to proceed with the upgrading of Part 91 for large and turbine-powered multi engine airplanes is an important threshold step in the FAA policy to remove, to the extent possible, those differences in the safety standards that a primarily economic in nature and result in unnecessary restrictions or limitations on aircraft operators. In accordance with that policy the need for different, or additional safety standards for corporate operations should be resolved on the basis of safety, rather than economics or juristic semantics. Safetywise, we have determined that neither the relationship of the corporations nor the type of compensation received for the services rendered should be relevant or controlling under the standards of the new Subpart [F] for the various corporate kinds of operations that do not involve common carriage. (37 FR 14758).

In order to make this change in policy clear to all interested persons, [§91.501(b)] includes a list of the kinds of operations that may be conducted under Subpart [F]. In addition, [§91.501(c)] of Subpart [F] expressly provides that charges covering the normal operating expenses of the aircraft and salary of the crew may be made under a time sharing or interchange agreement as defined in that section. This policy also applies to a corporation regardless of its relationship, if any, to the corporation for which the carriage is conducted. Accordingly, the application of Subpart [F] to a corporate operator will no longer be dependent upon whether that operator is a parent or subsidiary corporation, or a member of a conglomerate. It should be noted, however, that if a corporation is established solely for the purpose of providing transportation to the parent corporation, a subsidiary, or other corporation, the foregoing policy does not apply. In that case, the primary business of the corporation operating the airplane is transportation and the carriage of persons or goods for any other corporation, for a fee or charge of any kind would require the corporation operating the airplane to hold a commercial operator certificate under Part 121 or 135, as appropriate.

Some of the commentators requested expansion or the applicability of Subpart [F] to permit a jointly owned airplane to be operated under the safety standards of that subpart when the flight crew is furnished and employed by one of the joint owners. In regard to such operations we have concluded that if the flight crew is employed and furnished by one of the joint owners and continues in the employ of that owner when the airplane is used by another joint owner, it will be presumed that the joint owner employing and furnishing the flight crew is the operator of the airplane within the meaning of the Federal Aviation Regulations. Unless otherwise agreed to by the owners, he is responsible for compliance with the safety regulations applicable to that flight, even though the joint owner using the airplane at the particular time has the authority to specify the destination of the flight and the persons or cargo that may be carried on that flight. Safetywise, we perceive no reason under those circumstances to require the joint owner, as the operator of that airplane, to hold a commercial operator certificate. Accordingly, [§91.501(c)] has been amended to permit such operations to be conducted under Subpart [F]. If any charge is made by the operator in excess of the normal operating expenses of the flight, including fuel, oil, hangar and landing fees, and salary of the crew, the operation, of course, may not be conducted under Subpart [F]. When the charges are made, the operator must hold a commercial operator certificate and conduct the operation under the provisions of Part 121 or 35, as appropriate.

The carriage of persons on an airplane for the purpose of selling to them land, goods, or other property (including franchises) was described in the preamble to NPRM 71-32 as a corporate aircraft operation. However, the preamble did not further articulate the FAA policy in regard to such operations when conducted as an incident to the business of the corporation operating the aircraft. In recent years there has been an increase in the use of corporate aircraft for the carriage of prospective customers, especially as an incident to the business of real estate development and sales. It has been the policy of the FAA to permit the corporation to transport those customers on its aircraft without holding a commercial operator certificate, so long as no charge in made for the transportation and common carriage is not involved. It is our opinion that this policy should be continued without change. Accordingly, [§91.501(b)(9)] of the rule as adopted herein expressly permits the carriage of prospective customers under the rules of Subpart [F]. However, no charge of any kind may be made for that carriage, regardless of whether the charge represents the customer's pro rata operating expenses for the flight, or a loss. To permit a charge of any kind for the carriage of the customers would require constant surveillance and time consuming investigations by FAA inspectors to determine if the charge represents an amount that is permitted under the regulations, or is in fact considered compensation as that term is used in the definition of a commercial operator. Moreover, it should be noted that such operations may, under certain circumstances, result in the carriage of persons as a common carrier for compensation or hire. In that event, the person operating the airplane may be required to hold a certificate of public convenience and necessity or other appropriate economic authority from the Civil Aeronautics Board in addition to an air carrier operating certificate from the Administrator.

The preamble to NPRM 71-32 stated that a GENOT was issued by the FAA to make it clear that a "manufacturer" or "aircraft sales company" did not need a commercial operator certificated to demonstrate aircraft in flight to a prospective customer when that customer is charged a fee to defray the normal operating expenses of the flight, including fuel, oil, hangar or landing fees, and salary of the flight crew. In our judgment the authorization should be equally applicable to the owner of the aircraft regardless of whether he is a manufacturer or aircraft salesman. For this reason the language of [§91.501(b)(3)], as proposed in the notice, did not limit such authorization to a "manufacturer" or "aircraft sales company." Since there were no objections to that proposal, the rule as adopted herein permits such customer demonstrations by the owner of the airplane as well as the manufacturer, or sales company.

Inasmuch as the foregoing policies permit a greater use of corporate aircraft under joint ownership, time sharing, and interchange agreements, it appears desirable to restate herein the FAA policy in regard to the operation of an airplane under those agreements when they constitute a wet lease (the lease of an aircraft with a flight crew). When the lessor furnishes both the aircraft and flight crew, there is a presumption that the operational control and safety responsibility for the aircraft remains in the hands of the lessor during the lease agreement and he becomes the operator of the aircraft as that term is used in the Federal Aviation Regulations. This policy conforms with the policy recently adopted by the Civil Aeronautics Board in those cases involving the lease of aircraft with crew by foreign air carriers of other foreign persons.

In view of the comments received in response to the Notice, another change in the applicability of Subpart [F] was made. This change involved the carriage of goods or property on an airplane as an incident to a business other than transportation. Although it has been the policy of the FAA to permit a manufacturer to carry his materials from one factory to another for processing into a finished product to a customer or a distributor if a charge, direct or indirect, was made for such transportation. While this limitation rested upon a proper legal interpretation of the term compensation, it is no longer necessary under the safety standards of Subpart [F]. Accordingly, under the rules as adopted herein, the FAA will permit the carriage of property (other than mail) on an airplane operated by a person in the furtherance of a business (other than transportation), when the carriage is incidental to that business and no charge is made for that carriage in excess of the normal operating expenses of the flight. Although this charge in policy permits a greater use of an airplane as an incident to a business or profession, it does not change the FAA policy in regard to the carriage of goods or property by airplane when such carriage is the primary business of the operator of that airplane. When such carriage is in fact a major enterprise in itself, it may not be conducted by any person unless he holds an operating certificate under Part 121 or 135, as appropriate. (14 CFR Part 218, as amended by ER-716; 36 FR 23146).

The FAA received over 35 comments in response to Notice 72-28. All but one favored adoption of the proposed amendments to Subpart [F] of Par 91. However, most of the commentators favoring adoption recommended that the list of permissible charges in proposed [§91.501(d)] be changed so as to specifically permit charging for expenses that could be attributed to a particular flight, although they are not incurred as a direct result of that flight in that they are incurred irrespective of whether or not the flight is conducted. Such expenses include (1) salaries of flight crews employed by the aircraft operator, (2) aircraft depreciation, (3) insurance premiums (hull and liability), (4) crew training costs, and (5) maintenance costs. In this regard, a number of means were suggested by commentators whereby these expenses could be recovered as charges for a particular flight.

With respect to the proposal in the Notice that a charge equal to 100 percent of the cost of the fuel for the flight be allowed instead of a specific computation of these expenses, a number of commentators contended that such a provision would not, in many cases, permit recovery of all of the expenses resulting from the operation of the aircraft. However, the FAA believes, based on the information available to it, that the allowance of such charge would provide for the recovery by the operator of an amount that would reasonably attributed thereto. This would, at the same time, relieve the FAA of the administrative burden of verifying in detail the various methods used by operators to compute those expenses, in order to ensure that a profit is not made. Accordingly, [§91.501(d)(10)], as adopted, allows an additional charge equal to 100 percent of the expenses listed in [§91.501(d)(1)], and does not provide for authorization by the Administrator of any other charge.

It should be noted that, although the FAA does not foresee compliance with [§91.501(d)] causing an unreasonable burden on any operator, individual operators who believe that the uniqueness of their particular situation justifies a specific charge not provided for in subparagraph (d) may, of course, petition for an appropriate exemption in accordance with the procedures contained in Part 11.

The National Air Transportation Conference, Inc., in its comment on the Notice, suggested that the word "registered" be inserted before the word "owners" in proposed [§91.501(c)(3)], in order to prevent abuse of this provision through attempts to conceal the sale of air transportation under the guise of temporary ownership of an aircraft. The FAA agrees with this comment. Section 47.3(b)(1) provides that no person may operated an aircraft that is eligible for registration under section 501 of the Federal Aviation Act of 1958, unless that aircraft has been registered by its owner. Accordingly, proposed [§91.501(c)(3)], as adopted, is clarified by inserting the word "registered" before the words "joint owners" wherever they appear. (38 FR 19024).

CROSS REFERENCES

Previous designation: 91.181. 91.23, Truth-in-Leasing Clause Requirement in Leases and Conditional Sales Contracts; 91.321, Carriage of Candidates in Federal Elections; 91.409, Inspections.

ADVISORY CIRCULARS

AC 91-38A *Large and Turbine-Powered Multi-engine Airplanes* (1978).

AC 91-37A *Truth in Leasing* (1978).

AC 120-12A *Private Carriage Versus Common Carriage of Persons and Property* (1986).

CASES

Flight crew salary and other unlisted charges for the operations to which 91.501(d) applied could be charged provided such charges did not exceed 100% percent of the charges for fuel, oil, lubricants and other additives. *Administrator v. Bowen*, NTSB Order No. EA-3351 (1991).

The pilot's operations did not conform to the requirements of §91.501, in that they failed to meet the threshold requirement of not being in "common carriage." The four elements of common carriage are: (1) a holding out of a willingness to (2) transport persons or property (3) from place to place (4) for compensation. The administrative law judge found in this case, and the Board agreed, that there was a "direct, open, obvious solicitation of business for an on-demand air charter," i.e., a "holding out" therefore "common carriage." *Administrator v. Woolsey*, NTSB Order No. EA-3391 (1991).

The operator carried cargo, which had to be transported expeditiously, for a good and valued customer, but did not charge for the flight, and the expectation of future business was sufficient to render the flight one for compensation or hire. The Board also found that [§91.501(b)(7)] did not apply to this flight because carriage of auto parts was not "incidental" to the operator's business, which directly involved air transportation. *Administrator v. Towner*, 5 NTSB 1348 (1986).

Provision of air transportation by a hotel or resort to its facilities as part of its general operations, even at no charge, has been held to be common carriage. *Las Vegas Hacienda v. CAB*, 298 F.2d 430 (9th Cir. 1962) cert. denied 360 U.S. 851 (1962).

An order of emergency revocation was reduced to a 90 day suspension where a pilot who had performed demonstration flights under FAR 91.501 and the National Business Aviation Association (NBAA) exemption was accused of offering illegal charter services. The NTSB believed the pilot's explanation of the demonstration flights, but affirmed a suspension because the pilot failed to follow the exact requirements of the NBAA exemption, and in fact, had not read the exemption. *Administrator v. Tsosie*, EA-4679 (1998).

FAA CHIEF COUNSEL OPINIONS

May a company executive reimburse the company for personal use of a company aircraft and crew?

> The answer is no. You advised that your client, Charles Schwab & Co., Inc. (the "Company") leases without crew, an airplane ("the airplane") covered by the applicability of Subpart F. The airplane is used by the Company for usual corporate purposes including transportation of officials, employees and guests of the Company.

> §91.501(d) provides, in pertinent part, as follows: "The following may be charged, as expenses of a specific flight, for transportation as authorized by paragraphs (b)(3) and (7) and (c) (1) of this section: . . .."

> Paragraph (b)(3) addresses demonstration of an airplane to prospective customers. Paragraph (b)(7) allows carriage of property under certain circumstances. It does not apply to carriage of persons. We believe it is clear that neither of these paragraphs applies to the carriage you describe. Paragraph (c)(1) defines "time sharing agreement." Please note that a lease is involved in a time sharing agreement. There is no indication that the carriage you describe takes place pursuant to a time sharing agreement.

> The paragraph that applies to the carriage of officials, employees, and guests of a company is (b)(5). It reads as follows: "Carriage of officials, employees, guests, and property of a company on an airplane operated by that company, or the parent or a subsidiary of the parent when carriage is within the scope of, and incidental to, the business of the company(other than transportation by air) and no charge, assessment or fee is made for the carriage in excess of the cost of owning, operating and maintaining the airplane, <u>except that no charge of any kind may be made for the carriage of a guest of a company, when the carriage is not within the scope of, and incidental to, the business of that company</u>." (emphasis supplied.)

> Agency interpretations of this language have held that no charge may be made when officials, employees, and guests are carried on a company airplane for vacation, pleasure trip, or similar purposes. Their presence on the airplane is not considered to be within the scope of, and incidental to, the company's business.

> Your letter contains extensive arguments and theories designed to persuade us that Charles Schwab Company should be allowed to charge Mr. Schwab when he is carried for vacation pleasure or similar purposes. We have considered each argument and theory. Without intending to detract from your eloquence, we must advise you that we do not agree. It may very well be that the Company wants to maintain prompt communications with Mr. Schwab when he is on pleasure trips. That desire, however, does not alter that fact that he is traveling for pleasure. As stated, the Agency's interpretations have held that such carriage is not within the scope of, and incidental to, the company's business. The ability of the Company to communicate with him is no way dependent upon charging him for carriage for such purposes.

You also mentioned IRS considerations. Please be advised that interpretation and application of aviation safety regulations is not dependent on, or affected by, what may be consistent with IRS regulations.

We noticed your reference to an operations company that Charles Schwab & Co., Inc. uses to perform maintenance and operation of the airplane. We also note that you state that control of operation of the airplane is under Charles Schwab & Co., Inc. We do not make a finding regarding whether or not the Company has "operational control" of the operation of the airplane. (See 14 CFR §1.1). Whether or not the Company has operational control of its airplane depends upon an analysis of all the facts relevant to its operation. One of the elements to be considered is the written agreement between the operations company and the Charles Schwab Company and how the parties implement this agreement. The local Flight Standards District Office, in this case the FSDO at Burlingame, together with the Assistant Chief Counsel for the Western-Pacific region, should review all pertinent factors bearing on operational control.

A person has operational control if that person exercises complete control over the phases of aircraft operation requiring aviation expertise. Operate, with respect to aircraft, means use, cause to use or authorize to use aircraft for the purpose . . . of air navigation including the piloting of aircraft with or without the right of legal control (as owner, lessee, or otherwise). (8-2-93).

Under [§91.501(c)(2)] an interchange agreement provides for the leasing of airplanes on an equal time basis only. Flight time cannot be calculated on the basis of dollars rather than hours. If one airplane (Airplane A) is more expensive to operate than another (Airplane B), this would not justify more flight time on Airplane A. An interchange agreement could provide for payment by the owner of Airplane B to the owner of Airplane A to equalize the costs associated with operating the two airplanes. (8-17-90).

FAR 91.501(b)(5) permits recovery of the specified types of expenses for airplanes operated by a **company**. The regulation does not permit recovery of such expenses when an airplane is operated by an individual, as contrasted with a company. (7-13-90).

When "flight department companies" are organized solely for the purpose of owning and operating aircraft, they do not fall within the coverage of [§91.501] since the regulation requires that transportation by air be "incidental" to the company's business. (8-8-89).

There is no objection to a lessee, who has exclusive control of an aircraft, entering into a time sharing agreement with a third party. (9-9-85).

The provisions of [§91.501(b)(5)] apply only where there is a parent-subsidiary corporate structure. It does not apply in the case of "sister corporations." (7-16-85), (4-1-75).

[Editor's Note: "Sister corporations" exist where companies, separately organized, are owned by the same individual (not a corporation). Two corporations owned by the same corporation are part of a parent-subsidiary corporate structure and may operate pursuant to §91.501(b)(5).]

The term "parent," as used in [§91.501(b)(5)], was intended to apply only to a company or corporation and not to a natural person. Thus a natural person with a controlling interest in certain corporations, would not be deemed a "parent" under the regulation and the corporation that owns the aircraft would not qualify as a "subsidiary of the parent." (1-2-79).

The charges allowed under [§91.501(d)] must be those directly related to the specific flight. Average fuel consumption and average fuel price cannot be used in determining the charge. (7-11-85).

Under [§91.501(c)(2)] an "interchange agreement" must provide for "equal" time, not "equivalent" time. The difference in cost of operating the airplane for equal times can be covered by the terms of the agreement provided the charge does not exceed the difference between the cost of owning, operating and maintaining the two airplanes. (7-11-85).

FAR [§91.501(b)(6)] does not authorize carriage of property in an airplane operated under a "time sharing" agreement and there is no other authorization for carriage of property on airplanes operated pursuant to a "time sharing agreement." (3-19-84).

For those charges listed in [§91.501(d)] to be recoverable, the party recovering the charges must be a corporation. [§91.501(b)(6)] limits the imposition of charges listed in Subsection (d) of [§91.501] to flights involving company officials, employees, and guests. (10-29-80).

 [§91.501(d)(2)] allows a charge to be made to cover per diem expenses for crew positioning and travel expenses for the crew, if the costs would not have been incurred had the flight not been made. (10-31-78).

The provisions of [§91.501] are not guidelines for determining whether or not a particular operation is for compensation or hire. The section simply provides exceptions for certain types of commercial operations, allowing them to be conducted under the rules of [Subpart F] of Part 91 instead of Parts 121, 129, 135 and 137, when common carriage is not involved. (6-15-77).

The phrase "prospective customer" in [§91.501(b)(3)] cannot be limited to prospective purchasers, but must be interpreted to allow charges specified in [§91.501(d)] to be recovered from prospective lessees. (2-13-76).

May a corporation accept reimbursement from a government official?

> §91.501(b)(5) allows a company to carry only its employees, property, officials, and guests without being certified as a commercial operator, as long as no reimbursement is made to the company for travel that is not within the scope of, and incidental to, the business of the company. Reimbursement to the company is limited to actual operating expenses, and no profit is contemplated. §91.501(b)(5) applies because the questions raise issues of reimbursement to a corporation for carriage of a government official as a guest on a corporate aircraft.

> The word "officials" in the first line of the §91.501(b)(5) means company officials and not government officials. A government official can only be classified as a guest in §91.501(b)(5). The first test, therefore, is whether the carriage of a government official as a guest reasonably can be considered to be "within the scope of, and incidental to, the business of the company." If so, the company may be reimbursed, not to exceed the cost of owning, operating, and maintaining the airplane.

> If the travel of the government official as a guest aboard a corporate aircraft is not "within the scope of, and incidental to, the business of the company," receipt by the company of any remuneration, compensation or benefit for the carriage triggers the requirement to hold an appropriate FAA operating certificate.

> One way to make a showing that a company trip which includes governmental employees as guests would be a Board of Directors' resolution and opinion of the company's general counsel which fully explains why that carriage is "within the scope of, and incidental to, the business of the company." Another would be correspondence between the government agency and the company explaining the purpose of the trip.

It is not enough alone for the Government and the company to be both separately interested in the same thing, or to be going to the same destination, or both, for the carriage of a guest to be considered "within the scope of, and incidental to, the business of the company." Mutual interest is not enough. The government's interest may well run counter to the interests of the company. Nor does a desire on the part of the government to reimburse for transportation, to avoid the appearance of impropriety, mean that carriage by the company is automatically "within the scope of, and incidental to, the business of the company," so that payment can be accepted. (6-10-92).

In your letter you say that you own a light twin engine airplane. At various times friends have asked you to fly them to business appointments or vacation destinations. You do not wish to obtain a Part 135 certificate, and you propose several plans which would allow your airplane to be used by others with your personal involvement kept to a minimum.

The first plan you mention is an exclusive lease of your airplane to a local business, except for times when you would be using it personally. You would lease the airplane at a break-even rate, and the lessee would select the pilot of their choice. Occasionally, the business could hire you as a pilot, but there would be no obligation to do so.

Your letter seems to reflect a fear that this transaction may label you as a commercial operator, and that by charging only a break even amount to lease the airplane you may avoid this result.

§1.1 defines a commercial operator as "a person who, for compensation or hire, engages in the carriage by aircraft in air commerce of persons or property other than as an air carrier ..." There is no relationship between the amount you charge per hour to lease your airplane and whether or not you are a commercial operator. There is also no prohibition to your leasing your airplane as you describe. This would be called a dry lease, where only the airplane is leased. If a flight crew is provided with the leased airplane, it is called a wet lease, and questions of operational control come to the fore, generally requiring air carrier certification. If you arranged the lease and then arranged your subsequent hiring as pilot to fly a trip, this would be regarded as a sham to avoid the Part 135 certification requirements. (9-23-91).

The president of a large company, operating strictly under Part 91, sends his corporate jet to pick up potential customers for a business meeting at his headquarters. Following the meeting a contract is signed which results in the sale of a franchise (or property). Was this acceptable under §91.501(b)(9), even though the flight was made with the "expectation of compensation" in that the company hoped to make a sale?

As long as no charge was made for the flight itself, this is permissible under §91.501(b)(9). (4-19-93).

When two companies enter into an interchange agreement, and the first company's aircraft is more expensive to operate than the second company's aircraft the first company may not recoup or "equal up" the costs by flying more hours on the second companies aircraft. Under an interchange agreement, as defined, the lease agreement must provide for an equal flight time exchange, but allows the person having the airplane that is more expensive to own, operate, and maintain, to charge the person having the other airplane an amount that may not exceed the difference between the cost of owning, operating, and maintaining the two airplanes. (4-19-93).

91.503 FLYING EQUIPMENT AND OPERATING INFORMATION

(a)   The pilot in command of an airplane shall ensure that the following flying equipment and aeronautical charts and data, in current and appropriate form, are accessible for each flight at the pilot station of the airplane:

(1)   A flashlight having at least two size "D" cells, or the equivalent, that is in good working order.

(2)   A cockpit checklist containing the procedures required by paragraph (b) of this section.

(3)   Pertinent aeronautical charts.

(4)   For IFR, VFR over-the-top, or night operations, each pertinent navigational enroute, terminal area, and approach and letdown chart.

(5)   In the case of multi-engine airplanes, one-engine inoperative climb performance data.

(b)   Each cockpit checklist must contain the following procedures and shall be used by the flight crewmembers when operating the airplane:

(1)   Before starting engines.

(2)   Before takeoff.

(3)   Cruise.

(4)   Before landing.

(5)   After landing.

(6)   Stopping engines.

(7)   Emergencies.

(c)   Each emergency cockpit checklist procedure required by paragraph (b)(7) of this section must contain the following procedures, as appropriate:

(1)   Emergency operation of fuel, hydraulic, electrical, and mechanical systems.

(2)   Emergency operation of instruments and controls.

(3)   Engine inoperative procedures.

(4)   Any other procedures necessary for safety.

(d)   The equipment, charts, and data prescribed in this section shall be used by the pilot in command and other members of the flight crew, when pertinent.

EXPLANATION

The requirements of this section are in addition to those set forth in FAR 91.9.

CROSS REFERENCES

Previous designation: 91.183. 91.9, Civil Aircraft Flight Manual, Marking and Placard Requirements.

ADVISORY CIRCULARS

AC 91-38A *Large and Turbine-Powered Multi-engine Airplanes* (1978).

91.505 FAMILIARITY WITH OPERATING LIMITATIONS AND EMERGENCY EQUIPMENT

(a)   Each pilot in command of an airplane shall, before beginning a flight, become familiar with the Airplane Flight Manual for that airplane, if one is required, and with any placards, listings, instrument markings, or any combination thereof, containing each operating limitation prescribed for that airplane by the Administrator, including those specified in §91.9(b).

(b)   Each required member of the crew shall, before beginning a flight, become familiar with the emergency equipment installed on the airplane to which that crewmember is assigned and with the procedures to be followed for the use of that equipment in an emergency situation.

EXPLANATION

The requirements of this section are in addition to those set forth in FAR 91.9.

CROSS REFERENCES

Previous designation: 91.185. 91.9, Civil aircraft flight manual, marking, and placard requirements.

ADVISORY CIRCULARS

AC 91-38A *Large and Turbine-Powered Multi-engine Airplanes* (1978).

91.507 EQUIPMENT REQUIREMENTS: OVER-THE-TOP, OR NIGHT VFR OPERATIONS

No person may operate an airplane over-the-top or at night under VFR unless that airplane is equipped with the instruments and equipment required for IFR operations under §91.205(d) and one electric landing light for night operations. Each required instrument and item of equipment must be in operable condition.

EXPLANATION

"Operable condition" means that instruments and equipment are operating as intended by the manufacturer.

Under 91.205(d), a landing light is required for night flight if the aircraft is being operated for hire. 91.507 requires a landing light for all night operations.

CROSS REFERENCES

Previous designation: 91.187. 91.205(d), Powered Civil Aircraft with Standard Category U.S. Airworthiness Certificates: Instrument and Equipment Requirements.

ADVISORY CIRCULARS

AC 91-38A *Large and Turbine-Powered Multi-engine Airplanes* (1978).

91.509 SURVIVAL EQUIPMENT FOR OVERWATER OPERATIONS

(a)   No person may take off an airplane for a flight over water more than 50 nautical miles from the nearest shore unless that airplane is equipped with a life preserver or an approved flotation means for each occupant of the airplane.

(b)   No person may take off an airplane for a flight over water more than 30 minutes flying time or 100 nautical miles from the nearest shore unless it has on board the following survival equipment:

    (1)   A life preserver, equipped with an approved survivor locator light, for each occupant of the airplane.

    (2)   Enough life rafts (each equipped with an approved survivor locator light) of a rated capacity and buoyancy to accommodate the occupants of the airplane.

    (3)   At least one pyrotechnic signaling device for each life raft.

    (4)   One self-buoyant, water-resistant, portable emergency radio signaling device that is capable of transmission on the appropriate emergency frequency or frequencies and not dependent upon the airplane power supply.

    (5)   A lifeline stored in accordance with §25.1411(g) of this chapter.

(c)   The required life rafts, life preservers, and signaling devices must be installed in conspicuously marked locations and easily accessible in the event of a ditching without appreciable time for preparatory procedures.

(d)   A survival kit, appropriately equipped for the route to be flown, must be attached to each required life raft.

(e)   As used in this section, the term shore means that area of the land adjacent to the water which is above the high water mark and excludes land areas which are intermittently under water.

EXPLANATION

The prescribed equipment is required only for a planned or intended flight over water beyond the distances or time specified. Flights beyond the distances or time specified, due to ATC vector or route change to avoid adverse weather, without required equipment are not violations of FAR 91.509.

FAR 91.509 recognizes that most equipment required by this regulation is usually rented and installed on the airplane for the specific flight so the specific location of the equipment is not mandated, but its location must be conspicuously marked and easily accessible.

According to AC 91-38A, the following equipment meets the provisions of FAR 91.509(FAR Part 37 was dropped from the FARs after AC 91-38A was published, but some equipment may still be marked in reference to Part 37):

    a.   **Flotation equipment** requirements for individuals may be met by using:

        (1)   Flotation devices approved under FAR 37.178, and marked TSO-C72b.
        (2)   Flotation devices approved under FAR 37.123, and marked TSO-C13c.

    b.   **Life preserver** requirements may be met by using:

        (1)   Life preservers (not other devices) approved under FAR 37.178, and marked TSO-C72b.
        (2)   Life preservers approved under FAR 37.123, and marked TSO-C85.

c.   **Survivor locator light** requirements may be met by lights approved under FAR 37.191, and marked TSO-C85.

d.   **The life raft** requirements may be met by using:

(1)   Life rafts approved under FAR 37.122, and marked TSO-C12c.
(2)   Life rafts approved under FAR 37.176, and marked TSO-C70.

e.   **Pyrotechnic signaling devices** that have been accepted by an agency of the U.S. Government for sea rescue purposes are recommended for use in complying with FAR 91.509(b)(3).

f.   **Emergency locator transmitters** which are marked TSO-C91 and are of the "automatic deployable type," as described in FAR 37.200(b)(4), are recommended for use in complying with FAR 91.509(b)(4).

CROSS REFERENCES

Previous designation: 91.189. 25.1411(g), Safety Equipment, Life Line Storage Provisions; 25.1415, Ditching Equipment.

ADVISORY CIRCULARS

AC 91-38A *Large and Turbine-Powered Multi-engine Airplanes* (1978).

AC 91-70 *Oceanic Operations, an Authorization Guide to Oceanic Operations* (1994).

AC 120-47 *Survival Equipment for Use in Overwater Operations* (1987).

AC 121-6, *Portable Battery-Powered Megaphones* (1966).

91.511 RADIO EQUIPMENT FOR OVERWATER OPERATIONS

(a)   Except as provided in paragraphs (c), (d), and (f) of this section, no person may take off an airplane for a flight over water more than 30 minutes flying time or 100 nautical miles from the nearest shore unless it has at least the following operable equipment:
  (1)   Radio communication equipment appropriate to the facilities to be used and able to transmit to, and receive from, any place on the route, at least one surface facility:
    (i)   Two transmitters.
    (ii)   Two microphones.
    (iii) Two headsets or one headset and one speaker.
    (iv)   Two independent receivers.
  (2)   Appropriate electronic navigational equipment consisting of at least two independent electronic navigation units capable of providing the pilot with the information necessary to navigate the airplane within the airspace assigned by air traffic control. However, a receiver that can receive both communications and required navigational signals may be used in place of a separate communications receiver and a separate navigational signal receiver or unit.

(b)   For the purposes of paragraphs (a)(1)(iv) and (a)(2) of this section, a receiver or electronic navigation unit is independent if the function of any part of it does not depend on the functioning of any part of another receiver or electronic navigation unit.

(c)   Notwithstanding the provisions of paragraph (a) of this section, a person may operate an airplane on which no passengers are carried from a place where repairs or replacement cannot be made to a place where they can be made, if not more than one of each of the dual items of radio communication and navigational equipment specified in paragraphs (a)(1)(I) through (iv) and (a)(2) of this section malfunctions or becomes inoperative.

(d)   Notwithstanding the provisions of paragraph (a) of this section, when both VHF and HF communications equipment are required for the route and the airplane has two VHF transmitters and two VHF receivers for communications, only one HF transmitter and one HF receiver is required for communications.

(e)   As used in this section, the term "shore" means that area of the land adjacent to the water which is above the high-water mark and excludes land areas which are intermittently under water.

(f)   Notwithstanding the requirements in paragraph (a)(2) of this section, a person may operate in the Gulf of Mexico, the Caribbean Sea, and the Atlantic Ocean west of a line which extends from 44° 47' 00" N / 67° 00' 00" W to 39° 00' 00" N / 67° 00' 00" W to 38° 30' 00" N / 60° 00' 00" W south along the 60° 00' 00" W longitude line to the point where the line intersects with the northern coast of South America, when:

(1)   A single long-range navigation system is installed, operational, and appropriate for the route; and

(2)   Flight conditions and the aircraft's capabilities are such that no more than a 30-minute gap in two-way radio very high frequency communications is expected to exist.

EXPLANATION

The prescribed equipment is required only for a planned or intended flight over water beyond the distances or time specified. Flights beyond the distances or time specified, due to ATC vector or route change to avoid adverse weather, without required equipment are not violations of FAR 91.511.

CROSS REFERENCES

Previous designation: 91.191.

ADVISORY CIRCULARS

AC 91-38A *Large and Turbine-Powered Multi-engine Airplanes* (1978).

AC 91-49 *General Aviation Procedures for Flight in North Atlantic Minimum Navigation Performance Specifications Airspace* (1977).

AC 91-70 *Oceanic Operations, an Authorization Guide to Oceanic Operations* (1994).

91.513 EMERGENCY EQUIPMENT

(a) No person may operate an airplane unless it is equipped with the emergency equipment listed in this section:

(b) Each item of equipment —
   (1) Must be inspected in accordance with §91.409 to ensure its continued serviceability and immediate readiness for its intended purposes;
   (2) Must be readily accessible to the crew;
   (3) Must clearly indicate its method of operation; and
   (4) When carried in a compartment or container, must have that compartment or container marked as to contents and date of last inspection.

(c) Hand fire extinguishers must be provided for use in crew, passenger, and cargo compartments in accordance with the following:
   (1) The type and quantity of extinguishing agent must be suitable for the kinds of fires likely to occur in the compartment where the extinguisher is intended to be used.
   (2) At least one hand fire extinguisher must be provided and located on or near the flight deck in a place that is readily accessible to the flight crew.
   (3) At least one hand fire extinguisher must be conveniently located in the passenger compartment of each airplane accommodating more than six but less than 31 passengers, and at least two hand fire extinguishers must be conveniently located in the passenger compartment of each airplane accommodating more than 30 passengers.
   (4) Hand fire extinguishers must be installed and secured in such a manner that they will not interfere with the safe operation of the airplane or adversely affect the safety of the crew and passengers. They must be readily accessible and, unless the locations of the fire extinguishers are obvious, their stowage provisions must be properly identified.

(d) First aid kits for treatment of injuries likely to occur in flight or in minor accidents must be provided.

(e) Each airplane accommodating more than 19 passengers must be equipped with a crash axe.

(f) Each passenger-carrying airplane must have a portable battery-powered megaphone or megaphones readily accessible to the crewmember assigned to direct emergency evacuation, installed as follows:
   (1) One megaphone on each airplane with a seating capacity of more than 60 but less than 100 passengers, at the most rearward location in the passenger cabin where it would be readily accessible to a normal flight attendant seat. However, the Administrator may grant a deviation from the requirements of this subparagraph if the Administrator finds that a different location would be more useful for evacuation of persons during an emergency.
   (2) On each airplane with a seating capacity of 100 or more passengers, one megaphone installed at the forward end and one installed at the most rearward location where it would be readily accessible to a normal flight attendant seat.

EXPLANATION

This rule requires that the emergency equipment be readily accessible to the crew, and it is advisable that it be readily accessible to the passengers as well. Close attention to FAR 91.513 is required, because the requirements change according to the airplane configuration (i.e. number of seats) and use in the flight involved (i.e. Part 91 flights vs. Part 135 flights).

CROSS REFERENCES

Previous designation: 91.193. 91.409 Inspections.

ADVISORY CIRCULARS

AC 91-38A *Large and Turbine-Powered Multi-engine Airplanes* (1978).

AC 20-42C *Hand Fire Extinguishers for Use on Aircraft* (1984).

AC 121-6 *Portable Battery-Powered Megaphones* (1966).

91.515 FLIGHT ALTITUDE RULES

(a) Notwithstanding §91.119, and except as provided in paragraph (b) of this section, no person may operate an airplane under VFR at less than —
   (1) One thousand feet above the surface, or 1,000 feet from any mountain, hill, or other obstruction to flight, for day operations; and
   (2) The altitudes prescribed in §91.177, for night operations.
(b) This section does not apply —
   (1) During takeoff or landing;
   (2) When a different altitude is authorized by a waiver to this section under subpart J of this part; or
   (3) When a flight is conducted under the special VFR weather minimums of §91.157 with an appropriate clearance from ATC.

EXPLANATION

Day operations, under VFR, over other than congested areas must be conducted at or above 1,000 feet above the surface, and 1,000 feet from any mountain, hill, or other obstruction to flight. Deviations are allowed if a lower altitude is necessary for takeoff or landing, a waiver has been issued by the FAA, or a special VFR clearance has been issued by ATC.

Where necessary, a waiver from the altitude restrictions may be requested from the FAA under FAR Part 91, Subpart J.

The increase from 500 to 1,000 feet in other than congested areas is based on the fact that the subpart applies to large and turbo-jet multi-engine aircraft.

CROSS REFERENCES

Previous designation: 91.195. 91.119, Minimum Safe Altitudes: General; 91.157, Special VFR Weather Minimums; 91.177, Minimum Altitudes for IFR Operations; 91.901-91.905, Waivers.

ADVISORY CIRCULARS

AC 91-38A *Large and Turbine-Powered Multi-engine Airplanes* (1978).

91.517 PASSENGER INFORMATION

(a) Except as provided in paragraph (b) of this section, no person may operate an airplane carrying passengers unless it is equipped with signs that are visible to passengers and flight attendants to notify them when smoking is prohibited and when safety belts must be fastened. The signs must be so constructed that the crew can turn them on and off. They must be turned on during airplane movement on the surface, for each takeoff, for each landing, and when otherwise considered to be necessary by the pilot in command.

(b) The pilot in command of an airplane that is not required, in accordance with applicable aircraft and equipment requirements of this chapter, to be equipped as provided in paragraph (a) of this section shall ensure that the passengers are notified orally each time that it is necessary to fasten their safety belts and when smoking is prohibited.

(c) If passenger information signs are installed, no passenger or crewmember may smoke while any "no smoking" sign is lighted nor may any passenger or crewmember smoke in any lavatory.

(d) Each passenger required by §91.107(a)(3) to occupy a seat or berth shall fasten his or her safety belt about him or her and keep it fastened while any "fasten seat belt" sign is lighted.

(e) Each passenger shall comply with instructions given him or her by crewmembers regarding compliance with paragraphs (b), (c), and (d) of this section.

EXPLANATION

This requirement should be one of the items on the pre-takeoff checklist used by the pilot in command.

CROSS REFERENCES

Previous designation: 91.197. 91.107, Use of Safety Belts.

ADVISORY CIRCULARS

AC 91-38A *Large and Turbine-Powered Multi-engine Airplanes* (1978).

CASES

A passenger violated both §91.517(d) and (e) by refusing to fasten his seat belt while the seat belt sign was illuminated and refusing to do so after being asked by the flight attendant. For these violations he was assessed a $1,700 penalty. The Law Judge stated in brief that a passenger may not decide which orders to follow or substitute his judgement for that of the crew's. *FAA v. Stout*, FAA Order No. 98-12 (6-16-1998).

91.519 PASSENGER BRIEFING

(a)   Before each takeoff the pilot in command of an airplane carrying passengers shall ensure that all passengers have been orally briefed on —
     (1)   Smoking: Each passenger shall be briefed on when, where, and under what conditions smoking is prohibited. This briefing shall include a statement, as appropriate, that the Federal Aviation Regulations require passenger compliance with lighted passenger information signs and no smoking placards, prohibit smoking in lavatories, and require compliance with crewmember instructions with regard to these items;
     (2)   Use of safety belts and shoulder harnesses: Each passenger shall be briefed on when, where, and under what conditions it is necessary to have his or her safety belt and, if installed, his or her shoulder harness fastened about him or her. This briefing shall include a statement, as appropriate, that Federal Aviation Regulations require passenger compliance with the lighted passenger sign and/or crewmember instructions with regard to these items;
     (3)   Location and means for opening the passenger entry door and emergency exits;
     (4)   Location of survival equipment;
     (5)   Ditching procedures and the use of flotation equipment required under §91.509 for a flight over water; and
     (6)   The normal and emergency use of oxygen equipment installed on the airplane.
(b)   The oral briefing required by paragraph (a) of this section shall be given by the pilot in command or a member of the crew, but need not be given when the pilot in command determines that the passengers are familiar with the contents of the briefing. It may be supplemented by printed cards for the use of each passenger containing —
     (1)   A diagram of, and methods of operating, the emergency exits; and
     (2)   Other instructions necessary for use of emergency equipment.
(c)   Each card used under paragraph (b) must be carried in convenient locations on the airplane for the use of each passenger and must contain information that is pertinent only to the type and model airplane on which it is used.

EXPLANATION

The oral briefing and passenger cards cannot be general in nature, but must be for the specific type and model of aircraft.

This requirement should be included on the appropriate checklist for all operations since it is a good operating practice.

CROSS REFERENCES

Previous designation: 91.199. 91.107, Use of Safety Belts; 91.509, Survival Equipment for Overwater Operations.

ADVISORY CIRCULARS

AC 91-38A *Large and Turbine-Powered Multi-engine Airplanes* (1978).

AC 91-62A *Use of Child Seats in Aircraft* (1992).

91.521 SHOULDER HARNESS

(a) No person may operate a transport category airplane that was type certificated after January 1, 1958, unless it is equipped at each seat at a flight deck station with a combined safety belt and shoulder harness that meets the applicable requirements specified in §25.785 of this chapter, except that —
   (1) Shoulder harnesses and combined safety belt and shoulder harnesses that were approved and installed before March 6, 1980, may continue to be used; and
   (2) Safety belt and shoulder harness restraint systems may be designed to the inertia load factors established under the certification basis of the airplane.

(b) No person may operate a transport category airplane unless it is equipped at each required flight attendant seat in the passenger compartment with a combined safety belt and shoulder harness that meets the applicable requirements specified in §25.785 of this chapter, except that —
   (1) Shoulder harnesses and combined safety belt and shoulder harnesses that were approved and installed before March 6, 1980, may continue to be used; and
   (2) Safety belt and shoulder harness restraint systems may be designed to the inertia load factors established under the certification basis of the airplane.

CROSS REFERENCES

Previous designation: 91.200. 25.785, Seats, Berths, Litters, Safety Belts and Shoulder Harnesses; 91.105, Flight Crewmembers at Stations.

ADVISORY CIRCULARS

AC 91-38A *Large and Turbine-Powered Multi-engine Airplanes* (1978).

FAA CHIEF COUNSEL OPINIONS

Where nine DC-9-32 aircraft, with U.S. registration were being operated entirely outside the United States by Alitalia Airlines, compliance with [91.521] was not required since that requirement was inconsistent with the applicable regulations of the foreign country where the aircraft is operated or Annex 2 to the Convention on International Civil Aviation 2-16-83. [Editor's Note: The foregoing applies in the case of all regulations with the exception of §91.307(b), 91.309, 91.323 and 91.711. (See 91.703(a)(3))].

91.523 CARRY-ON-BAGGAGE

No pilot in command of an airplane having a seating capacity of more than 19 passengers may permit a passenger to stow his baggage aboard that airplane except —
(a) In a suitable baggage or cargo storage compartment, or as provided in §91.525; or
(b) Under a passenger seat in such a way that it will not slide forward under crash impacts severe enough to induce the ultimate inertia forces specified in §25.561(b)(3) of this chapter, or the requirements of the regulations under which the airplane was type certificated. Restraining devices must also limit sideward motion of under-seat baggage and be designed to withstand crash impacts severe enough to induce sideward forces specified in §25.561 (b)(3) of this chapter.

CROSS REFERENCES

Previous designation: 91.201. 25.561(b)(3), Emergency Landing Conditions; 91.525, Carriage of Cargo.

ADVISORY CIRCULARS

AC 91-38A *Large and Turbine-Powered Multi-engine Airplanes* (1978).

AC 121-29B *Carry-On Baggage* (2000).

91.525 CARRIAGE OF CARGO

(a) No pilot in command may permit cargo to be carried in any airplane unless —
   (1)   It is carried in an approved cargo rack, bin, or compartment installed in the airplane;
   (2)   It is secured by means approved by the Administrator; or
   (3)   It is carried in accordance with each of the following:
      (i)   It is properly secured by a safety belt or other tiedown having enough strength to eliminate the possibility of shifting under all normally anticipated flight and ground conditions.
      (ii)   It is packaged or covered to avoid possible injury to passengers.
      (iii)   It does not impose any load on seats or on the floor structure that exceeds the load limitation for those components.
      (iv)   It is not located in a position that restricts the access to or use of any required emergency or regular exit, or the use of the aisle between the crew and the passenger compartment.
      (v)   It is not carried directly above seated passengers.
(b) When cargo is carried in cargo compartments that are designed to require the physical entry of a crewmember to extinguish any fire that may occur during flight, the cargo must be loaded so as to allow a crewmember to effectively reach all parts of the compartment with the contents of a hand fire extinguisher.

EXPLANATION

The carriage of cargo generally falls into two classifications, all cargo operations and cargo/passenger operations. Cargo location, packaging, and security are major concerns when cargo and passengers occupy the same compartments.

CROSS REFERENCES

Previous designation: 91.203.

ADVISORY CIRCULARS

AC 91-38A *Large and Turbine-Powered Multi-engine Airplanes* (1978).

CASES

An airplane crashed on takeoff because the holding pens for the cattle on board were improperly installed, and the cattle had moved too far forward in the cargo compartment. The NTSB determined that the pilots were justified in relying on the loading agent, because under the circumstances, the pilots would not have been able to see if the pens had been properly installed, because the cattle had already been loaded when the pilots arrived. *Administrator v. Dickman and Roman*, 3 NTSB 2252 (1980).

91.527 OPERATING IN ICING CONDITIONS

(a)   No pilot may take off an airplane that has —
   (1)   Frost, snow, or ice adhering to any propeller, windshield, or powerplant installation or to an airspeed, altimeter, rate of climb, or flight attitude instrument system;
   (2)   Snow or ice adhering to the wings or stabilizing or control surfaces; or
   (3)   Any frost adhering to the wings or stabilizing or control surfaces, unless that frost has been polished to make it smooth.
(b)   Except for an airplane that has ice protection provisions that meet the requirements in section 34 of Special Federal Aviation Regulation No. 23, or those for transport category airplane type certification, no pilot may fly —
   (1)   Under IFR into known or forecast moderate icing conditions; or
   (2)   Under VFR into known light or moderate icing conditions unless the aircraft has functioning de-icing or anti-icing equipment protecting each propeller, windshield, wing, stabilizing or control surface, and each airspeed, altimeter, rate of climb, or flight attitude instrument system.
(c)   Except for an airplane that has ice protection provisions that meet the requirements in section 34 of Special Federal Aviation Regulation No. 23, or those for transport category airplane type certification, no pilot may fly an airplane into known or forecast severe icing conditions.
(d)   If current weather reports and briefing information relied upon by the pilot in command indicate that the forecast icing conditions that would otherwise prohibit the flight will not be encountered during the flight because of changed weather conditions since the forecast, the restrictions in paragraphs (b) and (c) of this section based on forecast conditions do not apply.

EXPLANATION

Subsection (d) provides another reason for continually monitoring all weather reporting sources and not just checking the forecasted weather.

CROSS REFERENCES

Previous designation: 91.209. 91.103, Preflight Action; Special Federal Aviation Regulation (SFAR) §23.34, Ice Protection.

ADVISORY CIRCULARS

AC 00-6A *Aviation Weather* (1975).

AC 00-45E *Aviation Weather Services* (1999).

AC 91-6A *Water, Slush and Snow on the Runway* (1978).

AC 91-13C *Cold Weather Operation of Aircraft* (1979).

AC 91-38A *Large and Turbine-Powered Multi-engine Airplanes* (1978).

AC 91-51A *Effect of Icing on Aircraft Control and Airplane Deice and Anti-Ice Systems* (1996).

AERONAUTICAL INFORMATION MANUAL

Meteorology, Para. 7-1-1 through 7-1-31.

91.529 FLIGHT ENGINEER REQUIREMENTS

(a)   No person may operate the following airplanes without a flight crewmember holding a current flight engineer certificate:

   (1)   An airplane for which a type certificate was issued before January 2, 1964, having a maximum certificated takeoff weight of more than 80,000 pounds.

   (2)   An airplane type certificated after January 1, 1964, for which a flight engineer is required by the type certification requirements.

(b)   No person may serve as a required flight engineer on an airplane unless, within the preceding 6 calendar months, that person has had at least 50 hours of flight time as a flight engineer on that type airplane or has been checked by the Administrator on that type airplane and is found to be familiar and competent with all essential current information and operating procedures.

EXPLANATION

This requirement for a flight engineer is the same as Part 121.

CROSS REFERENCES

Previous designation: 91.211. Part 63, Subpart B, Flight Engineers; 121.387, Flight Engineer.

ADVISORY CIRCULARS

AC 91-38A *Large and Turbine-Powered Multi-engine Airplanes* (1978).

FAA CHIEF COUNSEL OPINIONS

There is no maximum age limit prescribed by the Federal Aviation Regulations for persons serving as a flight engineer including those serving in Part 91 or Part 121 operations. (11-8-90).

A flight engineer who has received 50 hours of training in a Boeing 707 aircraft, while accompanied by a qualified, current, "type rated" 707 flight engineer is not considered qualified under [91.529(b)]. The flight crewmember must have served as a "required" flight engineer, not as a mere observer or trainee, to comply with the regulation. (4-14-77).

91.531 SECOND IN COMMAND REQUIREMENTS

(a)   Except as provided in paragraph (b) of this section, no person may operate the following airplanes without a pilot who is designated as second in command of that airplane;

   (1)   A large airplane, except that a person may operate an airplane certificated under SFAR 41 without a pilot who is designated as second in command if that airplane is certificated for operation with one pilot.

   (2)   A turbojet-powered multi-engine airplane for which two pilots are required under the type certification requirements for that airplane.

   (3)   A commuter category airplane, except that a person may operate a commuter category airplane notwithstanding paragraph (a)(1) of this section, that has a passenger seating configuration, excluding pilot seats, of nine or less without a pilot who is designated as second in command if that airplane is type certificated for operations with one pilot.

(b)   The Administrator may issue a letter of authorization for the operation of an airplane without compliance with the requirements of paragraph (a) of this section if that airplane is designed for and type certificated with only one pilot station. The authorization contains any conditions that the Administrator finds necessary for safe operation.

(c)   No person may designate a pilot to serve as second in command, nor may any pilot serve as second in command, of an airplane required under this section to have two pilots unless that pilot meets the qualifications for second in command prescribed in §61.55 of this chapter.

EXPLANATION

Subsection (b) provides relief from the second-in-command requirement in situations where the aircraft has only one pilot station.

CROSS REFERENCES

Previous designation: 91.213. 61.55, Second In Command Qualifications; Special Federal Aviation Regulation (SFAR) 41.

ADVISORY CIRCULARS

AC 91-38A *Large and Turbine-Powered Multi-engine Airplanes* (1978).

CASES

In the absence of a letter of authorization from the FAA, the enactment of FAR 91.213 in 1973 (the predecessor of 91.531) canceled the effectiveness of any aircraft manual provisions which authorized the operation of the aircraft without a second in command. *Administrator v. Staffney*, 2 NTSB 1815 (1975).

91.533 FLIGHT ATTENDANT REQUIREMENTS

(a)   No person may operate an airplane unless at least the following number of flight attendants are on board the airplane:
    (1)   For airplanes having more than 19 but less than 51 passengers on board, one flight attendant.
    (2)   For airplanes having more than 50 but less than 101 passengers on board, two flight attendants.
    (3)   For airplanes having more than 100 passengers on board, two flight attendants plus one additional flight attendant for each unit (or part of a unit) of 50 passengers above 100.

(b)   No person may serve as a flight attendant on an airplane when required by paragraph (a) of this section unless that person has demonstrated to the pilot in command familiarity with the necessary functions to be performed in an emergency or a situation requiring emergency evacuation and is capable of using the emergency equipment installed on that airplane.

EXPLANATION

While not required, it is recommended that a standardized checklist be prepared for use by the pilot in command in making the determination required by subsection (b).

While not required, it is recommended that a briefing book or manual be prepared, for use by the flight attendants, describing emergency procedures; location, function, and operation of emergency and survival equipment; etc.

CROSS REFERENCES

Previous designation: 91.215. 121.417, Crewmember Emergency Training.

ADVISORY CIRCULARS

AC 91-38A *Large and Turbine-Powered Multi-engine Airplanes* (1978).

91.535 STOWAGE OF FOOD, BEVERAGE, AND PASSENGER SERVICE EQUIPMENT DURING AIRCRAFT MOVEMENT ON THE SURFACE, TAKEOFF, AND LANDING

(a) No operator may move an aircraft on the surface, take off, or land when any food, beverage, or tableware furnished by the operator is located at any passenger seat.

(b) No operator may move an aircraft on the surface, take off, or land unless each food and beverage tray and seat back tray table is secured in its stowed position.

(c) No operator may permit an aircraft to move on the surface, take off, or land unless each passenger serving cart is secured in its stowed position.

(d) No operator may permit an aircraft to move on the surface, take off, or land unless each movie screen that extends into the aisle is stowed.

(e) Each passenger shall comply with instructions given by a crewmember with regard to compliance with this section.

INTENTIONALLY

LEFT

BLANK

INTENTIONALLY

LEFT

BLANK

SUBPART G — ADDITIONAL EQUIPMENT AND OPERATING REQUIREMENTS FOR LARGE AND TRANSPORT CATEGORY AIRCRAFT

91.601 APPLICABILITY

This subpart applies to operation of large and transport category U.S.-registered civil aircraft.

CROSS REFERENCES

Previous designation: New. Part 1, §1.1, "Category" and "Large Aircraft;" Part 25, Airworthiness Standards: Transport Category Airplanes; Part 29, Airworthiness Standards: Transport Category Rotorcraft.

91.603 AURAL SPEED WARNING DEVICE

No person may operate a transport category airplane in air commerce unless that airplane is equipped with an aural speed warning device that complies with §25.1303 (c)(1).

EXPLANATION

This regulation was adopted to make clear that an aural speed warning device is a continuing requirement for all operations in air commerce with a transport category aircraft.

CROSS REFERENCES

Previous designation: 91.49. 25.1303, Flight and Navigation Instruments.

91.605 TRANSPORT CATEGORY CIVIL AIRPLANE WEIGHT LIMITATIONS

(a)   No person may take off any transport category airplane (other than a turbine- engine-powered airplane certificated after September 30, 1958) unless —
   (1)   The takeoff weight does not exceed the authorized maximum takeoff weight for the elevation of the airport of takeoff;
   (2)   The elevation of the airport of takeoff is within the altitude range for which maximum takeoff weights have been determined;
   (3)   Normal consumption of fuel and oil in flight to the airport of intended landing will leave a weight on arrival not in excess of the authorized maximum landing weight for the elevation of that airport; and
   (4)   The elevations of the airport of intended landing and of all specified alternate airports are within the altitude range for which maximum landing weights have been determined.

(b)   No person may operate a turbine-engine-powered transport category airplane certificated after September 30, 1958, contrary to the Airplane Flight Manual, or take off that airplane unless —

   (1)   The takeoff weight does not exceed the takeoff weight specified in the Airplane Flight Manual for the elevation of the airport and for the ambient temperature existing at the time of takeoff;

   (2)   Normal consumption of fuel and oil in flight to the airport of intended landing and to the alternate airports will leave a weight on arrival not in excess of the landing weight specified in the Airplane Flight Manual for the elevation of each of the airports involved and for the ambient temperatures expected at the time of landing;

   (3)   The takeoff weight does not exceed the weight shown in the Airplane Flight Manual to correspond with the minimum distances required for takeoff, considering the elevation of the airport, the runway to be used, the effective runway gradient, the ambient temperature and wind component at the time of takeoff, and, if operating limitations exist for the minimum distances required for takeoff from wet runways, the runway surface condition (dry or wet). Wet runway distances associated with grooved or porous friction course runways, if provided in the Airplane Flight Manual, may be used only for runways that are grooved or treated with a porous friction course (PFC) overlay, and that the operator determines are designed, constructed, and maintained in a manner acceptable to the Administrator.

   (4)   Where the takeoff distance includes a clearway, the clearway distance is not greater than one-half of —

      (I)   The takeoff run, in the case of airplanes certificated after September 30, 1958, and before August 30, 1959; or

      (ii)   The runway length, in the case of airplanes certificated after August 29, 1959.

(c)   No person may take off a turbine-engine-powered transport category airplane certificated after August 29, 1959, unless, in addition to the requirements of paragraph (b) of this section —

   (1)   The accelerate-stop distance is no greater than the length of the runway plus the length of the stopway (if present); and

   (2)   The takeoff distance is no greater than the length of the runway plus the length of the clearway (if present); and

   (3)   The takeoff run is no greater than the length of the runway.

EXPLANATION

"Turbine engine-powered" includes both turbojets and turboprops.

CROSS REFERENCES

Previous designation: 91.37. 91.9, Civil Aircraft Flight Manual, Marking and Placard Requirements; 91.103, Preflight Action.

CASES

The captain of a Boeing 727 was cited for failing to follow the Electrical System Smoke or Fire Emergency Procedures in the airplane flight manual in violation of [91-605(b)]. *Administrator v. Raney*, 2 NTSB 1543 (75).

The captain of a Boeing 727 was cited for applying reverse thrust on all three engines, a procedure which was not authorized by the airplane flight manual and caused the pilot to lose directional control and swerve off the runway. *Administrator v. Cook*, 2 NTSB 952 (1974).

FAA CHIEF COUNSEL OPINIONS

Your hypotheticals generally involve a Boeing 767 aircraft which lands at a weight in excess of its Maximum Structural Landing Weight but below both its Landing Field Length Weight and Maximum Climb Limit Landing Weight. The weights come from the Airplane Flight Manual for the aircraft. Your hypothetical further assumes that the pilot does not declare an emergency, that the aircraft cannot jettison fuel in flight, and that maintenance personnel inspect the aircraft in accordance with its approved maintenance program and approve it for return to service before it takes off again.

You ask whether the air carrier in your hypothetical would be in compliance with Sections 91.605, 121.173, 121.195 or any other Federal Aviation Regulations (FAR).

The air carrier in your hypothetical may be in violation of Sections 91.605(b) and 91.9(a) of the Federal Aviation Regulations. Section 91.605(b) says that "no person may operate a turbine-engine powered transport category airplane certificated after September 30, 1958, contrary to the Airplane Flight Manual. . .." §91.9(a), a more general regulation, says that "no person may operate a civil aircraft without complying with the operating limitations specified in the approved Airplane or Rotorcraft Flight Manual. . .."

The pilot in your hypothetical violates these regulations because the Airplane Flight Manual does not permit overweight landings under the circumstances you describe. The air carrier also violates these sections if it causes or authorizes the overweight landing to occur (FAR §1.1, General Definitions, see "Operate" and "Person"). Procedures regarding overweight landings in the air carrier's Operation Manual are obviously important in determining whether the air carrier, as well as the pilot, is in violation of these sections of the regulations.

The air carrier in your hypothetical does not violate §121.195 of the Federal Aviation Regulations (§121.173 incorporates §121.195.) This Section says that "No person operating a turbine engine powered transport category airplane may take off that airplane at such a weight that (allowing for normal consumption of fuel and oil in flight to the destination or alternate airport) the weight of the airplane on arrival would exceed the landing weight set forth in the Airplane Flight Manual. . .." The aircraft in your hypothetical is heading for Europe and would be within weight limits upon landing were the flight to proceed as planned. The landing you describe at JFK is unintended. JFK is not the "destination." Neither the pilot nor the air carrier therefore, violates these sections.

You asked whether our interpretation would change if the aircraft in your hypothetical had fuel dumping capabilities and whether, under such circumstances, the pilot would be required to jettison fuel before landing. The pilot would not be required to jettison fuel but would be required, nevertheless, to conform to the landing weight restrictions of the Airplane Flight Manual. For purposes of complying with the Federal Aviation Regulations, whether the pilot jettison fuel or burns fuel off is up to the pilot. So long as the aircraft is within its weight limits when it lands, neither the pilot nor the air carrier is in violation of the regulations cited by you in your letter. (3-26-93).

91.607 EMERGENCY EXITS FOR AIRPLANES CARRYING PASSENGERS FOR HIRE

(a) Notwithstanding any other provision of this chapter, no person may operate a large airplane (type certificated under the Civil Air Regulations effective before April 9, 1957) in passenger-carrying operations for hire, with more than the number of occupants —

    (1) Allowed under Civil Air Regulations §4b. 362(a), (b), and (c) as in effect on December 20, 1951; or

    (2) Approved under Special Civil Air Regulations SR-387, SR-389, SR-389A, or SR-389B, or under this section as in effect.

        However, an airplane type listed in the following table may be operated with up to the listed number of occupants (including crewmembers) and the corresponding number of exits (including emergency exits and doors) approved for the emergency exit of passengers or with an occupant-exit configuration approved under paragraph (b) or (c) of this section.

Airplane type	Maximum number of occupants including all crewmembers	Corresponding number of exits authorized for passenger use
B-307	61	4
B-377	96	9
C-46	67	4
CV-240	53	6
CV-340 and CV-440	53	6
DC-3	35	4
DC-3 (Super)	39	5
DC-4	86	5
DC-6	87	7
DC-6B	112	11
L-18	17	3
L-049, L-649, L-749	87	7
L-1049 series	96	9
M-202	53	6
M-404	53	7
Viscount 700 series	53	7

(b) Occupants in addition to those authorized under paragraph (a) of this section may be carried as follows:

    (1) For each additional floor-level exit at least 24 inches wide by 48 inches high, with an unobstructed 20-inch-wide access aisleway between the exit and the main passenger aisle, 12 additional occupants.

    (2) For each additional window exit located over a wing that meets the requirements of the airworthiness standards under which the airplane was type certificated or that is large enough to inscribe an ellipse 19 x 26 inches: eight additional occupants.

    (3)   For each additional window exit that is not located over a wing but that otherwise complies with paragraph (b)(2) of this section, five additional occupants.

    (4)   For each airplane having a ratio (as computed from the table in paragraph (a) of this section) of maximum number of occupants to number of exits greater than 14:1, and for each airplane that does not have at least one full-size, door-type exit in the side of the fuselage in the rear part of the cabin, the first additional exit must be a floor-level exit that complies with paragraph (b)(1) of this section and must be located in the rear part of the cabin on the opposite side of the fuselage from the main entrance door. However, no person may operate an airplane under this section carrying more than 115 occupants unless there is such an exit on each side of the fuselage in the rear part of the cabin.

(c)   No person may eliminate any approved exit except in accordance with the following:

    (1)   The previously authorized maximum number of occupants must be reduced by the same number of additional occupants authorized for that exit under this section.

    (2)   Exits must be eliminated in accordance with the following priority schedule: First, non-over-wing window exits; second, over-wing window exits; third, floor-level exits located in the forward part of the cabin; fourth, floor-level exits located in the rear of the cabin.

    (3)   At least one exit must be retained on each side of the fuselage regardless of the number of occupants.

    (4)   No person may remove any exit that would result in a ratio of maximum number of occupants to approved exits greater than 14:1.

(d)   This section does not relieve any person operating under part 121 of this chapter from complying with §121.291.

EXPLANATION

This regulation applies to passenger carrying operations for hire. Therefore, it would apply to any operations under Part 91, Subpart F, for which any charge is made (Refer to FAR 91.501).

The difference in the number of passengers allowed to be carried for each additional floor level exit and window exit is based on the fact that window-type exits are less effective than door-type exits.

For operations conducted under Part 91, there is no requirement for a demonstration of evacuation procedures as in Part 121.

CROSS REFERENCES

Previous designation: 91.47. 121.291, Demonstration of Emergency Evacuation Procedures; 91.501, Applicability.

91.609 FLIGHT RECORDERS AND COCKPIT VOICE RECORDERS

(a)   No holder of an air carrier operating certificate or an operating certificate may conduct any operation under this part with an aircraft listed in the holder's operations specifications or current list of aircraft used in air transportation unless that aircraft complies with any applicable flight recorder and cockpit voice recorder requirements of the part under which its certificate is issued except that the operator may —

    (1)   Ferry an aircraft with an inoperative flight recorder or cockpit voice recorder from a place where repair or replacement cannot be made to a place where they can be made;

(2)   Continue a flight as originally planned, if the flight recorder or cockpit voice recorder becomes inoperative after the aircraft has taken off;

(3)   Conduct an airworthiness flight test during which the flight recorder or cockpit voice recorder is turned off to test it or to test any communications or electrical equipment installed in the aircraft; or

(4)   Ferry a newly acquired aircraft from the place where possession of it is taken to a place where the flight recorder or cockpit voice recorder is to be installed.

(b)   Notwithstanding paragraphs (c) and (e) of this section, an operator other than the holder of an air carrier or a commercial operator certificate may —

    (1)   Ferry an aircraft with an inoperative flight recorder or cockpit voice recorder from a place where repair or replacement cannot be made to a place where they can be made;

    (2)   Continue a flight as originally planned if the flight recorder or cockpit voice recorder becomes inoperative after the aircraft has taken off;

    (3)   Conduct an airworthiness flight test during which the flight recorder or cockpit voice recorder is turned off to test it or to test any communications or electrical equipment installed in the aircraft;

    (4)   Ferry a newly acquired aircraft from a place where possession of it was taken to a place where the flight recorder or cockpit voice recorder is to be installed; or

    (5)   Operate an aircraft:

        (i)   For not more than 15 days while the flight recorder and/or cockpit voice recorder is inoperative and/or removed for repair provided that the aircraft maintenance records contain an entry that indicates the date of failure, and a placard is located in view of the pilot to show that the flight recorder or cockpit voice recorder is inoperative.

        (ii)   For not more than an additional 15 days, provided that the requirements in paragraph (b)(5)(I) are met and that a certificated pilot or a certificated person authorized to return an aircraft to service under §43.7 of this chapter, certifies in the aircraft maintenance records that additional time is required to complete repairs or obtain a replacement unit.

(c)   No person may operate a U.S. civil registered, multi-engine, turbine-powered airplane or rotorcraft having a passenger seating configuration, excluding any pilot seats of 10 or more that has been manufactured after October 11, 1991, unless it is equipped with one or more approved flight recorders that utilize a digital method of recording and storing data and a method of readily retrieving that data from the storage medium, that are capable of recording the data specified in appendix E to this part, for an airplane, or appendix F to this part, for a rotorcraft, of this part within the range, accuracy, and recording interval specified, and that are capable of retaining no less than 8 hours of aircraft operation.

(d)   Whenever a flight recorder, required by this section, is installed, it must be operated continuously from the instant the airplane begins the takeoff roll or the rotorcraft begins lift-off until the airplane has completed the landing roll or the rotorcraft has landed at its destination.

(e)   Unless otherwise authorized by the Administrator, after October 11, 1991, no person may operate a U.S. civil registered multi-engine, turbine-powered airplane or rotorcraft having a passenger seating configuration of six passengers or more and for which two pilots are required by type certification or operating rule unless it is equipped with an approved cockpit voice recorder that:

(1)   Is installed in compliance with §23.1457(a) (1) and (2), (b), (c), (d), (e), (f), and (g); §25.1457(a) (1) and (2), (b), (c), (d), (e), (f), and (g); §27.1457(a) (1) and (2), (b), (c), (d), (e), (f), and (g); or §29.1457(a) (1) and (2), (b), (c), (d), (e), (f), and (g) of this chapter, as applicable; and

(2)   Is operated continuously from the use of the check list before the flight to completion of the final checklist at the end of the flight.

(f)   In complying with this section, an approved cockpit voice recorder having an erasure feature may be used, so that at any time during the operation of the recorder, information recorded more than 15 minutes earlier may be erased or otherwise obliterated.

(g)   In the event of an accident or occurrence requiring immediate notification to the National Transportation Safety Board under part 830 of its regulations that results in the termination of the flight, any operator who has installed approved flight recorders and approved cockpit voice recorders shall keep the recorded information for at least 60 days or, if requested by the Administrator or the Board, for a longer period. Information obtained from the record is used to assist in determining the cause of accidents or occurrences in connection with the investigation under part 830. The Administrator does not use the cockpit voice recorder record in any civil penalty or certificate action.

EXPLANATION

At no time may the aircraft be operated for more than 30 days with the flight recorder or cockpit voice recorder inoperative.

If an operation is conducted under the authorization of a Minimum Equipment List (MEL) and a letter of authorization issued by the FAA, the operator must operate in accordance with the MEL and the letter of authorization, even if the requirements are more restrictive than those found in 91.609. [Editor's Note: The FAA is evaluating a change to the preamble of the Master MEL to provide relief for operations conducted under Part 91.]

Flight recorder records can be used by the FAA in enforcement actions. The cockpit voice recorder record can not be used in civil penalty or certificate actions.

CROSS REFERENCES

Previous designation: 91.35. Part 91 Appendix E, Airplane Flight Recorder Specifications; Part 91 Appendix F, Helicopter Flight Recorder Specifications; 121.359, Cockpit Voice Recorder; 135.151, Cockpit Voice Recorder; NTSB Part 830, Rules Pertaining To The Notification and Reporting of Aircraft Accidents or Incidents and Overdue Aircraft, and Preservation of Aircraft Wreckage, Mail, Cargo and Records.

ADVISORY CIRCULARS

AC 20-141 *Airworthiness and Operational Approval of Digital Flight Data Recorder Systems* (1999).

AC No. 25.1457-1A *Cockpit Voice Recorder Installation* (1969).

91.611   AUTHORIZATION FOR FERRY FLIGHT WITH ONE ENGINE INOPERATIVE

(a)   *General.* The holder of an air carrier operating certificate or an operating certificate issued under part 125 may conduct a ferry flight of a four-engine airplane or a turbine-engine-powered airplane equipped with three engines, with one engine inoperative, to a base for the purpose of repairing that engine subject to the following:

(1)   The airplane model has been test flown and found satisfactory for safe flight in accordance with paragraph (b) or (c) of this section, as appropriate. However, each operator who before November 19, 1966 has shown that a model of airplane with an engine inoperative is satisfactory for safe flight by a test flight conducted in accordance with performance data contained in the applicable Airplane Flight Manual under paragraph (a)(2) of this section need not repeat the test flight for that model.

(2)   The approved Airplane Flight Manual contains the following performance data and the flight is conducted in accordance with that data:

   (i)   Maximum weight.
   (ii)   Center of gravity limits.
   (iii)   Configuration of the inoperative propeller (if applicable).
   (iv)   Runway length for takeoff (including temperature accountability).
   (v)   Altitude range.
   (vi)   Certificate limitations.
   (vii)   Ranges of operational limits.
   (viii)   Performance information.
   (ix)   Operating procedures.

(3)   The operator has FAA approved procedures for the safe operation of the airplane, including specific requirements for —

   (i)   Limiting the operating weight on any ferry flight to the minimum necessary for the flight plus the necessary reserve fuel load;
   (ii)   A limitation that takeoffs must be made from dry runways unless, based on a showing of actual operating takeoff techniques on wet runways with one engine inoperative, takeoffs with full controllability from wet runways have been approved for the specific model aircraft and included in the Airplane Flight Manual;
   (iii)   Operations from airports where the runways may require a takeoff or approach over populated areas; and
   (iv)   Inspection procedures for determining the operating condition of the operative engines.

(4)   No person may take off an airplane under this section if —

   (I)   The initial climb is over thickly populated areas; or
   (ii)   Weather conditions at the takeoff or destination airport are less than those required for VFR flight.

(5)   Persons other than required flight crewmembers shall not be carried during the flight.

(6)   No person may use a flight crewmember for flight under this section unless that crewmember is thoroughly familiar with the operating procedures for one-engine inoperative ferry flight contained in the certificate holder's manual and the limitations and performance information in the Airplane Flight Manual.

(b)   *Flight tests; reciprocating-engine-powered airplanes.* The airplane performance of a reciprocating-engine-powered airplane with one engine inoperative must be determined by flight test as follows:

(1)   A speed not less than 1.3 V_{S1} must be chosen at which the airplane may be controlled satisfactorily in a climb with the critical engine inoperative (with its propeller removed or in a configuration desired by the operator and with all other engines operating at the maximum power determined in paragraph (b)(3) of this section.

(2)   The distance required to accelerate to the speed listed in paragraph (b)(1) of this section and to climb to 50 feet must be determined with —

   (i)   The landing gear extended;

   (ii)   The critical engine inoperative and its propeller removed or in a configuration desired by the operator; and

   (iii)   The other engines operating at not more than maximum power established under paragraph (b)(3) of this section.

(3)   The takeoff, flight, and landing procedures, such as the approximate trim settings, method of power application, maximum power, and speed must be established.

(4)   The performance must be determined at a maximum weight not greater than the weight that allows a rate of climb of at least 400 feet per minute in the enroute configuration set forth In §25.67(d) of thls chapter In effect on January 31, 1977, at an altltude of 5,000 feet.

(5)   The performance must be determined using temperature accountability for the takeoff field length, computed in accordance with §25.61 of this chapter in effect on January 31, 1977.

(c)   *Flight tests: Turbine-engine-powered airplanes.* The airplane performance of a turbine-engine-powered airplane with one engine inoperative must be determined by flight tests, including at least three takeoff tests in accordance with the following:

(1)   Takeoff speeds V_R and V_2, not less than the corresponding speeds under which the airplane was type certificated under §25.107 of this chapter, must be chosen at which the airplane may be controlled satisfactorily with the critical engine inoperative (with its propeller removed or in a configuration desired by the operator, if applicable) and with all other engines operating at not more than the power selected for type certification as set forth in §25.101 of this chapter.

(2)   The minimum takeoff field length must be the horizontal distance required to accelerate and climb to the 35-foot height at V_2 speed (including any additional speed increment obtained in the tests) multiplied by 115 percent, and determined with —

   (i)   The landing gear extended;

   (ii)   The critical engine inoperative and its propeller removed or in a configuration desired by the operator (if applicable); and

   (iii)   The other engine operating at not more than the power selected for type certification as set forth in §25.101 of this chapter.

(3)   The takeoff, flight, and landing procedures such as the approximate trim setting, method of power application, maximum power, and speed must be established. The airplane must be satisfactorily controllable during the entire takeoff run when operated according to these procoduroc.

(4)   The performance must be determined at a maximum weight not greater than the weight determined under §25.121(c) of this chapter but with —

   (i)   The actual steady gradient of the final takeoff climb requirement not less than 1.2 percent at the end of the takeoff path with two critical engines inoperative; and

   (ii)   The climb speed not less than the two-engine inoperative trim speed for the actual steady gradient of the final takeoff climb prescribed by paragraph (c)(4)(I) of this section.

(5)   The airplane must be satisfactorily controllable in a climb with two critical engines inoperative. Climb performance may be shown by calculations based on, and equal in accuracy to, the results of testing.

(6)   The performance must be determined using temperature accountability for takeoff distance and final takeoff climb computed in accordance with §25.101 of this chapter.
For the purposes of paragraphs (c)(4) and (5), "two critical engines" means two adjacent engines on one side of an airplane with four engines, and the center engine and one outboard engine on an airplane with three engines.

EXPLANATION

An operator that does not hold a Part 121 or Part 125 operating certificate may make application under 21.197 for a special flight authorization (ferry permit) when he/she desires to conduct one-engine inoperative ferry flights.

CROSS REFERENCES

Previous designation: 91.45.

CASES

On a one-engine inoperative ferry flight with three company mechanics on board, [91.611(a)(5)] was violated, because the mechanics were not "required crewmembers," which must be pilots, flight engineers, or flight navigators assigned to duty in an aircraft during flight time. *Administrator v. South Pacific Island Airways, Inc.*, 5 NTSB 2001 (1987).

91.613 MATERIALS FOR COMPARTMENT INTERIORS

No person may operate an airplane that conforms to an amended or supplemental type certificate issued in accordance with SFAR No. 41 for a maximum certificated takeoff weight in excess of 12,500 pounds unless within 1 year after issuance of the initial airworthiness certificate under that SFAR the airplane meets the compartment interior requirements set forth in §25.853(a), (b), (b-1), (b-2), and (b-3) of this chapter in effect on September 26, 1978.

EXPLANATION

This regulation requires that, for all material used in compartment interiors, the requirements imposed by Part 25 for transport category aircraft be met within one year after the aircraft is issued an airworthiness certificate when the aircraft conforms to an amended or supplemental type certificate issued under Special Federal Aviation Regulation No. 41.

CROSS REFERENCES

Previous designation: 91.58. 25.853, Compartment Interiors.

ADVISORY CIRCULARS

AC No. 25.853-1 *Flammability Requirements For Aircraft Seat Cushions* (1986).

INTENTIONALLY

LEFT

BLANK

INTENTIONALLY

LEFT

BLANK

SUBPART H — FOREIGN AIRCRAFT OPERATIONS AND OPERATIONS OF U.S.–REGISTERED CIVIL AIRCRAFT OUTSIDE OF THE UNITED STATES

91.701 APPLICABILITY

(a)	This subpart applies to the operations of civil aircraft of U.S. registry outside of the United States and the operations of foreign civil aircraft within the United States.

(b)	Section 91.702 of this subpart also applies to each person on board an aircraft operated as follows:

(1)	A U.S. registered civil aircraft operated outside the United States;

(2	Any aircraft operated outside the United States—

(i)	That has its next scheduled destination or last place of departure in the United States if the aircraft next lands in the United States; or

(ii)	If the aircraft lands in the United States with the individual still on the aircraft regardless of whether it was a scheduled or otherwise planned landing site.

EXPLANATION

Pilots and operators should be aware that aircraft can and will be seized for nonpayment of landing and navigation fees. There are no statutes of limitation or filing deadlines on these claims. They are claims against the aircraft itself, which means that the aircraft may be seized even though the debt was owed by a previous owner or operator. Because the foreign countries are not required to file a notice of lien, there is no central place to check regarding the existence of any lien.

91.702 PERSONS ON BOARD

Section 91.11 of this part (Prohibitions on interference with crewmembers) applies to each person on board an aircraft.

91.703 OPERATIONS OF CIVIL AIRCRAFT OF U.S. REGISTRY OUTSIDE OF THE UNITED STATES

(a)	Each person operating a civil aircraft of U.S. registry outside of the United States shall —

(1)	When over the high seas, comply with annex 2 (Rules of the Air) to the Convention on International Civil aviation and with §§91.117(c), 91.127, 91.129, and 91.131;

(2)	When within a foreign country, comply with the regulations relating to the flight and maneuver of aircraft there in force;

(3)	Except for §§91.307(b), 91.309, 91.323, and 91.711, comply with this part so far as it is not inconsistent with applicable regulations of the foreign country where the aircraft is operated or annex 2 of the Convention on International Civil Aviation; and

(4)	When operating within airspace designated as Minimum Navigation Performance Specifications (MNPS) airspace, comply with §91.705. when operating within airspace designated as Reduced Vertical Separation Minimum (RVSM) airspace, comply with §91.706.

(b)	Annex 2 to the Convention on International Civil Aviation, Ninth Edition--July 1990, with Amendments through Amendment 32 effective February 19, 1996, to which reference is made a part hereof as provided in 5 U.S.— §552 and pursuant to 1 CFR part 51. Annex 2 (including a complete historic file of changes thereto) is available for public inspection at the Rules Docket, AGC-200, Federal Aviation Administration, 800 Independence Avenue SW., Washington, DC

20591; or at the Office of the Federal Register, 800 North Capitol Street, NW., Suite 700, Washington, DC. In addition, Annex 2 may be purchased from the International Civil Aviation Organization (Attention: Distribution Officer), P.O. Box 400, Succursale, Place de L'Aviation Internationale, 1000 Sherbrooke Street West, Montreal, Quebec, Canada H3A 2R2.

EXPLANATION

While the U.S. has not extended its geographic boundaries beyond 3 nautical miles from the U.S. coast, in December 1988, by Presidential Proclamation, the territorial sovereignty of the United States government for international purposes was extended to 12 miles from the coast of the United States. With the issuance of the proclamation, the airspace between 3 and 12 miles was no longer a part of the high seas. Accordingly, the FAR was amended to extend controlled airspace and the applicability of the flight rules to the airspace overlying the waters between 3 and 12 miles.

PREAMBLE

Various countries throughout the world have adopted the ICAO Annex 6 requirements discussed below for ACAS II equipage in their airspace. In some major areas, countries and regions have adopted accelerated equipage compliance dates. Because 14 CFR 91.703 requires United States operators to comply with the regulations of the countries in which they are operating, the ACAS II equipage requirements of foreign countries have already required United States operators to plan to equip with Version 7.0.

Section 91.703 is entitled "Operations of civil aircraft of U.S. registry outside of the United States". Paragraph 91.703(a)(2) states that each person operating a civil aircraft of U.S. registry outside the United States shall "when within a foreign country, comply with the regulations relating to the flight and maneuver of aircraft there in force".

ICAO Annex 6 Standards for ACAS II Equipage.

ICAO Annex 6 (Operation of Aircraft), part 1 (International Commercial Air Transport--Aeroplanes), paragraph 6.18 contains standards calling for TCAS II, Version 7.0 (ACAS II) equipage for specified aircraft by January 1, 2003. Specifically, it states that all turbine-engined aircraft with a maximum certified take-off mass (gross weight) that exceeds 15,000 kg (33,000 pounds) or authorized to carry more than 30 passengers shall be equipped with ACAS II by January 1, 2003. Annex 6 also calls for all aircraft to be equipped with a pressure altitude reporting transponder that operates in accordance with the relevant provisions of ICAO Annex 10. (66 FR 63891).

CROSS REFERENCES

Previous designation: 91.1. 61.3, Requirement for Certificates, Ratings, and Authorizations; 91.117(c) Aircraft Speed; 91.130 Operations in Class C Airspace; 91.307(b) Parachutes and Parachuting; 91.309, Towing: Gliders; 91.323, Increased Maximum Certificated Weights for Certain Airplanes Operating in Alaska; 91.705, Operations Within the North Atlantic Minimum Navigation Performance Specifications Airspace; 91.711, Special Rules For Foreign Civil Aircraft; Annex 2 (Rules of the Air) to the Convention on International Civil Aviation.

ADVISORY CIRCULARS

AC 90-79 *Recommended Practices and Procedures For Use of Electronic Long-Range Navigation Equipment* (1980).

AC 90-96 *Approval of U.S. Operators and Aircraft to Operate Under Instrument Flight Rules (IFR) in European Airspace Designated for Basic Area Navigation (BRNAV/RNP-5)* (1998).

AC 91-49 *General Aviation Procedures For Flight In North Atlantic Minimum Navigation Performance Specifications Airspace* (1977).

AC 91-70 *Oceanic Operations* (1994).

AERONAUTICAL INFORMATION MANUAL

Flights Outside the United States and U.S. Territories, Para. 5-1-9;
Airways and Route Systems, Para. 5-3-4(d).

CASES

An aircraft owner received suspension for allowing his airplane to be operated without a current annual inspection in the United Kingdom. *Administrator v. Morse*, EA-3766 (1992).

A violation of [91.703(a)(1)] occurred when a captain drifted 170 miles off course between Honolulu, Hawaii, and Los Angeles, California (over the "high seas"). *Administrator v. Anderson*, 4 NTSB 1069 (1983).

In the case where a check airman failed to report that engine temperatures were exceeded during a stall recovery on an Air Jamaica flight from Florida to Jamaica, and subsequently flew the aircraft on to several other destinations, the Board reinstated the order of revocation sought by the Administrator. The stall occurred during an airline flight with (screaming) passengers aboard. *Administrator v. Carter*, EA-4765 (1999).

FAA CHIEF COUNSEL OPINIONS

When operating a U.S. registered airplane within Israel, this FAR requires only that the pilot hold an Israeli pilot certificate and evidence of current medical qualification for that license issued by Israel. This FAR does not permit the pilot, the holder of an Israeli airman certificate, to operate the aircraft outside Israel. (1-28-85).

When a U.S. registered aircraft is operated in Israel the pilot shall comply with the Israeli regulations relating to flight and maneuver of the aircraft. [91.703(a)(3)] provides that, with certain exceptions, Part 91 must be complied with insofar as it is not inconsistent with the applicable regulations of the foreign country. [91.203 and 91.7] require that no person may operate a U.S. registered aircraft unless it has within it an appropriate and current airworthiness certificate, and is in an airworthy condition. Under 21.181, the airworthiness certificate is effective only as long as maintenance, preventive maintenance, and alterations are performed in accordance with the FAR. Therefore, a U.S. registered aircraft operated in Israel must be maintained in accordance with the U.S. standards. (1-28-85).

Under Italian regulations aircraft are not required to be equipped with the combined safety belt and shoulder harness prescribed by [91.521] or with the restraining devices to limit sideward motion of under-seat baggage as required by [91.523]. Also, Italian regulations require a 30 minute fuel reserve plus fuel for certain contingencies as compared to the 45 minute reserve required by [91.167(a)(3)]. Since the cited sections of the FAR are inconsistent with the applicable Italian regulations and the concerned U.S. registered DC-9 airplanes are operated entirely outside the U.S., under the provisions of [91.703(a)(3), 91.167(a)(3), (91.521 and (91.523)] are not applicable to the operation of these aircraft. (2-16-83).

91.705 OPERATIONS WITHIN AIRSPACE DESIGNATED AS MINIMUM NAVIGATION PERFORMANCE SPECIFICATION AIRSPACE.

(a) Except as provided in paragraph (b) of this section, no person may operate a civil aircraft of U.S. registry in airspace designated as Minimum Navigation Performance Specifications airspace unless—
  (1) The aircraft has approved navigation performance capability that complies with the requirements of appendix C of this part; and
  (2) The operator is authorized by the Administrator to perform such operations.
(b) The Administrator may authorize a deviation from the requirements of this section in accordance with Section 3 of appendix C to this part.

EXPLANATION

The purpose of this regulation is to meet the standards adopted by the International Civil Aviation Organization (ICAO) to permit a more efficient use of this airspace.

The FAA publishes *North Atlantic MNPS Airspace Operations Manual* to assist pilots and dispatchers. For answers to questions about MNPS airspace, call Anderson Davie, FAA Navigation Specialist (415) 876-2771. Pilots planning to use the MNPS airspace should contact the FAA well in advance of the proposed flight, so that a Letter of Authorization can be obtained in a timely manner.

FAR 91.705 does not require that a copy of a deviation from FAR Part 91, Appendix C, Section 3, be carried on board the aircraft. However, the inspector should encourage the operator to carry a copy of the deviation in the aircraft to prevent any problems that might possibly arise from a ramp inspection away from the operator's principal base.

CROSS REFERENCES

Previous designation: 91.20. 91.901-91.905, Waivers; Appendix C, Part 91.

ADVISORY CIRCULARS

AC 25-4 *Inertial Navigation Systems* (1966).

AC 90-79 *Recommended Practices and Procedures For Use of Electronic Long-Range Navigation Equipment* (1980).

AC 91-49 *General Aviation Procedures For Flight In the North Atlantic Minimum Navigation Performance Specifications Airspace* (1977).

AC 91-70 *Oceanic Operations* (1994).

North Atlantic International General Aviation Operations Manual (1990) [An FAA publication]

CASES

If an aircraft is not NAT-MNPS airspace qualified, a deviation must be obtained from ATC before it can be operated in that airspace. The issuance of a flight dispatch by the air carrier does not obviate the need for such deviation. *Administrator v. Hampton*, 5 NTSB 2410 (1987).

91.706 OPERATIONS WITHIN AIRSPACE DESIGNED AS REDUCED VERTICAL SEPARATION MINIMUM AIRSPACE.

(a)   Except as provided in paragraph (b) of this section, no person may operate a civil aircraft of U.S. registry in airspace designated as Reduced Vertical Separation Minimum (RVSM) airspace unless:

   (1)   The operator and the operator's aircraft comply with the requirements of appendix G of this part; and

   (2)   The operator is authorized by the Administrator to the conduct such operations.

(b)   The Administrator may authorize a deviation from the requirements of this section in accordance with Section 5 of appendix G to this part.

EXPLANATION

This 1997 rule allows the vertical separation minimum to be reduced from 2,000 feet to 1,000 feet between FL 290 and FL 410 in certain designated airspace. This rule was intended to increase the number of available flight levels, enhance airspace capacity, permit operators to fly more fuel/time efficient tracks and altitudes, and enhance air traffic controller flexibility by increasing the number of available flight levels, while maintaining an equivalent level of safety.

The FAA publishes *North Atlantic MNPS Airspace Operations Manual* to assist pilots and dispatchers. For answers to questions about MNPS airspace, call Anderson Davie, FAA Navigation Specialist (415) 876-2771(West Coast), or David Maloy, FAA Navigation Specialist (516) 228-8040, ext. 229 (East Coast). Pilots planning to use the MNPS airspace should contact the FAA well in advance of the proposed flight, so that a Letter of Authorization can be obtained in a timely manner. FAA Order 8400.12, *Required Navigation Performance 10 (RNP-10) Operational Approval* provides guidance for West Coast and Alaskan Letters of Authorization.

Interim Guidance 91-RVSM, located at URL www.faa.gov/ats/ato/150_docs/igchg-pg.doc, provides detailed guidance for operators and aircraft manufacturers to follow when developing programs intended to meet the requirements of section 91.706 and part 91, appendix G.

PREAMBLE

To help operators prepare to comply with the requirements of this rule, the FAA has prepared two documents. The first is Interim Guidance Material on the Approval of Operators/Aircraft for RVSM Operations (91-RVSM). This document contains guidance for the approval of aircraft and operators to conduct RVSM operations. It is based on the ICAO manual on RVSM. It was developed in the NATSPG forum by technical and operational experts from the FAA, the European Joint Airworthiness Authorities (JAA), the aircraft manufacturers, and pilot associations. The FAA is taking steps to publish it as an advisory circular (AC). In the interim, a copy of 91-RVSM may be obtained by contacting Mr. Roy Grimes, AFS-400, Technical Programs Division, Flight Standards Service, Federal Aviation Administration, 800 Independence Avenue, SW., Washington, DC 20591, telephone (202) 267-3734.

The second document is a Flight Standards Handbook Bulletin (HBAT) 97-02 entitled Approval of Aircraft and Operators for Flight in Airspace Above Flight Level 290 Where 1,000 Foot Vertical Separation Minimum Is Applied, and has been distributed through Flight Standards offices.

The interim guidance material describes methods of complying with the airworthiness approval, maintenance program approval, and operations approval requirements in the rule. It discusses timing, process, and maintenance and operations material that the operator should submit for FAA review and evaluation normally at least 60 days before the planned operation in RVSM airspace. Operators under Title 14, Code of Federal Regulations (14 CFR) part 91 receive FAA approval in the form of a letter of authorization, and operators under 14 CFR parts 121, 125, and 135 receive operations specifications approval.

The HBAT contains background information on RVSM, directs inspectors to use the Interim Guidance 91-RVSM for operator approval, and contains specific direction on issuing operating authority.

Current Requirements

In the Federal Aviation Regulations, 14 CFR 91.179(b)(3) establishes the 2,000 ft minimum separation in domestic airspace by requiring that flights in uncontrolled airspace at and above FL 290 on easterly magnetic courses (zero degrees through 179 degrees) be conducted at 4,000 ft intervals, starting at FL 290, (e.g., FL 290, 330, or 370). West-bound flights (magnetic courses of 180 degrees through 359 degrees) must be conducted at 4,000 ft intervals beginning at FL 310 (e.g., FL 310, 350, or 390). Flights in controlled airspace must be conducted at an altitude assigned by ATC.

For operations within a foreign country, 14 CFR 91.703 requires compliance with that country's regulations. For operations over the high seas outside the United States, 14 CFR 91.703 requires that aircraft of U.S. registry comply with Annex 2 (Rules of the Air) to the Convention on International Civil Aviation. Annex 2, amendment 32, effective February 19, 1996, reflects the planned change from 2,000 feet to 1,000 feet vertical separation for Instrument Flight Rules (IFR) traffic between FL 290 and FL 410, based on appropriate airspace designation, international agreements, and conformance with specified conditions. By this amendment, Annex 2, through amendment 32, is incorporated by reference in '91.703(b).

Regulatory requirements for operations within the NAT MNPS by U.S.-registered aircraft are contained in 14 CFR 91.705. The regulation states that the aircraft must have approved navigation performance capability that meets specified requirements, and that the operator have authorization from the Administrator for operations in the NAT MNPS.

The NAT MNPS is addressed in greater detail in appendix C to Part 91, Operations in the North Atlantic (NAT) Minimum Navigation Performance Specifications (MNPS) Airspace. The appendix defines the airspace geographically and sets minimum navigation performance capability requirements.

General Discussion of the Amendment

This rule allows operations of civil aircraft of U.S. registration outside the U.S. in airspace where a 1,000 foot vertical separation is applied, based on improvements in altitude-keeping technology. These improvements include:

- Introduction of the air data computer (ADC), which provides an automatic means of correcting the known static source error of aircraft to improve aircraft altitude measurement capability.
- Development of altimeters with enhanced transducers or double aneroids for computing altitude.

Under this amendment, airspace or routes in which RVSM is applied are considered special qualification airspace. Both the operator and the specific types of aircraft that the operator intends to use in RVSM airspace would have to be approved by the appropriate FAA office before the operator conducts flights in RVSM airspace.

Implementation of a 1,000 foot vertical separation standard above FL 290 offers substantial operational benefits to operators, including:

- Greater availability of the most fuel-efficient altitudes. In the RVSM environment, aircraft are able to fly closer to their optimum altitude at initial level off and through step climbing to the optimum altitude during the enroute phase.
- Greater availability of the most time- and fuel-efficient tracks and routes (and an increased probability of obtaining these tracks and routes). Operators often are not cleared on the track or route that was filed due to demand for the optimum routes, and resultant traffic congestion on those routes. RVSM allows ATC to accommodate a greater number of aircraft on a given track or route. More time- and fuel-efficient tracks or routes would therefore be available to more aircraft.
- Increased controller flexibility. RVSM gives ATC greater flexibility to manage traffic by increasing the number of flight levels on each track or route.
- Enhanced safety in the lateral dimension. Studies indicate that RVSM produces a wider distribution of aircraft among different tracks and altitudes, resulting in less exposure to aircraft at adjacent separation standards. RVSM reduces the number of occasions when two aircraft pass each other separated by a single separation standard (e.g., 60 nm laterally). The benefit to safety is that, should an aircraft enter, as a result of gross navigation error, onto an adjacent track, and another aircraft is on that track, there is an increased probability that the two aircraft would be flying at different flight levels.

NATSPG has agreed to change the floor and ceiling of MNPS airspace to FL 285 and FL 420. This change will enable the application of RVSM between FL 290 and FL 410, inclusive. The FAA does not consider this to be a substantive change.

Specific guidance on how to meet the requirements is available in Interim Guidance Material 91-RVSM, which addresses various aspects of RVSM requirements, including maintenance and operations programs. Operators can obtain authorization for RVSM from their local Flight Standards District Office (FSDO) or Certificate Management Office. Approval of aircraft may be given for aircraft groups or for individual aircraft. In the former case, the FAA expects that operators would need to enlist the assistance of the aircraft manufacturers to develop the necessary data on the aircraft group. In the latter case, the operator would work with the FAA to determine the accuracy of the altitude-keeping equipment on the individual aircraft.

This amendment results in more stringent vertical navigation standards in oceanic airspace; the standards will be applied in other airspace above FL 290 as they are designated as RVSM airspace in the future. In NAT MNPS airspace, aircraft and operators that do not meet the vertical navigation requirements of RVSM will be accommodated in 4 ways C

(1) RVSM will be implemented in stages. In Stage 1, RVSM approval will be required when operating between FL 33 to FL 370 inclusive. Unapproved operators will have the option of flying at FL 310 and below or FL 390 and above. The staged implementation plan was adopted to give operators more time and flexibility in their planning to gain RVSM approval (Note: NATSPG will evaluate user needs before implementing a second stage that applies RVSM requirements to other flight levels.).

(2)   Unapproved operators will be allowed to climb or descend in MNPS airspace through flight levels where RVSM is applied to operate at FL's where RVSM is not applied.

(3)   The operator may be authorized to deviate from RVSM requirements in accordance with the provisions of Appendix G, Section 5. Though it is not intended to be the routine mode of operation, this section does enable an operator that has not been RVSN approved (or an aircraft with an RVSM required system temporarily inoperative) to fly in MNPS airspace where RVSM is applied provided request is made in advance and ATC determines that appropriate separation can be applied without imposing a burden on other operators.

(4)   When RVSM is applied to all flight levels in MNPS airspace (FL 290 to 410 inclusive), the operator not wishing to gain RVSM approval will retain the option of crossing the North Atlantic at FL's above or below airspace where RVSM requirements apply. Such an operator will be able to fly at FL 280 and below or FL 430 and above. The FAA has determined that these are reasonable and adequate means to accommodate the transition to RVSM requirements, particularly for general aviation operators.

The Interim Guidance is intended to be applicable for RVSM aircraft and operator approval in continental, oceanic, and remote airspace. The FAA expects that RVSM eventually will be applied in other airspace, including the Pacific region, Europe, and eventually even U.S. airspace. The rule establishes requirements for operation of U.S. registered aircraft outside the U.S. in any airspace designated for RVSM; it specifically establishes that the NAT MNPS airspace is an area where RVSM may be applied. (62 FR 17483-17486).

CROSS REFERENCES

91.703, Operations of Civil Aircraft of U.S. Registry Outside of the United States; 91.705, Operations within Airspace designated as Minimum Navigation Performance Specification Airspace; Appendix G, Part 91.

ADVISORY CIRCULARS

AC 25-4 *Inertial Navigation Systems* (1966).

AC 90-79 *Recommended Practices and Procedures For Use of Electronic Long-Range Navigation Equipment* (1980).

AC 91-70 *Oceanic Operations* (1994).

North Atlantic International General Aviation Operations Manual (1990) [An FAA publication]

91.707 FLIGHTS BETWEEN MEXICO OR CANADA AND THE UNITED STATES

Unless otherwise authorized by ATC, no person may operate a civil aircraft between Mexico or Canada and the United States without filing an IFR or VFR flight plan, as appropriate.

CROSS REFERENCES

Previous designation: 91.84. 91.153 VFR Flight Plan: Information Required; 91.169, IFR Flight Plan: Information Required; 91.901-91.905, Waivers.

AERONAUTICAL INFORMATION MANUAL

Flights Outside the United States and U.S. Territories, Para. 5-1-9;
Airways and Route Systems, Para. 5-3-4(d).

91.709 OPERATIONS TO CUBA

No person may operate a civil aircraft from the United States to Cuba unless —
(a)   Departure is from an international airport of entry designated in §6.13 of the Air Commerce Regulations of the Bureau of Customs (19 CFR 6.13); and
(b)   In the case of departure from any of the 48 contiguous States or the District of Columbia, the pilot in command of the aircraft has filed —
    (1)   A DVFR or IFR flight plan as prescribed in §99.11 or 99.13 of this chapter; and
    (2)   A written statement, within 1 hour before departure, with the Office of Immigration and Naturalization Service at the airport of departure, containing —
        (i)   All information in the flight plan;
        (ii)   The name of each occupant of the aircraft;
        (iii) The number of occupants of the aircraft; and
        (iv)   A description of the cargo, if any.
    This section does not apply to the operation of aircraft by a scheduled air carrier over routes authorized in operations specifications issued by the Administrator.

EXPLANATION

This regulation does not speak to over-flights of Cuba. Prior to undertaking such a flight, a pilot should review the International Flight Manual, Part 99 and Annex 2 to ICAO.

CROSS REFERENCES

Previous designation: 91.101. Part 99, Security Control of Air Traffic; International Flight Information Manual; 19 C.F.R. 122.151-122.158, Flights To and From Cuba, U.S. Customs Service, Treasury Department.

AERONAUTICAL INFORMATION MANUAL

Transponder Operation, Para. 4-1-19(f)(3);
Flight Plan-VFR Flights, Para. 5-1-4(a);
Flight Plan-Defense VFR (DVFR) Flights, Para. 5-1-5;
Flights Outside the United States and U.S. Territories, Para. 5-1-9;
Airways and Route Systems, Para. 5-3-4(d);
National Security, Para. 5-6-1;
ADIZ Boundaries and Designated Mountainous Areas, Para. 5-6-5;
Preflight Briefing, Para. 7-1-4.

91.711 SPECIAL RULES FOR FOREIGN CIVIL AIRCRAFT

(a)   *General.* In addition to the other applicable regulations of this part, each person operating a foreign civil aircraft within the United States shall comply with this section.

(b)   *VFR.* No person may conduct VFR operations which require two-way radio communications under this part unless at least one crewmember of that aircraft is able to conduct two-way radio communications in the English language and is on duty during that operation.

(c)   *IFR.* No person may operate a foreign civil aircraft under IFR unless —
    (1)   That aircraft is equipped with —
        (i)   Radio equipment allowing two-way radio communication with ATC when it is operated in controlled airspace; and
        (ii)   Radio navigational equipment appropriate to the navigational facilities to be used;
    (2)   Each person piloting the aircraft —
        (i)   Holds a current United States instrument rating or is authorized by his foreign airman certificate to pilot under IFR; and
        (ii)   Is thoroughly familiar with the United States enroute, holding, and letdown procedures; and
    (3)   At least one crewmember of that aircraft is able to conduct two-way radiotelephone communications in the English language and that crewmember is on duty while the aircraft is approaching, operating within, or leaving the United States.

(d)   *Over water.* Each person operating a foreign civil aircraft over water off the shores of the United States shall give flight notification or file a flight plan in accordance with the Supplementary Procedure for the ICAO region concerned.

(e)   *Flight at and above FL 240.* If VOR navigational equipment is required under paragraph (c)(1)(ii) of this section, no person may operate a foreign civil aircraft within the 50 states and the District of Columbia at or above FL 240, unless the aircraft is equipped with distance measuring equipment (DME) capable of receiving and indicating distance information from the VORTAC facilities to be used. When DME required by this paragraph fails at and above FL 240, the pilot in command of the aircraft shall notify ATC immediately and may then continue operations at and above FL 240 to the next airport of intended landing at which repairs or replacement of the equipment can be made. However, paragraph (e) of this section does not apply to foreign civil aircraft that are not equipped with DME when operated for the following purposes and if ATC is notified prior to each takeoff:
    (1)   Ferry flights to and from a place in the United States where repairs or alterations are to be made.
    (2)   Ferry flights to a new country of registry.
    (3)   Flight of a new aircraft of U.S. manufacture for the purpose of —
        (i)   Flight testing the aircraft;
        (ii)   Training foreign flight crews in the operation of the aircraft; or
        (iii)   Ferrying the aircraft for export delivery outside the United States.
    (4)   Ferry, demonstration, and test flight of an aircraft brought to the United States for the purpose of demonstration or testing the whole or any part thereof.

EXPLANATION

Prior to the operation of a foreign civil aircraft within the United States, the provisions of 14 C.F.R. Part 375, Navigation of Foreign Civil Aircraft Within the United States, should be reviewed and complied with.

CROSS REFERENCES

Previous designation: 91.43. 61.3, Requirements For Certificates, Ratings, and Authorizations; Part 34, Fuel Venting and Exhaust Emission Requirements for Turbine Engine Powered Aircraft; Part 91, Subpart I, Operating Noise Limits; 14 C.F.R. Part 375, Navigation of Foreign Civil Aircraft Within the United States.

91.713 OPERATION OF CIVIL AIRCRAFT OF CUBAN REGISTRY

No person may operate a civil aircraft of Cuban registry except in controlled airspace and in accordance with air traffic clearance or air traffic control instructions that may require use of specific airways or routes and landings at specific airports.

EXPLANATION

A person operating a civil aircraft of Cuban registry within the United States must operate in controlled airspace, and, whether operating IFR or VFR, must obtain an ATC clearance.

CROSS REFERENCES

Previous designation: 91.103. 61.3, Requirements For Certificates, Ratings, and Authorizations; 91.901-91.905, Waivers.

91.715 SPECIAL FLIGHT AUTHORIZATIONS FOR FOREIGN CIVIL AIRCRAFT

(a) Foreign civil aircraft may be operated without airworthiness certificates required under §91.203 if a special flight authorization for that operation is issued under this section. Application for a special flight authorization must be made to the Flight Standards Division Manager or Aircraft Certification Directorate Manager of the FAA region in which the applicant is located or to the region within which the U.S. point of entry is located. However, in the case of an aircraft to be operated in the U.S. for the purpose of demonstration at an air show, the application may be made to the Flight Standards Division Manager or Aircraft Certification Directorate Manager of the FAA region in which the air show is located.

(b) The Administrator may issue a special flight authorization for a foreign civil aircraft subject to any conditions and limitations that the Administrator considers necessary for safe operation in the U.S. airspace.

(c) No person may operate a foreign civil aircraft under a special flight authorization unless that operation also complies with part 375 of the Special Regulations of the Department of Transportation (14 CFR 375).

EXPLANATION

This regulation provides a means whereby an aircraft purchased from a U.S. manufacturer in the United States and immediately registered in a foreign country, but not yet issued an airworthiness certificate by that country, can be flown from the factory to another facility in the U.S. for interior modification, etc.

CROSS REFERENCES

Previous designation: 91.28. 91.203, Civil Aircraft: Certificates Required; 14 C.F.R. Part 375, Navigation of Foreign Civil Aircraft Within the United States.

ADVISORY CIRCULARS

AC 20-65 *U.S. Airworthiness Certificates and Authorizations for Operation of Domestic and Foreign Aircraft* (1969).

INTENTIONALLY

LEFT

BLANK

INTENTIONALLY

LEFT

BLANK

SUBPART I — OPERATING NOISE LIMITS

91.801 APPLICABILITY: RELATION TO PART 36

(a) This subpart prescribes operating noise limits and related requirements that apply, as follows, to the operation of civil aircraft in the United States

    (1) Sections 91.803, 91.805, 91.807, 91.809, and 91.811 apply to civil subsonic turbojet airplanes with maximum weights of more than 75,000 pounds and —

        (i) If U.S. registered, that have standard airworthiness certificates; or

        (ii) If foreign registered, that would be required by this chapter to have a U.S. standard airworthiness certificate in order to conduct the operations intended for the airplane were it registered in the United States. Those sections apply to operations to or from airports in the United States under this part and parts 121, 125, 129, and 135 of this chapter.

    (2) Section 91.813 applies to U.S. operators of civil subsonic turbojet airplanes covered by this subpart. That section applies to operators operating to or from airports in the United States under this part and parts 121, 125, and 135, but not to those operating under part 129 of this chapter.

    (3) Sections 91.803 and 91.819, and 91.821 apply to U.S. registered civil supersonic airplanes having standard airworthiness certificates and to foreign-registered civil supersonic airplanes that, if registered in the United States, would be required by this chapter to have U.S. standard airworthiness certificates in order to conduct the operations intended for the airplane. Those sections apply to operations under this part and under parts 121, 125, 129, and 135 of this chapter.

(b) Unless otherwise specified, as used in this subpart "part 36" refers to 14 CFR part 36, including the noise levels under appendix C of that part, notwithstanding the provisions of that part excepting certain airplanes from the specified noise requirements. For purposes of this subpart, the various stages of noise levels, the terms used to describe airplanes with respect to those levels, and the terms "subsonic airplane" and "supersonic airplane" have the meanings specified under part 36 of this chapter. For purposes of this subpart, for subsonic airplanes operated in foreign air commerce in the United States, the Administrator may accept compliance with the noise requirements under annex 16 of the International Civil Aviation Organization when those requirements have been shown to be substantially compatible with, and achieve results equivalent to those achievable under part 36 for that airplane. Determinations made under these provisions are subject to the limitations of §36.5 of this chapter as if those noise levels were part 36 noise levels.

(c) Sections 91.851 through 91.877 of this subpart prescribe operating noise limits and related requirements that apply to any civil subsonic turbojet airplane with a maximum certificated weight of more than 75,000 pounds operating to or from an airport in the 48 contiguous United States and the District of Columbia under this part, part 121, 125, 129, or 135 of this chapter on and after September 25, 1991.

(d) Section 91.877 prescribes reporting requirements that apply to any civil subsonic turbojet airplane with a maximum weight of more than 75,000 pounds operated by an air carrier or foreign air carrier between the contiguous United States and the State of Hawaii, between the State of Hawaii and any point outside of the 48 contiguous United States, or between the islands of Hawaii in turnaround service, under part 121 or 129 of this chapter on or after November 5, 1990.

EXPLANATION

This regulation implements the provisions of the various noise abatement policies and statutes including the Airport Noise and Capacity Act of 1990 [49 U.S.C. App. §2151 et. seq.]. The provisions of 91.851 through 91.875 are applicable to all civil subsonic turbojet airplanes with a maximum certificated weight of over 75,000 pounds except those operating under an experimental airworthiness certificate.

Aircraft which are operated in foreign air commerce in the United States, and are in compliance with Annex 16 of the International Civil Aviation Organization (ICAO) — The FAA will determine whether the ICAO requirements are substantially compatible with, and will achieve results equivalent to those achievable under FAR Part 36 on a plane-by-plane basis.

PREAMBLE

The changes described below may appear to conflict with various portions of the noise transition regulations currently codified at 14 CFR 91.801 through 91.877. However, the new provisions state that the regulations are to be considered modified where they conflict with any new statutory provisions. The FAA is aware that the statutory change is not apparent to anyone reading the regulations, and plans to change the regulations through appropriate rulemaking within the next year.

Experimental Certificates

Turbojet airplanes over 75,000 pounds that operate under an experimental airworthiness certificate have been excepted from the law. The requirement that aircraft over 75,000 pounds meet Stage 3 noise levels no longer applies to airplanes with experimental airworthiness certificates. These airplanes may continue to be flown after December 31, 1999, without further action by the operator or by the FAA. The prohibition on non-Stage 3 operation continues to apply to all airplanes operating under any other type of airworthiness certificate.

Nonrevenue Stage 2 Operations

The revised law now permits a range of nonrevenue Stage 2 operations to occur after December 31, 1999. Any operator of a Stage 2 airplane over 75,000 pounds may operate that airplane in the contiguous United States for the following purposes:
- Sell, lease or scrap the airplane
- Obtain modifications to meet Stage 3 noise levels
- Obtain scheduled heavy maintenance or significant modifications
- Deliver the airplane to a lessee or return it to a lessor
- Park or store the airplane
- Prepare the airplane for any of these events

With regard to these listed uses, operators are advised to note the following:
(1) Nonrevenue flight is a shorthand term. Whether you are a commercial or noncommercial operator, Stage 2 operations are restricted to the purposes listed above only. No "dual purposes" are allowed. For example, you may not operate a Stage 2 airplane for one of the listed purposes and also transport a company official or company goods, or accomplish any action in furtherance of company business. Nonrevenue service means that the flight does not generate any revenue for carrying passengers or cargo.
(2) Operators moving a Stage 2 airplane to location where Stage 3 modifications may be obtained must provide a copy of the modification contract to the FAA with the application for a special flight authorization. For the other purposes, documentation of the activity may be required depending on the circumstances presented.

(3)   "Scheduled heavy maintenance" means a "C" or "D" check. The FAA interprets the statutory language to mean that operators of Stage 2 airplanes may not request a special flight authorization to accomplish routine light maintenance actions in the United States.

(4)   Similarly, "significantly modifications" is interpreted as those that require specialized knowledge or equipment not readily available elsewhere, or is not practicable to obtain outside the United States. All requests claiming significant modifications will be reviewed individually.

(5)   No Stage 1 operations of covered airplanes are permitted for any reason.

Special Flight Authorizations

The FAA is implementing the provisions of the law that allow nonrevenue flights by issuing special flight authorizations. An operator of a Stage 2 airplane that wishes to operate in the contiguous United States for any of the purposes listed in the revised statute (and above) may apply to the FAA's Office of Environment and Energy (AEE) for a special flight authorization. The applicant must file in advance. Applications are due 30 days in advance of the planned flight and must provide the information necessary for the FAA to determine that the planned flight is within the limits prescribed in the law.

Any Stage 2 airplane (not otherwise excepted from the law), that operates for any reason after December 31, 1999, without a special flight authorization, will be considered in violation of the law. The operator may be subject to civil penalties (including a fine of up to $11,000 per flight) or other remedial actions, including cease and desist orders. Once granted, the special flight authorization must be carried on board the airplane during the authorized flight. Similar to other special flight authorization, only flight crew members are permitted on board the airplane during the flight. Further, the special flight authorizations issued by AEE are for noise only. They are not substitutes for any other authorization or ferry permit that may be required for airworthiness or other reasons, such as those granted under 14 CFR §21.199 or §43.3.

To simplify the application process, the FAA has developed a form that lists the information that the applicant must supply. Use of this form is not mandatory; it is intended to simplify the process. The form does contain important reminders about the use of special flight authorizations. In some cases, more information than is requested on the form may be necessary for the FAA to determine whether a special flight authorization can be issued.

The form has received OMB approval for information collection and can be obtained on the FAA's web site (http://www.aee.faa.gov/noise/aee100_files/sfa_operatorform.pdf) or by fax or mail by contacting the Office of Environment and Energy at the number listed in the For Further Information Contact section above. The form is also reproduced below.

Given the short notice of these changes and procedures necessitated by the recent passage of the legislation, the FAA will make every attempt to satisfy the needs of affected operators of Stage 2 airplanes in a timely manner. Operators of Stage 2 airplanes that have any questions concerning their rights or requirement under the new statutory language are encouraged to contact the FAA as soon as possible.

Request for Special Flight Authorization Stage 2 Airplane Over 75,000 Pounds

1. Applying Operator:
   (a) Operator's Name:
   (b) Address:
   (c) City:
   (d) State and zip code:
   (e) Country:
   (f) Contact Name:
   (g) Contact Phone Number:
   (h) Contact Fax Number:
   (i) Contact E-mail Address:
2. Airplane:
   (a) Airplane Make, Model, and Series:
   (b) Registration Number (including country of registration):
   (c) Serial Number:
   (d) Current Noise Certification (check one):
       ____ Stage 1   ____ Stage 2
3. Purpose (check one and fill in appropriate fields):
   ____ (a) Sell, lease or use the airplane outside the contiguous 48 States;
   ____ (b) Scrap the airplane;
   ____ (c) Obtain modifications to the airplane to meet Stage 3 noise levels (copy of modification contract required with this application);
   ____ (d) Perform scheduled heavy maintenance or significant modifications on the airplane at a maintenance facility in the contiguous 48 States. Maintenance (check all applicable):
       ____ 'C' Check
       ____ 'D' Check
       ____ Other significant modifications (describe):
   ____ (e) Deliver the airplane to a lessee (include name and address of both parties below);
   ____ (f) Return the airplane to the lessor (include name and address of both parties below);
   ____ (g) Prepare or park or store the airplane in anticipation of any of the activities described in (a) through (e) (include name and location of storage or maintenance facility):

       Company's Name:
       Company's Location:

4. Flights:
   (a) Dates (approximate start and end dates);
   (b) Describe each flight (origin and destination). Designate if fuel stop only.
       Flight 1:
       Flight 2:
       ...
       Flight __:

5. Fill in number of persons on board in the appropriate boxes (up to 5 persons total).
   ____ Pilot   ____ Officer   ____ Flight Engineer   ____ Maintenance/Tech Representative

6. Other information:

Note: This form is an application for a special flight authorization only. It may not be used to fly an airplane. It must be submitted to the FAA, which will issue a special flight authorization based on the information submitted.

When issued, the Special Flight Authorization must be carried on board the airplane during the authorized flight. Persons on board are limited to flightcrew only. A Special Flight Authorization issued pursuant to this application is for noise only, and may not be used as a substitute for other ferry permit or authorization that may be required for airworthiness or other purposes, such as 14 CFR §21.199 or §43.3. (64 FR 70571).

CROSS REFERENCES

Previous designation: 91.301. 14 C.F.R. Part 36; 49 U.S.C. App. §2151 et.seq.

ADVISORY CIRCULARS

AC 36-1G *Noise Levels for U.S. Certificated and Foreign Aircraft* (1997).

AC 36-2C *Measured Or Estimated (Uncertified) Airplane Noise Levels* (1986).

AC 36-3G *Estimated Airplane Noise Levels in A-Weighted Decibels* (1996).

AC 36-4B *Noise Certification Handbook* (1988).

AC 91-53A *Noise Abatement Departure Profiles* (1993).

AC 91-66 *Noise Abatement for Helicopters* (1987).

AC 150/5020-1 *Noise Control and Compatibility Planning For Airports* (1983).

FAA CHIEF COUNSEL OPINIONS

Alaskan Operations:

Question — Since operations in the state of Alaska are not affected by either the nonaddition rule (§91.855) or the phased transition rules (§§91.865 91.867), are operators that operate exclusively in Alaska exempt from §§91.851 through 91.875?

> Response — No. Each operator of a large Stage 2 airplane is subject to the transition rules, including the nonaddition rule and the reporting requirements of §91.875. Each operator of a covered airplane must establish its base level and report its compliance. §91.801(c) indicates that the operating noise limits and related requirements codified in §§91.851 through 91.875 apply to:

Any civil subsonic turbojet airplane with a maximum certificated weight of more than 75,000 pounds operating to or from an airport in the 48 contiguous United States and the District of Columbia under this part [Part 91], Part 121, 125, 129, or 135 of this chapter on and after September 25, 1991.

The fact that an operator restricts operation of its airplanes to Alaska is not relevant to coverage. It is true, however, that the operation of Stage 2 airplanes in Alaska is not affected by the statutory prohibition or the interim compliance requirements. At this time, the FAA foresees allowing operators of affected airplanes that operate solely outside the contiguous United States to amend their operations specifications to remove these airplanes from operation in the contiguous United States. Any airplane that is restricted to operation outside the non-contiguous United States may be used to achieve compliance with the statutorily mandated restriction on the operation of Stage 2 airplanes.

The FAA realizes that operators that operate solely in Alaska (or other locations outside the contiguous United States) fall into a special category as far as the transition to an all Stage 3 fleet. While these operators must be treated the same as other domestic operators, they nonetheless present a special case since their Stage 2 airplanes are not restricted from their usual flight areas. For this reason, all operators are required to establish a base level and phase into an all Stage 3 fleet of airplanes operating in the contiguous United States. Any operator may comply with the transition requirements by removing its Stage 2 airplanes from operation in the contiguous United States.

While §91.857 addresses the operation of Stage 2 airplanes that are "imported" into the noncontiguous United States, these same provisions would apply to any currently operated airplane that an operator wishes to remove from operation in the contiguous United States. Thus, an operator may take advantage of §91.857(a) to change its operation specifications to meet the interim compliance dates, as necessary, and may use §91.857(b) to obtain a special flight authorization to operate a restricted Stage 2 airplane into the contiguous United States for the purpose of maintenance. (10-13-92).

91.803 PART 125 OPERATORS: DESIGNATION OF APPLICABLE REGULATIONS

For airplanes covered by this subpart and operated under part 125 of this chapter, the following regulations apply as specified:
(a) For each airplane operation to which requirements prescribed under this subpart applied before November 29, 1980, those requirements of this subpart continue to apply.
(b) For each subsonic airplane operation to which requirements prescribed under this subpart did not apply before November 29, 1980, because the airplane was not operated in the United States under this part or part 121, 129, or 135 of this chapter, the requirements prescribed under §§91.805, 91.809, 91.811, and 91.813 of this subpart apply.
(c) For each supersonic airplane operation to which requirements prescribed under this subpart did not apply before November 29, 1980, because the airplane was not operated in the United States under this part or Part 121, 129, or 135 of this chapter, the requirements of §§91.819 and 91.821 of this subpart apply.
(d) For each airplane required to operate under part 125 for which a deviation under that part is approved to operate, in whole or in part, under this part or parts 121, 129, or 135 of this chapter, notwithstanding the approval, the requirements prescribed under paragraphs (a), (b), and (c) of this section continue to apply.

EXPLANATION

Aircraft, operated under Parts 91, 121, 123, 129 and 135, that became subject to Part 125 on its effective date, remain subject to the particular noise requirements that were applicable to them prior to the effective date of Part 125.

CROSS REFERENCES

Previous designation: 91.302. 91.805, Final Compliance: Subsonic Airplanes; 91.809, Replacement Airplanes; 91.811, Service to Small Communities Exemption: Two-Engine, Subsonic Airplanes; 91.813, Compliance Plans and Status: U.S. Operators of Subsonic Airplanes; 91.819, Civil Supersonic Airplanes That Do Not Comply With Part 36; 91.821, Civil Supersonic Airplanes: Noise Limits; 14 C.F.R. Part 36; 49 U.S.C. App. §2151 et.seq.

ADVISORY CIRCULARS

AC 36-1G *Noise Levels for U.S. Certificated and Foreign Aircraft* (1997).

AC 36-2C *Measured Or Estimated (Uncertified) Airplane Noise Levels* (1980).

AC 36-3G *Estimated Airplane Noise Levels in A-Weighted Decibels* (1996).

AC 36-4B *Noise Certification Handbook* (1988).

AC 91-53A *Noise Abatement Departure Profiles* (1993).

AC 91-66 *Noise Abatement for Helicopters* (1987).

AC 150/5020-1 *Noise Control and Compatibility Planning For Airports* (1983).

91.805 FINAL COMPLIANCE: SUBSONIC AIRPLANES

Except as provided in §§91.809 and 91.811, on and after January 1, 1985, no person may operate to or from an airport in the United States any subsonic airplane covered by this subpart unless that airplane has been shown to comply with Stage 2 or Stage 3 noise levels under part 36 of this chapter.

CROSS REFERENCES

Previous designation: 91.303. 91.809, Replacement Airplanes; 91.811, Service to Small Communities Exemption: Two-Engine, Subsonic Airplanes; 14 C.F.R. Part 36; 49 U.S.C. App. §2151 et.seq.

ADVISORY CIRCULARS

AC 36-1G *Noise Levels for U.S. Certificated and Foreign Aircraft* (1997).

AC 36-2C *Measured Or Estimated (Uncertified) Airplane Noise Levels* (1986).

AC 36-3G *Estimated Airplane Noise Levels in A-Weighted Decibels* (1996).

AC 36-4B *Noise Certification Handbook* (1988).

AC 91-53A *Noise Abatement Departure Profiles* (1993).

AC 91-66 *Noise Abatement for Helicopters* (1987).

AC 150/5020-1 *Noise Control and Compatibility Planning For Airports* (1983).

91.807 PHASED COMPLIANCE UNDER PARTS 121, 125 and 135: SUBSONIC AIRPLANES

(a)   *General.* Each person operating airplanes under Part 121, 125, or 135 of this chapter, as prescribed under §91.803 of this subpart, regardless of the state of registry of the airplane, shall comply with this section with respect to subsonic airplanes covered by this subpart.

(b)   *Compliance schedule.* Except for airplanes shown to be operated in foreign air commerce under paragraph (c) of this section or covered by an exemption (including those issued under §91.811), airplanes operated by U.S. operators in air commerce in the United States must be shown to comply with Stage 2 or Stage 3 noise levels under part 36 of this chapter, in accordance with the following schedule, or they may not be operated to or from airports in the United States:

   (1)   By January 1, 1981 —

       (i)   At least one quarter of the airplanes that have four engines with no bypass ratio or with a bypass ratio less than two; and

       (ii)   At least half of the airplanes powered by engines with any other bypass ratio or by another number of engines.

   (2)   By January 1, 1983 —

       (i)   At least one-half of the airplanes that have four engines with no bypass ratio or with a bypass ratio less than two; and

       (ii)   All airplanes powered by engines with any other bypass ratio or by another number of engines.

(c)   *Apportionment of airplanes.* For purposes of paragraph (b) of this section, a person operating airplanes engaged in domestic and foreign air commerce in the United States may elect not to comply with the phased schedule with respect to that portion of the airplanes operated by that person shown, under an approved method of apportionment, to be engaged in foreign air commerce in the United States.

EXPLANATION

The method of apportionment in the case of aircraft engaged in domestic and foreign air commerce must be approved by the FAA.

CROSS REFERENCES

Previous designation: 91.305. 91.803, Part 125 Operators: Designation of Applicable Regulations; 91.811, Service to Small Communities Exemption: Two-Engine, Subsonic Airplanes; 14 C.F.R. Part 36; 49 U.S.C. App. §2151 et.seq.

ADVISORY CIRCULARS

AC 36-1G *Noise Levels for U.S. Certificated and Foreign Aircraft* (1997).

AC 36-2C *Measured Or Estimated (Uncertified) Airplane Noise Levels* (1986).

AC 36-3G *Estimated Airplane Noise Levels in A-Weighted Decibels* (1996).

AC 36-4B *Noise Certification Handbook* (1988).

AC 91-53A *Noise Abatement Departure Profiles* (1993).

AC 91-66 *Noise Abatement for Helicopters* (1987).

AC 150/5020-1 *Noise Control and Compatibility Planning For Airports* (1983).

91.809 REPLACEMENT AIRPLANES

A Stage 1 airplane may be operated after the otherwise applicable compliance dates prescribed under §§91.805 and 91.807 if, under an approved plan, a replacement airplane has been ordered by the operator under a binding contract as follows:
(a)   For replacement of an airplane powered by two engines, until January 1, 1986, but not after the date specified in the plan, if the contract is entered into by January 1, 1983, and specifies delivery before January 1, 1986, of a replacement airplane which has been shown to comply with Stage 3 noise levels under part 36 of this chapter.
(b)   For replacement of an airplane powered by three engines, until January 1, 1985, but not after the date specified in the plan, if the contract is entered into by January 1, 1983, and specifies delivery before January 1, 1985, of a replacement airplane which has been shown to comply with Stage 3 noise levels under part 36 of this chapter.
(c)   For replacement of any other airplane, until January 1, 1985, but not after the date specified in the plan, if the contract specifies delivery before January 1, 1985, of a replacement airplane which —
(1)   Has been shown to comply with Stage 2 or Stage 3 noise levels under part 36 of this chapter prior to issuance of an original standard airworthiness certificate; or
(2)   Has been shown to comply with Stage 3 noise levels under part 36 of this chapter prior to issuance of a standard airworthiness certificate other than original issue.

(d)   Each operator of a Stage 1 airplane for which approval of a replacement plan is requested under this section shall submit to the Director, Office of Environment and Energy, an application constituting the proposed replacement plan (or revised Plan) that contains the information specified under this paragraph and which is certified (under penalty of 18 U.S.C. 1001) as true and correct. Each application for approval must provide information corresponding to that specified in the contract, upon which the FAA may rely in considering its approval, as follows:
   (1)   Name and address of the applicant.
   (2)   Aircraft type and model and registration number for each airplane to be replaced under the plan.
   (3)   Aircraft type and model of each replacement airplane.
   (4)   Scheduled dates of delivery and introduction into service of each replacement airplane.
   (5)   Names and addresses of the parties to the contract and any other persons who may effectively cancel the contract or otherwise control the performance of any party.
   (6)   Information specifying the anticipated disposition of the airplanes to be replaced.
   (7)   A statement that the contract represents a legally enforceable, mutual agreement for delivery of an eligible replacement airplane.
   (8)   Any other information or documentation requested by the Director, Office of Environment and Energy, reasonably necessary to determine whether the plan should be approved.

EXPLANATION

In the case of the certification required by 91.809(d) anyone knowingly and willingly making a false or fraudulent statement or representation is subject to being fined and/or imprisoned as provided in 18 U.S.C. §1001.

CROSS REFERENCES

Previous designation: 91.306. 91.805, Final Compliance: Subsonic Airplanes; 91.807, Phased Compliance Under Parts 121, 125 and 135: Subsonic Airplanes; 14 C.F.R. Part 36; 49 U.S.C. App. §2151 et.seq.

ADVISORY CIRCULARS

AC 36-1G *Noise Levels for U.S. Certificated and Foreign Aircraft* (1997).

AC 36-2C *Measured Or Estimated (Uncertified) Airplane Noise Levels* (1986).

AC 36-3G *Estimated Airplane Noise Levels in A-Weighted Decibels* (1996).

AC 36-4B *Noise Certification Handbook* (1988).

AC 91-53A *Noise Abatement Departure Profiles* (1993).

AC 91-66 *Noise Abatement for Helicopters* (1987).

AC 150/5020-1 *Noise Control and Compatibility Planning For Airports* (1983).

91.811 SERVICE TO SMALL COMMUNITIES EXEMPTION: TWO-ENGINE, SUBSONIC AIRPLANES

(a) A Stage 1 airplane powered by two engines may be operated after the compliance dates prescribed under §§91.805, 91.807, and 91.809, when, with respect to that airplane, the Administrator issues an exemption to the operator from the noise level requirements under this subpart. Each exemption issued under this section terminates on the earliest of the following dates:

 (1) For an exempted airplane sold, or otherwise disposed of, to another person on or after January 1, 1983, on the date of delivery to that person;

 (2) For an exempted airplane with a seating configuration of 100 passenger seats or less, on January 1, 1988.

 (3) For an exempted airplane with a seating configuration of more than 100 passenger seats, on January 1, 1985.

(b) For purpose of this section, the seating configuration of an airplane is governed by that shown to exist on December 1, 1979, or an earlier date established for that airplane by the Administrator.

CROSS REFERENCES

Previous designation: 91.307. 91.805, Final Compliance: Subsonic Airplanes; 91.807, Phased Compliance Under Parts 121, 125 and 135: Subsonic Airplanes; 91.809, Replacement Airplanes; 14 C.F.R. Part 36; 49 U.S.C. App. §2151 et.seq.

ADVISORY CIRCULARS

AC 36-1G *Noise Levels for U.S. Certificated and Foreign Aircraft* (1997).

AC 36-2C *Measured Or Estimated (Uncertified) Airplane Noise Levels* (1986).

AC 36-3G *Estimated Airplane Noise Levels in A-Weighted Decibels* (1996).

AC 36-4B *Noise Certification Handbook* (1988).

AC 91-53A *Noise Abatement Departure Profiles* (1993).

AC 91-66 *Noise Abatement for Helicopters* (1987).

AC 150/5020-1 *Noise Control and Compatibility Planning For Airports* (1983).

91.813 COMPLIANCE PLANS AND STATUS: U.S. OPERATORS OF SUBSONIC AIRPLANES

(a)   Each U.S. operator of a civil subsonic airplane covered by this subpart (regardless of the state of registry) shall submit to the Director, Office of Environment and Energy, in accordance with this section, the operator's current compliance status and plan for achieving and maintaining compliance with the applicable noise level requirements of this subpart. If appropriate, an operator may substitute for the required plan a notice, certified as true (under penalty of 18 U.S.C. 1001) by that operator, that no change in the plan or status of any airplane affected by the plan has occurred since the date of the plan most recently submitted under this section.

(b)   Each compliance plan, including each revised plan, must contain the information specified under paragraph (c) of this section for each airplane covered by this section that is operated by the operator. Unless otherwise approved by the Administrator, compliance plans must provide the required plan and status information as it exists on the date 30 days before the date specified for submission of the plan. Plans must be certified by the operator as true and complete (under penalty of 18 U.S.C. 1001) and be submitted for each airplane covered by this section on or before 90 days after initially commencing operation of airplanes covered by this section, whichever is later, and thereafter —

(1)   Thirty days after any change in the operator's fleet or compliance planning decisions that has a separate or cumulative effect on 10 percent or more of the airplanes in either class of airplanes covered by §91.807(b); and

(2)   Thirty days after each compliance date applicable to that airplane under this subpart, and annually thereafter through 1985, or until any later date for that airplane prescribed under this subpart, on the anniversary of that submission date, to show continuous compliance with this subpart.

(c)   Each compliance plan submitted under this section must identify the operator and include information regarding the compliance plan and status for each airplane covered by the plan as follows:

(1)   Name and address of the airplane operator.

(2)   Name and telephone number of the person designated by the operator to be responsible for the preparation of the compliance plan and its submission.

(3)   The total number of airplanes covered by this section and in each of the following classes and subclasses:

(i)   For airplanes engaged in domestic air commerce —

(A)   Airplanes powered by four turbojet engines with no bypass ratio or with a bypass ratio less than two.

(B)   Airplanes powered by engines with any other bypass ratio or by another number of engines; and

(C)   Airplanes covered by an exemption issued under §91.811 of this subpart.

(ii)   For airplanes engaged in foreign air commerce under an approved apportionment plan —

(A)   Airplanes powered by four turbojet engines with no bypass ratio or with a bypass ratio less than two;

(B)   Airplanes powered by engines with any other bypass ratio or by another number of engines; and

(C)   Airplanes covered by an exemption issued under §91.811 of this subpart.

(4)   For each airplane covered by this section —
(i)   Aircraft type and model;
(ii)   Aircraft registration number;
(iii)   Aircraft manufacturer serial number;
(iv)   Aircraft powerplant make and model;
(v)   Aircraft year of manufacture;
(vi)   Whether part 36 noise level compliance has been shown, "Yes/No";
(vii)   The appropriate code prescribed under paragraph (c)(5) of this section which indicates the acoustical technology installed, or to be installed, on the airplane;
(viii) For airplanes on which acoustical technology has been or will be applied, following the appropriate code entry, the actual or scheduled month and year of installation on the airplane;
(ix)   For DC-8 and B-707 airplanes operated in domestic U.S. air commerce which have been or will be retired from service in the United States without replacement between January 24, 1977, and January 1, 1985, the appropriate code prescribed under paragraph (c)(5) of this section followed by the actual or scheduled month and year of retirement of the airplane from service;
(x)   For DC-8 and B-707 airplanes operated in foreign air commerce in the United States which have been or will be retired from service in the United States without replacement between April 14, 1980, and January 1, 1985, the appropriate code prescribed under paragraph (c)(5) of this section followed by the actual or scheduled month and year of retirement of the airplane from service;
(xi)   For airplanes covered by an approved replacement plan under §91.807(c) of this subpart, the appropriate code prescribed under paragraph (c)(5) of this section followed by the scheduled month and year for replacement of the airplane;
(xii)   For airplanes designated as "engaged in foreign commerce" in accordance with an approved method of apportionment under §91.807(c) of this subpart, the appropriate code prescribed under paragraph (c)(5) of this section;
(xiii) For airplanes covered by an exemption issued to the operator granting relief from noise level requirements of this subpart, the appropriate code prescribed under paragraph (c)(5) of this section followed by the actual or scheduled month and year of expiration of the exemption and the appropriate code and applicable dates which indicate the compliance strategy planned or implemented for the airplane.
(xiv)   For all airplanes covered by this section, the number of spare shipsets of acoustical components needed for continuous compliance and the number available on demand to the operator in support of those airplanes; and
(xv)   For airplanes for which none of the other codes prescribed under paragraph (c)(5) of this section describes either the technology applied or to be applied to the airplane in accordance with the certification requirements under parts 21 and 36 of this chapter, or the compliance strategy or methodology following the code "OTH," enter the date of any certificate action and attach an addendum to the plan explaining the nature and the extent of the certificated technology, strategy, or methodology employed, with reference to the type certificate documentation.

(5) TABLE OF ACOUSTICAL TECHNOLOGY/STRATEGY CODES

Code	Airplane type/ model	Certificated technology
A	B-707-120B; B-707-320B/C; B-720B	Quiet nacelles + 1-ring.
B	B-727-100	Double wall fan duct treatment.
C	B-727-200	Double wall fan duct treatment (pre-January 1977 installations and amended type certificate).
D	B-727-200; B-737-100; B-737-200	Quiet nacelles + double wall fan duct treatment
E	B-747-100 (pre-December 1971); B-747-200 (pre-December 1971)	Fixed lip inlets + sound absorbing material treatment.
F	DC-8	New extended inlet and bullet with treatment + fan duct treatment areas.
G	DC-9	P-36 sound absorbing material treatment kit.
H	BAC-111-200	Silencer kit (BAC Acoustic Report 522).
I	BAC-111-400	Silencer kit (BAC Acoustic Report 598)
J	B-707; DC-8	Reengined with high bypass ratio turbojet engines + quiet nacelles (if certificated under stage 3 noise level requirements).

REP-   For airplanes covered by an approved replacement plan under §91.807(c) of this subpart.

EFC-   For airplanes designated as "engaged in foreign commerce" in accordance with an approved method of apportionment under §91.811 of this subpart.

RET-   For DC-8 and B-707 airplanes operated in domestic U.S. air commerce and retired from service in the United States without replacement between January 24, 1977, and January 1, 1985.

RFC-   For DC-8 and B-707 airplanes operated by U.S. operators in foreign air commerce in the United States and retired from service in the United States without replacement between April 14, 1980, and January 1, 1985.

EXD-   For airplanes exempted from showing compliance with the noise level requirements of this subpart.

OTH-   For airplanes for which no other prescribed code describes either the certificated technology applied or to be applied to the airplane, or the compliance strategy or methodology. (An addendum must explain the nature and extent of technology, strategy, or methodology and reference the type certificate documentation.)

EXPLANATION

This regulation sets forth the information that must be submitted with compliance plans and status reports.

CROSS REFERENCES

Previous designation: 91.308. 91.807, Phased Compliance Under Parts 121, 125 and 135: Subsonic Airplanes; 91.811, Service to Small Communities Exemption: Two-Engine, Subsonic Airplanes; 14 C.F.R. Part 36; 18 U.S.C. §1001; 49 U.S.C. App. §2151 et.seq.

ADVISORY CIRCULARS

AC 36-1G *Noise Levels for U.S. Certificated and Foreign Aircraft* (1997).

AC 36-2C *Measured Or Estimated (Uncertified) Airplane Noise Levels* (1986).

AC 36-3G *Estimated Airplane Noise Levels in A-Weighted Decibels* (1996).

AC 36-4B *Noise Certification Handbook* (1988).

AC 91-53A *Noise Abatement Departure Profiles* (1993).

AC 91-66 *Noise Abatement for Helicopters* (1987).

AC 150/5020-1 *Noise Control and Compatibility Planning For Airports* (1983).

91.815 AGRICULTURAL AND FIRE FIGHTING AIRPLANES: NOISE OPERATING LIMITATIONS

(a)   This section applies to propeller-driven, small airplanes having standard airworthiness certificates that are designed for "agricultural aircraft operations" (as defined in §137.3 of this chapter, as effective on January 1, 1966) or for dispensing fire fighting materials.

(b)   If the Airplane Flight Manual, or other approved manual material, information, markings, or placards for the airplane indicate that the airplane has not been shown to comply with the noise limits under part 36 of this chapter, no person may operate that airplane, except —

(1)   To the extent necessary to accomplish the work activity directly associated with the purpose for which it is designed;

(2)   To provide flight crewmember training in the special purpose operation for which the airplane is designed; and

(3)   To conduct "nondispensing aerial work operations" in accordance with the requirements under §137.29(c) of this chapter.

CROSS REFERENCES

Previous designation: [New]. 137.3, Definition of Terms; 137.29, General; 14 C.F.R. Part 36.

ADVISORY CIRCULARS

AC 137-1 *Agricultural Aircraft Operations* (1965).

AC 36-1G *Noise Levels for U.S. Certificated and Foreign Aircraft* (1997).

AC 36-2C *Measured Or Estimated (Uncertified) Airplane Noise Levels* (1986).

AC 36-3G *Estimated Airplane Noise Levels in A-Weighted Decibels* (1996).

AC 36-4B *Noise Certification Handbook* (1988).

AC 91-53A *Noise Abatement Departure Profiles* (1993).

AC 91-66 *Noise Abatement for Helicopters* (1987).

AC 150/5020-1 *Noise Control and Compatibility Planning For Airports* (1983).

91.817 CIVIL AIRCRAFT SONIC BOOM

(a)   No person may operate a civil aircraft in the United States at a true flight Mach number greater than 1 except in compliance with conditions and limitations in an authorization to exceed Mach 1 issued to the operator under appendix B of this part.

(b)   In addition, no person may operate a civil aircraft for which the maximum operating limit speed M_{mo} exceeds a Mach number of 1, to or from an airport in the United States, unless —

   (1)   Information available to the flight crew includes flight limitations that ensure that flights entering or leaving the Unites States will not cause a sonic boom to reach the surface within the United States; and

   (2)   The operator complies with the flight limitations prescribed in paragraph (b)(1) of this section or complies with conditions and limitations in an authorization to exceed Mach 1 issued under appendix B of this part.

CROSS REFERENCES

Previous designation: [New]. 14 C.F.R. Part 91 Appendix B; 14 C.F.R. Part 36; 49 U.S.C. App. §2151 et.seq.

ADVISORY CIRCULARS

AC 36-1G *Noise Levels for U.S. Certificated and Foreign Aircraft* (1997).

AC 36-2C *Measured Or Estimated (Uncertified) Airplane Noise Levels* (1986).

AC 36-3G *Estimated Airplane Noise Levels in A-Weighted Decibels* (1996).

AC 36-4B *Noise Certification Handbook* (1988).

AC 91-53A *Noise Abatement Departure Profiles* (1993).

AC 91-66 *Noise Abatement for Helicopters* (1987).

AC 150/5020-1 *Noise Control and Compatibility Planning For Airports* (1983).

91.819 CIVIL SUPERSONIC AIRPLANES THAT DO NOT COMPLY WITH PART 36

(a) *Applicability.* This section applies to civil supersonic airplanes that have not been shown to comply with the Stage 2 noise limits of Part 36 in effect on October 13, 1977, using applicable trade-off provisions, and that are operated in the United States after July 31, 1978.

(b) *Airport use.* Except in an emergency, the following apply to each person who operates a civil supersonic airplane to or from an airport in the United States:

   (1) Regardless of whether a type design change approval is applied for under part 21 of this chapter, no person may land or take off an airplane covered by this section for which the type design is changed, after July 31, 1978, in a manner constituting an "acoustical change" under §21.93, unless the acoustical change requirements of part 36 are complied with.

   (2) No flight may be scheduled, or otherwise planned, for takeoff or landing after 10 p.m. and before 7 a.m. local time.

CROSS REFERENCES

Previous designation: 91.309. 14 C.F.R. Part 21; 14 C.F.R. Part 36.

ADVISORY CIRCULARS

AC 36-1G *Noise Levels for U.S. Certificated and Foreign Aircraft* (1997).

AC 36-2C *Measured Or Estimated (Uncertified) Airplane Noise Levels* (1986).

AC 36-3G *Estimated Airplane Noise Levels in A-Weighted Decibels* (1996).

AC 36-4B *Noise Certification Handbook* (1988).

AC 91-53A *Noise Abatement Departure Profiles* (1993).

AC 91-66 *Noise Abatement for Helicopters* (1987).

AC 150/5020-1 *Noise Control and Compatibility Planning For Airports* (1983).

91.821 CIVIL SUPERSONIC AIRPLANES: NOISE LIMITS

Except for Concorde airplanes having flight time before January 1, 1980, no person may operate in the United States a civil supersonic airplane that does not comply with the Stage 2 noise limits of part 36 in effect on October 13, 1977, using applicable trade-off provisions.

EXPLANATION

This regulation exists essentially to give "grandfather" rights to the original Concorde to operate in the United States.

CROSS REFERENCES

Previous designation: 91.331.

91.851 DEFINITIONS

For the purposes of §§91.851 through 91.877 of this subpart:

Contiguous United States means the area encompassed by the 48 contiguous United States and the District of Columbia.

Fleet means those civil subsonic turbojet airplanes with a maximum certificated weight of more than 75,000 pounds that are listed on an operator's operations specifications as eligible for operation in the contiguous United States.

Import means a change in ownership of an airplane from a non-U.S. person to a U.S. person when the airplane is brought into the United States for operation.

Operations specifications means an enumeration of airplanes by type, model, series, and serial number operated by the operator or foreign air carrier on a given day, regardless of how or whether such airplanes are formally listed or designated by the operator.

Owner means any person that has indicia of ownership sufficient to register the airplane in the United States pursuant to part 47 of this chapter.

New entrant means an air carrier or foreign air carrier that, on or before November 5, 1990, did not conduct operations under part 121, or 129 of this chapter using an airplane covered by this subpart to or from any airport in the contiguous United States, but that initiates such operation after that date.

Stage 2 noise levels mean the requirements for Stage 2 noise levels as defined in part 36 of this chapter in effect on November 5, 1990.

Stage 3 noise levels mean the requirements for Stage 3 noise levels as defined in part 36 of this chapter in effect on November 5, 1990.

Stage 2 airplane means a civil subsonic turbojet airplane with a maximum certificated weight of 75,000 pounds or more that complies with Stage 2 noise levels as defined in part 36 of this chapter.

Stage 3 airplane means a civil subsonic turbojet airplane with a maximum certificated weight of 75,000 pounds or more that complies with Stage 3 noise levels as defined in part 36 of this chapter.

EXPLANATION

These definitions only apply to FARs 91.853 through 91.875.

Even though other FARs do not require an operator to maintain a list of airplanes being used as part of its operations specifications, such a list is required to comply with FARs 91.853 through 91.875.

CROSS REFERENCES

Previous designation: [New].

91.853 FINAL COMPLIANCE: CIVIL SUBSONIC AIRPLANES

Except as provided in §91.873, after December 31, 1999, no person shall operate to or from any airport in the contiguous United States any airplane subject to §91.801(c) of this subpart, unless that airplane has been shown to comply with Stage 3 noise levels.

EXPLANATION

The final compliance date of December 31, 1999 does not apply to aircraft operating to or from any airport outside the 48 contiguous states and the District of Columbia, i.e. Hawaii, Alaska, Puerto Rico or any of the possessions of the United States.

Even if the compliance date seems to apply to an aircraft under this regulation, a waiver may be available under 91.873.

CROSS REFERENCES

Previous designation: [New]. 91.801, Applicability: Relation to Part 36; 91.851, Definitions; 91.873, Waivers From Final Compliance.

91.855 ENTRY AND NONADDITION RULE

No person may operate any airplane subject to §91.801(c) of this subpart to or from an airport in the contiguous United States unless one or more of the following apply:
(a) The airplane complies with Stage 3 noise levels.
(b) The airplane complies with Stage 2 noise levels and was owned by a U.S. person on and since November 5, 1990. Stage 2 airplanes that meet these criteria and are leased to foreign airlines are also subject to the return provisions of paragraph (e) of this section.
(c) The airplane complies with Stage 2 noise levels, is owned by a non-U.S. person, and is the subject of a binding lease to a U.S. person effective before and on September 25, 1991. Any such airplane may be operated for the term of the lease in effect on that date, and any extensions thereof provided for in that lease.
(d) The airplane complies with Stage 2 noise levels and is operated by a foreign air carrier.
(e) The airplane complies with Stage 2 noise levels and is operated by a foreign operator other than for the purpose of foreign air commerce.
(f) The airplane complies with Stage 2 noise levels and—
  (1) On November 5, 1990, was owned by:
    (i)   A corporation, trust, or partnership organized under the laws of the United States or any State (including individual States, territories,
    possessions, and the District of Columbia);
    (ii)   An individual who is a citizen of the United States; or
    (iii) An entity owned or controlled by a corporation, trust, partnership, or individual described in paragraph (f)(1)(I) or (ii) of this section; and
  (2) Enters into the United States not later than 6 months after the expiration of a lease agreement (including any extensions thereof) between an owner described in paragraph (f)(1) of this section and a foreign airline.

(g) The airplane complies with Stage 2 noise levels and was purchased by the importer under a written contract executed before November 5, 1990.

(h) Any Stage 2 airplane described in this section is eligible for operation in the contiguous United States only as provided under §91.865 or 91.867.

EXPLANATION

This regulation describes the categories of airplanes that can be operated in the contiguous United States on and after September 25, 1991.

While a Stage 2 airplane that was operated as part of an operator's fleet on November 5, 1990, may subsequently be leased outside the United States, its later return will not count as an addition to a U.S. operator's base level.

91.855(f)(2) refers to leases to foreign airlines, not just foreign air carriers.

It is the ownership status, not the location of the airplane, on November 5, 1990, that is the determining factor.

CROSS REFERENCES

Previous designation: [New]. 14 C.F.R. Part 47; 91.801, Applicability: Relation to Part 36; 91.851, Definitions; 91.861, Base Level; 91.865, Phased Compliance For Operators With Base Level; 91.867, Phased Compliance for New Entrants.

ADVISORY CIRCULARS

AC 36-1G *Noise Levels for U.S. Certificated and Foreign Aircraft* (1997).

AC 36-2C *Measured Or Estimated (Uncertified) Airplane Noise Levels* (1986).

AC 36-3G *Estimated Airplane Noise Levels in A-Weighted Decibels* (1996).

AC 36-4B *Noise Certification Handbook* (1988).

AC 91-53A *Noise Abatement Departure Profiles* (1993).

AC 91-66 *Noise Abatement for Helicopters* (1987).

AC 150/5020-1 *Noise Control and Compatibility Planning For Airports* (1983).

FAA CHIEF COUNSEL OPINIONS

Return of Foreign-leased Airplanes:

Question — If a U.S.-owned Stage 2 airplane is leased to a non-U.S. operator, must it physically return to the United States within six months after expiration of the lease before being released to qualify under the return rule of §91.855(f)?

> Response — No. Nothing in the language or legislative history of ANCA §9309 suggests that physical contact with U.S. soil is necessary to make a leased airplane returnable, nor does any practical argument exist for such a requirement. This applies to any number of successive leases to the same or other non-U.S. airline so long as no more than six months elapse between the end of one lease period and the beginning of the next.
>
> The FAA cautions that the eligibility of a Stage 2 airplane to return after a foreign lease in no way confers any operational status as far as the phased transition requirements of Part 91 are concerned. Any operator that chooses to use a returned Stage 2 airplane to conduct operations in the contiguous United States must ensure that the airplane fits in the operator's fleet requirements under §91.865 or §91.867. (10-13-92).

Alaskan Operations: [See opinion under §91.801]

Dual-Certificated 747-100 Aircraft:

Question — Since a number of Boeing 747-100 airplanes were originally certificated to operate as either Stage 2 or Stage 3 airplanes, what is the status of these airplanes under the phased transition rules (§91.865 or §91.867)?

> Response — Until notified, the FAA considers all dual-certificated Boeing 747-100 airplanes to be Stage 2 airplanes for noise compliance purposes. Each operator of these airplanes may choose to permanently reclassify these airplanes as Stage 3 to count them toward compliance with the Stage 3 transition rules.
>
> This reclassification involves changes in the airplane flight manual to delete the parameters that describe Stage 2 operation, and the addition of the placard in the affected airplane indicating that the airplane may not be flown in Stage 2 configuration. In addition, the FAA will require each operator to submit a written statement identifying the reclassified airplane and certifying that the airplane will not afterward be flown as a Stage 2 airplane to or from a point in the contiguous United States.
>
> The only exception to this permanent reclassification is in the case of leased airplanes. The lessee of a dual-certified 747 will be allowed to make the Stage 3 reclassification election effective for the length of the airplane lease. This exception provides that no lessor/owner or a dual certificated 747 is bound irrevocably by the action of its lessee, while the lessee retains the flexibility to continue operation of the airplane in a configuration that is compatible with its needs under the Stage 3 transition.
>
> While notice to the FAA must be made in writing, there is no precise form in which the owner or operator must declare its actions to reclassify an individual airplane. The FAA is looking into the development of an optional form for this purpose. The FAA anticipates that operators would file these certifications at the time it submits its annual report, but they may be filed at any time. This form, or any such written certification from an owner or operator, will not fulfill any other recordkeeping requirement made necessary by changes to the airplane flight manual or the airplane itself. (10-13-92).

Airplanes Leased From Non-U.S. Entities:

Question — §91.855(c) allows for the operation of Stage 2 airplanes that were leased by non-U.S. owners to U.S. operators before September 25, 1991. May a wholly owned U.S. subsidiary of a non-U.S. corporation take advantage of this provision?

> Response — If the wholly owned U.S. subsidiary has established a voting trust to register its airplanes in the United States, it may not claim that it leased the airplane as a non-U.S. entity under §91.855(c). The voting trust means that the subsidiary's airplanes are considered U.S.-owned. If the trust acquired a Stage 2 airplane before November 5, 1990, it may lease the airplane to another U.S. entity to operate in the contiguous United States without restriction. If a Stage 2 airplane was acquired after November 5, 1990, by a subsidiary, the airplane could not be leased to a U.S. operator for operation in the contiguous United States because of the nonaddition rule. (10-13-92).

Question — For a Stage 2 airplane operating under the leasing provisions of §91.855(c), may that airplane be sold to another non-U.S. entity and continue to operate subject to that lease? May it be sold to a U.S. entity and continue to operate subject to the lease?

> Response — If a Stage 2 airplane is owned by a non-U.S. entity and transferred to another non-U.S. entity subject to a lease to a U.S. operator, the airplane may continue to operate under §91.855(c). The FAA will not view the continuation of the lease as a violation of §91.855(c), as though a new lease from a non-U.S. entity were occurring.
>
> This allowance presumes that the airplane is sold subject to the express terms of the existing lease. Any change in the terms of the lease at the time of the sale would be considered a new lease from a foreign entity. Any extensions of that lease would be limited to the terms in the original lease. Once the lease expires, the airplane may not be operated in the contiguous United States by a U.S. operator.
>
> Conversely, a non-U.S. owned Stage 2 airplane that is currently leased by a U.S. operator may not continue to operate if the airplane is sold to a U.S. entity. Stage 2 airplanes purchased by a U.S. entity after November 4, 1990, are prohibited from operating in the contiguous United States. To allow a newly purchased airplane to continue operation based on the original lease from the non-U.S. entity is clearly prohibited by the terms of the statutory nonaddition rule. If the airplane is allowed to transfer to a U.S. entity and is allowed to continue operating subject to the lease, the transfer would serve as a means around the nonaddition rule. By protecting the lease, the receiving U.S. entity would be purchasing an airplane that, without the lease, would be prohibited from operation in the contiguous United States.
>
> The continued operation of this airplane, if sold to a U.S. entity, could be viewed as consistent with the nonaddition rule since it does not increase the amount of Stage 2 noise in the United States — the airplane is already operating here. However, a change to U.S. ownership thwarts the very intent of Congress in codifying the nonaddition rule: to limit the liability of all U.S. owners of Stage 2 airplanes to that which existed on November 5, 1990. While it may be argued that limiting operation to the length of the lease would not effect any change as far as operation of Stage 2 airplanes, the new U.S. owner would enjoy a benefit unavailable to most others, and that benefit would have been gained by a means that clearly violates the nonaddition rule.

The anomaly that arises from this situation was recognized by the FAA at the time the regulations were promulgated, and is caused by the difference between the statutory cutoff for importation of Stage 2 airplanes and the regulatory cutoff for leasing non-U.S. airplanes. The anomaly resulted when the FAA "closed the loophole" of leased non-U.S. airplanes. The FAA concluded that the September 25, 1991, cutoff date was the only viable alternative to declaring those leases void retroactively, since they were expressly limited by the ANCA.

The FAA will not now interpret the rule in a manner that would, in effect, violate the spirit of the legislation by allowing the continued operation of these leased airplanes should they become U.S.-owned. Allowing this operation could easily lead to numerous sales of leased non-U.S. Stage 2 airplanes, effectively foiling the purposes of the nonaddition rule and unfairly favoring those who already have the advantage of a previously-leased Stage 2 airplane. Further, allowing these operations would place upon the FAA the burden of monitoring leases to which it is not a party and over which it exercises no control. (10-13-92).

Base Level: [See opinions under §91.861]

91.857 STAGE 2 OPERATIONS OUTSIDE OF THE 48 CONTIGUOUS UNITED STATES, AND AUTHORIZATION FOR MAINTENANCE.

An operator of a Stage 2 airplane that is operating only between points outside the contiguous United States on or after November 5, 1990, shall:
(a)   Include in its operations specifications a statement that such airplane may not be used to provide air transportation to or from any airport in the contiguous United States.
(b)   Obtain a special flight authorization to operate that airplane into the contiguous United States for the purpose of maintenance. The special flight authorization must include a statement indicating that this regulation is the basis for the authorization.

EXPLANATION

This regulation applies to airplanes purchased by a U.S. owner from a foreign owner after November 5, 1990, for U.S. operation. When used for air transportation, these airplanes may only be operated outside the contiguous United States.

A "ferry" permit may be obtained to operate such an airplane to the contiguous United States, but only for maintenance purposes.

CROSS REFERENCES

Previous designation: [New].

FAA CHIEF COUNSEL OPINIONS

Alaskan Operations: [See opinion under §91.801]

91.859 MODIFICATION TO MEET STAGE 3 NOISE LEVELS

For an airplane subject to §91.801(c) of this subpart and otherwise prohibited from operation to or from an airport in the contiguous United States by §91.855, any person may apply for a special flight authorization for that airplane to operate in the contiguous United States for the purpose of obtaining modification to meet Stage 3 noise levels.

EXPLANATION

The FAA will be issuing a Special Federal Aviation Regulation (SFAR) describing the procedures for obtaining the special flight authorization referred to in this regulation. Until the SFAR is issued, anyone desiring a special flight authorization may seek an exemption from FAR 91.855 in accordance with FAR 11.25, Provisions For Rulemaking Exemption.

CROSS REFERENCES

Previous designation: [New]. 11.25, Provisions For Rulemaking Exemption; 91.855, Entry and Nonaddition Rule.

ADVISORY CIRCULARS

AC 36-1G *Noise Levels for U.S. Certificated and Foreign Aircraft* (1997).

AC 36-2C *Measured Or Estimated (Uncertified) Airplane Noise Levels* (1986).

AC 36-3G *Estimated Airplane Noise Levels in A-Weighted Decibels* (1996).

AC 36-4B *Noise Certification Handbook* (1988).

AC 91-53A *Noise Abatement Departure Profiles* (1993).

AC 91-66 *Noise Abatement for Helicopters* (1987).

AC 150/5020-1 *Noise Control and Compatibility Planning For Airports* (1983).

91.861 BASE LEVEL

(a) *U.S. Operators.* The base level of a U.S. operator is equal to the number of owned or leased Stage 2 airplanes subject to §91.801(c) of this subpart that were listed on that operator's operations specifications for operations to or from airports in the contiguous United States on any one day selected by the operator during the period January 1, 1990, through July 1, 1991, plus or minus adjustments made pursuant to paragraphs (a)(1) and (2).
  (1) The base level of a U.S. operator shall be increased by a number equal to the total of the following—
    (i) The number of Stage 2 airplanes returned to service in the United States pursuant to §91.855(f);
    (ii) The number of Stage 2 airplanes purchased pursuant to §91.855(g); and
    (iii) Any U.S. operator base level acquired with a Stage 2 airplane transferred from another person under §91.863.
  (2) The base level of a U.S. operator shall be decreased by the amount of U.S. operator base level transferred with the corresponding number of Stage 2 airplanes to another person under §91.863.
(b) *Foreign air carriers.* The base level of a foreign air carrier is equal to the number of owned or leased Stage 2 airplanes that were listed on that carrier's U.S. operations specifications on any one day during the period January 1, 1990, through July 1, 1991, plus or minus any adjustments to the base levels made pursuant to paragraphs (b)(1) and (2).
  (1) The base level of a foreign air carrier shall be increased by the amount of foreign air carrier base level acquired with a Stage 2 airplane from another person under §91.863.
  (2) The base level of a foreign air carrier shall be decreased by the amount of foreign air carrier base level transferred with a Stage 2 airplane to another person under §91.863.
(c) New entrants do not have a base level.

EXPLANATION

This regulation describes how operators established their base levels.

New entrants, having no base level, must meet the requirements of FAR 91.867.

CROSS REFERENCES

Previous designation: [New]. 91.801, Applicability: Relation to Part 36; 91.851, Definitions; 91.855, Entry and Nonaddition Rule; 91.863, Transfers of Stage 2 Airplanes With Base Level; 91.867, Phased Compliance for New Entrants.

ADVISORY CIRCULARS

AC 36-1G *Noise Levels For Certificated and Foreign Aircraft* (1997).

AC 36-2C *Measured Or Estimated (Uncertified) Airplane Noise Levels* (1986).

AC 36-3G *Estimated Airplane Noise Levels in A-Weighted Decibels* (1996).

AC 36-4B *Noise Certification Handbook* (1988).

AC 91-53A *Noise Abatement Departure Profile* (1993).

AC 91-66 *Noise Abatement for Helicopters* (1987).

AC 150/5020-1 *Noise Control and Compatibility Planning For Airports* (1983).

FAA CHIEF COUNSEL OPINIONS

Base Level:

Question — Can base level be held by anyone other than an operator of Stage 2 airplanes?

> Response — Yes. Base level is created by operators (or others in certain other circumstances) because it is based on the number of Stage 2 airplanes on their operations specifications as a chosen day. Base level is thus held by an operator until the operator decides to transfer it.

> §91.863 does not specify either who may hold base level, or who makes the decision whether base level will transfer in a given transaction. Because base level may be transferred to nonoperators, the FAA has no way of knowing the parties involved in any individual transfer. Once an operator establishes its base level, it holds that base level until it decides to transfer all or part of the base level with the corresponding airplanes. The FAA's statement in the preamble to the final rule establishes the starting point by saying that base level established with leased airplanes stays with the operator.

> The decision on whether the base level will transfer thus belongs to the party that holds the base level and airplanes before the transaction. In a chain of airplane transfers together with base level, any party may choose to transfer the airplanes and retain the base level. (10-13-92).

Question — May a transfer of base level be made now for an airplane transfer that occurred before the issuance of §91.863?

> Response — Yes. Since the establishment of base level was a "look back," the FAA currently allows the transfer of base level for airplane sales or lease returns made after the transferring owner/operator established its base level. These transactions are to be negotiated by the parties to the airplane transfer and are to be reported pursuant to §91.863(c).

> The transferring parties must report the original date of the airplane transfer. The related base level transfer will be valid only if the airplane transfer occurred after the date established by the transferring party as its base level date. Airplane transfers that predate the establishment of the transferring party's base level would be invalid since no base level had yet been established to transfer.

> The FAA anticipates that this "look back" procedure may not exist indefinitely. After gaining more experience with base level transfers and the complexity of tracking base level, the agency may decide that after a certain date, no further "look back" transactions will be approved. If made, the FAA will publish a notice of this decision before the cutoff date. (10-13-92).

Question — If an airplane is returned by a lessee to the lessor without base level, and the airplane is subsequently re-leased without base level, may the subsequent lessee obtain the base level from the original lessee without the involvement of the lessor under §91.863(a)?

Response — No. This transfer is prohibited under §91.863. Base level may only transfer with a Stage 2 airplane and cannot "leapfrog" an intervening transferee of the Stage 2 airplane. Base level does not attach to an individual airplane and follow wherever the airplane goes. Base level may be transferred only with a Stage 2 airplane, and may be either (1) retransferred with the subject airplane, (2) retained by the receiving party, or (3) transferred with another Stage 2 airplane of the receiver's choosing. Base level may transfer only at the discretion of the parties to individual Stage 2 airplane transfers.

In the situation described in the question, the original lessor may choose to hold onto its base level from the transferred airplanes, transfer the base level with other Stage 2 airplanes, or transfer the base level to the recipient of the subject Stage 2 airplanes, its lessor. The subsequent transferee of the airplanes is not eligible to receive base level directly from the original lessee because it did not obtain the airplanes from the original lessee. (10-13-92).

Question — Can a bankrupt operator hold base level even though it has no valid use of it? Does base level automatically transfer to the lessor of an aircraft when the operator/lessee has declared bankruptcy and returned the airplane to the lessor?

Response — A bankrupt operator may validly hold base level. The transition rule makes no provision for the FAA to decide that base level may only be held by operators that have a "valid" use for it. If that were true, then a logical extension of that premise would allow base level to be held only by viable operators, since no one else will ever need it for compliance purposes. When the FAA decided to make base level transferable, it did so to facilitate the trade in Stage 2 airplanes and with the intent that these transfers would be negotiated between the parties to the transfer. At no time did the FAA anticipate having any decision making authority over whether base level would transfer in an individual transaction. The FAA reserved only the right to approve transfers pursuant to its policies and deny the use of base level for compliance if the transfers involved compromise the transition goals.

The creation of base level is unrelated to the provision of the Bankruptcy Code that deals with the disposition of the original lease of an airplane. Unless that original lease included the airplane's base level in its provisions, the lessor has no right to demand its transfer. The FAA does not view the retention of base level by any party validly holding it to diminish the value of any airplane when the base level was not part of the original transaction, and the base level is validly in the possession of the holder.

Base level is established by the fact that an airplane appeared on an operator's operations specification on the date the operator chose to establish its base level. Base level is otherwise severable at the discretion of the holder. §1110 of the Bankruptcy Code appears irrelevant to the discussion of base level since base level does not "attach" to the airplane itself, nor become part of the leased property.

Accordingly, the FAA will not interpret the rule to require the "automatic" transfer of base level from an operator that has ceased operations to the lessor of its airplanes. To do so would violate the policy established in the final rule that the decision to transfer base level remains with the party holding it at the time an airplane is transferred. To require transfers in the case of operators that have filed for bankruptcy would further involve the FAA in a matter over which it has no control. The transfer of base level may well be viewed by a bankruptcy court as a disposition of an operator's assets, a matter in which the FAA will play no role.

Base level, as a concept, was created by the Federal Aviation Administration (FAA) as a means to track the compliance of operators in their transition to an all Stage 3 fleet. This is the reason that base level is presumed to remain with the operator when a leased airplane is returned to a lessor, unless the parties otherwise agree and inform the FAA of the transfer. Compliance is required by the operators, not by the lessor of the airplanes. If an operator chooses the phaseout method of compliance, it demonstrates its compliance by the base level it holds. The FAA will not interpret any of the transition regulations to take away base level from an operator without its consent. (10-13-92).

Question — If an aircraft is held "in reserve" by one operator for another operator's occasional use, may it be counted in the base level of the operator for who it is held in reserve?

Response — §91.861 allows each operator to choose the date on which it establishes its base level. Only airplanes that appeared on an operator's operations specifications on the date chosen may be counted. A Stage 2 airplane that was on an operator's operations specifications on the day the operator chooses its base level may be included, even if the airplane was returned subsequently to the lessor.

Airplanes that are held in reserve for use but that did not appear on operations specifications on the date chosen to establish base level may not be counted in establishing base level. The right to count those airplanes and the responsibility for them under the transition rule belong to another entity. The reserved airplane may continue to be used after the first interim compliance date provided that the operator otherwise meets the criteria of the transition rules as to the number of Stage 2 airplanes eligible for operation in the contiguous United States. (10-13-92).

Question — Can base level be leased?

Response — Yes. §91.863(a) states that base level may be transferred only with a corresponding number of Stage 2 airplanes. By choosing the word "transfer," the FAA intended that all airplane transactions be included. The FAA specifically foresaw the inclusion of base level in the lease of Stage 2 airplanes, with the base level "leased" as part of the deal.

The FAA anticipated that the final disposition of the base level would appear in the lease agreement, whether it would be returned to lessor or retained by lessee. The regulation was written so as not to preclude any transaction involving the transfer of the airplane from including a disposition of the base level that is available to transfer with it. (10-13-92).

Question — Does leased base level return automatically to lessor at the end of a lease?

Response — No. While return of base level may be a term of the lease, there is no automatic transfer in FAA records.

At present, if a Stage 2 airplane was leased to an operator at the time the operator established its base level (between January 1, 1990 and July 1, 1991), then the base level is presumed to stay with the operator at the termination of the lease. This may be changed by an amendment to the lease concerning base level as negotiated by the parties.

For any other airplane that was the subject of a lease agreement dated after July 1, 1991, if the lease agreement is silent as to the base level, it is assumed that no base level was transferred as part of the lease; there is no presumption that the lessor had any base level to transfer. Again, this may be amended at the agreement of the parties to the lease.

The FAA has determined that this disposition of "leased" base level is the most consistent with other base level concepts and is the fairest to all parties. Operators need to be able to rely on their base level, which they were allowed to establish based on their individual circumstances. After the period for choosing the base level date closed, however, operators can have no such expectation and the forces of the market take over.

Further, this interpretation addresses the possibility that a lessee might refuse to sign a recordation of transfer of base level. Either the lessee created the base level itself, in which case it is presumed retained, or base level must be subject of the lease itself. If a lessee refuses to honor the terms of a lease agreement, the FAA presumes that the lessor would pursue its legal remedies under the contract, a situation that does not involve the FAA.

Moreover, no "automatic" statute will be presumed for reporting purposes. The FAA will not assume the responsibility for tracking the expiration of leases that would transfer base level back to the lessor. There are several circumstances under which a lease agreement might end. The FAA is not a party to these agreements and presumes no knowledge of them, nor will the FAA assume the responsibility to monitor individual leases.

As to the terms and conditions of the lease, the FAA has no expectations. The FAA considers the transfer of base level at the inception of the lease to be covered under §91.863(c), a transfer that must be reported to the FAA. At present, the FAA expects only the information required by that section, plus the fact that the reported base level is part of the lease transaction. Accordingly, the transfer back to the lessor at the termination of the lease must also be reported as a transfer of base level under §91.863(c). During the term of the lease, the base level will appear as being held by the lessee.

FAA will take no other action under the lease, including enforcement of the terms of the lease regarding the base level. The parties to the transaction are expected to protect themselves. At no time will the FAA accept the lease document as a report of base level transfer, nor accept any responsibility for staying abreast of the terms of the lease over which it has no interest or control. For this reason, the original transfer and return of leased base level are considered separate base level transactions for FAA reporting purposes.

Further, since base level can only be "transferred" with a Stage 2 airplane, base level alone cannot be leased or sold, and the transaction in base level must be coincident with the transfer of airplane, whether by lease or sale. The terms of the lease or sale cannot provide for the base level to transfer before or after the lease begins or ends or the sale is consummated by transfer of the airplane. The only exception is the FAA's current policy of allowing transfers of base level to "look back" to airplane transfers made before the regulations were promulgated. (10-13-92).

Question — Can a lessee of an airplane with base level sublease the base level?

Response — As indicated previously, the FAA presumes that the terms of any lease of base level would establish the rights of the lessee with regard to the use of the leased base level. The regulation does not specifically restrict any transfer of base level, as long as it accompanies the transfer of a Stage 2 airplane. (10-13-92).

Question — Does §91.861 allow every U.S.-owned Stage 2 airplane that was leased to a foreign entity to increase a U.S. operator's base level when it returns, regardless of when the airplane was leased to the non-U.S. entity?

Response — No. The FAA interprets §91.861 as allowing a U.S.-owned Stage 2 airplane to increase the base level of a U.S. operator when the airplane returns from a foreign lease within six months of the expiration of that lease. However, the limiting factor in this rule is not when the airplane was leased to the non-U.S. entity, but whether the airplane had previously been used by a U.S. operator to establish base level.

For example, if a Stage 2 airplane was originally leased to a non-U.S. entity before January 1, 1990, then it may return to the United States and increase the base level of the operator that buys or leases it. However, for airplanes leased to non-U.S. entities after January 1, 1990, further base level may only be established if the airplane was not used to established base level before it left the United States, i.e., was not on the operations specifications of a U.S. operator at the time that operator established its base level.

This limitation is essential to the integrity of the base level concept. If the airplane had already been used to establish base level domestically, it will not be allowed to generate base level domestically again. Were this permitted, the FAA anticipates that a steady market in short-term leases non-U.S. entities would arise solely to create new base level upon return of the airplanes. This overcreation of base level directly contradicts both the goals of the legislation and the purposes behind the creation of the base level concept.

The statutory allowance in 49 U.S.C. 2158(c) is not rendered meaningless by this interpretation. The legislation states that a U.S.-owned airplane returning from a non-U.S. lessee within six months of the end of that lease shall not be considered an imported airplane for purposes of the nonaddition rule. This provision allows these airplanes to escape the operating limitation imposed by the nonaddition rule, in case there was any question as to their status. The status of those airplanes in connection with the regulatory base level system is a separate consideration. In creating the base level system, the FAA was well aware that the mere ability to operate domestically is meaningless without the right to do so. Accordingly, a returning airplane is allowed to increase the base level of the U.S. operator that subsequently operates it, as long as it was not used in the prior establishment of base level.

This interpretation is not inconsistent with the FAA's statement that an airplane may be leased at any time and still return if it does so within six months of the end of the lease. In drafting this statement, the FAA was aware that the statutory ability to return as a U.S.-owned airplane did not guarantee the unconditional right to fly the airplane until the 1999 statutory deadline. For that reason, the actual right to return is presented in §91.855 and the establishment of base level is presented in §91.861. The Congress left the FAA to establish the method by which Stage 2 airplanes would be phased out of operation. To interpret §2158 of the Airport Noise and Capacity Act of 1990 as an unrestricted right to operate at every return would result in returned airplanes having a higher status that those that stayed in the United States, an interpretation that the FAA is confident was not the intent of Congress in its inclusion of the import limitation in 49 U.S.C. 2158(c).

Nor does the FAA consider this interpretation inconsistent with the fact that one airplane may have been used to establish base level for two or more operators by virtue of its appearance on the operations specifications of two or more operators. The FAA knew this situation could occur, and accounted for it when the rule was written. However, the FAA recognizes that the number of these occurrences is limited and that they cannot occur again. Further, the transfers that occurred during the base level establishment period were done without knowledge of the base level system, and therefore cannot be interpreted as an attempt to manipulate that system. Finally, instances of base level being created by two U.S. operators does not carry the possibility of constant overcreation, since the situation can on longer occur.

The FAA will not allow an expansion of this concept that results in the unlimited creation of base level by the manipulation of short-term foreign leases by persons familiar with the system. If the airplane already created base level by its presence on a U.S. operator's operations specifications, its ability to create base level is exhausted. The underlying theme of the base level system is one-per-Stage-2-airplane. The exception noted above prevents U.S. operators from being harmed by a system they did not know would exist later. This harm is not imposed on a U.S. owner whose airplane was used to establish base level and now has full knowledge of the system. (10-13-92).

Question — Will the FAA establish a "safe harbor" of base level that results from bankruptcy or liquidation transfers, with these transfers free from the review function established in §91.863(d)?

Response — The FAA will not make these types of decisions on individual transfers, whether in the context of an interpretation or at the time of an individual transfer. The FAA views this as the equivalent of a request for a "no action" statement as is sometimes issued by other federal agencies, but which the FAA does not use.

As indicated in the preamble to the final rule and reiterated in the question, the FAA has reserved the right to review any transaction or series of transactions that appear to have been made to avoid compliance with the regulations. That series of transactions may take place over time, and the FAA will not make individual determinations that insulate a transaction from any later transfers.

The FAA understands that this review function may cause some transferring parties to lack a sense of finality in a transfer. However, the FAA has [no] intention of scrutinizing every simple transaction or imputing bad intent upon the parties to every transaction. While several ways of circumventing the base level rules were foreseen, the agency is sure that not every permutation was considered. Accordingly, §91.863 was inserted to give the agency the ultimate right of review when abuse is suspected.

For these same reasons, the FAA will not create a "safe harbor" of base level transactions that result from transfers made pursuant to bankruptcy or liquidation actions. It appears that the concern is if one "bad" transfer is identified, all related transfers of base level will be invalidated for compliance purposes. The FAA does not anticipate that, in the case of a suspect transaction, every related transaction would be found tainted. While it is impossible to judge every possible future transaction in a vacuum, parties may presume that a transfer mandated by a bankruptcy court would be difficult to challenge retroactively. (10-13-92).

Question — Is the beneficiary of a trust able to acquire base level in a transaction even though the airplane actually transfers between owner-trustee and a lessee?

Response — For several reasons, these transfers will not be allowed. Acceptance of these circumstances would require that an entity not even party to the transfer of the airplane be designated as the transferee of base level. This is expressly denied by the language of the regulation that indicates that base level transfers must accompany the transfer of a Stage 2 airplane. To allow this transfer would be to deny the right of the owner-trustee that is expressed in the regulation.

Second, by allowing this transaction, the FAA would be responsible for determining the identity of the trust beneficiary in an arrangement to which the FAA is not a party. The FAA will not assume this liability. Further, the FAA must be able to easily track the ownership of the base level and the subject airplane. Presumably, a transfer of base level to the beneficiary would result in another transfer by the beneficiary, although at neither time would the beneficiary transfer a Stage 2 airplane. The FAA will not allow a third party uninvolved in the transfer of Stage 2 airplanes to trade in base level; to do so would violate the reasons of the prohibition that was built into the regulation.

Finally, allowing the transfer of base level to a beneficiary would be in direct opposition to the interpretation concerning leased base level. Transactions in base level are not allowed to skip over any transferee of the subject airplane, regardless of the financing circumstances of an individual airplane.

The FAA does not consider the problem faced in the transfer of a Stage 2 aircraft held in trust to be insurmountable. As we have indicated previously, any person may hold or transfer base level as long is it is transferred with a Stage 2 airplane. Although the transfer process may involve more pieces of paper than would otherwise be desired, the FAA will consider any unique multiparty transfer documentation as long as the transfer does not violate the basic policies expressed here and in the regulations. (10-13-92).

Question — Must an airplane be on a transferring party's operations specifications for the transfer to include base level?

Response — No. The transferring party need only have the legal right to transfer a Stage 2 airplane (and actually accomplish the transfer) to transfer base level with that airplane. Anyone is allowed to hold base level, or transfer it with a Stage 2 airplane, but only operators have operations specifications. The only use of operations specifications with regard to base level is the initial establishment of base level by an operator. Base level is created only by an airplane's appearance on an operator's operations specifications (or other limited circumstances under §91.855) on the date chosen by the operator. The subsequent transfer of an airplane with base level is unrelated to its appearance on any operator's operations specifications at the time of the transfer. (10-13-92).

91.863 TRANSFERS OF STAGE 2 AIRPLANES WITH BASE LEVEL

(a) Stage 2 airplanes may be transferred with or without the corresponding amount of base level. Base level may not be transferred without the corresponding number of Stage 2 airplanes.

(b) No portion of a U.S. operator's base level established under §91.861 (a) may be used for operations by a foreign air carrier. No portion of a foreign air carrier's base level established under §91.861(b) may be used for operations by a U.S. operator.

(c) Whenever a transfer of Stage 2 airplanes with base level occurs, the transferring and acquiring parties shall, within 10 days, jointly submit written notification of the transfer to the FAA, Office of Environment and Energy. Such notification shall state:

(1) The names of the transferring and acquiring parties;

(2) The name, address, and telephone number of the individual responsible for submitting the notification on behalf of the transferring and acquiring parties;

(3) The total number of Stage 2 airplanes transferred, listed by airplane type, model, series, and serial number;

(4) The corresponding amount of base level transferred and whether it is U.S. operator or foreign air carrier base level; and

(5) The effective date of the transaction.

(d) If, taken as a whole, a transaction or series of transactions made pursuant to this section does not produce an increase or decrease in the number of Stage 2 airplanes for either the acquiring or transferring operator, such transaction or series of transactions may not be used to establish compliance with the requirements of §91.865.

EXPLANATION

Transactions under this regulation will be watched carefully to ensure that they are not shams used to achieve compliance either in the reduction of Stage 2 airplanes or a change in the fleet mix.

CROSS REFERENCES

Previous designation: [New]. 91.851, Definitions; 91.861, Base Level; 91.865, Phased Compliance For Operators With Base Level.

ADVISORY CIRCULARS

AC 36-1G *Noise Levels for U.S. Certificated and Foreign Aircraft* (1997).

AC 36-2C *Measured Or Estimated (Uncertified) Airplane Noise Levels* (1986).

AC 36-3G *Estimated Airplane Noise Levels in A-Weighted Decibels* (1996).

AC 36-4B *Noise Certification Handbook* (1988).

AC 91-53A *Noise Abatement Departure Profiles* (1993).

AC 91-66 *Noise Abatement for Helicopters* (1987).

AC 150/5020-1 *Noise Control and Compatibility Planning For Airports* (1983).

FAA CHIEF COUNSEL OPINIONS

Base Level: [See opinions under §91.861]

91.865 PHASED COMPLIANCE FOR OPERATORS WITH BASE LEVEL

Except as provided in paragraph (a) of this section, each operator that operates an airplane under part 91, 121, 125, 129, or 135 of this chapter, regardless of the national registry of the airplane, shall comply with paragraph (b) or (d) of this section at each interim compliance date with regard to its subsonic airplane fleet covered by §91.801(c) of this subpart.

(a) This section does not apply to new entrants covered by §91.867 or to foreign operators not engaged in foreign air commerce.

(b) Each operator that chooses to comply with this paragraph pursuant to any interim compliance requirement shall reduce the number of Stage 2 airplanes it operates that are eligible for operation in the contiguous United States to a maximum of:
   (1) After December 31, 1994, 75 percent of the base level held by the operator;
   (2) After December 31, 1996, 50 percent of the base level held by the operator;
   (3) After December 31, 1998, 25 percent of the base level held by the operator.

(c) Except as provided under §91.871, the number of Stage 2 airplanes that must be reduced at each compliance date contained in paragraph (b) of this section shall be determined by reference to the amount of base level held by the operator on that compliance date as calculated under §91.861.

(d) Each operator that chooses to comply with this paragraph pursuant to any interim compliance requirement shall operate a fleet that consists of:
   (1) After December 31, 1994, not less than 55 percent Stage 3 airplanes;
   (2) After December 31, 1996, not less than 65 percent Stage 3 airplanes;
   (3) After December 31, 1998, not less than 75 percent Stage 3 airplanes.

(e) Calculations resulting in fractions may be rounded to permit the continued operation of the next whole number of Stage 2 airplanes.

EXPLANATION

This regulation provides two methods of achieving phased compliance. The operator can phase out Stage 2 airplanes or achieve a specific percentage of Stage 3 airplanes in its fleet.

Each operator must maintain the compliance it reported at the previous compliance date when they switch from one compliance method to another.

An operator using the fleet mix (FAR 91.865(d)) method may increase the Stage 2 airplanes it operates only if it adds enough Stage 3 airplanes to maintain the required percentage.

CROSS REFERENCES

Previous designation: [New]. 91.801, Applicability: Relation to Part 36; 91.851, Definitions; 91.867, Phased Compliance for New Entrants; 91.875 Annual Progress Reports.

ADVISORY CIRCULARS

AC 36-1G *Noise Levels for U.S. Certificated and Foreign Aircraft* (1997).

AC 36-2C *Measured Or Estimated (Uncertified) Airplane Noise Levels* (1986).

AC 36-3G *Estimated Airplane Noise Levels in A-Weighted Decibels* (1996).

AC 36-4B *Noise Certification Handbook* (1988).

AC 91-53A *Noise Abatement Departure Profiles* (1993).

AC 91-66 *Noise Abatement for Helicopters* (1987).

AC 150/5020-1 *Noise Control and Compatibility Planning For Airports* (1983).

91.867 PHASED COMPLIANCE FOR NEW ENTRANTS

(a)   New entrant U.S. air carriers.
    (1)   A new entrant initiating operations under part 121 of this chapter on or before December 31, 1994, may initiate service without regard to the percentage of its fleet composed of Stage 3 airplanes.
    (2)   After December 31, 1994, at least 25 percent of the fleet of a new entrant must comply with Stage 3 noise levels.
    (3)   After December 31, 1996, at least 50 percent of the fleet of a new entrant must comply with Stage 3 noise levels.
    (4)   After December 31, 1998, at least 75 percent of the fleet of a new entrant must comply with Stage 3 noise levels.
(b)   New entrant foreign air carriers.
    (1)   A new entrant foreign air carrier initiating part 129 operations on or before December 31, 1994, may initiate service without regard to the percentage of its fleet composed of Stage 3 airplanes.
    (2)   After December 31, 1994, at least 25 percent of the fleet on U.S. operations specifications of a new entrant foreign air carrier must comply with Stage 3 noise levels.
    (3)   After December 31, 1996, at least 50 percent of the fleet on U.S. operations specifications of a new entrant foreign air carrier must comply with Stage 3 noise levels.
    (4)   After December 31, 1998, at least 75 percent of the fleet on U.S. operations specifications of a new entrant foreign air carrier must comply with Stage 3 noise levels.
(c)   Calculations resulting in fractions may be rounded to permit the continued operation of the next whole number of Stage 2 airplanes.

CROSS REFERENCES

Previous designation: [New]. 91.851, Definitions.

ADVISORY CIRCULARS

AC 36-1G *Noise Levels for U.S. Certificated and Foreign Aircraft* (1997).

AC 36-2C *Measured Or Estimated (Uncertified) Airplane Noise Levels* (1986).

AC 36-3G *Estimated Airplane Noise Levels in A-Weighted Decibels* (1996).

AC 36-4B *Noise Certification Handbook* (1988).

AC 91-53A *Noise Abatement Departure Profiles* (1993).

AC 91-66 *Noise Abatement for Helicopters* (1987).

AC 150/5020-1 *Noise Control and Compatibility Planning For Airports* (1983).

91.869 CARRY-FORWARD COMPLIANCE

(a) Any operator that exceeds the requirements of paragraph (b) of §91.865 of this part on or before December 31, 1994, or on or before December 31, 1996, may claim a credit that may be applied at a subsequent interim compliance date.

(b) Any operator that eliminates or modifies more Stage 2 airplanes pursuant to §91.865(b) than required as of December 31, 1994, or December 31, 1996, may count the number of additional Stage 2 airplanes reduced as a credit toward—

    (1) The number of Stage 2 airplanes it would otherwise be required to reduce following a subsequent interim compliance date specified in §91.865(b); or

    (2) The number of Stage 3 airplanes it would otherwise be required to operate in its fleet following a subsequent interim compliance date to meet the percentage requirements specified in §91.865(d).

EXPLANATION

Carry-forward compliance credits can be used even if the operator decides to use a different method of compliance, i.e. fleet-mix instead of Stage 2 reduction.

Carry-forward compliance credits cannot be transferred to another operator.

The carry-forward compliance credit does not expire, but it cannot be used to achieve compliance with the 85% fleet mix required to apply for a waiver from the final compliance date, because that is a statutory requirement and cannot be affected by regulation.

CROSS REFERENCES

Previous designation: [New]. 91.851, Definitions; 91.865, Phased Compliance For Operators With Base Level; 91.873, Waivers From Final Compliance.

ADVISORY CIRCULARS

AC 36-1G *Noise Levels for U.S. Certificated and Foreign Aircraft* (1997).

AC 36-2C *Measured Or Estimated (Uncertified) Airplane Noise Levels* (1986).

AC 36-3G *Estimated Airplane Noise Levels in A-Weighted Decibels* (1996).

AC 36-4B *Noise Certification Handbook* (1988).

AC 91-53A *Noise Abatement Departure Profiles* (1993).

AC 91-66 *Noise Abatement for Helicopters* (1987).

AC 150/5020-1 *Noise Control and Compatibility Planning For Airports* (1983).

91.871 WAIVERS FROM INTERIM COMPLIANCE REQUIREMENTS

(a) Any U.S. operator or foreign air carrier subject to the requirements of §91.865 or 91.867 of this subpart may request a waiver from any individual compliance requirement.

(b) Applications must be filed with the Secretary of Transportation at least 120 days prior to the compliance date from which the waiver is requested.

(c) Applicants must show that a grant of waiver would be in the public interest, and must include in its application its plans and activities for modifying its fleet, including evidence of good faith efforts to comply with the requirements of §91.865 or §91.867. The application should contain all information the applicant considers relevant, including, as appropriate, the following:
   (1) The applicant's balance sheet and cash flow positions;
   (2) The composition of the applicant's current fleet; and
   (3) The applicant's delivery position with respect to new airplanes or noise-abatement equipment.

(d) Waivers will be granted only upon a showing by the applicant that compliance with the requirements of §§91.865 or 91.867 at a particular interim compliance date is financially onerous, physically impossible, or technologically infeasible, or that it would have an adverse effect on competition or on service to small communities.

(e) The conditions of any waiver granted under this section shall be determined by the circumstances presented in the application, but in no case may the term extend beyond the next interim compliance date.

(f) A summary of any request for a waiver under this section will be published in the Federal Register, and public comment will be invited. Unless the Secretary finds that circumstances require otherwise, the public comment period will be at least 14 days.

EXPLANATION

This regulation contains procedures and information required to be submitted by U.S. and foreign operators when requesting a waiver from the interim compliance requirement.

A timely submission is important because certain procedural requirements must be met before a final decision can be made.

The existence and availability of noise abatement retrofit equipment will be an important factor in the consideration of application for interim waivers.

CROSS REFERENCES

Previous designation: [New]. 91.865, Phased Compliance For Operators With Base Level; 91.867, Phased Compliance For New Entrants.

ADVISORY CIRCULARS

AC 36-1G *Noise Levels for U.S. Certificated and Foreign Aircraft* (1997).

AC 36-2C *Measured Or Estimated (Uncertified) Airplane Noise Levels* (1986).

AC 36-3G *Estimated Airplane Noise Levels in A-Weighted Decibels* (1996).

AC 36-4B *Noise Certification Handbook* (1988).

AC 91-53A *Noise Abatement Departure Profiles* (1993).

AC 91-66 *Noise Abatement for Helicopters* (1987).

AC 150/5020-1 *Noise Control and Compatibility Planning For Airports* (1983).

91.873 WAIVERS FROM FINAL COMPLIANCE

(a)   A U.S. air carrier may apply for a waiver from the prohibition contained in §91.853 for its remaining Stage 2 airplanes, provided that, by July 1, 1999, at least 85 percent of the airplanes used by the carrier to provide service to or from an airport in the contiguous United States will comply with the Stage 3 noise levels.

(b)   An application for the waiver described in paragraph (a) of this section must be filed with the Secretary of Transportation no later than January 1, 1999. Such application must include a plan with firm orders for replacing or modifying all airplanes to comply with Stage 3 noise levels at the earliest practicable time.

(c)   To be eligible to apply for the waiver under this section, a new entrant U.S. air carrier must initiate service no later than January 1, 1999, and must comply fully with all provisions of this section.

(d)	The Secretary may grant a waiver under this section if the Secretary finds that granting such waiver is in the public interest. In making such a finding, the Secretary shall include consideration of the effect of granting such waiver on competition in the air carrier industry and the effect on small community air service, and any other information submitted by the applicant that the Secretary considers relevant.

(e)	The term of any waiver granted under this section shall be determined by the circumstances presented in the application, but in no case will the waiver permit the operation of any Stage 2 airplane covered by this subchapter in the contiguous United States after December 31, 2003.

(f)	A summary of any request for a waiver under this section will be published in the Federal Register, and public comment will be invited. Unless the secretary finds that circumstances require otherwise, the public comment period will be at least 14 days.

EXPLANATION

This regulation sets forth the waiver provision relating to final compliance as set forth in the Airport Noise And Capacity Act of 1990.

No waiver can be granted that allows operation of any Stage 2 airplane beyond December 31, 2003.

An 85% Stage 3 fleet, achieved by use of carry-forward compliance credits, will not be accepted as meeting the requirement for seeking a waiver from the final compliance date.

CROSS REFERENCES

Previous designation: [New]. 91.851, Definitions; 91.853, Final Compliance: Civil Subsonic Airplanes; 91.869, Carry-Forward Compliance.

ADVISORY CIRCULARS

AC 36-1G *Noise Levels for U.S. Certificated and Foreign Aircraft* (1997).

AC 36-2C *Measured Or Estimated (Uncertified) Airplane Noise Levels* (1986).

AC 36-3G *Estimated Airplane Noise Levels in A-Weighted Decibels* (1996).

AC 36-4B *Noise Certification Handbook* (1988).

AC 91-53A *Noise Abatement Departure Profiles* (1993).

AC 91-66 *Noise Abatement for Helicopters* (1987).

AC 150/5020-1 *Noise Control and Compatibility Planning For Airports* (1983).

91.875 ANNUAL PROGRESS REPORTS

(a) Each operator subject to §91.865 or §91.867 of this chapter shall submit an annual report to the FAA, Office of Environment and Energy, on the progress it has made toward complying with the requirements of that section. Such reports shall be submitted no later than 45 days after the end of a calendar year. All progress reports must provide the information through the end of the calendar year, be certified by the operator as true and complete (under penalty of 18 U.S.C. 1001), and include the following information:

   (1) The name and address of the operator;

   (2) The name, title, and telephone number of the person designated by the operator to be responsible for ensuring the accuracy of the information in the report;

   (3) The operator's progress during the reporting period toward compliance with the requirements of §91.853, §91.865 or §91.867. For airplanes on U.S. operations specifications, each operator shall identify the airplanes by type, model, series, and serial number.

      (i) Each Stage 2 airplane added or removed from operation or U.S. operations specifications (grouped separately by those airplanes acquired with and without base level);

      (ii) Each Stage 2 airplane modified to Stage 3 noise levels (identifying the manufacturer and model of noise abatement retrofit equipment;

      (iii) Each Stage 3 airplane on U.S. operations specifications as of the last day of the reporting period; and

      (iv) For each Stage 2 airplane transferred or acquired, the name and address of the recipient or transferor; and, if base level was transferred, the person to or from whom base level was transferred or acquired pursuant to Section 91.863 along with the effective date of each base level transaction, and the type of base level transferred or acquired.

(b) Each operator subject to §91.865 or §91.867 of this chapter shall submit an initial progress report covering the period from January 1, 1990, through December 31, 1991, and provide:

   (1) For each operator subject to §91.865:

      (i) The date used to establish its base level pursuant to §91.861(a); and

      (ii) a list of those Stage 2 airplanes (by type, model, series and serial number) in its base level, including adjustments made pursuant to §91.861 after the date its base level was established.

   (2) For each U.S. operator:

      (i) A plan to meet the compliance schedules in §91.865 or §91.867 and the final compliance date of §91.853, including the schedule for delivery of replacement Stage 3 airplanes or the installation of noise abatement retrofit equipment; and

      (ii) A separate list (by type, model, series, and serial number) of those airplanes included in the operator's base level, pursuant to §91.861(a)(1)(l) and (ii), under the categories "returned" or "purchased," along with the date each was added to its operations specifications.

(c) Each operator subject to §91.865 or §91.867 of this chapter shall submit subsequent annual progress reports covering the calendar year preceding the report and including any changes in the information provided in paragraphs (a) and (b) of this section; including the use of any carry-forward credits pursuant to §91.869.

(d) An operator may request, in any report, that specific planning data be considered proprietary.

(e)   If an operator's actions during any reporting period cause it to achieve compliance with §91.853, the report should include a statement to that effect. Further progress reports are not required unless there is any change in the information reported pursuant to paragraph (a) of this section.

(f)   For each U.S. operator subject to §91.865, progress reports submitted for calendar years 1994, 1996, and 1998, shall also state how the operator achieved compliance with the requirements of that section, i.e.—

   (1)   By reducing the number of Stage 2 airplanes in its fleet to no more than the maximum permitted percentage of its base level under §91.865(b), or

   (2)   By operating a fleet that consists of at least the minimum required percentage of Stage 3 airplanes under §91.865(d).

EXPLANATION

This regulation describes the reports that must be made to the FAA Office of Environment and Energy. The Progress Reports are based on calendar years.

CROSS REFERENCES

Previous designation: [New]. 91.851, Definitions; 91.853, Final Compliance: Civil Subsonic Airplanes; 91.861, Base Level; 91.865, Phased Compliance For Operators With Base Level; 91.867, Phased Compliance For New Entrants.

ADVISORY CIRCULARS

AC 36-1G *Noise Levels for U.S. Certificated and Foreign Aircraft* (1997).

AC 36-2C *Measured Or Estimated (Uncertified) Airplane Noise Levels* (1986).

AC 36-3G *Estimated Airplane Noise Levels in A-Weighted Decibels* (1996).

AC 36-4B *Noise Certification Handbook* (1988).

AC 91-53A *Noise Abatement Departure Profiles* (1993).

AC 91-66 *Noise Abatement for Helicopters* (1987).

AC 150/5020-1 *Noise Control and Compatibility Planning For Airports* (1983).

91.877 ANNUAL REPORTING OF HAWAIIAN OPERATIONS

(a)   Each air carrier or foreign air carrier subject to §91.865 or §91.867 of this part that conducts operations between the contiguous United States and the State of Hawaii, between the State of Hawaii and any point outside of the contiguous United States, or between the islands of Hawaii in turnaround service, on or since November 5, 1990, shall include in its annual report the information described in paragraph (c) of this section.

(b)   Each air carrier or foreign air carrier not subject to §91.865 or §91.867 of this part that conducts operations between the contiguous U.S. and the State of Hawaii, between the State of Hawaii and any point outside of the contiguous United States, or between the islands of Hawaii in turnaround service, on or since November 5, 1990, shall submit an annual report to the FAA, Office of Environment and Energy, on its compliance with the Hawaiian operations provisions of 49 U.S.C. 47528. Such reports shall be submitted no later than 45 days after the end of a calendar year. All progress reports must provide the information through the end of the calendar year, be certified by the operator as true and complete (under penalty of 18 U.S.C. 1001), and include the following information—

    (1)   The name and address of the air carrier or foreign air carrier;

    (2)   The name, title, and telephone number of the person designated by the air carrier or foreign air carrier to be responsible for ensuring the accuracy of the information in the report; and

    (3)   The information specified in paragraph (c) of this section.

(c)   The following information must be included in reports filed pursuant to this section —

    (1)   For operations conducted between the contiguous United States and the State of Hawaii —

        (i)   The number of Stage 2 airplanes used to conduct such operations as of November 5, 1990;

        (ii)   Any change to that number during the calendar year being reported, including the date of such change;

    (2)   For air carrier that conduct inter-island turnaround service in the State of Hawaii —

        (i)   The number of Stage 2 airplanes used to conduct such operations as of November 5, 1990;

        (ii)   Any change to that number during the calendar year being reported, including the date of such change;

        (iii)   For an air carrier that provided inter-island turnaround service within the State of Hawaii on November 5, 1990, the number reported under paragraph (c)(2)(I) of this section may include all Stage 2 airplanes with a maximum certificated takeoff weight of more than 75,000 pounds that were owned or leased by the air carrier on November 5, 1990, regardless of whether such airplanes were operated by that air carrier or foreign air carrier on that date.

    (3)   For operations conducted between the State of Hawaii and a point outside the contiguous United States —

        (i)   The number of Stage 2 airplanes used to conduct such operations as of November 5, 1990; and

        (ii)   Any change to that number during the calendar year being reported, including the date of such change.

(d)   Reports or amended reports for years predating this regulation are required to be filed concurrently with the next annual report.

EXPLANATION

This rule establishes the reporting requirements for aircraft operated within the State of Hawaii or between the State of Hawaii and points outside the contiguous United States on and since November 5, 1990. Each affected operator will need to report the number of Stage 2 airplanes it operated in either described operation since November 5, 1990, and any changes in the number since that time. This reporting requirement is needed to ensure compliance with the 1991 amendment to the Airport Noise and Capacity Act of 1990 (49 U.S.C. 47521 et seg.).

PREAMBLE

The changes described below may appear to conflict with various portions of the noise transition regulations currently codified at 14 CFR 91.801 through 91.877. However, the new provisions state that the regulations are to be considered modified where they conflict with any new statutory provisions. The FAA is aware that the statutory change is not apparent to anyone reading the regulations, and plans to change the regulations through appropriate rulemaking within the next year.

Hawaiian Operators

Certain operators of Stage 2 airplanes in Hawaii are now allowed to bring their Stage 2 airplanes to the contiguous United States for maintenance or major alterations. This change to the statute permits these flights without further action by the operators or by the FAA.

Nonrevenue Stage 2 Operations

The revised law now permits a range of nonrevenue Stage 2 operations to occur after December 31, 1999. Any operator of a Stage 2 airplane over 75,000 pounds may operate that airplane in the contiguous United States for the following purposes:

- Sell, lease or scrap the airplane
- Obtain modifications to meet Stage 3 noise levels
- Obtain scheduled heavy maintenance or significant modifications
- Deliver the airplane to a lessee or return it to a lessor
- Park or store the airplane
- Prepare the airplane for any of these events

With regard to these listed uses, operators are advised to note the following:

(1) Nonrevenue flight is a shorthand term. Whether you are a commercial or noncommercial operator, Stage 2 operations are restricted to the purposes listed above only. No "dual purposes" are allowed. For example, you may not operate a Stage 2 airplane for one of the listed purposes and also transport a company official or company goods, or accomplish any action in furtherance of company business. Nonrevenue service means that the flight does not generate any revenue for carrying passengers or cargo.

(2) Operators moving a Stage 2 airplane to location where Stage 3 modifications may be obtained must provide a copy of the modification contract to the FAA with the application for a special flight authorization. For the other purposes, documentation of the activity may be required depending on the circumstances presented.

(3) "Scheduled heavy maintenance" means a "C" or "D" check. The FAA interprets the statutory language to mean that operators of Stage 2 airplanes may not request a special flight authorization to accomplish routine light maintenance actions in the United States.

(4) Similarly, "significantly modifications" is interpreted as those that require specialized knowledge or equipment not readily available elsewhere, or is not practicable to obtain outside the United States. All requests claiming significant modifications will be reviewed individually.

(5) No Stage 1 operations of covered airplanes are permitted for any reason.

Special Flight Authorizations

The FAA is implementing the provisions of the law that allow nonrevenue flights by issuing special flight authorizations. An operators of a Stage 2 airplane that wishes to operate in the contiguous United States for any of the purposes listed in the revised statute (and above) may apply to the FAA's Office of Environment and Energy (AEE) for a special flight authorization. The applicant must file in advance. Applications are due 30 days in advance of the planned flight and must provide the information necessary for the FAA to determine that the planned flight is within the limits prescribed in the law. (64 FR 70571).

CROSS REFERENCES

Previous designation: [New]. 91.851, Definitions; 91.853, Final Compliance: Civil Subsonic Airplanes; 91.861, Base Level; 91.865, Phased Compliance For Operators With Base Level; 91.867, Phased Compliance For New Entrants; 91.875, Annual Progress Reports.

ADVISORY CIRCULARS

AC 36-1G *Noise Levels for U.S. Certificated and Foreign Aircraft* (1997).

AC 36-2C *Measured Or Estimated (Uncertified) Airplane Noise Levels* (1986).

AC 36-3G *Estimated Airplane Noise Levels in A-Weighted Decibels* (1996).

AC 36-4B *Noise Certification Handbook* (1988).

AC 91-53A *Noise Abatement Departure Profiles* (1993).

AC 91-66 *Noise Abatement for Helicopters* (1987).

AC 150/5020-1 *Noise Control and Compatibility Planning For Airports* (1983).

INTENTIONALLY

LEFT

BLANK

INTENTIONALLY

LEFT

BLANK

SUBPART J — WAIVERS

91.903 POLICY AND PROCEDURES

(a) The Administrator may issue a certificate of waiver authorizing the operation of aircraft in deviation from any rule listed in this subpart if the Administrator finds that the proposed operation can be safely conducted under the terms of that certificate of waiver.

(b) An application for a certificate of waiver under this part is made on a form and in a manner prescribed by the Administrator and may be submitted to any FAA office.

(c) A certificate of waiver is effective as specified in that certificate of waiver.

EXPLANATION

A person intending to request a waiver should do so well in advance of the intended operation (at least 30 days) because the conditions placed on the waiver by the FAA may require some adjustments in the operation. A waiver will only be issued for a short time period for a specific operation or series of related operations. Any long-term or continuing need for regulatory relief must be petitioned for under the provisions of FAR 11.25, Provisions For Rulemaking Exemption.

In the case of regulations in Part 91 which are not listed in this regulation, a person may seek authorization to operate an aircraft in deviation from any regulation by seeking an exemption. The procedures for seeking an exemption are set forth in FAR 11.25. To obtain an exemption, it must be shown that an equivalent level of safety will be maintained and the issuance of the exemption is in the public interest.

CROSS REFERENCES

Previous designation: 91.63. 11.61, May I ask FAA to adopt, amend, or repeal a regulation, or grant relief from the requirements of a current regulation? And 11.63, How and to whom do I submit my petition for rulemaking or petition for exemption?

ADVISORY CIRCULARS

AC 91-72 *Waivers of Provisions of Title 14 of the Code of Federal Regulations Part 91* (1996).

91.905 LIST OF RULES SUBJECT TO WAIVERS

Sec.

91.107	Use of safety belts.
91.111	Operating near other aircraft.
91.113	Right-of-way rules: Except water operations.
91.115	Right-of-way rules: Water operations.
91.117	Aircraft speed.
91.119	Minimum safe altitudes: General.
91.121	Altimeter settings.
91.123	Compliance with ATC clearances and instructions.
91.125	ATC light signals.
91.126	Operating on or in the vicinity of an airport in Class G airspace.
91.127	Operating on or in the vicinity of an airport in Class E airspace.
91.129	Operations in Class D airspace.
91.130	Operations in Class C airspace.
91.131	Operations in Class B airspace.
91.133	Restricted and prohibited areas.
91.135	Operations in Class A airspace.
91.137	Temporary flight restrictions.
91.141	Flight restrictions in the proximity of the Presidential and other parties.
91.143	Flight limitation in the proximity of space flight operations.
91.153	VFR flight plan: Information required.
91.155	Basic VFR weather minimums.
91.157	Special VFR weather minimums.
91.159	VFR cruising altitude or flight level.
91.169	IFR flight plan: Information required.
91.173	ATC clearance and flight plan required.
91.175	Takeoff and landing under IFR.
91.177	Minimum altitudes for IFR operations.
91.179	IFR cruising altitude or flight level.
91.181	Course to be flown.
91.183	IFR radio communications.
91.185	IFR operations: Two-way radio communications failure.
91.187	Operation under IFR in controlled airspace: Malfunction reports.
91.209	Aircraft lights.
91.303	Aerobatic flights.
91.305	Flight test areas.
91.311	Towing: Other than under §91.309.
91.313(e)	Restricted category civil aircraft: Operating limitations.
91.515	Flight altitude rules.
91.705	Operations within the North Atlantic Minimum Navigation Performance Specifications Airspace.
91.707	Flights between Mexico or Canada and the United States.
91.713	Operation of civil aircraft of Cuban registry.

CROSS REFERENCES

Previous designation: [New]. 11.61, May I ask FAA to adopt, amend, or repeal a regulation, or grant relief from the requirements of a current regulation? And 11.63, How and to whom do I submit my petition for rulemaking or petition for exemption?

ADVISORY CIRCULARS

AC 91-72 *Waivers of Provisions of Title 14 of the Code of Federal Regulations Part 91* (1996).

INTENTIONALLY

LEFT

BLANK

APPENDIX D
AIRPORTS/LOCATIONS: SPECIAL OPERATING RESTRICTIONS

Section 1. Locations at which the requirements of § 91.215(b)(2) apply.

The requirements of § 91.215(b)(2) apply below 10,000 feet above the surface within a 30-nautical-mile radius of each location in the following list:

Atlanta, GA (The William B. Hartsfield Atlanta International Airport)
Baltimore, MD (Baltimore Washington International Airport)
Boston, MA (General Edward Lawrence Logan International Airport)
Chantilly, VA (Washington Dulles International Airport)
Charlotte, NC (Charlotte/Douglas International Airport)
Chicago, IL Chicago-O'Hare International Airport)
Cleveland, OH (Cleveland-Hopkins International Airport)
Covington, KY (Cincinnati Northern Kentucky International Airport)
Dallas, TX (Dallas/Fort Worth Regional Airport)
Denver, CO (Denver International Airport)
Detroit, MI (Metropolitan Wayne County Airport)
Honolulu, HI (Honolulu International Airport)
Houston, TX (George Bush Intercontinental Airport/Houston)
Kansas City, KS (Mid-Continent International Airport)
Las Vegas, NV (McCarran International Airport)
Los Angeles, CA (Los Angeles International Airport)
Memphis, TN (Memphis International Airport)
Miami, FL (Miami International Airport)
Minneapolis, MN (Minneapolis-St. Paul International Airport)
Newark, NJ (Newark International Airport)
New Orleans, LA (New Orleans International Airport-Moisant Field)
New York, NY (John F. Kennedy International Airport)
New York, NY (LaGuardia Airport)
Orlando, FL (Orlando International Airport)
Philadelphia, PA (Philadelphia International Airport)
Phoenix, AZ (Phoenix Sky Harbor International Airport)
Pittsburgh, PA (Greater Pittsburgh International Airport)
St. Louis, MO (Lambert-St. Louis International Airport)
Salt Lake City, UT (Salt Lake City International Airport)
San Diego, CA (San Diego International Airport)
San Francisco, CA (San Francisco International Airport)
Seattle, WA (Seattle-Tacoma International Airport)
Tampa, FL (Tampa International Airport)
Washington, DC (Ronald Reagan Washington National Airport and Andrews Air Force Base, MD)

Section 2. Airports at which the requirements of § 91.215(b)(5)(ii) apply. [Reserved]

Section 3. Locations at which fixed-wing Special VFR operations are prohibited.

The Special VFR weather minimums of § 91.157 do not apply to the following airports:

Atlanta, GA (The William B. Hartsfield Atlanta International Airport)
Baltimore, MD (Baltimore/Washington International Airport)
Boston, MA (General Edward Lawrence Logan International Airport)
Buffalo, NY (Greater Buffalo International Airport)
Chicago, IL (Chicago-O'Hare International Airport)
Cleveland, OH (Cleveland-Hopkins International Airport)
Columbus, OH (Port Columbus International Airport)
Covington, KY (Cincinnati Northern Kentucky International Airport)
Dallas, TX (Dallas/Fort Worth Regional Airport)
Dallas, TX (Love Field)
Denver, CO (Denver International Airport)
Detroit, MI (Metropolitan Wayne County Airport)
Honolulu, HI (Honolulu International Airport)
Houston, TX (George Bush Intercontinental Airport/Houston)
Indianapolis, IN (Indianapolis International Airport)
Los Angeles, CA (Los Angeles International Airport)
Louisville, KY (Standiford Field)
Memphis, TN (Memphis International Airport)
Miami, FL (Miami International Airport)
Minneapolis, MN (Minneapolis-St. Paul International Airport)
Newark, NJ (Newark International Airport)
New York, NY (John F. Kennedy International Airport)
New York, NY (LaGuardia Airport)
New Orleans, LA (New Orleans International Airport-Moisant Field)
Philadelphia, PA (Philadelphia International Airport)
Pittsburgh, PA (Greater Pittsburgh International Airport)
Portland, OR (Portland International Airport)
San Francisco, CA (San Francisco International Airport)
Seattle, WA (Seattle-Tacoma International Airport)
St. Louis, MO (Lambert-St. Louis International Airport)
Tampa, FL (Tampa International Airport)
Washington, DC (Ronald Reagan Washington National Airport and Andrews Air Force Base, MD)

Section 4. Locations at which solo student pilot activity is not permitted.

Pursuant to § 91.131(b)(2), solo student pilot operations are not permitted at any of the following airports.

Atlanta, GA (The William B. Hartsfield Atlanta International Airport)
Boston, MA (General Edward Lawrence Logan International Airport)
Chicago, IL (Chicago-O'Hare International Airport)
Dallas, TX (Dallas/Fort Worth Regional Airport)
Los Angeles, CA (Los Angeles International Airport)
Miami, FL (Miami International Airport)
Newark, NJ (Newark International Airport)
New York, NY (John F. Kennedy International Airport)
New York, NY (LaGuardia Airport)
San Francisco, CA (San Francisco International Airport)
Washington, DC (Washington National Airport)
Andrews Air Force Base, MD

INTENTIONALLY

LEFT

BLANK

APPENDIX G
OPERATIONS IN REDUCED VERTICAL SEPARATION MINIMUM (RVSM) AIRSPACE

Section 1. Definitions

Reduced Vertical Separation Minimum (RVSM) Airspace. Within RVSM airspace, air traffic control (ATC) separates aircraft by a minimum of 1,000 feet vertically between flight level (FL) 290 and FL 410 inclusive. RVSM airspace is special qualification airspace; the operator and the aircraft used by the operator must be approved by the Administrator. Air-traffic control notifies operators of RVSM by providing route planning information. Section 8 of this appendix identifies airspace where RVSM may be applied.

RVSM Group Aircraft. Aircraft within a group of aircraft, approved as a group by the Administrator, in which each of the aircraft satisfy each of the following:

(a) The aircraft have been manufactured to the same design, and have been approved under the same type certificate, amended type certificate, or supplemental type certificate.
(b) The static system of each aircraft is installed in a manner and position that is the same as those of the other aircraft in the group. The same static source error correction is incorporated in each aircraft of the group.
(c) The avionics units installed in each aircraft to meet the minimum RVSM equipment requirements of this appendix are:
    (1) Manufactured to the same manufacturer specification and have the same part number; or
    (2) Of a different manufacturer or part number, if the applicant demonstrates that the equipment provides equivalent system performance.

RVSM Nongroup Aircraft. An aircraft that is approved for RVSM operations as an individual aircraft.

RVSM Flight envelope. An RVSM flight envelope includes the range of Mach number, weight divided by atmospheric pressure ratio, and altitudes over which an aircraft is approved to be operated in cruising flight within RVSM airspace. RVSM flight envelopes are defined as follows:
(a) The full RVSM flight envelope is bounded as follows:
    (1) The altitude flight envelope extends from FL 290 upward to the lowest altitude of the following:
        (i) FL 410 (the RVSM altitude limit);
        (ii) The maximum certificated altitude for the aircraft; or
        (iii) The altitude limited by cruise thrust, buffet, or other flight limitations.
    (2) The airspeed flight envelope extends:
        (i) From the airspeed of the slats/flaps-up maximum endurance (holding) airspeed, or the maneuvering airspeed, whichever is lower;
        (ii) To the maximum operating airspeed (Vmo/Mmo), or airspeed limited by cruise thrust buffet, or other flight limitations, whichever is lower.
    (3) All permissible gross weights within the flight envelopes defined in paragraphs (1) and (2) of this definition.

(b)   The basic RVSM flight envelope is the same as the full RVSM flight envelope except that the airspeed flight envelope extends:
   (1)   From the airspeed of the slats/flaps-up maximum endurance (holding) airspeed, or the maneuver airspeed, whichever is lower;
   (2)   To the upper Mach/airspeed boundary defined for the full RVSM flight envelope, or a specified lower value not less than the long-range cruise Mach number plus .04 Mach, unless further limited by available cruise thrust, buffet, or other flight limitations.

Section 2. Aircraft Approval

(a)   An operator may be authorized to conduct RVSM operations if the Administrator finds that its aircraft comply with this section.
(b)   The applicant for authorization shall submit the appropriate data package for aircraft approval. The package must consist of at least the following:
   (1)   An identification of the RVSM aircraft group or the nongroup aircraft;
   (2)   A definition of the RVSM flight envelopes applicable to the subject aircraft;
   (3)   Documentation that establishes compliance with the applicable RVSM aircraft requirements of this section; and
   (4)   The conformity tests used to ensure that aircraft approved with the data package meet the RVSM aircraft requirements.
(c)   Altitude-keeping equipment: All aircraft. To approve an aircraft group or a nongroup aircraft, the Administrator must find that the aircraft meets the following requirements:
   (1)   The aircraft must be equipped with two operational independent altitude measurement systems.
   (2)   The aircraft must be equipped with at least one automatic altitude control system that controls the aircraft altitude --
      (i)   Within a tolerance band of ±65 feet about an acquired altitude when the aircraft is operated in straight and level flight under nonturbulent, nongust conditions; or
      (ii)   Within a tolerance band of ±130 feet under nonturbulent, nongust conditions for aircraft for which application for type certification occurred on or before April 9, 1997 that are equipped with an automatic altitude control system with flight management/performance system inputs.
   (3)   The aircraft must be equipped with an altitude alert system that signals an alert when the altitude displayed to the flight crew deviates from the selected altitude by more than:
      (i)   ±300 feet for aircraft for which application for type certification was made on or before April 9, 1997; or
      (ii)   ±200 feet for aircraft for which application for type certification is made after April 9, 1997.
(d)   Altimetry system error containment: Group aircraft for which application for type certification was made on or before April 9, 1997. To approve group aircraft for which application for type certification was made on or before April 9, 1997, the Administrator must find that the altimetry system error (ASE) is contained as follows:
   (1)   At the point in the basic RVSM flight envelope where mean ASE reaches its largest absolute value, the absolute value may not exceed 80 feet.
   (2)   At the point in the basic RVSM flight envelope where mean ASE plus three standard deviations reaches its largest absolute value, the absolute value may not exceed 200 feet.

(3)   At the point in the full RVSM flight envelope where mean ASE reaches its largest absolute value, the absolute value may not exceed 120 feet.

(4)   At the point in the full RVSM flight envelope where mean ASE plus three standard deviations reaches its largest absolute value, the absolute value may not exceed 245 feet.

(5)   Necessary operating restrictions. If the applicant demonstrates that its aircraft otherwise comply with the ASE containment requirements, the Administrator may establish an operating restriction on that applicant's aircraft to restrict the aircraft from operating in areas of the basic RVSM flight envelope where the absolute value of mean ASE exceeds 80 feet, and/or the absolute value of mean ASE plus three standard deviations exceeds 200 feet; or from operating in areas of the full RVSM flight envelope where the absolute value of the mean ASE exceeds 120 feet and/or the absolute value of the mean ASE plus three standard deviations exceeds 245 feet.

(e)   Altimetry system error containment: Group aircraft for which application for type certification is made after April 9, 1997. To approve group aircraft for which application for type certification is made after April 9, 1997, the Administrator must find that the altimetry system error (ASE) is contained as follows:

(1)   At the point in the full RVSM flight envelope where mean ASE reaches its largest absolute value, the absolute value may not exceed 80 feet.

(2)   At the point in the full RVSM flight envelope where mean ASE plus three standard deviations reaches its largest absolute value, the absolute value may not exceed 200 feet.

(f)   Altimetry system error containment: Nongroup aircraft. To approve a nongroup aircraft, the Administrator must find that the altimetry system error (ASE) is contained as follows:

(1)   For each condition in the basic RVSM flight envelope, the largest combined absolute value for residual static source error plus the avionics error may not exceed 160 feet.

(2)   For each condition in the full RVSM flight envelope, the largest combined absolute value for residual static source error plus the avionics error may not exceed 200 feet.

(g)   Traffic Alert and Collision Avoidance System (TCAS) Compatibility With RVSM Operations: All aircraft. After March 31, 2002, unless otherwise authorized by the Administrator, if you operate an aircraft that is equipped with TCAS II in RVSM airspace, it must be a TCAS II that meets TSO C-119b (Version 7.0), or a later version.

(h)   If the Administrator finds that the applicant's aircraft comply with this section, the Administrator notifies the applicant in writing.

Section 3. Operator Authorization

(a)   Authority for an operator to conduct flight in airspace where RVSM is applied is issued in operations specifications or a Letter of Authorization, as appropriate. To issue an RVSM authorization, the Administrator must find that the operator's aircraft have been approved in accordance with Section 2 of this appendix and that the operator complies with this section.

(b) An applicant for authorization to operate within RVSM airspace shall apply in a form and manner prescribed by the Administrator. The application must include the following:

(1) An approved RVSM maintenance program outlining procedures to maintain RVSM aircraft in accordance with the requirements of this appendix. Each program must contain the following:

(i) Periodic inspections, functional flight tests, and maintenance and inspection procedures, with acceptable maintenance practices, for ensuring continued compliance with the RVSM aircraft requirements.

(ii) A quality assurance program for ensuring continuing accuracy and reliability of test equipment used for testing aircraft to determine compliance with the RVSM aircraft requirements.

(iii) Procedures for returning noncompliant aircraft to service.

(2) For an applicant who operates under part 121 or 135, initial and recurring pilot training requirements.

(3) Policies and Procedures. An applicant who operates under part 121 or 135 shall submit RVSM policies and procedures that will enable it to conduct RVSM operations safely.

(c) Validation and Demonstration. In a manner prescribed by the Administrator, the operator must provide evidence that:

(1) It is capable to operate and maintain each aircraft or aircraft group for which it applies for approval to operate in RVSM airspace; and

(2) Each pilot has an adequate knowledge of RVSM requirements, policies, and procedures.

Section 4. RVSM Operations

(a) Each person requesting a clearance to operate within RVSM airspace shall correctly annotate the flight plan filed with air traffic control with the status of the operator and aircraft with regard to RVSM approval. Each operator shall verify RVSM applicability for the flight planned route through the appropriate flight planning information sources.

(b) No person may show, on the flight plan filed with air traffic control, an operator or aircraft as approved for RVSM operations, or operate on a route or in an area where RVSM approval is required, unless:

(1) The operator is authorized by the Administrator to perform such operations; and

(2) The aircraft has been approved and complies with the requirements of Section 2 of this appendix.

Section 5. Deviation Authority Approval

The Administrator may authorize an aircraft operator to deviate from the requirements of § 91.706 for a specific flight in RVSM airspace if that operator has not been approved in accordance with Section 3 of this appendix, and if:

(a) The operator submits an appropriate request with the air traffic control center controlling the airspace, (request should be made at least 48 hours in advance of the operation unless prevented by exceptional circumstances); and

(b) At the time of filing the flight plan for that flight, ATC determines that the aircraft may be provided appropriate separation and that the flight will not interfere with, or impose a burden on, the operations of operators who have been approved for RVSM operations in accordance with Section 3 of this appendix.

Section 6. Reporting Altitude-Keeping Errors

Each operator shall report to the Administrator each event in which the operator's aircraft has exhibited the following altitude-keeping performance:

(a)   Total vertical error of 300 feet or more;
(b)   Altimetry system error of 245 feet or more; or
(c)   Assigned altitude deviation of 300 feet or more.

Section 7. Removal or Amendment of Authority

The Administrator may amend operations specifications to revoke or restrict an RVSM authorization, or may revoke or restrict an RVSM letter of authorization, if the Administrator determines that the operator is not complying, or is unable to comply, with this appendix or subpart H of this part. Examples of reasons for amendment, revocation, or restriction include, but are not limited to, an operator's:

(a)   Committing one or more altitude-keeping errors in RVSM airspace;
(b)   Failing to make an effective and timely response to identify and correct an altitude-keeping error; or
(c)   Failing to report an altitude-keeping error.

Section 8. Airspace Designation

(a)   RVSM in the North Atlantic.
       (1)   RVSM may be applied in the NAT in the following ICAO Flight Information Regions (FIRs): New York Oceanic, Gander Oceanic, Sondrestrom FIR, Reykjavik Oceanic, Shanwick Oceanic, and Santa Maria Oceanic.
       (2)   RVSM may be effective in the Minimum Navigation Performance Specification (MNPS) airspace within the NAT. The MNPS airspace within the NAT is defined by the volume of airspace between FL 285 and FL 420 (inclusive) extending between latitude 27 degrees north and the North Pole, bounded in the east by the eastern boundaries of control areas Santa Maria Oceanic, Shanwick Oceanic, and Reykjavik Oceanic and in the west by the western boundaries of control areas Reykjavik Oceanic, Gander Oceanic, and New York Oceanic, excluding the areas west of 60 degrees west and south of 38 degrees 30 minutes north.
(b)   RVSM in the Pacific. (1) RVSM may be applied in the Pacific in the following ICAO Flight Information Regions (FIRs): Anchorage Arctic, Anchorage Continental, Anchorage Oceanic, Auckland Oceanic, Brisbane, Edmonton, Honiara, Los Angeles, Melbourne, Nadi, Naha, Nauru, New Zealand, Oakland, Oakland Oceanic, Port Moresby, Seattle, Tahiti, Tokyo, Ujung Pandang and Vancouver.
(c)   RVSM in the West Atlantic Route System (WATRS). RVSM may be applied in the New York FIR portion of the West Atlantic Route System (WATRS). The area is defined as beginning at a point 38°30' N / 60°00' W direct to 38°30' N / 69°15' W direct to 38°20' N / 69°57' W direct to 37°31' N / 71°41' W direct to 37°13' N / 72°40' W direct to 35°05' N / 72°40' W direct to 34°54' N / 72°57' W direct to 34°29' N / 73°34' W direct to 34°33' N / 73°41' W direct to 34°19' N / 74°02' W direct to 34°14' N / 73°57' W direct to 32°12' N / 76°49' W direct to 32°20' N / 77°00' W direct to 28°08' N / 77°00' W direct to 27°50' N / 76°32' W direct to 27°50' N / 74°50' W direct to 25°00' N / 73°21' W direct to 25°00' 05' N / 69°13' 06' W direct to 25°00' N / 69°07' W direct to 23°30' N / 68°40' W direct to 23°30' N / 60°00' W to the point of beginning.

INTENTIONALLY

LEFT

BLANK

FEDERAL AVIATION REGULATIONS

PART 141 — PILOT SCHOOLS

TABLE OF CONTENTS

SUBPART A — GENERAL

SUBPART B — PERSONNEL, AIRCRAFT, AND FACILITIES REQUIREMENTS

TABLE OF CONTENTS

SUBPART C — TRAINING COURSE OUTLINE AND CURRICULUM

SUBPART D — EXAMINING AUTHORITY

SUBPART E — OPERATING RULES

TABLE OF CONTENTS

SUBPART F — RECORDS

INTENTIONALLY

LEFT

BLANK

SUBPART A — GENERAL

141.1 APPLICABILITY

This part prescribes the requirements for issuing pilot school certificates, provisional pilot school certificates, and associated ratings, and the general operating rules applicable to a holder of a certificate or rating issued under this part.

EXPLANATION

Part 141 prescribes comprehensive training course requirements for pilot schools. Students are not required to learn to fly in a school certified under Part 141, but students who choose a Part 141 school have lower flight time requirements than students who learn to fly under Part 61.

Call the National Air Transportation Association at (703) 845-9000 for information on the Department of Veterans Affairs Flight Training Assistance Program.

CROSS REFERENCES

141.3, Certificate Required; 141.5, Requirements for a Pilot School Certificate; 141.7, Provisional Pilot School Certificate.

ADVISORY CIRCULARS

AC 141-1A *Pilot School Certification* (1993).

141.3 CERTIFICATE REQUIRED

No person may operate as a certificated pilot school without, or in violation of, a pilot school certificate or provisional pilot school certificate issued under this part.

EXPLANATION

A flight instructor is not required to have a Part 141 certificate or join a certificated school in order to give flight instruction. This regulation simply prohibits anyone from fraudulently advertising that a school is certificated when it is not.

ADVISORY CIRCULARS

AC 141-1A *Pilot School Certification* (1993).

141.5 REQUIREMENTS FOR A PILOT SCHOOL CERTIFICATE

An applicant may be issued a pilot school certificate with associated ratings if the applicant:
(a) Completes the application for a pilot school certificate on a form and in a manner prescribed by the Administrator;
(b) Holds a provisional pilot school certificate, issued under this part, for at least 24 calendar months preceding the month in which the application for a pilot school certificate is made;
(c) Meets the applicable requirements of subparts A through C of this part for the school ratings sought; and
(d) Has trained and recommended for pilot certification and rating tests, within 24 calendar months preceding the month the application is made for the pilot school certificate, at least 10 students for a knowledge or practical test for a pilot certificate, flight instructor certificate, ground instructor certificate, an additional rating, an end-of-course test for a training course specified in appendix K to this part, or any combination of those tests, and at least 80 percent of all tests administered were passed on the first attempt.

EXPLANATION

A brand-new pilot school is not eligible for a "pilot school certificate." It must apply for a "provisional pilot school certificate" as defined in §141.7.

A certificated pilot school that, after 24 months, does not meet the recent training experience requirements of FAR §141.5 but meets all other requirements may apply for a provisional pilot school certificate.

The holder of a provisional pilot school certificate that does not meet the recent training experience requirement (24 months) prior to the expiration of its certificate may not apply for a new certificate for a period of 180 days from the expiration date of the expired certificate.

PREAMBLE

Because of the size of some part 141-approved schools, the FAA does not have sufficient personnel resources to respond to all the demands that would be generated by this proposal. In addition, the FAA considers designated examiners to be representatives of the Administrator, rather than employees of a school, when they are conducting practical tests. This does not preclude these examiners from otherwise being employed by a school. To prevent confusion, the FAA has deleted from paragraph (d)(i) the following language: "a test that was conducted by an FAA inspector or an examiner who is not an employee of the school", and replaced this language with "the required test". In addition, the FAA reformatted this section and added the phrase "or any combination of those tests," to reflect the FAA's intent with respect to pass rates. Except for these changes, the final rule is adopted as proposed. (62 FR 16278).

CROSS REFERENCES

Part 141, Subpart A – General; Subpart B - Personnel, Aircraft, and Facilities Requirements; Subpart C - Training Course Outline and Curriculum.

ADVISORY CIRCULARS

AC 141-1A *Pilot School Certification* (1993).

141.7 PROVISIONAL PILOT SCHOOL CERTIFICATE

An applicant that meets the applicable requirements of subparts A, B, and C of this part, but does not meet the recent training activity requirements of §141.5(d) of this part, may be issued a provisional pilot school certificate with ratings.

EXPLANATION

A brand-new pilot school must start with a "provisional pilot school certificate." Those interested in buying an existing certificated pilot school should be aware of the requirements of §141.17(b). Refer to explanation under §141.5 for other comments on provisional pilot school certificates.

CROSS REFERENCES

Part 141, Subpart A – General; Subpart B - Personnel, Aircraft, and Facilities Requirements; Subpart C - Training Course Outline and Curriculum; 141.17, Duration of Certificate and Examining Authority.

ADVISORY CIRCULARS

AC 141-1A *Pilot School Certification* (1993).

141.9 EXAMINING AUTHORITY

An applicant is issued examining authority for its pilot school certificate if the applicant meets the requirements of subpart D of this part.

CROSS REFERENCES

Part 141, Subpart A – General; Subpart B - Personnel, Aircraft, and Facilities Requirements; Subpart C - Training Course Outline and Curriculum; Subpart D - Examining Authority; 141.17, Duration of Certificate and Examining Authority.

ADVISORY CIRCULARS

AC 141-1A *Pilot School Certification* (1993).

141.11 PILOT SCHOOL RATINGS

(a)   The ratings listed in paragraph (b) of this section may be issued to an applicant for:

    (1)   A pilot school certificate, provided the applicant meets the requirements of §141.5 of this part; or

    (2)   A provisional pilot school certificate, provided the applicant meets the requirements of §141.7 of this part.

(b)   An applicant may be authorized to conduct the following courses:

    (1)   *Certification and rating courses.* (Appendixes A through J).

        (i)   Recreational pilot course.

        (ii)   Private pilot course.

        (iii)   Commercial pilot course.

        (iv)   Instrument rating course.

        (v)   Airline transport pilot course.

        (vi)   Flight instructor course.

        (vii)   Flight instructor instrument course.

        (viii) Ground instructor course.

        (ix)   Additional aircraft category or class rating course.

        (x)   Aircraft type rating course.

    (2)   *Special preparation courses.* (Appendix K).

        (i)   Pilot refresher course.

        (ii)   Flight instructor refresher course.

        (iii)   Ground instructor refresher course.

        (iv)   Agricultural aircraft operations course.

        (v)   Rotorcraft external-load operations course.

        (vi)   Special operations course.

        (vii)   Test pilot course.

    (3)   *Pilot ground school course.* (Appendix L).

EXPLANATION

If a rating is denied, an applicant may reapply at any time for an Air Agency Certificate or rating in the same manner prescribed for the initial application. At the inspector's discretion, reinspection of previously approved areas may not be necessary. However, a complete inspection will probably be required if more than 120 days have elapsed since the previous inspection.

A pilot school may apply to have a rating deleted simply by sending a letter to the certificate-holding FAA district office, signed by a person authorized to sign for the school. The rating may not be deleted immediately if the FAA has initiated, or is contemplating, enforcement action against the school.

CROSS REFERENCES

141.13, Application For Issuance, Amendment, or Renewal; 141.17, Duration of Certificate and Examining Authority; 141.23 Advertising Limitations; 141.27, Renewal of Certificates and Ratings.

ADVISORY CIRCULARS

AC 141-1A *Pilot School Certification* (1993).

141.13 APPLICATION FOR ISSUANCE, AMENDMENT, OR RENEWAL

(a) Application for an original certificate and rating, an additional rating, or the renewal of a certificate under this part must be made on a form and in a manner prescribed by the Administrator.

(b) Application for the issuance or amendment of a certificate or rating must be accompanied by two copies of each proposed training course curriculum for which approval is sought.

EXPLANATION

AC 141-1 *Pilot School Certification* sets forth specific procedures for issuance, amendment or renewal of pilot school certificates, and gives instructions on how to complete FAA Form 8420-8 (OMB 04-R0204). See §141.27, Renewal of Certificates and Ratings for information about the renewal process.

CROSS REFERENCES

141.17, Duration of Certificate and Examining Authority; 141.27, Renewal of Certificates and Ratings; Part 141, Subpart C - Training Course Outline and Curriculum.

ADVISORY CIRCULARS

AC 141-1A *Pilot School Certification* (1993).

141.17 DURATION OF CERTIFICATE AND EXAMINING AUTHORITY

(a) Unless surrendered, suspended, or revoked, a pilot school's certificate or a provisional pilot school's certificate expires:
   (1) On the last day of the 24th calendar month from the month the certificate was issued;
   (2) Except as provided in paragraph (b) of this section, on the date that any change in ownership of the school occurs;
   (3) On the date of any change in the facilities upon which the school's certificate is based occurs; or
   (4) Upon notice by the Administrator that the school has failed for more than 60 days to maintain the facilities, aircraft, or personnel required for any one of the school's approved training courses.

(b) A change in the ownership of a pilot school or provisional pilot school does not terminate that school's certificate if, within 30 days after the date that any change in ownership of the school occurs:
   (1) Application is made for an appropriate amendment to the certificate, and
   (2) No change in the facilities, personnel, or approved training courses is involved.

(c) An examining authority issued to the holder of a pilot school certificate expires on the date that the pilot school certificate expires, or is surrendered, suspended, or revoked.

EXPLANATION

When a certified school changes its name only, with no change in ownership, facilities, instructor personnel, or training courses, a new certificate will be issued in the new name, with the same certificate number, ratings and original expiration date. An inspection by the FAA is not required.

The holder of pilot school air agency certificate may request cancellation of the certificate or a rating at any time. The request should be submitted to the certificate-holding district office in writing, with the air agency certificate to be canceled. The request must be signed by the person(s) authorized to sign for the certificate holder. If the FAA has taken or is contemplating enforcement action against the certificate, the cancellation must be approved by the FAA Regional Counsel's office.

CROSS REFERENCES

141.13, Application for Issuance, Amendment, or Renewal; 141.27, Renewal of Certificates and Ratings.

ADVISORY CIRCULARS

AC 141-1A *Pilot School Certification* (1993).

141.18 CARRIAGE OF NARCOTIC DRUGS, MARIJUANA, AND DEPRESSANT OR STIMULANT DRUGS OR SUBSTANCES

If the holder of a certificate issued under this part permits any aircraft owned or leased by that holder to be engaged in any operation that the certificate holder knows to be in violation of §91.19(a) of this chapter, that operation is a basis for suspending or revoking the certificate.

CROSS REFERENCES

91.19, Carriage of Narcotic Drugs, Marihuana, and Depressant or Stimulant Drugs or Substances.

141.19 DISPLAY OF CERTIFICATE

(a) Each holder of a pilot school certificate or a provisional pilot school certificate must display that certificate in a place in the school that is normally accessible to the public and is not obscured.
(b) A certificate must be made available for inspection upon request by:
    (1) The Administrator;
    (2) An authorized representative of the National Transportation Safety Board; or
    (3) A Federal, State, or local law enforcement officer.

EXPLANATION

A pilot school is not required to surrender its certificate unless the FAA issues an order of suspension or revocation.

141.21 INSPECTIONS

Each holder of a certificate issued under this part must allow the Administrator to inspect its personnel, facilities, equipment, and records to determine the certificate holder's:
(a) Eligibility to hold its certificate;
(b) Compliance with 49 U.S.C. 40101 et seq., formerly the Federal Aviation Act of 1958, as amended; and
(c) Compliance with the Federal Aviation Regulations.

EXPLANATION

Inspections may occur at the following times:

(1) Initial certification;
(2) Certificate renewal;
(3) Transfer of ownership;
(4) Change of main base;
(5) Upon application of the school for an additional rating(s); and
(6) When the FSDO deems an inspection necessary to ensure compliance with the Training Course Outline (TCO) and other requirements of the FARs.

Inspections for the purpose of certification, renewal, transfer of ownership or change of base are made at a time agreeable to the school and the FAA. However, inspections made by the FAA to determine compliance with the training course outline or the FARs may be "unscheduled."

An FAA inspection may include the following:

(1) Administer practical tests to the chief flight instructors and any assistant chief flight instructors.
(2) Inspect the applicant's record keeping system for compliance with the FARs. The importance of complete and accurate record keeping is often emphasized by the FAA.
(3) Conduct an aircraft conformity inspection.
(4) Conduct a base inspection.
(5) Inspect satellite bases.
(6) Inspect ground trainers, training aids, and other equipment.

CROSS REFERENCES

141.13, Application for Issuance, Amendment, or Renewal; 141.27, Renewal of Certificates and Ratings.

ADVISORY CIRCULARS

AC 141-1A *Pilot School Certification* (1993).

141.23 ADVERTISING LIMITATIONS

(a)   The holder of a pilot school certificate or a provisional pilot school certificate may not make any statement relating to its certification and ratings that is false or designed to mislead any person contemplating enrollment in that school.

(b)   The holder of a pilot school certificate or a provisional pilot school certificate may not advertise that the school is certificated unless it clearly differentiates between courses that have been approved under part 141 of this chapter and those that have not been approved under part 141 of this chapter.

(c)   The holder of a pilot school certificate or a provisional pilot school certificate must promptly remove:

(1)   From vacated premises, all signs indicating that the school was certificated by the Administrator; or

(2)   All indications (including signs), wherever located, that the school is certificated by the Administrator when its certificate has expired or has been surrendered, suspended, or revoked.

EXPLANATION

Pilot school advertising must clearly differentiate between courses that have been approved and those that have not. The FAA does not expect a pilot school to resort to negative advertising and list every course which has **not** been approved. However, each training course which has been approved should be clearly stated, along with a clarification that **only** those courses have been approved.

If a certificate expires, or is surrendered, suspended, or revoked, the school is required to remove all indications that the school was certified by the FAA. This includes all advertising mediums, such as billboards, radio, television, and the removal of all signs.

If an FAA-approved school moves from one location to another, it is required to promptly remove all signs from its old premises indicating that the school was certificated by the FAA at that location.

CROSS REFERENCES

141.19, Display of Certificate.

ADVISORY CIRCULARS

AC 141-1A *Pilot School Certification* (1993).

141.25 BUSINESS OFFICE AND OPERATIONS BASE

(a)   Each holder of a pilot school or a provisional pilot school certificate must maintain a principal business office with a mailing address in the name shown on its certificate.

(b)   The facilities and equipment at the principal business office must be adequate to maintain the files and records required to operate the business of the school.

(c)   The principal business office may not be shared with, or used by, another pilot school.

(d)   Before changing the location of the principal business office or the operations base, each certificate holder must notify the FAA Flight Standards District Office having jurisdiction over the area of the new location, and the notice must be:

   (1)   Submitted in writing at least 30 days before the change of location; and

   (2)   Accompanied by any amendments needed for the certificate holder's approved training course outline.

(e)   A certificate holder may conduct training at an operations base other than the one specified in its certificate, if:

   (1)   The Administrator has inspected and approved the base for use by the certificate holder; and

   (2)   The course of training and any needed amendments have been approved for use at that base.

EXPLANATION

141.25(a): The purpose of a principal business office is to provide a specific location for required school files and records, and a location from which the operation of the school business is conducted. This requirement should not be construed to mean that all school functions, such as scheduling flights, training functions, etc., must be conducted at the principal business office. While this regulation does not require that a "business office" be a room with four walls and a door, the regulation does prohibit the sharing with or use by another pilot school of that business office; therefore, the business office should be conspicuously isolated by walls or partitions to ensure separation from another pilot school's activity. The business office should be located so that required school files and student training records can be kept up to date and available to students and instructors.

141.25(b): Written notice of a proposed change of location should be submitted on a new application, FAA Form 8420-8. The notice of a change must be accompanied by necessary amendments to approved TCO's.

CROSS REFERENCES

141.15, Location of Facilities; 141.21, Inspections; 141.43, Pilot Briefing Areas.

ADVISORY CIRCULARS

AC 141-1A *Pilot School Certification* (1993).

141.26 TRAINING AGREEMENTS

A training center certificated under part 142 of this chapter may provide the training, testing, and checking for pilot schools certificated under part 141 of this chapter, and is considered to meet the requirements of part 141, provided—
(a) There is a training agreement between the certificated training center and the pilot school;
(b) The training, testing, and checking provided by the certificated training center is approved and conducted under part 142;
(c) The pilot school certificated under part 141 obtains the Administrator's approval for a training course outline that includes the training, testing, and checking to be conducted under part 141 and the training, testing, and checking to be conducted under part 142; and
(d) Upon completion of the training, testing, and checking conducted under part 142, a copy of each student's training record is forwarded to the part 141 school and becomes part of the student's permanent training record.

EXPLANATION

Contact your FSDO for information about obtaining FAA approval for a training course outline that includes training, checking and testing by a Part 142 training center pursuant to a training agreement.

141.27 RENEWAL OF CERTIFICATES AND RATINGS

(a) *Pilot school.*
   (1) A pilot school may apply for renewal of its school certificate and ratings within 30 days preceding the month the pilot school's certificate expires, provided the school meets the requirements prescribed in paragraph (a)(2) of this section for renewal of its certificate and ratings.
   (2) A pilot school may have its school certificate and ratings renewed for an additional 24 calendar months if the Administrator determines the school's personnel, aircraft, facility and airport, approved training courses, training records, and recent training ability and quality meet the requirements of this part.
   (3) A pilot school that does not meet the renewal requirements in paragraph (a)(2) of this section, may apply for a provisional pilot school certificate if the school meets the requirements of §141.7 of this part.
(b) *Provisional pilot school.*
   (1) Except as provided in paragraph (b)(3) of this section, a provisional pilot school may not have its provisional pilot school certificate or the ratings on that certificate renewed.
   (2) A provisional pilot school may apply for a pilot school certificate and associated ratings provided that school meets the requirements of §141.5 of this part.
   (3) A former provisional pilot school may apply for another provisional pilot school certificate, provided 180 days have elapsed since its last provisional pilot school certificate expired.

EXPLANATION

A pilot school or provisional pilot school certificate, and any ratings or examining authority on that certificate, expires at the end of the twenty-fourth month after the month in which it was issued.

Application for renewal is made by submitting two copies of FAA Form 8420-8, Application For Pilot School Certificate. A school may apply for the renewal of any or all ratings it holds, or it may also apply for the addition of a new rating. Examining authority should be renewed at the same time the school certificate is renewed.

A school must meet the same requirements for renewal as for original certification. Therefore, upon receipt of an application for renewal, the FSDO may conduct the same evaluation of qualifications and inspection of facilities as required for original certification. However, if the FSDO is very familiar with the school's operation or has recently inspected it, there may be no need for an extensive reinspection nor for reexamination of instructors.

PREAMBLE

The FAA acknowledges the commenter's concern, and points out that the requirement in §141.5 that tests be conducted by an FAA inspector or an examiner who is not an employee of the school has been withdrawn from the final rule. The proposed rule is adopted as proposed with minor editorial and format changes. (62 FR 16279).

CROSS REFERENCES

141.5, Pilot School Certificate; 141.7, Provisional Pilot School Certificate; 141.9, Examining Authority; 141.13, Application for Issuance, Amendment, or Renewal; 141.17, Duration of Certificate and Examining Authority; 141.21, Inspections.

ADVISORY CIRCULARS

AC 141-1A *Pilot School Certification* (1993).

INTENTIONALLY

LEFT

BLANK

SUBPART B — PERSONNEL, AIRCRAFT, AND FACILITIES REQUIREMENTS

141.31 APPLICABILITY

(a) This subpart prescribes:
   (1) The personnel and aircraft requirements for a pilot school certificate or a provisional pilot school certificate; and
   (2) The facilities that a pilot school or provisional pilot school must have available on a continuous basis.
(b) As used in this subpart, to have continuous use of a facility, including an airport, the school must have:
   (1) Ownership of the facility or airport for at least 6 calendar months after the date the application for initial certification and on the date of renewal of the school's certificate is made; or
   (2) A written lease agreement for the facility or airport for at least 6 calendar months after the date the application for initial certification and on the date of renewal of the school's certificate is made.

EXPLANATION

The "continuous use" requirement can be met if the school has a written agreement showing that it has continuous use of those facilities for six months at the time of certification or renewal of its certificate.

CROSS REFERENCES

141.5, Requirements for a Pilot School Certificate; 141.7, Provisional Pilot School Certificate.

ADVISORY CIRCULARS

AC 141-1A *Pilot School Certification* (1993).

141.33 PERSONNEL

(a) An applicant for a pilot school certificate or for a provisional pilot school certificate must meet the following personnel requirements:
   (1) Each applicant must have adequate personnel, including certificated flight instructors, certificated ground instructors, or holders of a commercial pilot certificate with a lighter-than-air rating, and a chief instructor for each approved course of training who is qualified and competent to perform the duties to which that instructor is assigned.
   (2) If the school employs dispatchers, aircraft handlers, and line and service personnel, then it must instruct those persons in the procedures and responsibilities of their employment.
   (3) Each instructor to be used for ground or flight training must hold a flight instructor certificate, ground instructor certificate, or commercial pilot certificate with a lighter-than-air rating, as appropriate, with ratings for the approved course of training and any aircraft used in that course.

(b)   An applicant for a pilot school certificate or for a provisional pilot school certificate must designate a chief instructor for each of the school's approved training courses, who must meet the requirements of §141.35 of this part.

(c)   When necessary, an applicant for a pilot school certificate or for a provisional pilot school certificate may designate a person to be an assistant chief instructor for an approved training course, provided that person meets the requirements of §141.36 of this part.

(d)   A pilot school and a provisional pilot school may designate a person to be a check instructor for conducting student stage checks, end-of-course tests, and instructor proficiency checks, provided:

   (1)   That person meets the requirements of §141.37 of this part; and

   (2)   That school has a student enrollment of at least 50 students at the time designation is sought.

(e)   A person, as listed in this section, may serve in more than one position for a school, provided that person is qualified for each position.

EXPLANATION

Each school is required to ensure that the dispatchers, service personnel, or other persons assigned responsibilities with the school are adequately trained in the procedures and responsibilities of their employment. Compliance with this requirement may be accomplished through verbal instruction, manuals, or any other means chosen by the school. The FAA may evaluate any personnel at any time to determine that they have been instructed in their responsibilities and are competent to perform their duties.

Qualified personnel may serve in more than one capacity with the school. For example, a school may wish to use a flight instructor as a dispatcher or a ground instructor.

PREAMBLE

The FAA did not intend to mandate the employment of the personnel listed in paragraph (a)(2), only that, if employed, they be properly trained. The final rule modifies this language. The final rule also includes references in paragraph (a)(1) and (a)(3) to commercial pilots with a lighter-than-air-rating. In response to the commenter's concerns regarding paragraph (d), the FAA notes that the rule explicitly requires a student enrollment of at least 50 students at the time designation is sought. The FAA has determined that 50 students is the maximum for which one chief instructor or assistant chief instructor could reasonably provide checks, and, therefore, permits a pilot school or provisional pilot school to designate check instructors for conducting student stage checks, end-of-course tests, and instructor proficiency checks.

The proposed rule is adopted with these changes and other minor editorial changes. (62 FR 16279).

CROSS REFERENCES

141.35, Chief Instructor Qualifications; 141.36, Assistant Chief Instructor Qualifications; 141.79, Flight Training; 141.81, Ground Training; 141.83, Quality of Training; 141.85, Chief Instructor Responsibilities; 141.87, Change of Chief Instructor.

ADVISORY CIRCULARS

AC 141-1A *Pilot School Certification* (1993).

141.35 CHIEF INSTRUCTOR QUALIFICATIONS

(a)   To be eligible for designation as a chief instructor for a course of training, a person must meet the following requirements:
   (1)   Hold a commercial pilot certificate or an airline transport pilot certificate, and, except for a chief instructor for a course of training solely for a lighter-than-air rating, a current flight instructor certificate. The certificates must contain the appropriate aircraft category and class ratings for the category and class of aircraft used in the course and an instrument rating, if an instrument rating is required for enrollment in the course of training.
   (2)   Meet the pilot-in-command recent flight experience requirements of §61.57 of this chapter;
   (3)   Pass a knowledge test on—
      (i)   Teaching methods;
      (ii)   Applicable provisions of the "Aeronautical Information Manual";
      (iii) Applicable provisions of parts 61, 91, and 141 of this chapter; and
      (iv)   The objectives and approved course completion standards of the course for which the person seeks to obtain designation.
   (4)   Pass a proficiency test on instructional skills and ability to train students on the flight procedures and maneuvers appropriate to the course;
   (5)   Except for a course of training for gliders, balloons, or airships, the chief instructor must meet the applicable requirements in paragraphs (b), (c), and (d) of this section; and
   (6)   A chief instructor for a course of training for gliders, balloons, or airships is only required to have 40 percent of the hours required in paragraphs (b) and (d) of this section.
(b)   For a course of training leading to the issuance of a recreational or private pilot certificate or rating, a chief instructor must have:
   (1)   At least 1,000 hours as pilot in command; and
   (2)   Primary flight training experience, acquired as either a certificated flight instructor or an instructor in a military pilot flight training program, or a combination thereof, consisting of at least—
      (i)   2 years and a total of 500 flight hours; or
      (ii)   1,000 flight hours.
(c)   For a course of training leading to the issuance of an instrument rating or a rating with instrument privileges, a chief instructor must have:
   (1)   At least 100 hours of flight time under actual or simulated instrument conditions;
   (2)   At least 1,000 hours as pilot in command; and
   (3)   Instrument flight instructor experience, acquired as either a certificated flight instructor-instrument or an instructor in a military pilot flight training program, or a combination thereof, consisting of at least—
      (i)   2 years and a total of 250 flight hours; or
      (ii)   400 flight hours.
(d)   For a course of training other than those leading to the issuance of a recreational or private pilot certificate or rating, or an instrument rating or a rating with instrument privileges, a chief instructor must have:
   (1)   At least 2,000 hours as pilot in command; and
   (2)   Flight training experience, acquired as either a certificated flight instructor or an instructor in a military pilot flight training program, or a combination thereof, consisting of at least—
      (i)   3 years and a total of 1,000 flight hours; or
      (ii)   1,500 flight hours.
   (e)   To be eligible for designation as chief instructor for a ground school course, a person must have 1 year of experience as a ground school instructor at a certificated pilot school.

EXPLANATION

§141.35 contains references to "primary" flight training. Historically, old Part 141 used this same term to describe flight instruction given to private pilots.

Schools should keep in mind that approved courses of training that combine both basic and instrument flying schools, such as an unlimited type rating, would require a chief flight instructor or his assistant to meet more than one general requirement listed under §141.35 or §141.36.

A chief flight instructor or assistant chief flight instructor is designated by a pilot school when a school applies for and receives a certification in a particular course of training. The pilot school applicant designates the chief flight instructor or assistant chief flight instructor, by name, in the training course outline for each course. The chief flight instructor practical test includes both an oral examination and a check ride. Any applicant should fill out FAA Form 8710-1 Airman Certificate and/or Rating Application. The applicant should mark the "other" box and type "Application For Chief Flight Instructor Proficiency Check" at the top of the form. The oral exam and check ride will be conducted by an FAA inspector, so applicants are well-advised to make sure that the aircraft that they plan to use is airworthy and that all documents are up to date and in the aircraft.

If the inspector determines that the chief flight instructor applicant's performance does not meet the minimum standards appropriate to the certificate held, the training course outline for the school may not be approved until an acceptable chief flight instructor is designated. Failure of a practical test by an assistant chief flight instructor is not grounds for disapproval of the training course outline; however, the training course outline cannot include the assistant chief flight instructor's name until the practical test has been passed.

An applicant who has failed the chief flight instructor practical test may apply for a retest. If the retest is accomplished within 60 days, only the portion of the test that was unsatisfactory needs to be repeated. If reexamination is delayed beyond 60 days, the entire test must be satisfactorily accomplished.

CROSS REFERENCES

141.11, Pilot School Ratings; 141.36, Assistant Chief Instructor Qualifications; 141.53, Approved Procedures for a Training Course: General; 141.55, Training Course Contents; 141.79, Flight Training; 141.81, Ground Training; 141.83, Quality of Training; 141.85, Chief Instructor Responsibilities; 141.87, Change of Chief Instructor; 141.101, Training Records.

ADVISORY CIRCULARS

AC 141-1A *Pilot School Certification* (1993).

141.36 ASSISTANT CHIEF INSTRUCTOR QUALIFICATIONS

(a)   To be eligible for designation as an assistant chief instructor for a course of training, a person must meet the following requirements:
(1)   Hold a commercial pilot or an airline transport pilot certificate and, except for the assistant chief instructor for a course of training solely for a lighter-than-air rating, a current flight instructor certificate. The certificates must contain the appropriate aircraft category, class, and instrument ratings if an instrument rating is required by the course of training for the category and class of aircraft used in the course;
(2)   Meet the pilot-in-command recent flight experience requirements of §61.57 of this chapter;
(3)   Pass a knowledge test on—
(i)   Teaching methods;
(ii)   Applicable provisions of the "Aeronautical Information Manual";
(iii)   Applicable provisions of parts 61, 91, and 141 of this chapter; and
(iv)   The objectives and approved course completion standards of the course for which the person seeks to obtain designation.
(4)   Pass a proficiency test on the flight procedures and maneuvers appropriate to that course; and
(5)   Meet the applicable requirements in paragraphs (b), (c) and (d) of this section. However, an assistant chief instructor for a course of training for gliders, balloons, or airships is only required to have 40 percent of the hours required in paragraphs (b) and (d) of this section.
(b)   For a course of training leading to the issuance of a recreational or private pilot certificate or rating, an assistant chief instructor must have:
(1)   At least 500 hours as pilot in command; and
(2)   Flight training experience, acquired as either a certificated flight instructor or an instructor in a military pilot flight training program, or a combination thereof, consisting of at least—
(i)   1 year and a total of 250 flight hours; or
(ii)   500 flight hours.
(c)   For a course of training leading to the issuance of an instrument rating or a rating with instrument privileges, an assistant chief flight instructor must have:
(1)   At least 50 hours of flight time under actual or simulated instrument conditions;
(2)   At least 500 hours as pilot in command; and
(3)   Instrument flight instructor experience, acquired as either a certificated flight instructor-instrument or an instructor in a military pilot flight training program, or a combination thereof, consisting of at least—
(i)   1 year and a total of 125 flight hours; or
(ii)   200 flight hours.
(d)   For a course of training other than one leading to the issuance of a recreational or private pilot certificate or rating, or an instrument rating or a rating with instrument privileges, an assistant chief instructor must have:
(1)   At least 1,000 hours as pilot in command; and
(2)   Flight training experience, acquired as either a certificated flight instructor or an instructor in a military pilot flight training program, or a combination thereof, consisting of at least—
(i)   1-1/2 years and a total of 500 flight hours; or
(ii)   750 flight hours.
(e)   To be eligible for designation as an assistant chief instructor for a ground school course, a person must have 6 months of experience as a ground school instructor at a certificated pilot school.

EXPLANATION

An FAA approved pilot school may designate one or more assistant chief flight instructors for a course(s) of training. The assistant chief flight instructor must meet the requirements of §141.35, since the assistant is expected to act for the chief flight instructor in the chief flight instructor's absence. The FAA will approve the use of assistant chief flight instructors when approving individual training course outlines.

The failure of a practical test by an assistant chief instructor is not grounds for disapproval of a training course outline; however, the training course outline cannot include the assistant chief flight instructor's name until the practical test has been passed. Refer to §141.35 for tips about the practical test.

The chief instructor may delegate duties to the assistant chief flight instructor or, if there is no assistant chief flight instructor, to another instructor in that course; however, the ultimate responsibility for each function remains with the chief flight instructor. Examples of duties which would be appropriate for delegation would be the certification of training records, and the conduct of stage checks (with the exception of final stage checks, which **must** be given by the chief instructor or assistant chief instructor). Delegation ensures that the instruction can still be given in a course of training when the chief instructor is ill, is on vacation, or otherwise unable to perform the duties temporarily.

CROSS REFERENCES

141.5, Requirements for a Pilot School Certificate; 141.7, Provisional Pilot School Certificate; 141.11, Pilot School Ratings; 141.35, Chief Instructor Qualifications; 141.53, Approved Procedures for a Training Course: General; 141.55, Training Course Contents; 141.79, Flight Training; 141.81, Ground Training, 141.83, Quality of Training; 141.85, Chief Instructor Responsibilities; 141.87, Change of Chief Instructor; 141.101, Training Records.

ADVISORY CIRCULARS

AC 141-1A *Pilot School Certification* (1993).

141.37 CHECK INSTRUCTOR QUALIFICATIONS

(a)   To be designated as a check instructor for conducting student stage checks, end-of-course tests, and instructor proficiency checks under this part, a person must meet the eligibility requirements of this section:

    (1)   For checks and tests that relate to either flight or ground training, the person must pass a test, given by the chief instructor, on—

        (i)   Teaching methods;

        (ii)   Applicable provisions of the "Aeronautical Information Manual";

        (iii)   Applicable provisions of parts 61, 91, and 141 of this chapter; and

        (iv)   The objectives and course completion standards of the approved training course for the designation sought.

(2)   For checks and tests that relate to a flight training course, the person must—
    (i)   Meet the requirements in paragraph (a)(1) of this section;
    (ii) Hold a commercial pilot certificate or an airline transport pilot certificate and, except for a check instructor for a course of training for a lighter-than-air rating, a current flight instructor certificate. The certificates must contain the appropriate aircraft category, class, and instrument ratings for the category and class of aircraft used in the course;
    (iii) Meet the pilot-in-command recent flight experience requirements of §61.57 of this chapter; and
    (iv) Pass a proficiency test, given by the chief instructor or assistant chief instructor, on the flight procedures and maneuvers of the approved training course for the designation sought.
(3)   For checks and tests that relate to ground training, the person must—
    (i)   Meet the requirements in paragraph (a)(1) of this section;
    (ii) Except for a course of training for a lighter-than-air rating, hold a current flight instructor certificate or ground instructor certificate with ratings appropriate to the category and class of aircraft used in the course; and
    (iii) For a course of training for a lighter-than-air rating, hold a commercial pilot certificate with a lighter-than-air category rating and the appropriate class rating.
(b) A person who meets the eligibility requirements in paragraph (a) of this section must:
    (1)   Be designated, in writing, by the chief instructor to conduct student stage checks, end-of-course tests, and instructor proficiency checks; and
    (2)   Be approved by the FAA Flight Standards District Office having jurisdiction over the school.
(c) A check instructor may not conduct a stage check or an end-of-course test of any student for whom the check instructor has:
    (1)   Served as the principal instructor; or
    (2)   Recommended for a stage check or end-of-course test.

EXPLANATION

This rule was added with the 1997 amendment.

PREAMBLE

References to medical certificate requirements in this section have been deleted from the final rule. For further discussion, see the analysis of §61.23. After further review, the FAA has decided to permit the assistant chief to give a proficiency test. The assistant chief instructor was included as an individual able to give proficiency tests because, the FAA has determined that an assistant chief instructor has the qualifications necessary to give proficiency tests to check instructors. The final rule reflects this change. (62 FR 16280).

141.38 AIRPORTS

(a)   An applicant for a pilot school certificate or a provisional pilot school certificate must show that he or she has continuous use of each airport at which training flights originate.

(b)   Each airport used for airplanes and gliders must have at least one runway or takeoff area that allows training aircraft to make a normal takeoff or landing under the following conditions at the aircraft's maximum certificated takeoff gross weight:

    (1)   Under wind conditions of not more than 5 miles per hour;

    (2)   At temperatures in the operating area equal to the mean high temperature for the hottest month of the year;

    (3)   If applicable, with the powerplant operation, and landing gear and flap operation recommended by the manufacturer; and

    (4)   In the case of a takeoff—

        (i)   With smooth transition from liftoff to the best rate of climb speed without exceptional piloting skills or techniques; and

        (ii)   Clearing all obstacles in the takeoff flight path by at least 50 feet.

(c)   Each airport must have a wind direction indicator that is visible from the end of each runway at ground level;

(d)   Each airport must have a traffic direction indicator when:

    (1)   The airport does not have an operating control tower; and

    (2)   UNICOM advisories are not available.

(e)   Except as provided in paragraph (f) of this section, each airport used for night training flights must have permanent runway lights;

(f)   An airport or seaplane base used for night training flights in seaplanes is permitted to use adequate nonpermanent lighting or shoreline lighting, if approved by the Administrator.

EXPLANATION

Each airport must have a wind indicator that is visible from the ends of each runway at ground level. However, a current FAA policy interpretation states that if an airport's wind indicator cannot be seen from each runway end at ground level but the aircraft has a radio, and the airport has a unicom, an operating control tower, a flight service station, or other air traffic facilities which can provide wind information of an advisory nature, the airport is acceptable for use by an approved pilot's school.

141.38(c): A wind "T," tetrahedron, or similar device, may be a "landing direction indicator" that is manually set and not necessarily a "wind direction indicator" which moves with the wind.

141.38(d): When required, the traffic direction indicator must show the direction of traffic patterns for all runways regardless of landing or take-off direction.

141.38(e): Landing area outline lights, water area boundary lights, or temporary lighting such as flare pots, or deployed portable electric runway lighting systems do not meet the requirements of this subsection.

CROSS REFERENCES

141.5, Requirements for a Pilot School Certificate; 141.7, Provisional Pilot School Certificate; 141.91, Satellite Bases.

ADVISORY CIRCULARS

AC 141-1A *Pilot School Certification* (1993).

AERONAUTICAL INFORMATION MANUAL

Visual Indicators at Uncontrolled Airports without an Operating Control Tower, Para. 4-3-3.

141.39 AIRCRAFT

An applicant for a pilot school certificate or provisional pilot school certificate, must show that each aircraft used by that school for flight training and solo flights meets the following requirements:

(a) Each aircraft must be registered as a civil aircraft in the United States;

(b) Each aircraft must be certificated with a standard airworthiness certificate or a primary airworthiness certificate, unless the Administrator determines that due to the nature of the approved course, an aircraft not having a standard airworthiness certificate or primary airworthiness certificate may be used,

(c) Each aircraft must be maintained and inspected in accordance with the requirements under subpart E of part 91 of this chapter that apply to aircraft operated for hire;

(d) Each aircraft used in flight training must have at least two pilot stations with engine-power controls that can be easily reached and operated in a normal manner from both pilot stations; and

(e) Each aircraft used in a course involving IFR en route operations and instrument approaches must be equipped and maintained for IFR operations. For training in the control and precision maneuvering of an aircraft by reference to instruments, the aircraft may be equipped as provided in the approved course of training.

EXPLANATION

If an aircraft is not owned by a school, the school should show, through appropriate documentation, that it has a use agreement (lease) with the owner. However, an exclusive use lease is not required. A lease that would allow the school to make the aircraft available for students to meet the training course objectives meets the intent of a TCO approval. The FAA does not require that the lease be for a specified minimum period of time.

Training aircraft must be certificated in the standard airworthiness category, except aircraft used for a course of training in agricultural operations, external load operations, and aerial work operations; such as banner towing, sky writing, etc. In such courses, the school may use aircraft certificated in the restricted category. No other special airworthiness certificate is accepted by the FAA.

Each aircraft used by a school for flight training must be inspected and maintained in accordance with §91.169(b), (which applies to aircraft used to give flight instruction for hire), 91.169(c)(2), or 91.169(d) or (e).

This requires aircraft used in an approved course of training to have 100-hour and annual inspections or be maintained under a procedure described under §91.169(c)(2). It should be clearly understood that these inspection requirements include aircraft used for dual instruction, solo, and pilot-in-command flights.

When a student enrolled in an approved school provides an aircraft for personal use in an approved course, that aircraft must meet the requirements of the training aircraft described in the appropriate training course outline. In addition, that aircraft must meet the same inspection requirements as aircraft operated by the approved school. If the approved training syllabus requires flights under instrument flight rules, the aircraft used must be one in which instrument flight is authorized by its operating limitations and by its equipment. If the approved training syllabus requires only simulated IFR operations, the aircraft must be equipped and maintained for IFR operations. However, IFR operations need not be authorized by its operating limitations. An aircraft not completely equipped for IFR operations may be used for instruction in the control and precise maneuvering of an aircraft by reference to instruments if it is approved in the training course outline. For example, an airplane need only be equipped with appropriate flight instruments needed for the basic instrument portion of a course.

PREAMBLE

Commenters' concerns over the proposed inspection program were noted. Upon reviewing the issue, the FAA has decided not to adopt the proposal in the final rule. The inspection program was not proposed for other operations that engage in similar types of training under part 61, and would have increased costs with no commensurate safety benefit. The FAA has determined that compliance with subpart E of part 91 ensures an adequate level of safety. Furthermore, the proposal placed part 141 schools at an unwarranted economic disadvantage. The concerns of HAI, NBAA, and others, regarding aircraft used for instrument training, also were considered. In response, the FAA has modified the requirement to apply only to aircraft used in a course involving IFR en route operations and instrument approaches. In response to comments on the required accessibility of flight controls, the words "flight controls" have been deleted to accommodate throwover yokes. The reference to "two-place aircraft" has been changed to "two-pilot stations" to include training in balloons.

References to the proposed term "supervised pilot in command" have been replaced by "solo" as discussed in the analysis of §61.1. The FAA also renumbered this section in the final rule.

The rule is adopted with these changes. (62 FR 16280 - 16281).

CROSS REFERENCES

141.5, Requirements for a Pilot School Certificate; 141.7, Provisional Pilot School Certificate; 141.75, Aircraft Requirements.

ADVISORY CIRCULARS

AC 141-1A *Pilot School Certification* (1993).

FAA CHIEF COUNSEL OPINIONS

A Part 141 certificate school does not have to **own** any aircraft but it must have **use of** aircraft that will be used in each course. The aircraft to be used by a Part 141 school, whether the school owns the aircraft or has a "use agreement" with an aircraft supplier, must be inspected by a local FAA agent to make sure the aircraft meets the specific requirements under §141.39. Although a Part 141 school does not have to have continuous use of an aircraft, it must at all times have evidence of its ability to have access to aircraft that will be used in each course. A Part 141 certificated school that neither owns nor has use of aircraft would not be in compliance with the FAR. An exclusive use agreement for aircraft is not required, but some form of use agreement is needed. (6-22-92).

141.41 FLIGHT SIMULATORS, FLIGHT TRAINING DEVICES, AND TRAINING AIDS

An applicant for a pilot school certificate or a provisional pilot school certificate must show that its flight simulators, flight training devices, training aids, and equipment meet the following requirements:

(a) *Flight simulators.* Each flight simulator used to obtain flight training credit allowed for flight simulators in an approved pilot training course curriculum must—

    (1) Be a full-size aircraft cockpit replica of a specific type of aircraft, or make, model, and series of aircraft;

    (2) Include the hardware and software necessary to represent the aircraft in ground operations and flight operations;

    (3) Use a force cueing system that provides cues at least equivalent to those cues provided by a 3 degree freedom of motion system;

    (4) Use a visual system that provides at least a 45-degree horizontal field of view and a 30-degree vertical field of view simultaneously for each pilot; and

    (5) Have been evaluated, qualified, and approved by the Administrator.

(b) *Flight training devices.* Each flight training device used to obtain flight training credit allowed for flight training devices in an approved pilot training course curriculum must—

    (1) Be a full-size replica of instruments, equipment panels, and controls of an aircraft, or set of aircraft, in an open flight deck area or in an enclosed cockpit, including the hardware and software for the systems installed that is necessary to simulate the aircraft in ground and flight operations;

    (2) Need not have a force (motion) cueing or visual system; and

    (3) Have been evaluated, qualified, and approved by the Administrator.

(c) *Training aids and equipment.* Each training aid, including any audiovisual aid, projector, tape recorder, mockup, chart, or aircraft component listed in the approved training course outline, must be accurate and appropriate to the course for which it is used.

EXPLANATION

This regulation prescribes the requirements for ground trainers that may be used to obtain the maximum flight training credit allowed for ground trainers in an approved pilot training course.

PREAMBLE

The FAA recently published Amendment No. 61-100. The FAA has revised the title of this section to include flight simulators and revised the section to conform with the definitions of "flight simulator" and "flight training device" as set forth in that rule. The proposed rule is adopted with these changes. Those flight training devices previously approved under the provisions of this section may continue to be used, provided that they continue to meet the design criteria and functional requirements for which they were originally approved. (62 FR 16281).

CROSS REFERENCES

141.5, Requirements for a Pilot School Certificate; 141.7, Provisional Pilot School Certificate; 61.51, Pilot Logbooks; 61.109, Private Pilot: Aeronautical Experience.

ADVISORY CIRCULARS

AC 141-1A *Pilot School Certification* (1993).

141.43 PILOT BRIEFING AREAS

(a) An applicant for a pilot school certificate or provisional pilot school certificate must show that the applicant has continuous use of a briefing area located at each airport at which training flights originate that is:
  (1) Adequate to shelter students waiting to engage in their training flights;
  (2) Arranged and equipped for the conduct of pilot briefings; and
  (3) Except as provided in paragraph (c) of this section, for a school with an instrument rating or commercial pilot course, equipped with private landline or telephone communication to the nearest FAA Flight Service Station.
(b) A briefing area required by paragraph (a) of this section may not be used by the applicant if it is available for use by any other pilot school during the period it is required for use by the applicant.
(c) The communication equipment required by paragraph (a)(3) of this section is not required if the briefing area and the flight service station are located on the same airport, and are readily accessible to each other.

EXPLANATION

The requirement that a school have continuous use of a briefing area at each airport at which training flights originate means that schools do not need to have pilot briefing areas at destination airports used for cross-country flight training.

141.43(a): To meet this requirement, the FAA suggests that the equipment should include tables of adequate size to lay out aeronautical charts for planning purposes, and a chalkboard. In addition, if a flight service station or weather bureau is not conveniently available, the school must provide a telephone line for flight service briefings and/or access to DUAT or another aviation weather service.

141.43(b): There is no objection to other pilots using the briefing facilities, provided orderly school functions are maintained. However, no other school may use the area.

CROSS REFERENCES

141.5, Requirements for a Pilot School Certificate; 141.7, Provisional Pilot School Certificate; 141.25, Business Office and Operations Base; 141.55, Training Course Contents; 141.89, Maintenance of Personnel, Facilities and Equipment.

ADVISORY CIRCULARS

AC 141-1A *Pilot School Certification* (1993).

141.45 GROUND TRAINING FACILITIES

An applicant for a pilot school or provisional pilot school certificate must show that:
(a) Each room, training booth, or other space used for instructional purposes is heated, lighted, and ventilated to conform to local building, sanitation, and health codes; and
(b) The training facility is so located that the students in that facility are not distracted by the training conducted in other rooms, or by flight and maintenance operations on the airport.

EXPLANATION

The FAA recognizes that pilot training methods differ from other kinds of training. Pilot schools enroll students with widely varying backgrounds, goals, and varying degrees of motivation and aviation experience. For this reason, it is understandable that it is not always possible to schedule large classes for ground training at one time. Individual instruction is often necessary for maximum benefit to a particular student. Therefore, it is anticipated that FAA-approved schools will use classrooms, small isolated rooms, training booths, or other areas with an instructor or training aid, as appropriate. All ground instructional facilities are subject to approval under §141.55(a).

CROSS REFERENCES

141.5, Requirements for a Pilot School Certificate; 141.7, Provisional Pilot School Certificate; 141.43, Pilot Briefing Areas; 141.55, Training Course Contents; 141.89, Maintenance of Personnel, Facilities and Equipment.

ADVISORY CIRCULARS

AC 141-1A *Pilot School Certification* (1993).

INTENTIONALLY

LEFT

BLANK

SUBPART C — TRAINING COURSE OUTLINE AND CURRICULUM

141.51 APPLICABILITY

This subpart prescribes the curriculum and course outline requirements for the issuance of a pilot school certificate or provisional pilot school certificate and ratings.

CROSS REFERENCES

141.5, Requirements for a Pilot School Certificate; 141.7, Provisional Pilot School Certificate.

ADVISORY CIRCULARS

AC 141-1A *Pilot School Certification* (1993).

141.53 APPROVAL PROCEDURES FOR A TRAINING COURSE: GENERAL

(a) *General.* An applicant for a pilot school certificate or provisional pilot school certificate must obtain the Administrator's approval of the outline of each training course for which certification and rating is sought.

(b) *Application.*
  (1) An application for the approval of an initial or amended training course must be submitted in duplicate to the FAA Flight Standards District Office having jurisdiction over the area where the school is based.
  (2) An application for the approval of an initial or amended training course must be submitted at least 30 days before any training under that course, or any amendment thereto, is scheduled to begin.
  (3) An application for amending a training course must be accompanied by two copies of the amendment.

(c) *Training courses.*
  (1) A training course submitted for approval prior to August 4, 1997 may, if approved, retain that approval until 1 year after August 4, 1997.
  (2) An applicant for a pilot school certificate or provisional pilot school certificate may request approval of the training courses specified in §141.11(b) of this part.

EXPLANATION

Training course outline (TCO) approval may be granted for initial certification of the school, for amendment of a course, or for addition of a course to an existing school certificate. Each course of training requires a separate TCO. Approval of a TCO would result in placing the course on the air agency certificate and list of approved courses for the school. This entitles the school to train and certify pilots for that particular rating. Addition of or amendment to a TCO for an already certified school constitutes an amendment of the air agency certificate held by the school.

When a training course outline has been approved by the FAA Flight Standards District Office (FSDO), the original copy will be returned to the school with each page marked "FAA Approved," signed, and dated by the principal operations inspector (POI) or manager of the FSDO having jurisdiction over the school. If there is no change to the curriculum of a commercially developed syllabus, only the first page will be stamped "FAA Approved."

When amendment of an approved training course outline is submitted for approval, the FSDO will review the proposed changes and, if they are satisfactory, sign, date, and return the original pages of the amendment(s) to the school. Use FAA Form 8420-8 for an application for the approval of an initial or amended TCO.

A school may elect to purchase a commercially developed syllabus and present it for FAA approval. These syllabi (such as Jeppesen Sanderson) have been reviewed at the national level, but none have been given approval. Approval must come from the local FSDO. The school should fully understand the objectives and the standards of the syllabus and be able to actually give training as described. Once a commercially developed syllabus has been approved by the FSDO, a school may use the syllabus as approved. However, if modifications are made, the FSDO must approve the modifications.

The producer of a commercially developed syllabus may choose to change the syllabus. If a pilot school wishes to amend its syllabus accordingly, it must obtain FSDO approval. The syllabus used by the school must be the same as that used by the students. Therefore, schools should be alert to changes in course content by producers of commercial syllabi.

CROSS REFERENCES

141.5, Requirements for a Pilot School Certificate; 141.7, Provisional Pilot School Certificate; 141.55, Training Course Contents; 141.57, Special Curricula.

ADVISORY CIRCULARS

AC 141-1A *Pilot School Certification* (1993).

141.55 TRAINING COURSE: CONTENTS

(a) Each training course for which approval is requested must meet the minimum curriculum requirements in accordance with the appropriate appendix of this part.

(b) Except as provided in paragraphs (d) and (e) of this section, each training course for which approval is requested must meet the minimum ground and flight training time requirements in accordance with the appropriate appendix of this part.

(c) Each training course for which approval is requested must contain:

(1) A description of each room used for ground training, including the room's size and the maximum number of students that may be trained in the room at one time;

(2) A description of each type of audiovisual aid, projector, tape recorder, mockup, chart, aircraft component, and other special training aids used for ground training;

(3) A description of each flight simulator or flight training device used for training;

(4) A listing of the airports at which training flights originate and a description of the facilities, including pilot briefing areas that are available for use by the school's students and personnel at each of those airports;

(5) A description of the type of aircraft including any special equipment used for each phase of training;

(6)   The minimum qualifications and ratings for each instructor assigned to ground or flight training; and

(7)   A training syllabus that includes the following information —

    (i)   The prerequisites for enrolling in the ground and flight portion of the course that include the pilot certificate and rating (if required by this part), training, pilot experience, and pilot knowledge;

    (ii)   A detailed description of each lesson, including the lesson's objectives, standards, and planned time for completion;

    (iii)   A description of what the course is expected to accomplish with regard to student learning;

    (iv)   The expected accomplishments and the standards for each stage of training; and

    (v)   A description of the checks and tests to be used to measure a student's accomplishments for each stage of training.

(d)   A pilot school may request and receive initial approval for a period of not more than 24 calendar months for any of the training courses of this part without specifying the minimum ground and flight training time requirements of this part, provided the following provisions are met:

(1)   The school holds a pilot school certificate issued under this part and has held that certificate for a period of at least 24 consecutive calendar months preceding the month of the request;

(2)   In addition to the information required by paragraph (c) of this section, the training course specifies planned ground and flight training time requirements for the course;

(3)   The school does not request the training course to be approved for examining authority, nor may that school hold examining authority for that course; and

(4)   The practical test or knowledge test for the course is to be given by —

    (i)   An FAA inspector; or

    (ii)   An examiner who is not an employee of the school.

(e)   A certificated pilot school may request and receive final approval for any of the training courses of this part without specifying the minimum ground and flight training time requirements of this part, provided the following conditions are met:

(1)   The school has held initial approval for that training course for at least 24 calendar months.

(2)   The school has —

    (i)   Trained at least 10 students in that training course within the preceding 24 calendar months and recommended those students for a pilot, flight instructor, or ground instructor certificate or rating; and

    (ii)   At least 80 percent of those students passed the practical or knowledge test, or any combination thereof, on the first attempt, and that test was given by —

       (A)   An FAA inspector; or

       (B)   An examiner who is not an employee of the school.

(3)   In addition to the information required by paragraph (c) of this section, the training course specifies planned ground and flight training time requirements for the course.

(4)   The school does not request that the training course be approved for examining authority nor may that school hold examining authority for that course.

EXPLANATION

Part 141 does not require that a school specify maximum course times. All time parameters listed in a training course outline (TCO) or syllabus are minimum times. However, if a school submits a TCO which includes a maximum course time for that school, the following may be used as a general guide:

(1)   For all courses of training, except those for turbo-jet type ratings, 20 percent over the course of time prescribed in the curricula in the Appendixes of FAR Part 141.

(2)   For turbo-jet type ratings, 100 percent over the course time prescribed in Appendix F of FAR Part 141.

(3)   For courses of training where a corresponding curriculum is not prescribed in the Appendixes of FAR Part 141, the FAA inspector should use his or her best judgment.

Each TCO must contain a training syllabus which is a "building block" progression of learning with provisions for regular review and evaluation at prescribed stages.

Each applicant should be encouraged to develop training syllabi in a format similar to that used in Appendix A of Advisory Circular 141.1 *Pilot School Certification*.

The training syllabus must contain any prerequisites necessary for enrollment in the course; for example, minimum pilot certificates and ratings, if any, and the required class of medical certificate or statement of no medical deficiency (required for glider or balloon courses only). In addition, it must contain any training, pilot experience, or special knowledge required for enrollment in the course.

In addition, the training syllabus must contain a description of each lesson, including its objectives and standards, and the measurable unit of student accomplishment or learning to be derived from the lesson or course. The syllabus must include stages of training and the completion standards for each stage. Course, stage, and lesson objectives should be stated in relation to the performance expected of the student.

Each course, stage, lesson objective, and completion standard should meet the following criteria.

(a)   Overall objectives should describe what students are expected to know or be able to do at the end of a particular course, stage or lesson. They should be stated as terms of desired student learning outcomes.

(b)   Course objectives should state in broad terms the knowledge and skill goals to be reached by the student at the end of the course.

(c)   Stage objectives should be more limited and state desired student goals in specific areas of knowledge and skill.

(d)   Lesson objectives should clearly specify desired student outcomes for each lesson and should be consistent with the objective of the stage and course.

Although Part 141 recognizes the ability of a certificated school to develop its own courses of training, the school may elect to purchase a commercially developed syllabus and present it for FSDO approval. When evaluating the school's use of a commercially developed syllabus, the reviewing inspector will determine if the school can actually give the training in the manner described in the syllabus, and whether the syllabus completely supports the curriculum upon which it is based.

PREAMBLE

141.55(d): In implementing this proposal, the FAA intends to monitor the approval process to ensure that a uniform national standard is maintained. FAA has added language to paragraph (d)(3) to clarify that a school may not hold examining authority for a training course conducted under this paragraph. Regarding HAI's concerns, if a school is unable to meet the training activity requirements of part 141 it would not be allowed to hold a pilot school certificate. Therefore, the rule is adopted as proposed.

141.55(e): The FAA has added language to paragraph (e)(4) to clarify that a school may not hold examining authority for a training course conducted under this paragraph because the FAA's philosophy has been to maintain a system of checks and balances to ensure that the schools providing training do not have a conflict of interest with respect to the administering of the practical test. Therefore, in response to the commenter's question, all students must be examined by an FAA inspector or an examiner who is not an employee of the school.

The FAA deleted proposed paragraph (f) from the final rule because, after further review, the FAA has determined that this paragraph is unnecessary. The proposal is adopted with the changes discussed above, and other minor editorial changes. (62 FR 16282).

CROSS REFERENCES

141.5, Requirements for a Pilot School Certificate; 141.7, Provisional Pilot School Certificate; 141.53, Approval Procedures for a Training Course: General; 141.57, Special Curricula.

ADVISORY CIRCULARS

AC 141-1A *Pilot School Certification* (1993).

141.57 SPECIAL CURRICULA

An applicant for a pilot school certificate or provisional pilot school certificate may apply for approval to conduct a special course of airman training for which a curriculum is not prescribed in the appendixes of this part, if the applicant shows that the training course contains features that could achieve a level of pilot proficiency equivalent to that achieved by a training course prescribed in the appendixes of this part or the requirements of part 61 of this chapter.

EXPLANATION

An original and two copies of a proposed special curriculum must be submitted along with a cover letter requesting FAA approval at least 60 days before the training is scheduled to begin. FAA approval or denial should be accomplished within 30 days to allow the school sufficient time to develop a training course outline based on the special curriculum. When a special curriculum is approved, each page of the original and office copies should be dated and signed by the FAA principal operations inspector.

CROSS REFERENCES

141.5, Requirements for a Pilot School Certificate; 141.7, Provisional Pilot School Certificate; 141.53, Approval Procedures for a Training Course: General; 141.55, Training Course Contents.

INTENTIONALLY

LEFT

BLANK

SUBPART D — EXAMINING AUTHORITY

141.61 APPLICABILITY

This subpart prescribes the requirements for the issuance of examining authority to the holder of a pilot school certificate, and the privileges and limitations of that examining authority.

EXPLANATION

A pilot school may request flight test examining authority, knowledge test examining authority, or both, for a course of training. Without flight test examining authority, final pilot certification is conducted by an FAA inspector, or a designated pilot examiner. Without knowledge test examining authority, knowledge tests for certificates or ratings must be given by an FAA testing center, through a designated knowledge test examiner.

CROSS REFERENCES

141.63, Examining Authority Qualification Requirements; 141.65, Privileges; 141.67, Limitations and Reports.

ADVISORY CIRCULARS

AC 141-1A *Pilot School Certification* (1993).

141.63 EXAMINING AUTHORITY QUALIFICATION REQUIREMENTS

(a) A pilot school must meet the following prerequisites to receive initial approval for examining authority:
   (1) The school must complete the application for examining authority on a form and in a manner prescribed by the Administrator;
   (2) The school must hold a pilot school certificate and rating issued under this part;
   (3) The school must have held the rating in which examining authority is sought for at least 24 consecutive calendar months preceding the month of application for examining authority;
   (4) The training course for which examining authority is requested may not be a course that is approved without meeting the minimum ground and flight training time requirements of this part; and
   (5) Within 24 calendar months before the date of application for examining authority, that school must meet the following requirements—
      (i) The school must have trained at least 10 students in the training course for which examining authority is sought and recommended those students for a pilot, flight instructor, or ground instructor certificate or rating; and
      (ii) At least 90 percent of those students passed the required practical or knowledge test, or any combination thereof, for the pilot, flight instructor, or ground instructor certificate or rating on the first attempt, and that test was given by—
         (A) An FAA inspector; or
         (B) An examiner who is not an employee of the school.

(b)   A pilot school must meet the following requirements to retain approval of its examining authority:

    (1)   The school must complete the application for renewal of its examining authority on a form and in a manner prescribed by the Administrator;

    (2)   The school must hold a pilot school certificate and rating issued under this part;

    (3)   The school must have held the rating for which continued examining authority is sought for at least 24 calendar months preceding the month of application for renewal of its examining authority; and

    (4)   The training course for which continued examining authority is requested may not be a course that is approved without meeting the minimum ground and flight training time requirements of this part.

EXPLANATION

141.63(a): Application for examining authority is made in duplicate on FAA Form 8420-8, Application for Pilot School Certificate, and sent to the FAA District Office having jurisdiction over the area in which the school is located. When examining authority is requested for flight testing privileges only, the applicant must enter the words, "Flight Only", on the application immediately after the title of the course or courses. If examining authority is requested for written testing privileges only, the applicant must enter the words, "Written Only," on the application immediately after the title of the course or courses. When examining authority is requested for both flight and written testing privileges, the applicant must place an "X" in the appropriate box beside the title of the course; no other wording is necessary.

Only the holder of a pilot school certificate may apply for authority to conduct written and/or practical tests of their own graduates for the issuance of pilot certificates and ratings without further testing by the FAA. The authority to test graduates for airline transport pilot or flight instructor certificates or turbojet type ratings is not authorized under FAR Part 141.

141.63(b)(2): This eligibility requirement is not a continuing requirement after examining authority is issued or renewed to the applicant. The pilot school is not required to maintain their "90% pass rate" for the duration of the pilot school certificate.

PREAMBLE

After reviewing the comments, the FAA continues to believe that it is important to prohibit pilot schools that train to standard from possessing examining authority. Permitting these schools to have examining authority would not provide an adequate system of checks and balances. The proposal is adopted with minor editorial changes. (62 FR 16282).

CROSS REFERENCES

141.65, Privileges; 141.67, Limitations and Reports; 141.83, Quality of Training.

ADVISORY CIRCULARS

AC 141-1A *Pilot School Certification* (1993).

141.65 PRIVILEGES

A pilot school that holds examining authority may recommend a person who graduated from its course for the appropriate pilot, flight instructor, or ground instructor certificate or rating without taking the FAA knowledge test or practical test in accordance with the provisions of this subpart.

EXPLANATION

When a student has graduated from a pilot ground school course under an examining authority, that student is issued a graduation certificate that will be accepted as evidence of meeting the aeronautical knowledge requirements (written test) appropriate to the course from which the student graduated. A graduation certificate is valid for 24 months from the date of graduation, just like normal written test results. When a graduate of a pilot ground school course graduates from an appropriate flight course under an examining authority, that student becomes an applicant for a certificate or rating in accordance with §61.71(b). The student must apply within 90 days after graduation to the FAA for the certificate or rating which the student seeks. If the student does not apply for the issuance of a certificate or rating within 90 days, the student must meet all the requirements of FAR Part 61.

CROSS REFERENCES

141.67, Limitations and Reports; 61.71, Graduates of Certificated Flying Schools: Special Rules.

ADVISORY CIRCULARS

AC 141-1A *Pilot School Certification* (1993).

141.67 LIMITATIONS AND REPORTS

A pilot school that holds examining authority may only recommend the issuance of a pilot, flight instructor, or ground instructor certificate and rating to a person who does not take an FAA knowledge test or practical test, if the recommendation for the issuance of that certificate or rating is in accordance with the following requirements:
(a) The person graduated from a training course for which the pilot school holds examining authority.
(b) Except as provided in this paragraph, the person satisfactorily completed all the curriculum requirements of that pilot school's approved training course. A person who transfers from one part 141 approved pilot school to another part 141 approved pilot school may receive credit for that previous training, provided the following requirements are met:
    (1) The maximum credited training time does not exceed one-half of the receiving school's curriculum requirements;
    (2) The person completes a knowledge and proficiency test conducted by the receiving school for the purpose of determining the amount of pilot experience and knowledge to be credited;
    (3) The receiving school determines (based on the person's performance on the knowledge and proficiency test required by paragraph (b)(2) of this section) the amount of credit to be awarded, and records that credit in the person's training record;

(4)   The person who requests credit for previous pilot experience and knowledge obtained the experience and knowledge from another part 141 approved pilot school and training course; and

(5)   The receiving school retains a copy of the person's training record from the previous school.

(c)   Tests given by a pilot school that holds examining authority must be approved by the Administrator and be at least equal in scope, depth, and difficulty to the comparable knowledge and practical tests prescribed by the Administrator under part 61 of this chapter.

(d)   A pilot school that holds examining authority may not use its knowledge or practical tests if the school:

(1)   Knows, or has reason to believe, the test has been compromised; or

(2)   Is notified by an FAA Flight Standards District Office that there is reason to believe or it is known that the test has been compromised.

(e)   A pilot school that holds examining authority must maintain a record of all temporary airman certificates it issues, which consist of the following information:

(1)   A chronological listing that includes—

(i) The date the temporary airman certificate was issued;

(ii)   The student to whom the temporary airman certificate was issued, and that student's permanent mailing address and telephone number;

(iii)   The training course from which the student graduated;

(iv)   The name of person who conducted the knowledge or practical test;

(v)   The type of temporary airman certificate or rating issued to the student; and

(vi)   The date the student's airman application file was sent to the FAA for processing for a permanent airman certificate.

(2)   A copy of the record containing each student's graduation certificate, airman application, temporary airman certificate, superseded airman certificate (if applicable), and knowledge test or practical test results; and

(3)   The records required by paragraph (e) of this section must be retained for 1 year and made available to the Administrator upon request. These records must be surrendered to the Administrator when the pilot school ceases to have examining authority.

(f)   Except for pilot schools that have an airman certification representative, when a student passes the knowledge test or practical test, the pilot school that holds examining authority must submit that student's airman application file and training record to the FAA for processing for the issuance of a permanent airman certificate.

EXPLANATION

141.67(d): A procedure for monitoring answer sheets should be established as a part of the overall plan for ensuring the tests are not compromised. If the same questions are missed, or a student who has shown a poor understanding during class receives an abnormally high grade, then the school knows or has reason to believe that the test has been "compromised." Instructors, students, and the general public should not be allowed to use question selection sheets for study or discussion purposes, nor copy any portion of the question selection sheets.

PREAMBLE

141.67(a), (b), (c), and (d): After review of the proposed rule, the FAA has changed the references in paragraphs (d)(1) and (d)(2) from "knowledge test" to "test" to make the language consistent with the introductory language of paragraph (d).

141.67(f): Upon further review, the FAA has decided to delete the 7-day requirement from the final rule. The FAA notes that the schools should submit the required documents to the FAA in a timely fashion. The FAA also has retained the existing requirement for a school to submit a graduate's training record. In the final rule, the FAA added the training record to the list of documents that must be submitted after a student passes the knowledge test or practical test. The proposal is adopted with minor editorial changes. (62 FR 16282 - 16283).

CROSS REFERENCES

141.65, Privileges; 141.101, Training Records.

ADVISORY CIRCULARS

AC 141-1A *Pilot School Certification* (1993).

INTENTIONALLY

LEFT

BLANK

SUBPART E — OPERATING RULES

141.71 APPLICABILITY

This subpart prescribes the operating rules applicable to a pilot school or provisional pilot school certificated under the provisions of this part.

ADVISORY CIRCULARS

AC 141-1A *Pilot School Certification* (1993).

141.73 PRIVILEGES

(a)   The holder of a pilot school certificate or a provisional pilot school certificate may advertise and conduct approved pilot training courses in accordance with the certificate and any ratings that it holds.

(b)   A pilot school that holds examining authority for an approved training course may recommend a graduate of that course for the issuance of an appropriate pilot, flight instructor, or ground instructor certificate and rating, without taking an FAA knowledge test or practical test, provided the training course has been approved and meets the minimum ground and flight training time requirements of this part.

EXPLANATION

This regulation is limited by the restrictions on examining authority set forth in §141.65.

CROSS REFERENCES

141.23, Advertising Limitations; 141.65, Privileges; 141.67, Limitations and Reports.

ADVISORY CIRCULARS

AC 141-1A *Pilot School Certification* (1993).

141.75 AIRCRAFT REQUIREMENTS

The following items must be carried on each aircraft used for flight training and solo flights:
(a)   A pretakeoff and prelanding checklist; and
(b)   The operator's handbook for the aircraft, if one is furnished by the manufacturer, or copies of the handbook if furnished to each student using the aircraft.

EXPLANATION

141.75(a): The requirement for a checklist defining the terms of "pretakeoff" and "prelanding" is broad and considers less complicated aircraft. However, it is always a good operating practice to expand upon checklists as aircraft become more complicated. Even though an aircraft is relatively uncomplicated, teaching the use of a more complex checklist is an excellent means of forming the habit in students of using a checklist.

The operating handbook may include a checklist, and while these checklists may be useful in developing new printed checklists, they are not desirable for use as a checklist by themselves. Normally, such handbooks are not readily available to the pilot, and during emergency procedure training or during a natural emergency, particularly when there is only one pilot aboard the aircraft, he or she would be required to fly the aircraft and at the same time, search through a book for the checklist.

CROSS REFERENCES

141.39, Aircraft.

ADVISORY CIRCULARS

AC 141-1A *Pilot School Certification* (1993).

141.77 LIMITATIONS

(a)   The holder of a pilot school certificate or a provisional pilot school certificate may not issue a graduation certificate to a student, or recommend a student for a pilot certificate or rating, unless the student has:
(1)   Completed the training specified in the pilot school's course of training; and
(2)   Passed the required final tests.
(b)   Except as provided in paragraph (c) of this section, the holder of a pilot school certificate or a provisional pilot school certificate may not graduate a student from a course of training unless the student has completed all of the curriculum requirements of that course;
(c)   A student may be given credit towards the curriculum requirements of a course for previous pilot experience and knowledge, provided the following conditions are met:
(1)   If the credit is based upon a part 141-approved training course, the credit given that student for the previous pilot experience and knowledge may be 50 percent of the curriculum requirements and must be based upon a proficiency test or knowledge test, or both, conducted by the receiving pilot school;

(2)   If the credit is not based upon a part 141-approved training course, the credit given that student for the previous pilot experience and knowledge shall not exceed more than 25 percent of the curriculum requirements and must be based upon a proficiency test or knowledge test, or both, conducted by the receiving pilot school;

(3)   The receiving school determines the amount of course credit to be transferred under paragraph (c)(1) or paragraph (c)(2) of this section, based on a proficiency test or knowledge test, or both, of the student; and

(4)   Credit for training specified in paragraph (c)(1) or paragraph (c)(2) of this section may be given only if the previous provider of the training has certified in writing, or other form acceptable to the Administrator as to the kind and amount of training provided, and the result of each stage check and end-of-course test, if applicable, given to the student.

EXPLANATION

With the 1997 amendment, when a student transfers from one FAA-approved school to another, 50% of the curriculum requirements obtained in the previous course of training may be credited in all or part by the receiving school. The receiving school should determine the amount of credits to be allowed based upon a proficiency test or knowledge test, or both. A student who enrolls in a course of training may be credited for not more than 25% of the curriculum requirements for knowledge and experience gained in a non-Part 141 flight school. In any case, the amount of credit for previous training allowed, whether received from an FAA-approved school or other source, should be placed in the student's enrollment record at the time of enrollment. When a student transfers from one FAA-approved school to another, or terminates his training for any reason, he or she must be given, upon request, a transcript of the results of his or her participation in the course of training which was interrupted. The transcript should include at least the following:

a.   The name of the school that gave the training, including the school's certificate number.

b.   Kind and amount of training given (dual, solo, ground school, ground trainer time, etc.).

c.   The kind of training course involved.

PREAMBLE

The FAA acknowledges the concerns of HAI and other commenters. The FAA notes that the provisions for the transfer of credits set forth in the proposed rule restate the existing requirements. However, in response to these concerns, the final rule includes a provision to allow for up to 25 percent credit for pilot experience and knowledge that was not obtained in a part 141-approved training course. The proposal is adopted with this change, and other minor editing and formatting changes. (62 FR 16283).

141.79 FLIGHT TRAINING

(a) No person other than a certificated flight instructor or commercial pilot with a lighter-than-air rating who has the ratings and the minimum qualifications specified in the approved training course outline may give a student flight training under an approved course of training.

(b) No student pilot may be authorized to start a solo practice flight from an airport until the flight has been approved by a certificated flight instructor or commercial pilot with a lighter-than-air rating who is present at that airport.

(c) Each chief instructor and assistant chief instructor assigned to a training course must complete, at least once every 12 calendar months, an approved syllabus of training consisting of ground or flight training, or both, or an approved flight instructor refresher course.

(d) Each certificated flight instructor or commercial pilot with a lighter-than-air rating who is assigned to a flight training course must satisfactorily complete the following tasks, which must be administered by the school's chief instructor, assistant chief instructor, or check instructor:

    (1) Prior to receiving authorization to train students in a flight training course, must—

        (i) Accomplish a review of and receive a briefing on the objectives and standards of that training course; and

        (ii) Accomplish an initial proficiency check in each make and model of aircraft used in that training course in which that person provides training; and

    (2) Every 12 calendar months after the month in which the person last complied with the requirements of paragraph (d)(1)(ii) of this section, accomplish a recurrent proficiency check in one of the aircraft in which the person trains students.

EXPLANATION

141.79(b): Solo cross-country flights, when properly dispatched from the originating airport, would be considered to have approval for the entire flight. However, if the student should be delayed en route because of unexpected weather or mechanical delays, the school should arrange for another instructor based at the point of delay to redispatch the flight, or have a school instructor dispatch the flight by telephone. Cross-country flights should be made to airports specified in the appropriate training course outline. Emergency handling can be accomplished by pre-arrangement with other schools or fixed based operators.

141.79(c): This requirement may be met by attending an approved flight instructor refresher course (FIRC). It may be a two-day course or a home study course, provided it is an FAA-approved FIRC. The Jeppesen Sanderson 16-hour CFI Renewal Program was fully approved to meet the requirements of §141.79(c) on a continuous annual basis on November 15, 1995. This permits the chief and assistant chief instructor to meet the total annual training requirements using this program year after year provided the local FAA Flight Standards District Office (FSDO) concurs. This is a change from the original approval which had certain limitations prior to November 15, 1995.

141.79(d): The flight instructor need not be given a flight check in each type of aircraft annually.

PREAMBLE

The final rule includes references to commercial pilots with a lighter-than-air rating in paragraphs (a), (b), and (d). With regard to HAI's comment, the rule does not require the chief or assistant chief flight instructors to attend a commercially sponsored refresher training course. It has always been the FAA's position that schools could develop their own refresher training for chief instructors or assistant chief flight instructors. These courses may be submitted to the FAA for approval. Regarding the proposal for the assistant chief instructor to receive annual training, the FAA believes that in light of the responsibilities and duties of the assistant chief instructor it is necessary to require that person to maintain currency and proper qualification.

The proposed rule is adopted with these changes, and editing and formatting changes.
(62 FR 16283 - 16284).

CROSS REFERENCES

141.33, Personnel; 141.35, Chief Instructor Qualifications; 141.36, Assistant Chief Instructor Qualifications; 141.83, Quality of Training; 141.85, Chief Instructor Responsibilities, 141.87, Change of Chief Instructor.

ADVISORY CIRCULARS

AC 141-1A *Pilot School Certification* (1993).

141.81 GROUND TRAINING

(a)   Except as provided in paragraph (b) of this section, each instructor who is assigned to a ground training course must hold a flight or ground instructor certificate, or a commercial pilot certificate with a lighter-than-air rating, with the appropriate rating for that course of training.

(b)   A person who does not meet the requirements of paragraph (a) of this section may be assigned ground training duties in a ground training course, if:
  (1)   The chief instructor who is assigned to that ground training course finds the person qualified to give that training; and
  (2)   The training is given while under the supervision of the chief instructor or the assistant chief instructor who is present at the facility when the training is given.

(c)   An instructor may not be used in a ground training course until that instructor has been briefed on the objectives and standards of that course by the chief instructor, assistant chief instructor, or check instructor.

EXPLANATION

141.81(b): FAA policy indicates that the chief instructor, assistant chief instructor, or another instructor designated by the chief instructor must be present at the school and in the classroom during instruction by uncertificated ground instructors. Certificated ground and flight instructors do not have to be as closely supervised as uncertificated ground instructors. For certificated ground and flight instructors, the chief instructor need only be available for consultation at the school's base of operation.

CROSS REFERENCES

141.33, Personnel; 141.35, Chief Instructor Qualifications; 141.36, Assistant Chief Instructor Qualifications; 141.41, Flight Simulators, Flight Training Devices and Training Devices; 141.43, Pilot Briefing Areas; 141.45, Ground Training Facilities; 141.83, Quality of Training; 141.85, Chief Instructor Responsibilities; 141.87, Change of Chief Instructor; 141.91, Satellite Bases.

ADVISORY CIRCULARS

AC 141-1A *Pilot School Certification* (1993).

FAA CHIEF COUNSEL OPINION

The provisions of §141.81 apply at the satellite base as well as at the main operating base. (10-17-78).

141.83 QUALITY OF TRAINING

(a)   Each pilot school or provisional pilot school must meet the following requirements:
  (1)   Comply with its approved training course; and
  (2)   Provide training of such quality that meets the requirements of §141.5(d) of this part.
(b)   The failure of a pilot school or provisional pilot school to maintain the quality of training specified in paragraph (a) of this section may be the basis for suspending or revoking that school's certificate.
(c)   When requested by the Administrator, a pilot school or provisional pilot school must allow the FAA to administer any knowledge test, practical test, stage check, or end-of-course test to its students.
(d)   When a stage check or end-of-course test is administered by the FAA under the provisions of paragraph (c) of this section, and the student has not completed the training course, then that test will be based on the standards prescribed in the school's approved training course.
(e)   When a practical test or knowledge test is administered by the FAA under the provisions of paragraph (c) of this section, to a student who has completed the school's training course, that test will be based upon the areas of operation approved by the Administrator.

CROSS REFERENCES

141.63, Application and Qualification; 141.21, Inspections.

ADVISORY CIRCULARS

AC 141-1A *Pilot School Certification* (1993).

FAA CHIEF COUNSEL OPINION

The 80% pass rate requirement contained in §141.83 is a continuing requirement even after a pilot school certificate is issued. (12-8-87).

141.85 CHIEF INSTRUCTOR RESPONSIBILITIES

(a)   Each person designated as a chief instructor for a pilot school or provisional pilot school shall be responsible for:
   (1)   Certifying each student's training record, graduation certificate, stage check and end-of-course test report, recommendation for course completion, and application;
   (2)   Ensuring that each certificated flight instructor, certificated ground instructor, or commercial pilot with a lighter-than-air rating passes an initial proficiency check prior to that instructor being assigned instructing duties in the school's approved training course, and thereafter that the instructor passes a recurrent proficiency check every 12 calendar months after the month in which the initial test was accomplished;
   (3)   Ensuring that each student accomplishes the required stage checks and end-of-course tests in accordance with the school's approved training course; and
   (4)   Maintaining training techniques, procedures, and standards for the school that are acceptable to the Administrator.
(b)   The chief instructor or an assistant chief instructor must be available at the pilot school or, if away from the pilot school, be available by telephone, radio, or other electronic means during the time that training is given for an approved training course.
(c)   The chief instructor may delegate authority for conducting stage checks, end-of-course tests, and flight instructor proficiency checks to the assistant chief instructor or a check instructor.

EXPLANATION

141.85(a)(1): When giving a stage or final test, "student recommendations," should be complete and definitive with respect to additional training needed, if any.

141.85(b): Availability by means of telephone, radio, or other electronic means while away from the premises of the flight school, does not satisfy the requirements of §141.81(b)(2).

CROSS REFERENCES

141.35, Chief Instructor Qualifications; 141.79, Flight Training; 141.83, Quality of Training; 141.101, Training Records.

ADVISORY CIRCULARS

AC 141-1A *Pilot School Certification* (1993).

141.87 CHANGE OF CHIEF INSTRUCTOR

Whenever a pilot school or provisional pilot school makes a change of designation of its chief instructor, that school:
(a) Must immediately provide the FAA Flight Standards District Office that has jurisdiction over the area in which the school is located with written notification of the change;
(b) May conduct training without a chief instructor for that training course for a period not to exceed 60 days while awaiting the designation and approval of another chief instructor;
(c) May, for a period not to exceed 60 days, have the stage checks and end-of-course tests administered by:
    (1) The training course's assistant chief instructor, if one has been designated;
    (2) The training course's check instructor, if one has been designated;
    (3) An FAA inspector; or
    (4) An examiner.
(d) Must, after 60 days without a chief instructor, cease operations and surrender its certificate to the Administrator; and
(e) May have its certificate reinstated, upon:
    (1) Designating and approving another chief instructor;
    (2) Showing it meets the requirements of §141.27(a)(2) of this part; and
    (3) Applying for reinstatement on a form and in a manner prescribed by the Administrator.

EXPLANATION

When the instructor for a particular course of training changes, the certificate holder must apply to amend the appropriate training course outline, and, therefore, the air agency certificate. The holder of the school certificate is responsible for the maintenance of training records, the issuance of graduation certificates, and the general operation of the school during any change of chief instructor.

CROSS REFERENCES

141.13, Application for Issuance, Amendment, or Renewal; 141.27, Renewal of Certificates and Ratings; 141.53, Approval Procedures for a Training Course: General; 141.55, Training Course Contents.

ADVISORY CIRCULARS

AC 141-1A *Pilot School Certification* (1993).

141.89 MAINTENANCE OF PERSONNEL, FACILITIES, AND EQUIPMENT

The holder of a pilot school certificate or provisional pilot school certificate may not provide training to a student who is enrolled in an approved course of training unless:
(a)   Each airport, aircraft, and facility necessary for that training meets the standards specified in the holder's approved training course outline and the appropriate requirements of this part; and
(b)   Except as provided in §141.87 of this part, each chief instructor, assistant chief instructor, check instructor, or instructor meets the qualifications specified in the holder's approved course of training and the appropriate requirements of this part.

CROSS REFERENCES

141.53, Approval Procedures for a Training Course: General; 141.55, Training Course Contents; 141.87, Change of Chief Instructor.

ADVISORY CIRCULARS

AC 141-1A *Pilot School Certification* (1993).

141.91 SATELLITE BASES

The holder of a pilot school certificate or provisional pilot school certificate may conduct ground training or flight training in an approved course of training at a base other than its main operations base if:
(a)   An assistant chief instructor is designated for each satellite base, and that assistant chief instructor is available at that base or, if away from the premises, by telephone, radio, or other electronic means during the time that training is provided for an approved training course;
(b)   The airport, facilities, and personnel used at the satellite base meet the appropriate requirements of subpart B of this part and its approved training course outline;
(c)   The instructors are under the direct supervision of the chief instructor or assistant chief instructor for the appropriate training course, who is readily available for consultation in accordance with §141.85(b) of this part; and
(d)   The FAA Flight Standards District Office having jurisdiction over the area in which the school is located is notified in writing if training is conducted at a base other than the school's main operations base for more than 7 consecutive days.

EXPLANATION

141.91(c): The FAA has interpreted this in accordance with §141.81. It is not intended to require additional supervision of flight or ground instructors when they are instructing at the satellite base. The provisions of §141.81 apply at the satellite base as well as the main operations base.

CROSS REFERENCES

141.81, Ground Training; 141.85, Chief Instructor Responsibilities.

ADVISORY CIRCULARS

AC 141-1A *Pilot School Certification* (1993).

FAA CHIEF COUNSEL OPINION

§141.91(c) appears to require instructors at a satellite base to be under the "direct supervision" of the chief instructor. This provision would therefore contradict §141.81 which requires direct supervision only for ground instructors who do not hold a flight or ground instructor's certificate with an appropriate rating. §141.91(c), however, must be interpreted in the light of §141.81. It is not intended to require additional supervision of persons with flight or ground instructor certificates when they are teaching at a satellite base. The provisions of §141.81 apply at the satellite base as well as at the main operations base. (10-17-78).

141.93 ENROLLMENT

(a) The holder of a pilot school certificate or a provisional pilot school certificate must, at the time a student is enrolled in an approved training course, furnish that student with a copy of the following:
   (1) A certificate of enrollment containing—
      (i) The name of the course in which the student is enrolled; and
      (ii) The date of that enrollment.
   (2) A copy of the student's training syllabus.
   (3) A copy of the safety procedures and practices developed by the school that describe the use of the school's facilities and the operation of its aircraft. Those procedures and practices shall include training on at least the following information—
      (i) The weather minimums required by the school for dual and solo flights;
      (ii) The procedures for starting and taxiing aircraft on the ramp;
      (iii) Fire precautions and procedures;
      (iv) Redispatch procedures after unprogrammed landings, on and off airports;
      (v) Aircraft discrepancies and approval for return-to-service determinations;
      (vi) Securing of aircraft when not in use;
      (vii) Fuel reserves necessary for local and cross-country flights;
      (viii) Avoidance of other aircraft in flight and on the ground;
      (ix) Minimum altitude limitations and simulated emergency landing instructions; and
      (x) A description of and instructions regarding the use of assigned practice areas.
(b) The holder of a pilot school certificate or provisional pilot school certificate must maintain a monthly listing of persons enrolled in each training course offered by the school.

EXPLANATION

The enrollment certificates are required to be mailed promptly because some approved training courses are very short and provide a minimum time for the FAA to conduct possible inspections of the training.

PREAMBLE

The FAA inadvertently omitted existing paragraph (a)(3). This requirement is retained in the final rule. The proposed rule is adopted with this change. (62 FR 16284).

CROSS REFERENCES

141.21, Inspections; 141.77, Limitations; 141.101, Training Records.

ADVISORY CIRCULARS

AC 141-1A *Pilot School Certification* (1993).

141.95 GRADUATION CERTIFICATE

(a) The holder of a pilot school certificate or provisional pilot school certificate must issue a graduation certificate to each student who completes its approved course of training.

(b) The graduation certificate must be issued to the student upon completion of the course of training and contain at least the following information:
   (1) The name of the school and the certificate number of the school;
   (2) The name of the graduate to whom it was issued;
   (3) The course of training for which it was issued;
   (4) The date of graduation;
   (5) A statement that the student has satisfactorily completed each required stage of the approved course of training including the tests for those stages;
   (6) A certification of the information contained on the graduation certificate by the chief instructor for that course of training; and
   (7) A statement showing the cross-country training that the student received in the course of training.

PREAMBLE

The commenter's concerns are noted; however, the disputed language is a continuation of an existing requirement. Except for minor editing changes, the final rule is adopted as proposed.

CROSS REFERENCES

141.65, Privileges; 141.67, Limitations and Reports; 141.101, Training Records.

ADVISORY CIRCULARS

AC 141-1A *Pilot School Certification* (1993).

INTENTIONALLY

LEFT

BLANK

SUBPART F — RECORDS

141.101 TRAINING RECORDS

(a) Each holder of a pilot school certificate or provisional pilot school certificate must establish and maintain a current and accurate record of the participation of each student enrolled in an approved course of training conducted by the school that includes the following information:
   (1) The date the student was enrolled in the approved course;
   (2) A chronological log of the student's course attendance, subjects, and flight operations covered in the student's training, and the names and grades of any tests taken by the student; and
   (3) The date the student graduated, terminated training, or transferred to another school.

(b) The records required to be maintained in a student's logbook will not suffice for the record required by paragraph (a) of this section.

(c) Whenever a student graduates, terminates training, or transfers to another school, the student's record must be certified to that effect by the chief instructor.

(d) The holder of a pilot school certificate or a provisional pilot school certificate must retain each student record required by this section for at least 1 year from the date that the student:
   (1) Graduates from the course to which the record pertains;
   (2) Terminates enrollment in the course to which the record pertains; or
   (3) Transfers to another school.

(e) The holder of a pilot school certificate or a provisional pilot school certificate must make a copy of the student's training record available upon request by the student.

CROSS REFERENCES

141.25, Business Office and Operations Base; 141.67, Limitations and Reports; 141.77, Limitations; 141.85, Chief Instructor Responsibilities; 141.93, Enrollment; 141.95, Graduation Certificate.

ADVISORY CIRCULARS

AC 141-1A *Pilot School Certification* (1993).

INTENTIONALLY

LEFT

BLANK

APPENDIX A TO PART 141 — RECREATIONAL PILOT CERTIFICATION COURSE

1. *Applicability.* This appendix prescribes the minimum curriculum required for a recreational pilot certification course under this part, for the following ratings:
   (a) Airplane single-engine.
   (b) Rotorcraft helicopter.
   (c) Rotorcraft gyroplane.
2. *Eligibility for enrollment.* A person must hold a student pilot certificate prior to enrolling in the flight portion of the recreational pilot certification course.
3. *Aeronautical knowledge training.* Each approved course must include at least 20 hours of ground training on the following aeronautical knowledge areas, appropriate to the aircraft category and class for which the course applies:
   (a) Applicable Federal Aviation Regulations for recreational pilot privileges, limitations, and flight operations;
   (b) Accident reporting requirements of the National Transportation Safety Board;
   (c) Applicable subjects in the "Aeronautical Information Manual" and the appropriate FAA advisory circulars;
   (d) Use of aeronautical charts for VFR navigation using pilotage with the aid of a magnetic compass;
   (e) Recognition of critical weather situations from the ground and in flight, windshear avoidance, and the procurement and use of aeronautical weather reports and forecasts;
   (f) Safe and efficient operation of aircraft, including collision avoidance, and recognition and avoidance of wake turbulence;
   (g) Effects of density altitude on takeoff and climb performance;
   (h) Weight and balance computations;
   (i) Principles of aerodynamics, powerplants, and aircraft systems;
   (j) Stall awareness, spin entry, spins, and spin recovery techniques, if applying for an airplane single-engine rating;
   (k) Aeronautical decision making and judgment; and
   (l) Preflight action that includes—
       (1) How to obtain information on runway lengths at airports of intended use, data on takeoff and landing distances, weather reports and forecasts, and fuel requirements; and
       (2) How to plan for alternatives if the planned flight cannot be completed or delays are encountered.
4. *Flight training.*
   (a) Each approved course must include at least 30 hours of flight training (of which 15 hours must be with a certificated flight instructor and 3 hours must be solo flight training as provided in section No. 5 of this appendix) on the approved areas of operation listed in paragraph (c) of this section that are appropriate to the aircraft category and class rating for which the course applies, including:
       (1) Except as provided in §61.100 of this chapter, 2 hours of dual flight training to and at an airport that is located more than 25 nautical miles from the airport where the applicant normally trains, with at least three takeoffs and three landings; and
       (2) 3 hours of dual flight training in an aircraft that is appropriate to the aircraft category and class for which the course applies, in preparation for the practical test within 60 days preceding the date of the test.

(b)   Each training flight must include a preflight briefing and a postflight critique of the student by the flight instructor assigned to that flight.

(c)   Flight training must include the following approved areas of operation appropriate to the aircraft category and class rating—

    (1)   *For an airplane single-engine course*:
        (i)   Preflight preparation;
        (ii)   Preflight procedures;
        (iii)   Airport operations;
        (iv)   Takeoffs, landings, and go-arounds;
        (v)   Performance maneuvers;
        (vi)   Ground reference maneuvers;
        (vii)   Navigation;
        (viii)   Slow flight and stalls;
        (ix)   Emergency operations; and
        (x)   Postflight procedures.

    (2)   For a rotorcraft helicopter course:
        (i)   Preflight preparation;
        (ii)   Preflight procedures;
        (iii)   Airport and heliport operations;
        (iv)   Hovering maneuvers;
        (v)   Takeoffs, landings, and go-arounds;
        (vi)   Performance maneuvers;
        (vii)   Navigation;
        (viii)   Emergency operations; and
        (ix)   Postflight procedures.

    (3)   *For a rotorcraft gyroplane course*:
        (i)   Preflight preparation;
        (ii)   Preflight procedures;
        (iii)   Airport operations;
        (iv)   Takeoffs, landings, and go-arounds;
        (v)   Performance maneuvers;
        (vi)   Ground reference maneuvers;
        (vii)   Navigation;
        (viii)   Flight at slow airspeeds;
        (ix)   Emergency operations; and
        (x)   Postflight procedures.

5.   *Solo flight training.* Each approved course must include at least 3 hours of solo flight training on the approved areas of operation listed in paragraph (c) of section No. 4 of this appendix that are appropriate to the aircraft category and class rating for which the course applies.

6.   *Stage checks and end-of-course tests.*

(a)   Each student enrolled in a recreational pilot course must satisfactorily accomplish the stage checks and end-of-course tests, in accordance with the school's approved training course, consisting of the approved areas of operation listed in paragraph (c) of section No. 4 of this appendix that are appropriate to the aircraft category and class rating for which the course applies.

(b)   Each student must demonstrate satisfactory proficiency prior to receiving an endorsement to operate an aircraft in solo flight.

APPENDIX B TO PART 141 — PRIVATE PILOT CERTIFICATION COURSE

1. *Applicability.* This appendix prescribes the minimum curriculum for a private pilot certification course required under this part, for the following ratings:
    (a) Airplane single-engine.
    (b) Airplane multiengine.
    (c) Rotorcraft helicopter.
    (d) Rotorcraft gyroplane.
    (e) Powered-lift.
    (f) Glider.
    (g) Lighter-than-air airship.
    (h) Lighter-than-air balloon.
2. *Eligibility for enrollment.* A person must hold a recreational or student pilot certificate prior to enrolling in the flight portion of the private pilot certification course.
3. *Aeronautical knowledge training.*
    (a) Each approved course must include at least the following ground training on the aeronautical knowledge areas listed in paragraph (b) of this section, appropriate to the aircraft category and class rating:
        (1) 35 hours of training if the course is for an airplane, rotorcraft, or powered-lift category rating.
        (2) 15 hours of training if the course is for a glider category rating.
        (3) 10 hours of training if the course is for a lighter-than-air category with a balloon class rating.
        (4) 35 hours of training if the course is for a lighter-than-air category with an airship class rating.
    (b) Ground training must include the following aeronautical knowledge areas:
        (1) Applicable Federal Aviation Regulations for private pilot privileges, limitations, and flight operations;
        (2) Accident reporting requirements of the National Transportation Safety Board;
        (3) Applicable subjects of the "Aeronautical Information Manual" and the appropriate FAA advisory circulars;
        (4) Aeronautical charts for VFR navigation using pilotage, dead reckoning, and navigation systems;
        (5) Radio communication procedures;
        (6) Recognition of critical weather situations from the ground and in flight, windshear avoidance, and the procurement and use of aeronautical weather reports and forecasts;
        (7) Safe and efficient operation of aircraft, including collision avoidance, and recognition and avoidance of wake turbulence;
        (8) Effects of density altitude on takeoff and climb performance;
        (9) Weight and balance computations;
        (10) Principles of aerodynamics, powerplants, and aircraft systems;
        (11) If the course of training is for an airplane category or glider category rating, stall awareness, spin entry, spins, and spin recovery techniques;
        (12) Aeronautical decision making and judgment; and
        (13) Preflight action that includes—
            (i)   How to obtain information on runway lengths at airports of intended use, data on takeoff and landing distances, weather reports and forecasts, and fuel requirements; and
            (ii) How to plan for alternatives if the planned flight cannot be completed or delays are encountered.

4.   *Flight training.*
    (a)   Each approved course must include at least the following flight training, as provided in this section and section No. 5 of this appendix, on the approved areas of operation listed in paragraph (d) of this section, appropriate to the aircraft category and class rating:
        (1)   35 hours of training if the course is for an airplane, rotorcraft, powered-lift, or airship rating.
        (2)   6 hours of training if the course is for a glider rating.
        (3)   8 hours of training if the course is for a balloon rating.
    (b)   Each approved course must include at least the following flight training:
        (1)   *For an airplane single-engine course:* 20 hours of flight training from a certificated flight instructor on the approved areas of operation in paragraph (d)(1) of this section that includes at least—
            (i)   Except as provided in §61.111 of this chapter, 3 hours of cross-country flight training in a single-engine airplane;
            (ii)   3 hours of night flight training in a single-engine airplane that includes—
                (A)   One cross-country flight of more than 100-nautical-miles total distance; and
                (B)   10 takeoffs and 10 landings to a full stop (with each landing involving a flight in the traffic pattern) at an airport.
            (iii) 3 hours of instrument training in a single-engine airplane; and
            (iv)   3 hours of flight training in a single-engine airplane in preparation for the practical test within 60 days preceding the date of the test.
        (2)   *For an airplane multiengine course:* 20 hours of flight training from a certificated flight instructor on the approved areas of operation in paragraph (d)(2) of this section that includes at least—
            (i)   Except as provided in §61.111 of this chapter, 3 hours of cross-country flight training in a multiengine airplane;
            (ii)   3 hours of night flight training in a multiengine airplane that includes—
                (A)   One cross-country flight of more than 100-nautical-miles total distance; and
                (B)   10 takeoffs and 10 landings to a full stop (with each landing involving a flight in the traffic pattern) at an airport.
            (iii) 3 hours of instrument training in a multiengine airplane; and
            (iv)   3 hours of flight training in a multiengine airplane in preparation for the practical test within 60 days preceding the date of the test.
        (3)   *For a rotorcraft helicopter course:* 20 hours of flight training from a certificated flight instructor on the approved areas of operation in paragraph (d)(3) of this section that includes at least—
            (i)   Except as provided in §61.111 of this chapter, 3 hours of cross-country flight training in a helicopter.
            (ii)   3 hours of night flight training in a helicopter that includes—
                (A)   One cross-country flight of more than 50-nautical-miles total distance; and
                (B)   10 takeoffs and 10 landings to a full stop (with each landing involving a flight in the traffic pattern) at an airport.
            (iii) 3 hours of flight training in a helicopter in preparation for the practical test within 60 days preceding the date of the test.

(4) *For a rotorcraft gyroplane course:* 20 hours of flight training from a certificated flight instructor on the approved areas of operation in paragraph (d)(4) of this section that includes at least—
   (i) Except as provided in §61.111 of this chapter, 3 hours of cross country flight training in a gyroplane.
   (ii) 3 hours of night flight training in a gyroplane that includes—
      (A) One cross-country flight over 50-nautical-miles total distance; and
      (B) 10 takeoffs and 10 landings to a full stop (with each landing involving a flight in the traffic pattern) at an airport.
   (iii) 3 hours of flight training in a gyroplane in preparation for the practical test within 60 days preceding the date of the test.
(5) *For a powered-lift course:* 20 hours of flight training from a certificated flight instructor on the approved areas of operation in paragraph (d)(5) of this section that includes at least—
   (i) Except as provided in §61.111 of this chapter, 3 hours of cross-country flight training in a powered-lift;
   (ii) 3 hours of night flight training in a powered-lift that includes—
      (A) One cross-country flight of more than 100-nautical-miles total distance; and
      (B) 10 takeoffs and 10 landings to a full stop (with each landing involving a flight in the traffic pattern) at an airport.
   (iii) 3 hours of instrument training in a powered-lift; and
   (iv) 3 hours of flight training in a powered-lift in preparation for the practical test, within 60 days preceding the date of the test.
(6) For a glider course: 4 hours of flight training from a certificated flight instructor on the approved areas of operation in paragraph (d)(6) of this section that includes at least—
   (i) Five training flights in a glider with a certified flight instructor on the launch/tow procedures approved for the course and on the appropriate approved areas of operation listed in paragraph (d)(6) of this section; and
   (ii) Three training flights in a glider with a certified flight instructor in preparation for the practical test within 60 days preceding the date of the test.
(7) *For a lighter-than-air airship course:* 20 hours of flight training from a commercial pilot with an airship rating on the approved areas of operation in paragraph (d)(7) of this section that includes at least—
   (i) Except as provided in §61.111 of this chapter, 3 hours of cross-country flight training in an airship;
   (ii) 3 hours of night flight training in an airship that includes—
      (A) One cross-country flight over 25-nautical-miles total distance; and
      (B) Five takeoffs and five landings to a full stop (with each landing involving a flight in the traffic pattern) at an airport.
   (iii) 3 hours of instrument training in an airship; and
   (iv) 3 hours of flight training in an airship in preparation for the practical test within 60 days preceding the date of the test.

    (8) *For a lighter-than-air balloon course:* 8 hours of flight training, including at least five training flights, from a commercial pilot with a balloon rating on the approved areas of operation in paragraph (d)(8) of this section, that includes—

        (i) If the training is being performed in a gas balloon—

           (A) Two flights of 1 hour each;

           (B) One flight involving a controlled ascent to 3,000 feet above the launch site; and

           (C) Two flights in preparation for the practical test within 60 days preceding the date of the test.

        (ii) If the training is being performed in a balloon with an airborne heater—

           (A) Two flights of 30 minutes each;

           (B) One flight involving a controlled ascent to 2,000 feet above the launch site; and

           (C) Two flights in preparation for the practical test within 60 days preceding the date of the test.

(c) For use of flight simulators or flight training devices:

    (1) The course may include training in a flight simulator or flight training device, provided it is representative of the aircraft for which the course is approved, meets the requirements of this paragraph, and the training is given by an authorized instructor.

    (2) Training in a flight simulator that meets the requirements of §141.41(a) of this part may be credited for a maximum of 20 percent of the total flight training hour requirements of the approved course, or of this section, whichever is less.

    (3) Training in a flight training device that meets the requirements of §141.41(b) of this part may be credited for a maximum of 15 percent of the total flight training hour requirements of the approved course, or of this section, whichever is less.

    (4) Training in flight simulators or flight training devices described in paragraphs (c)(2) and (c)(3) of this section, if used in combination, may be credited for a maximum of 20 percent of the total flight training hour requirements of the approved course, or of this section, whichever is less. However, credit for training in a flight training device that meets the requirements of §141.41(b) cannot exceed the limitation provided for in paragraph (c)(3) of this section.

(d) Each approved course must include the flight training on the approved areas of operation listed in this paragraph that are appropriate to the aircraft category and class rating—

    (1) *For a single-engine airplane course:*

        (i)   Preflight preparation;

        (ii)   Preflight procedures;

        (iii) Airport and seaplane base operations;

        (iv) Takeoffs, landings, and go-arounds;

        (v)   Performance maneuvers;

        (vi) Ground reference maneuvers;

        (vii) Navigation;

        (viii) Slow flight and stalls;

        (ix) Basic instrument maneuvers;

        (x)   Emergency operations;

        (xi) Night operations, and

        (xii) Postflight procedures.

(2)   *For a multiengine airplane course*:
    (i)   Preflight preparation;
    (ii)   Preflight procedures;
    (iii) Airport and seaplane base operations;
    (iv) Takeoffs, landings, and go-arounds;
    (v)   Performance maneuvers;
    (vi) Ground reference maneuvers;
    (vii) Navigation;
    (viii) Slow flight and stalls;
    (ix) Basic instrument maneuvers;
    (x)   Emergency operations;
    (xi) Multiengine operations;
    (xii) Night operations; and
    (xiii) Postflight procedures.

(3)   *For a rotorcraft helicopter course*:
    (i)   Preflight preparation;
    (ii)   Preflight procedures;
    (iii) Airport and heliport operations;
    (iv) Hovering maneuvers;
    (v)   Takeoffs, landings, and go-arounds;
    (vi) Performance maneuvers;
    (vii) Navigation;
    (viii) Emergency operations;
    (ix) Night operations; and
    (x)   Postflight procedures.

(4)   *For a rotorcraft gyroplane course:*
    (i)   Preflight preparation;
    (ii)   Preflight procedures;
    (iii) Airport operations;
    (iv) Takeoffs, landings, and go-arounds;
    (v)   Performance maneuvers;
    (vi) Ground reference maneuvers;
    (vii) Navigation;
    (viii) Flight at slow airspeeds;
    (ix) Emergency operations;
    (x)   Night operations; and
    (xi) Postflight procedures.

(5)   *For a powered-lift course*:
    (i)   Preflight preparation;
    (ii)   Preflight procedures;
    (iii) Airport and heliport operations;
    (iv) Hovering maneuvers;
    (v)   Takeoffs, landings, and go-arounds;
    (vi) Performance maneuvers;
    (vii) Ground reference maneuvers;
    (viii) Navigation;
    (ix) Slow flight and stalls;
    (x)   Basic instrument maneuvers;
    (xi) Emergency operations;
    (xii) Night operations; and
    (xiii) Postflight procedures.

      (6)   For a glider course:
          (i)   Preflight preparation;
          (ii)   Preflight procedures;
          (iii) Airport and gliderport operations;
          (iv) Launches/tows, as appropriate, and landings;
          (v)   Performance speeds;
          (vi) Soaring techniques;
          (vii) Performance maneuvers;
          (viii) Navigation;
          (ix) Slow flight and stalls;
          (x)   Emergency operations; and
          (xi) Postflight procedures.
      (7)   *For a lighter-than-air airship course*:
          (i)   Preflight preparation;
          (ii)   Preflight procedures;
          (iii) Airport operations;
          (iv) Takeoffs, landings, and go-arounds;
          (v)   Performance maneuvers;
          (vi) Ground reference maneuvers;
          (vii) Navigation;
          (viii) Emergency operations; and
          (ix) Postflight procedures.
      (8)   *For a lighter-than-air balloon course*:
          (i)   Preflight preparation;
          (ii)   Preflight procedures;
          (iii) Airport operations;
          (iv) Launches and landings;
          (v)   Performance maneuvers;
          (vi) Navigation;
          (vii) Emergency operations; and
          (viii) Postflight procedures.

5.   *Solo flight training.* Each approved course must include at least the following solo flight training:
    (a) *For an airplane single-engine course:* 5 hours of solo flight training in a single-engine airplane on the approved areas of operation in paragraph (d)(1) of section No. 4 of this appendix that includes at least—
      (1)   One solo cross-country flight of at least 100 nautical miles with landings at a minimum of three points, and one segment of the flight consisting of a straight-line distance of at least 50 nautical miles between the takeoff and landing locations; and
      (2)   Three takeoffs and three landings to a full stop (with each landing involving a flight in the traffic pattern) at an airport with an operating control tower.

(b) *For an airplane multiengine course:* 5 hours of flight training in a multiengine airplane performing the duties of a pilot in command while under the supervision of a certificated flight instructor. The training must consist of the approved areas of operation in paragraph (d)(2) of section No. 4 of this appendix, and include at least—
  (1) One cross-country flight of at least 100 nautical miles with landings at a minimum of three points, and one segment of the flight consisting of a straight-line distance of at least 50 nautical miles between the takeoff and landing locations; and
  (2) Three takeoffs and three landings to a full stop (with each landing involving a flight in the traffic pattern) at an airport with an operating control tower.

(c) *For a rotorcraft helicopter course:* 5 hours of solo flight training in a helicopter on the approved areas of operation in paragraph (d)(3) of section No. 4 of this appendix that includes at least—
  (1) One solo cross-country flight of more than 50 nautical miles with landings at a minimum of three points, and one segment of the flight consisting of a straight-line distance of at least 25 nautical miles between the takeoff and landing locations; and
  (2) Three takeoffs and three landings to a full stop (with each landing involving a flight in the traffic pattern) at an airport with an operating control tower.

(d) *For a rotorcraft gyroplane course:* 5 hours of solo flight training in gyroplanes on the approved areas of operation in paragraph (d)(4) of section No. 4 of this appendix that includes at least—
  (1) One solo cross-country flight of more than 50 nautical miles with landings at a minimum of three points, and one segment of the flight consisting of a straight-line distance of at least 25 nautical miles between the takeoff and landing locations; and
  (2) Three takeoffs and three landings to a full stop (with each landing involving a flight in the traffic pattern) at an airport with an operating control tower.

(e) *For a powered-lift course:* 5 hours of solo flight training in a powered-lift on the approved areas of operation in paragraph (d)(5) of section No. 4 of this appendix that includes at least—
  (1) One solo cross-country flight of at least 100 nautical miles with landings at a minimum of three points, and one segment of the flight consisting of a straight-line distance of at least 50 nautical miles between the takeoff and landing locations; and
  (2) Three takeoffs and three landings to a full stop (with each landing involving a flight in the traffic pattern) at an airport with an operating control tower.

(f) *For a glider course:* Two solo flights in a glider on the approved areas of operation in paragraph (d)(6) of section No. 4 of this appendix, and the launch and tow procedures appropriate for the approved course.

(g) For a lighter-than-air airship course: 5 hours of flight training in an airship performing the duties of pilot in command while under the supervision of a commercial pilot with an airship rating. The training must consist of the approved areas of operation in paragraph (d)(7) of section No. 4 of this appendix.

(h) For a lighter-than-air balloon course: Two solo flights in a balloon with an airborne heater if the course involves a balloon with an airborne heater, or, if the course involves a gas balloon, at least two flights in a gas balloon performing the duties of pilot in command while under the supervision of a commercial pilot with a balloon rating. The training must consist of the approved areas of operation in paragraph (d)(8) of section No. 4 of this appendix, in the kind of balloon for which the course applies.

6. *Stage checks and end-of-course tests.*
    (a) Each student enrolled in a private pilot course must satisfactorily accomplish the stage checks and end-of-course tests in accordance with the school's approved training course, consisting of the approved areas of operation listed in paragraph (d) of section No. 4 of this appendix that are appropriate to the aircraft category and class rating for which the course applies.
    (b) Each student must demonstrate satisfactory proficiency prior to receiving an endorsement to operate an aircraft in solo flight.

APPENDIX C TO PART 141 — INSTRUMENT RATING COURSE

1. *Applicability.* This appendix prescribes the minimum curriculum for an instrument rating course and an additional instrument rating course, required under this part, for the following ratings:
    (a) Instrument—airplane.
    (b) Instrument—helicopter.
    (c) Instrument—powered-lift.
2. *Eligibility for enrollment.* A person must hold at least a private pilot certificate with an aircraft category and class rating appropriate to the instrument rating for which the course applies prior to enrolling in the flight portion of the instrument rating course.
3. *Aeronautical knowledge training.*
    (a) Each approved course must include at least the following ground training on the aeronautical knowledge areas listed in paragraph (b) of this section appropriate to the instrument rating for which the course applies:
        (1) 30 hours of training if the course is for an initial instrument rating.
        (2) 20 hours of training if the course is for an additional instrument rating.
    (b) Ground training must include the following aeronautical knowledge areas:
        (1) Applicable Federal Aviation Regulations for IFR flight operations;
        (2) Appropriate information in the "Aeronautical Information Manual";
        (3) Air traffic control system and procedures for instrument flight operations;
        (4) IFR navigation and approaches by use of navigation systems;
        (5) Use of IFR en route and instrument approach procedure charts;
        (6) Procurement and use of aviation weather reports and forecasts, and the elements of forecasting weather trends on the basis of that information and personal observation of weather conditions;
        (7) Safe and efficient operation of aircraft under instrument flight rules and conditions;
        (8) Recognition of critical weather situations and windshear avoidance;
        (9) Aeronautical decision making and judgment; and
        (10) Crew resource management, to include crew communication and coordination.
4. *Flight training.*
    (a) Each approved course must include at least the following flight training on the approved areas of operation listed in paragraph (d) of this section, appropriate to the instrument-aircraft category and class rating for which the course applies:
        (1) 35 hours of instrument training if the course is for an initial instrument rating.
        (2) 15 hours of instrument training if the course is for an additional instrument rating.
    (b) For the use of flight simulators or flight training devices—
        (1) The course may include training in a flight simulator or flight training device, provided it is representative of the aircraft for which the course is approved, meets the requirements of this paragraph, and the training is given by an authorized instructor.
        (2) Training in a flight simulator that meets the requirements of §141.41(a) of this part may be credited for a maximum of 50 percent of the total flight training hour requirements of the approved course, or of this section, whichever is less.
        (3) Training in a flight training device that meets the requirements of §141.41(b) of this part may be credited for a maximum of 40 percent of the total flight training hour requirements of the approved course, or of this section, whichever is less.
        (4) Training in flight simulators or flight training devices described in paragraphs (b)(2) and (b)(3) of this section, if used in combination, may be credited for a maximum of 50 percent of the total flight training hour requirements of the approved course, or of this section, whichever is less. However, credit for training in a flight training device that meets the requirements of §141.41(b) cannot exceed the limitation provided for in paragraph (b)(3) of this section.

(c)   Each approved course must include the following flight training—

(1)   *For an instrument airplane course:* Instrument training time from a certificated flight instructor with an instrument rating on the approved areas of operation in paragraph (d) of this section including at least one cross-country flight that—

(i)   Is in the category and class of airplane that the course is approved for, and is performed under IFR;

(ii) Is a distance of at least 250 nautical miles along airways or ATC-directed routing with one segment of the flight consisting of at least a straight-line distance of 100 nautical miles between airports;

(iii) Involves an instrument approach at each airport; and

(iv) Involves three different kinds of approaches with the use of navigation systems.

(2)   *For an instrument helicopter course:* Instrument training time from a certificated flight instructor with an instrument rating on the approved areas of operation in paragraph (d) of this section including at least one cross-country flight that—

(i)   Is in a helicopter and is performed under IFR;

(ii) Is a distance of at least 100 nautical miles along airways or ATC-directed routing with one segment of the flight consisting of at least a straight-line distance of 50 nautical miles between airports;

(iii) Involves an instrument approach at each airport; and

(iv) Involves three different kinds of approaches with the use of navigation systems.

(3)   *For an instrument powered-lift course:* Instrument training time from a certificated flight instructor with an instrument rating on the approved areas of operation in paragraph (d) of this section including at least one cross-country flight that—

(i)   Is in a powered-lift and is performed under IFR;

(ii) Is a distance of at least 250 nautical miles along airways or ATC-directed routing with one segment of the flight consisting of at least a straight-line distance of 100 nautical miles between airports;

(iii) Involves an instrument approach at each airport; and

(iv) Involves three different kinds of approaches with the use of navigation systems.

(d)   Each approved course must include the flight training on the approved areas of operation listed in this paragraph appropriate to the instrument aircraft category and class rating for which the course applies:

(1)   Preflight preparation;

(2)   Preflight procedures;

(3)   Air traffic control clearances and procedures;

(4)   Flight by reference to instruments;

(5)   Navigation systems;

(6)   Instrument approach procedures;

(7)   Emergency operations; and

(8)   Postflight procedures.

5.   *Stage checks and end-of-course tests.* Each student enrolled in an instrument rating course must satisfactorily accomplish the stage checks and end-of-course tests, in accordance with the school's approved training course, consisting of the approved areas of operation listed in paragraph (d) of section No. 4 of this appendix that are appropriate to the aircraft category and class rating for which the course applies.

APPENDIX D TO PART 141 — COMMERCIAL PILOT CERTIFICATION COURSE

1. *Applicability.* This appendix prescribes the minimum curriculum for a commercial pilot certification course required under this part, for the following ratings:
   (a) Airplane single-engine.
   (b) Airplane multiengine.
   (c) Rotorcraft helicopter.
   (d) Rotorcraft gyroplane.
   (e) Powered-lift.
   (f) Glider.
   (g) Lighter-than-air airship.
   (h) Lighter-than-air balloon.

2. *Eligibility for enrollment.* A person must hold the following prior to enrolling in the flight portion of the commercial pilot certification course:
   (a) At least a private pilot certificate; and
   (b) If the course is for a rating in an airplane or a powered-lift category, then the person must:
       (1) Hold an instrument rating in the aircraft that is appropriate to the aircraft category rating for which the course applies; or
       (2) Be concurrently enrolled in an instrument rating course that is appropriate to the aircraft category rating for which the course applies, and pass the required instrument rating practical test prior to completing the commercial pilot certification course.

3. *Aeronautical knowledge training.*
   (a) Each approved course must include at least the following ground training on the aeronautical knowledge areas listed in paragraph (b) of this section, appropriate to the aircraft category and class rating for which the course applies:
       (1) 35 hours of training if the course is for an airplane category rating or a powered-lift category rating.
       (2) 65 hours of training if the course is for a lighter-than-air category with an airship class rating.
       (3) 30 hours of training if the course is for a rotorcraft category rating.
       (4) 20 hours of training if the course is for a glider category rating.
       (5) 20 hours of training if the course is for a lighter-than-air category with a balloon class rating.
   (b) Ground training must include the following aeronautical knowledge areas:
       (1) Federal Aviation Regulations that apply to commercial pilot privileges, limitations, and flight operations;
       (2) Accident reporting requirements of the National Transportation Safety Board;
       (3) Basic aerodynamics and the principles of flight;
       (4) Meteorology, to include recognition of critical weather situations, windshear recognition and avoidance, and the use of aeronautical weather reports and forecasts;
       (5) Safe and efficient operation of aircraft;
       (6) Weight and balance computations;
       (7) Use of performance charts;
       (8) Significance and effects of exceeding aircraft performance limitations;
       (9) Use of aeronautical charts and a magnetic compass for pilotage and dead reckoning;
       (10) Use of air navigation facilities;

(11) Aeronautical decision making and judgment;

(12) Principles and functions of aircraft systems;

(13) Maneuvers, procedures, and emergency operations appropriate to the aircraft;

(14) Night and high-altitude operations;

(15) Descriptions of and procedures for operating within the National Airspace System; and

(16) Procedures for flight and ground training for lighter-than-air ratings.

4.   *Flight training.*

(a)   Each approved course must include at least the following flight training, as provided in this section and section No. 5 of this appendix, on the approved areas of operation listed in paragraph (d) of this section that are appropriate to the aircraft category and class rating for which the course applies:

(1)   120 hours of training if the course is for an airplane or powered-lift rating.

(2)   155 hours of training if the course is for an airship rating.

(3)   115 hours of training if the course is for a rotorcraft rating.

(4)   6 hours of training if the course is for a glider rating.

(5)   10 hours of training and 8 training flights if the course is for a balloon rating.

(b)   Each approved course must include at least the following flight training:

(1)   *For an airplane single-engine course:* 55 hours of flight training from a certificated flight instructor on the approved areas of operation listed in paragraph (d)(1) of this section that includes at least—

(i)   5 hours of instrument training in a single-engine airplane;

(ii)   10 hours of training in a single-engine airplane that has retractable landing gear, flaps, and a controllable pitch propeller, or is turbine-powered;

(iii)   One cross-country flight in a single-engine airplane of at least a 2-hour duration, a total straight-line distance of more than 100 nautical miles from the original point of departure, and occurring in day VFR conditions;

(iv)   One cross-country flight in a single-engine airplane of at least a 2-hour duration, a total straight-line distance of more than 100 nautical miles from the original point of departure, and occurring in night VFR conditions; and

(v)   3 hours in a single-engine airplane in preparation for the practical test within 60 days preceding the date of the test.

(2)   *For an airplane multiengine course:* 55 hours of flight training from a certificated flight instructor on the approved areas of operation listed in paragraph (d)(2) of this section that includes at least—

(i)   5 hours of instrument training in a multiengine airplane;

(ii)   10 hours of training in a multiengine airplane that has retractable landing gear, flaps, and a controllable pitch propeller, or is turbine-powered;

(iii)   One cross-country flight in a multiengine airplane of at least a 2-hour duration, a total straight-line distance of more than 100 nautical miles from the original point of departure, and occurring in day VFR conditions;

(iv)   One cross-country flight in a multiengine airplane of at least a 2-hour duration, a total straight-line distance of more than 100 nautical miles from the original point of departure, and occurring in night VFR conditions; and

(v)   3 hours in a multiengine airplane in preparation for the practical test within 60 days preceding the date of the test.

(3) *For a rotorcraft helicopter course:* 30 hours of flight training from a certificated flight instructor on the approved areas of operation listed in paragraph (d)(3) of this section that includes at least—
(i)   5 hours of instrument training;
(ii) One cross-country flight in a helicopter of at least a 2-hour duration, a total straight-line distance of more than 50 nautical miles from the original point of departure and occurring in day VFR conditions;
(iii) One cross-country flight in a helicopter of at least a 2-hour duration, a total straight-line distance of more than 50 nautical miles from the original point of departure, and occurring in night VFR conditions; and
(iv) 3 hours in a helicopter in preparation for the practical test within 60 days preceding the date of the test.

(4) *For a rotorcraft gyroplane course:* 30 hours of flight training from a certificated flight instructor on the approved areas of operation listed in paragraph (d)(4) of this section that includes at least—
(i)   5 hours of instrument training;
(ii) One cross-country flight in a gyroplane of at least a 2-hour duration, a total straight line distance of more than 50 nautical miles from the original point of departure, and occurring in day VFR conditions;
(iii) One cross-country flight in a gyroplane of at least a 2-hour duration, a total straight-line distance of more than 50 nautical miles from the original point of departure, and occurring in night VFR conditions; and
(iv) 3 hours in a gyroplane in preparation for the practical test within 60 days preceding the date of the test.

(5) *For a powered-lift course:* 55 hours of flight training from a certificated flight instructor on the approved areas of operation listed in paragraph (d)(5) of this section that includes at least—
(i)   5 hours of instrument training in a powered-lift;
(ii) One cross-country flight in a powered-lift of at least a 2-hour duration, a total straight-line distance of more than 100 nautical miles from the original point of departure, and occurring in day VFR conditions;
(iii) One cross-country flight in a powered-lift of at least a 2-hour duration, a total straight-line distance of more than 100 nautical miles from the original point of departure, and occurring in night VFR conditions; and
(iv) 3 hours in a powered-lift in preparation for the practical test within 60 days preceding the date of the test.

(6) *For a glider course:* 4 hours of flight training from a certificated flight instructor on the approved areas of operation in paragraph (d)(6) of this section, that includes at least—
(i)   Five training flights in a glider with a certificated flight instructor on the launch/tow procedures approved for the course and on the appropriate approved areas of operation listed in paragraph (d)(6) of this section; and
(ii) Three training flights in a glider with a certificated flight instructor in preparation for the practical test within the 60 days preceding the date of the test.

(7)   *For a lighter-than-air airship course:* 55 hours of flight training in airships from a commercial pilot with an airship rating on the approved areas of operation in paragraph (d)(7) of this section that includes at least—
  (i)   3 hours of instrument training in an airship;
  (ii)   One cross-country flight in an airship of at least a 1-hour duration, a total straight-line distance of more than 25 nautical miles from the original point of departure, and occurring in day VFR conditions; and
  (iii) One cross-country flight in an airship of at least a 1-hour duration, a total straight-line distance of more than 25 nautical miles from the original point of departure, and occurring in night VFR conditions; and
  (iv)   3 hours in an airship, in preparation for the practical test within 60 days preceding the date of the test.

(8)   *For a lighter-than-air balloon course:* Flight training from a commercial pilot with a balloon rating on the approved areas of operation in paragraph (d)(8) of this section that includes at least—
  (i)   If the course involves training in a gas balloon:
    (A)   Two flights of 1 hour each;
    (B)   One flight involving a controlled ascent to at least 5,000 feet above the launch site; and
    (C)   Two flights in preparation for the practical test within 60 days preceding the date of the test.
  (ii)   If the course involves training in a balloon with an airborne heater:
    (A)   Two flights of 30 minutes each;
    (B)   One flight involving a controlled ascent to at least 3,000 feet above the launch site; and
    (C)   Two flights in preparation for the practical test within 60 days preceding the date of the test.

(c)   For the use of flight simulators or flight training devices:
  (1)   The course may include training in a flight simulator or flight training device, provided it is representative of the aircraft for which the course is approved, meets the requirements of this paragraph, and is given by an authorized instructor.
  (2)   Training in a flight simulator that meets the requirements of §141.41(a) of this part may be credited for a maximum of 30 percent of the total flight training hour requirements of the approved course, or of this section, whichever is less.
  (3)   Training in a flight training device that meets the requirements of §141.41(b) of this part may be credited for a maximum of 20 percent of the total flight training hour requirements of the approved course, or of this section, whichever is less.
  (4)   Training in the flight training devices described in paragraphs (c)(2) and (c)(3) of this section, if used in combination, may be credited for a maximum of 30 percent of the total flight training hour requirements of the approved course, or of this section, whichever is less. However, credit for training in a flight training device that meets the requirements of §141.41(b) cannot exceed the limitation provided for in paragraph (c)(3) of this section.

(d) Each approved course must include the flight training on the approved areas of operation listed in this paragraph that are appropriate to the aircraft category and class rating—

    (1) *For an airplane single-engine course*:
        (i) Preflight preparation;
        (ii) Preflight procedures;
        (iii) Airport and seaplane base operations;
        (iv) Takeoffs, landings, and go-arounds;
        (v) Performance maneuvers;
        (vi) Navigation;
        (vii) Slow flight and stalls;
        (viii) Emergency operations;
        (ix) High-altitude operations; and
        (x) Postflight procedures.

    (2) *For an airplane multiengine course*:
        (i) Preflight preparation;
        (ii) Preflight procedures;
        (iii) Airport and seaplane base operations;
        (iv) Takeoffs, landings, and go-arounds;
        (v) Performance maneuvers;
        (vi) Navigation;
        (vii) Slow flight and stalls;
        (viii) Emergency operations;
        (ix) Multiengine operations;
        (x) High-altitude operations; and
        (xi) Postflight procedures.

    (3) *For a rotorcraft helicopter course*:
        (i) Preflight preparation;
        (ii) Preflight procedures;
        (iii) Airport and heliport operations;
        (iv) Hovering maneuvers;
        (v) Takeoffs, landings, and go-arounds;
        (vi) Performance maneuvers;
        (vii) Navigation;
        (viii) Emergency operations;
        (ix) Special operations; and
        (x) Postflight procedures.

    (4) *For a rotorcraft gyroplane course*:
        (i) Preflight preparation;
        (ii) Preflight procedures;
        (iii) Airport operations;
        (iv) Takeoffs, landings, and go-arounds;
        (v) Performance maneuvers;
        (vi) Navigation;
        (vii) Flight at slow airspeeds;
        (viii) Emergency operations; and
        (ix) Postflight procedures.

(5) *For a powered-lift course*:
   (i)   Preflight preparation;
   (ii)   Preflight procedures;
   (iii) Airport and heliport operations;
   (iv) Hovering maneuvers;
   (v)   Takeoffs, landings, and go-arounds;
   (vi) Performance maneuvers;
   (vii) Navigation;
   (viii) Slow flight and stalls;
   (ix) Emergency operations;
   (x)   High altitude operations;
   (xi) Special operations; and
   (xii) Postflight procedures.
(6) *For a glider course*:
   (i)   Preflight preparation;
   (ii)   Preflight procedures;
   (iii) Airport and gliderport operations;
   (iv) Launches/tows, as appropriate, and landings;
   (v)   Performance speeds;
   (vi) Soaring techniques;
   (vii) Performance maneuvers;
   (viii) Navigation;
   (ix) Slow flight and stalls;
   (x)   Emergency operations; and
   (xi) Postflight procedures.
(7) *For a lighter-than-air airship course*:
   (i)   Fundamentals of instructing;
   (ii)   Technical subjects;
   (iii) Preflight preparation;
   (iv) Preflight lessons on a maneuver to be performed in flight;
   (v)   Preflight procedures;
   (vi) Airport operations;
   (vii) Takeoffs, landings, and go-arounds;
   (viii) Performance maneuvers;
   (ix) Navigation;
   (x)   Emergency operations; and
   (xi) Postflight procedures.
(8) *For a lighter-than-air balloon course*:
   (i)   Fundamentals of instructing;
   (ii)   Technical subjects;
   (iii) Preflight preparation;
   (iv) Preflight lesson on a maneuver to be performed in flight;
   (v)   Preflight procedures;
   (vi) Airport operations;
   (vii) Launches and landings;
   (viii) Performance maneuvers;
   (ix) Navigation;
   (x)   Emergency operations; and
   (xi) Postflight procedures.

5. *Solo training.* Each approved course must include at least the following solo flight training:

(a) *For an airplane single-engine course:* 10 hours of solo flight training in a single-engine airplane on the approved areas of operation in paragraph (d)(1) of section No. 4 of this appendix that includes at least—

(1) One cross-country flight, if the training is being performed in the State of Hawaii, with landings at a minimum of three points, and one of the segments consisting of a straight-line distance of at least 150 nautical miles;

(2) One cross-country flight, if the training is being performed in a State other than Hawaii, with landings at a minimum of three points, and one segment of the flight consisting of a straight-line distance of at least 250 nautical miles; and

(3) 5 hours in night VFR conditions with 10 takeoffs and 10 landings (with each landing involving a flight with a traffic pattern) at an airport with an operating control tower.

(b) *For an airplane multiengine course:* 10 hours of flight training in a multiengine airplane performing the duties of pilot in command while under the supervision of a certificated flight instructor. The training must consist of the approved areas of operation in paragraph (d)(2) of section No. 4 of this appendix, and include at least—

(1) One cross-country flight, if the training is being performed in the State of Hawaii, with landings at a minimum of three points, and one of the segments consisting of a straight-line distance of at least 150 nautical miles;

(2) One cross-country flight, if the training is being performed in a State other than Hawaii, with landings at a minimum of three points and one segment of the flight consisting of straight-line distance of at least 250 nautical miles; and

(3) 5 hours in night VFR conditions with 10 takeoffs and 10 landings (with each landing involving a flight with a traffic pattern) at an airport with an operating control tower.

(c) *For a rotorcraft helicopter course:* 10 hours of solo flight training in a helicopter on the approved areas of operation in paragraph (d)(3) of section No. 4 of this appendix that includes at least—

(1) One cross-country flight with landings at a minimum of three points and one segment of the flight consisting of a straight-line distance of at least 50 nautical miles from the original point of departure; and

(2) 5 hours in night VFR conditions with 10 takeoffs and 10 landings (with each landing involving a flight with a traffic pattern) at an airport with an operating control tower.

(d) *For a rotorcraft-gyroplane course:* 10 hours of solo flight training in a gyroplane on the approved areas of operation in paragraph (d)(4) of section No. 4 of this appendix that includes at least—

(1) One cross-country flight with landings at a minimum of three points, and one segment of the flight consisting of a straight-line distance of at least 50 nautical miles from the original point of departure; and

(2) 5 hours in night VFR conditions with 10 takeoffs and 10 landings (with each landing involving a flight with a traffic pattern) at an airport with an operating control tower.

(e) *For a powered-lift course:* 10 hours of solo flight training in a powered-lift on the approved areas of operation in paragraph (d)(5) of section No. 4 of this appendix that includes at least—

(1) One cross-country flight, if the training is being performed in the State of Hawaii, with landings at a minimum of three points, and one segment of the flight consisting of a straight-line distance of at least 150 nautical miles;

       (2)   One cross-country flight, if the training is being performed in a State other than Hawaii, with landings at a minimum of three points, and one segment of the flight consisting of a straight-line distance of at least 250 nautical miles; and

       (3)   5 hours in night VFR conditions with 10 takeoffs and 10 landings (with each landing involving a flight with a traffic pattern) at an airport with an operating control tower.

  (f)   *For a glider course:* 5 solo flights in a glider on the approved areas of operation in paragraph (d)(6) of section No. 4 of this appendix.

  (g)   *For a lighter-than-air airship course:* 10 hours of flight training in an airship, while performing the duties of pilot in command while under the supervision of a commercial pilot with an airship rating. The training must consist of the approved areas of operation in paragraph (d)(7) of section No. 4 of this appendix and include at least—

       (1)   One cross-country flight with landings at a minimum of three points, and one segment of the flight consisting of a straight-line distance of at least 25 nautical miles from the original point of departure; and

       (2)   5 hours in night VFR conditions with 10 takeoffs and 10 landings (with each landing involving a flight with a traffic pattern).

  (h)   *For a lighter-than-air balloon course:* Two solo flights if the course is for a hot air balloon rating, or, if the course is for a gas balloon rating, at least two flights in a gas balloon, while performing the duties of pilot in command under the supervision of a commercial pilot with a balloon rating. The training shall consist of the approved areas of operation in paragraph (d)(8) of section No. 4 of this appendix, in the kind of balloon for which the course applies.

6.   *Stage checks and end-of-course tests.*

  (a)   Each student enrolled in a commercial pilot course must satisfactorily accomplish the stage checks and end-of-course tests, in accordance with the school's approved training course, consisting of the approved areas of operation listed in paragraph (d) of section No. 4 of this appendix that are appropriate to aircraft category and class rating for which the course applies.

  (b)   Each student must demonstrate satisfactory proficiency prior to receiving an endorsement to operate an aircraft in solo flight.

APPENDIX E TO PART 141 — AIRLINE TRANSPORT PILOT CERTIFICATION COURSE

1. *Applicability.* This appendix prescribes the minimum curriculum for an airline transport pilot certification course under this part, for the following ratings:
   (a)   Airplane single-engine.
   (b)   Airplane multiengine.
   (c)   Rotorcraft helicopter.
   (d)   Powered-lift.
2. *Eligibility for enrollment.* Prior to enrolling in the flight portion of the airline transport pilot certification course, a person must:
   (a)   Meet the aeronautical experience requirements prescribed in subpart G of part 61 of this chapter for an airline transport pilot certificate that is appropriate to the aircraft category and class rating for which the course applies;
   (b)   Hold at least a commercial pilot certificate and an instrument rating;
   (c)   Meet the military experience requirements under §61.73 of this chapter to qualify for a commercial pilot certificate and an instrument rating, if the person is a rated military pilot or former rated military pilot of an Armed Force of the United States; or
   (d)   Hold either a foreign airline transport pilot license or foreign commercial pilot license and an instrument rating, if the person holds a pilot license issued by a contracting State to the Convention on International Civil Aviation.
3. *Aeronautical knowledge areas.*
   (a)   Each approved course must include at least 40 hours of ground training on the aeronautical knowledge areas listed in paragraph (b) of this section, appropriate to the aircraft category and class rating for which the course applies.
   (b)   Ground training must include the following aeronautical knowledge areas:
      (1)   Applicable Federal Aviation Regulations of this chapter that relate to airline transport pilot privileges, limitations, and flight operations;
      (2)   Meteorology, including knowledge of and effects of fronts, frontal characteristics, cloud formations, icing, and upper-air data;
      (3)   General system of weather and NOTAM collection, dissemination, interpretation, and use;
      (4)   Interpretation and use of weather charts, maps, forecasts, sequence reports, abbreviations, and symbols;
      (5)   National Weather Service functions as they pertain to operations in the National Airspace System;
      (6)   Windshear and microburst awareness, identification, and avoidance;
      (7)   Principles of air navigation under instrument meteorological conditions in the National Airspace System;
      (8)   Air traffic control procedures and pilot responsibilities as they relate to en route operations, terminal area and radar operations, and instrument departure and approach procedures;
      (9)   Aircraft loading; weight and balance; use of charts, graphs, tables, formulas, and computations; and the effects on aircraft performance;
      (10) Aerodynamics relating to an aircraft's flight characteristics and performance in normal and abnormal flight regimes;
      (11) Human factors;
      (12) Aeronautical decision making and judgment; and
      (13) Crew resource management to include crew communication and coordination.

4.   *Flight training.*
     (a)   Each approved course must include at least 25 hours of flight training on the approved areas of operation listed in paragraph (c) of this section appropriate to the aircraft category and class rating for which the course applies. At least 15 hours of this flight training must be instrument flight training.
     (b)   For the use of flight simulators or flight training devices—
           (1)   The course may include training in a flight simulator or flight training device, provided it is representative of the aircraft for which the course is approved, meets the requirements of this paragraph, and the training is given by an authorized instructor.
           (2)   Training in a flight simulator that meets the requirements of §141.41(a) of this part may be credited for a maximum of 50 percent of the total flight training hour requirements of the approved course, or of this section, whichever is less.
           (3)   Training in a flight training device that meets the requirements of §141.41(b) of this part may be credited for a maximum of 25 percent of the total flight training hour requirements of the approved course, or of this section, whichever is less.
           (4)   Training in flight simulators or flight training devices described in paragraphs (b)(2) and (b)(3) of this section, if used in combination, may be credited for a maximum of 50 percent of the total flight training hour requirements of the approved course, or of this section, whichever is less. However, credit for training in a flight training device that meets the requirements of §141.41(b) cannot exceed the limitation provided for in paragraph (b)(3) of this section.
     (c)   Each approved course must include flight training on the approved areas of operation listed in this paragraph appropriate to the aircraft category and class rating for which the course applies:
           (1)   Preflight preparation;
           (2)   Preflight procedures;
           (3)   Takeoff and departure phase;
           (4)   In-flight maneuvers;
           (5)   Instrument procedures;
           (6)   Landings and approaches to landings;
           (7)   Normal and abnormal procedures;
           (8)   Emergency procedures; and
           (9)   Postflight procedures.
5.   *Stage checks and end-of-course tests.*
     (a)   Each student enrolled in an airline transport pilot course must satisfactorily accomplish the stage checks and end-of-course tests, in accordance with the school's approved training course, consisting of the approved areas of operation listed in paragraph (c) of section No. 4 of this appendix that are appropriate to the aircraft category and class rating for which the course applies.
     (b)   Each student must demonstrate satisfactory proficiency prior to receiving an endorsement to operate an aircraft in solo flight.

APPENDIX F TO PART 141 — FLIGHT INSTRUCTOR CERTIFICATION COURSE

1. *Applicability.* This appendix prescribes the minimum curriculum for a flight instructor certification course and an additional flight instructor rating course required under this part, for the following ratings:
    (a) Airplane single-engine.
    (b) Airplane multiengine.
    (c) Rotorcraft helicopter.
    (d) Rotorcraft gyroplane.
    (e) Powered-lift.
    (f) Glider category.
2. *Eligibility for enrollment. A person must hold the following prior to enrolling in the flight portion of* the flight instructor or additional flight instructor rating course:
    (a) A commercial pilot certificate or an airline transport pilot certificate, with an aircraft category and class rating appropriate to the flight instructor rating for which the course applies; and
    (b) An instrument rating or privilege in an aircraft that is appropriate to the aircraft category and class rating for which the course applies, if the course is for a flight instructor airplane or powered-lift instrument rating.
3. *Aeronautical knowledge training.*
    (a) Each approved course must include at least the following ground training in the aeronautical knowledge areas listed in paragraph (b) of this section:
        (1) 40 hours of training if the course is for an initial issuance of a flight instructor certificate; or
        (2) 20 hours of training if the course is for an additional flight instructor rating.
    (b) Ground training must include the following aeronautical knowledge areas:
        (1) The fundamentals of instructing including—
            (i) The learning process;
            (ii) Elements of effective teaching;
            (iii) Student evaluation and testing;
            (iv) Course development;
            (v) Lesson planning; and
            (vi) Classroom training techniques.
        (2) The aeronautical knowledge areas in which training is required for—
            (i) A recreational, private, and commercial pilot certificate that is appropriate to the aircraft category and class rating for which the course applies; and
            (ii) An instrument rating that is appropriate to the aircraft category and class rating for which the course applies, if the course is for an airplane or powered-lift aircraft rating.
    (c) A student who satisfactorily completes 2 years of study on the principles of education at a college or university may be credited with no more than 20 hours of the training required in paragraph (a)(1) of this section.

4. *Flight training.*
   (a) Each approved course must include at least the following flight training on the approved areas of operation of paragraph (c) of this section appropriate to the flight instructor rating for which the course applies:
       (1) 25 hours, if the course is for an airplane, rotorcraft, or powered-lift rating; and
       (2) 10 hours, which must include 10 flights, if the course is for a glider category rating.
   (b) For the use of flight simulators or flight training devices:
       (1) The course may include training in a flight simulator or flight training device, provided it is representative of the aircraft for which the course is approved, meets the requirements of this paragraph, and the training is given by an authorized instructor.
       (2) Training in a flight simulator that meets the requirements of §141.41(a) of this part, may be credited for a maximum of 10 percent of the total flight training hour requirements of the approved course, or of this section, whichever is less.
       (3) Training in a flight training device that meets the requirements of §141.41(b) of this part, may be credited for a maximum of 5 percent of the total flight training hour requirements of the approved course, or of this section, whichever is less.
       (4) Training in flight simulators or flight training devices described in paragraphs (b)(2) and (b)(3) of this section, if used in combination, may be credited for a maximum of 10 percent of the total flight training hour requirements of the approved course, or of this section, whichever is less. However, credit for training in a flight training device that meets the requirements of §141.41(b) cannot exceed the limitation provided for in paragraph (b)(3) of this section.
   (c) Each approved course must include flight training on the approved areas of operation listed in this paragraph that are appropriate to the aircraft category and class rating for which the course applies—
       (1) *For an airplane—single-engine course*:
           (i) Fundamentals of instructing;
           (ii) Technical subject areas;
           (iii) Preflight preparation;
           (iv) Preflight lesson on a maneuver to be performed in flight;
           (v) Preflight procedures;
           (vi) Airport and seaplane base operations;
           (vii) Takeoffs, landings, and go-arounds;
           (viii) Fundamentals of flight;
           (ix) Performance maneuvers;
           (x) Ground reference maneuvers;
           (xi) Slow flight, stalls, and spins;
           (xii) Basic instrument maneuvers;
           (xiii) Emergency operations; and
           (xiv) Postflight procedures.

(2) *For an airplane—multiengine course:*
   (i)   Fundamentals of instructing;
   (ii) Technical subject areas;
   (iii) Preflight preparation;
   (iv) Preflight lesson on a maneuver to be performed in flight;
   (v) Preflight procedures;
   (vi) Airport and seaplane base operations;
   (vii) Takeoffs, landings, and go-arounds;
   (viii) Fundamentals of flight;
   (ix) Performance maneuvers;
   (x) Ground reference maneuvers;
   (xi) Slow flight and stalls;
   (xii) Basic instrument maneuvers;
   (xiii) Emergency operations;
   (xiv) Multiengine operations; and
   (xv) Postflight procedures.

(3) *For a rotorcraft—helicopter course:*
   (i)   Fundamentals of instructing;
   (ii) Technical subject areas;
   (iii) Preflight preparation;
   (iv) Preflight lesson on a maneuver to be performed in flight;
   (v) Preflight procedures;
   (vi) Airport and heliport operations;
   (vii) Hovering maneuvers;
   (viii) Takeoffs, landings, and go-arounds;
   (ix) Fundamentals of flight;
   (x) Performance maneuvers;
   (xi) Emergency operations;
   (xii) Special operations; and
   (xiii) Postflight procedures.

(4) *For a rotorcraft—gyroplane course:*
   (i)   Fundamentals of instructing;
   (ii) Technical subject areas;
   (iii) Preflight preparation;
   (iv) Preflight lesson on a maneuver to be performed in flight;
   (v) Preflight procedures;
   (vi) Airport operations;
   (vii) Takeoffs, landings, and go-arounds;
   (viii) Fundamentals of flight;
   (ix) Performance maneuvers;
   (x) Flight at slow airspeeds;
   (xi) Ground reference maneuvers;
   (xii) Emergency operations; and
   (xiii) Postflight procedures.

      (5)   *For a powered-lift course:*
          (i)   Fundamentals of instructing;
          (ii)   Technical subject areas;
          (iii) Preflight preparation;
          (iv) Preflight lesson on a maneuver to be performed in flight;
          (v)   Preflight procedures;
          (vi) Airport and heliport operations;
          (vii) Hovering maneuvers;
          (viii) Takeoffs, landings, and go-arounds;
          (ix) Fundamentals of flight;
          (x)   Performance maneuvers;
          (xi) Ground reference maneuvers;
          (xii) Slow flight and stalls;
          (xiii) Basic instrument maneuvers;
          (xiv) Emergency operations;
          (xv) Special operations; and
          (xvi) Postflight procedures.
      (6)   *For a glider course:*
          (i)   Fundamentals of instructing;
          (ii)   Technical subject areas;
          (iii) Preflight preparation;
          (iv) Preflight lesson on a maneuver to be performed in flight;
          (v)   Preflight procedures;
          (vi) Airport and gliderport operations;
          (vii) Tows or launches, landings, and go-arounds, if applicable;
          (viii) Fundamentals of flight;
          (ix) Performance speeds;
          (x)   Soaring techniques;
          (xi) Performance maneuvers;
          (xii) Slow flight, stalls, and spins;
          (xiii) Emergency operations; and
          (xiv) Postflight procedures.
5.   *Stage checks and end-of-course tests.*
     (a)   Each student enrolled in a flight instructor course must satisfactorily accomplish the stage checks and end-of-course tests, in accordance with the school's approved training course, consisting of the appropriate approved areas of operation listed in paragraph (c) of section No. 4 of this appendix appropriate to the flight instructor rating for which the course applies.
     (b)   In the case of a student who is enrolled in a flight instructor-airplane rating or flight instructor-glider rating course, that student must have:
         (1)   Received a logbook endorsement from a certificated flight instructor certifying the student received ground and flight training on stall awareness, spin entry, spins, and spin recovery procedures in an aircraft that is certificated for spins and is appropriate to the rating sought; and
         (2)   Demonstrated instructional proficiency in stall awareness, spin entry, spins, and spin recovery procedures.

APPENDIX G TO PART 141 — FLIGHT INSTRUCTOR INSTRUMENT (FOR AN AIRPLANE, HELICOPTER, OR POWERED-LIFT INSTRUMENT INSTRUCTOR RATING, AS APPROPRIATE) CERTIFICATION COURSE

1. *Applicability.* This appendix prescribes the minimum curriculum for a flight instructor instrument certification course required under this part, for the following ratings:
   (a) Flight Instructor Instrument—Airplane.
   (b) Flight Instructor Instrument—Helicopter.
   (c) Flight Instructor Instrument—Powered-lift aircraft.
2. *Eligibility for enrollment.* A person must hold the following prior to enrolling in the flight portion of the flight instructor instrument course:
   (a) A commercial pilot certificate or airline transport pilot certificate with an aircraft category and class rating appropriate to the flight instructor category and class rating for which the course applies; and
   (b) An instrument rating or privilege on that flight instructor applicant's pilot certificate that is appropriate to the flight instructor instrument rating (for an airplane-, helicopter-, or powered-lift-instrument rating, as appropriate) for which the course applies.
3. *Aeronautical knowledge training.*
   (a) Each approved course must include at least 15 hours of ground training on the aeronautical knowledge areas listed in paragraph (b) of this section, appropriate to the flight instructor instrument rating (for an airplane-, helicopter-, or powered-lift-instrument rating, as appropriate) for which the course applies:
   (b) Ground training must include the following aeronautical knowledge areas:
       (1) The fundamentals of instructing including:
           (i) The learning process;
           (ii) Elements of effective teaching;
           (iii) Student evaluation and testing;
           (iv) Course development;
           (v) Lesson planning; and
           (vi) Classroom training techniques.
       (2) The aeronautical knowledge areas in which training is required for an instrument rating that is appropriate to the aircraft category and class rating for the course which applies.
4. *Flight training.*
   (a) Each approved course must include at least 15 hours of flight training in the approved areas of operation of paragraph (c) of this section appropriate to the flight instructor rating for which the course applies.
   (b) For the use of flight simulators or flight training devices:
       (1) The course may include training in a flight simulator or flight training device, provided it is representative of the aircraft for which the course is approved for, meets requirements of this paragraph, and the training is given by an instructor.
       (2) Training in a flight simulator that meets the requirements of §141.41(a) of this part, may be credited for a maximum of 10 percent of the total flight training hour requirements of the approved course, or of this section, whichever is less.
       (3) Training in a flight training device that meets the requirements of §141.41(b) of this part, may be credited for a maximum of 5 percent of the total flight training hour requirements of the approved course, or of this section, whichever is less.

(4) Training in flight simulators or flight training devices described in paragraphs (b)(2) and (b)(3) of this section, if used in combination, may be credited for a maximum of 10 percent of the total flight training hour requirements of the approved course, or of this section, whichever is less. However, credit for training in a flight training device that meets the requirements of §141.41(b) cannot exceed the limitation provided for in paragraph (b)(3) of this section.

(c) An approved course for the flight instructor-instrument rating must include flight training on the following approved areas of operation that are appropriate to the instrument-aircraft category and class rating for which the course applies:

(1) Fundamentals of instructing;

(2) Technical subject areas;

(3) Preflight preparation;

(4) Preflight lesson on a maneuver to be performed in flight;

(5) Air traffic control clearances and procedures;

(6) Flight by reference to instruments;

(7) Navigation systems;

(8) Instrument approach procedures;

(9) Emergency operations; and

(10) Postflight procedures.

5. *Stage checks and end-of-course tests.* Each student enrolled in a flight instructor instrument course must satisfactorily accomplish the stage checks and end-of-course tests, in accordance with the school's approved training course, consisting of the approved areas of operation listed in paragraph (c) of section No. 4 of this appendix that are appropriate to the flight instructor instrument rating (for an airplane-, helicopter-, or powered-lift-instrument rating, as appropriate) for which the course applies.

APPENDIX H TO PART 141 — GROUND INSTRUCTOR CERTIFICATION COURSE

1. *Applicability.* This appendix prescribes the minimum curriculum for a ground instructor certification course and an additional ground instructor rating course, required under this part, for the following ratings:
   (a)   Ground Instructor—Basic.
   (b)   Ground Instructor—Advanced.
   (c)   Ground Instructor—Instrument.
2. *Aeronautical knowledge training.*
   (a)   Each approved course must include at least the following ground training on the knowledge areas listed in paragraphs (b), (c), (d), and (e) of this section, appropriate to the ground instructor rating for which the course applies:
      (1)   20 hours of training if the course is for an initial issuance of a ground instructor certificate; or
      (2)   10 hours of training if the course is for an additional ground instructor rating.
   (b)   Ground training must include the following aeronautical knowledge areas:
      (1)   Learning process;
      (2)   Elements of effective teaching;
      (3)   Student evaluation and testing;
      (4)   Course development;
      (5)   Lesson planning; and
      (6)   Classroom training techniques.
   (c)   Ground training for a basic ground instructor certificate must include the aeronautical knowledge areas applicable to a recreational and private pilot.
   (d)   Ground training for an advanced ground instructor rating must include the aeronautical knowledge areas applicable to a recreational, private, commercial, and airline transport pilot.
   (e)   Ground training for an instrument ground instructor rating must include the aeronautical knowledge areas applicable to an instrument rating.
   (f)   A student who satisfactorily completed 2 years of study on the principles of education at a college or university may be credited with 10 hours of the training required in paragraph (a)(1) of this section.
3. *Stage checks and end-of-course tests.* Each student enrolled in a ground instructor course must satisfactorily accomplish the stage checks and end-of-course tests, in accordance with the school's approved training course, consisting of the approved knowledge areas in paragraph (b), (c), (d), and (e) of section No. 2 of this appendix appropriate to the ground instructor rating for which the course applies.

APPENDIX I TO PART 141 — ADDITIONAL AIRCRAFT CATEGORY OR CLASS RATING COURSE

1. *Applicability.* This appendix prescribes the minimum curriculum for an additional aircraft category rating course or an additional aircraft class rating course required under this part, for the following ratings:
    (a) Airplane single-engine.
    (b) Airplane multiengine.
    (c) Rotorcraft helicopter.
    (d) Rotorcraft gyroplane.
    (e) Powered-lift.
    (f) Glider.
    (g) Lighter-than-air airship.
    (h) Lighter-than-air balloon.
2. *Eligibility for enrollment.* A person must hold the level of pilot certificate for the additional aircraft category and class rating for which the course applies prior to enrolling in the flight portion of an additional aircraft category or additional aircraft class rating course.
3. *Aeronautical knowledge training.* Each approved course for an additional aircraft category rating or additional aircraft class rating must include the ground training time requirements and ground training on the aeronautical knowledge areas that are specific to that aircraft category and class rating and pilot certificate level for which the course apples as required in appendix A, B, D, or E of this part, as appropriate.
4. *Flight training.*
    (a) Each approved course for an additional aircraft category rating or additional aircraft class rating must include the flight training time requirements and flight training on the areas of operation that are specific to that aircraft category and class rating and pilot certificate level for which the course applies as required in appendix A, B, D, or E of this part, as appropriate.
    (b) For the use of flight simulators or flight training devices:
        (1) The course may include training in a flight simulator or flight training device, provided it is representative of the aircraft for which the course is approved, meets the requirements of this paragraph, and the training is given by an authorized instructor.
        (2) Training in a flight simulator that meets the requirements of §141.41(a) of this part may be credited for a maximum of 30 percent of the total flight training hour requirements of the approved course, or of this section, whichever is less.
        (3) Training in a flight training device that meets the requirements of §141.41(b) of this part may be credited for a maximum of 20 percent of the total flight training hour requirements of the approved course, or of this section, whichever is less.
        (4) Training in the flight simulators or flight training devices described in paragraphs (b)(2) and (b)(3) of this section, if used in combination, may be credited for a maximum of 30 percent of the total flight training hour requirements of the approved course, or of this section, whichever is less. However, credit for training in a flight training device that meets the requirements of §141.41(b) cannot exceed the limitation provided for in paragraph (c)(3) of this section.

5.   *Stage checks and end-of-course tests.*
   - (a) Each student enrolled in an additional aircraft category rating course or an additional aircraft class rating course must satisfactorily accomplish the stage checks and end-of-course tests, in accordance with the school's approved training course, consisting of the approved areas of operation in section No. 4 of this appendix that are appropriate to the aircraft category and class rating for which the course applies at the appropriate pilot certificate level.
   - (b) Each student must demonstrate satisfactory proficiency prior to receiving an endorsement to operate an aircraft in solo flight.

APPENDIX J TO PART 141 — AIRCRAFT TYPE RATING COURSE, FOR OTHER THAN AN AIRLINE TRANSPORT PILOT CERTIFICATE

1. *Applicability.* This appendix prescribes the minimum curriculum for an aircraft type rating course other than an airline transport pilot certificate, for:
    (a) A type rating in an airplane category—single-engine class.
    (b) A type rating in an airplane category—multiengine class.
    (c) A type rating in a rotorcraft category—helicopter class.
    (d) A type rating in a powered-lift category.
    (e) Other aircraft type ratings specified by the Administrator through the aircraft type certificate procedures.
2. *Eligibility for enrollment.* Prior to enrolling in the flight portion of an aircraft type rating course, a person must hold at least a private pilot certificate and:
    (a) An instrument rating in the category and class of aircraft that is appropriate to the aircraft type rating for which the course applies, provided the aircraft's type certificate does not have a VFR limitation; or
    (b) Be concurrently enrolled in an instrument rating course in the category and class of aircraft that is appropriate to the aircraft type rating for which the course applies, and pass the required instrument rating practical test concurrently with the aircraft type rating practical test.
3. *Aeronautical knowledge training.*
    (a) Each approved course must include at least 10 hours of ground training on the aeronautical knowledge areas listed in paragraph (b) of this section, appropriate to the aircraft type rating for which the course applies.
    (b) Ground training must include the following aeronautical areas:
        (1) Proper control of airspeed, configuration, direction, altitude, and attitude in accordance with procedures and limitations contained in the aircraft's flight manual, checklists, or other approved material appropriate to the aircraft type;
        (2) Compliance with approved en route, instrument approach, missed approach, ATC, or other applicable procedures that apply to the aircraft type;
        (3) Subjects requiring a practical knowledge of the aircraft type and its powerplant, systems, components, operational, and performance factors;
        (4) The aircraft's normal, abnormal, and emergency procedures, and the operations and limitations relating thereto;
        (5) Appropriate provisions of the approved aircraft's flight manual;
        (6) Location of and purpose for inspecting each item on the aircraft's checklist that relates to the exterior and interior preflight; and
        (7) Use of the aircraft's prestart checklist, appropriate control system checks, starting procedures, radio and electronic equipment checks, and the selection of proper navigation and communication radio facilities and frequencies.
4. *Flight training.*
    (a) Each approved course must include at least:
        (1) Flight training on the approved areas of operation of paragraph (c) of this section in the aircraft type for which the course applies; and
        (2) 10 hours of training of which at least 5 hours must be instrument training in the aircraft for which the course applies.

(b)	For the use of flight simulators or flight training devices:
(1)	The course may include training in a flight simulator or flight training device, provided it is representative of the aircraft for which the course is approved, meets requirements of this paragraph, and the training is given by an authorized instructor.
(2)	Training in a flight simulator that meets the requirements of §141.41(a) of this part, may be credited for a maximum of 50 percent of the total flight training hour requirements of the approved course, or of this section, whichever is less.
(3)	Training in a flight training device that meets the requirements of §141.41(b) of this part, may be credited for a maximum of 25 percent of the total flight training hour requirements of the approved course, or of this section, whichever is less.
(4)	Training in the flight simulators or flight training devices described in paragraphs (b)(2) and (b)(3) of this section, if used in combination, may be credited for a maximum of 50 percent of the total flight training hour requirements of the approved course, or of this section, whichever is less. However, credit training in a flight training device that meets the requirements of §141.41(b) cannot exceed the limitation provided for in paragraph (b)(3) of this section.
(c)	Each approved course must include the flight training on the areas of operation listed in this paragraph, that are appropriate to the aircraft category and class rating for which the course applies:
(1)	*A type rating for an airplane—single-engine course*:
(i)	Preflight preparation;
(ii)	Preflight procedures;
(iii)	Takeoff and departure phase;
(iv)	In-flight maneuvers;
(v)	Instrument procedures;
(vi)	Landings and approaches to landings;
(vii)	Normal and abnormal procedures;
(viii)	Emergency procedures; and
(ix)	Postflight procedures.
(2)	*A type rating for an airplane—multiengine course*:
(i)	Preflight preparation;
(ii)	Preflight procedures;
(iii)	Takeoff and departure phase;
(iv)	In-flight maneuvers;
(v)	Instrument procedures;
(vi)	Landings and approaches to landings;
(vii)	Normal and abnormal procedures;
(viii)	Emergency procedures; and
(ix)	Postflight procedures.
(3)	*A type rating for a powered-lift course*:
(i)	Preflight preparation;
(ii)	Preflight procedures;
(iii)	Takeoff and departure phase;
(iv)	In-flight maneuvers;
(v)	Instrument procedures;
(vi)	Landings and approaches to landings;
(vii)	Normal and abnormal procedures;
(viii)	Emergency procedures; and
(ix)	Postflight procedures.

    (4)   *A type rating for a rotorcraft—helicopter course*:
        (i)   Preflight preparation;
        (ii) Preflight procedures;
        (iii) Takeoff and departure phase;
        (iv) In-flight maneuvers;
        (v) Instrument procedures;
        (vi) Landings and approaches to landings;
        (vii) Normal and abnormal procedures;
        (viii) Emergency procedures; and
        (ix) Postflight procedures.
    (5)   *Other aircraft type ratings specified by the Administrator through aircraft type certificate procedures*:
        (i)   Preflight preparation;
        (ii) Preflight procedures;
        (iii) Takeoff and departure phase;
        (iv) In-flight maneuvers;
        (v) Instrument procedures;
        (vi) Landings and approaches to landings;
        (vii) Normal and abnormal procedures;
        (viii) Emergency procedures; and
        (ix) Postflight procedures.

5.   *Stage checks and end-of-course tests.*
    (a) Each student enrolled in an aircraft type rating course must satisfactorily accomplish the stage checks and end-of-course tests, in accordance with the school's approved training course, consisting of the approved areas of operation that are appropriate to the aircraft type rating for which the course applies at the airline transport pilot certificate level; and
    (b) Each student must demonstrate satisfactory proficiency prior to receiving an endorsement to operate an aircraft in solo flight.

APPENDIX K TO PART 141 — SPECIAL PREPARATION COURSES

1. *Applicability.* This appendix prescribes the minimum curriculum for the special preparation courses that are listed in §141.11 of this part.
2. *Eligibility for enrollment.* Prior to enrolling in the flight portion of a special preparation course, a person must hold a pilot certificate, flight instructor certificate, or ground instructor certificate that is appropriate for the exercise of the operating privileges or authorizations sought.
3. *General requirements.*
    (a) To be approved, a special preparation course must:
        (1) Meet the appropriate requirements of this appendix; and
        (2) Prepare the graduate with the necessary skills, competency, and proficiency to exercise safely the privileges of the certificate, rating, or authorization for which the course is established.
    (b) An approved special preparation course must include ground and flight training on the operating privileges or authorization sought, for developing competency, proficiency, resourcefulness, self-confidence, and self-reliance in the student.
4. *Use of flight simulators or flight training devices.*
    (a) The approved special preparation course may include training in a flight simulator or flight training device, provided it is representative of the aircraft for which the course is approved, meets requirements of this paragraph, and the training is given by an authorized instructor.
    (b) Training in a flight simulator that meets the requirements of §141.41(a) of this part, may be credited for a maximum of 10 percent of the total flight training hour requirements of the approved course, or of this section, whichever is less.
    (c) Training in a flight training device that meets the requirements of §141.41(b) of this part, may be credited for a maximum of 5 percent of the total flight training hour requirements of the approved course, or of this section, whichever is less.
    (d) Training in the flight simulators or flight training devices described in paragraphs (b) and (c) of this section, if used in combination, may be credited for a maximum of 10 percent of the total flight training hour requirements of the approved course, or of this section, whichever is less. However, credit for training in a flight training device that meets the requirements of §141.41(b) cannot exceed the limitation provided for in paragraph (c) of this section.
5. *Stage check and end-of-course tests.* Each person enrolled in a special preparation course must satisfactorily accomplish the stage checks and end-of-course tests, in accordance with the school's approved training course, consisting of the approved areas of operation that are appropriate to the operating privileges or authorization sought, and for which the course applies.
6. *Agricultural aircraft operations course.* An approved special preparation course for pilots in agricultural aircraft operations must include at least the following—
    (a) 25 hours of training on:
        (1) Agricultural aircraft operations;
        (2) Safe piloting and operating practices and procedures for handling, dispensing, and disposing agricultural and industrial chemicals, including operating in and around congested areas; and
        (3) Applicable provisions of part 137 of this chapter.
    (b) 15 hours of flight training on agricultural aircraft operations.

7. *Rotorcraft external-load operations course.* An approved special preparation course for pilots of external-load operations must include at least the following—
   (a) 10 hours of training on:
       (1) Rotorcraft external-load operations;
       (2) Safe piloting and operating practices and procedures for external-load operations, including operating in and around congested areas; and
       (3) Applicable provisions of part 133 of this chapter.
   (b) 15 hours of flight training on external-load operations.

8. *Test pilot course.* An approved special preparation course for pilots in test pilot duties must include at least the following—
   (a) Aeronautical knowledge training on:
       (1) Performing aircraft maintenance, quality assurance, and certification test flight operations;
       (2) Safe piloting and operating practices and procedures for performing aircraft maintenance, quality assurance, and certification test flight operations;
       (3) Applicable parts of this chapter that pertain to aircraft maintenance, quality assurance, and certification tests; and
       (4) Test pilot duties and responsibilities.
   (b) 15 hours of flight training on test pilot duties and responsibilities.

9. *Special operations course.* An approved special preparation course for pilots in special operations that are mission-specific for certain aircraft must include at least the following—
   (a) Aeronautical knowledge training on:
       (1) Performing that special flight operation;
       (2) Safe piloting operating practices and procedures for performing that special flight operation;
       (3) Applicable parts of this chapter that pertain to that special flight operation; and
       (4) Pilot in command duties and responsibilities for performing that special flight operation.
   (b) Flight training:
       (1) On that special flight operation; and
       (2) To develop skills, competency, proficiency, resourcefulness, self-confidence, and self-reliance in the student for performing that special flight operation in a safe manner.

10. *Pilot refresher course.* An approved special preparation pilot refresher course for a pilot certificate, aircraft category and class rating, or an instrument rating must include at least the following—
   (a) 4 hours of aeronautical knowledge training on:
       (1) The aeronautical knowledge areas that are applicable to the level of pilot certificate, aircraft category and class rating, or instrument rating, as appropriate, that pertain to that course;
       (2) Safe piloting operating practices and procedures; and
       (3) Applicable provisions of parts 61 and 91 of this chapter for pilots.
   (b) 6 hours of flight training on the approved areas of operation that are applicable to the level of pilot certificate, aircraft category and class rating, or instrument rating, as appropriate, for performing pilot-in-command duties and responsibilities.

11. *Flight instructor refresher course.* An approved special preparation flight instructor refresher course must include at least a combined total of 16 hours of aeronautical knowledge training, flight training, or any combination of ground and flight training on the following—
  (a) Aeronautical knowledge training on:
    (1) The aeronautical knowledge areas of part 61 of this chapter that apply to student, recreational, private, and commercial pilot certificates and instrument ratings;
    (2) The aeronautical knowledge areas of part 61 of this chapter that apply to flight instructor certificates;
    (3) Safe piloting operating practices and procedures, including airport operations and operating in the National Airspace System; and
    (4) Applicable provisions of parts 61 and 91 of this chapter that apply to pilots and flight instructors.
  (b) Flight training to review:
    (1) The approved areas of operations applicable to student, recreational, private, and commercial pilot certificates and instrument ratings; and
    (2) The skills, competency, and proficiency for performing flight instructor duties and responsibilities.
12. *Ground instructor refresher course.* An approved special preparation ground instructor refresher course must include at least 16 hours of aeronautical knowledge training on:
  (a) The aeronautical knowledge areas of part 61 of this chapter that apply to student, recreational, private, and commercial pilots and instrument rated pilots;
  (b) The aeronautical knowledge areas of part 61 of this chapter that apply to ground instructors;
  (c) Safe piloting operating practices and procedures, including airport operations and operating in the National Airspace System; and
  (d) Applicable provisions of parts 61 and 91 of this chapter that apply to pilots and ground instructors.

APPENDIX L TO PART 141 — PILOT GROUND SCHOOL COURSE

1. *Applicability.* This appendix prescribes the minimum curriculum for a pilot ground school course required under this part.
2. *General requirements.* An approved course of training for a pilot ground school must include training on the aeronautical knowledge areas that are:
    (a) Needed to safely exercise the privileges of the certificate, rating, or authority for which the course is established; and
    (b) Conducted to develop competency, proficiency, resourcefulness, self-confidence, and self-reliance in each student.
3. *Aeronautical knowledge training requirements.* Each approved pilot ground school course must include:
    (a) The aeronautical knowledge training that is appropriate to the aircraft rating and pilot certificate level for which the course applies; and
    (b) An adequate number of total aeronautical knowledge training hours appropriate to the aircraft rating and pilot certificate level for which the course applies.
4. *Stage checks and end-of-course tests.* Each person enrolled in a pilot ground school course must satisfactorily accomplish the stage checks and end-of-course tests, in accordance with the school's approved training course, consisting of the approved areas of operation that are appropriate to the operating privileges or authorization that graduation from the course will permit and for which the course applies.

NATIONAL TRANSPORTATION SAFETY BOARD

PART 830 - RULES PERTAINING TO THE NOTIFICATION
AND REPORTING OF AIRCRAFT ACCIDENTS OR INCIDENTS AND
OVERDUE AIRCRAFT, AND PRESERVATION OF AIRCRAFT
WRECKAGE, MAIL, CARGO, AND RECORDS

TABLE OF CONTENTS

SUBPART A — GENERAL

SUBPART B — INITIAL NOTIFICATION OF AIRCRAFT ACCIDENTS, INCIDENTS, AND OVERDUE AIRCRAFT

SUBPART C — PRESERVATION OF AIRCRAFT WRECKAGE, MAIL CARGO, AND RECORDS

SUBPART D — REPORTING OF AIRCRAFT ACCIDENTS, INCIDENTS, AND OVERDUE AIRCRAFT

INTENTIONALLY

LEFT

BLANK

SUBPART A — GENERAL

830.1 APPLICABILITY

This part contains rules pertaining to:
(a) Initial notification and later reporting of aircraft incidents and accidents and certain other occurrences in the operation of aircraft, wherever they occur, when they involve civil aircraft of the United States; when they involve certain public aircraft, as specified in this part, wherever they occur; and when they involve foreign civil aircraft where the events occur in the United States, its territories, or its possessions.
(b) Preservation of aircraft wreckage, mail, cargo, and records involving all civil and certain public aircraft accidents, as specified in this part, in the United States and its territories or possessions.

EXPLANATION

These reporting requirements apply to civil aircraft of United States registration both within and outside the United States.

These reporting requirements apply to all public aircraft except those operated by the Armed Services and Intelligence Agencies.

The preservation requirements of §830.10 apply to all civil aircraft in the United States, but not to United States registered aircraft outside the United States, its territories or possessions.

A failure to comply with this part can subject a person to a civil penalty of not to exceed $1000 per day for each day the violation continues. If in doubt, call the NTSB **immediately** for assistance.

CROSS REFERENCES

91.25, Aviation Safety Reporting Program: Prohibition Against Use of Reports For Enforcement Purposes; §701(a) of the Federal Aviation Act of 1958, as amended (40 U.S.C. §1443(a)), Aircraft Accident Investigations; Accidents Involving Civil Aircraft: General Duties; §901(a)(1)(A) of the Federal Aviation Act of 1958, as amended (49 U.S.C. §1471(a)(1)(A)), Penalties; Civil Penalties: Safety, Economic, and Postal Offenses; Chapter 5, Investigation, Annex 13, Aircraft Accident Investigation, to the Convention on International Civil Aviation.

ADVISORY CIRCULARS

AC 00-46C *Aviation Safety Reporting Program* (1985).

AC 120-30A *Reporting Requirements of Air Carriers, Commercial Operators, Travel Clubs, and Air Traffic Operators of Large and Small Aircraft* (1976).

AERONAUTICAL INFORMATION MANUAL

Aviation Safety Reporting Program, Para. 7-6-1;
Aircraft Accident and Incident Reporting, Para. 7-6-2;
Near Midair Collision Reporting, Para. 7-6-3.

830.2 DEFINITIONS

As used in this part the following words or phrases are defined as follows:

"Aircraft accident" means an occurrence associated with the operation of an aircraft which takes place between the time any person boards the aircraft with the intention of flight and all such persons have disembarked, and in which any person suffers death or serious injury, or in which the aircraft receives substantial damage.

"Civil aircraft" means any aircraft other than a public aircraft.

"Fatal injury" means any injury which results in death within 30 days of the accident.

"Incident" means an occurrence other than an accident, associated with the operation of an aircraft, which affects or could affect the safety of operations.

"Operator" means any person who causes or authorizes the operation of an aircraft, such as the owner, lessee, or bailee of an aircraft.

"Public aircraft" means an aircraft used only for the United States Government, or an aircraft owned and operated (except for commercial purposes) or exclusively leased for at least 90 continuous days by a government other than the United States Government, including a State, the District of Columbia, a territory or possession of the United States, or a political subdivision of that government. "Public aircraft" does not include a government-owned aircraft transporting property for commercial purposes and does not include a government-owned aircraft transporting passengers other than: transporting (for other than commercial purposes) crewmembers or other persons aboard the aircraft whose presence is required to perform, or is associated with the performance of, a governmental function such as firefighting, search and rescue, law enforcement, aeronautical research, or biological or geological resource management; or transporting (for other than commercial purposes) persons aboard the aircraft if the aircraft is operated by the Armed Forces or an intelligence agency of the United States. Notwithstanding any limitation relating to use of the aircraft for commercial purposes, an aircraft shall be considered to be a public aircraft without regard to whether it is operated by a unit of government on behalf of another unit of government pursuant to a cost reimbursement agreement, if the unit of government on whose behalf the operation is conducted certifies to the Administrator of the Federal Aviation Administration that the operation was necessary to respond to a significant and imminent threat to life or property (including natural resources) and that no service by a private operator was reasonably available to meet the threat.

"Serious injury" means any injury which: (1) requires hospitalization for more than 48 hours, commencing within 7 days from the date the injury was received; (2) results in a fracture of any bone (except simple fractures of fingers, toes, or nose); (3) causes severe hemorrhages, nerve, muscle, or tendon damage; (4) involves any internal organ; or (5) involves second- or third-degree burns, or any burns affecting more than 5 percent of the body surface.

"Substantial damage" means damage or failure which adversely affects the structural strength, performance, or flight characteristics of the aircraft, and which would normally require major repair or replacement of the affected component. Engine failure or damage limited to an engine if only one engine fails or is damaged, bent fairings or cowling, dented skin, small punctured holes in the skin or fabric, ground damage to rotor or propeller blades, and damage to landing gear, wheels, tires, flaps, engine accessories, brakes, or wingtips are not considered "substantial damage" for the purpose of this part.

EXPLANATION

These definitions apply only to these NTSB regulations.

ADVISORY CIRCULARS

AC 00-46C *Aviation Safety Reporting Program* (1985).

AC 120-30A *Reporting Requirements of Air Carriers, Commercial Operators, Travel Clubs, and Air Traffic Operators of Large and Small Aircraft* (1976).

AERONAUTICAL INFORMATION MANUAL

Aviation Safety Reporting Program, Para. 7-6-1;
Aircraft Accident and Incident Reporting, Para. 7-6-2;
Near Midair Collision Reporting, Para. 7-6-3.

NTSB DECISIONS

Where an aircraft was parked in its customary location, the affected employee was outside the airliner itself and any injury that occurred was caused by the jet blast of an airliner operated by another carrier, the operator of the parked aircraft would not have a duty under Part 830 to report the occurrence as it was not associated with the operation of that aircraft. (1-22-92). (Editor's Note: The opinion contained a caution to the effect that the Board itself had not ruled on the precise question because most reporting determinations are made at the field level by regional staff.)

SUBPART B — INITIAL NOTIFICATION OF AIRCRAFT ACCIDENTS, INCIDENTS, AND OVERDUE AIRCRAFT

830.5 IMMEDIATE NOTIFICATION

The operator of any civil aircraft, or any public aircraft not operated by the Armed Forces or an intelligence agency of the United States, or any foreign aircraft shall immediately, and by the most expeditious means available, notify the nearest National Transportation Safety Board (Board) field office[1] when:

(a)   An aircraft accident or any of the following listed incidents occur:
   (1)   Flight control system malfunction or failure;
   (2)   Inability of any required flight crewmember to perform his normal flight duties as a result of injury or illness;
   (3)   Failure of structural components of a turbine engine excluding compressor and turbine blades and vanes;
   (4)   In-flight fire; or
   (5)   Aircraft collide in flight.
   (6)   Damage to property, other than the aircraft, estimated to exceed $25,000 for repair (including materials and labor) or fair market value in the event of total loss, whichever is less.
   (7)   For large multiengine aircraft (more than 12,500 pounds maximum certificated takeoff weight):
      (i)   In-flight failure of electrical systems which requires the sustained use of an emergency bus powered by a back-up source such as a battery, auxiliary power unit, or air-driven generator to retain flight control or essential instruments;
      (ii)   In-flight failure of hydraulic systems that results in sustained reliance on the sole remaining hydraulic or mechanical system for movement of flight control surfaces;
      (iii) Sustained loss of the power or thrust produced by two or more engines; and
      (iv)   An evacuation of an aircraft in which an emergency egress system is utilized.
(b)   An aircraft is overdue and is believed to have been involved in an accident.

[1] The Board field offices are listed under U.S. Government in the telephone directories of the following cities: Anchorage, AK, Atlanta, GA, West Chicago, IL, Denver, CO, Arlington, TX, Gardena (Los Angeles), CA, Miami, FL, Parsippany, NJ (metropolitan New York, NY), Seattle, WA, and Washington, DC.

EXPLANATION

While an operator must immediately notify the nearest National Transportation Safety Board field office if any incidents described in (a)(1) through (a)(7) occur, a **report** is required only if requested by an authorized representative of the Board.

CROSS REFERENCES

91.25, Aviation Safety Reporting Program: Prohibition Against Use of Reports For Enforcement Purposes; 830.15, Reporting of Aircraft Accidents, Incidents, and Overdue Aircraft: Reports and Statements to be Filed.

ADVISORY CIRCULARS

AC 00-46C *Aviation Safety Reporting Program* (1985).

AC 120-30A *Reporting Requirements of Air Carriers, Commercial Operators, Travel Clubs, and Air Traffic Operators of Large and Small Aircraft* (1976).

AERONAUTICAL INFORMATION MANUAL

Aviation Safety Reporting Program, Para. 7-6-1;
Aircraft Accident and Incident Reporting, Para. 7-6-2;
Near Midair Collision Reporting, Para. 7-6-3.

830.6 INFORMATION TO BE GIVEN IN NOTIFICATION

The notification required in §830.5 shall contain the following information, if available:
(a) Type, nationality, and registration marks of the aircraft;
(b) Name of owner, and operator of the aircraft;
(c) Name of the pilot-in-command;
(d) Date and time of the accident;
(e) Last point of departure and point of intended landing of the aircraft;
(f) Position of the aircraft with reference to some easily defined geographical point;
(g) Number of persons aboard, number killed, and number seriously injured;
(h) Nature of the accident, the weather and the extent of damage to the aircraft, so far as is known; and
(i) A description of any explosives, radioactive materials, or other dangerous articles carried.

EXPLANATION

While accurate and complete information on all aspects is essential, in the case of items described in (i), you should be as detailed as possible and, if necessary, provide follow-up information as received.

CROSS REFERENCES

91.25, Aviation Safety Reporting Program: Prohibition Against Use of Reports For Enforcement Purposes; 830.5, Initial Notification of Aircraft Accidents, Incidents, and Overdue Aircraft: Immediate Notification.

ADVISORY CIRCULARS

AC 00-46C *Aviation Safety Reporting Program* (1985).

AC 120-30A *Reporting Requirements of Air Carriers, Commercial Operators, Travel Clubs, and Air Traffic Operators of Large and Small Aircraft* (1976).

AERONAUTICAL INFORMATION MANUAL

Aviation Safety Reporting Program, Para. 7-6-1;
Aircraft Accident and Incident Reporting, Para. 7-6-2;
Near Midair Collision Reporting, Para. 7-6-3.

SUBPART C — PRESERVATION OF AIRCRAFT WRECKAGE, MAIL, CARGO, AND RECORDS

830.10 PRESERVATION OF AIRCRAFT WRECKAGE, MAIL, CARGO, AND RECORDS

(a) The operator of an aircraft involved in an accident or incident for which notification must be given is responsible for preserving to the extent possible any aircraft wreckage, cargo, and mail aboard the aircraft, and all records, including all recording mediums of flight, maintenance, and voice recorders, pertaining to the operation and maintenance of the aircraft and to the airmen until the Board takes custody thereof or a release is granted pursuant to §831.12(b).

(b) Prior to the time the Board or its authorized representative takes custody of aircraft wreckage, mail, or cargo, such wreckage, mail, or cargo may not be disturbed or moved except to the extent necessary:

   (1) To remove persons injured or trapped;

   (2) To protect the wreckage from further damage, or

   (3) To protect the public from injury.

(c) Where it is necessary to move aircraft wreckage, mail or cargo, sketches, descriptive notes, and photographs shall be made, if possible, of the original position and condition of the wreckage and any significant impact marks.

(d) The operator of an aircraft involved in an accident or incident shall retain all records, reports, internal documents and memoranda dealing with the accident or incident, until authorized by the Board to the contrary.

EXPLANATION

The wreckage, mail, cargo, or records will not be released until an authorized representative of the Board has determined that the Board has no further need for same.

In the case of an accident not involving fatalities, of a small aircraft, the actual investigation of the accident may be made by Federal Aviation Administration inspectors with the National Transportation Safety Board making the probable cause determination.

CROSS REFERENCES

91.25, Aviation Safety Reporting Program: Prohibition Against Use of Reports For Enforcement Purposes; 831.2(b), Aircraft Accident/Incident Investigation Procedures: Access to and Release of Wreckage, Records, Mail and Cargo.

ADVISORY CIRCULARS

AC 00-46C *Aviation Safety Reporting Program* (1985).

AC 120-30A *Reporting Requirements of Air Carriers, Commercial Operators, Travel Clubs, and Air Traffic Operators of Large and Small Aircraft* (1976).

AERONAUTICAL INFORMATION MANUAL

Aviation Safety Reporting Program, Para. 7-6-1;
Aircraft Accident and Incident Reporting, Para. 7-6-2;
Near Midair Collision Reporting, Para. 7-6-3.

SUBPART D — REPORTING OF AIRCRAFT ACCIDENTS, INCIDENTS, AND OVERDUE AIRCRAFT

830.15 REPORTS AND STATEMENTS TO BE FILED

(a) Reports. The operator of a civil, public (as specified in §830.5), or foreign aircraft shall file a report on Board Form 6120.12 (OMB No. 3147-0001)[2] within 10 days after an accident, or after 7 days if an overdue aircraft is still missing. A report on an incident for which immediate notification is required by §830.5(a) shall be filed only as requested by an authorized representative of the Board.

(b) Crewmember statement. Each crewmember, if physically able at the time the report is submitted, shall attach a statement setting forth the facts, conditions, and circumstances relating to the accident or incident as they appear to him. If the crewmember is incapacitated, he shall submit the statement as soon as he is physically able.

(c) Where to file the reports. The operator of an aircraft shall file any report with the field office of the Board nearest the accident or incident.

[2]Forms are obtainable from the Board field offices (see footnote 1), the National Transportation Safety Board, Washington, D.C. 20594, and the Federal Aviation Administration Flight Standards District Office.

EXPLANATION

Your attorney should review any statement you prepare before you submit it to the NTSB.

CROSS REFERENCES

91.25, Aviation Safety Reporting Program: Prohibition Against Use of Reports For Enforcement Purposes; 830.5(a), Initial Notification of Aircraft Accidents, Incidents, and Overdue Aircraft: Immediate Notification.

ADVISORY CIRCULARS

AC 00-46C *Aviation Safety Reporting Program* (1985).

AC 120-30A *Reporting Requirements of Air Carriers, Commercial Operators, Travel Clubs, and Air Traffic Operators of Large and Small Aircraft* (1976).

AERONAUTICAL INFORMATION MANUAL

Aviation Safety Reporting Program, Para. 7-6-1;
Aircraft Accident and Incident Reporting, Para. 7-6-2;
Near Midair Collision Reporting, Para. 7-6-3.

INTENTIONALLY

LEFT

BLANK

A

B

C

D

AD-1

...ATION WEATHER 2ND EDITION

...ost comprehensive, award-winning aviation weather book just got better. New 480-page hard ...edition is extensively updated with the last METAR, TAF, and Graphic Weather Products from ...45E, Aviation Weather Services. Over 500 full-color illustrations and photographs present detailed ...al in an uncomplicated way. International weather considerations are included as well as ...nt/incident information to add relevance to the weather data. Expanded coverage of icing, weather ...ls, and flight planning. Review questions with answers at the end of the book. All new ...ded appendices cover common conversions, weather reports, forecasts, and charts, ...l as domestic and international METAR, TAF, and graphic weather products. ...letely new Instructor's Guide available on CD-ROM, which includes AC00-45E, ...on Weather Services (professors only).

NUMBER JS319010 $54.95

AVIATION HISTORY BY JEPPESEN

Announcing one of the most significant books on aviation history that has been published to date. Aviation History is an exciting new full-color book that gives both new and experienced pilots a unique perspective on international aviation history. Each of the ten chapters is packed with information, containing over 950 photographs and color graphics. Aviation History explores the question "what was aviation" from its birth in Annonay, France, in 1783, to the exhilarating accomplishments in space. Through personal profiles, you are able to meet the people who made significant contributions to aviation. You will explore historical evidence and see how historians use the artifacts of aviation to confirm what happened. 636 pages.

ITEM NUMBER JS319008 $69.95

...HE FEDERAL RULE BOOKS

...R/AIM Manual

...ellent study or reference source. Complete pilot/controller glossary. Changes conveniently indicated. ...ides FAR Parts 1, 43, 61, 67, 71, 73, 91, 97, 119, 133, 135, 141, 142, HMR 175 and NTSB 830. Use ...cial study lists to direct students to appropriate FARs. Check student's understanding of FARs with ...rcise questions tailored for Private, Instrument, Commercial and Helicopter.

...M NUMBER JS314550 $16.95

...EE UPDATE SUMMARY ON THE WEB AT WWW.JEPPESEN.COM

...panded FAR/AIM CD-ROM with FARs Explained by Kent Jackson

The Federal Aviation Regulations are an integral part of aeronautical training. This CD contains applicable portions of Parts 1, 13, 21, 23, 27, 33, 34, 35, 39, 43, 45, 47, 61, 65, 67, 71, 73, 91, 97, 108, 119, 125, 133, 135, 141, 142, 145 (old & new), 147, 183, HMR 175 and NTSB 830. Search the regulations by part or by keyword or phrase. The FAR/AIM CD-ROM contains: FARs, FARs Explained by Kent Jackson, FAR Exercises, the AIM and the Pilot Controller Glossary. Also includes SFARs and Maintenance Advisory Circulars as well as FAA-E-8082-11. Includes both Pilot and Maintenance Regulations. Offered with a revision service that includes two updated FAR/AIM CD-ROMs following the FAA AIM revisions each January and July. System requirements: PC with 486 or faster processor, 2x CD-ROM drive, Windows 95, 98, NT, ME and 2000.

ITEM NUMBER JS206350 FAR/AIM CD-ROM $25.95
ITEM NUMBER JS206443 FAR/AIM CD-ROM AND REVISION SERVICE $60.95

FREE UPDATES ON THE WEB AT WWW.JEPPESEN.COM

VISIT YOUR JEPPESEN DEALER OR CALL 1-800-621-5377
MAKE SURE TO CHECK OUT OUR WEB PAGE AT HTTP://WWW.JEPPESEN.COM
PRICES SUBJECT TO CHANGE.

stop
wasting

time.

FliteStar™ is desktop flight planning so powerful you **spend more time flying, less time planning.** Whatever your flight planning needs, FliteStar is **fast, accurate,** comprehensive and **convenient.**

FliteStar gives you **real-time, online access** to multiple sources of **advanced weather graphics,** customizable enroute plate options that include the convenience of route profile and Navlog information printed at the bottom of the strip charts, airport inform-ation, continental U.S. FBO data, available **international and regional coverage** and more.

FliteStar's exclusive VectorPlus Mapping Tech-nology gives you infinitely **scalable, crisp images every time.** And all this **extraordinary power** is available in all three versions - VFR, IFR and Corporate.

Stop wasting time. Spend more time flying and less time planning - **with FliteStar!**

For more information about
FliteStar, visit us
on the internet at
www.jeppesen.com

or call us:

1-800-621-5377
or 303-799-9090
(Western Hemisphere)

+49 6102 5070
(Eastern Hemisphere)

+61 3 9706 0022 (Australasia)

JEPPESEN.
OnBoard

JEPPESEN
Making Every Mission Possible

CAPTAIN BAG

...ed for the ultimate in versatility. Each Captain Bag contains two detachable headset bags, which ... connected together to form a separate bag. The removable Transceiver/GPS bag can be ...d or fastened to the side of the flight bag with heavy-duty buttons. The roomy interior has a ...adjustable divider that can hold four Jeppesen binders. The exterior front pocket can be ...ed to reveal a convenient storage space to help pilots organize their supplies. Two large ...d storage pockets can hold pilot accessories. Carry your supplies in comfort with a wide ...ned shoulder strap, fully-padded 600 denier poly. 12"x22 1/2"x8"

...UMBER JS621214 (BLACK) $139.95
...UMBER JS621251 (BLUE) $139.95

THE NAVIGATOR BAG

The ultimate choice for convenience and flexibility. Each Navigator Bag includes all of the features and benefits of the Captain Bag, except the removable Transceiver/GPS bag and the two zippered exterior storage pockets. Instead, it includes two exterior pockets for easy access to Section Charts. 12"x22 1/2"x8"

ITEM NUMBER JS621213 (BLACK) $99.95
ITEM NUMBER JS621250 (BLUE) $99.95

...E STUDENT PILOT

...at first bag for the student pilot. Numerous outside ...ets organize charts, flight computer, fuel tester, plotter, pens and pencils, flashlight and much more. ...fortable, wide removable shoulder strap; double zipper opening for easy access. Reinforced bottom. ...structed with durable PVC backed 600 denier poly. 10"x5 1/2"x17"

...NUMBER JS621212 (BLACK ONLY) $41.95

THE AVIATOR BAG

Slightly smaller than our Navigator Bag, but still spacious enough for all of your flight materials. Includes one exterior front pocket as well as detachable headset and transceiver cases. Constructed with durable PVC backed 600 denier poly. 15"x6 1/2"x12"

ITEM NUMBER JS621252 (BLACK ONLY) $79.95

...HE PROTECTOR HEADSET BAGS

...ly padded 600 denier poly for extra protection. Snap-On handle grip for comfort. Large enough to fit the ANR ...adsets. single and dual configuaration. 12"x2 3/4"x8"

...M NUMBER SINGLE JS621220 (BLACK ONLY) $17.95
...M NUMBER DUAL JS621219 (BLACK ONLY) $35.95

balanced
training

Jeppesen Academy Training

Jeppesen Academy offers the training you need, **when and where you want it.**

Instructor-led classes deliver training on subjects ranging from flight operations and planning to maintenance information services to navigation and airspace. **Innovative new multimedia programs** deliver courses with the convenience and flexibility that technology and the Internet has to offer.

Whether you need instructor-led classes, our innovative multimedia courses, or a combination of the two, Jeppesen Academy provides airlines and flight departments **cost-effective training solutions.** Designed to support Part 121, 135 and 91 operations, Jeppesen Academy training can be tailored to **conveniently deliver** the training you require.

Call Jeppesen Academy today to learn more about our **balanced training solutions.**

Customized, high-quality training for little as **$70 per pilot, per year!**

Call us today:

+1 (303) 328 4423
Jeppesen Academy, U.S.

+49 6102 5070
Jeppesen Academy,
Frankfurt

+44 (0) 1293 842432
Jeppesen Academy, U.K.

PSHADES

Flip-Up Training Glasses

Replaces bulky, hard-to-use instrument training hoods • Improved design for better student/instructor interaction • Cockpit proven design works conveniently under headsets • Universal adjusting strap reduces pressure on ears and temples • Velcro™ strap fits comfortably • Flip-up lens allows convenient IFR/VFR flight transition • High quality polycarbonate lens is impact resistant.

ITEM NUMBER JS404311 $24.95

FLIGHT TIME RECORD KEEPING MADE EASY

Beginner or professional, maintaining accurate records of your flight time, aircraft and conditions is a must. Jeppesen logbooks provide a permanent record of your flying history.

PROFESSIONAL PILOT LOGBOOK

The book the pros use. Aviation's most popular professional logbook can handle 10 years of data. It includes simplified pilot and aircraft annual summaries. The quality construction matches the professional look of the Airway Manual binders. The gold signature strip allows you to personalize the cover with your own signature.
(Size: 6¾"x11¼")
ITEM NUMBER JS506050 $24.95

FLITELOG® LOGBOOK

#1 Rated Computer Logbook–Runs on both IBM and Macintosh

FliteLog gives you excellent flexibility with a traditional paper logbook feel (modeled after our Professional Pilot Logbook). Flitelog is shipped with common, predefined columns to get you going fast while also giving you the benefit of adding your own columns, changing column widths and column headings. You even have the option to hide or view columns. The Automatic Currency reminder ensures you will not overlook important currency requirements such as flight experience and medical requirements. FliteLogs's pilot profile feature makes it easy for you to make timely logbook entries and help you keep on top of your record keeping.

FLITELOG (WINDOWS)
ITEM NUMBER JM301592 $89.00

it's so
easy.

JeppChart Training Online

JeppChart Training Online just made learning **what you wanted to know** about Jeppesen's world-famous charts **a whole lot easier** – via the Internet. You can't beat the convenience. Just log on and begin. Wherever you are. Whenever you want.

Whether you're an experienced pilot or a beginning student, you'll appreciate the **interactivity, greater depth and detail** the lessons include. Graded feedback from the exercises tells you exactly what you know, what you don't, and where you need to spend more time. The program is also **updated periodically as changes occur.**

JeppChart Training Online lets you train **when you want, where you want.** And once you sign up, you have unlimited access for 90 days. Becoming a JeppChart **expert** couldn't be easier.

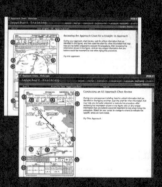

To find out how to make your **JeppChart Training** this easy, visit us on the internet at **www.jeppesen.com**

or call us:

1-800-621-5377
or 303-799-9090
(Western Hemisphere)

+49 6102 5070
(Eastern Hemisphere)

+61 3 9706 0022 (Australasia)

AWARD of Distinction

JEPPESEN
Making Every Mission Possible

charting

new courses.

Digital Charting Solutions

Jeppesen continues to set the standard for accurate and up-to-date flight information. We are leading the way with innovative digital charting solutions that can give your operation distinct advantages in **performance, safety, and overall effectiveness.**

Whether you use JeppView, JeppView FliteDeck, or our digital charts in an integrated avionics system, our goal is to provide you **the highest level** of convenience and capability now and in the future.

When it comes to **mission critical flight information**, it's nice to know you have Jeppesen OnBoard.

For more information about **Jeppesen digital charts** visit us on the internet at **www.jeppesen.com**

or call us:

1-800-621-5377
or 303-799-9090
(Western Hemisphere)

+49 6102 5070
(Eastern Hemisphere)

+61 3 9706 0022 (Australasia)

JEPPESEN
Making Every Mission Possible